Philosophy
of
Sex and Love
A Reader

Edited by
Robert Trevas
Arthur Zucker
Donald Borchert
Ohio University

D1280072

Library of Congress Cataloging-in-Publication Data

Philosophy of sex and love : a reader / edited by Robert Trevas,
    Arthur Zucker, Donald Borchert.
        p.   cm.
    Includes bibliographical references.
    ISBN 0–02–312431–8
    1. Love.   2. Sex.   I. Trevas, Robert.   II. Zucker, Arthur (date).
    III. Borchert, Donald M. (date).
    BD436.P46   1997
176—dc20   96–31845
                                                                CIP

This book was set in Times Roman by The Composing Room of Michigan, Inc.

Acquisitions editor: Angela Stone
Editorial production/supervision
        and interior design: F. Hubert
Manufacturing buyer: Lynn Pearlman

Printed in the United States of America

ISBN 0-02-312431-8

Prentice-Hall International (UK) Limited, London
Prentice-Hall of Australia Pty. Limited, Sydney
Prentice-Hall Canada Inc., Toronto
Prentice-Hall Hispanoamericana, S.A., Mexico
Prentice-Hall of India Private Limited, New Delhi
Prentice-Hall of Japan, Inc., Tokyo
Pearson Education Asia Pte. Ltd., Singapore
Editoria Prentice-Hall do Brasil, Ltda., Rio De Janeiro

Contents

CHAPTER 2

The Debate Between Sex With Love Versus Sex Without Love 63

CHAPTER 3

Feminist Critiques of Sex and Love 92

CHAPTER 4

Marriage 124

CHAPTER 5

Adultery 168

CHAPTER 8

Homosexuality 260

CHAPTER 9

Pornography 285

CHAPTER 10

Sexual Harassment and Rape   325

APPENDIX A

Contemporary Religious Discussions   394

APPENDIX B

Psychology and Sex   429

Preface

THE INTEREST OF COLLEGE STUDENTS IN THE PHILOSOPHY OF SEX AND LOVE is burgeoning. The topics of this subfield of philosophy—marriage, adultery, prostitution, homosexuality, pornography, sexual harassment etc.—involve issues that matter a great deal to students as they seek to come to terms with love and sex in their own lives.

We have prepared this book with these students in mind. More than twenty years ago, we introduced a course on the philosophy of sex and love into the curriculum at Ohio University. From the outset, student demand for this course far surpassed the available seats. Indeed, frequently we have had between two and three hundred "close-outs" for a particular offering of the course. From the beginning we have searched in vain for a textbook that examined not only current discussions of sex and love but also discussed the historical roots of contemporary discussions in ancient Greek philosophy, the biblical tradition, medieval Christendom, and modern secular psychology. In addition, we desired a text that combined primary sources with significant editorial comments that elucidate the material in a balanced fashion. Finding no such text, we decided several years ago to prepare one ourselves.

One of the greatest challenges we encountered was the need to be selective. There is a veritable plethora of engaging material from diverse cultures that is relevant to the philosophy of sex and love. We decided to focus primarily on material drawn from diverse sources ranging from the philosophical writings of ancient Greece to the theological discussions in contemporary Islam, Judaism, Protestantism, and Roman Catholicism to help elucidate current discussions in so-called Western civilization. Accordingly, mountains of interesting and important material would have to be left unexplored such as the philosophical analysis of pleasure, the literature on romantic love, the sutras of the Indian tradition, the powerful debate on female circumcision, and so forth.

The more than sixty primary sources we have included represent diverse and frequently competing perspectives. All of the sources are reader friendly. While some of our authors hold strong views and are strident in their criticism of others, we have tried very hard to provide a hearing for the opposition and to insert editorial comments in such a way that readers are always challenged to make up their own minds and to become authentic voices in their own right rather than mere echoes of others.

We are grateful to the countless students who have engaged us through the years in edifying discourse about the philosophy of sex and love. As any college teacher knows, the learning process at its best is always two-way. We also wish to extend our appreciation to our colleagues in the Philosophy Department at Ohio University for providing a congenial place to teach, think, learn, and write, especially to the departmental secretaries, Christina Dalesandry, Alice Donohoe, and Penny Schall, whose strength and skills have lifted many burdens—both great and small—from our shoulders. Thanks must be expressed also to the fine professionals at Prentice Hall, especially Frank Hubert, without whose expertise our project could not have been completed. Finally, we wish to thank our families, our children, and our spouses, but especially our spouses—Harriet, Laurie, and Mary Ellen—for their patience, insight, and editorial assistance during the course of this project.

We genuinely hope that those who explore the philosophy of sex and love through this book will achieve greater clarity about the topics discussed, will develop respect for positions that differ from their own, and will embrace those views—both old and new—that seem to have the strongest warrant.

ROBERT TREVAS
ARTHUR ZUCKER
DONALD M. BORCHERT
Ohio University
Athens, Ohio

The Philosophy of Sex and Love

THE PHILOSOPHY OF SEX AND LOVE emerged as a relatively new discipline in the late 1960s with the publication of Thomas Nagel's seminal article, "Sexual Perversion."[1] Since many of the substantial concerns of this discipline focused on moral and ethical issues, early anthology writers found it convenient to classify different types of sexual philosophies. Before beginning your study of the readings, it may be interesting and fruitful for you to reflect and determine which, if any, classification most closely resembles your own current view of the subject. Such reflection may provide you with a rudimentary understanding of alternative philosophies and also offer some insight into your own attitudes and beliefs.

In their analysis of sexual philosophies, writers initially broke down the subject into *three* major categories with reference to the morality of various sexual activities.

The *conservative* view may be described as the philosophy that considers sexual acts to be morally permissible only if they occur within the confines of a legitimate marriage and are for the purpose of procreation. Thus, not only are all premarital and extramarital sexual interactions deemed to be morally wrong but even sex for pleasure within marriage is considered objectionable.

The *moderate* or "sex-with-love" approach considers sexual interactions to be morally permissible if they occur between consenting adults, do no unjustified harm to others, and include a loving and/or committed relationship. When these factors are present, premarital sexual acts may be permissible, as may be nonmarital sexual acts and, under some circumstances, extramarital sexual activities such as those taking place in an open marriage. On the other hand, affectionless sex, such as prostitution or one-nighters, would be regarded as immoral.

The *liberal* philosophy construes all sexual acts as morally neutral taken by themselves. There is nothing inherently right or wrong in any particular sexual interaction. However, sexual acts may be judged as morally wrong, not because they are sexual, but because they may violate rationally justified moral rules such as, "Don't cause needless suffering," "Don't lie or deceive," "Don't coerce or exploit another," "Don't deprive another of their human rights," etc. Thus, the liberal makes moral judgments about sexual interactions not because there is a unique sexual morality, but because there is morality that applies to sexual matters as well as other issues. For example, rape is immoral not because it is sexual,

[1]*The Journal of Philosophy* 66, no. 1 (January 16, 1969).

but because it unjustly harms another. As a consequence, the liberal may countenance a wide variety of sexual activities, such as casual and recreational sex, one-nighters, promiscuous sex, sex with prostitutes, communal sex, etc., just as long as no justified moral rules are violated.

As the discussion of the philosophy of sex and love developed, it became apparent that two additional categories would be helpful in describing the wide variety of views presented in the literature: the *ultraconservative* and the *ultraliberal*.

The *ultraconservative* position holds that all sex, even within a formal marriage, is either inherently shameful or morally wrong. The most notable classical formulation of this view is found in St. Augustine's *City of God*. More recent exponents are found among many contemporary radical or lesbian feminists who oppose heterosexual sex, e.g., Ti-Grace Atkinson, Andrea Dworkin, Charlotte Bunch, etc., and interestingly, Marxists who perceive sexual activities in capitalistic institutions. Thus, Marxists regard a woman's sexual activities within a bourgeois marriage as a crass form of prostitution.

The *ultraliberal* view contends that all sexual activities are morally permissible— no if's, and's, or but's. All moral rules are nothing but the human-made conventions of unimaginative people. The main exponent of this philosophy was the Marquis de Sade (1740–1814), who held that all sexual desires, be they to have sex with children, to cause another pain, or to take another by force, sprang from nature. This being the case, it is natural and permissible to act on such desires.

Although it is advisable to avoid the philosophical vice of multiplying classifications beyond practical necessity, over the last decade or so, two additional important subcategories have moved to the forefront—"important" because it has become obvious that a considerable number of people within our culture have adopted them as legitimate options: the *neoconservative* and the *neoliberal* (or "sex-with-like") approaches.

The *neoconservative* approach appears as a subcategory under the conservative philosophy. In both religious and secular versions, the neoconservative maintains that sexual activity outside of marriage is immoral. However, unlike the conservative, the neoconservative argues that sex within marriage need not be confined to procreation, and sex is allowed for the purpose of pleasure, affection and intimacy. Moreover, the nature of acceptable sexual acts is broader. Since the conservative insists that sex must be tied to procreation, only noncontraceptive sexual intercourse is acceptable. The neoconservative, on the other hand, does not find other forms of sexual activity, such as oral-genital sex, to be immoral so long as they remain within the context of marriage.

Under the liberal category falls the *neoliberal* or "sex-with-like" position, which fills the gap between the moderate "sex-with-love" approach and the liberal view. Unlike the former, it does not demand love and/or deep commitment, but contra the liberal, it does require some degree of genuine affection for one's partner. Some literary examples of sexual behavior that would be condemned under this category are portrayed in *A Clockwork Orange* and *Clan of the Cave Bear*. Some forms of recreational sex, promiscuity, prostitution, etc., would also be condemned.

One of the benefits of studying sexual philosophy is to allow us, through exposure to a variety of alternative belief systems, to consider new possibilities and options for ourselves as well as to gain a deeper understanding of that philosophy we already hold. Moreover, we become better equipped for participating in the public discourse about issues that impact our social well-being. Surely the human experience of sex and love is one of those issues.

The chapters that follow begin with an historical overview of some of the seminal thinkers, beginning with Plato and Aristotle and ending with Erich Fromm and Alexander

Comfort, who have helped shape contemporary discussions in the philosophy of sex and love. Then we examine nine of the major topics treated in the philosophy of sex and love. In each of these chapters an engaging, and at times heated, debate will be encountered. You will be challenged to understand the debate and to adjudicate the competing claims. To assist you in meeting this challenge, it might be helpful to keep two questions in mind.

First, "Are the key concepts that figure in the discussion clearly defined?" Conceptual clarity is enormously important and cannot be taken for granted. We will discover that even such common terms as "love," "marriage," "natural," and "perverse" need conceptual clarification. Without such clarification, we cannot be sure that all of us are discussing the same issue. But getting things clear is not enough. Clarity helps us to understand the claims being made. We must also assess those claims. That leads us to the next question.

Second, "What justification is there for the claim being made?" In the readings that follow, many claims or propositions will be presented as candidates for our belief. Before we accept a particular proposition, however, and make it one of our beliefs, it would be wise to ask what reasons, if any, exist to commend that proposition to us.

Some of the propositions we encounter will be primarily about matters of fact; others will be chiefly about matters of value. Claims about matters of fact can usually be checked up on by an appeal to the way the world is. For example, if someone claims that homosexuality is a genetically determined condition, then we would look to the science of genetics to tell us if that is the way the world is. Even though genetics at present may not be able to answer our question decisively, the route to verify or falsify the claim is clearly via an appeal to the facts.

But where do claims about matters of value find their justification? If someone claims that homosexuality is immoral and somebody else claims that it is not, how shall we adjudicate the dispute? Here the route is not so clear. Presumably, claims about the morality or immorality of things can be checked up on by an appeal to some sort of standard for assessing people and their actions. But it is very difficult to gain universal agreement on what that standard should be. Shall we agree with those who judge actions morally on the basis of their consequences? If we do, what are the desirable consequences for which we should be looking? Pleasure? Happiness? The Good? If so, whose pleasure? Whose happiness? Whose Good? Or shall we concur with those who judge actions morally on the basis of conformity to certain moral rules? If so, which rules? Or shall we side with those who claim that the morality of actions depends on doing one's duty? But then we face the task of spelling out what precisely is the content of our duty. Is duty defined as the moral commands of reason? The commands of God? The commands of society?

With these questions we have moved from the specific issues in the philosophy of sex and love (such as the nature and morality of adultery) to the broad issues of moral theory. It is not necessary for us to settle all the questions of moral theory before we can investigate and discuss the issues in the philosophy of sex and love. What is needed, however, is for us to be aware of these deep issues of moral justification and to recognize that careful and thoughtful people find themselves embracing different moral theories for justifying the ethical judgments they make in the philosophy of sex and love. Just as there is not simply one intellectually respectable sexual philosophy, even so there is not just one legitimate moral theory capable of justifying one's moral judgments.

Philosophy is one of those disciplines where one question might yield several answers that have equal warrant. To be sure, multiple well-justified answers to the same question could be regarded as a serious disadvantage in some situations. For example, if you are trying to land an aircraft in foggy conditions, you don't want multiple equally warranted declarations as to the position of the glide slope or the altitude of the landing strip. In philosophy, however, we celebrate competing and well-supported claims because it means that the intellectual dialogue about these questions is ongoing, unfinished. For example, consider the question, "Is marriage morally right?" Your first response might be, "Why, of course!" But after pondering the question a little longer you might think of circumstances under which marriage might be immoral. Or take the issue of adultery. Is it morally wrong? Here, too, you might be inclined to say, "Definitely!" Yet after further consideration you might imagine scenarios where adultery would be morally permitted. Very few final, absolute answers to pressing moral questions are available. Most of our answers, when considered further, need qualification. But is not this element of ambiguity and uncertainty in moral matters precisely what we would expect if we humans are truly free in some important sense, if we are free to explore and assess alternative futures? Perhaps such uncertainty is the burden and joy of freedom.

While we may not be able to reach universal agreement about which moral theory is best and which answer to a specific moral question is the most strongly justified, nevertheless we can commit ourselves to the ongoing task of sharpening our critical faculties and entering into the public discourse on the important issues of sex and love. We can try to discern what basis for making moral judgments a particular author is assuming, and then ask if that author's judgments seem to follow from that basis. Furthermore, we can ask what the outcome would be if we assumed a different basis. In so doing, we might find ourselves becoming more enlightened about our own moral judgments in these matters, and also a little more patient with those who differ from us.

As you proceed now to read and analyze the articles that follow, we hope you will critically examine the reasons supporting each of these positions and struggle to develop a philosophy of sex and love that, when examined fully and rationally, will not only best suit you personally but will also promote the welfare of society as a whole.

CHAPTER 1

Historical Overview

W HILE THE PHILOSOPHY OF SEX AND LOVE is a relatively new subfield of philosophy, critical reflection about sex and love occupied human minds as far back as the ancient Greeks and beyond. Because our contemporary views on sex and love have been influenced by the thoughts of our predecessors, a clearer understanding of the current scene will be facilitated if we review briefly some of the major past reflections on this topic. Limitations of space do not allow us to hear all the important voices that have been raised throughout the centuries on sex and love. Needing to be selective, therefore, we have focused on only four out of many perspectives: the ancient Greek, the biblical, the medieval, and some modern clinical views. As we turn to a consideration of the ancient Greek view, it is important to remember that even within these four perspectives we have once again of necessity been selective in the writings chosen to represent a particular point of view.

ANCIENT GREEK VIEWS
Plato

Plato, one of the giants of the Greek philosophical tradition, was born of an aristocratic family in Athens about 428 B.C., two years after the death of Pericles, under whom the Golden Age of Athenian culture (461–431 B.C.) flourished. It was the time when Herodotus compiled history, Aeschylus and Sophocles wrote tragedies, Aristophanes composed comedies, and Phidias carved incomparable sculptures. Symbolic of this Golden Age was the reconstruction of the Acropolis under Pericles with its new Parthenon, a majestic temple dedicated to the goddess Athena, whose magnificent statue, carved in gold and ivory by Phidias and erected in the Parthenon, reminded citizens and strangers alike that Athenian prosperity and splendor, including their triumph over the Persians in a protracted struggle, were gifts of the gods.

As democracy developed in Athens, political success frequently depended upon one's ability to influence the citizenry through eloquent speeches. Accordingly, the Sophists (itinerant scholars who popularized knowledge and offered lessons in rhetoric) were sought out by young Athenians who wanted to develop techniques of persuasion and refutation to match their political ambitions. Socrates (ca. 470–399 B.C.), the teacher of Plato, was no

The selections from the *Symposium* are taken from *Symposium of Plato,* translated by Tom Griffith (Berkeley: University of California Press, 1989), 181b,c,d; 183d,e; 184d,e; 185b,c; 191d,e; 192c; 193a; 199c; 200a–201c; 204d–205a; 205e–207a,d; 208e–209c; 210a–212b. Used by permission of the University of California Press.

stranger to these arts of persuasion, and neither was Plato. Indeed, both of them were masters of these arts and passed them on to their students.

One of the formal methods used and taught by rhetoricians set two debaters, a questioner and an answerer, against each other. The answerer set forth a claim, or thesis, which the questioner challenged. The questions would generally be phrased to elicit either a "Yes" or "No" answer. The goal of the questioner's *elenchus,* or interrogation, was destruction of the opponent's views: showing that the answerer's thesis either was false or contained logical flaws. The goal of the answerer, of course, was to respond in such a way that the thesis would stand unrefuted. Plato adopted various forms of this method of debate in a number of his dialogues, including the *Symposium* from which the selections below have been taken.

Plato presented his philosophical ideas in about two dozen dialogues including *The Republic.* In his dialogues Plato's chief spokesperson is generally Socrates, who questions a variety of contemporary interlocutors. In the *Symposium* Socrates serves as both a questioner and an answerer as Plato sets forth his views on sex and love.

By teaching young Athenians the techniques of refutation, Socrates placed in their hands a powerful weapon with which they could attack the heralded wisdom of the leaders of society. Such attacks, in addition to his own assaults on the presumed knowledge of the authorities, engendered animosity among the powerful that eventually led to his trial and execution around 399 B.C. Sometime after the death of Socrates, in approximately 385 B.C., Plato in Athens, with the assistance of Theatetus (a mathematician) and perhaps Eudoxus (an astronomer and mathematician), founded the Academy, a minicollege offering lectures on diverse subjects. One of the students who attended the Academy was Aristotle, the other representative of the ancient Greek tradition we have selected for consideration. Plato died in 347 B.C. at the age of 81.

Plato's *Symposium* is probably the first philosophical discussion of love in European literature. The setting for the dialogue is a dinner party given by a young writer of tragedies, Agathon, to celebrate his victory in a dramatic contest held in Athens in 416 B.C. The Greek word *symposion* from which the title of the dialogue is taken, literally means "drinking together," thereby indicating that while eating and entertainment were aspects of such a party, heavy drinking was the main business of the affair. Thus, as soon as the celebrants at Agathon's party had completed the preliminary activities of eating and so forth, they directed their attention to the matter of drinking. They decided, however, to be rather temperate in their drinking on this occasion because some of them were still feeling the effects of a heavy drinking party the previous night. In addition, they agreed to devote themselves to an evening of conversation in which each of them would make a speech in honor of the Greek god Eros, whose praises humans had heretofore neglected to sing.

The Greek word *eros,* which can be translated as "desire" or "love," refers to intense attachment and desire, frequently to sexual desire and to the god (Eros) who personified that state of attachment and desire. The standard Greek word for "love," however, is *philia,* which can apply to the relations between nations as well as the feelings one has for a parent, child, close friend, spouse or lover.

Whether or not this *symposion* ever took place or, if it did, whether or not the account of it is accurate, are matters of scholarly interest that need not concern us here. What is important for us is that as the speakers in turn praise Eros we are given a window from which to view the ideas about sex and love entertained by a number of ancient Athenians, especially Plato.

Before considering the individual speeches in praise of Eros, it is important to recognize that the sexual love discussed in the *Symposium* is primarily pederasty, a practice condoned in ancient Athens. It was socially acceptable for an older man to seek sexual gratification from an adolescent boy. Such a liaison could coexist comfortably within the conventional relationships of a heterosexual marriage. The older man, the "lover," was supposed to win the boy, the "beloved," but only after the boy had resisted the advances of the man. While the older man was expected to enjoy the pleasure of the sexual act, it was regarded as unseemly and depraved for the boy to enjoy himself at the same time. In addition, it was assumed that the "lover" would be an ethical and intellectual mentor for the boy until the boy reached adulthood, at which time the homosexual relationship would end and the boy would become a "friend" instead of a "beloved."

The first speech, offered by Phaedrus, celebrates pederasty, a benefit brought to humankind by Eros, "created first of the Gods." Phaedrus observes, "I can see nothing better in life for a young boy, as soon as he is old enough, than finding a good lover, nor for a lover than finding a boy friend" (178c). This relationship between a man and a boy inspires both of them to virtuous deeds: The man would not want to be seen doing evil deeds in the sight of the boy he loves; nor would the boy want his admirer to see him behaving badly. Indeed, the intense desire of a lover and his beloved to look virtuous in the eyes of each other is so likely to generate courage and loyalty that Phaedrus suggested that an army made up entirely of such pairs of homosexual lovers would be virtually invincible.

The next person to speak is Pausanias, Agathon's lover. He distinguishes Common Eros from Heavenly Eros and prefers the latter to the former:

> The [Common] Eros . . . is, in all senses of the word, common, and quite haphazard in his operation. This is the love of the man in the street. For a start, he is as likely to fall in love with women as with boys. Secondly, he falls in love with their bodies rather than their minds. Thirdly, he picks the most unintelligent people he can find, since all he's interested in is the sexual act. He doesn't care whether it's done in the right way or not. That is why the effect of this Eros is haphazard—sometimes good, sometimes the reverse. This love [is] . . . composed equally of the female and male elements.
>
> The other [Heavenly] Eros . . . is composed solely of the male element, with none of the female (so it is the love of boys we are talking about), and in the second place is older, and hence free from lust. In consequence, those inspired by this love turn to the male, attracted by what is naturally stronger and of superior intelligence. And even among those who love boys you can tell the ones whose love is purely heavenly. They only fall in love with boys old enough to think for themselves—in other words, with boys who are nearly grown up.   (181b, c, d)

Clearly, Pausanias regards males to be naturally stronger and smarter than females and values most highly the pederasty of Heavenly Eros that focuses on the love of the mind. He continues,

> So love is neither right nor wrong in itself. Done rightly, it is right; done wrongly, it is wrong. It is wrong if you satisfy the wrong person, for the wrong reasons, and right if you satisfy the right person, for the rights reasons. The wrong person is the common love I was talking about—the one who loves the body rather than the mind. His love is not lasting, since *what* he loves is not lasting either. As soon as the youthful bloom of the body (which is what he loves) starts to fade, he 'spreads his wings and is off,' as they say, making a mockery of all his speeches and promises. On the other hand, the man who loves a boy for his good character will stick to him for life, since he has attached himself to what is lasting. . . .
>
> So it can only be regarded as right for a boy to satisfy his lover if both these conditions are satisfied—both the lover's behaviour, and the boy's desire for wisdom and

goodness. Then the lover and the boy have the same aim, and each has the approval of convention—the lover because he is justified in performing any service he chooses for a boy who satisfies him, the boy because he is justified in submitting, in any way he will, to the man who can make him wise and good. So if the lover has something to offer in the way of sound judgment and moral goodness, and if the boy is eager to accept this contribution to his education and growing wisdom, then, and only then, this favourable combination makes it right for a boy to satisfy his lover. In no other situation is it right. . . .

   So it is absolutely correct for boys to satisfy their lovers, if it is done in pursuit of goodness. This is the love which . . . is itself heavenly, and of great value to state and individual alike, since it compels both lover and boy to devote a lot of attention to their own moral improvement.   (183d, e; 184d, e; 185b, c)

Eryximachus, a medical doctor, is the next to celebrate Eros. He commends Pausanias for distinguishing Common Eros from Heavenly Eros, vulgar from noble love, but criticizes the narrowness of his perspective. Eros, Eryximachus argues, is neither found only in human hearts nor aroused only by human beauty. Extending the meaning of "love" to include "attraction" and even "harmony," he is able to claim that eros is aroused by many things and is found throughout nature and is responsible for benefits in such diverse fields as medicine, music, and meteorology.

   The next speaker, Aristophanes, a writer of comedies, offers a bold, speculative myth concerning the origin of human sexuality and the nature of love. Originally, says Aristophanes, humans were of three sexes: male, female, and male-female. Each of these primordial humans had twice as many limbs and organs as humans today. In addition, they had remarkable strength, vigor, and ambition, so much so, that they made an assault on the gods. To weaken and punish them, Zeus cut these humans in half. Accordingly, these humans and their descendants yearn for reunion with their original other half. This yearning or desire for reunion is eros, love. Aristophanes declares,

   We're all looking for our 'other half.' Men who are a fragment of the common sex (the one called hermaphrodite), are womanisers, and most adulterers are to be found in this category. Similarly, women of this type are nymphomaniacs and adulteresses. On the other hand, women who are part of an original woman pay very little attention to men. Their interest is in women; Lesbians are found in this class and those who are part of a male pursue what is male. . . . People like this are clearly inclined to have boy friends or (as boys) inclined to have lovers, because they always welcome what is akin. . . . So that's the explanation; it's because our original nature was as I have described, and because we were once complete. And the name of this desire and pursuit of completeness is Eros, or love. Formerly, as I say, we were undivided, but now we've been split up by god for our misdeeds. . . .   (191d, e; 192c; 193a)

With his myth Aristophanes seems to be claiming that sexual orientation, whether homosexual or heterosexual, is a matter of divine decree rather than a matter of human choice. Is he implying that homosexual love and heterosexual love are both completely natural? Furthermore, is he anticipating the modern romantic notion that love draws together two unique individuals and unites them as one person?

   Agathon, the young tragic poet who is both the object of Pausanias' love and also the host of the dinner party, takes his turn and describes the nature of Eros by listing his specific characteristics. He is the most blessed, the most beautiful, and the best of the gods. He is very young, very delicate, and very supple. He is just, virtuous, courageous, and wise. Agathon's description of Eros has set the stage for Socrates.

Socrates begins with an interrogation of Agathon:

Well, my dear Agathon, I liked the beginning of your speech. You said the first thing to do was to reveal the nature of Eros; after that his achievements. I think that was an excellent starting point. . . .

SOCRATES: Try . . . to answer my question about Eros. Is Eros love of nothing, or of something?

AGATHON: Of something, certainly.

SOCRATES: Good. Hold on to that answer. Keep it in mind, & make a mental note what it is that Eros is love of. But first tell me this; this thing which Eros is love of, does he desire it, or not?

AGATHON: Certainly.

SOCRATES: And does he possess that which he desires & loves, or not?

AGATHON: Probably not.

SOCRATES: I'm not interested in probability, but in certainty. Consider this proposition: anything which desires something desires what it does not have, and it only desires when it is lacking something. This proposition, Agathon, seems to me to be absolutely certain. How does it strike you?

AGATHON: Yes, it seems certain to me too.

SOCRATES: Quite right. So would a big man want to be big, or a strong man want to be strong?

AGATHON: No, that's impossible, given what we have agreed so far.

SOCRATES: Because if he possesses these qualities, he cannot also lack them.

AGATHON: True.

SOCRATES: So if a strong man wanted to be strong, or a fast runner to be fast, or a healthy man to be healthy—but perhaps I'd better explain what I'm on about. I'm a bit worried that you may think that people like this, people having these qualities, can also want the qualities which they possess. So I'm trying to remove this misapprehension. If you think about it, Agathon, people cannot avoid possession of whichever of these qualities they do possess, whether they like it or not. So obviously there's no point in desiring to do so. When anyone says, 'I'm in good health, and I also desire to be in good health,' or 'I am rich & also desire to be rich,' i.e. 'I desire those things which I already have,' then we should answer him: 'what you want is to go on possessing, in the future, the wealth, health, or strength you possess now, since you have them now, like it or not. So when you say you desire what you've already got, are you sure you don't just mean you want to continue to possess in the future what you possess now?' Would he deny this?

AGATHON: No, he would agree.

SOCRATES: But isn't this a question of desiring what he doesn't already have in his possession—i.e. the desire that what he does have should be safely & permanently available to him in the future?

AGATHON: Yes, it is.

SOCRATES: So in this, or any other, situation, the man who desires something desires what is not available to him, and what he doesn't already have in his possession. And what he neither has nor himself is—that which he lacks—this is what he wants and desires.

AGATHON: Absolutely.

SOCRATES: Right then, let's agree on the argument so far. Eros has an existence of his own; he is in the first place love of something, and secondly, he is love of that which he is without.

AGATHON: Yes.

SOCRATES: Keeping that in mind, just recall what you said were the objects of Eros, in your speech. I'll remind you, if you like. I think what you said amounted to this: trouble among the gods was ended by their love of beauty, since there could be no love of what is ugly. Isn't that roughly what you said?

AGATHON: Yes, it is.

SOCRATES: And a very reasonable statement, too, my friend. And this being so, Eros must have an existence as love of beauty, & not love of ugliness, mustn't he?

AGATHON: Yes.

SOCRATES: But wasn't it agreed that he loves what he lacks, and does not possess?

AGATHON: Yes, it was.

SOCRATES: So Eros lacks, and does not possess, beauty.

AGATHON: That is the inevitable conclusion.

SOCRATES: Well then, do you describe as beautiful that which lacks beauty and has never acquired beauty?

AGATHON: No.

SOCRATES: If that is so, do you still maintain that Eros is beautiful?

AGATHON: I rather suspect, Socrates, that I didn't know what I was talking about.

SOCRATES: It sounded marvellous, for all that, Agathon. Just one other small point. Would you agree that what is good is also beautiful?

AGATHON: Yes, I would.

SOCRATES: So if Eros lacks beauty, and if what is good is beautiful, then Eros would lack what is good also.

AGATHON: I can't argue with you, Socrates. Let's take it that it is as you say. (199c; 200a–201c)

Clearly Agathon was mistaken about the nature of love. He had described love in terms of the object of love (namely, goodness, beauty, wisdom, etc.) rather than focusing upon what love is in the lover: a desire, a longing for something not possessed. Socrates admits that he had at one time spoken about love as Agathon had, but that he had been corrected and instructed by Diotima, a priestess from the city of Mantineia. Socrates recalls Diotima as saying,

Socrates . . . your views on Eros revealed a quite common mistake. You thought that Eros was what was loved, rather than the lover. That is why you thought Eros was beautiful. After all, what we love really *is* beautiful and delicate, perfect and delightful. . . . [Moreover,] we would classify wisdom as very beautiful, and Eros is love of what is beautiful, so it necessarily follows that Eros is a love of wisdom. (204c,b)

Do the previous speakers who extol homosexual pederasty regard females as less worthy objects of love than males? Would they agree with Pausanias (Agathon's lover) who indicates that Heavenly Eros turns from the female to the male who is naturally stronger and of superior intelligence? In the light of these previous speeches, is it not interesting that

Plato portrays his premier spokesperson, Socrates, as being instructed by Diotima, a *woman*? Would not Pausanias have difficulty depreciating the intelligence of Diotima when she is heralded by Socrates as "an expert" on love as well as on "many other" subjects?

We turn now to some of Socrates' recollections of the conversation he had with Diotima and the instruction he received from her. Diotima begins,

> Now let's imagine someone asking us, 'Why is Eros love of the beautiful, Socrates and Diotima?' Let me put it more clearly: what is it that the lover of beauty desires?'
> 'To possess it.'
> 'That prompts the further question, what good does it do someone to possess beauty?'
> 'I don't quite know how to give a quick answer to that question.'
> 'Well, try a different question, about goodness rather than beauty: Socrates, what does the lover of goodness want?'
> 'To possess it.'
> 'What good will it do him to possess it?'
> 'That's easier. It will make him happy.'
> 'Yes, because those who are happy are happy because they possess what is good. The enquiry seems to have reached a conclusion, and there is no need to ask the further question, 'If someone wants to be happy, why does he want to be happy?''
> 'True.' . . .
> 'There is a theory that lovers are people in search of their other half. But according to my theory, love is not love of a half, nor of a whole, unless it is good. . . . the good is the only object of human love, as I think you will agree.'
> 'Yes, I certainly do agree.'
> 'Can we say, then, quite simply, that men love the good?'
> 'Yes.'
> 'And presumably we should add that they want to possess the good?'
> 'Yes, we should.'
> 'And not merely to possess it, but to possess it for ever.'
> 'That also.'
> 'In short, then, love is the desire for permanent possession of the good.'
> 'Precisely.'
> 'If this is always the object of our desire, what is the particular manner of pursuit, and the particular sphere of activity, in which enthusiasm & effort qualify for the title 'love'? What is this activity? Do you know?'
> 'No, I don't. That's why I find your knowledge so impressive. In fact, I've kept coming to see you, because I want an answer to just that question.'
> 'Very well, I'll tell you. The activity we're talking about is the use of what is beautiful for the purpose of reproduction, whether physical or mental.'
> 'I'm no good at riddles. I don't understand what you mean.'
> 'I'll try to make myself clearer. Reproduction, Socrates, both physical and mental, is a universal human activity. At a certain age our nature desires to give birth. To do so, it cannot employ an ugly medium, but insists on what is beautiful. Sexual intercourse between man and woman is this reproduction. So there is the divine element, this germ of immortality, in mortal creatures—i.e. conception and begetting. These cannot take place in an uncongenial medium, and ugliness is uncongenial to everything divine, while beauty is congenial. Therefore procreation has Beauty as its midwife and its destiny, which is why the urge to reproduce becomes gentle and happy when it comes near

beauty: then conception & begetting become possible. By contrast, when it comes near ugliness it becomes sullen and offended, it contracts, withdraws, and shrinks away and does not beget. It stifles the reproductive urge, and is frustrated. So in anyone who is keen (one might almost say bursting) to reproduce, beauty arouses violent emotion, because beauty can release its possessor from the agony of reproduction. Your opinion, Socrates, that love is desire for beauty, is mistaken.'

'What is the correct view, then?'

'It is the desire to use beauty to beget and bear offspring.'

'Perhaps.'

'Certainly! And why to beget? Because begetting is, by human standards, something eternal and undying. So if we were right in describing love as the desire always to possess the good, then the inevitable conclusion is that we desire immortality as well as goodness. On this argument, love must be desire for immortality as much as for beauty.'

. . . What is mortal tries, to the best of its ability, to be everlasting and immortal. It does this in the only way it can, by always leaving a successor to replace what decays. . . .

Those whose creative urge is physical tend to turn to women, & pursue Eros by this route. The production of children gains them, as they imagine, immortality and a name and happiness for themselves, for all time. In others the impulse is mental or spiritual—people who are creative mentally, much more than physically. They produce what you would expect the mind to conceive and produce. And what is that? Thought, and all other human excellence. All poets are creators of this kind, & so are those artists who are generally regarded as inventive. However, under the general heading 'thought,' by far the finest and most important item is the art of political and domestic economy, what we call good judgment, and justice.

Someone who, right from his youth, is mentally creative in these areas, when he is ready, and the time comes, feels a strong urge to give birth, or beget. So he goes around, like everyone else, searching, as I see it, for a medium of beauty in which he can create. He will never create in an ugly medium. So in his desire to create he is attracted to what is physically beautiful rather than ugly. But if he comes across a beautiful, noble, well-formed mind, then he finds the combination particularly attractive. He'll drop everything & embark on long conversations about goodness, with such a companion, trying to teach him about the nature & behaviour of the good man. Now that he's made contact with someone beautiful, and made friends with him, he can produce and bring to birth what he long ago conceived. Present or absent, he keeps it in mind, and joins with his friends in bringing his conception to maturity. In consequence such people have a far stronger bond between them than there is between the parents of children; and they form much firmer friendships, because they are jointly responsible for finer, & more lasting, offspring. (204d–205a; 205e–207a, d; 208e–209c)

Loving goodness in order to possess it for the sake of happiness, desiring to possess goodness forever, seeking immortality through reproduction, creating offspring physically and spiritually—these are some of the themes Diotima has discussed. Finally she describes the ladder of love that the mature lover ascends, beginning first with the pursuit of physical beauty and reaching eventually a breathtaking vision of beauty itself. She observes,

The true follower of this subject must begin, as a young man, with the pursuit of physical beauty. In the first place, if his mentor advises him properly, he should be attracted, physically, to one individual; at this stage his offspring are beautiful discussions & conversations. Next he should realise that the physical beauty of one body is akin to that of any other body, and that if he's going to pursue beauty of appearance, it's the height of folly not to regard the beauty which is in all bodies as one and the same. This insight will convert him into a lover of all physical beauty, and he will become less obsessive in his pursuit of his one former passion, as he realises its unimportance.

The next stage is to put a higher value on mental than on physical beauty. The right qualities of mind, even in the absence of any great physical beauty, will be enough to awaken his love & affection. He will generate the kind of discussions which are improving to the young. The aim is that, as the next step, he should be compelled to contemplate the beauty of customs and institutions, to see that all beauty of this sort is related, and consequently to regard physical beauty as trivial.

From human institutions his teacher should direct him to knowledge, so that he may, in turn, see the beauty of different types of knowledge. Whereas before, in servile & contemptible fashion, he was dominated by the individual case, loving the beauty of a boy, or a man, or a single human activity, now he directs his eyes to what is beautiful in general, as he turns to gaze upon the limitless ocean of beauty. Now he produces many fine and inspiring thoughts and arguments, as he gives his undivided attention to philosophy. Here he gains in strength and stature until his attention is caught by that one special knowledge—the knowledge of a beauty which I will now try to describe to you. So pay the closest possible attention.

When a man has reached this point in his education in love, studying the different types of beauty in correct order, he will come to the final end and goal of this education. Then suddenly he will see a beauty of a breathtaking nature. Socrates, the beauty which is the justification of all his efforts so far. It is eternal, neither coming to be nor passing away, neither increasing nor decreasing. Moreover it is not beautiful in part, and ugly in part, nor is it beautiful at one time, and not at another; nor beautiful in some respects, but not in others; nor beautiful here and ugly there, as if beautiful in some people's eyes, but not in others. It will not appear to him as the beauty of a face, or hands, or anything physical—nor as an idea or branch of knowledge, nor as existing in any determinate place, such as a living creature, or the earth, or heaven, or anywhere like that. It exists for all time, by itself and with itself, unique. All other forms of beauty derive from it, but in such a way that their creation or destruction does not strengthen or weaken it, or affect it in any way at all. If a man progresses (as he will do, if he goes about his love affairs in the right way) from the lesser beauties, & begins to catch sight of this beauty, then he is within reach of the final revelation. Such is the experience of the man who approaches, or is guided towards, love in the right way, beginning with the particular examples of beauty, but always returning from them to the search for that one beauty. He uses them like a ladder, climbing from the love of one person to love of two; from two to love of all physical beauty; from physical beauty to beauty in human behavior; thence to beauty in subjects of study; from them he arrives finally at that branch of knowledge which studies nothing but ultimate beauty. Then at last he understands what true beauty is.

That, if ever, is the moment, my dear Socrates, when a man's life is worth living, as he contemplates beauty itself. Once seen, it will not seem to you to be a good such as gold, or fashionable clothes, or the boys and young men who have such an effect on you now when you see them. You, and any number of people like you, when you see your boyfriends and spend all your time with them, are quite prepared (or would be, if it were possible) to go without food & drink, just looking at them and being with them. But suppose it were granted to someone to see beauty itself quite clearly, in its pure, undiluted form—not clogged up with human flesh and colouring, and a whole lot of other worthless and corruptible matter. No, imagine he were able to see the divine beauty itself in its unique essence. Don't you think he would find it a wonderful way to live, looking at it, contemplating it as it should be contemplated, and spending his time in its company? It cannot fail to strike you that only then will it be possible for him, seeing beauty as it should be seen, to produce, not likenesses of goodness (since it is no likeness he has before him), but the real thing (since he has the real thing before him); and that this producing, and caring for, real goodness earns him the friendship of the gods and makes him, if anyone, immortal.'

There you are, then, Phaedrus and the rest of you. That's what Diotima said to me, & I, for one, find it convincing.   (210a–212b)

The final speech in the *Symposium* is not in honor of Eros, but in praise of Socrates. Alcibiades, at one time an object of Socrates' love, arrives at the party just after Socrates had completed his speech. Drunk and boisterous, Alcibiades contradicts the popular view of Socrates as "someone who fancies attractive men, spends all his time with them, [and] finds them irresistible." Instead, says Alcibiades, Socrates is "a model of restraint." Alcibiades continues, "It makes no difference at all how attractive you are, he has an astonishing contempt for that kind of thing. Similarly with riches, or any of the other so-called advantages we possess. He regards all possessions as worthless, and us humans as insignificant" (216d). Indeed, Alcibiades confesses that his attempt to seduce Socrates was a humiliating failure.

Is Plato, perhaps through the mouth of Alcibiades, indicating that Socrates had learned well his lesson in love from Diotima? That he was seeking the spiritual delight of knowing beauty itself rather than the physical pleasure of homosexual satisfaction? That Socrates had united the theory and practice of Platonic love?

ANCIENT GREEK VIEWS
Aristotle

We turn now to consider the thought of Plato's most famous student, Aristotle. He was born in 384 B.C. in the city of Stagira in Thrace, the son of the physician to the king of Macedon. At the age of seventeen, Aristotle went to Athens to study at Plato's Academy where he remained for twenty years, enjoying an ongoing philosophical dialogue with Plato. When Plato died in 347 B.C., Aristotle left the Academy because he did not see eye to eye with its new director (Plato's nephew, Speusippus). After several years of travelling, Aristotle settled down as the tutor of the thirteen-year-old son of King Philip II of Macedon. The young prince ascended the throne in 335 B.C. and embarked on a course of conquest that eventually won him the title of Alexander the Great. At the same time, Aristotle returned to Athens where he established his own school called the Lyceum or Peripatos. When Alexander died in 323 B.C., Athenian reaction to Macedonian domination was so strong that Aristotle took refuge in Chalcis where he died in poor health the next year.

Aristotle differed from his teacher Plato on a number of important issues, a chief one of which was the Platonic theory of forms. Plato apparently first outlined this theory in the passages of the *Symposium* (which we have already reviewed) where Diotima describes the

The selection from *Rhetoric* 1381a 1–5 is reprinted from *The Oxford Translation of Aristotle,* edited by W. D. Ross, Vol. II (1925). Used by permission of Oxford University Press. The selections from *Nicomachean Ethics* (1156a6–1157b4; 1158b12–29; 1160b23–1161a29; 1162a–1162b4; 1168a28–1169b2) are reprinted from *The Oxford Translation of Aristotle,* edited by W. D. Ross (1925). Used by permission of Oxford University Press.

ladder of love that the mature lover climbs, starting with attraction toward one physically beautiful body, then toward another and another, until the lover seeks and gazes upon beauty itself. Diotima observes,

> Such is the experience of the man who approaches, or is guided towards, love in the right way, beginning with the particular examples of beauty, but always returning from them to the search for that one beauty. He uses them like a ladder, climbing from the love of one person to love of two; from two to love of all physical beauty; from physical beauty to beauty in human behaviour; thence to beauty in subjects of study; from them he arrives finally at that branch of knowledge which studies nothing but ultimate beauty. Then at least he understands what true beauty is. (211b–c)

But *where* is this "ultimate," "true" beauty to which the mature lover ascends, and upon which he or she gazes? Ultimate beauty is seen not with physical eyes but with the eyes of the mind. It is an eternal idea or form which all beautiful things more or less approximate. According to Plato, there are many such ideas or forms. There is, for example, the idea of an absolutely straight line which all "straight" lines drawn by humans more or less approximate. Then, too, there is perfect goodness and perfect justice. Also, there is oak tree-ness, catness, dogness, etc. These forms, Plato thought, populate a real, eternal, changeless, permanent world to which the human mind can ascend through intellectual moves analogous to climbing the ladder of love. This eternal world stands in sharp contrast to the temporal and transient world of specific entities that flourish, fade, and pass away. Beautiful objects come and go, but the idea of beauty abides forever. Oak trees come and go, but the idea of oak treeness abides forever.

Aristotle rejected Plato's dualistic notion of an eternal world of forms juxtaposed to a temporal world of changing entities. For him there is but one world: the world in which we live and develop and change. For Aristotle, all entities in this world (except God) are striving to actualize their potentialities. In so doing, they are seeking, striving, and desiring to be like God, who alone is fully actualized (even though they might not be conscious of their Godlike quest). Accordingly, instead of projecting the goal of human desire and love to be the contemplation of the eternal world of forms, especially the form of true beauty, Aristotle sets forth as the major goal of human desire and striving the actualization of human potentialities in this temporal world of change. The focus of love for Aristotle becomes not the abstract, timeless form of beauty but the concrete, temporal relationships of humans to each other. Aristotle's key term in this regard is *philia,* which many scholars translate as "friendship." Some commentators, however, think that "friendship" blunts the robust nature of Aristotle's Greek and that "love" would be a better translation.

Let us turn to the definition of *philia* that Aristotle provides for us in his treatise called *Rhetoric.* Aristotle writes,

> We will begin by defining friendship and friendly feeling. We may describe friendly feeling towards any one as wishing for him what you believe to be good things, not for your own sake but for his, and being inclined, so far as you can, to bring these things about. A friend is one who feels thus and excites these feelings in return: those who think they feel thus towards each other think themselves friends. This being assumed, it follows that your friend is the sort of man who shares your pleasure in what is good and your pain in what is unpleasant, for your sake and for no other reason. (1381a1–5)

Does not Aristotle's concern seem to be far removed from Plato's ladder of love? And does not the benevolent attitude of friendly feeling seem to be quite different from the egocentric attitude of Plato's mature lover in pursuit of the satisfying vision of perfect beauty?

In another major treatise, *Nicomachean Ethics,* Aristotle analyzes friendship in great detail. He begins with the declaration that without friends life would not be worth living, and proceeds to distinguish three kinds of friendship based on three different motives: the love of pleasure, the love of advantage or usefulness, and the love of moral goodness.

There are therefore three kinds of friendship, equal in number to the things that are lovable; for with respect to each there is a mutual and recognized love, and those who love each other wish well to each other in that respect in which they love one another. Now those who love each other for their utility do not love each other for themselves but in virtue of some good which they get from each other. So too with those who love for the sake of pleasure; it is not for their character that men love ready-witted people, but because they find them pleasant. Therefore those who love for the sake of utility love for the sake of what is good for *themselves,* and those who love for the sake of pleasure do so for the sake of what is pleasant to *themselves,* and not in so far as the other is the person loved but in so far as he is useful or pleasant. And thus these friendships are only incidental; for it is not as being the man he is that the loved person is loved, but as providing some good or pleasure. Such friendships, then, are easily dissolved, if the parties do not remain like themselves; for if the one party is no longer pleasant or useful the other ceases to love him.

Now the useful is not permanent but is always changing. Thus when the motive of the friendship is done away, the friendship is dissolved, inasmuch as it existed only for the ends in question. This kind of friendship seems to exist chiefly between old people (for at that age people pursue not the pleasant but the useful) and, of those who are in their prime or young, between those who pursue utility. And such people do not live much with each other either; for sometimes they do not even find each other pleasant; therefore they do not need such companionship unless they are useful to each other; for they are pleasant to each other only in so far as they rouse in each other hopes of something good to come. Among such friendships people also class the friendship of host and guest. On the other hand the friendship of young people seems to aim at pleasure; for they live under the guidance of emotion, and pursue above all what is pleasant to themselves and what is immediately before them; but with increasing age their pleasures become different. This is why they quickly become friends and quickly cease to be so; their friendship changes with the object that is found pleasant, and such pleasure alters quickly. Young people are amorous too; for the greater part of the friendship of love depends on emotion and aims at pleasure; this is why they fall in love and quickly fall out of love, changing often within a single day. But these people do wish to spend their days and lives together; for it is thus that they attain the purpose of their friendship.

Perfect friendship is the friendship of men who are good, and alike in virtue; for these wish well alike to each other *qua* good, and they are good in themselves. Now those who wish well to their friends for their sake are most truly friends; for they do this by reason of their own nature and not incidentally; therefore their friendship lasts as long as they are good—and goodness is an enduring thing. And each is good without qualification and to his friend, for the good are both good without qualification and useful to each other. So too they are pleasant; for the good are pleasant both without qualification and to each other, since to each his own activities and others like them are pleasurable, and the actions of the good *are* the same or like. And such a friendship is as might be expected permanent, since there meet in it all the qualities that friends should have. For all friendship is for the sake of good or of pleasure—good or pleasure either in the abstract or such as will be enjoyed by him who has the friendly feeling—and is based on a certain resemblance; and to a friendship of good men all the qualities we have named belong in virtue of the nature of the friends themselves; for in the case of this kind of friendship the other qualities also are alike in both friends, and that which is good without qualification is also without qualification pleasant, and these are the most lovable qualities. Love and friendship therefore are found most and in their best form between such men.

But it is natural that such friendships should be infrequent; for such men are rare. Further, such friendship requires time and familiarity; as the proverb says, men cannot know each other till they have 'eaten salt together'; nor can they admit each other to friendship or be friends till each has been found lovable and been trusted by each. Those who quickly show the marks of friendship to each other wish to be friends, but are not friends unless they both are lovable and know the fact; for a wish for friendship may arise quickly, but friendship does not.

This kind of friendship, then, is perfect both in respect of duration and in all other respects, and in it each gets from each in all respects the same as, or something like what, he gives; which is what ought to happen between friends. Friendship for the sake of pleasure bears a resemblance to this kind; for good people too *are* pleasant to each other. So too does friendship for the sake of utility; for the good are also useful to each other. Among men of these inferior sorts too, friendships are most permanent when the friends get the same thing from each other (e.g. pleasure), and not only that but also from the same source, as happens between ready-witted people, not as happens between lover and beloved. For these do not take pleasure in the same things, but the one in seeing the beloved and the other in receiving attentions from his lover; and when the bloom of youth is passing the friendship sometimes passes too (for the one finds no pleasure in the sight of the other, and the other gets no attentions from the first); but many lovers on the other hand are constant, if familiarity has led them to love each other's characters, these being alike. But those who exchange not pleasure but utility in their amour are both less truly friends and less constant. Those who are friends for the sake of utility part when the advantage is at an end; for they were lovers not of each other but of profit.

For the sake of pleasure or utility, then, even bad men may be friends of each other, or good men of bad, or one who is neither good nor bad may be a friend to any sort of person, but for their own sake clearly only good men can be friends; for bad men do not delight in each other unless some advantage come of the relation.

The friendship of the good too and this alone is proof against slander; for it is not easy to trust any one's talk about a man who has long been tested by oneself; and it is among good men that trust and the feeling that 'he would never wrong me' and all the other things that are demanded in true friendship are found. In the other kinds of friendship, however, there is nothing to prevent these evils arising.

For men apply the name of friends even to those whose motive is utility, in which sense states are said to be friendly (for the alliances of states seem to aim at advantage), and to those who love each other for the sake of pleasure, in which sense children are called friends. Therefore we too ought perhaps to call such people friends, and say that there are several kinds of friendship—firstly and in the proper sense that of good men *qua* good, and by analogy the other kinds; for it is in virtue of something good and something akin to what is found in true friendship that they are friends, since even the pleasant is good for the lovers of pleasure. But these two kinds of friendship are not often united, nor do the same people become friends for the sake of utility and of pleasure; for things that are only incidentally connected are not often coupled together.

Friendship being divided into these kinds, bad men will be friends for the sake of pleasure or of utility, being in this respect like each other, but good men will be friends for their own sake, i.e. in virtue of their goodness. These, then, are friends without qualification; the others are friends incidentally and through a resemblance to these. (1156a6–1157b4)

Of the three kinds of friendship, then, the most perfect is the one between persons who resemble each other in goodness and who wish well to each other for the sake of each other. Such friendship based on moral goodness obviously involves pleasure and usefulness. Those who are good and noble find both delight and profit in each other. But delight and profit, pleasure and usefulness do not form the foundation of this kind of friendship.

Aristotle goes on to discuss additional features of friendship, including friendship which "involves an inequality between the parties, e.g. that of father to son and in general of elder to younger, that of man to wife and in general that of ruler to subject" (1158b11–15). Between such unequal persons, friendship is based on proportional love; that is, the better of the two, the more useful of the two, the more pleasurable of the two, should receive more love than he or she gives. Aristotle writes,

> But there is another kind of friendship, viz. that which involves an inequality between the parties, e.g. that of father to son and in general of elder to younger, that of man to wife and in general that of ruler to subject. And these friendships differ also from each other; for it is not the same that exists between parents and children and between rulers and subjects, nor is even that of father to son the same as that of son to father, nor that of husband to wife the same as that of wife to husband. For the virtue and the function of each of these is different, and so are the reasons for which they love; the love and the friendship are therefore different also. Each party, then, neither gets the same from the other, nor ought to seek it; but when children render to parents what they ought to render to those who brought them into the world, and parents render what they should to their children, the friendship of such persons will be abiding and excellent. In all friendships implying inequality the love also should be proportional, i.e. the better should be more loved than he loves, and so should the more useful, and similarly in each of the other cases; for when the love is in proportion to the merit of the parties, then in a sense arises equality, which is certainly held to be characteristic of friendship. (1158b12–29)

For Aristotle, every association of persons presents the possibility of friendship. Accordingly, he includes in his discussion of friendship a brief description of the basic forms of government and their perversions: monarchy, whose perversion is tyranny; aristocracy, whose perversion is oligarchy; and timocracy (or polity), whose perversion is democracy. He proceeds to find resemblances to these forms of government in the prevailing relationships in households:

> One may find resemblances to the constitutions and, as it were, patterns of them even in households. For the association of a father with his son bears the form of monarchy, since the father cares for his children; and this is why Homer calls Zeus 'father'; it is the ideal of monarchy to be paternal rule. But among the Persians the rule of the father is tyrannical; they use their sons as slaves. Tyrannical too is the rule of a master over slaves; for it is the advantage of the master that is brought about in it. Now this seems

to be a correct form of government, but the Persian type is perverted; for the modes of rule appropriate to different relations are diverse. The association of man and wife seems to be aristocratic; for the man rules in accordance with his worth, and in those matters in which a man should rule, but the matters that befit a woman he hands over to her. If the man rules in everything the relation passes over to oligarchy; for in doing so he is not acting in accordance with their respective worth, and not ruling in virtue of his superiority. Sometimes, however, women rule, because they are heiresses; so their rule is not in virtue of excellence but due to wealth and power, as in oligarchies. The association of brothers is like timocracy; for they are equal, except in so far as they differ in age; hence if they differ *much* in age, the friendship is no longer of the fraternal type. Democracy is found chiefly in masterless dwellings (for here every one is on an equality), and in those in which the ruler is weak and every one has license to do as he pleases.

Each of the constitutions may be seen to involve friendship just in so far as it involves justice. The friendship between a king and his subjects depends on an excess of benefits conferred; for he confers benefits on his subjects if being a good man he cares for them with a view to their well-being, as a shepherd does for his sheep (whence Homer called Agamemnon 'shepherd of the peoples'). Such too is the friendship of a father, though this exceeds the other in the greatness of the benefits conferred; for he is responsible for the existence of his children, which is thought the greatest good, and for their nurture and upbringing. These things are ascribed to ancestors as well. Further, by nature a father tends to rule over his sons, ancestors over descendants, a king over his subjects. These friendships imply superiority of one party over the other, which is why ancestors are honoured. The justice therefore that exists between persons so related is not the same on both sides but is in every case proportioned to merit; for that is true of the friendship as well. The friendship of man and wife, again, is the same that is found in an aristocracy; for it is in accordance with virtue—the better gets more of what is good, and each gets what befits him; and so, too, with the justice in these relations. The friendship of brothers is like that of comrades; for they are equal and of like age, and such persons are for the most part like in their feelings and their character. Like this, too, is the friendship appropriate to timocratic government; for in such a constitution the ideal is for the citizens to be equal and fair; therefore rule is taken in turn, and on equal terms; and the friendship appropriate here will correspond. (1160b23–1161a29)

In summation of the three kinds of friendship, Aristotle says,

There are three kinds of friendship, as we said at the onset of our inquiry, and in respect of each some are friends on an equality and others by virtue of a superiority (for not only can equally good men become friends but a better man can make friends with a worse, and similarly in friendships of pleasure or utility the friends may be equal or unequal in the benefits they confer). This being so, equals must effect the required equalization on a basis of equality in love and in all other respects, while unequals must render what is in proportion to their superiority or inferiority.   (1162a34–1162b4)

Aristotle proceeds to address a series of issues pertaining to friendship that the thoughtful reader might raise. One of those issues is the matter of self-love. Some of Aristotle's contemporaries viewed it negatively as blameworthy. Others regarded it positively as praiseworthy. Which is it? Aristotle responds by clarifying the concept of self-love in order to show in what sense self-love may be regarded as noble and praiseworthy.

The question is also debated, whether a man should love himself most, or some one else. People criticize those who love themselves most, and call them self-lovers, using this as an epithet of disgrace, and a bad man seems to do everything for his own sake, and the more so the more wicked he is—and so men reproach him, for instance, with doing nothing of his own accord—while the good man acts for honour's sake, and the more so the better he is, and acts for his friend's sake, and sacrifices his own interest.

But the facts clash with these arguments, and this is not surprising. For men say that one ought to love best one's friend, and a man's best friend is one who wishes well to the object of his wish for his sake, even if no one is to know of it; and these attributes are found most of all in a man's attitude towards himself, and so are all the other attributes by which a friend is defined; for, as we have said, it is from this relation that all the characteristics of friendship have extended to our neighbours. All the proverbs, too, agree with this, e.g. 'a single soul,' and 'what friends have is common property,' and 'friendship is equality,' and 'charity begins at home'; for all these marks will be found most in a man's relation to himself; he is his own best friend and therefore ought to love himself best. It is therefore a reasonable question, which of the two views we should follow; for both are plausible.

Perhaps we ought to mark off such arguments from each other and determine how far and in what respects each view is right. Now if we grasp the sense in which each school uses the phrase 'lover of self,' the truth may become evident. Those who use the term as one of reproach ascribe self-love to people who assign to themselves the greater share of wealth, honours, and bodily pleasures; for these are what most people desire, and busy themselves about as though they were the best of all things, which is the reason, too, why they become objects of competition. So those who are grasping with regard to these things gratify their appetites and in general their feelings and the irrational element of the soul; and most men are of this nature (which is the reason why the epithet has come to be used as it is—it takes its meaning from the prevailing type of self-love, which is a bad one); it is just, therefore, that men who are lovers of self in this way are reproached for being so. That it is those who give themselves the preference in regard to objects of this sort that most people usually call lovers of self is plain; for if a man were always anxious that he himself, above all things, should act justly, temperately, or in accordance with any other of the virtues, and in general were always to try to secure for himself the honourable course, no one will call such a man a lover of self or blame him.

But such a man would seem more than the other a lover of self; at all events he assigns to himself the things that are noblest and best, and gratifies the most authoritative element in himself and in all things obeys this; and just as a city or any other systematic whole is most properly identified with the most authoritative element in it, so is a man; and therefore the man who loves this and gratifies it is most of all a lover of self. Besides, a man is said to have or not to have self-control according as his reason has or has not the control, on the assumption that this is the man himself; and the things men have done on a rational principle are thought most properly their own acts and voluntary acts. That this is the man himself, then, or is so more than anything else, is plain, and also that the good man loves most this part of him. Whence it follows that he is most truly a lover of self, of another type than that which is a matter of reproach, and as different from that as living according to a rational principle is from living as passion dictates, and desiring what is noble from desiring what seems advantageous. Those, then, who busy themselves in an exceptional degree with noble actions all men approve and praise; and if *all* were to strive towards what is noble and strain every nerve to do the noblest deeds, everything would be as it should be for the common weal, and every one would secure for himself the goods that are greatest, since virtue is the greatest of goods.

Therefore the good man should be a lover of self (for he will both himself profit by doing noble acts, and will benefit his fellows), but the wicked man should not; for he will hurt both himself and his neighbours, following as he does evil passions. For the wicked man, what he does clashes with what he ought to do, but what the good man ought to do he does; for reason in each of its possessors chooses what is best for itself, and the good man obeys his reason. It is true of the good man too that he does many acts for the sake of his friends and his country, and if necessary dies for them; for he will throw away both wealth and honours and in general the goods that are objects of competition, gaining for himself nobility; since he would prefer a short period of intense pleasure to a long one of mild enjoyment, a twelve-month of noble life to many years of humdrum existence, and one great and noble action to many trivial ones. Now those who die for others doubtless attain this result; it is therefore a great prize that they choose for themselves. They will throw away wealth too on condition that their friends will gain more; for while a man's friend gains wealth he himself achieves nobility; he is therefore assigning the greater good to himself. The same too is true of honour and office; all these things he will sacrifice to his friend; for this is noble and laudable for himself. Rightly then is he thought to be good, since he chooses nobility before all else. But he may even give up actions to his friend; it may be nobler to become the cause of his friend's acting than to act himself. In all the actions, therefore, that men are praised for, the good man is seen to assign to himself the greater share in what is noble. In this sense, then, as has been said, a man should be a lover of self; but in the sense in which most men are so, he ought not.   (1168a28–1169b2)

For Aristotle, then, a person's relationship with his or her friend is built upon that person's relationship with himself or herself. In truly loving oneself, one seeks what is good and noble for oneself, and that implies seeking what is good and noble for others, especially for one's friend. One would be justified in saying that, for Aristotle, one's friend is in fact an *alter ego*.

Although this overview of Aristotle's view of *philia* (friendship or love) is brief, it is sufficient to show that the focus of his discussion of love is not Plato's abstract, timeless form of beauty, but rather the concrete, temporal, multifaceted relationship of friendship. While we might find his emphasis on the personal relationships in this world of change and struggle to be welcome, nevertheless some of us might find a number of features in his discussion troublesome. For example, is his notion of perfect friendship an elitist view that limits perfect friendship to but a few members of society? Does not his view of the friendship between a husband and a wife suggest a male dominance with a subordination of women that many of us would find objectionable today? Furthermore, while his definition of *philia* in *Rhetoric* seems to be strongly altruistic and other-centered, nevertheless his discussion of the three kinds of friendship in *Nicomachean Ethics* seems to involve a distinct egoistic emphasis. Is that consistent? Or does *Nicomachean Ethics* present a more realistic blend of the altruistic and egoistic tendencies that are at work in any human loving relationship? Finally, what about a person's loving someone who is not a source of pleasure for that person, not a bundle of utilities for that person, and not a paragon of virtue for anyone? That is to say, what about loving someone simply for their own sake in the sense of loving them not for their attractiveness but simply for their inherent humanity with its potentiality for goodness and nobility? To this final question Aristotle's answer might go something like this: Because friendship is based on the three things that are lovable (namely, pleasure, utility, and virtue), where none of these is present in a person, that person is unlovable and cannot be looked upon as a friend. A radically different answer, however, would be given by the biblical tradition in which love for those who are "unlovable" in the Aristotelian sense is a major emphasis. To a consideration of that tradition we now turn.

BIBLICAL VIEWS: HEBRAIC
Hosea

The Hebrew scriptures have a rich variety of passages that portray sex and love, ranging from the story of love and betrayal in the case of Samson and Delilah (Judges 16:4–22) to the account of adultery and murder in the case of King David and Bathsheba (2 Samuel 11:1–27). The story we have selected from the Hebrew scriptures to display the biblical view of love is also a tale of love, marriage, and betrayal. It is the story of the prophet Hosea and his adulterous wife, Gomer. We have chosen it because the author of the story, presumably Hosea, sees in his domestic relationship a microcosm of Israel's relationship to God, and at the heart of both relationships is a distinctively biblical love that has come to be called agapaic. Before we explore the nature of this love through an examination Hosea's story, it is necessary to comment briefly on the overall human drama depicted in the Bible that forms the background for Hosea's interpretation of his marriage and love.

Although the Hebrew Bible is a minilibrary of thirty-nine different books, and although it was written over the course of more than five centuries, those thirty-nine books seem to contain a unifying story. It is a story that chronicles the origin and development of the nation of Israel, but not simply as the account of the exploits of kings and queens, the fury of clashing armies, the rewards of military victory, and the agonies of defeat. Infused throughout this tale of political and socioeconomic development is the theme that God is working in the midst of Israel's rise as a nation to accomplish a special purpose. That purpose, seldom seen by kings but frequently grasped by prophets, seems to be the creation of a human community where God is honored, neighbors are loved, justice is present, and *shalom* (peace) covers the land like the waters cover the sea. To accomplish that purpose God selected the children of Israel to be his servant.

As the biblical narrative unfolds, we are told that Abraham was summoned by God to leave his homeland in Mesopotamia and to journey to a promised land where God would fashion his descendants into a great nation through whom all the families of earth would be blessed. Accordingly, around 1750 B.C. Abraham set out in search of the promised land, which turned out to be Canaan, a rather narrow strip of land stretching along the Mediterranean Sea from Mt. Lebanon in the north to the Negeb Desert in the south. There Abraham settled, as did his son Isaac, his grandson Jacob (also referred to as "Israel"), and their descendants, until a famine drove Jacob and his family southward into Egypt in search of food. The children of Israel flourished in Egypt until the Pharaoh enslaved them to serve as laborers in his vast building projects. Their bondage was harsh, and they cried out to the God of their fathers (Abraham, Isaac, and Jacob) to deliver them from their suffering. We are told that God in response summoned Moses to mastermind their escape, their Exodus from Egypt, around 1290 B.C. Their goal was to return to the land of Canaan, the land of their ancestors, a land flowing with milk and honey. Entry into Canaan, however, was blocked by the current inhabitants, and the Israelites were forced to wander in the desert for many years before they were able to effect a successful invasion. While in the desert, Moses brought them to the foot of Mt. Sinai where he supervised the Israelites as they entered into a Covenant with their God, Yahweh. In the ceremony at Mt. Sinai, Yahweh told the Israelites that he had selected them for a special purpose and had brought them, as it were, "on eagles' wings" out of Egypt. Yahweh offered them the opportunity to be his "kingdom of priests," his "holy nation," through whom he would achieve his divine purposes. Yahweh would dwell among his people with the benefits of security and prosperity that would accompany his presence. On their part, the Israelites were summoned to unwavering allegiance to Yahweh and unfaltering obedience to his commandments (classically summarized in the Decalogue or Ten Commandments).

Moses, however, died before the Israelites gained access to Canaan. The task of guiding them into Canaan fell on the shoulders of Joshua, an able military leader, who engineered the establishment of settlements among the inhabitants of Canaan. For many years the Israelites were unable to neutralize the constant military threat posed by the indigenous Canaanites. In addition, Canaanite polytheistic religion with its emphasis on sexual fertility rites represented an attractive alternative to the Israelite faith with its exclusive worship of Yahweh and obedience to his moral commands. While the Canaanite military threat was gradually reduced by the increasing Israelite military prowess especially evident in the establishment of the Davidic monarchy around 1000 B.C., the challenge from Canaanite religion remained an appealing and powerful option for centuries. Under King David and his son Solomon, the nation reached its zenith of power and influence. However, the political ineptitude of Solomon's son, Rehoboam, led to the splitting of David's domain into the northern kingdom of Israel with its capital in Samaria and the southern kingdom of Judah with its capital in Jerusalem.

In both the northern and southern kingdoms the children of Israel vacillated in their devotion to Yahweh and the Mosaic Covenant. In times of prosperity many would forget the God of the Exodus and ignore the ethical demands laid upon the children of Israel by the Covenant. Yahweh was shunted aside in favor of the Canaanite fertility gods (the Baalim), and love and justice were buried in materialistic greed. Prophets in both the north and the south declared divine judgment upon this apostasy and immorality. When adversity would strike, the Israelites would frequently repent and call upon Yahweh to deliver them from their current misfortunes even as he had delivered their ancestors from bondage in Egypt so long ago. As infidelity to the Mosaic Covenant became more entrenched among the Israelites, prophetic voices became more strident. In the 8th century B.C. Amos and Hosea in the north and Isaiah and Micah in the south declared the impending judgment of Yahweh upon his people. That judgment, we are told, was exacted by the brutal Assyrian armies that annihilated the northern kingdom in 722 B.C. and severely punished the southern kingdom. Apostasy and immorality continued, however, in the southern kingdom and Hebrew prophets again warned of divine judgment. This time the tool of God's wrath was the Babylonian army, which destroyed Jerusalem in 586 B.C. and carried the leading citizens of Judah into exile in Babylon. Babylon, in turn, was conquered by Cyrus the Great, king of Persia, who issued an edict in 538 B.C. allowing the exiled Jews to return to Jerusalem to rebuild their city and temple. From this time forth, the children of Israel gave unyielding loyalty to Yahweh and to the Mosaic Covenant.

That the Jewish faith did not disappear with the destruction of Jerusalem and the subsequent exile in Babylon is due in no small measure to the fact that the great Hebrew prophets not only declared doom and destruction upon generation after generation of unfaithful people, but they also proclaimed a message of hope rooted in the firm belief that while Yahweh the Lord of creation and history could use kings and armies to shape his people, he would never let those forces of destruction completely annihilate his people because that would mean the defeat of Yahweh himself. Such a defeat was incommensurable with the prophetic vision.

With this background in mind, we can now turn to the distinctive prophetic message that Hosea declared to the northern kingdom of Israel around 745 B.C., only two decades before the Assyrian armies rolled over that kingdom like a tidal wave and washed it away forever.

Although Hosea is one of the most difficult biblical texts to interpret because of its mixture of poetry and prose patched together with glaring inconsistencies and puzzling metaphors, the parallel between Hosea's marriage and the "marriage" or covenant between Yahweh and his people is strikingly clear. Hosea married a woman named Gomer who proved to be unfaithful. Scholars differ on whether she was a wanton woman before he married her or whether she became so later. The important point is that their marriage was rocked by an infidelity that mirrored the unfaithfulness of the children of Israel to Yahweh. Hosea gave his children names that declared God's judgment on the sins of Israel. He named their firstborn, a son, "Jezreel" to declare that even as Jehu had established his rule over Israel by means of a bloody coup in the Valley of Jezreel, so his current descendants sitting on the throne would perish in that same Valley. Their second child, a little girl, was named "Lo-ruhamah" (meaning "not pitied") to symbolize the fact that God's pity for Israel was now exhausted and that devastating judgment was on the horizon. Their third child, another son, was named "Lo-ammi" (meaning "not my people"), which affirmed the fact that the covenant bond between Yahweh and his people had been totally shattered. Here are the words of Hosea:

THIS IS THE BEGINNING OF THE LORD'S message by Hosea. He said, Go, take a wanton for your wife and get children of her wantonness; for like a wanton this land is unfaithful to the LORD. So he went and took Gomer, a worthless woman; and she conceived and bore him a son. And the LORD said to him,

> Call him Jezreel, for in a little while
> I will punish the line of Jehu for the
>   blood shed in Jezreel
>   and put an end to the kingdom of
>   Israel.
>   On that day
> I will break Israel's bow in the Vale
>   of Jezreel.

She conceived again and bore a daughter, and the LORD said to him,

> Call her Lo-ruhamah;
> for I will never again show love to
>   Israel,
>   never again forgive them.

After weaning Lo-ruhamah, she conceived and bore a son; and the LORD said,

> Call him Lo-ammi;
>   for you are not my people,
> and I will not be your God.

(Hosea 1:2–9)

Hosea begs his children to plead with their mother to abandon her lovers:

> Plead my cause with your mother;
> is she not my wife and I her
>   husband?
> Plead with her to forswear those
>   wanton looks,
> to banish the lovers from her bosom.
>   Or I will strip her and expose her
>   naked as the day she was born;
> I will make her bare as the wilderness,

> parched as the desert,
> and leave her to die of thirst.
>   I will show no love for her
>   children;
> they are the offspring of
>   wantonness,
> and their mother is a wanton.

(Hosea 2:2–5)

Neither the entreaties of Hosea nor the pleading of his children are able to convince Gomer to give up her wanton ways, and she apparently leaves home in pursuit of her lovers. The next view we are given of Hosea's troubled marriage is a scene in which he buys back his unfaithful wife for fifteen pieces of silver and a quantity of barley and wine. Presumably he is compensating either a paramour for the loss of his mistress or a master for the loss of his slave. Hosea is determined to bring Gomer home in order to rescue her from her wantonness and perhaps to win back for his children a mother and for himself a wife:

The LORD said to me,

Go again and love a woman
   loved by another man, an adultress,
and love her as I, the LORD, love
   the Israelites
although they resort to other gods
   and love the raisin-cakes offered to
     their idols.

So I got her back for fifteen pieces of silver, a homer of barley and a measure of wine; and I said to her,

Many a long day you shall live in
   my house
   and not play the wanton,
and have no intercourse with a man,
   nor I with you.

(Hosea 3:1–3)

Perhaps Hosea reasoned that if his love for Gomer transcended her infidelity, then God's love for his people would be just as strong, if not stronger, than his. If so, would not Yahweh always be true to the covenant even though his people forsook him one generation after another? Or perhaps Hosea reasoned in the opposite direction. Did Hosea discern a strength in God's love for his people that became a model for his own relationship to his unfaithful wife? Regardless of which relationship was the model for the other, the parallel between the two is what is important because both relationships reveal the kind of love that continues to love even when the loved one becomes unlovely.

Listen to the agonizing words of betrayed love that Hosea puts in the mouth of Yahweh, a God who judges but refuses to give up on his unfaithful people. In the passages below, Hosea adds to the metaphor of betrayed marital love the metaphor of parental love to characterize Yahweh's love for Israel. Hosea uses the name "Ephraim," one of the major northern tribes, to refer to the northern kingdom of Israel:

O Ephraim, how shall I deal with
   you?
How shall I deal with you, Judah?
Your loyalty to me is like the
   morning mist,
like dew that vanishes early.
Therefore have I lashed you through
   the prophets
   and torn you to shreds with my
     words;
loyalty is my desire, not sacrifice,
   not whole-offerings but the
     knowledge of God.

(Hosea 6:4–6)

When Israel was a boy, I loved
   him;
I called my son out of Egypt;

but the more I called, the further
   they went from me;
  they must needs sacrifice to the
    Baalim
    and burn offerings before carved
     images.
It was I who taught Ephraim to
   walk,
   I who had taken them in my
    arms;
but they did not know that I harnessed
   them in leading-strings
and led them with bonds of love—
that I had lifted them like a little
   child to my cheek,
that I have bent down to feed them.
Back they shall go to Egypt,
the Assyrian shall be their king;

for they have refused to return
to me.
The sword shall be swung over
their blood-spattered altars
and put an end to the prattling
priests
and devour my people in return
for all their schemings,
bent on rebellion as they are.
Though they call on their high god,
even when he will not reinstate
them.
How can I give you up, Ephraim,
how surrender you, Israel?
How can I make you like Admah
or treat you as Zeboyim?
My heart is changed within me,
my remorse kindles already.

I will not let loose my fury,
I will not turn round and destroy
Ephraim;
for I am God and not a man,
the Holy One in your midst;
I will not come with threats like a
roaring lion.
No; when I roar, I who am God,
my sons shall come with speed out
of the west.
They will come speedily, flying like
birds out of Egypt,
like pigeons from Assyria,
and I will settle them in their
own homes.
This is the very word of the LORD.
(Hosea 11:1–11)

Through his metaphors of marital and parental love, Hosea was the first to identify love as Yahweh's motive for selecting Israel to be his covenant people. Set within the context of the Covenant, which was rooted in a divine initiative that chose Israel without regard for Israel's merits, this love took on an unconditional aspect. Yahweh's love for Israel did not originate in, and its continuance did not depend on, Israel's lovableness. Yahweh's love seems to have been rooted in his purpose, which involved employing Israel as his servant to create a righteous human community. Implicit in the unconditional nature of this love, both Hosea's and Yahweh's, is the assumption that such love will eventually transform the loved one from a state of unfaithfulness to a new fidelity. This unconditional love with transforming possibilities became a major theme in the Christian view of love depicted in the New Testament. To a consideration of that view we now turn.

BIBLICAL VIEWS: CHRISTIAN
St. Paul

Christianity was born within Judaism. The God of Jesus and his early disciples was the God of Abraham, Isaac, and Jacob, the God of the Mosaic Covenant. The Bible of Jesus and his followers was the Hebrew Bible, which included the writings of Hosea and the other prophets. It is not surprising, therefore, that the early Christians interpreted the life of Jesus within the context of Yahweh's purposeful action and with the aid of themes already articulated in the Hebrew Bible. One of the major biblical themes used by the early Christians was divine love. Jesus was portrayed as being sent by divine love to summon humankind to turn from its religious apostasy and moral decay, to accept God's forgiving love, and to pursue a life of righteousness, love, and justice. Jesus was presented as an incarnate model of divine love that all his disciples were called to follow. As God loved humankind through Jesus the Christ, so humans were challenged to love each other. And the kind of love envisaged was the unconditional love that harbors transforming possibilities about which Hosea spoke. This kind of love in modern time has come to be referred to as "agapaic," from the Greek words for love (the verb *agapan,* and the noun *agape*) that were widely used in the Greek language current at the time of Jesus.

There are many passages from the Christian scriptures that could be selected to display agapaic love. Some of them focus on the agapaic deeds of Jesus such as his washing the disciples' feet at the Last Supper. Others offer commentary on the nature of love, as in the Epistles of John. We have chosen for review a classic exposition of agapaic love found in the thirteenth chapter of Paul's first letter to the church at Corinth. Before examining the Pauline text let us look briefly at the historical setting in which Paul wrote this letter.

Following the crucifixion of Jesus, his followers experienced certain events which led them to believe that Jesus had been raised from the dead by God and that this risen Christ, prior to his ascension into heaven, had commissioned them to go into all parts of the world to proclaim the message that the life, death, and resurrection of Jesus were all part of Yahweh's longstanding purpose to create a human community where God is honored, neighbors are loved, justice is present, and *shalom* (peace) covers the land like the waters cover the sea. Such a community was called the reign or kingdom of God. The early Christians apparently believed that God had inaugurated his reign with the ministry of Jesus the Christ and that the return of the risen Christ was imminent, at which time God's kingly rule would be established triumphantly over all humankind. With an understandable sense of urgency, the early Christians shared their views with their fellow Jews. While some of their compatriots were convinced by their message, others were unconvinced, and still others began to persecute them. One of the zealous persecutors of these early Jewish Christians was a learned young Jew with Roman citizenship, Saul of Tarsus. Saul, however, following a dramatic spiritual experience en route to persecute the Christians in Damascus, was converted to Christianity. Subsequently, his name was changed to Paul and he became the most famous of early Christian missionaries, carrying the message of God's love for humankind to the Gentile world. From city to city throughout the Mediterranean world Paul went preaching his message, converting Jews and Gentiles to the faith, and gathering the new converts in each city into a worshipping community called a church. To maintain contact with the churches he had founded and to offer them guidance as he moved from city to city, Paul initiated a rather extensive letter writing campaign. His letters, delivered in person by his aides, addressed specific issues that were relevant to a particular person, church, or group of churches in a region. Thirteen letters ascribed to Paul are included among the twenty-seven literary pieces that make up the New Testament.

Corinth, the location of the church to which Paul addressed the letter we are considering, was a Greek city of early origin that stretches back at least a thousand years prior to Paul's establishing a church there. Located strategically on an isthmus that separated the harbor at Lechaeum on the Corinthian Gulf from the harbor at Cenchreae on the Saronic Gulf, Corinth became an important commercial center. It was probably the capital of the Roman province of Achaia, which would further enhance its importance. In addition, Corinth was famous for its courtesans, evidenced by the Greek verb *Korinthiazomai,* meaning "to practice fornication." It appears that Corinth was not only a center of commerce and government but also a veritable "Sin City" of ancient Greece.

Given the Corinthian environment, it is not surprising that in his letter Paul had to deal with such issues as Christians who were involved in bitter factional struggles, who were permitting a sexual practice (namely, a man involved in a relationship with his stepmother) that was disallowed by both Roman and Jewish law, who were hauling each other before local magistrates to settle disputes, and who were wondering what implications their Christian faith had for sex, celibacy, marriage, and commercial food that had been consecrated to pagan deities. Having addressed all of these concerns, Paul focused his attention on the matter of "spiritual gifts." Apparently the Corinthian Christians were debating the relative importance of their diverse capacities. What is the appropriate pecking order for prophets, teachers, miracle-workers, healers, counselors, ecstatic speakers, etc.? Who is superior to whom? Which spiritual gift should be most highly prized? In response to such questions, Paul pens his famous "hymn" on Christian agapaic love. Here are Paul's words:

> Now you are Christ's body, and each of you a limb or organ of it. Within our community God has appointed, in the first place apostles, in the second place prophets, thirdly teachers; then miracle-workers, then those who have gifts of healing, or ability to help others or power to guide them, or the gift of ecstatic utterance of various kinds. Are all apostles? all prophets? all teachers? Do all work miracles? Have all gifts of healing? Do all speak in tongues of ecstasy? Can all interpret them? The higher gifts are those you should aim at.
>
> And now I will show you the best way of all.
>
> I may speak in tongues of men or of angels, but if I am without love, I am a sounding gong or a clanging cymbal. I may have the gift of prophecy, and know every hidden truth; I may have faith strong enough to move mountains; but if I have no love, I am nothing. I may dole out all I possess, or even give my body to be burnt, but if I have no love, I am none the better.
>
> Love is patient; love is kind and envies no one. Love is never boastful, nor conceited, nor rude; never selfish, not quick to take offence. Love keeps no score of wrongs; does not gloat over other men's sins, but delights in the truth. There is nothing love cannot face; there is no limit to its faith, its hope, and its endurance.
>
> Love will never come to an end. Are there prophets? their work will be over. Are there tongues of ecstasy? they will cease. Is there knowledge? it will vanish away; for our knowledge and our prophecy alike are partial, and the partial vanishes when wholeness comes. When I was a child, my speech, my outlook, and my thoughts were all childish. When I grew up, I had finished with childish things. Now we see only puzzling reflections in a mirror, but then we shall see face to face. My knowledge now is partial; then it will be whole, like God's knowledge of me. In a word, there are three things that last for ever: faith, hope, and love; but the greatest of them all is love.

(I Corinthians 12:27–13:13)

In understanding Paul's view of agapaic love it is important to note that Paul was a Christocentric thinker, as were most if not all of the New Testament writers. That means that the controlling center of his theological thinking was Jesus the Christ, who was regarded as the agapaic love of God in human flesh, a loving person who did not stop loving those who were trying to destroy him on a cross. Accordingly, Paul's challenge to the Corinthian Christians to exemplify love is in effect a summons to them to model themselves after Jesus the Christ.

Having held up the ideal of agapaic love to the Corinthians, Paul goes on to discuss the practice of ecstatic utterance (or speaking in tongues) as well as the matter of life after death in the light of the resurrection of Jesus the Christ. He ends his letter with the following greeting:

> This greeting is in my own hand—PAUL.
> If anyone does not love the Lord, let him be outcast.
> *Marana tha*—Come, O Lord!
> The grace of the Lord Jesus Christ be with you.
> My love to you all in Christ Jesus. Amen.

(I Corinthians 16:21–24)

Such, then, is agapaic love in the biblical tradition: love that is unconditional in the sense that its origin and continuance does not depend on the lovableness of the person loved; love that can transform the person loved; love that is exemplified in God's relationship to humankind and that humans are summoned to display toward each other. Unlike Platonic *eros,* this agapaic love is "down-to-earth" and pragmatic. And unlike Aristotelian friendship, this agapaic love does not depend on the lovableness of the loved one.

While presenting a lofty ideal, agapaic love does elicit a number of troublesome questions. Is unconditional love perhaps an impossible ideal for human beings? It might be acceptable to think of God as exhibiting such love, but can human beings realistically be expected to love equally (an implication of the unconditional nature of that love) the Adolph Hitlers and the Mother Theresas of the world? Then, too, if agapaic love is an impossible ideal, is it not likely to foster deep psychological problems in those who attempt to achieve the impossible? Furthermore, is Nietzsche correct in suggesting that love which does not evoke love in response is a weak and degrading love? Suppose the agapaist replied that it is in the very nature of an ideal to be an impossible possibility. That is to say, an ideal is impossible in the sense that it cannot be completely achieved; but it is possible in the sense that it can serve as a guide for human action. Would that reply answer adequately our questions? Are there additional questions that need to be put to the agapaist?

MEDIEVAL VIEWS
Augustine

So far we have reviewed representatives of the Greek and biblical traditions. In turning now to two major thinkers of the medieval tradition, Augustine and Aquinas, we encounter blends of Greek and biblical thought. Both of these thinkers tried to interpret, commend, and defend Christian doctrine with the aid of Greek philosophy. Augustine drew support from Platonic ideas inasmuch as Neoplatonism was prominent during his day. Aquinas, several centuries later, utilized Aristotelian themes because a revival of interest in Aristotelianism was taking place in his day. Given this synthesizing of Greek and biblical themes, it is not surprising that the views of sex and love championed by Augustine and Aquinas exhibit the blending of these two traditions. Let us consider first the Augustinian synthesis.

Augustine's intellectual odyssey is probably best described using his own comment that human hearts "are restless until they rest in God." For Augustine, love's desire is not satisfied until the object of that love is God. Born in A.D. 354 in the North African village of Tagaste, Augustine wandered restlessly from one philosophical school to another until he arrived at Christianity where his intellectual quest came to "rest." In his journey to Christianity, the youthful Augustine was attracted by the theater in Carthage with its poetry and

The selections from Augustine's "On the Morals of the Catholic Church," Chapters III, VI, and XV are from *The Basic Writings of St. Augustine,* translated by R. Stothert. Copyright © 1948 by Random House, Inc. Reprinted by permission of Random House, Inc. The selections from Augustine's *The City of God* Book XIV, Chapters XVI, XVIII, XXI, XXVI, and XXVIII are from *The City of God,* translated by Marcus Dods. Copyright © 1950 by Random House, Inc. Reprinted by permission of Random House, Inc. The selections from Augustine's *The Good of Marriage,* Chapters 3, 6, 8, 9 were translated by Charles T. Wilcox and are taken from *The Father of the Church,* Vol. 15 (New York: Fathers of the Church, Inc., 1955). Used by permission of Catholic University of America Press.

love affairs. He took on a mistress who, when he was eighteen years of age, bore him a son, whom he named Adeodatus ("Given of God").

His passion for the theater was transferred to philosophy when he read Cicero's *Hortensius* (a book now lost). His thirst for philosophic wisdom was temporarily satisfied by the Manichaean world view. Founded in the third century A.D. by the prophet-martyr Manes, Manichaeism blended strands of Zoroastrianism, Greek philosophy, and Christian doctrine into a dualistic world view that captivated the young Augustine. The Manichaeans taught that there were two major deities: the Good God of Light and the Evil God of Darkness. These gods and their respective cohorts had been struggling with each other for aeons, and their conflict eventually spilled over into the creation of this world where elements of light and darkness continued to struggle with each other. Human beings became important battle fields of these cosmic forces. In each human the forces of good (usually identified with spirit and the life of the intellect) were locked in a battle for supremacy with the forces of evil (usually identified with matter and bodily drives). The Manichaeans called upon humans to bring their bodily passions under the control of their intellects and thereby contribute to the victory of the Good God of Light over the Evil God of Darkness. Gradually, Augustine not only became disillusioned with Manichaean professions of moral purity, but he also found their dualism to be philosophically untenable. While Augustine rejected Manichaeism as he moved forward in his intellectual journey, he seems to have carried with him the Manichaean depreciation of the body in favor of the spirit, a depreciation that was further nourished by his study of Neoplatonism.

From Carthage, Augustine went to Rome where he flirted momentarily with skepticism, and then to Milan where he was introduced to the works of Plotinus, a central figure in the revival of Platonism during the third century A.D., whose philosophy was far more coherent, consistent, and compelling than that of the Manichaeans. Among other things, Plotinus taught that a transcendent immaterial source called "the One" or "the Good" (some later Neoplatonists referred to the One as "God") produced a series of beings that are progressively less unified, weaker, and more imperfect than the One. Humankind is one of the series that emanated from the One. Humans are intelligent spirits temporarily housed in earthly bodies. Their chief goal is to find their way back to the divine world from which they originally proceeded, a search whose culmination is a mystical union of the human with the One. This union with the One is achievable here and now if a person yields to the driving power of love, to the urge for perfect union with the One that the One placed in all of us. Reminiscent of Plato's ladder of love, Plotinus declared that through meditation on the beauty of objects in this lower world of nature and art, plus an appropriate measure of moral discipline, humans can awaken to their higher natures and return to the true goal of their desires: union with the One, the Good. Here, again, is a depreciation of the material world in favor of a higher spiritual world, a depreciation that Augustine seems to have carried with him into the synthesis he eventually constructed.

As he explored one philosophical perspective after another, the Christian faith was always in the background inasmuch as Augustine's mother, a devout Christian, was constantly praying for her son and repeatedly urging him to forsake his mistresses and receive baptism into the Christian faith. The Christian perspective moved into the foreground while Augustine was in Milan. There, influenced by Ambrose (the Bishop of Milan) and others, Augustine explored Neoplatonism and the Christian faith concurrently. Augustine soon discovered that the Christian faith he had scorned while a Manichaean was a mere caricature of the real faith. Moreover, he learned that Platonic philosophy and Christian doctrine were remarkably compatible. Augustine's intellectual quest was being satisfied by what he saw as the reasonableness of Christianity. The more difficult struggle was at the level of the will.

For years Augustine had been charmed by the sexual pleasures of his mistresses. At one point in his younger days he had prayed, "Give me chastity and continency, only not yet." At Milan the monastic ideal being advocated by Ambrose stood in sharp contrast to the life of sexual pleasure Augustine so enjoyed. In a remarkable conversion scene reported by Augustine in the *Confessions* (his lengthy autobiography), we are told how he finally gained the strength to sever his ties with his mistresses and to prepare himself for Christian baptism. Following his conversion, in one treatise after another Augustine worked out his synthesis of biblical and Neoplatonic themes. Augustine died in A.D. 430, having served as the Bishop of Hippo in his native north Africa for thirty-five years.

Central to Augustine's synthesis was his view of love (*amor*). For Augustine, all human love is desire for happiness, a quest for one's self-fulfilling good. Moreover, as a person loves, so he or she becomes. If one's love is fixed upon mutable, changeable things, then one's love changes as those things change. Ultimately, such love, the lover and the loved thing, perish. If, however, one's love is fixed upon that which is immutable, changeless, and eternal (namely, God), then one's love can endure forever. For Augustine, sin is simply misdirected love: love directed toward created goods instead of toward the Creator of those goods. In accordance with the focus of their love, humankind is divided into two cities: the Earthly City and the Heavenly City. The first City is populated by humans whose love is directed toward various good but mutable things in this world, especially toward the self. Their love (*amor*) is combined with pride (*superbia*) inasmuch as they are attempting to achieve happiness in a self-sufficient way, relying on their own resourcefulness. Such love, which Augustine labels *cupiditas* (cupidity or avarice), is self-defeating because it seeks permanent happiness through attachment to impermanent things. The second City is populated by those who love God preeminently and primarily. Their love (*amor*) is combined with humility (*humilitas*) because with no pretense of self-sufficiency they are relying upon God's love manifest in Christ to be the ground of their happiness. Such love, which satisfies permanently the human thirst for happiness, Augustine calls *caritas* (charity). Throughout his treatises, Augustine held firmly to the belief that all things, insofar as they have being at all, are good because they have been created by a good God. Evil arises in God's creation only when intelligent beings of their own free will direct their love away from God toward the created goods of this world.

Let us now turn to Augustine's comments on happiness, which involves possessing and loving one's chief good, namely, God:

> How then, according to reason, ought man to live? We all certainly desire to live happily; and there is no human being but assents to this statement almost before it is made. But the title happy cannot, in my opinion, belong either to him who has not what he loves, whatever it may be, or to him who has what he loves if it is hurtful, or to him who does not love what he has, although it is good in perfection. For one who seeks what he cannot obtain suffers torture, and one who has got what is not desirable is cheated, and one who does not seek for what is worth seeking for is diseased. Now in all these cases the mind cannot but be unhappy, and happiness and unhappiness cannot reside at the same time in one man; so in none of these cases can the man be happy. I find, then, a fourth case, where the happy life exists—when that which is man's chief good is both loved and possessed. For what do we call enjoyment but having at hand the objects of love? And no one can be happy who does not enjoy what is man's chief good, nor is there any one who enjoys this who is not happy. We must then have at hand our chief good, if we think of living happily.
>
> (*On the Morals of the Catholic Church,* Chap. III)

Following after God is the desire of happiness; to reach God is happiness itself. We follow after God by loving Him; we reach Him, not by becoming entirely what He is, but in nearness to Him, and in wonderful and immaterial contact with Him, and in being inwardly illuminated and occupied by His truth and holiness. He is light itself; we get enlightenment from Him. The greatest commandment, therefore, which leads to happy life, and the first, is this: "Thou shalt love the Lord thy God with all thy heart, and soul, and mind." For to those who love the Lord all things issue in good. Hence Paul adds shortly after, "I am persuaded that neither death, nor life, nor angels, nor virtue, nor things present, nor things future, nor height, nor depth, nor any other creature, shall be able to separate us from the love of God, which is in Christ Jesus our Lord." If, then, to those who love God all things issue in good, and if, as no one doubts, the chief or perfect good is not only to be loved, but to be loved so that nothing shall be loved better, as is expressed in the words, "With all thy soul, with all thy heart, and with all thy mind," who, I ask, will not at once conclude, when these things are all settled and most surely believed, that our chief good which we must hasten to arrive at in preference to all other things is nothing else than God? And then, if nothing can separate us from His love, must not this be surer as well as better than any other good?

(*On the Morals of the Catholic Church,* Chap. XI)

As to virtue leading us to a happy life, I hold virtue to be nothing else than perfect love of God. For the fourfold division of virtue I regard as taken from four forms of love. For these four virtues (would that all felt their influence in their minds as they have their names in their mouths!), I should have no hesitation in defining them: that temperance is love giving itself entirely to that which is loved; fortitude is love readily bearing all things for the sake of the loved object; justice is love serving only the loved object, and therefore ruling rightly; prudence is love distinguishing with sagacity between what hinders it and what helps it. The object of this love is not anything, but only God, the chief good, the highest wisdom, the perfect harmony. So we may express the definition thus: that temperance is love keeping itself entire and incorrupt for God; fortitude is love bearing everything readily for the sake of God; justice is love serving God only, and therefore ruling well all else, as subject to man; prudence is love making a right distinction between what helps it towards God and what might hinder it.

(*On the Morals of the Catholic Church,* Chap. XV)

Instead of possessing and loving their chief good, humankind since the Fall of Adam and Eve has loved things instead of God. Human love has been misdirected, sinful. Yet some humans, with the aid of divine grace, have redirected their love to God. Thus, two cities can be discerned: one earthly, the other heavenly:

Accordingly, two cities have been formed by two loves: the earthly by the love of self, even to the contempt of God; the heavenly by the love of God, even to the contempt of self. The former, in a word, glories in itself, the latter in the Lord. For the one seeks glory from men; but the greatest glory of the other is God, the witness of conscience. The one lifts up its head in its own glory; the other says to its God, "Thou art my glory, and the lifter up of mine head." In the one, the princes and the nations it subdues are ruled by the love of ruling; in the other, the princes and the subjects serve one another in love, the latter obeying, while the former take thought for all. The one delights in its own strength, represented in the persons of its rulers; the other says to its God, "I will love Thee, O Lord, my strength."

(*The City of God,* Book XIV, Chap. XXVIII)

Misdirected love or sin corrupts all human relations, according to Augustine. Even the classic virtues of the Greek tradition were deemed by him to be nothing more than splendid vices apart from the appropriate love of God. Especially pertinent to the philosophy of sex and love is Augustine's claim that sexual intercourse was forever tainted by lust after the Fall of Adam and Eve in the Garden of Eden. First, Augustine describes the nature of lust:

> Although, therefore, lust may have many objects, yet when no object is specified, the word lust usually suggests to the mind the lustful excitement of the organs of generation. And thus lust not only takes possession of the whole body and outward members, but also makes itself felt within, and moves the whole man with a passion in which mental emotion is mingled with bodily appetite, so that the pleasure which results is the greatest of all bodily pleasures. So possessing indeed is this pleasure, that at the moment of time in which it is consummated, all mental activity is suspended. What friend of wisdom and holy joys, who being married, but knowing, as the apostle says, "how to possess his vessel in sanctification and honor, not in the disease of desire, as the Gentiles who know not God," would not prefer, if this were possible, to beget children without this lust, so that in this function of begetting offspring the members created for this purpose should not be stimulated by the heat of lust, but should be actuated by his volition, in the same way as his other members serve him for their respective ends? But even those who delight in this pleasure are not moved to it at their own will, whether they confine themselves to lawful or transgress to unlawful pleasures; but sometimes this lust importunes them in spite of themselves, and sometimes fails them when they desire to feel it, so that though lust rages in the mind, it stirs not in the body. Thus, strangely enough, this emotion not only fails to obey the legitimate desire to beget offspring, but also refuses to serve lascivious lust; and though it often opposes its whole combined energy to the soul that resists it, sometimes also it is divided against itself, and while it moves the soul, leaves the body unmoved.

> *(The City of God,* Book XIV, Chap. XVI)

Next, Augustine claims that shame attends all post-Fall sexual intercourse and is indicative of its tainted, lustful nature:

> Lust requires for its consummation darkness and secrecy; and this not only when unlawful intercourse is desired, but even such fornication as the earthly city has legalized. Where there is no fear of punishment, these permitted pleasures still shrink from the public eye. Even where provision is made for this lust, secrecy also is provided; and while lust found it easy to remove the prohibitions of law, shamelessness found it impossible to lay aside the veil of retirement. For even shameless men call this shameful; and though they love the pleasure, dare not display it. What! does not even conjugal intercourse, sanctioned as it is by law for the propagation of children, legitimate and honorable though it be, does it not seek retirement from every eye? Before the bridegroom fondles his bride, does he not exclude the attendants, and even the paranymphs, and such friends as the closest ties have admitted to the bridal chamber? The greatest master of Roman eloquence says, that all right actions wish to be set in the light, *i.e.,* desire to be known. This right action, however, has such a desire to be known, that yet it blushes to be seen. Who does not know what passes between husband and wife that children may be born? Is it not for this purpose that wives are married with such ceremony? And yet, when this well-understood act is gone about for the procreation of children, not even the children themselves, who may already have been born to them, are

suffered to be witnesses. This right action seeks the light, in so far as it seeks to be known, but yet dreads being seen. And why so, if not because that which is by nature fitting and decent is so done as to be accompanied with a shame-begetting penalty of sin?

(*The City of God,* Book XIV, Chap. XVIII)

. . . it was after sin that lust began. It was after sin that our nature, having lost the power it had over the whole body, but not having lost all shame, perceived, noticed, blushed at, and covered it.

(*The City of God,* Book XIV, Chap. XXI)

Nevertheless this lust, of which we at present speak, is the more shameful on this account, because the soul is therein neither master of itself, so as not to lust at all, nor of the body, so as to keep the members under the control of the will; for if they were thus ruled, there should be no shame. But now the soul is ashamed that the body, which by nature is inferior and subject to it, should resist its authority.

(*The City of God,* Book XIV, Chap. XXIII)

Notice that, for Augustine, the shamefulness of lust seems to reside in the fact that lust seizes control of the human being, dethroning the rational soul and allowing the inferior body to reign. Pre-Fall sexual intercourse for procreation, however, could have been free of lust. Augustine attempts to describe such lust-free sexual intercourse between Adam and Eve:

In Paradise, then, man lived as he desired so long as he desired what God had commanded. He lived in the enjoyment of God, and was good by God's goodness; he lived without any want, and had it in his power so to live eternally. He had food that he might not hunger, drink that he might not thirst, the tree of life that old age might not waste him. There was in his body no corruption, nor seed of corruption, which could produce in him any unpleasant sensation. He feared no inward disease, no outward accident. Soundest health blessed his body, absolute tranquility his soul. As in Paradise there was no excessive heat or cold, so its inhabitants were exempt from the vicissitudes of fear and desire. No sadness of any kind was there, nor any foolish joy; true gladness ceaselessly flowed from the presence of God, who was loved out of a pure heart, and a good conscience, and faith unfeigned. The honest love of husband and wife made a sure harmony between them. Body and spirit worked harmoniously together, and the commandment was kept without labor. No languor made their leisure wearisome; no sleepiness interrupted their desire to labor.

In such happy circumstances and general human well-being we should be far from suspecting that offspring could not have been begotten without the disease of lust, but those parts, like all the rest, would be set in motion at the command of the will; and without the seductive stimulus of passion, with calmness of mind and with no corrupting of the integrity of the body, the husband would lie upon the bosom of his wife. Nor ought we not to believe this because it cannot be proved by experiment. But rather, since no wild heat of passion would arouse those parts of the body, but a spontaneous power, according to the need, would be present, thus must we believe that the male semen could have been introduced into the womb of the wife with the integrity of the female genital organ being preserved, just as now, with that same integrity being safe, the menstrual flow of blood can be emitted from the womb of a virgin. To be sure, the seed could be introduced in the same way through which the menses can be emitted. In order that not the groans of labor-pain should relax the female organs for parturition, but rather the impulse of the fully developed foetus, thus not the eager desire of lust, but the normal exercise of the will, should join the male and female for breeding and conception.

(The City of God, Book XIV, Chap. XXVI)

Although lust is even present in marriage, Augustine considers marriage to be a good. Why? Here is his reply:

This does not seem to me to be a good solely because of the procreation of children, but also because of the natural companionship between the two sexes. Otherwise, we could not speak of marriage in the case of old people, especially if they had either lost their children or had begotten none at all. But, in a good marriage, although one of many years, even if the ardor of youths has cooled between man and woman, the order of charity still flourishes between husband and wife. They are better in proportion as they begin the earlier to refrain by mutual consent from sexual intercourse, not that it would afterwards happen of necessity that they would not be able to do what they wished, but that it would be a matter of praise that they had refused beforehand what they were able to do. If, then, there is observed that promise of respect and of services due to each other by either sex, even though both members weaken in health and become almost corpse-like, the chastity of souls rightly joined together continues the purer, the more it has been proved, and the more secure, the more it has been calmed.

Marriage has also this good, that carnal or youthful incontinence, even if it is bad, is turned to the honorable task of begetting children, so that marital intercourse makes something good out of the evil of lust. Finally, the concupiscence of the flesh, which parental affection tempers, is repressed and becomes inflamed more modestly. For a kind of dignity prevails when, as husband and wife they unite in the marriage act, they think of themselves as mother and father.

(The Good of Marriage, Chap. 3)

Notice in the above quotation that Augustine deems it praiseworthy if a married couple by mutual consent refrain from sexual intercourse while they still have sexual drives. Indeed, Augustine values celibacy above marriage and sexual intercourse. He writes,

For this reason it is a good to marry, since it is a good to beget children, to be the mother of a family; but it is better not to marry, since it is better for human society itself not to have need of marriage. For, such is the present state of the human race that not only some who do not check themselves are taken up with marriage, but many are wanton and given over to illicit intercourse. Since the good Creator draws good out of their evils, there is no lack of numerous progeny and an abundance of generation whence holy friendships might be sought out.

(The Good of Marriage, Chap. 9)

. . . marriage and continence are two goods, the second of which is better. . . . but freedom from all sexual intercourse is both an angelic ideal here, and remains forever.

(The Good of Marriage, Chap. 8)

Given what Augustine has already said about sexual intercourse and lust, it is not surprising that he finds sexual intercourse only for the sake of pleasure to be highly problematic, even within the bonds of marriage:

Furthermore, in the more immoderate demand of the carnal debt, which the Apostle enjoined on them not as a command but conceded as a favor, to have sexual intercourse even without the purpose of procreation, although evil habits impel them to such intercourse, marriage protects them from adultery and fornication. For this is not permitted because of the marriage, but because of the marriage it is pardoned. Therefore, married people owe each other not only the fidelity of sexual intercourse for the purpose of procreating children—and this is the first association of the human race in this mortal life—but also the mutual service, in a certain measure, of sustaining each other's weakness, for the avoidance of illicit intercourse, so that, even if perpetual continence is pleasing to one of them, he may not follow this urge except with the consent of the other. In this case, 'The wife has not authority over her body, but the husband; the husband likewise has not authority over his own body, but the wife.' So, let them not deny either to each other, what the man seeks from matrimony and the woman from her husband, not for the sake of having children but because of weakness and incontinence, lest in this way they fall into damnable seductions through the temptations of Satan because of the incontinence of both or of one of them.

In marriage, intercourse for the purpose of generation has no fault attached to it, but for the purpose of satisfying concupiscence, provided with a spouse, because of the marriage fidelity, it is a venial sin; adultery or fornication, however, is a mortal sin. And so, continence from all intercourse is certainly better than marital intercourse itself which takes place for the sake of begetting children.

(The Good of Marriage, Chap. 6)

Such, then, are Augustine's view on sex and love. No doubt he thought that he was articulating views that were consistent with the biblical tradition. Yet does he not seem to spiritualize the human love of God in Platonic fashion to the extent that concrete loving human relationships are depreciated? Furthermore, is not his elevating the spiritual soul above the material body with its passions and drives akin to the views of Manichaeism and Neoplatonism? Could he really mount a convincing case that the biblical tradition preferred celibacy to marriage and that it branded all sexual intercourse except for procreation as sinful? Here, too, is not Augustine closer to Manichaeism and Neoplatonism than to the biblical tradition? Or, to psychologize a little, is it perhaps the case that Augustine's views on sex and love reflect more his own tormented soul (caught between the celibacy of the monastic ideal and the joy of sex with his mistresses) than a sound interpretation of the biblical tradition?

Yet for generations to come Christendom looked at Augustine as a paradigm of piety and an authoritative interpreter and defender of biblical doctrine. In many respects that authority was not misplaced. Indeed, for example, his theodicy became a classic defence of God's omnipotence and goodness in the face of human suffering; his *Confessions* became a classic of devotional literature; his multivolume *The City of God* was a masterpiece of early Christian historical writing; and his criticism of skepticism foreshadowed almost verbatim the famous dictum "*Cogito, ergo sum*" formulated by Descartes more than a thousand years later. Impressive, to be sure! Yet his writings also contributed to the subordination of marriage compared with celibacy and to the depreciation of sexual activity that dominated the Church for centuries. His views on sex and love have survived in various Christian groups to the present day, views which have been subjected to severe criticism by Christian and non-Christian thinkers alike. Critics claim that his depreciation of the material body and human sexual drives is incompatible with the biblical view of the goodness of creation. Critics also see him as a classic advocate of a Puritanistic sexual ethic that stifles legitimate human drives and leads to diverse psychological problems. Can something be said in Augustine's defense?

Let us turn now to another medieval synthesis of Greek and biblical themes: the thought of Thomas Aquinas.

MEDIEVAL VIEWS
Aquinas

Eight centuries after the death of Augustine, Thomas Aquinas was born in A.D. 1225 in Roccasecca, near Naples, Italy. His father belonged to the Lombard nobility and his mother to Norman nobility. His paternal grandmother was the sister of Frederick Barbarossa. At the age of five, he was sent for education to the Benedictine monastery of Monte Cassino, and about ten years later to the University of Naples to complete his studies. While in Naples he became acquainted with a newly established monastic order, the Dominicans, and determined to join their ranks. In 1244 he received the habit of the Dominican order, an initiation strongly opposed by his mother. Whereas Augustine's mother would have been delighted by such religious seriousness in her son, Thomas's mother dispatched his brothers to rescue him from the Dominicans. His brothers succeeded in doing so and held him captive for more than a year in Roccasecca. At this time, we are told that his brothers introduced a beautiful young woman into the room where Thomas was sleeping in order to tempt him away from monasticism. Thomas, however, seized a flaming torch and drove the temptress from his cell. During his confinement Thomas observed the rites of his religious Order, converted his sister, and even softened the heart of his mother. When he eventually escaped he pursued advanced studies in theology in Paris and Cologne. At the age of thirty-one he was awarded the mastership in theology, and entered a career of teaching, writing, and controversy. Early in 1274 he was summoned by Pope Gregory X to the Council he had convoked at Lyons, but became ill on the journey and died in the monastery of Santa Maria at Fossanova in northern Italy.

Barely fifty years after Thomas's death, Pope John XXII, on July 18, 1323, canonized him, thereby recognizing the contribution his life and thought had made to Christendom. Five centuries later, the authoritative nature of St. Thomas's writings was firmly established when Pope Leo XIII in his encyclical letter *Aeterni Patris* (August 4, 1879) urged the teachers of the Roman Catholic Church to follow the example of St. Thomas Aquinas in their theologizing. Leo XIII's high praise for Aquinas was reiterated by subsequent prelates, and St. Thomas is widely regarded today in the Roman Catholic Church as the Angelic Doctor, the theologian par excellence. What he wrote, therefore, regarding sex and love so many years ago is enormously important on the contemporary scene.

The work from which the following selections have been taken is Aquinas's classic *Summa Theologica,* a massive, multivolume work that covers virtually every conceivable Christian doctrinal issue in exhaustive detail. With a thoroughgoing knowledge of the Bible as well as Aristotle and Augustine and countless other thinkers, Aquinas shaped his synthesis of Aristotelian and biblical themes. As you read the selections below, try to discern any Aristotelian and Augustinian influences that might be present. We have chosen mater-

The selections from Thomas Aquinas are taken from his *Summa Theologica,* translated by Fathers of the English Dominican Province, 3 vols. (New York: Benziger Brothers, Inc., 1947) Pt. I–II: Q. 72, Art. 5; Pt. II–II: Q. 23, Art. 1, 7; Q. 24, Art. 2, 3, 4, 12; Q. 25, Art. 1, 3, 5, 6, 8, 10, 11; Q. 151, Art. 1; Q. 152, Art. 1, 4, 5; Q. 153, Art. 1, 2, 3, 5; Q. 154, Art. 1, 11; Suppl.: Q. 41, Art. 1, 3; Q. 42, Art. 3; Q. 49, Art. 1, 2; Q. 49, Art. 6. Used by permission of Benziger Publishing Co., a Division of Glencoe-McGraw Hill Publishing Co.

ial to illustrate Thomas's views on charity, chastity, lust, and marriage. When Aquinas mentions "the Philosopher," he is referring to Aristotle.

Turning to charity, then, Aquinas identifies charity as the friendship of the human being for God, that is, the love between the human and God that is based on mutual sharing and communication. For Aquinas, the ultimate and principal good of the human being is the enjoyment of God to which friendship with God or charity leads:

> According to the Philosopher, not every love has the character of friendship, but that love which is together with benevolence, when, to wit, we love someone so as to wish good to him. If, however, we do not wish good to what we love, but wish its good for ourselves, (thus we are said to love wine, or a horse, or the like) it is love not of friendship, but of a kind of concupiscence. For it would be absurd to speak of having friendship for wine or for a horse.
>
> Yet neither does well-wishing suffice for friendship, for a certain mutual love is requisite, since friendship is between friend and friend: and this well-wishing is founded on some kind of communication.
>
> Accordingly, since there is a communication between man and God, inasmuch as He communicates His happiness to us, some kind of friendship must needs be based on this same communication. . . . The love which is based on this communication, is charity: wherefore it is evident that charity is the friendship of man for God.   (Pt. II–II, Q. 23, Art. 1)
>
> The ultimate and principal good of man is the enjoyment of God. . . .   (Pt. II–II, Q. 23, Art. 7)

Charity, according to Aquinas, is a gift of God. It is in humans by divine "infusion" of the third person of the Trinity, the Holy Ghost. It increases as one moves closer to God, but can be lost through a mortal sin that so disorders the soul that the soul turns away from God, thereby blocking, so to speak, the flow of charity from God:

> As stated above, charity is a friendship of man for God, founded upon the fellowship of everlasting happiness. Now this fellowship is in respect, not of natural, but of gratuitous gifts. . . .
>
> Therefore charity can be in us neither naturally, nor through acquisition by the natural powers, but by the infusion of the Holy Ghost, Who is the love of the Father and the Son, and the participation of Whom in us is created charity. . .   (Pt. II–II, Q. 24, Art. 2)
>
> . . . the quantity of charity depends . . . only on the will of Holy Ghost Who divides His gifts according as He will.   (Pt. II–II, Q. 24, Art. 3)
>
> The charity of a wayfarer can increase. For we are called wayfarers by reason of our being on the way to God, Who is the last end of our happiness. In this way we advance as we get nigh to God, Who is approached, not by steps of the body but by the affections of the soul: and this approach is the result of charity, since it unites man's mind to God. Consequently it is essential to the charity of a wayfarer that it can increase, for it if could not, all further advance along the way would cease.   (Pt. II–II, Q. 24, Art. 4)
>
> Now it is evident that through every mortal sin which is contrary to God's commandments, an obstacle is placed to the outpouring of charity, since from the very fact that a man chooses to prefer sin to God's friendship, which requires that we should obey His will, it follows that the habit of charity is lost at once through one mortal sin.   (Pt. II–II, Q. 24, Art. 12)

. . . when the soul is so disordered by sin as to turn away from its last end, viz. God, to Whom it is united by charity, there is mortal sin; but when it is disordered without turning away from God, there is venial sin.   (Pt. I–II, Q. 72, Art. 5)

Aquinas confronts the question: What in addition to God is to be loved out of charity?

One's Neighbor?

Now the aspect under which our neighbor is to be loved, is God, since what we ought to love in our neighbor is that he may be in God. Hence it is clear that it is specifically the same act whereby we love God, and whereby we love our neighbor. Consequently the habit of charity extends not only to the love of God, but also to the love of our neighbor.   (Pt. II–II, Q. 25, Art. 1)

Irrational Creatures?

Charity is a kind of friendship. Now the love of friendship is twofold: first, there is the love for the friend to whom our friendship is given, secondly, the love for those good things which we desire for our friend. With regard to the first, no irrational creature can be loved out of charity; and for three reasons. Two of these reasons refer in a general way to friendship, which cannot have an irrational creature for its object: first because friendship is towards one to whom we wish good things, while, properly speaking, we cannot wish good things to an irrational creature, because it is not competent, properly speaking, to possess good, this being proper to the rational creature which, through its free-will, is the master of its disposal of the good it possesses. . . . Secondly, because all friendship is based on some fellowship in life; since nothing is so proper to friendship as to live together, as the Philosopher proves. Now irrational creatures can have no fellowship in human life which is regulated by reason. Hence friendship with irrational creatures is impossible, except metaphorically speaking. The third reason is proper to charity, for charity is based on the fellowship of everlasting happiness, to which the irrational creature cannot attain. Therefore we cannot have the friendship of charity towards an irrational creature.

Nevertheless we can love irrational creatures out of charity, if we regard them as the good things that we desire for others, in so far, to wit, as we wish for their preservation, to God's honor and man's use; thus too does God love them out of charity.   (Pt. II–II, Q. 25, Art. 3)

One's Body?

Now the nature of our body was created not by an evil principle, as the Manicheans pretend, but by God. Hence we can use it for God's service. . . . Consequently, out of the love of charity with which we love God, we ought to love our bodies also; but we ought not to love the evil effects of sin and the corruption of punishment; we ought rather, by the desire of charity, to long for the removal of such things.   (Pt. II–II, Q. 25, Art. 5)

Sinners?

Two things may be considered in the sinner, his nature and his guilt. According to his nature, which he has from God, he has a capacity for happiness, on the fellowship of which charity is based . . . wherefore we ought to love sinners, out of charity, in respect of their nature.

On the other hand their guilt is opposed to God, and is an obstacle to happiness. Wherefore, in respect of their guilt whereby they are opposed to God, all sinners are to be hated. . . .   (Pt. II–II, Q. 25, Art. 6)

Our Enemies?

Love of one's enemies may be understood in three ways. First, as though we were to love our enemies as such: this is perverse, and contrary to charity, since it implies love of that which is evil in another.

Secondly, love of one's enemies may mean that we love them as to their nature, but in general: and in this sense charity requires that we should love our enemies, namely, that in loving God and our neighbor, we should not exclude our enemies from the love given to our neighbor in general.

Thirdly, love of one's enemies may be considered as specially directed to them, namely, that we should have a special movement of love towards our enemies. Charity does not require this absolutely. . . . Nevertheless charity does require this, in respect of our being prepared in mind, namely, that we should be ready to love our enemies individually, if the necessity were to occur.   (Pt. II–II, Q. 25, Art. 8)

Angels?

The friendship of charity is founded upon the fellowship of everlasting happiness, in which men share in common with the angels. . . . It is therefore evident that the friendship of charity extends also to the angels.   (Pt. II–II, Q. 25, Art. 10)

Demons?

In the sinner, we are bound, out of charity, to love his nature, but to hate his sin. But the name of demon is given to designate a nature deformed by sin, wherefore demons should not be loved out of charity. . . . [Yet] we love irrational creatures out of charity, in as much as we wish them to endure, to give glory to God, and be useful to man . . . and in this way too we can love the nature of the demons even out of charity, in as much as we desire those spirits to endure, as to their natural gifts, unto God's glory.   (Pt. II–II, Q. 25, Art. 11)

Many philosophers have a penchant for drawing fine distinctions. That Aquinas is one of them is evidenced in the material cited so far from the *Summa Theologica*. In the next subtopic of his discussion of charity, the "order of charity," Thomas prioritizes whom one should love. Space limitations allow us only to list the issues he treats under this subtopic, but even the list reveals his proclivity for the art of fine distinctions. Here are the questions he addresses:

Whether God ought to be loved more than our neighbor?

Whether, out of charity, man is bound to love God more than himself?

Whether, out of charity, man ought to love himself more than his neighbor?

Whether a man ought to love his neighbor more than his own body?

Whether we ought to love one neighbor more than another?

Whether we ought to love those who are better more than those who are more closely united to us?

Whether we ought to love more those who are connected with us by ties of blood?

Whether a man ought, out of charity, to love his children more than his father?

Whether a man ought to love his mother more than his father?

Whether a man ought to love his wife more than his father and mother?

Whether a man ought to love more his benefactor than one he has benefited?

Whether the order of charity endures in heaven?

As Aquinas continues to discuss charity, he next examines the primary act of charity, which is love and its effects, namely, joy, peace, mercy, beneficence, almsgiving, and fraternal correction. His discussion exhibits his usual careful reasoning and minute distinctions. We will, however, not discuss these additional subtopics in the hope that his view of charity is already sufficiently clear for the purpose of this book. Let us, instead, move on to a consideration of his views on chastity.

To begin, Aquinas identifies chastity as a virtue:

> Chastity takes its name from the fact that reason *chastises* concupiscence, which, like a child, needs curbing, as the Philosopher states. Now the essence of human virtue consists in being something moderated by reason. . . . Therefore it is evident that chastity is a virtue.   (Pt. II–II, Q. 151, Art. 1)

Virginity is a part of chastity and is characterized as follows:

> Virginity takes its name apparently from *viror* (freshness), and just as a thing is described as fresh and retaining its freshness, so long as it is not parched by excessive heat, so too, virginity denotes that the person possessed thereof is unseared by the heat of concupiscence which is experienced in achieving the greatest bodily pleasure which is that of sexual intercourse. Hence, Ambrose says that virginal chastity is integrity free of pollution.   (Pt. II–II, Q. 152, Art. 1)

For Aquinas, virginity is clearly more excellent than marriage:

> According to Jerome the error of Jovinian consisted in holding virginity not to be preferable to marriage. This error is refuted above all by the example of Christ Who both chose a virgin for His mother, and remained Himself a virgin. . . . It is also refuted by reason, both because a Divine good takes precedence of a human good, and because the good of the soul is preferable to the good of the body, and again because the good of the contemplative life is better than that of the active life. Now virginity is directed to the good of the soul in respect of the contemplative life, which consists in thinking on the things of God, whereas marriage is directed to the good of the body, namely the bodily increase of the human race, and belongs to the active life, since the man and woman who embrace the married life have to think on the things of the world as the Apostle says. Without doubt therefore virginity is preferable to conjugal continence. (Pt. II–II, Q. 152, Art. 4)

> . . . virginity is most excellent, namely in the genus of chastity, since it surpasses the chastity both of widowhood and of marriage.   (Pt. II–II, Q. 152, Art. 5)

The vice that is contrary to chastity is lust. With characteristic precision, Aquinas unpacks this vice:

As Isidore says, a lustful man is one who is debauched with pleasures. Now venereal pleasures above all debauch a man's mind. Therefore lust is especially concerned with such like pleasures.   (Pt. II–II. Q. 153, Art. 1)

A person's mind is debauched by venereal (that is, sexual) pleasures when the ordering of reason in sexual acts is subverted. Reason tells us that the purpose of sexual intercourse is the procreation of children. When the goal of sexual activity becomes venereal pleasure instead of procreation, the ordering of reason is subverted and lust is present:

A sin, in human acts, is that which is against the order of reason. Now the order of reason consists in its ordering everything to its end in a fitting manner. Wherefore it is no sin if one, by the dictate of reason, makes use of certain things in a fitting manner and order for the end to which they are adapted, provided this end be something truly good. Now just as the preservation of the bodily nature of one individual is a true good, so, too, is the preservation of the nature of the human species a very great good. And just as the use of food is directed to the preservation of life in the individual, so is the use of venereal acts directed to the preservation of the whole human race. Hence Augustine says: "What food is to a man's well being, such is sexual intercourse to the welfare of the whole human race." Wherefore just as the use of food can be without sin, if it be taken in due manner and order, as required for the welfare of the body, so also the use of venereal acts can be without sin, provided they be performed in due manner and order, in keeping with the end of human procreation.   (Pt. II–II, Q. 153, Art. 2)

Now lust consists essentially in exceeding the order and mode of reason in the matter of venereal acts. Wherefore without any doubt lust is a sin.   (Pt. II–II, Q. 153, Art. 3)

When the lower powers are strongly moved toward their objects, the result if that the higher powers are hindered and disordered in their acts. Now the effect of the vice of lust is that the lower appetite, namely the concupiscible, is most vehemently intent on its object, to wit, the object of pleasure, on account of the vehemence of the pleasure. Consequently the higher powers, namely the reason and the will, are most grievously disordered by lust.

Now the reason has four acts in matters of action. First there is simple understanding, which apprehends some end as good, and this act is hindered by lust. . . . In this respect we have *blindness of heart.* The second act is counsel about what is to be done for the sake of the end: and this is also hindered by the concupiscence of lust. . . . In this respect there is *rashness.* . . . The third act is judgment about the things to be done, and this again is hindered by lust. . . . In this respect there is *thoughtlessness.* The fourth act is the reason's command about the thing to be done, and this also is impeded by lust, in so far as through being carried away by concupiscence, a man is hindered from doing what his reason ordered to be done. To this *inconstancy* must be referred. . . .

On the part of the will there results a twofold inordinate act. One is the desire for the end, to which we refer *self-love,* which regards the pleasure which a man desires inordinately, while on the other hand there is *hatred of God,* by reason of His forbidding the desired pleasure. The other act is the desire for the things directed to the end. With regard to this there is *love of this world,* whose pleasures a man desires to enjoy, while on the other hand there is *despair of a future world,* because through being held back by carnal pleasures he cares not to obtain spiritual pleasures, since they are distasteful to him.   (Pt. II–II, Q. 153, Art. 5)

Aquinas proceeds to identify and describe six types of lust, each of which is not in accord with right reason:

As stated above, the sin of lust consists in seeking venereal pleasure not in accordance with right reason. This may happen in two ways. First, in respect of the matter wherein his pleasure is sought; secondly, when, whereas there is due matter, other due circumstances are not observed. . . .

Now this same matter may be discordant with right reason in two ways. First, because it is inconsistent with the end of the venereal act. In this way, as hindering the begetting of children, there is the *vice against nature,* which attaches to every venereal act from which generation cannot follow; and, as hindering the due upbringing and advancement of the child when born, there is *simple fornication,* which is the union of an unmarried man with an unmarried woman. Secondly, the matter wherein the venereal act is consummated may be discordant with right reason in relation to other persons; and this in two ways. First, with regard to the woman, with whom a man has connection, by reason of due honor not being paid to her; and thus there is *incest,* which consists in the misuse of a woman who is related by consanguinity or affinity. Secondly, with regard to the person under whose authority the woman is placed: and if she be under the authority of a husband, it is *adultery,* if under the authority of her father, it is *seduction,* in the absence of violence, and *rape* if violence be employed.   (Pt. II–II, Q. 154, Art. 1)

In addition, Aquinas discusses four types of lust that fall under the rubric of "unnatural vice." By "pollution" in the passage below Aquinas seems to be referring to sexual climax, and in this case with respect to masturbation:

Wherever there occurs a special kind of deformity whereby the venereal act is rendered unbecoming, there is a determinate species of lust. This may occur in two ways: First, through being contrary to right reason, and this is common to all lustful vices; secondly, because, in addition, it is contrary to the natural order of the venereal act as becoming to the human race: and this is called *the unnatural vice.* This may happen in several ways. First, by procuring pollution, without any copulation, for the sake of venereal pleasure: this pertains to the sin of *uncleanness* which some call *effeminacy.* Secondly, by copulation with a thing of undue species, and this is called *bestiality.* Thirdly, by copulation with an undue sex, male with male, or female with female . . . and this is called the *vice of sodomy.* Fourthly, by not observing the natural manner of copulation, either as to undue means, or as to other monstrous and bestial manners of copulation.   (Pt. II–II, Q. 154, Art. 11)

Let us consider finally the topic of marriage or matrimony. Here, again, Aquinas's discussion is precise and thorough, covering over one hundred large pages in the *Summa.* And, once again, we can only sample his thinking. We have already seen that Aquinas considers virginity to be more excellent than marriage and that sexual intercourse is appropriately ordered by reason when it is conducted within the bonds of marriage and for the purpose of procreation, not for the purpose of pleasure. Marriage, he now tells us, is "natural," not in the sense that nature requires and compels it, but in the sense that nature inclines us to it and it comes to pass through the exercise of free will. Note the two purposes he assigns to marriage and the gender-based division of labor in marriage he assumes:

Matrimony is natural because natural reason inclines thereto in two ways. First, in relation to the principal end of matrimony, namely to good of the offspring. For nature intends not only the begetting of offspring, but also its education and development until it reach the perfect state of man as man, and that is the state of virtue. Hence, according to the Philosopher, we derive three things from our parents, namely *existence, nourishment,* and *education.* Now a child cannot be brought up and instructed unless it have certain and definite parents, and this would not be the case unless there were a tie between the man and a definite woman, and it is in this that matrimony consists. Secondly, in relation to the secondary end of matrimony, which is the mutual services which married persons render one another in household matters. For just as natural reason dictates that men should live together, since one is not self-sufficient in all things concerning life, for which reason man is described as being naturally inclined to political society, so too among those works that are necessary for human life some are becoming to men, others to women. Wherefore nature inculcates that society of man and woman which consists in matrimony. These two reasons are given by the Philosopher. (Suppl. Q. 41, Art. 1)

Although Aquinas has devalued marriage compared to virginity, he refuses to call procreation within marriage a sinful act:

If we suppose the corporeal nature to be created by the good God, we cannot hold that those things which pertain to the preservation of the corporeal nature and to which nature inclines, are altogether evil; wherefore, since the inclination to beget an offspring whereby the specific nature is preserved is from nature, it is impossible to maintain that the act of begetting children is altogether unlawful. . . .

The shamefulness of concupiscence that always accompanies the marriage act is a shamefulness not of guilt, but of punishment inflicted for the first sin, inasmuch as the lower powers and the members do not obey reason. . . .

Properly speaking, a thing is said to be excused when it has some appearance of evil, and yet is not evil, or not evil as it seems, because some things excuse wholly, others in part. And since the marriage act, by reason of the corruption of concupiscence, has the appearance of an inordinate act, it is wholly excused by the marriage blessing, so as not to be sin.   (Suppl. Q. 41, Art. 3)

Marriage confers grace that can be a remedy for concupiscence by curbing it and the additional concupiscible acts that frequently follow from it:

A remedy can be employed against concupiscence in two ways. First, on the part of concupiscence by repressing it in its root, and thus matrimony affords a remedy by the grace given therein. Secondly, on the part of its act, and this is two ways: first, by depriving the act to which concupiscence inclines of its outward shamefulness, and this is done by the marriage blessings which justify carnal concupiscence; secondly, by hindering the shameful act, which is done by the very nature of the act; because concupiscence, being satisfied by the conjugal act, does not incline so much to other wickedness. . . . For though the works congenial to concupiscence are in themselves of a nature to increase concupiscence, yet in so far as they are directed according to reason they repress concupiscence, because like acts result in like dispositions and habits.   (Suppl. Q. 42, Art. 3)

Because marriage involves vehement pleasure in sexual intercourse and anxious concern for temporal things that subvert reason (which is unfitting), marriage needs to be "excused" or made "right" by certain goods which accrue from marriage. Those goods are three in number: offspring, faith (or fidelity), and sacrament (that is, a sanctifying remedy against sin offered to humankind under sensible signs):

No wise man should allow himself to lose a thing except for some compensation in the shape of an equal or better good. Wherefore for a thing that has a loss attached to it to be eligible, it needs to have some good connected with it, which by compensating for that loss makes that thing ordinate and right. Now there is a loss of reason incidental to the union of man and woman, both because the reason is carried away entirely on account of the vehemence of the pleasure, so that it is unable to understand anything at the same time, as the Philosopher says; and again because of the tribulation of the flesh which such persons have to suffer from solicitude for temporal things. Consequently the choice of this union cannot be made ordinate except by certain compensations whereby that same union is righted; and these are the goods which excuse marriage and make it right.   (Suppl. Q. 49, Art. 1)

Matrimony is instituted both as an office of nature and as a sacrament of the Church. As an office of nature it is directed by two things, like every other virtuous act. One of these is required on the part of the agent and is the intention of the due end, and thus the *offspring* is accounted a good of matrimony; the other is required on the part of the act, which is good generically through being about a due matter; and thus we have *faith,* whereby a man has intercourse with his wife and with no other woman. Besides this it has a certain goodness as a sacrament, and this is signified by the very word *sacrament.* (Suppl. Q. 49, Art. 2)

Aquinas returns to the issue of sexual intercourse in marriage for the sake of pleasure rather than for procreation. While such intercourse is still sinful, Aquinas draws a fine distinction regarding two different ways a man can approach his wife in the sexual act, which enables him to distinguish sex for pleasure's sake that is a mortal sin from sex for pleasure's sake that is a venial sin:

If pleasure be sought in such a way as to exclude the honesty of marriage, so that, to wit, it is not as a wife but as woman that man treats his wife, and that he is ready to use her in the same way if she were not his wife, it is a mortal sin; wherefore such a man is said to be too ardent a lover of his wife, because his ardor carries him away from the goods of marriage. If, however, he seek pleasure within the bounds of marriage, so that it would not be sought in another than his wife, it is a venial sin.   (Suppl. Q. 49, Art. 6)

Aquinas goes on to examine in great detail additional subtopics of marriage: the marriage of slaves; the impediments to marriage such as consanguinity, affinity, impotence, and insanity; adoption; the marriage of believers to unbelievers; wife-murder; fornication; divorce and remarriage; the plurality of wives; bigamy; illegitimate children, etc. While space limitations prevent us from exploring all of these issues, we trust that his general views on charity, chastity, lust, and marriage are quite clear from the material already cited.

Like Augustine, Aquinas believed his portrayal of the issues relating to the philosophy of sex and love was consistent with the biblical perspective. And many Christians, especially within the Roman Catholic Church as illustrated by Leo XIII's *Aeterni Patris,* would agree with him. Yet there are critics who would raise the same basic question they would pose to Augustine: Does not his depreciation of the body with its drives and pleasures reflect the influence of a Greek dualism that exalted the spiritual soul at the expense of the material body? Furthermore, does not Aquinas overintellectualize love through overanalysis and finer and finer distinctions to the end that the creative unexpectedness of agapaic love is lost? Moreover, is it really clear that the biblical tradition and/or rational argument declare that virginity is more excellent than marriage, and that sexual gratification is not one of the goods of marriage? The shadow cast by the thought of Augustine and Aquinas is long, stretching into today's world. Those who live in that shadow have some challenging questions to address. What might they say?

MODERN SECULAR VIEWS
Erich Fromm

The biblical tradition and Greek philosophy (especially as it is represented by Plato and Aristotle) had a feature in common that probably facilitated the blending of the traditions that Augustine and Aquinas were able to achieve. That feature is referred to by some scholars as the breaking of the ancient world's mythopoeic mode of thinking. For many ancient people nature was the enchanted dwelling place of the divine, and the exploits of these divine beings were described in mythopoetry. In some mythopoetry, natural phenomena were personified as divine beings that interacted with human beings. Both the biblical tradition and Greek philosophy disenchanted nature, removed the divine from nature, and set the divine in a transcendent domain vis-à-vis nature. Accordingly, the transcendent Platonic Idea of the Good in which all things participated was readily identifiable by Augustine with the Holy God of scripture, and the Aristotelian First Cause of all things, the Unmoved Mover responsible for all motion, was easily equated by Aquinas with the transcendent biblical Creator.

This disenchantment of nature not only facilitated the Augustinian and Thomistic syntheses but also encouraged the development of technology and science because a disenchanted nature was a far less daunting object for investigation and experimentation than was a nature inhabited by gods. As modern science developed and became the paradigm pathway to knowledge, a disenchanted nature was replaced by a secularized nature in which the divine was not simply relocated to a transcendent realm but was virtually removed from any significant relationship to nature. For some moderns, this secularized nature seemed to support atheism. For others, a secularized nature called for a revision of traditional theology in such a way that God, for example, was viewed as now teaching humankind that it could "get along without him" in managing the affairs of the world. And for all of us, modern secularization means that the liberation of human thought from theological and religious tutelage is a powerful current on the contemporary scene. This liberation is particularly evident in the philosophy of sex and love where, unlike Augustine and Aquinas, contemporary thinking is not constrained by religious presuppositions. To illustrate this liberation from religious tutelage, the two contemporary thinkers we have selected are Erich Fromm and Alexander Comfort. The former offers a nonreligious view of love and the latter a nonreligious view of sex. That does not mean that their views are antireligious. Indeed, a case could be made, for example, that they are compatible in certain basic features with the biblical perspective.

Turning first to Erich Fromm, he was born in Frankfurt, Germany, on March 23, 1900. After receiving his PhD from the University of Heidelberg in 1922 he pursued additional studies at the University of Munich and the Psychoanalytic Institute in Berlin. For several years he lectured at the Psychoanalytic Institute in Frankfurt and at the Institute for Social Research in the University of Frankfurt. Beginning in 1934 he held various lectureships and teaching positions at institutions in the United States, including Columbia University, Bennington College, Yale, Michigan State University, the New School of Social Research, and the American Institute for Psychoanalysis. He taught for a number of years at the National

University of Mexico, and in 1974 he moved to Switzerland where he continued to work until his death on March 18, 1980. Fromm wrote a number of books, including *Escape from Freedom* (1941), *Man for Himself* (1947), *Psychoanalysis and Religion* (1950), *The Sane Society* (1955), and *The Art of Loving* (1956), in which he offered an account of the emergence of the modern human being whose deep psychological problems can only be resolved through productive love. The selections included below are all taken from *The Art of Loving* while the editorial comments draw on material from his other writings as well.

At the outset, let us review briefly Fromm's account of the development of the troubled modern human being. In primordial times, the ancestors of human beings, like all other animals, enjoyed an unreflective oneness with nature. Instinct guided their actions. In the course of evolution, however, human beings were deprived of instinct and torn away from the primary bonds which united them with animals and nature. They developed reason and imagination, which facilitated self-awareness, a basic aspect of human freedom. They became aware of themselves as distinct from the rest of nature. Through imagination they were able to project themselves into the future and to select one of several possible futures to follow. They were able to imagine future pleasures and triumphs as well as future pains and failures. They became aware of themselves and their openness to the future. They also became aware of their separateness, aloneness, and isolation from nature. This awareness of isolation became so distressing that humans developed new ties, namely the various facets of culture, to bind themselves to each other and to the rest of nature.

Fromm sees the emergent isolation of humankind mirrored in the birth and development of each individual. At birth a baby is thrust from the security of its mother's womb. The basic primary ties with the mother grow weaker as the child becomes aware of being a separate entity. Along with its growing sense of isolation the child develops a corresponding sense of self-strength.

Such isolation experienced within modern European and American societies was intensified by socioeconomic and political developments. During the Middle Ages society was structured so that each person had an assigned position. Although opportunity to rise out of that role was restricted, movement within that role was less restrained. While lacking social mobility, the medieval person did possess security and meaningful belongingness. With the emergence of Renaissance individualism, new dimensions of social freedom appeared as the stratified medieval society was shattered, but meaningful belongingness was replaced by a sense of isolation. Similarly, capitalism opened new opportunities for freedom, but its alienating features exacerbated the sense of isolation. Modern society, then, affects the individual in two ways: On the one hand, people have become more independent, self-reliant and critical; on the other hand, they have become more isolated, alone, and afraid.

Fromm sees the contemporary individual facing a basic alternative: Either one can seek to reestablish the primary bonds (long ago broken when reason and imagination replaced instinct) through escape mechanisms that sacrifice individuality and integrity; or one can strive to relate spontaneously and creatively to the world. Fromm identifies five kinds of escape mechanisms people employ to transcend isolation and escape from freedom's self-awareness: authoritarianism (in both its masochistic and sadistic expressions), destructiveness, withdrawal, self-aggrandizement, and automaton conformity. These mechanisms yield their users a fragile security, but at the high cost of one's individuality and integrity.

The alternative to escape mechanisms for dealing with painful isolation is spontaneous, creative activity that is rooted in self-acceptance, that is to say, in the recognition that the growth and realization of a person's individuality is an end that must never be subordinated to any other purpose. Spontaneous activity has two components: love and work. Love, which is the foremost element, is not the love of losing the self in another person, nor the love of possessing another, but the love of spontaneously affirming others, of uniting with others while preserving one's own integrity. Work, the other element, is not the work of compulsive activity undertaken to escape freedom's self-awareness, nor the work of striving to dominate nature (expressed partly in worship of, and partly in enslavement by, human products), but the work of creative activity in which the human becomes one with nature through shaping and cooperating with nature in the pursuit of human well-being.

Fromm admits that this ideal of love and work has never been realized on a very large scale, but claims that it could be if two "revolutions" occurred. The first revolution is a restoration of humanistic ethics which, according to Fromm, exalts humans as the only legitimate authors of values and norms for human action, as well as the only effective agents for achieving human well-being. Humanistic ethics stand in sharp contrast to authoritarian ethics, such as religious ethics, which impose on humankind divinely authored goals that can only be accomplished with divine intervention.

The second revolution needed for genuine love and work to flourish is a political change: the institution of democratic socialism in which the individual's sense of powerlessness is overcome through active participation in the social process.

In his book *The Art of Loving,* Fromm describes in detail the nature of the love he would like to see flourish under the aegis of humanistic ethics and democratic socialism. First of all he points out that love is an *art:*

> Is love an art? Then it requires knowledge and effort. Or is love a pleasant sensation, which to experience is a matter of chance, something one "falls into" if one is lucky? This little book is based on the former premise, while undoubtedly the majority of people today believe in the latter. (p. 1)

> The process of learning an art can be divided conveniently into two parts: one, the mastery of the theory; the other, the mastery of the practice. . . . But . . . there is a third factor necessary to becoming a master in any art—the mastery of the art must be a matter of ultimate concern; there must be nothing else in the world more important than the art. This holds true for music, for medicine, for carpentry—and for love. (p. 5)

The fundamental human problem is how to deal with the distressing awareness of one's isolation. Neither work nor orgiastic fusion nor conformity is an adequate solution:

> The unity achieved in productive work is not interpersonal; the unity achieved in orgiastic fusion is transitory; the unity achieved by conformity is only pseudo-unity. Hence, they are only partial answers to the problem of existence. The full answer lies in the achievement of interpersonal union, of fusion with another person, in *love.* (p. 18)

Love has several distinctive features. First, it involves the union of persons while preserving their integrity as individual persons:

> In contrast to symbiotic union, mature *love* is *union under the condition of preserving one's integrity,* one's individuality. *Love is an active power in man;* a power which breaks through the walls which separate man from his fellow men, which unites him with others; love makes him overcome the sense of isolation and separateness, yet it permits him to be himself, to retain his integrity. In love the paradox occurs that two beings become one and yet remain two. (pp. 20–21)

Second, love is an activity that involves primarily giving, not receiving:

> Spinoza . . . differentiates . . . between active and passive affects, "actions" and "passions." In the exercise of an active effect, man is free, he is the master of his affect; in the exercise of a passive affect, man is driven, the object of motivations of which he himself is not aware. Thus Spinoza arrives at the statement that virtue and power are one and the same. Envy, jealousy, ambition, any kind of greed are passions; love is an action, the practice of a human power, which can be practiced only in freedom and never as the result of a compulsion.
>
> Love is an activity, not a passive affect; it is a "standing in," not a "falling for." In the most general way, the active character of love can be described by stating that love is primarily *giving,* not receiving. . . . Giving is the highest expression of potency. In the very act of giving, I experience my strength, my wealth, my power. This experience of heightened vitality and potency fills me with joy. I experience myself as overflowing, spending, alive, hence as joyous. Giving is more joyous than receiving, not because it is a deprivation, but because in the act of giving lies the expression of my aliveness. (pp. 22–23)

Third, love produces love, or it isn't love:

> The most important sphere of giving . . . is not that of material things, but lies in the specifically human realm. What does one person give to another? He gives of himself . . . of his life. This does not necessarily mean that he sacrifices his life for the other— but that he gives him of that which is alive in him; he gives him of his joy, of his interest, of his understanding, of his knowledge, of his humor, of his sadness—of all expressions and manifestations of that which is alive in him. In thus giving of his life, he enriches the other person, he enhances the other's sense of aliveness by enhancing his own sense of aliveness. He does not give in order to receive; giving is in itself exquisite joy. But in giving he cannot help bringing something to life in the other person, and this which is brought to life reflects back to him; in truly giving, he cannot help receiving that which is given back to him. Giving implies to make the other person a giver also and they both share in the joy of what they have brought to life. In the act of giving something is born, and both persons involved are grateful for the life that is born for both of them. Specifically with regard to love this means: love is a power which produces love; impotence is the inability to produce love. This thought has been beautifully expressed by Marx: " . . . If you love without calling forth love, that is, if your love as such does not produce love, if by means of an *expression of life* as a loving person you do not make of yourself a *loved person,* then your love is impotent, a misfortune." (pp. 24–25)

Fourth, love involves a cluster of four very closely related attitudes: care, responsibility, respect, and knowledge:

Care

> That love implies *care* is most evident in a mother's love for her child. No assurance of her love could strike us as sincere if we saw her lacking in care for the infant, if she neglected to feed it, to bathe it, to give it physical comfort. . . . *Love is the active concern for the life and the growth of that which we love.* Where this active concern is lacking, there is no love. (p. 26)

Responsibility

Care and concern imply another aspect of love; that of *responsibility*. Today responsibility is often meant to denote duty, something imposed upon one from the outside. But responsibility, in its true sense, is an entirely voluntary act; it is my response to the needs, expressed or unexpressed, of another human being. To be "responsible" means to be able and ready to "respond." (pp. 27–28)

Respect

Responsibility could easily deteriorate into domination and possessiveness, were it not for a third component of love, *respect*. Respect is not fear and awe; it denotes, in accordance with the root of the word (*respicere* = to look at), the ability to see a person as he is, to be aware of his unique individuality. Respect means the concern that the other person should grow and unfold as he is. Respect, thus, implies the absence of exploitation. I want the loved person to grow and unfold for his own sake, and in his own ways, and not for the purpose of serving me. . . . If I love the other person, I feel one with him or her, but with him *as he is,* not as I need him to be as an object for my use. It is clear that respect is possible only if *I* have achieved independence; if I can stand and walk without needing crutches, without having to dominate and exploit anyone else. Respect exists only on the basis of freedom: "l'amour est l'enfant de la liberté" as an old French song says; love is the child of freedom, never that of domination. (p. 28)

Knowledge

To respect a person is not possible without *knowing* him; care and responsibility would be blind if they were not guided by knowledge. Knowledge would be empty if it were not motivated by concern. There are many layers of knowledge; the knowledge which is an aspect of love is one which does not stay at the periphery, but penetrates to the core. . . .

Knowledge has one more, and a more fundamental, relation to the problem of love. The basic need to fuse with another person so as to transcend the prison of one's separateness is closely related to another specifically human desire, that to know the "secret of man." While life in its merely biological aspects is a miracle and a secret, man in his human aspects is an unfathomable secret to himself—and to his fellow man. We know ourselves, and yet even with all the efforts we may make, we do not know ourselves. We know our fellow man, and yet we do not know him, because we are not a thing, and our fellow man is not a thing. The further we reach into the depth of our being, or someone else's being, the more the goal of knowledge eludes us. Yet we cannot help desiring to penetrate into the secret of man's soul, into the innermost nucleus which is "he." (p. 29)

There is one way, a desperate one, to know the secret: it is that of complete power over another person . . . which transforms him into a thing, our thing, our possession. The ultimate degree of this attempt to know lies in the extremes of sadism, the desire and ability to make a human being suffer; to torture him, to force him to betray his secret in his suffering. (p. 30)

The other path to knowing "the secret" is love. Love is active penetration of the other person, in which my desire to know is stilled by union. In the act of fusion I know you,

I know myself, I know everybody—and I "know" nothing. I know in the only way knowledge of that which is alive is possible for man—by experience of union—not by any knowledge our thought can give. . . . Love is the only way of knowledge, which in the act of union answers my quest. In the act of loving, of giving myself, in the act of penetrating the other person, I find myself, I discover myself, I discover us both, I discover man. . . . The only way of full knowledge lies in the *act* of love: this act transcends thought, it transcends words. It is the daring plunge into the experience of union. (pp. 30–31)

While Fromm deploys terms (such as fusion, penetration, and union) in this description of love's knowledge that remind one of sexual intercourse, it is not primarily sexual intercourse that he has in mind. Rather, he is referring to all the diverse acts of love in which persons open themselves to each other and experience a bonding of themselves to each other. Now he moves on to discuss biological union and sexual intercourse. Notice Fromm's reference to a myth we encountered earlier in Plato's *Symposium* when Aristophanes told how the desire for erotic reunion of male and female arose:

Thus far I have spoken of love as the overcoming of human separateness, as the fulfillment of the longing for union. But above the universal, existential need for union rises a more specific, biological one: the desire for union between the masculine and feminine poles. The idea of this polarization is most strikingly expressed in the myth that originally man and woman were one, that they were cut in half, and from then on each male has been seeking for the lost female part of himself in order to unite again with her. (The same idea of the original unity of the sexes is also contained in the Biblical story of Eve being made from Adam's rib, even though in this story, in the spirit of patriarchalism, woman is considered secondary to man.) The meaning of the myth is clear enough. Sexual polarization leads man to seek union in a specific way, that of union with the other sex. The polarity between the male and female principles exists also *within* each man and each woman. Just as physiologically man and woman each have hormones of the opposite sex, they are bisexual also in the psychological sense. They carry in themselves the principle of receiving and of penetrating, of matter and of spirit. Man—and woman—finds union within himself only in the union of his female and his male polarity. This polarity is the basis for all creativity.

The male-female polarity is also the basis for interpersonal creativity. This is obvious biologically in the fact that the union of sperm and ovum is the basis for the birth of a child. But in the purely psychic realm it is not different; in the love between man and woman, each of them is reborn. (The homosexual deviation is a failure to attain this polarized union, and thus the homosexual suffers from the pain of never-resolved separateness, a failure, however, which he shares with the average heterosexual who cannot love.)

The same polarity of the male and female principle exists in nature; not only, as is obvious in animals and plants, but in the polarity of the two fundamental functions, that of receiving and that of penetrating. It is the polarity of the earth and rain, of the river and the ocean, of night and day, of darkness and light, of matter and spirit. (p. 33–34)

In summing up the distinctive features of love, Fromm emphasizes that love is primarily an attitude, an orientation of character rather than a relationship to a specific person:

Love is not primarily a relationship to a specific person; it is an *attitude,* an *orientation* of *character* which determines the relatedness of a person to the world as a whole, not toward one "object" of love. If a person loves only one other person and is indifferent to the rest of his fellow men, his love is not love but a symbiotic attachment, or an enlarged egotism. Yet, most people believe that love is constituted by the object, not by the faculty. In fact, they even believe that it is a proof of the intensity of their love when they do not love anybody except the "loved" person. . . . Because one does not see that love is an activity, a power of the soul, one believes that all that is necessary to find is the right object—and that everything goes by itself afterward. This attitude can be compared to that of a man who wants to paint but who, instead of learning the art, claims that he has just to wait for the right object, and that he will paint beautifully when he finds it. If I truly love one person I love all persons, I love the world, I love life. If I can say to somebody else, "I love you," I must be able to say, "I love in you everybody, I love through you the world, I love in you also myself."

Saying that love is an orientation which refers to all and not to one does not imply, however, the idea that there are no differences between various types of love, which depend on the kind of object which is loved. (pp. 46–47)

Fromm goes on to distinguish six types of love based on the kind of object that is loved:

Brotherly Love

The most fundamental kind of love, which underlies all types of love, is *brotherly love*. By this I mean the sense of responsibility, care, respect, knowledge of any other human being, the wish to further his life. This is the kind of love the Bible speaks of when it says: love thy neighbor as thyself. Brotherly love is love for all human beings; it is characterized by its very lack of exclusiveness. If I have developed the capacity for love, then I cannot help loving my brothers. In brotherly love there is the experience of union with all men, of human solidarity, of human at-onement. Brotherly love is based on the experience that we all are one. . . .

Brotherly love is love between equals: but, indeed, even as equals we are not always "equal"; inasmuch as we are human, we are all in need of help. (p. 47)

Motherly Love

Motherly love by its very nature is unconditional. Mother loves the newborn infant because it is her child, not because the child has fulfilled any specific expectation. (p. 41)

Motherly love . . . is unconditional affirmation of the child's life and his needs. . . . Affirmation of the child's life has two aspects; one is the care and responsibility absolutely necessary for the preservation of the child's life and his growth. The other aspect goes further than mere preservation. It is the attitude which instills in the child a love for living, which gives him the feeling: it is good to be alive, it is good to be a little boy or girl, it is good to be on this earth! (p. 49)

But the child must grow. It must emerge from mother's womb, from mother's breast; it must eventually become a completely separate human being. The very essence of motherly love is to care for the child's growth, and that means to want the child's separation from herself. Here lies the basic difference to erotic love. In erotic love, two people who were separate become one. In motherly love, two people who were one become separate. The mother must not only tolerate, she must wish and support the child's separation. It is only at this stage that motherly love becomes such a difficult task, that it requires unselfishness, the ability to give everything and to want nothing but the happiness of the loved one. It is also at this stage that many mothers fail in their task of motherly love. The narcissistic, the domineering, the possessive woman can succeed in being a "loving" mother as long as the child is small. Only the really loving woman, the woman who is happier in giving than in taking, who is firmly rooted in her own existence, can be a loving mother when the child is in the process of separation. (pp. 51–52)

Fatherly Love

Fatherly love is conditional love. Its principle is "I love you *because* you fulfill my expectations, because you do your duty, because you are like me." In conditional fatherly love we find . . . a negative and a positive aspect. The negative aspect is the very fact that fatherly love has to be deserved, that it can be lost if one does not do what is expected. In the nature of fatherly love lies the fact that obedience becomes the main virtue, that disobedience is the main sin—and its punishment the withdrawal of fatherly love. The positive side is equally important. Since his love is conditioned, I can do something to acquire it, I can work for it; his love is not outside of my control as motherly love is.

The mother's and the father's attitudes toward the child correspond to the child's own needs. The infant needs mother's unconditional love and care physiologically as well as psychically. The child, after six, begins to need father's love, his authority and guidance. Mother has the function of making him secure in life, father has the function of teaching him, guiding him to cope with those problems with which the particular society the child has been born into confronts him. (p. 43)

Erotic Love

Brotherly love is love among equals; motherly love is love for the helpless. Different as they are from each other, they have in common that they are by their very nature not restricted to one person. If I love my brother, I love all my brothers; if I love my child, I love all my children; no, beyond that, I love all children, all that are in need of my help. In contrast to both types of love is *erotic love;* it is the craving for complete fusion, for union with one other person. It is by its very nature exclusive and not universal; it is also perhaps the most deceptive form of love there is.

First of all, it is often confused with the explosive experience of "falling" in love, the sudden collapse of the barriers which existed until that moment between two strangers. But . . . this experience of sudden intimacy is by its very nature short-lived. After the stranger has become an intimately known person there are no more barriers to be overcome, there is no more sudden closeness to be achieved. . . . For them intimacy is established primarily through sexual contact. Since they experience the separateness of the other person primarily as physical separateness, physical union means overcoming separateness.

Beyond that, there are other factors which to many people denote the overcoming of separateness. To speak of one's own personal life, one's hopes and anxieties, to show oneself with one's childlike or childish aspects, to establish a common interest vis-à-vis the world—all this is taken as overcoming separateness. Even to show one's anger, one's hate, one's complete lack of inhibition is taken for intimacy. . . . But all these types of closeness tend to become reduced more and more as time goes on. The consequence is one seeks love with a new person, with a new stranger. Again the stranger is transformed into an "intimate" person, again the experience of falling in love is exhilarating and intense, and again it slowly becomes less and less intense, and ends in the wish for a new conquest, a new love—always with the illusion that the new love will be different from the earlier ones. These illusions are greatly helped by the deceptive character of sexual desire.

Sexual desire aims at fusion—and is by no means only a physical appetite, the relief of a painful tension. But sexual desire can be stimulated by the anxiety of aloneness, by the wish to conquer or be conquered, by vanity, by the wish to hurt and even to destroy, as much as it can be stimulated by love. It seems that sexual desire can easily blend with and be stimulated by any strong emotion, of which love is only one. Because sexual desire is in the minds of most people coupled with the idea of love, they are easily misled to conclude that they love each other when they want each other physically. Love can inspire the wish for sexual union; in this case the physical relationship is lacking in greediness, in a wish to conquer or to be conquered, but is blended with tenderness. If the desire for physical union is not stimulated by love, if erotic love is not also brotherly love, it never leads to union in more than an orgiastic, transitory sense. Sexual attraction creates, for the moment, the illusion of union, yet without love this "love" leaves strangers as far apart as they were before. . . .

In erotic love there is an exclusiveness which is lacking in brotherly love and motherly love. . . . Frequently the exclusiveness of erotic love is misinterpreted as meaning possessive attachment. . . . Erotic love is exclusive, but it loves in the other person all of mankind, all that is alive. It is exclusive only in the sense that I can fuse myself fully and intensely with one person only. Erotic love excludes the love for others only in the sense of erotic fusion, full commitment in all aspects of life—but not in the sense of deep brotherly love.

Erotic love, if it is love, has one premise. That I love from the essence of my being—and experience the other person in the essence of his or her being. In essence, all human beings are identical. We are all part of One; we are One. This being so, it should not make any difference whom we love. Love should be essentially an act of will, of decision to commit my life completely to that of one other person. This is, indeed, the rationale behind the idea of the insolubility of marriage. . . . To love somebody is not just a strong feeling—it is a decision, it is a judgment, it is a promise. If love were only a feeling, there would be no basis for the promise to love each other forever. A feeling comes and it may go. How can I judge that it will stay forever, when my act does not involve judgment and decision?

Taking these views into account one may arrive at the position that love is exclusively an act of will and commitment, and that therefore fundamentally it does not matter who the two persons are. Whether the marriage was arranged by others, or the result of individual choice, once the marriage is concluded, the act of will should guarantee the continuation of love. This view seems to neglect the paradoxical character of human nature and of erotic love. We are all One—yet every one of us is a unique, unduplicable entity. . . . Both views then, that of erotic love as completely individual attraction, unique between two specific persons, as well as the other view that erotic love is nothing but an act of will, are true—or, as it may be put more aptly, the truth is neither this nor that. (pp. 52–57)

Self-Love

It is a widespread belief that, while it is virtuous to love others, it is sinful to love oneself. . . .

Before we start the discussion of the psychological aspects of selfishness and self-love, the logical fallacy in the notion that love for others and love for oneself are mutually exclusive should be stressed. If it is a virtue to love my neighbor as a human being, it must be a virtue—and not a vice—to love myself, since I am a human being too. . . .

We have come to the basic psychological premises on which the conclusions of our argument are built. Generally, these premises are as follows: not only others, but we ourselves are the "object" of our feelings and attitudes; the attitudes toward others and toward ourselves, far from being contradictory, are basically *conjunctive*. With regard to the problem under discussion this means: love of others and love of ourselves are not alternatives. On the contrary, an attitude of love toward themselves will be found in all those who are capable of loving others. *Love,* in principle, *is indivisible as far as the connection between "objects" and one's own self is concerned.* Genuine love is an expression of productiveness and implies care, respect, responsibility and knowledge. It is not an "affect" in the sense of being affected by somebody, but an active striving for the growth and happiness of the loved person, rooted in one's own capacity to love.

To love somebody is the actualization and concentration of the power to love. The basic affirmation contained in love is directed toward the beloved person as an incarnation of essentially human qualities. Love of one person implies love of man as such. The kind of "division of labor," as William James calls it, by which one loves one's family but is without feeling for the "stranger," is a sign of a basic inability to love. Love of man is not, as is frequently supposed, an abstraction coming after the love for a specific person, but it is its premise, although genetically it is acquired in loving specific individuals. . . . *The affirmation of one's own life, happiness, growth, freedom is rooted in one's capacity to love.* . . . If an individual is able to love productively, he loves himself too; if he can love *only* others, he cannot love at all. . . .

The *selfish* person is interested only in himself, wants everything for himself, feels no pleasure in giving, but only in taking. . . . He can see nothing but himself; he judges everyone and everything from its usefulness to him; he is basically unable to love. Does not this prove that concern for others and concern for oneself are unavoidable alternatives? This would be so if selfishness and self-love were identical. But that assumption is the very fallacy which has led to so many mistaken conclusions concerning our problem. *Selfishness and self-love, far from being identical, are actually opposites.* The selfish person does not love himself too much but too little; in fact he hates himself. This lack of fondness and care for himself, which is only one expression of his lack of productiveness, leaves him empty and frustrated. He is necessarily unhappy and anxiously concerned to snatch from life the satisfactions which he blocks himself from attaining. He seems to care too much for himself, but actually he only makes an unsuccessful attempt to cover up and compensate for his failure to care for his real self. (pp. 57–61)

Love of God

It has been stated above that the basis for our need to love lies in the experience of separateness and the resulting need to overcome the anxiety of separateness by the experience of union. The religious form of love, that which is called the love of God, is, psychologically speaking, not different. It springs from the need to overcome separateness and to achieve union. . . .

In all theistic religions, whether they are polytheistic or monotheistic, God stands for the highest value, the most desirable good. Hence, the specific meaning of God depends on what is the most desirable good for a person. . . . (p. 63)

The truly religious person, if he follows the essence of the monotheistic idea, does not pray for anything, does not expect anything from God; he does not love God as a child loves his father or his mother; he has acquired the humility of sensing his limitations, to the degree of knowing that he knows nothing about God. God becomes to him a symbol in which man, at an earlier stage of his evolution, has expressed the totality of that which man is striving for, the realm of the spiritual world, of love, truth and justice. He has faith in the principles which "God" represents; he thinks truth, lives love and justice, and considers all of his life only valuable inasmuch as it gives him the chance to arrive at an ever fuller unfolding of his human powers—as the only reality that matters, as the only object of "ultimate concern"; and, eventually, he does not speak about God—nor even mention his name. To love God, if he were going to use this word, would mean, then, to long for the attainment of the full capacity to love, for the realization of that which "God" stands for in oneself. . . .

Having spoken of the love of God, I want to make it clear that I myself do not think in terms of a theistic concept, and that to me the concept of God is only a historically conditioned one, in which man has expressed his experience of his higher powers, his longing for truth and for unity at a given historical period. (pp. 71–72)

Recall that for Fromm love is an art, and that if one wishes to master an art, one must learn the theory and master the practice of the art. Thus, having completed his discussion of the theory of love, Fromm comments on mastering its practice. He notes four techniques that are common to the mastery of any art: discipline, concentration, patience, and supreme concern for mastering the art. In addition, the art of loving requires the transcendence of narcissism (inordinate focusing upon one's own concerns); the development of rational faith in oneself, in others, and in the power of one's love to produce love in others; the exercising of courage that stakes everything on one's supreme values; and the pursuit of productive activity which is made possible in a society shaped by democratic socialism.

Such, then, is Fromm's secularized view of love. It is a view that has widespread appeal on the contemporary scene. That attractiveness may be due in part to its addressing the current sense of isolation and aloneness, its inclusion of agapaic brotherly love, its loftiness as an ideal, and its lack of religious prerequisites. Yet his view does have some troubling features.

To begin, is his ideal of love so lofty that it is in fact unrealistic and unrealizable? For example, does it seem realistic to say that genuine love requires me to be able to say in all honesty that in loving someone (namely, my child, sexual partner, brother, sister, parent, etc.) I am loving everybody? Who could possibly live up to such a mandate? Furthermore, is it convincing to say that love to be love must produce love in return? Consider the affection a mother provides for an infant that dies before it can return to the mother a love that harbors care, responsibility, respect, and knowledge. Would we want to say that such a mother's affection was not love because it did not evoke a response of love in the infant?

Moving now to a deeper problem, one can wonder whether Fromm's concept of love is really a coherent concept at all. Recall that Fromm's basic assumption is that love is the solution to the isolation produced in persons not only by evolutionary development but also by birth and social conditioning. Accordingly, at the heart of Fromm's view is the notion that love is a self-interested fusion of one person with another in order to transcend painful isolation. But does not that notion build into his view of love a strong egoistic bent? And how can such egoism be reconciled with the robust altruism he requires of all genuine love? For example, while Fromm asserts that love to be love must love in the loved one all humankind, his advice regarding the practice of love extols an enlightened self-interest that shuns certain "bad company." He writes,

> I should add here that just as it is important to avoid trivial conversation, it is important to avoid bad company. By bad company I do not refer only to people who are vicious and destructive; one should avoid their company because their orbit is poisonous and depressing. I mean also the company of zombies, of people whose soul is dead, although their body is alive; of people whose thoughts and conversation are trivial; who chatter instead of talk, and who assert cliché opinions instead of thinking. However, it is not always possible to avoid the company of such people, nor even necessary. If one does not react in the expected way—that is, in clichés and trivialities—but directly and humanly, one will often find that such people change their behavior, often helped by the surprise effected by the shock of the unexpected. (pp. 113–114)

Is it not perhaps the case that human experience is richly diverse and ambiguous and that all of us exhibit egoistic and altruistic tendencies? If so, is not Fromm asking the concept "love" to do too much when he builds into it such diverse and conflicting human responses? Furthermore, is not Fromm stretching the concept of love beyond appropriate limits by having it include human actions ranging from sexual attraction to motherly affection? A defender of Fromm might reply that love is a pervasive and paradoxical phenomenon in which polar opposites exist in tension, and that the concept of love must reflect these tensions. The critic might, however, insist that Fromm's concept of love needs to be clarified, redefined, and delimited with greater precision. If one took the critic seriously at this point, how would one proceed? What descriptors could one use and what limits should one set? A promising technique for identifying appropriate descriptors for a concept is to select a number of specific, diverse events that unquestionably exemplify the concept and then to try to isolate the major commonalities in those diverse events. Such commonalities might then become the descriptors for the concept. What commonalities would such an analysis of a variety of generally agreed-upon acts of love yield? This would not be an easy task, but becoming clear about the meaning of love is an important part of the philosophy of sex and love.

MODERN SECULAR VIEWS
Alexander Comfort

Many and diverse voices can be heard in contemporary discussions of the philosophy of sex and love. In some of them we can discern accents from the Greek tradition; in others the influence of the biblical tradition. In some we can note the tones of medieval Christendom; in others the timbre of modern secularity. Fromm and Comfort illustrate modern secularity, the liberation of thought from religious tutelage. Fromm speaks of love. Comfort talks about sex. Neither writer feels constrained by religious commitments.

Alexander Comfort was born in London, England, on February 10, 1920. He studied at Cambridge and London Universities and holds the PhD, DSc, and MD degrees. He has served on the faculty of several institutions, including Stanford University in the Department of Psychiatry from 1974 to 1983, and the University of California Medical School at

From *The New Joy of Sex* by Alexander Comfort (New York: Crown Publishers, Inc., 1991), pp. 6–11, 34–35, 38. Used by permission of Reed Consumers Books Ltd., London, England.

Irvine in the Department of Pathology from 1976 to 1978. He has published books of poems and essays as well as several novels and many technical works. Probably his most widely read work is his series on the joy of sex: *The Joy of Sex: A Cordon Bleu Guide to Lovemaking* (1972), *More Joy: A Lovemaking Companion to the Joy of Sex* (1987), and *The New Joy of Sex* (1991).

Comfort's first version of the joy of sex was published shortly after a major sexual revolution had taken root in Western society. Facilitated by secularization and biomedical advances relating to sexual activity, a new openness to public discourse about sex appeared. In print, photography, and movies sex was discussed and portrayed with increasing realistic candor. Comfort comments about this revolution in the Preface to his 1991 version, *The New Joy of Sex*. He writes,

> I first wrote this book nearly 20 years and over 8,000,000 copies ago. I am a physician and human biologist for whom the natural history of human sexuality is of as much interest as the rest of human natural history. As with the rest of human natural history, I had notes on it. My wife encouraged me to bring biology into medicine, and my old medical school had no decent textbook to teach a human sexuality course.
>
> JOY was compiled and, very importantly, illustrated, just after the end of that daft and extraordinary non-statute in Western society, the Sexual Official Secrets Act. For at least two hundred years the description, and above all the depiction, of this most familiar and domestic group of activities, and of almost everything associated with them, had been classified. When, in the sixteenth century, Giulio Romano engraved his weightily classical pictures showing sixteen ways of making love, and Aretino wrote poems to go with them, a leading ecclesiastic opined that the artist deserved to be crucified. The public apparently thought otherwise ('Why,' said Aretino, 'should we not look upon that which pleases us most?') and *Aretin's Postures* have circulated surreptitiously ever since, but even in 1950's Britain the existence of pubic hair was artistically classified: it has to be airbrushed out to provide a smooth and featureless surface.
>
> People today, who never experienced the freeze on sexual information, won't appreciate the proportions of the transformation when it ended—it was like ripping down the Iron Curtain. My immediate predecessor in writing about domestic sex, Dr. Eustace Chesser, was (unsuccessfully) prosecuted for his low-key unillustrated book *Love Without Fear,* and even in 1972 there was still some remaining doubt whether JOY would be banned by the Thought Police. It wasn't.
>
> The main aim of 'sexual bibliotherapy' (writing books like this one) was to undo some of the mischief caused by guilt, misinformation and no-information. . . . One can now read books and see pictures devoted to sexual behavior almost without limitation in democratic countries, but it takes more than 20 years and a turnover of generations to undo centuries of misinformation; and of the material released by the new glasnost about sex, much is anxious or hostile or over the top. . . .
>
> Sexual behavior probably changes remarkably little over the years—sexual revolutions and moral backlashes chiefly affect the degree of frankness or reticence about what people do in private: the main contributor to any sexual revolution in our own time, insofar as it affects behavior, has not been frankness but the advent of reliable contraception, which makes it possible to separate the reproductive and recreational uses of sexuality. (*The New Joy of Sex,* pp. 6–7. Subsequent citations will be from this 1991 edition unless otherwise noted.)

This separation of the reproductive and recreational uses of sex, made possible by reliable contraception, is a radical departure from the way Aquinas and his followers within the Roman Catholic Church view things. Recall that for Thomas Aquinas virginity is preferable to marriage, sexual intercourse is warranted only for the purpose of reproduction, and sexual gratification per se is depreciated. Consonant with the thinking of Aquinas, the Roman Catholic leadership for years has opposed modern contraceptive technology. Comfort, however, celebrates contraception because it frees sexual activity from reproduction and allows it to be fully recreational, joyfully playful. Comfort continues,

> It is only recently, as ethology has replaced psychoanalytic theory, that counselors have come to realize that sex, besides being a serious interpersonal matter, is a deeply rewarding form of play (their clients sense this but got little encouragement). Children are not encouraged to be embarrassed about their play: adults often have been and are still. So long as play is not hostile, cruel, unhappy or limiting, they need not be.
>
> One of the most important uses of play is in expressing a healthy awareness of sexual equality. This involves letting both sexes take turns in controlling the game; sex is no longer what men do to women and women are supposed to enjoy. Sexual interaction is sometimes a loving fusion, sometimes a situation where each is a 'sex object'— maturity in sexual relationships involves balancing, rather than denying, the personal and the impersonal aspects of physical arousal. Both are essential and built-in to humans. For anyone who is short on either of these elements, play is the way to learn; men learn to stop domineering and trying to perform, women that they can take control in the give and take of the game rather than by nay-saying. If they achieve this, Man and Woman are one another's best friends in the very sparks they strike from one another. (p. 7)

In keeping with his view that sexual activity should be a playful, joyful experience, Comfort selects a gourmet cookbook metaphor to characterize his discussion of sex. Becoming adept at gourmet cooking requires study and effort: The same can be said about becoming skilled at "Cordon Bleu Sex." Comfort writes,

> Chef-grade cooking doesn't happen naturally: it starts at the point where people know how to prepare and enjoy food, are curious about it and willing to take trouble preparing it, read recipe hints, and find they are helped by one or two detailed techniques. It's hard to make mayonnaise by trial and error, for instance. Cordon Bleu sex, as we define it, is exactly the same situation—the extra one can get from comparing notes, using some imagination, trying way-out or new experiences, when one already is making satisfying love and wants to go on from there. (p. 8)

Comfort makes it clear that the high quality gourmet sex that he has in mind is always linked with love:

> The people we are addressing are the adventurous and uninhibited lovers who want to find the limits of their ability to enjoy sex. That means we take some things for granted—having intercourse naked and spending time over it; being able and willing to make it last, up to a whole afternoon on occasion; having privacy and washing facilities; not being scared of things like genital kisses; not being obsessed with one sexual trick to the exclusion of all others, and, of course, loving each other.
>
> This book is about love as well as sex as the title implies: you don't get high quality sex on any other basis—either you love each other before you come to want it, or, if you happen to get it, you love each other because of it, or both. No point in arguing this, but just as you can't cook without heat you can't make love without feedback (which may be the reason we say 'make love' rather than 'make sex'). Sex is the one

place where we today can learn to treat people as people. Feedback means the right mixture of stop and go, tough and tender, exertion and affection. This comes by empathy and long mutual knowledge. Anyone who expects to get this in a first attempt with a stranger is an optimist, or a neurotic—if he does, it is what used to be called love at first sight, and isn't expendable: 'skill,' or variety are no substitutes. Also one can't teach tenderness. (p. 9)

The starting point of all lovemaking is close bodily contact. Love has been defined as the harmony of two souls and the contact of two epidermes. It is also, from our infancy, the starting point of human relationships and needs. Our culture ('Anglo-Saxon'), after several centuries of intense taboos on many such contacts—between friends, between males—which are used by other cultures, has cut down 'intimacy' based on bodily contact to parent-child and lover-lover situations. We're getting over this taboo, or at least the part which has spilled over into baby-raising and explicit love-making, but coupled with our other cultural reservation, which says that play and fantasy are only safe for children, it has dealt us a bad hand for really full and personal sex. Our idea of sex wouldn't be recognizable to some other cultures, though our range of choice is the widest ever. For a start it's over-genital: 'sex' for our culture means putting the penis in the vagina. Man's whole skin is a genital organ. (p. 10)

There isn't too much point in crying over cultural spilt milk. Our sex repertoire has to be geared to us as we are, not to Trobriand Islanders (who have their own, different hangups). We need extensive sex play which is centered in intercourse and in doing things. At the same time we might as well plan our menu so that we learn to use the rest of our equipment. That includes our whole skin surface, our feelings of identity, aggression and so on, and all of our fantasy needs. Luckily, sex behavior in humans is enormously elastic (it has had to be, or we wouldn't be here), and also nicely geared to help us express most of the needs which society or our upbringing have corked up. Elaboration in sex is something we need rather specially (though it isn't confined to our sort of society) and it has the advantage that if we really make it work it makes us more, not less, receptive to each other as people. . . . There may be other places we can learn to express all of ourselves, and to do it mutually, but there aren't many. (pp. 10–11)

Comfort offers some additional comments on love and tenderness:

Love.   We use the same word for man-woman, mother-child, child-parent, and I-mankind relations—rightly, because they are a continuous spectrum. In talking about sexual relations, it seems right to apply it to any relationship in which there is mutual tenderness, respect and consideration—from a total interdependence where the death of one maims the other for years, to an agreeable night together. The intergrades are all love, all worthy, all part of human experience. Some meet the needs of one person, some of another—or of the same person at different times. That's really the big problem of sexual ethics, and it's basically a problem of self-understanding and of communication. You can't assume that your 'conditions of love' are applicable to, or accepted by, any other party; you can't assume that these won't be changed quite unpredictably in both of you by the experience of loving; you can't necessarily know your own mind. If you are going to love, these are risks you have to take, and don't depend simply on whether or not you have sex together—though that is such a potentially overwhelming experience that tradition is right in pinpointing it. Sometimes two people know each other very well, or think they've worked things out by discussion, and they may be right. But even so if it's dignifiable by the name of love it's potentially an open-ended experience. . . .

If sexual love can be—and it is—the supreme human experience, it must be also a bit hazardous. It can give us our best and our worst moments. In this respect it's like mountain climbing—over-timid people miss the whole experience; reasonably balanced and hardy people accept the risks for the rewards, but realize that there's a difference between this and being foolhardy. Love, moreover, involves someone else's neck beside your own. At least you can make as sure as may be that you don't exploit or injure someone—you don't take a novice climbing and abandon them halfway up when things get difficult. Getting them to sign a form of consent before they start isn't an answer either. There was a hell of a lot to be said for the English Victorian idea of not being a cad ('person devoid of finer or gentlemanly feelings'). A cad can be of either sex.

Marriage between two rival actor-managers, each trying to produce the other regardless, isn't love. The relationship between a prostitute and a casual client where, for reasons they don't quite get, real tenderness and respect occur, is. (pp. 34–35)

Tenderness. This, in fact, is what the whole book is about. It doesn't exclude extremely violent games (though many people neither need nor want these), but it does exclude clumsiness, heavy handedness, lack of feedback, spitefulness and non-rapport generally. Shown fully in the way you touch each other. What it implies at root is a constant awareness of what your partner is feeling, plus the knowledge of how to heighten that feeling, gently, toughly, slowly or fast, and this only comes from an inner state of mind between you. No really tender person can just turn over and go to sleep. Many if not most inexperienced men, and some women, are just naturally clumsy—either through haste, through anxiety, or through lack of sensing how the other sex feels. Men in general are harder-skinned than women—don't grab breasts, stick fingers into the vagina, handle female skin as if it was your own, or (and this goes for both sexes) misplace bony parts of your anatomy. More girls respond to very light than to very heavy stimulation—just brushing pubic or skin hairs will usually do far more than a whole-hand grab. At the same time don't be frightened—neither of you is made of glass. Women by contrast often fail to use enough pressure, especially in handwork, though the light, light variety is a sensation on its own. Start very gently, making full use of the skin surface, and work up. Stimulus toleration in any case increases with sexual excitement until even hard blows can become excitants (though not for everyone). This loss of pain sense disappears almost instantly with orgasm, so don't go on too long, and be extra gentle as soon as he or she has come.

If we could teach tenderness most of this book would be superseded by intuition. . . . Few people want to be in bed on any terms with a person who isn't basically tender, and most people are delighted to be in bed with the right person who is. The ultimate test is whether you can bear to find the person there when you wake up. If you are actually pleased, then you're onto the right thing. (p. 38)

Cordon Bleu Sex, then, is playful and joyful. It requires study and effort. It is inextricably linked with love, which is present in any relationship in which there is mutual tenderness, respect, consideration, and mutual feedback (that is to say, interpersonal communication for the enrichment of each other). And it involves a far richer range of activities than simply the penis in the vagina. Comfort goes on to discuss the two modes of sex: the "duet" and the "solo":

There are two modes of sex, the duet and the solo, and a good concert alternates between them. The duet is a cooperative effort aiming at simultaneous orgasm, or at least one orgasm each, and complete, untechnically planned let-go. This in fact needs skill, and can be built up from more calculated 'love-play' until doing the right thing for both of you becomes fully automatic. This is the basic sexual meal. The solo, by contrast, is when one partner is the player and the other the instrument. The aim of the player is to produce results on the other's pleasure experience as extensive, unexpected and generally wild as his or her skill allows—to blow them out of themselves. The player doesn't lose control, though he or she can get wildly excited by what is happening to the other. The instrument does lose control—in fact, with a responsive instrument and a skillful performer, this is the concerto situation—if it ends in an uncontrollable ensemble, so much the better. All the elements of music and the dance get into this scene—rhythm, mounting tension, tantalization, even actual aggression. . . . (p. 11)

Having set forth these general conditions for gourmet sex, Comfort discusses in detail more than one hundred entries appearing on his gourmet menu. If one pursued the various options recommended by Comfort, one's sexual activity would no doubt have the spice of variety. We need not examine, however, his menu further at this point because our space is limited and because we already have his perspective displayed sufficiently for the purposes of the philosophy of sex and love.

The fact that millions of copies of Comfort's menu for Cordon Bleu Sex have been sold suggests that his ideas are congenial to many people. Certainly, many will find his frank discussion of human sexual activity to be liberating. Also, his attempt to deliver sex from the depreciating stigmas attached to it by a Western tradition heavily influenced by Platonism, Augustinianism, and Thomism will be welcomed by many. Furthermore, his insistence that sex, to be the finest sex, must be linked with love will be seen by many as a humanizing and responsible position.

Yet some worrisome questions need to be addressed. First of all, what would Comfort say to those who claimed that sex without love is really a superior pleasure to sex with love? Furthermore, is not Comfort's concept of love rather ill-formed compared to Fromm's? And if Fromm's concept of love ran into the problem of its meaning being blurred by applying it to too many diverse human experiences, would not Comfort's concept of love encounter the same predicament?

A deeper problem arises, however, when one questions the warrant for the menu for Cordon Bleu Sex. Comfort does not address the question of warrant head-on; but his discussion seems to imply an appeal to what is natural. Comfort seems to believe that humans are programmed by nature for sexual pleasure; that a study of the ways that they can and do gain sexual pleasure reveals a rich variety; and that this variety is natural and must be freed from the past and present constraints of bigots and censors. But the appeal to what is natural is fraught with problems, as we shall see in a subsequent chapter. Is not cruelty also "natural"? What warrant does Comfort have for preferring sex with tenderness to sex with cruelty? What could Comfort say to a Marquis de Sade who would claim that sadistic sexual pleasure is superior to wimpy Cordon Bleu Sex?

CHAPTER 2

The Debate Between
Sex With Love
Versus
Sex Without Love

IN CONTEMPORARY PHILOSOPHICAL LITERATURE, an intriguing debate has arisen concerning the value of sex with love versus the value of sex without love. Traditionally, the disvalue of sex without love has been assumed. Even those who see sex as a positive value would add that sex with love is superior. At first blush, it would appear that the question of sex with love versus sex without love is easily determined by empirical measures such as attitude polls and interviews. For example, a particular survey could indicate that a large percentage of females prefer sex when it occurs within a loving relationship, whereas most males prefer sex primarily for the physical pleasure.

Those who have traditionally opted for the superiority of sex with love may be troubled by certain empirical claims such as those of prominent sex researchers William H. Masters, Virginia E. Johnson, and Robert G. Kolodny, who report:

> There is no evidence, however, that sex is always or usually better if you are in love. We have worked with hundreds of loving, committed relationships where the sexual interaction was in shambles and with hundreds of people who deeply enjoyed sex without being in love.   (*Human Sexuality*, p. 237)

However, even if data are compiled regarding the pleasure or enjoyment of sex in such relationships, does that settle the major aspects of the debate between the value of sex with love as against sex without love?

Many philosophers, theologians, and moralists do not believe the question ends with current statements of such facts, but rather, they remain interested in larger evaluative issues at many levels as well as from a variety of perspectives. What is the value of sex with or without love when all things are reflectively and critically examined from a wider point of view? Does the fact that someone desires or enjoys something at a given time establish that it is really *desirable* or worthy of enjoyment? Should sexual experiences be examined and evaluated as isolated events, disconnected from other important aspects of one's life, including one's relationships with family, friends, and communities? Many liberals, such as Russell Vannoy, do urge us to view sex for its own sake; that is, for its own unique and inherent value. In their view, sex is similar to other human activities, such as eating, playing tennis, and reading, and should be enjoyed for its own sake without the mystification and symbolism of love and marriage.

Deeper underlying value conflicts can also be found between the advocates of the superiority of sex with love and the supporters of sex without love. For example, the debate could extend into disputes over what constitutes "the good life." One view could be characterized as the "smorgasbord" ideal, in which the good life consists in the maximization and enjoyment of a wide variety of human experiences that need not be anchored in any particular overarching life plan or overriding dominant goal. On the other hand, others may view the good life from a more monistic perspective, where there is a dominant plan and some all-important goal. For thinkers such as Peter Bertocci, such a goal would consist in following a natural progression culminating in the dominant ideal of marriage-family-community. Accordingly, activities such as sex are evaluated with reference to whether they contribute or detract from the attainment of the higher and more important values of marriage, family, and community. For such theorists, it is not the empirical facts of the pleasures of sex that are paramount, but rather the extent to which sexual experiences foster love and its progression to the higher values of marriage, family, and community. The debate continues as thinkers such as Vannoy view Bertocci's dominant ideal as a mere conservative preference for one kind of lifestyle that may not be the best life for all or even most people. In fact, as we shall see below, Vannoy will argue that the love that acts as the catalyst for Bertocci's love progression to the higher values is not the noble and benign thing it has been portrayed to be. Rather, such love is beset with fatal contradictions that do not promote the best in human relationships. Furthermore, such love is said to interfere with satisfying sexual relationships.

The opposing positions in the sex-with-love versus sex-without-love debate may further reflect still another conflict—a conflict among human needs. The human needs of security and emotional attachment may contradict the needs for independence, adventure, and novelty. Thus, people who have sex with love may be assigning primary value to the need for security, whereas those who adopt the sex-without-love approach may decide in favor of adventure and novelty. Is the choice between security and novelty irreconcilable or is it another false dilemma? Can using one's powers of critical reflection lead to an appropriate compromise? For example, can one achieve a life with a secure and stable sexual relationship combined with an adventurous or novel occupational life, or a steady and secure work life combined with a novel and adventurous sex life, or any other variations of security and novelty within an individual's lifestyle?

So far, we have mentioned only some *general* value questions regarding the goodness of sex with and without love. However, many philosophers and theologians have focused on the *moral* aspects of such sexual experiences. Some view sex without love as immoral on various grounds. For example, it is contended that in sex without love, one partner egoistically views the other as a mere instrument or means to one's own satisfaction. The use or manipulation of another for one's selfish purposes is a direct violation of the Kantian moral principle, "Always treat humanity, whether in your own person or that of another, as an end and never as a means only." For Kant, the use of another is the antithesis of a genuine regard for the other as a valuable autonomous being to be respected for his or her own sake. Others will see sex without love as morally problematic insofar as it is likely to cause harm to others; that is, the pain suffered from being left in the lurch, lied to, or physically abused, etc.

Liberals, on the other hand, will argue that such charges against sex without love reflect a false dualism. One may respect and be generous to one's partner even if one is not in love with him or her. Moreover, many lovers do not treat their partners as ends in themselves. And it cannot be emphasized too strongly that those involved in a sex-with-love relationship may still be selfish, inconsiderate, and violent toward their partners. (Thousands of spousal abuse cases provide vivid examples of this.)

Still another interesting problem in this debate has been suggested by some evolutionary psychologists, anthropologists, and sex researchers; that is, the question of the value of sex with love versus sex without love may assume that both genders experience love and sex in the same way when it can be strongly argued that males and females sense sex and love differently. We shall see in Lillian Rubin's comments that for women generally, sex with love is more satisfying and enjoyable, and for men generally, the physical aspects may determine the value of the sexual experience. This, if true, would raise another cogent philosophical issue: Are these facts consistent and unalterable givens that must be accepted, or is it possible through social developments to change the way we experience sex? Some feminists, for example, argue that both the male and female sexual experience may be strongly determined by the patriarchal culture that conditions each sex to accept certain gender roles and to have attitudinal and behavioral traits that facilitate these roles. Moreover, it is argued that through rational reflection, one may be able to choose freely the manner in which sexuality can be experienced.

Having outlined a few of the philosophical concerns of the sex-with-love versus sex-without-love debate, we shall now turn to some more in-depth explorations of the issue. First, Peter Bertocci presents a traditional defense of the superiority of sex with love; then Russell Vannoy offers a contemporary assault on the traditional view, as well as his own argument for the superiority of sex without love. Finally, we take a brief look at Lillian Rubin's observations concerning male-female sexual experience.

SEX WITH LOVE

One popular current philosophical view is that sex is like any other human appetite or activity and ought to be pursued as an end in itself, the end of obtaining uniquely sexual pleasures. Bertocci squarely attacks this view in the following selection. He contends that sex for sex's sake falls far short of an enriching, joyful, and significant human experience. When disconnected from some of the highest human values of love, marriage, family, and community, sex becomes an egoistic, short-lived, and impoverishing experience.

According to Bertocci, to be most fulfilling, sex needs to subserve and foster love, which has its own laws of progression; that is, love leads to marriage, the creation of children, and the betterment of society. When sex serves love's progression and is an expression of these higher human values, it becomes one of human life's greatest and most satisfying experiences.

---

from The Human Venture in Sex, Love, and Marriage

PETER A. BERTOCCI

The Human Experience of Sex

When a person decides that he is going to get all he can out of sex *as sex,* he is driven into an almost endless progression: he must find a new fancy, a new variety of sexual experience, real or imaginary, for he soon tires of the last mode of sexual exploration. Having made sex an end in itself, as a miser makes money an end in itself, or as a glutton makes food an end in itself, there is nothing

From *The Human Venture in Sex, Love, and Marriage* by Peter A. Bertocci (New York: Association Press, 1949), pp. 47–61.

more to do but seek some more thrilling or novel sexual experience. Many sexual perverts are products of this chase for new forms of pleasure. They teach us that sexual expression for its own sake brings diminishing returns. I am not, of course, trying to say that every incontinent person becomes a sex pervert, but he invites trouble for himself and others when he tries to find in sex what sex as such cannot give him. Sex experience for its own sake, and certainly when the other person is simply "used," hardens the arteries of tender feeling. Though sexual perversion is by no means a necessary result, the loss of tenderness and sympathy, let alone self-confidence, is a tremendous price to pay for sex pleasure.

On the other hand, sex is an increasing source of personal enrichment when dedicated to objectives other than mere self-satisfaction. The fact of human experience seems to be that persons enjoy deeper, more lasting, and more profound satisfaction when the normal experience of sex lust is not primarily an end in itself but a symbolic expression of other values. This, after all, is true not only about sex but about other desires also. We enjoy eating at a banquet in honor of a friend more than eating in solitude. Before elaborating this theme, several remarks must be made about a counter-theme that has pervaded, sometimes quite subtly, much thinking about the functioning of sex in human life.

There is a tendency to think of sex in human experience as a continuation of the sex function in animals. Man's life, including sex, is more complicated but not essentially different from that of the higher animals. The prevalence of this view has sometimes led us to suppose that sex education is hardly necessary since at the right time the biological organism will react effectively and appropriately as it does among animals. Thinking of man as a complicated animal, we falsely reasoned that his sex behavior is as mechanical and automatic with him as it is with animals. Indeed, some of us added, to expect him to control himself sexually is like expecting an animal in heat to reject sexual advances. The best we can do, according to this view, is to realize that man is a higher animal and teach him enough of the physiology of sex to avoid disease.

This line of reasoning neglects the *human* significance of sex. Sex in the human is so interwoven with his total psychological being that, once allowance is made for some physiological similarities, the contrasts are more illuminating than the likenesses. To compare the sounds an animal makes with the poetry of word symbols gives some notion of the range of differences possible. The biological transaction of sexual intercourse in animals has at its best nowhere near the possible meaning that a similar biological transaction can have in human experience. Sex education has failed to make enough of the function of sex as human experience. In consequence we have talked as if the biology of sex measures its importance as a human function.

Consequently the argument against intercourse has emphasized the physical effects of sexual promiscuity, the danger of sexual diseases and of pregnancy. These must not be minimized, but they have played such a large part in the so-called "case for chastity" that both young and old have wondered, with justification, what possible case can be made against promiscuity once knowledge of the methods of disease prevention and contraceptives has been increased and disseminated. The concern of the military during World War II did not go beyond educating young men and women for physical efficiency. The general impression was left that sin is not in sexual intercourse but in the infection that may result from carelessness. We seemed to be bankrupt of really adequate reasons why human beings should abstain from promiscuity when they are confident that impregnation or venereal diseases can be prevented.

The situation will not be greatly changed until we become more fully aware of the conditions in human experience under which sexual intercourse makes its deepest contributions. Here we are clearly in the area of the interpretation of the value of sex as part of the meaning of life. If we cannot interpret the higher values of sex as clearly as we have explained physiological, and even psychological, details, we shall go on "expressing" sex and "avoiding frustration" when we might be finding, through sex experience, a creative human joy.

The Human Challenge in Love

The assumption at this stage of the argument is that love, marriage, and the home are among the supreme values of human existence; that the human beings who cannot enjoy the blessings that love, marriage, and the home bestow are relatively poverty-stricken. We shall try to show that the experience of sex may bless or endanger love, that it may bless or be a constant source of friction in marriage, that it may be a solid foundation for co-operative family life or a source of frustrating disharmony.

As already suggested, there is a "love progression" in human life. This progression is affected by the sexual progression, but it has its own laws. The love progression protects the satisfactions of sex, but sex, unless mastered, will endanger the progression of love and enslave the person. The individual in love invests his energies and abilities in joyous concern for the security and growth of another. He finds fulfillment of his own life in consecration to the needs and development of his beloved. As his love grows, his self-discipline increases with a view to insuring the happiness of his sweetheart. He rethinks and replans the goals of his life so that she may find opportunity and realization within them. "To love a person productively implies to care, to feel responsible for his life, not only for his physical existence, but for the growth and development of all his human powers."[1]

Loving, therefore, is a kind of growing. Love inspires one to live with at least one other person in mind. The circle of self-enjoyment grows into an ellipse in which the two poles are included. But, as Plato long ago reminded us, love is a suffering yearning for what one does not possess completely. The individual must refocus his mind and body, re-form his ideas and dreams, so that the good he wants for himself and for his sweetheart may be realized. Love means growth; it means work; it means moral progress. Thus *love, inclusive of sex, needs marriage to protect and nourish its values. And marriage, to be a most fruitful and inclusive experience which protects and nourishes the values of both love and sex, must be put to work in building a family and a society.* This is the inner progression of love.

It is evident that there will be many obstacles on the way to realizing personality and character built around love. The deception in the progression of love is just the opposite of that in the sex-ual progression. For now the individual will be tempted to stop short of more complete fulfillment. It will be easy to think that a sexual experience enjoyed by two persons will remain an adequate source of joy, that the pleasure of sex and love without marriage will endure, that marriage without commitment to objectives greater than the union of two married lovers will maintain a challenging equilibrium. For there is no doubt that sex lust usually brings pleasure sufficiently gratifying to seem entirely satisfactory, especially to those who do not know the quality of sex love. So also with this next step in the progression of love: sex love without marriage can bring so much satisfaction, at least for a time, that two persons may be tempted to forego the more complete satisfaction of married love. Then there are some who, having reached a high level of married love, may be tempted to forfeit the more creative experience that children and a home can bring.

Let the sexual act be the expression of the conscious desire and decision to become parents, and that act reaches its zenith in human feeling, inspiration, and fulfillment. It is almost foolish to try to make this experience clear to those who have not known it. Words that receive their content from other levels of sex experience are quite inadequate for this. Let two persons extend their love for each other into the tender and responsible decision to have and care for children, and they will find the meaning of the sexual experience immeasurably enriched.

Sex, love, marriage, family, and social responsibility are human ventures all along the line. The question is: Which venture brings completeness, invites to growth in character and personality, enables the individual to feel that he has accepted the role that his abilities allow in the achievement of a dependable social order? It is our thesis that love, including sex love, is the more radiant and satisfying when it becomes a means of communicating one's concern for the wider range of values that purposeful living together makes possible. Sex without love, love without marriage, and marriage without creative commitments to children (or the equivalent) are in constant danger of vanishing away. Persons disregard the laws of growth and development in human nature only to find that they have forfeited their heritage.

Love, at its best, is the supreme victory over parasitism and egoism. It is a unique fruition of human experience, so unique and so different from anything in the physical and biological world, that it stands as the richest product of human effort. It is not, however, a fruit which just comes with maturation. It will be no greater than the person in love; it will reflect and challenge the intelligence, emotion, and discipline dedicated to its development.

The Impetus of Love

A human being without love exists on a subhuman level. He may try to avoid responsibilities and cares while enjoying lesser satisfactions. But his nature is such that, once he has known what it means to be in love, life without love is a clanging cymbal. For to love is to change the directions of life; it is to center one's own satisfaction in the creative growth of another. It binds two persons into a unique relation in which they live for and with each other. It makes the difference between existing and living. Note how the lover says to his beloved that he had been only existing without her, and he never wants to go back to that!

Loving is a kind of wager with existence; it is a new level of existence that calls for the reorganization of one's being around a more inclusive objective—the life of the partner. It is no great wonder that to the person to whom love is new, life becomes "out of this world." It is a new adventure that involves new responsibilities. To find that another really cares without having to, that one's life is important and a source of enrichment to another, is reason enough for the intoxicating superlatives that fill the diaries of lovers. "I can't believe it. I thought nobody would ever find me important to happiness. I wonder if I can really make her happy. She deserves so much! I must never let her down, never give her one bad moment! Oh, it's so wonderful to be with her! Everything about her, from that delicate wave in her hair to the way she walks, makes me feel so proud and so humble." And so it goes on.

Love begins in that early attraction, develops as each finds more encouragement for his own values, more challenge in another's interests and needs and objectives. There are many things to do, to plan, to talk about and dream about, and they are much more interesting because two persons can enjoy them and find themselves interlocked by them. There is a surge of emotional energy—sometimes quiet, sometimes turbulent, always demanding—constantly seeking a new way, a more intimate and complete means of expressing itself. One cannot go on feeling this way day after day, can one? It seems more than one can bear—more than both lovers can bear—to be so close to each other spiritually, without expressing their unity physically. They hold hands tightly, they kiss meaningfully, they embrace almost as one, and feel a closer, a more symbolic psychological and spiritual unity. "How can it be wrong for two human beings who admire and respect each other as we do, who are committed to each other as we are, to follow what every pulse of mind and body urges?"

What two persons in love have not found themselves pondering this question? It is easy for one not in this situation to minimize its power until he is brought face to face with it as was the day that Judith and Harry came to see me. Both juniors in college, interested in sports, debating, "Y" work, and social questions, they had been going together for about a year. These were not just two wild-eyed "kids" whose hands unconsciously and naturally found each other. They looked tense and tired; they had come to the end of their emotional and philosophical rope. Had they been irresponsible young people, they would not have been there with the question Harry was ready to pose.

"Why shouldn't we express our love for each other, and stop bottling up our feelings? We don't want to live without each other, but we can't be married for at least two years. We've been told that sexual intercourse is not justified, and we both know that our parents would be bitterly disappointed if they knew that these thoughts even entered our heads. But here we are, feeling like society's scapegoats. This demand of our parents and of society is going to break up, if we let it, one of the most beautiful experiences in our lives. We want each other; we want to stop fighting each other's feelings. We know about contraceptives, and we know where we can get adequate medical advice in these matters. If a baby should come, we would make the adjustment and we'd love it. I can always quit school and get a job if it comes to that. We care for each other so much that we can take any eventuality in our stride, but we know we can't go on this way; we'll go stale! Maybe we're rationalizing, but isn't society rationalizing? Suppose there is a risk. Can you give a real reason for postponing the full expression of our love?"

Here, then, are two young people who stand at a peak of experience. For them life now means a certain quality of togetherness that heightens the value of their existence. If they live by the impetus of their dominant psychobiological impulses alone, they will go into an experience that in itself will transcend past peaks. It does no good to minimize that fact for, after all, it will be for them (two years earlier) the same symbol of spiritual unity that it would be after marriage. What can be said, indeed, that will meet them on their own grounds and be rationally satisfying?

The attitude of Judith and Harry weakens the criticism that appeals to the fear of pregnancy, to society's demand that children should be supported, and to other possible social consequences of premarital intercourse. If there is a case that will stand against sexual intercourse at their level of experience, it must spring from considerations as deep as is this spiritual demand for the fruition of sex love, and not merely sex lust. This is the challenge in Harry's and Judith's question. Our generation must give an answer to it. Let us make their case even stronger and assume that foolproof contraceptives are available. What makes it wrong for human beings to enjoy sexual intercourse when they love each other? Why intimate that love expressed in sexual intercourse without marriage is endangered while love expressed in sexual intercourse in marriage is not endangered?

The Place of Marriage in a Person's Life

It seems to me that no reasonable answer is possible without an understanding of the function of human marriage in psychological and ethical terms. Too many Judiths and Harrys, as well as their elders, conceive of marriage as an institution that justifies sexual intercourse and protects the children born thereby. For many young people the reason for sexual abstinence, especially if two persons love each other, would vanish if perfect contraception were assured. Let us turn our attention first to the broader and deeper roots of monogamous marriage. Once we reflect upon these, we can better appraise the place of sexual intercourse in life.[2]

Monogamous marriage is a testimony to the reasonable faith that two human beings can improve the quality of their lives to a degree not otherwise possible. Every person develops aims for his life. He may not be conscious of his aims or values, but for him they make life worth-while. Frequently he wants more than he is able to realize through his abilities in the situations confronting him. It is not easy to have dreams and then become aware of one's inability to work them out because of obstacles in oneself and in the environment. It is easy to lose faith in oneself, and in life itself, especially when growing up means a sharper awareness of good and evil, of hypocrisy in unexpected places, of human failures in kindness and forgiveness. Doubt about the value of ideals allows the maturing person to be less censorious of his own weakness. And yet he would like to believe that life holds promise, that he is not alone in the struggle for meaning. For him to find another engaged in the same struggle is to find a partner whose efforts throw light on his own. The sympathy and encouragement of the other dissolve the loneliness of spirit that roots in the fear that one's ideals may perhaps be mere dreams.

Can it be, indeed, that the inspiration and revival human beings find in falling in love springs from the realization that life will not have to be a kind of soliloquy at the deeper value centers in experience? To find another who is stirred by the same visions, who does not talk what is "ultimate nonsense" all the time, whose beliefs challengingly express one's ideals, and whose life is at least a partial incarnation of what we consider worth-while—this is to find one's life befriended and one's values at home right here and now in this person who walks, talks, smiles, and reflects them. There are, no doubt, problems with which each soul may simply have to walk alone or with God. But even at these moments to feel that another would, if possible, share that problem, is to feel more at home and confident in life. Others may help and feel close to one in many ways, but this sweetheart is willing to live through to the end.

If this suggests to some reader that the experience of being in love is analogous to vital religious experience, the comparison is aptly drawn. As we see it, the faith that there is Another who cares, cares in a degree and manner that no human being can adequately understand, is psychologically continuous with the yearning that one's deepest values find at least another sponsor in the world. Whether the belief in such a Personal Source of Values be true or untrue, for those who sincerely believe that God cares about their growth, there usually comes that peace *in* mind, that motivation of purpose, which keeps life steadfast in the pursuit of greater good. Many who do not find this dimension of spiritual incentive do discover in their love for another, and in another's love for them, a similar anchoring of their ideals and zest for their development.[3]

To state these things is to feel a certain audacity in the human venture in monogamy. For one suddenly realizes how preposterous seems the draft being made upon a human relation. Yet none of us can deny the existence of this yearning not to walk alone with one's values, to respect and serve the values of another, to find solace and inspiration in the course of one's weariness, a companion for one's joys, and a partner in one's crucial ideals. Nor can we deny that the person in love, when his love is more than lust, feels something akin to this poor description. When he marries he dedicates these feelings publicly and openly, vowing that he will continue to work with his beloved for the things that matter most as they understand them.

Unmarried persons are free from the awesome problem of creatively unifying two lives. They do not face the challenge of harmonizing complicated sets of value themes—the challenge of days, weeks, months, and years of responsibilities and opportunities, of dishes and dusting, of mending and buying, of earning and giving, of sickness and health, of meeting people and making friends, of working with and for others. Nor do they experience an incessant challenge to their resources of good humor and intelligence, of courage and good will, of patience and flexibility. The economy of effort that marriage makes possible at one point calls for a maximum of effort at many others, for one shares the other's concerns along with one's own. Even these brief suggestions should indicate that, while marriage takes root in vital yearnings, it also sets up as many problems as it promises to solve. Many of these problems, and others as complex, a human being has to face even without the comradeship of another. But the only thing worse than unhappy singleness is unhappy marriage. For now all burdens are complicated and the failure is more devastating. We are never surprised at the seemingly high rate of divorce, undesirable as it is for all concerned. Monogamous marriage is a high calling, fraught with real values and real dangers. The coming of children increases the sense of significance, the problems, the opportunities for mutual growth, and the burden of possible failure.

Are the values worth the risk? For those who would judge life by a balance sheet of pleasure and pain, the answer might be doubtful. The young lover, of course, has no doubt of the worth-whileness of the venture. He is no longer happy in his singleness, and he feels that existence has little to offer unless he and his dear one are united. But romantic illusions aside, and accepting the assumption that children *might* be reared in a better atmosphere than a family, is the marriage relation between two persons in itself desirable?

The answer may be briefly suggested by the questions: Is there any other relation between human beings (apart from parent and child) that calls for more kindness, sincerity, sensitivity to growth, courage, and patience, and that can yield so much peace of mind, zest for life, opportunity for sharing, intimacy of human feeling, and gracious generosity? Can any other human relation produce and develop such virtues and values in two persons? We shall need to say much more about the demands that a creative marriage makes upon two persons (Chapter Four). At this point we may affirm that the person who deliberately by-passes marriage is risking the loss of a supreme purpose and an inspiring joy. Within marriage there grows that love which is the goal of all other loves between human beings, the responsible sharing of the human adventure in purposeful living. Nor must we overlook the adventure in maturing of spirit that the rearing of children makes possible! Were not great values and great losses at stake, there would be little point in trying to answer the difficult question: Why should not two persons in sex love with each other, and who intend to marry, have sexual intercourse?

Notes

1. Fromm, Eric. *Man for Himself.* (New York: Farrar & Rinehart, 1947).

2. The conception of marriage that will be suggested here might be related to the many conceptions of the function of marriage explored by the anthropologist and sociologist. But our concern is to suggest an ethical norm for marriage that takes into adequate account, we hope, the forces present in the social matrix of Western civilization. While forms of marriage other than the monogamous may serve important social func-

tions in their particular social context, they hardly provide the conditions in which some of the finest values of life are protected. Rather than assert that other forms of marriage are just as good as monogamy, we would hold that monogamy best satisfies the needs of human beings, and that the sooner other societies can develop to the stage where monogamy is possible, the better it will be for all mankind. We cannot here do more than suggest the background of a conviction on a very involved problem, but those for whom we are writing are at least socially committed to monogamous marriage.

3. We have long wondered why many psychologists have not allowed such experiences of the lover to tell them something about human nature in its own terms before they decide to reduce it to a complicated form of infantile or childhood experience. Certainly the spiritual trauma, the struggle for security in one's values, is as significant as, and more observable than, the birth trauma.

Bertocci raises a crucial question when he asks, "Why should not two persons in sex love with each other, and who intend to marry, have sexual intercourse?" His answer, of course, would come from his eloquent and thoughtful defense of the traditional view that sex with love is far superior to sex without love. However, it is more accurate to characterize Bertocci's philosophy as the sex with love-marriage-children-home-approach, as becomes quite evident in his reply to the question of Judith and Harry.

It is clear that a major part of Bertocci's argument depends on his portrayal of romantic love.[1] Whereas Bertocci exhalts the value of love and its enriching influence on the human sexual experience, Vannoy, in the next selection, will subject this claim to rigorous criticism.

Another significant assumption that energizes Bertocci's argument is his portrayal of those who prefer sex without love as egoistical, selfish, inconsiderate persons who engage in subhuman, animalistic sex acts. He further reinforces this by use of the addiction model in which the sex-without-love lover is viewed as one who is enslaved by lust and in constant but futile pursuit of sexual satisfaction. Here again, we shall see Vannoy's endeavor to repudiate Bertocci's assumptions.

As we prepare to study Vannoy, we may consider several questions. For example, does Bertocci describe a rarely achieved ideal of the sex-love-marriage connection? Does love really proceed according to the "laws" Bertocci describes? Are there, in fact, any such laws at all? If so, how do we rationally discover and defend them? Is the love-sex connection actually experienced that way by people in a long-term marital relationship? Why do so many happily married people turn to sex therapy counselors or become involved in adulterous relationships?[2]

On the other hand, is Vannoy's portrayal of sex without love simply another rarely achieved ideal? One in which the participants are assumed to be humanistic, generous, caring persons, free from the ordinary anxieties, jealousies, insecurities, and other human frailties? Is Vannoy offering an accurate picture of "lovers" as egoistical seekers of personal satisfaction?

[1]Since Bertocci's concept of love is heavily influenced by Eric Fromm, it may be of interest to read Vannoy's critique of Fromm in *Sex Without Love,* pp. 159–166. Further material on the concept of love is provided in Chapter 1.

[2]For more discussion of adultery, see Chapter 5.

Could it be, notwithstanding Bertocci, that for some people, sex without love is a truly enriching and mutually enjoyable experience that is integrated with their other values to produce a meaningful and happy life? And could it be that for others, notwithstanding Vannoy, sex with love is equally rewarding and life enhancing? Could it be that for some humanistic and generous nonlovers, their sexual experiences may be shallow, disappointing, and of poor quality? Moreover, is it not plausible that for some people deeply in love and married to one another, their sexual lives are either relatively unimportant or of poor quality? Can married lovers experience sexual frustrations that may undermine the strength of their love and commitment?

With some of these questions in mind, let us turn to Russell Vannoy's "Sex Without Love."

SEX WITHOUT LOVE

Both moderates and conservatives contend that when sex is separated from love, it becomes impersonal, egoistic, manipulative, mechanical, and exploitive. Such exploitive sex contradicts the humanistic philosophy advocated by Russell Vannoy—a philosophy that emphasizes care and respect for others. By using another in a sexual encounter as a mere means for one's own selfish pleasures, that person is violating one of the strongest principles of Western morality—the Kantian precept, "Always treat humanity, whether in your own person or that of another, as an end and never as a means only."

In the following selections from Vannoy's provocative book, *Sex Without Love,* he develops a rigorous critique of the moderates' and conservatives' claims. First, Vannoy argues that the idea that sex with love is noble, altruistic, and beautiful but sex without love is selfish, animalistic, and impersonal is a fallacious dualism. Many lovers are selfish, exploitive, and abusive, and many humanistic nonlovers are caring, generous, and loving people. In the first selection, he argues that sex without love with a humanistic person can be just as rich, noble, meaningful, and caring as sex with love.

In the second part of his book, Vannoy engages in a lengthy critical examination of romantic love, in which he finds it to be riddled with fatal contradictions. In our final selection from Vannoy, he uses one of these contradictions—that is, altruism versus egoism—to support his view that sex without love is superior to sex with love. He concludes that lovers are really selfish and egoistic; therefore, sex with a generous and caring nonlover is a far superior experience.

from Sex With Love vs. Sex Without Love _____

RUSSELL VANNOY

1. The Difficulty of Combining Sex with Love

If anyone defends, say, a humanist philosophy of sexuality that upholds the dignity of the human person, must he draw the traditional distinction between "sheer lust," on the one hand, and the supposedly richer and more fulfilling experience of having sex with someone who is loved? *Love* is, to be sure, often a mere code word for marriage in

From *Sex Without Love* by Russell Vannoy (Buffalo, New York: Prometheus Books, 1980), pp. 7–17, 20–29.

some circles, but this surely need not be true for all sexual philosophies. Yet it might very well seem that respect for the human person would demand that a humanist roundly condemn sex without love. For is this not the sort of sex in which two partners have traditionally been said to be merely manipulating each other in order to satisfy their own selfish lusts and then quickly saying farewell? Instead of a deep form of communication between two human beings, in which each one is touched to the depths of his emotional core, there is, it is often claimed, a mere "contact between two epidermises," or a quick ejaculation where gratification is temporary at best.

The traditional claim that females feel themselves degraded by loveless sex is certainly confirmed by surveys in my own undergraduate class, "Philosophies of Love and Sex," taught to more than two thousand students over the past ten years. Nearly 80 percent of the young women in my surveys clearly preferred sex with someone who loved them. The young men, on the other hand, registered quite the opposite view; slightly less than 20 percent found deep emotional involvement to be of any significant importance.[1]

Would this prove that women are the true humanists in the world of sex, and that males cannot be relied upon to practice any such view?

Certainly distinguished male theorists of sexuality have widely argued that sex without love is vastly inferior to sex with a lover. It is well known that Freud, who regarded sex as essentially a mere release of sexual tension, nevertheless regarded the combination of tenderness and sensuality (which for him was rarely achieved) as the ultimate form of sexual fulfillment. C. H. and Winifred Whiteley make it perfectly clear that they feel sex with love is superior when they write: "Sex has beyond all the human experiences the power to exalt, to produce ecstasy, to give people the sense of being carried beyond themselves to a higher level of feeling—not, of course, when it is a mere physical tumescence, but when it is associated with love and delight in another person."[2]

Peter Koestenbaum, in *Existential Sexuality,* goes to great lengths to claim that sex without love fully qualifies as an "authentic choice," despite the fact that he refers to sex as a mere itch in the groin that yields momentary pleasure and nothing else.

He does not seem to be able to bring himself to say that sex without love is fully meaningful, and one wonders if he really does think that sex without love is as authentic a choice as sex with love:

> The problem of Rhoda and Ruth is the fragmentation of sex. Both expect sex to have *meaning* (other than pleasure) by itself. In fact sex has meaning only in connection with love. Meaning stands for integration: meaning refers to a total life and to the fulfillment of its potential. Both Rhoda and Ruth want ideal sex but search for it as if it were an isolated physical rather than a total being-experience.... Existential sex is a total, integral experience, one which is built on a foundation of existential *love.*[3]

If, however, one probes a bit more deeply into the precise nature of love and sex, the easy reconciliation between the two made by many writers encounters some glaring difficulties. One clue is given by Oswald Schwarz: "*Although totally different in nature,* sexual impulse and love are dependent on and complementary to, each other. In a perfect, fully mature human being only this inseparable fusion of sexual impulse and love exists." (Italics mine.)[4]

The problem raised by Schwarz's admission that love and sex are "totally different in nature" is, if valid, not easily resolved by merely saying they are "dependent on and complementary to each other." There is no a priori reason to think that things said to be totally different in nature are somehow going to complement each other—however much the differences may have been papered over by centuries of habit, conditioning, blindness to the more subtle differences between sex and love, the necessity of procreation, the maintenance of religious and social conventions, and so forth.

One example of a difficulty that confronts combining love and sex is that the attitudes we take toward a person when we wish to show our love may differ significantly from our mode of viewing a person sexually. James Barrel, for example, contrasts two different modes of viewing another person:

> The sexual excitement we feel is related to the way we look at the other person. To clarify the notion of the objectness viewing position, we shall contrast it with another position referred to as ten-

derness. When we feel tenderness we look at the other's body as a whole. Our gaze spends most of its time in the head area and *within* the body boundaries. However, this position involves penetration of the other beyond the object characteristics. The body is experienced as a whole rather than as separate parts. It is perceived as embedded in its natural environment. For example, the reflection of sunlight off the hair, the grass one is sitting on, or the creek that one is near, all facilitate the tenderness orientation. There is a desire to place one's arms around and embrace rather than to use one's arms as instruments to manipulate the other.[5]

By contrast with the tender or loving attitude, Barrel defines the "objectifying attitude" of sexual arousal in the following way:

> By contrast, in the objectness position we view the other as an object separate from and not embedded in the world. We see the body as consisting of parts; we see legs or bust rather than the total person. For the most part this objectifying gaze gives attention to the erogenous zones and body boundaries, avoiding the head and face (p. 99).

It is not clear from Barrel's paper whether he considers the tenderness and the objectifying orientation as merely alternative modes of sexual arousal, or whether he thinks they are incompatible with each other. There is, of course, the possibility that one might begin the act by first viewing the person as a whole and then moving gradually into the objectifying attitude. But it is clearly true that for many persons the "love attitude" and the sexual "objectifying attitude" could conflict because of the fundamentally different ways one views one's lover in the two modes. Switching from one attitude to the other could be very difficult, particularly if the lovers find it degrading to view each other as sex objects.[6]

But if they do come to see each other as sex objects, and if this is a necessary condition for sexual arousal, then the two lovers who have objectified each other would not vary one bit from two non-lovers who similarly view each other in this way. The only difference would be that in the former case a loving attitude may have preceded the sex act, while in the latter case there may be no such antecedent attitude. But once the lovers have switched from the loving to the objectifying attitude, love then has nothing to do with the act and they are sexually on a par with the non-lovers and can claim no superiority for their sex act because they also happen to love each other. For who thinks of love when one surrenders himself fully to lust and willingly becomes a sex object for another?

Perhaps the classic statement of the difference between love and sex is found in the writings of Theodore Reik, in which he tries to refute Freud's view that love is merely sublimated or "aim-inhibited" sex.

> Between love and sex are differences of such a decisive nature that it is very unlikely they could be, as psychoanalysis asserts, of the same origin and character. These differences are best realized when both phenomena are contrasted in their purest form; here are a few examples: sex is a biological urge, a product of chemistry within the organism; love is an emotional craving, a creation of individual imagination. In sex there is a drive to get rid of organic tension; in love there is a need to escape from the feeling of one's own inadequacy. In the first there is a quest for physical satisfaction; in the second there is a pursuit of happiness. One concerns the choice of a body. Sex has a general meaning; love a personal one. The first is a call from nature; the second from culture. Sex is common to men and beasts; love or romance is unknown to millions of people even now. Sex is indiscriminate; love is directed to a certain person. The one relaxes the muscles; the other opens the floodgates of personality. Also the sexually satisfied individual can feel love-starved. The sex drive is extinguished; there is a tension, a spasm, a release. The ultimate act of pleasure cannot later be recalled, just as the taste of a food cannot be vividly recalled. No such ultimate indifference to the object is to be observed in the phenomenon of love. Every word and every gesture of your sweetheart is deliciously remembered. Sex is dramatic; love is lyric. The object of sex is desired only during the short time of excitement and appears undesirable otherwise; the beloved person is the object of continued tenderness.[7]

One who defends sex with love might argue that the crude form of sex Reik discusses is precisely what results when love is divorced from sex. Yet, if the differences between sex and love are as drastic as Reik suggests, one wonders how one could possibly be an expression of the other. If one thinks that sex without love is "animalistic," then how does it suddenly become a satisfactory vehicle for expressing the tenderer emotions of love?

To be sure, sex that expresses love may become more tender and sensuous. But what then becomes of its cruder aspects, which so many participants desire? They regard anything else as insipid and excessively refined. Indeed, just how does a penis that is vigorously thrusting up and down in a vagina express anything at all, with the possible exception of dominance (which is hardly the same thing as love)? If one moves the penis slowly, is this an expression of love? The absurdity of this line of thinking is evident.

Can love and lust really be combined in a perfect harmony? Reik notes that when love and sex are united "it is sometimes difficult to know which of the needs has the lion's share, but they can usually clearly be separated in our perception."[8]

But if the two can be distinguished clearly, what then becomes of the perfect unity between the two, where they are said to form an indistinguishable unity that is richer than sex alone? Indeed, if one does surrender oneself to lust in the act, is there any awareness of some higher unity of love and lust? One's lust-clogged perceptions are hardly in a position to say that the purely lustful experience really was enriched by love; perhaps its ecstacy came from lust alone, and one only fancied that love made it better.

Furthermore, Reik himself suggests that there is no such thing as crude sex at all, that lust is a myth in human beings. "How is it possible to exclude the factor of emotion, to remove the influence of thoughts and fantasies connected with sex as we know it, to eliminate the effects of other drives? [Reik includes power and ego drives as part of human sexuality.] It seems that we can never reach the psychological expression in its crudest, most primitive form (p. 12)."

Although Reik speaks of the "factor of emotion," this certainly need not refer only to love; for there are many other emotions that can enrich sex other than just the emotion of love. Reik's admission, therefore, that there is really no such thing as sheer lust in human beings—what with all this psychological complexity, associations, and so forth—undercuts the familiar claim that the only alternative to sex with love is "sheer lust." For if sheer lust in human beings is a myth, this opens the intriguing possibility that there are richer, more complex forms of human sexuality that need not involve being with one's beloved at all.

Before proceeding to a hypothetical debate between those who want sex with a lover and those who defend sex with a person one is not emotionally involved with, it is important to recall the point that love, as well as sex, comes in many forms. Alan Lee's work, *The Colors of Love* (Toronto: New Press, 1973) has, for example, made a strong case for a pluralistic analysis of love. Each of his love types has quite different notions of what "good sex" is. Although Lee was not specifically concerned with the problem we face here, a closer analysis of what he discovered from his sociological studies of what is considered good sex by differing kinds of lovers gives cold comfort to those who think that love and sex invariably have a humanistic connection.

Lee's "eros" type, for example, seeks beauty and immediate and prolonged sensuous and sensual rapport; yet, while the *experience* of sex with such a type may be beautiful indeed, the insistence on high standards of beauty and sexual sophistication could generate anxiety (even during the sex act) as to whether one will be able to maintain the high standards the eros-type demands. Lee's "ludus" type is the playboy who regards sex as a game of conquest and seduction; whether the sex act itself is of any real importance to him is dubious indeed, and fidelity is out of the question. (His "ludic-eros" type merely combines the disadvantages of the two types.)

Lee's "manic" lover is perhaps the worst of all; the manic is so obsessively attached to his beloved, so lacking in a sense of self-worth, that his sex acts are generally an utter failure. The "storge" or "family man" type of lover lacks the romantic ecstasy of eros and sees sex largely as a routine matter for a quick relief of tension or for producing a family. "Pragma" has an obsession with performing sex according to the mechanical procedures outlined in sex manuals. Only one type—"storgic-eros"—

seems to fulfill the requirement of humanistic sex; he has idealism, personal warmth, tenderness, and a sense of self-sacrifice for the beloved's happiness. Yet Lee notes, without comment, that the storgic-eros type confines himself mostly to tender embraces, the gentler forms of affection that would hardly be satisfying to women who demand more intense forms of sensual gratification than he could provide.

2. Some Arguments for Sex With Love

Let us now imagine a hypothetical debate between a defender of sex with love and a defender of sex with a person one is not in love with. By *love* I shall mean the kind of affiliative love that suggests emotional ties deeper than just friendship, where there is usually fidelity of one partner to another. With such a love there is at least the theoretical possibility of marriage, although the partners may not be married or never will be married.

In order that the debate be fair and not plagued by narrow-minded arguments, both partners should be capable of an "authentic decision," as defined by Peter Koestenbaum in the Foreword; that is, it is a decision made with a minimum of external influences, a decision made deliberately and not unconsciously, a decision based on knowledge of the kind of person one uniquely is.

Further conditions for making a fair decision between sex with and without love would include:

- That one have an open mind and not see sex as so sinful that it can be redeemed only by love.
- That one should have no guilt or hangups about either love or sex. One should be open to the possibilities of both love and sensual pleasure.
- That one should have experienced both forms of sex—with and without love.
- That one should be a secure person, one who does not need to be "loved" in order to feel self-acceptance and self-respect. A man should also feel secure, in not needing to prove his virility with an endless string of sex acts with or without love. Furthermore, a woman who is secure will not be afraid to reveal herself to a non-lover.
- That one should have experienced stimulating, responsive, considerate partners in both love and non-love sexual relationships.

- That one have experienced both forms of sex in an equally favorable setting. It would hardly be fair to have one's ideas about sex with love shaped by love-making on a bearskin rug in a romantic, elegant setting, while one's experience of love without sex took place with a self-centered partner in the back seat of a car in some dingy section of town.
- That one have a clear awareness of just what it is one is enjoying in the act. Some partners don't really care for sex at all—it's just an excuse to enjoy the feeling of being loved and wanted. Such people are like those who pour spoons and spoons of cream and sugar in their coffee; they don't really enjoy coffee as coffee.
- That one be aware of the fact that sex can be a "loving act" even though one's partner may not be in love with you. Such an affair may last for one night or several months, but no permanence or fidelity is necessary. For example, such a partner, if he is a man, would show the woman courtesy and attention even though he might be a total stranger. Nor would he exploit the woman; he would give her as much or more than she gave him. This would indicate that a partner's having a good character is as decisive (and perhaps even more so) than his loving a woman.

Let us now consider some of the arguments in favor of sex with love.

- Perhaps the most common defense of sex with love is that it is deeply *personal.* One forms a unity not only with the body, but also with all the other aspects of what constitute a complete experience: the mental, emotional, and spiritual. One not only gives pleasure but receives pleasure in giving pleasure; one feels not only one's own pleasure but the pleasure of the beloved as well. And the experience is enriched by memories of prior satisfactions and the anticipation that the joys will continue. There is, for the woman, the knowledge that one has been chosen above all the rest—not the feeling that one's lover wanted just any woman. Sex with love is thus claimed to be a rich complex of mental, emotional, and physical attributes that are lacking in sex without love. Another way of putting this is that sex *as* sex is pleasure only; only love (as Koestenbaum argues) has *meaning* and can make sex a meaningful and rich experience as well as a pleasurable one.

• It follows from this that sex with a beloved would be very important for those who must be quite certain they aren't being treated as an object. But is it not true, the defender of sex without love might argue, that when one is in the throes of lust one is often said to become completely "embodied," that is, one has submitted conscious control of one's acts to bodily desires? But then it would seem that even in love one reaches a state where one has become a certain kind of object, as it were, that takes pleasure in being manipulated and surrendering to the wishes of the partner. What, then, would be the difference between sex with a lover and a non-lover, once both reach this objectified state? For, as I noted earlier, who thinks of *love* when they are overwhelmed by *lust?*

Perhaps, the defender of sex with love would reply, when one is embodied one does not become so totally divorced from all consciousness that one does not remain unaware that this partner is one's lover. Furthermore, there are those moments of foreplay and afterplay that precede and follow embodiment—clasping palms, stroking hair, holding each other tight, kissing tenderly, and so forth; and it might be argued that non-lovers skip these preliminaries or else do them in a crude way to arouse themselves instead of their partner. Yet lovers often do skip these preliminaries. One need only think of the millions of weary husbands who seek sex with their wives as a form of quick relief from their tensions. And a non-lover might very well engage in such foreplay as a way of expressing appreciation for the partner's beauty or as a way of expressing gratitude for having been selected as a sexual partner.

• Good sex is often something one would like to continue, maybe permanently with someone. Sex with a lover is often claimed to be more likely to lead to future emotional security; men and women don't have to worry constantly about whether or not they will find a new "one-night" stand. (This would be important as they grow older and find themselves rejected by "swinging singles.") Perhaps because the lover accepts the partner more for what he or she is (or perhaps because love is blind), it is claimed that the lover will be aroused by the partner at any age. (Perhaps love is a kind of eternal aphrodisiac—or is it that one is really making love to a *memory* of what the older

person once was and not to that person in the here and now?)

It should be noted, however, that the rejection of older single people by "swinging singles" is more a malady of our social mores than it is an inherent flaw in sex without love. Nor is it always true that sex with a non-lover is a mere one-night stand. Furthermore, the stability of sex *amongst* lovers depends on how they view each other; if they only love one another because of certain qualities that fade with age, then aging lovers are going to be rejected just as much as aging non-lovers. (One need only examine the divorce statistics to confirm this.)

• Even if one is not interested in emotional aspects and just wants good sex, it might be argued that a lover is still best at the purely physical level. Won't a lover put more of him or herself into the act and do his best to please the partner, knowing this is not just a one-night affair but involves someone whom he or she wants to please and to keep? He *selected* you, the argument goes, and selectivity implies *concern* for your happiness as well as his.

Furthermore, if you do happen to perform poorly one night, the lover won't dump you in the middle of the act. A lover is more forgiving of your failings, knowing from past experiences that this is just an off night for you.

However, given the statistics on the infrequency of orgasm among a large number of wives and the crudity of the sex practiced by the average "storge" lover, or man, as described earlier from Alan Lee's book, one wonders if the *average* lover is really as noble as the preceding description implies. Once again the key factors depend more on the partner's *sexual sophistication* and *innate generosity* than it does on whether that person happens to be one's beloved. Becoming a lover or a spouse does not—alas!—turn a man into a knight in shining armor or a woman into Queen Guinevere. *Indeed, it seems clear that one who is committed to humanistic principles as to the intrinsic worth of the individual person and who has some degree of ability to provide an exciting sexual experience will perform equally well and generously with a lover or non-lover.*

On the other hand, a selfish person who "falls in love" or who marries may (for a time) treat the beloved much more tenderly and generously than a mere sex object; but it is often a mark of selfish persons to treat their possessions with great care because they are proud to own them and because of the prospect of greater satisfaction received in return for such attention.

Indeed, if it is claimed that sex without love is selfish, how do we explain all those persons who engaged in sex *before* they fell in love? For if their sexual activity had been selfish, then it could never have contributed to their falling in love at all; for neither person would love someone whom they perceived as being primarily concerned with self-gratification of mere lust. Furthermore, even at the crudest physiological level, there is a kind of giving and receiving that need not be one-sided provided that the partners have mutually agreed to desire each other solely for simple sensual gratification. For to receive a man's penis, a female must "give" of her vagina, and vice versa. Thus, there is a kind of mutual give-and-take, even if only at the level of lust.

• It is sometimes argued that if all one wants is sex for sex's sake, and not as an expression of love, why not just masturbate? A clitoral orgasm, for example, is allegedly more intense than the vaginal orgasm produced by the thrusting of the male penis. Why do we seek out another person when we want the "best sex"? Isn't this because we want to unite with, relate to, communicate with another human being? If interpersonal communion is part of what is involved in the best sex, wouldn't the most profound and meaningful communication of this non-verbal, bodily type be with someone we love, someone who understands or who wants to understand us best, someone to whom we have something to say that mere words cannot convey? Sex would thus be a kind of body language, in which two lovers communicate emotions that lie beyond the powers of language to convey.[9]

When such communication is the central focus of the sex act, all the worries about premature ejaculation or simultaneous orgasm (or even whether one will have an orgasm) will disappear, whereas in sex without love performance and ejaculation are often said to be everything.

While this view has much to commend it, it is not clear why love needs to be the only beautiful thing that can be communicated by sex. For example, one can communicate gratification for having been selected to engage in such a beautiful experience, even though erotic love is absent. There is also the problem that emphasis on "communicating" emotion may direct attention from the sensual aspects of sex in which two persons surrender themselves to sexual feeling. The distraction is wondering if one is succeeding in communicating an emotion of some sort which the other may not even share or understand. Sex is complex enough without worrying about what or whether one's bodily language is actually communicating. Indeed, a penis thrusting up and down in a vagina may actually "communicate" dominance and aggression more than it does love, and this could disturb a sensitive person who is trying to communicate love, at least if he is doing it in a very self-conscious sort of way to show his intentions. Finally, there is the possibility that sex used primarily as a tool for communicating emotion would come to devalue the purely sensual aspects of sex.

• One student of mine argued in a paper that sex with love was clearly best for him since, for him, love is the "ultimate aphrodisiac" and that he is not aroused by someone he cannot love. But one wonders what "love" means in this context. Love is ordinarily defined as a love of the total person for his or her own sake alone. But when one speaks of love as an "aphrodisiac," can one really be sure that one is not merely responding in a lustful way to a complex of particular qualities the "loved" one is fortunate enough to possess (physical beauty, evidence of being sexually responsive and adept, and so forth)? Can he really be sure that he is loving his partner in some total sense that includes non-erotic as well as sexually stimulating qualities? If he claims that he loves all her other qualities as well, how does he know that this is not merely because he associates these qualities with the erotic ones which are really of primary significance to him? These questions arise because when love is described in aphrodisiacal terms, one wonders if it is not really being confused with lust—an all-too-common phenomenon.

• A further argument for sex with a lover that constantly recurs is the claim that a non-lover is too "insecure" to give himself in total fidelity to a loved one. But this sort of psychologizing can cut both ways, for it could equally well be argued that the one who insists on love is too insecure to give oneself to the adventure of having sex with a stranger. Actually, security has no necessary connection with someone who prefers one form of sex or the other. . . .

• • •

One of the most vigorous defenses of sex with love is found in Rollo May's *Love and Will* (New York: Dell Publishing Co., 1969). May's argument is the familiar claim that sex with love is "profoundly personal" while sex without love is impersonal and obsessed with techniques at the expense of spontaneity and emotional surrender. His development of this theme does, however, raise some important philosophical difficulties. "We have," he says, "to block something off, exact some effort to make it [sex] *not* personal" (p. 312). This suggests that sex will not be fully spontaneous, that one will always hold back some important element of oneself unless the act is *personal,* a term that May uses interchangeably with *love.* But with this rather broad use of the word *love,* sex could be a loving act and thus be profoundly personal, even though the partners were not "lovers," in the narrower sense of the word.

Furthermore, it is not clear that "blocking something off" or withholding some aspect of one's self (by which May means the absence of love) means that one will not totally surrender to those aspects of one's being that are relevant to sex *as sex; that* is, the total surrender to lustful feelings. Certainly love is not the only aphrodisiac, nor even necessarily the most powerful aphrodisiac for all persons; otherwise there would be no sex between non-lovers at all. Thus, one may be totally involved with another person in ways that are relevant to a mutually agreed upon sex act; the emotion of love may be absent, but it does not follow that the partners need treat each other in a cold, withdrawn manner that is merely an excuse to display sexual techniques.

May further argues that "for human beings the more powerful need is not for sex per se but for relationship, intimacy, acceptance, and affirmation" (p. 311). This, however, suggests that sex is being used to gratify those needs that are so often missing in an impersonal society, and one wonders if the relative brevity of the sex act can carry its share

of the burden that is placed on it to fulfill these needs. If one adopts the view that sex is primarily a mutually pleasurable experience, it is not clear that one who also expects sex to fulfill his needs for "relationship, intimacy, acceptance, and affirmation" is going to emerge with a very lasting feeling that these needs have been fulfilled. If one is repeatedly disappointed with sex for this reason, this would be a possible basis for a return to the old antisex attitudes the modern world thought it had overcome.

Another benefit that May claims for sex with love is that it fulfills our need to become totally absorbed with another person, to overcome our separateness and isolation. "The paradox of love is that it is the highest degree of awareness of the self as a person and the highest degree of absorption in another" (p. 311). The difficulty with this paradox is that it is not at all clear just how I become most aware of myself as a person while also seeking to lose myself in another. May seems to mean that my giving of myself totally and simultaneously receiving gratification of my deepest needs makes me more of a person, even though I am absorbed in another. He speaks of a resulting increased sense of self-awareness: "We normally emerge from the act of lovemaking with renewed vigor, a vitality that comes not from triumph or proof of one's strength but from the expansion of awareness" (p. 314). Yet, curiously enough, May sees this increased sense of self-awareness as contributing an element of sadness to the sex act.

> This sadness comes from the reminder that we have not succeeded absolutely in losing our separateness; and the infantile hope that we can recover the womb never becomes a reality. Even our increased self-awareness can also be a poignant reminder that none of us ever overcomes his loneliness completely. But by the replenished sense of our own personal significance in the love act itself, we can accept these limitations laid upon us by our human finiteness (p. 314).

It is, however, odd that someone who praises so highly our increased sense of self-awareness should add that this contributes sadness to the act. Despite the fact that he calls this need for total absorption infantile, it seems that what May thinks is most valuable is a total loss of self. He gives his highest praise, for example, to the moment of climax, where all sense of separateness between lover and beloved is lost (p. 316). May thus seems confused as to what value he wants to place on total absorption versus an increased sense of self-awareness. It is certainly not clear that everyone wants to totally lose himself in absorption with another in the sex act; for some, retaining conscious control over the sex act and directing or manipulating one's partner's feelings and actions can be as sexually exciting as a loss of identity and self-control. On the other hand, if the emphasis in sex is on total surrender to lustful feelings, to a sense of being identified with one's own on each other's bodies, it would seem this would provide the sense of total loss of self-consciousness he seems to be seeking. These latter things do not, of course, require love; indeed, one's concern for making sex also provide "relationship, intimacy, acceptance, and affirmation" by means of love may actually interfere with a total surrender of self to lustful feelings. For the more demands one makes of the sex act, the more self-conscious one may become about whether all these needs are being met.

Rollo May's most vigorous attack on what he takes to be current sexual trends occurs, however, in the chapter "Paradoxes of Sex and Love." He lists three paradoxes that he feels will eventually lead to society's turning against sex, a phenomenon that he calls the advent of a new form of Puritanism. The first paradox, he claims, is that emancipated sexual partners report that they are having more sex but somehow are enjoying it less. He thinks that there is a lack of feeling and passion, even though Victorian repression is gone. Indeed, he says that people feel guilty if they don't have enormous quantities of sex, and the female is made to feel guilty if she performs poorly and does not have a powerful orgasm that will impress her mate with her tremendous sexual potency.

The second paradox, according to May, is that there has been an overemphasis on sexual technique at the expense of spontaneity and passion. There develops a "mechanistic attitude towards love-making that goes along with alienation, feelings of loneliness, and depersonalization" (p. 43). There is, for example, the desperate attempt to so structure the sex act that the couple will achieve simultaneous orgasm. "I confess," May writes,

"that when people talk about the 'apocalyptic (simultaneous) orgasm,' I find myself wondering, why do they have to try so hard? What abyss of self-doubt, what inner void of loneliness, are they trying to cover up by this great concern for grandiose effects" (p. 44). What is missing in an act based on technique is "the sheer fact of intimacy . . . the meeting, the growing closeness with the excitement of not knowing where it will lead, the assertion of the self and the giving of the self" (p. 45). He notes that the "technical preoccupation robs the woman of what she wants most of all, physically and emotionally, namely the man's spontaneous abandon at the moment of climax" (p. 44).

The third paradox May labels the "new Puritanism." Whereas the traditional Puritanism sought to have love without falling into sex, the new form of Puritanism seeks to have sex without falling into love. The coldness that one associated with traditional Puritanism is now defined in terms of a withdrawal of feeling and passion, a new kind of duty to have sex whether one wants it or not, and the use of the body as a kind of sex machine that one carefully manipulates without daring to let oneself go in any kind of passionate commitment. May concludes by arguing that the sex machine who views himself as someone to be "turned on, adjusted, and steered" eventually loses the feeling he has either for himself or his partner. The loss of feeling, May argues, also eventually causes a loss of sexual appetite and ability. "The upshot of this self-defeating pattern is that in the long run *the lover who is most efficient will also be the one who is most impotent*" (p. 55).

What is the reason for the shift from love to technique that May deplores? Is the only alternative to sex with love that of becoming a heartless sex machine? Perhaps the answer to the first question is that we are or have been going through a transitional period, in which modern man felt obligated to be liberated, yet was still saddled with a subconscious distaste for sex inherited from his Victorian past. Thus, out of fear of a total surrender to lust, he withdraws into the use of technique, which permits him to go through the obligatory motions of being sexually active but without the attendant guilt of a full surrender to lust. (May himself suggests a similar sort of explanation, p. 52.)

May further suggests there may eventually be a withdrawal from an obsession with technique and a combination of lust with a meaningful love relationship. But his insistence on a commitment to love one's sex partner is probably an inheritance from our Puritan past that is still lurking in May's attitude. His constant theme that two persons who simply surrender themselves to each other's bodies are devoid of "intimacy" and "mutual give and take" is itself the old Puritanism described in a new language—no longer that of "sinful lust."

Can it not also be true that two people who are not in love can be totally absorbed in a union of lust and mutually gratify each other's needs, not just for momentary sexual release but for mutual acceptance of each other's worth as well? Those who are interested in sex for sex's sake often look for many things in a partner other than just the presence of sexual organs. Lust can be aroused by many features of a human being, including personality, intelligence, and physical attractiveness. Lust thus has its own kind of selectivity (except, of course, for the desperate), and it is not just love that confirms my worth to myself. Indeed, if I am secure in my own sense of self-worth, my need for the acceptance and intimacy that May insists sex must provide should not matter at all. Merely to be chosen as a desirable sexual partner should be enough.

Finally, May's insistence on the split between "surrender to each other" and "technique" is a false dualism that constantly recurs in books advocating sex with love. Technique need not be the cold, self-centered phenomenon it is often described as being. The skilled exercise of technique, provided it does not become an end in itself, can be an all-absorbing phenomenon that is very lustfully arousing. One need not become a cold, withdrawn sex machine, as May suggests happens when one places great emphasis on technique. Its exercise can be so spontaneously performed and so integrated into the sex act that technique itself becomes a kind of lustful—or even loving—phenomenon.

May's book, therefore, exhibits a total lack of understanding of the infinite possibilities for gratification that sex without love can offer. Furthermore, it is far from clear that everyone's deepest needs are those that May suggests or that sex with love can gratify the needs May lists. Finally, he seems unaware that sex can be a "loving act" without the two partners being bound to each other in some profound, enduring emotional commitment, which he suggests should lead to procreation. This seems a giveaway to May's underlying desire to return to a more traditional form of love-making.

3. Some Arguments for Sex Without Love

I shall now present some arguments to show that sex without love may be, in certain circumstances, superior to sex with a lover. Some quotations from my students' papers illustrate this view:

- "I get so hung up on giving pleasure—or trying to—to my beloved that I don't think of my own pleasure. And I wonder if my lover is asking himself, 'Is she really enjoying it or is she just trying to please me?'"

- "I prefer sex with just friends. There are no worries about possessiveness or jealousy. The lover wants him to be a part of you and for you to be a part of him—permanently, and with all others excluded. The deeper the relation went and the deeper the emotion became, the more I ceased to be a separate person."

- "My lover gets 'cocksure' and makes demands, and apparently says to himself, 'She'll understand. She's my lover, after all.' Sometimes I have to do it even when I'm not horny: am I being selfish and inconsiderate if I refuse or is he being selfish for asking me when he knows I don't want to? I haven't figured that one out yet. But things like that don't bug me when I'm having sex for a good time with a stranger."

- "In reality those who demand sex with love should say, 'I'm copping out. I don't really like sex at all . . . but, if I must have it I'll set limitations and only have sex with someone I love.' They don't really believe sex with love is better than loveless sex—they are only choosing the lesser of two evils."

- "Once you've shown a lover all you know about sex you will have to repeat. With a non-lover there is a new demonstration of yourself each time and a new experience of each other's approach each time."

- "When I have sex accompanied by love my conscience directs me to self-sacrifice. When I perform sex without love there is a kind of intoxicated splendor with life and the feeling of well-being which spontaneously arises in me; and it becomes easier to be gratified and to gratify the partner."

- "When two people just start dating they are more concerned with each other's feelings. There is the novelty of a new romance. But as the romance progresses each person seems to become less of an individual. They think of the other as being almost physically attached to them. They are one, and each has no individuality. One may begin to think the other has the same desires and needs in love-making, but they really don't. [This apparently refers to differences between male and female conceptions mentioned earlier.] The mate falls into the category of 'the person I married' or 'my girlfriend.' These people gradually appear as numbers or faceless entities to each other."

- "You choose a lover according to how you wish to be loved, and you choose a sex partner according to how you wish to be laid. There is no guarantee whatever that the person you love and the person whom you find most sexually desirable are one and the same. There are just certain things a lover may not be able to give you, and it may be good sex."

It is tempting to give a "Dear Abby" reply to these student comments and to say that they are immature persons who do not know what "true love" is (as if anyone really knows!). But while such objections may be valid in some cases, such replies usually sidestep any objections to sex with love by simply defining away any objections to love by saying that such difficulties do not really hold for true or mature love. Thus the perfection of sex with love is upheld by simply being made true by definition.

In a recent paper Lawrence Casler has argued that the *need* for love is based on personal insecurity, a need for sexual gratification, and a need to conform to societal norms dictating that those who are not loved are among the damned.[10] Casler does not seem to disapprove of love as such; a secure person possessed of self-respect would feel no need for it, even though he might very properly choose to love. But Casler's thesis, if correct, certainly shakes many forms of love at their foundations; indeed, it suggests that the fundamental requirement is a solid sense of self-worth. Perhaps this is what is needed to make sex a valid, fulfilling experience rather than "being in love."

Furthermore, it is clear that if someone is loved for the reasons Casler suggests, that person would simply be one who is *used* to overcome the lover's lack of self-worth; and such a person would be making overt or subconscious demands that could make the sex act most unfulfilling. Or if one did wish to continue such a relationship, one would have to keep the person weak or dependent in order for her or him to continue to have the *need* to be in love.

The most devastating attacks on love, however, have come from certain recent feminist writers, who argue that love is merely a kind of masochistic worship of a woman's oppressor, the male.[11] They certainly have a point. If women have been relegated to an inferior position down through the ages, what can one say of the genuineness of a love where one partner keeps the other "in her place," even though he has showered her with passionate love letters or exotic balcony or bedroom scenes? One can, after all, shower affection on puppies, but this is hardly a mature love between equals. That there is a kind of love possible for those one treats as inferiors shows that a mature love between equals is perhaps more a function of the character of the lovers than it is of emotional involvement. But then a non-lover who is also a person of character may show a woman much greater consideration than would her sexist husband.

If these charges against certain forms of love are valid, then one could hardly claim that such love somehow ennobles sex. Certainly such charges require a reply from the countless male writers who extol the beauty of love combined with sex.

Those who defend sex with a lover say that love expresses deep emotions for another person, whereas sex with a non-lover is superficial and crude. We have already seen that many husbands who in some sense love their wives are equally superficial and crude in the bedroom. That is, there is an important difference between (1) whether two people love each other; and (2) whether two people are capable of sexually satisfying each other, especially when the rose-colored glasses of the honeymoon are removed by time.

Certainly not all husbands (especially of Alan Lee's storge type) see sex or could even enjoy sex as an expression of anything. Using vigorous penile-vaginal intercourse to express the tenderer emotions of love would be for many people two different realms that are as difficult to relate as it would be difficult for a dancing fat lady to "express" grace.

Furthermore, for many persons, just bringing off the sex act on the physiological level is enough of a challenge, much less simultaneously worrying about whether one is also succeeding in expressing any emotions and thus possibly offending one's lover if one fails to express what was intended. And at the moment of orgasm one is so lost in the ecstasy of the moment—the familiar sense of momentarily being outside space and time—that it is not clear that one is in any mental condition to be aware of anything other than one's own ecstasy. (I am not thinking of the relatively infrequent phenomenon of simultaneous orgasm; here there could perhaps be a shared sense of joy, but this could hold for lovers and non-lovers alike.)

Is sex without love superficial, as compared with the unity of heart, mind, and body that is claimed to exist between sex and love? Suppose that at a San Francisco night club I find myself overwhelmed by an attraction for someone in both a sensual and sensuous sense. Such a person's beauty need not, of course, be physical. There are many things about this person which may stir my emotions, even though I may have no desire to become emotionally involved with her in the sense usually meant by erotic love. The experience is enriched by the beautiful setting, by the hopes of sharing an evening with her, by memories of previous encounters with such charming individuals, by the prospects of meeting her or someone like her again, by the thought of having sex with an utter stranger with whom I may have a unique and fresh experience of her and my sexual abilities, by the fact that she has been sensually aroused and has responded to my stare, and so forth. Is this merely a description of a ludic playboy on the prowl for a sex object? It could be, but it need not be. For people who are concerned with persons as persons can experience such rich complexity of thought, emotion, and sensuality as much as anyone else; and so long as the object of one's affec-

tions shares one's views, an evening may be spent together that can be totally free of mutual exploitation.

It can be an evening of sensuous eroticism that may continue for hours and include all the foreplay, afterplay, kisses, and caresses that actual lovers enjoy, perhaps done simply out of deep mutual admiration for each other's sensuous qualities and out of gratitude for having been chosen by the other for such an evening. Yet the pair may go their separate ways in the morning and never see each other again, perhaps because they prefer their own independence and singlehood to permanent emotional involvement and marriage. The claim, then, that sex with love is a rich, complex phenomenon and sex without involvement is a mere sensation in the groin is a fallacious dualism.

Indeed, if there were only a lustful attachment between two strangers who are not wholly sure of each other's motives, the evening might still be an exciting and rewarding one. Robert Solomon writes:

> The fact that excitement is essential to sexuality explains how it is that many people find danger highly sexual . . . (short of terror, which understandably kills sexual enthusiasm) . . . It allows us to understand one of the most apparent anomalies of our sexual behaviour, the fact that our most satisfying sexual encounters are often with strangers, where there are strong elements of tension—fear, insecurity, guilt, and anticipation. Conversely, sex may be least satisfying with those whom we love and know well and whose habits and reactions are extremely well known to us.[12]

Moralists have traditionally drawn a sharp either-or distinction between sex with a lover (hoping thereby to preserve the institution of marriage) and sex with a non-lover, which they picture as something crude, selfish, animalistic. The idea that sex can be a loving act and that even loveless sex can be fun under certain conditions, they never admit. They falsely think that the only loving, unselfish act can be between two people who are in love, married, or going to be married.

Perhaps the young female has been so conditioned by the value system which maintains that either one is in love or else it's going to be vicious and dirty, that she truly believes an encounter has been vicious and dirty when it may not have been so in reality. And perhaps the male has been conditioned in the same way. He says: "I don't love her, so this means I'm going to exploit her; for this is what society expects me to do with someone I don't love." But if he had not been conditioned to view sex without love as selfish and animalistic in the first place, perhaps his unselfish side could assert itself naturally and he could provide the woman with a loving act even though he wasn't romantically involved with her at all.

As I noted in an earlier section, one can hardly say that sex with love is always superior, since millions of husbands practice only a crude form of the sex act that leaves their wives unfulfilled. The reply might be that such husbands do not really love their wives. But perhaps the husband simply does not (and, indeed, could not) care for the kind of sex his wife does—perhaps females in general prefer sensuous eroticism and males in general prefer the lustier, more "manly" type of sex. The husband might defend his love for his wife by saying that lovers need not share mutual interests in all areas, that love is a give-and-take proposition, and that he shows his love for her in other ways to make up for his wife's lack of fulfillment in the bedroom. But if he can thus prove that he does love his wife, then sex with love is not going to be the best for females who are married to this type of man.

Is the person who feels that the only good sex is with a lover someone who feels that basically sex is dirty and can only be indulged in if it is done in a socially approved way (that is, it is only "nice" if it is bathed in the holy water of "love")? But, if deep down they think that sex without love is ugly or dirty or animalistic, then won't this perhaps unconscious attitude carry over even with a lover, and won't it be sensed? Will sex in such circumstances ever be open and spontaneous and guilt-free? If this is true, then only someone who can first enjoy sex for its own sake can really provide his beloved with a joyous experience.

There are, furthermore, certain things available to a non-lover that are often not available to a lover:

- There is the fun of seducing someone. One does not seduce a lover.

- One need not feel obligated to perform sexually except when one feels like it. But lovers often feel that they *owe* their beloveds the satisfaction of each other's needs even when they are not in the mood for sex.

- One can experiment with new partners or with new sex techniques without feeling guilt or fear of offending one's beloved. Furthermore, if sex is an appetite, as many claim, it seems odd to think that one could go through life satisfying an appetite in only one way. One's appetite for food cannot be permanently satisfied by hamburger, no matter how many different ways one tries to prepare it. Could not the same thing also be true of the sexual appetite? Isn't there a need for a variety of partners, and isn't our claim that we can be satisfied with one person forever a product of social conditioning used to preserve and protect the institution of marriage?

- One need not fear performing inadequately, ejaculating prematurely or not having an orgasm with a stranger whom you'll never see again. But if these things happen too often with a lover, one will feel that one has failed the loved one. This can be quite disheartening even if the lover is forgiving of one's faults.

- Perhaps the most basic difficulty of using sex to express love is that one is often merely using sex as a means to an end: expressing love, rather than enjoying sex for sex's sake. The focus tends to be on the emotions of love rather than lust itself. The sensual aspects of sex thus tend in many such cases to be sacrificed to tenderness, something which has its own worth and beauty, to be sure, but which may not be the central focus many sexual partners would prefer.

4. Summary and Conclusions

In this chapter I have tried to show that the old distinction between sex with a lover and crude, manipulative, exploitative sex (which I shall dub "loveless sex") is a false dualism, and further, that another type of sex is a loving act of mutual gratification and consideration without emotional commitment. In addition, I have tried to show that old distinctions between "noble and unselfish love" and "crude, selfish, simple lust," and between "warm and tender love" and "cold and mechanical" technique are vastly overdrawn in the traditional literature.

Who would win the argument between sex with love and sex without love? It is often argued that there is no winner in philosophical debates, and it may very well be true of this little debate also. Could it be that the preference for sex with love over sex without love is merely one of taste—tenderness versus raunchiness, predictability and security versus adventure and novelty, attachment versus independence? I am reminded of those who prefer their coffee straight and those who must have it mixed with cream and sugar. In each case something is gained and something is lost. The one who likes it only with cream and sugar will never savor coffee with its full "kick," and the one who likes it straight will never know how rich and sweet it tastes with cream and sugar.

Yet this conclusion is not really satisfactory either, for I have tried to show that there are forms of sex without love that are as rich in their own way as sex with love. (And I have also tried to show that many of those who prefer sex with love are really only interested in the "cream"—the feeling of being loved—and do not care for the coffee at all.)

Even if one is not able to decide the winner of such a debate, this chapter reveals that terms like *more meaningful, mature, wholesome,* and *richer* are not the exclusive domain of sex with love, if indeed they really do describe many such experiences at all to the exclusion of other forms of sexuality.

Notes

1. This, of course, raises grave implications for the viability of heterosexual love if the two sexes really do have such divergent views on sex. Perhaps one or the other of the sexes is suppressing his or her own views to please the other in order to have sex or love at all. And in a sexist society, there is little doubt which sex is suppressing its views. The interviews also confirmed the point that males tend to prefer quick, sensual, hard, direct sex whose primary goal is ejaculation; the females tend to prefer the more lengthy and tender and sophisticated approach that might be described as sensuous eroticism. One female noted, interestingly enough, that if you have a 160-pound male on top of you, you'd certainly want to be sure he'd respect you as a lover would!

2. C. H. and Winifred Whiteley, *Sex and Morals* (New York: Basic Books, 1967), p. 48.

3. Koestenbaum, *Existential Sexuality* (Englewood Cliffs, N.J.: Prentice Hall, 1974), p. 4.

4. Schwarz, *The Psychology of Sex* (Baltimore: Penguin Books, 1949), p. 21.

5. Barrel, "Sexual Arousal in the Objectifying Attitude," *Review of Existential Psychology and Psychiatry* 13, no. 1 (1974): 98–99.

6. Freud argued that one has difficulty in having sex with a loved one because one was severely scolded in childhood for having incestuous wishes for the mother. This causes a man to feel guilt in the presence of women when he grows up, and he is compelled to degrade them in his mind so they will not remind him of his beloved mother and thus arouse the subconscious feelings of guilt at violating the incest taboo. But perhaps the explanation for having difficulty with sexual intercourse with a loved one is much simpler. It is that when one objectifies the female (often a necessary condition for male arousal), one feels the same sort of horror when he finds a beloved object, such as a car, dismantled into its component parts. There is the further possibility that, when one reduces a female into her component sexual parts of breasts, vagina, rump, thighs, and so forth, such objectification of the female is somehow linked to *conquest* of her; and this could cause guilt feelings in a particularly sensitive male. (For does not one break up an object and destroy its wholeness in order to better conquer it, he might ask.) Freud's theory is expounded in greater detail in "The Most Prevalent Form of Degradation in Erotic Life," *Sexuality and the Psychology of Love* (New York: Collier Books, 1972), pp. 58–70.

7. Reik, *The Psychology of Sexual Relations* (New York: Grove Press, 1945), pp. 17–18. See also Reik, *A Psychologist Looks at Love* (New York: Lancer Books, 1944), pp. 31–36.

8. Reik, *Psychology of Sexual Relations*, p. 19.

9. See Robert Solomon, "Sex and Perversion," *Philosophy and Sex*, ed. Robert Baker and Frederick Elliston (Buffalo, NY: Prometheus Books, 1976), pp. 279–282.

10. Casler, "Toward a Re-Evaluation of Love," *Symposium on Love*, ed. Mary Ellen Curtin (New York: Behavioural Publications, 1973), pp. 1–36.

11. "The most common escape (from their imprisonment in the female role and the denial of their humanity) is the psychopathological condition of love. It is a euphoric state of fantasy in which the victim transforms her oppressor into her redeemer: she turns her natural hostility against herself—her consciousness—and sees her counterpart in contrast to herself as all powerful (as he is by now at her expense). The combination of his power, her self-hatred and the hope for a life that is self-justifying—the goal of all living creatures—results in a yearning for her stolen life—her self—that is the delusion and poignancy of love. 'Love' is the natural response of the victim to the rapist." Ti-Grace Atkinson, "Radical Feminism," *Notes from the Second Year: Women's Liberation* (Boston, 1969), pp. 36–37.

12. Solomon, "Sex and Perversion," p. 278.

In part two of Vannoy's book, he subjects the concept of love to a lengthy critical analysis. Vannoy claims that the concept of erotic love is not a viable one and that it is riddled with contradictions. Such contradictions produce constant mental anguish for lovers by creating conflicting desires within the lovers. Based on this analysis, Vannoy concludes, " . . . on the whole, sex with a humanistic non-lover is far preferable to sex with an erotic lover" (Vannoy, p. 219).

Our next author, Lillian Rubin, investigates the differences in the way that men and women experience love and sex.

SEX IS GENDERED

In the debate between the superiority of sex with love versus sex without love, there is an assumption that is often ignored—that the relation of sex and love is experienced the *same* by men and women. But is it plausible that sex is gendered? That is, do women and men perceive or experience sex and love differently?

In the following selection from Lillian Rubin's *Intimate Strangers,* she observes that there is in fact such a difference. For most women, their primary concerns in a sexual encounter are that it be intimate, relational, meaningful, and emotionally connected. For most males, sex is sought primarily for physical pleasure, although Rubin notes that for men sex often has a way of bringing out their other emotions afterwards.

from Intimate Strangers

LILLIAN B. RUBIN

Some analysts of society point to the culture, to the ideologies that have defined the limits of male and female sexuality. Certainly there's truth in that. There's no gainsaying that, through the ages of Western society, women's sexuality has come under attack, that there have been sometimes extreme pressures to control and confine it—even to deny its existence. There's no doubt either that we have dealt with male sexuality with much more ambivalence. On the one hand, it too has been the object of efforts at containment; on the other, we have acknowledged its force and power—indeed, built myth and monument in homage to what we have taken to be its inherently uncontrollable nature.

Such social attitudes about male and female sexuality, and the behavioral ideals that have accompanied them, not only shape our sexual behavior but affect our experience of our own sexuality as well. For culture both clarifies and mystifies. A set of beliefs is at once a way of seeing the world more clearly while, at the same time, foreclosing an alternative vision. When it comes to sex—precisely because it's such a primitive, elemental force—all societies seek some control over it and, therefore, the mystification is greater than the clarification. Thus, for example, Victorian women often convinced themselves that they had no sexual feelings even when the messages their bodies sent would have told them otherwise if they had been able to listen. And, even now, men often engage in compulsive sexual behavior that brings them little, if any, pleasure without allowing themselves to notice the joylessness of it. Both behaviors a response to cultural mandates, both creating dissonance, if not outright conflict, when inner experience is at odds with behavioral expectations.

The blueprint to which our sexuality conforms, then, is drawn by the culture. But that's not yet the whole story. The dictates of any society are reinforced by its institutional arrangements and mediated by the personal experience of the people who must live within them. And it's in that confluence of social arrangement and psychological response that we'll come to understand the basis of the sexual differences that so often divide us from each other.

For a woman, there's no satisfactory sex without an emotional connection; for a man, the two are more easily separable. For her, the connection generally must precede the sexual encounter:

> For me to be excited about making love, I have to feel close to him—like we're sharing something, not just living together.

For him, emotional closeness can be born of the sexual contact.

> It's the one subject we never get anywhere on. It's a lot easier for me to tell her what she wants to hear when I feel close, and that's when I get closest—when we're making love. It's kind of hard to explain it, but [trying to find the words] . . . well, it's when the emotions come roaring up.

The issues that divide them around intimacy in the relationship are nowhere to be seen more clearly than here. When she speaks of connection, she usually means intimacy that's born of some verbal expression, some sharing of thought and feeling:

> I want to know what he's thinking—you know, what's going on inside him—before we jump into bed.

For him, it's enough that they're in the same room.

> To me, it feels like there's a nice bond when we're together—just reading the paper or watching the tube or something like that. Then, when we go to bed, that's not enough for her.

The problem, then, is not *how* we talk to each other but *whether* we do so. And it's connected to what words and the verbal expression of emotion mean to us, how sex and emotion come together for each of us, and the fact that we experience the balance between the two so differently—all of which takes us again to the separation and individuation experiences of childhood.

For both boys and girls, the earliest attachment and the identification that grows from it are much larger, deeper, and more all-embracing than anything we, who have successfully buried that primitive past in our unconscious, can easily grasp. Their root is pure eros—that vital, life-giving force with which all attachment begins. The infant bathes in it. But we are a society of people who have learned to look on eros with apprehension, if not outright fear. For us, it is associated with passion, with sex, with forces that threaten to be out of our control. And we teach our young very early, and in ways too numerous to count, about the need to limit the erotic, about our fears that eros imperils civilization.

In the beginning, it's the same for children of either sex. As the child grows past the early symbiotic union with mother, as the boundaries of self begin to develop, the social norms about sexuality begin to make themselves felt. In conformity with those norms, the erotic and emotional are split one from the other, and the erotic takes on a more specifically sexual meaning.

But here the developmental similarities end. For a boy at this stage, it's the emotional component of the attachment to mother that comes under attack as he seeks to repress his identification with her. The erotic—or sexualized—aspect of the attachment is left undisturbed, at least in heterosexual men. To be sure, the incest taboo assures that future sexual *behavior* will take place with a woman other than mother. But the issue here is not behavior but the emotional structure that underlies it.

For a girl, the developmental requirement is exactly the opposite. For her, it's the erotic component of the attachment to a woman that must be denied and shifted later to a man; the larger emotional involvement and the identification remain intact.

This split between the emotional and the erotic components of attachment in childhood has deep and lasting significance for the ways in which we respond to relationships—sexual and otherwise—in adulthood. For it means that, for men, the erotic aspect of any relationship remains forever the most compelling, while, for women, the emotional component will always be the more salient. It's here that we can come to understand the depth of women's emotional connection to each other—the reasons why nonsexual friendships between women remain so central in their lives, so important to their sense of themselves and to their well-being. And it's here also that we can see why nonsexual relationships hold such little emotional charge for men.

It's not, as folklore has held, that a woman's sexual response is more muted than a man's, or that she doesn't need or desire sexual release the way a man does. But, because it's the erotic aspect of her earliest attachment that has to be repressed in childhood if a girl is later to form a sexual bond with a man, the explicitly sexual retains little *independent* status in her inner life. A man may lust after *women,* but a woman lusts after *a man.* For a woman, sex usually has meaning only in a relational context—perhaps a clue to why so many girls never or rarely masturbate in adolescence or early adulthood.

We might argue that the social proscriptions against masturbation alone could account for its insignificance in girls and young women. But boys, too, hear exhortations against masturbation—indeed, even today, many still are told tales of the horrors that will befall them. Yet, except to encourage guilt and secrecy, such injunctions haven't made much difference in its incidence among them.

It would be reasonable to assume that this is a response to the mixed message this society sends to men about their sexuality. On the one hand, they're expected to exercise restraint; on the other, there's an implicit understanding that we can't really count on them to do so—that, at base, male sexuality cannot be controlled, that, after all, boys will be boys.

Surely such differences in the ways in which male and female sexuality are viewed could account for some of the differences between the sexes in their patterns and incidence of masturbation. But I believe there's something else that makes the social prohibitions take so well with women. For with them, an emotional connection in a relationship generally is a stimulus, if not a precondition, for the erotic.

If women depend on the emotional attachment to call up the sexual, men rely on the sexual to spark the emotional, as these words from a forty-one-year-old man, married fourteen years, show:

> Having sex with her makes me feel much closer so it makes it easier to bridge the emotional gap, so to speak. It's like the physical sex opens up another door, and things and feelings can get expressed that I couldn't before.

For women, emotional attachments without sex are maintained with little difficulty or discomfort; for men, they're much more problematic. It's not that they don't exist at all, but that they're less common and fraught with many more difficulties and reservations.

This is the split that may help to explain why men tend to be fearful of homosexuality in a way that women are not. I don't mean by this that women welcome homosexual stirrings any more than men do. But, for women, the emotional and the erotic are separated in such a way that they can be intensely connected emotionally without fear that this will lead to a sexual connection. For men, where the emotional connection so often depends on a sexual one, a close emotional relationship with another man usually is experienced as a threat.

•   •   •

The fear that each of them experiences is an archaic one—the remnants of the separation-unity conflict of childhood that's brought to the surface again at the moment of sexual union. The response is patterned and predictable. He fears engulfment; she fears invasion. Their emotional history combines with cultural mandates about femininity and masculinity to prepare them each for their own side; their physiology does the rest.

For men, the repression of their first identification and the muting of *emotional* attachment that goes with it fit neatly with cultural proscriptions about manliness that require them to abjure the emotional side of life in favor of the rational. Sex, therefore, becomes the one arena where it is legitimate for men to contact their deeper feeling states and to express them. Indeed, all too often, the sex act carries most of the burden of emotional expression for men—a reality of their lives that may explain the urgency with which men so often approach sex. For, if sex is the main conduit through which inhibited emotions are animated, expressed, and experienced, then that imperative and compulsive quality that seems such a puzzle becomes understandable.

But the act of entry itself stirs old conflictual desires that must be contained. This is the moment a man hungers for, while it's also the instant of his greatest vulnerability. As a woman takes him into her body, there are both ecstasy and fear—the ecstasy of union with a woman once again; the fear of being engulfed by her, of somehow losing a part of himself that he's struggled to maintain through the years.

For a woman, the repression of her first *erotic* attachment is also a good fit with the cultural proscriptions against the free expression of her sexuality. But, in childhood, there was no need to make any assault on her first identification with mother and the deep emotional attachment that lay beneath it; no need, either, to differentiate herself as fully and firmly as was necessary for a male child. In adulthood, therefore, she remains concerned with the fluidity of her boundaries, on guard against their permeability—a concern that's activated most fully at the moment of penetration.

This is one of those moments in life when the distinction between fantasy and reality is blurred by the fact that the two actually look so much alike. With entry, her boundaries have been violated, her body invaded. It's just this that may explain why a woman so often avoids the sexual encounter—a common complaint in marriages— even when she will also admit to finding it pleasurable and gratifying once she gets involved. For there are both pleasure and pain—the pleasure of experiencing the union, the pain of the intrusion that violates her sometimes precarious sense of her own separateness. Together, these conflicting feelings often create an inertia about sex—not about an emotional connection but about a sexual one—especially when she doesn't feel as if there's enough emotional pay-off in it to make it worth the effort to overcome her resistance to stirring up the conflict again.

This conflict can be seen in its most unvarnished form in the early stages of relations between lesbians. There's a special kind of ecstasy in their sexual relationship just because it's with a woman—because in a woman's arms the boundaries of separateness fall, the dream of a return to the old symbiosis with mother is fulfilled. But the rapture can be short-lived, for the wish for symbiosis belongs to the infant, not the adult. Once achieved, therefore, ecstasy can give way to fear— fear of the loss of self, which is heightened beyond anything known in the sexual bond with a man.

There's anxiety about boundaries in heterosexual sex, of course. But there's also some measure of safety that exists in this union with one's opposite. For, although sex between a man and a woman can be an intensely intimate experience, there's a limit, a boundary between them that can't be crossed simply by virtue of the fact that they're woman and man. It may, indeed, be one of the aspects of sex with a man that a woman finds so seductive—the ability to satisfy sexual need while still retaining the integrity of a separate sense of self. For, in heterosexual sex, the very physical differences help to reassure us of our separateness while, at the same time, permitting a connection with another that's possible in no other act in human life.

• • •

As I write these pages, some questions begin to form in my mind. "Is all this," I wonder, "just another way of saying that women are less sexual than men? What about the women we see all around us today who seem to be as easy with their sexuality as men are, and as emotionally detached?"

Without doubt there are today—perhaps always have been—some women for whom sex and emotion are clearly split. But, when we look beneath the behavior of even the most sexually active woman, most of the time we'll see that it's not just sex that engages her. It's true that such a woman no longer needs to convince herself that she's in love in order to have a sexual relationship with a man. But the key word here is *relationship*— limited, yes, perhaps existing only in a transitory fantasy, but there for her as a reality. And, more often than not, such relationships, even when they are little more than fleeting ones, have meanings other than sexual for a woman. For the sexual stimulus usually is connected to some emotional attachment, however limited it may be. And what, at first glance, might seem simply to be a sexual engagement is, in reality, a search for something else.

We need only listen to women to hear them corroborate what I'm saying here. When asked what it is they get in their more casual sexual encounters, even those who consider themselves the most sexually liberated will generally admit that they're often not orgasmic in such transient relationships. "When I was single, I'd sleep with someone who appealed to me right away, no problems," said a recently married twenty-seven-year-old breezily. "Did you usually have orgasms in those relationships?" I asked her. Laughing, she replied, "Nope, that was reserved." "Reserved for what?" I wanted to know. Saucily, "For the guy who deserved it." "And what does that mean?" Finally, she became serious. "I guess it means I have to trust a guy before I can come with him—like I have to know there's some way of touching him emotionally and that I can trust him enough to let him into that part of me."

"What's in it for you?" I asked all the women who spoke this way. "Why get involved at all if it's not sexually gratifying?" Without exception, they said they engaged sexually because it was the only way they could get the other things they need from a man. "What things?" I wanted to know. The answer: Something that told of their need for relationship and attachment rather than sex. They spoke of wanting "hugging more than fucking," of how it "feels good to be connected for a little while." They talked almost urgently of the "need to be held," "to feel needed by someone," of how important it is that "there's someone to give something to and take something from."

It's true, men also will speak of the need to be held and hugged. But orgasm generally is not in question and hugging is seldom an end to be desired in and for itself. In fact, it's one of the most common complaints of women that, even in the context of a stable relationship, such tender physical contact becomes too quickly transformed into a prelude to sex. "Why can't he just be happy to hold me; why does it always have to lead to fucking?" a woman complains. "I hold her and we hug and cuddle; I like it and I like her to hold me, too. But there's a natural progression, isn't there?" her husband asks, mystified.

Having read the debate between Bertocci and Vannoy and perused some of Rubin's insights, we have been encouraged to reflect further on our own evaluations concerning the value of sex with love versus sex without love. Beginning with Vannoy, we might ask if he has successfully shown that traditional defenders of sex with love (such as Bertocci) have indeed presented us with a false dichotomy of sex with love and sex without love, one that would prejudice the case against sex without love.

Does this debate suggest another interesting question on the matter? Should we evaluate our sexual activities on a case-by-case basis or should we see each sexual encounter as it relates to the other projects in our lives at the time? If so, is there only one legitimate project—that of love-marriage-children-community? Can there not be alternative lifestyles or goals that may be enriching and satisfying for some people? While it might be more beneficial to society as a whole to promote a unified goal of a homogeneous lifestyle, is it possible that this lifestyle is not suitable for everyone, such as homosexuals, career-oriented couples, etc.? Would it also be feasible to presume that not everyone should be encouraged to marry and have children, such as drug abusers, alcoholics, batterers, etc.?[1]

While Bertocci grounds his view in one concept of love which is subject to the kind of criticism that Vannoy produces, doesn't Vannoy's attack on romantic love also present problems? Vannoy himself concludes in his chapter "Can One Define Love?"[2] that there is no acceptable objective definition of love and that it can mean *whatever* an individual means

---

[1]For an in-depth discussion of marriage, see Chapter 4.

[2]See *Sex Without Love*, Part II, Chapter 2.

by that term. But if this is true and there is no single meaning of the term "love," how can Vannoy produce arguments against love? Wouldn't it be necessary to define love in order to identify who the lovers are? How can one criticize a lover if one has no definition of love? How can one produce empirical evidence such as that of Alan Lee if we really have no definition of love at all?

Finally, with regard to Rubin, even if it were true that men and women experience sex differently, are we convinced that the answer to our debate is gender based, so that men and women will forever disagree?

CHAPTER 3

Feminist Critiques
of
Sex and Love

THERE IS NO ONE POSITION on any issue that can be identified as *the* feminist position. Following are some examples of feminist approaches to ethics, science, and surrogate motherhood.

Iris Murdoch was a professor of ethics at Oxford. Instead of writing articles in philosophy journals carefully dissecting concepts, she wrote novels. She felt that ethics could be understood only in the context of the unfolding of stories. Annette Baier, a professor of ethics at the University of Pittsburgh, does not write novels. Yet her current articles are unique, stressing as they often do her emphasis on the sterility of moral theory and the need to know the backgrounds of philosophers writing on ethics.

Barbara McClintock was a Nobel Prize-winning geneticist. Unlike other scientists in her field, she spoke of the need to have a "feeling for the organism." For example, corn, fruit flies, and guinea pigs should not be seen as mere objects for experimentation. To learn the most about them, one must feel for them and with them—or at least make the effort. This is not the vaunted objectivity one usually associates with science. Alison Jaggar writes that one cannot separate emotion from knowledge because science is full of emotion. We have just been lulled into not noticing it.

Some feminists believe that women have the right to bear children for others in any manner that they deem safe. Ruth Macklin, an ethicist at Albert Einstein University College of Medicine, (and some feminists) believe that a woman demeans herself when she asks to be let out of a surrogate mother contract because of emotional ties to the baby. On the other hand, some feminists argue that a surrogate mother ought to be allowed to break the surrogacy contract because of unexpected emotional ties. Not to allow this demeans and devalues women by undervaluing the importance of their real feelings as potential mothers. Carmel Shalev points out that not allowing surrogacy violates the freedom of women and thus demeans them (*Birth Power*, New Haven, CT: Yale University Press, 1989). Janice Raymond has argued that surrogate mothering demeans women by reducing them to the status of property; it objectifies them ("In the Matter of Baby M: Rejudged," *Reproductive and Genetic Engineering* 1, no. 2, pp. 175–181).

Is there a thread that runs through feminism? One such thread might be the search for a male-oriented bias in any already well-established discipline. After all, just about all our accepted disciplines have been created by and run by and for men. Why not expect that to make a difference? There need be no claim (but there very well might be) that a male-oriented approach is wrong, just that it is biased. Here is a clear example.

Ever since medicine used clinical trials (carefully controlled experiments) to establish the safety and efficacy of drug therapies, women have been excluded from being experimental subjects. The reason was twofold. One was that they might be pregnant or get pregnant and that drugs might harm the fetus. The other was that the physiology of a woman seemed so complex that it might confound the results. Is it any wonder, then, that virtually all drugs carry a warning that they may cause problems with pregnancy? Therefore, scientifically speaking, what is known about many drugs is just how they work on men. What this means is that when they are given to women, we are not really sure how they will work. Further, because of this, the evidence of drug efficacy and safety in women is anecdotal and thus untrustworthy. (The claim that anecdotes are untrustworthy might just be male dogma.)

A simpler example of male bias is Freud's never having discussed the importance of breast development in young girls. Another example of such male bias is pointed out by Carol Gilligan in her book *In A Different Voice* (Cambridge, MA: Harvard University Press, 1982). She says that in Piaget's account of moral judgment girls get four entries in the index and boys get none because to Piaget, "child" is *assumed* to be male. In the articles that follow, we will see feminists at work dissecting love and sexual behavior. This is the best way to get a feeling for feminism. They will argue that romantic love is a male invention; that to be free of male domination requires a special kind of existential liberation; that when properly understood, all intercourse is rape; that heterosexuality is just cultural happenstance; and that gender can be chosen. Two feminist novelists will then give their opinions on what makes perfect sex and why marriages are likely to be less than ideal from the standpoint of women.

In the chapter on sexual harassment and rape, we will also read the works of feminists. In all, we will see the gamut of feminists from those who are so very moderate in their views that many feminists do not consider them feminist at all (Roiphe on date rape) to those who seem quite extreme (Dworkin and Firestone).

ON ROMANTIC LOVE—A MALE INVENTION

To Firestone, romantic love is a male invention to oppress women. Without this kind of romantic love, she claims, our patriarchal culture would fall apart. Real romantic love, on the other hand, would be total mutual exchange. But this requires equality, something beyond our reach. Why is equality impossible to attain? Because men are in control of our culture and because of the way they are mothered. Add to this men's need to stay in control, and the result is men who cannot love the way that women would want them to love. No woman is valued for her real characteristics, as Plato would have required for true love. The result of mothering, according to Firestone, is that in order to love a woman, a man has to see that woman as better in an abstract way because men see particular women as inferior to men. To men, love is only ownership and control. Firestone asks, but only rhetorically, "Who needs it?"

Firestone depends a great deal on the psychological work of Theodore Reik. Does this strengthen or weaken her position? Perhaps other psychological theories would not support her views. Is Firestone committed, by using psychology as she does, to some sort of deterministic picture of human relationships? That is, even if she is right about the differences between how men and women "love," isn't it possible for men (and women) to change?

Are all loving relationships as Firestone characterizes them? In other words, if a man and woman denied that their relation fitted Firestone's characterization, would this show that she was wrong, or just that the couple really did not understand their relationship?

from Love: A Feminist Critique

SHULAMITH FIRESTONE

A book on radical feminism that did not deal with love would be a political failure. For love, perhaps even more than childbearing, is the pivot of women's oppression today. I realize this has frightening implications: Do we want to get rid of love?

The panic felt at any threat to love is a good clue to its political significance. Another sign that love is central to any analysis of women or sex psychology is its omission from culture itself, its relegation to "personal life." (And whoever heard of logic in the bedroom?) Yes, it is portrayed in novels, even metaphysics, but in them it is described, or better, recreated, not analyzed. Love has never been *understood,* though it may have been fully *experienced,* and that experience communicated.

There is reason for this absence of analysis: *Women and Love are underpinnings. Examine them and you threaten the very structure of culture.*

The tired question "What were women doing while men created masterpieces?" deserves more than the obvious reply: Women were barred from culture, exploited in their role of mother. Or its reverse: Women had no need for paintings since they created children. Love is tied to culture in much deeper ways than that. Men were thinking, writing, and creating, because women were pouring their energy into those men; women are not creating culture because they are preoccupied with love.

That women live for love and men for work is a truism. Freud was the first to attempt to ground this dichotomy in the individual psyche: the male child, sexually rejected by the first person in his at-

tention, his mother, "sublimates" his "libido"—his reservoir of sexual (life) energies—into long-term projects, in the hope of gaining love in a more generalized form; thus he displaces his need for love into a need for recognition. This process does not occur as much in the female; most women never stop seeking direct warmth and approval.

There is also much truth in the clichés that "behind every man there is a woman," and that "women are the power behind [read: voltage in] the throne." (Male) culture was built on the love of women, and at their expense. Women provided the substance of those male masterpieces; and for millennia they have done the work, and suffered the costs, of one-way emotional relationships the benefits of which went to men and to the work of men. So if women are a parasitical class living off, and at the margins of, the male economy, the reverse too is true: *(Male) culture was (and is) parasitical, feeding on the emotional strength of women without reciprocity.*

Moreover, we tend to forget that this culture is not universal, but rather sectarian, presenting only half the spectrum. The very structure of culture itself, as we shall see, is saturated with the sexual polarity, as well as being in every degree run by, for, and in the interests of male society. But while the male half is termed all of culture, men have not forgotten there is a female "emotional" half: They live it on the sly. As the result of their battle to reject the female in themselves (the Oedipus Complex as we have explained it) they are unable to take love seriously as a cultural matter; but they can't do without it altogether. Love is the underbelly of (male) culture just as love is the weak spot of every man, bent on proving his virility in that large male world of "travel and adventure." Women have always known how men need love, and how they deny this need. Perhaps this explains the peculiar contempt women so universally feel for men ("men are so dumb"), for they can see that men are posturing in the outside world.

I

How does this phenomenon "love" operate? Contrary to popular opinion, love is not altruistic. The initial attraction is based on curious admiration (more often today, envy and resentment) for the self-possession, the integrated unity, of the other and a wish to become part of this Self in some way (today, read: intrude or take over), to become important to that psychic balance. The self-containment of the other creates desire (read: a challenge); admiration (envy) of the other becomes a wish to incorporate (possess) its qualities. A clash of selves follows in which the individual attempts to fight off the growing hold over him of the other. Love is the final opening up to (or, surrender to the dominion of) the other. The lover demonstrates to the beloved how he himself would like to be treated. ("I tried so hard to make him fall in love with me that I fell in love with him myself.") Thus love is the height of selfishness: the self attempts to enrich itself through the absorption of another being. Love is being psychically wide-open to another. It is a situation of total emotional vulnerability. Therefore it must be not only the incorporation of the other, but an *exchange* of selves. Anything short of a mutual exchange will hurt one or the other party.

There is nothing inherently destructive about this process. A little healthy selfishness would be a refreshing change. Love between two equals would be an enrichment, each enlarging himself through the other: instead of being one, locked in the cell of himself with only his own experience and view, he could participate in the existence of another—an extra window on the world. This accounts for the bliss that successful lovers experience: Lovers are temporarily freed from the burden of isolation that every individual bears.

But bliss in love is seldom the case: For every successful contemporary love experience, for every short period of enrichment, there are ten destruc-

tive love experiences, post-love "downs" of much longer duration—often resulting in the destruction of the individual, or at least an emotional cynicism that makes it difficult or impossible ever to love again. Why should this be so, if it is not actually inherent in the love process itself?

Let's talk about love in its destructive guise—and why it gets that way, referring once more to the work of Theodore Reik. Reik's concrete observation brings him closer than many better minds to understanding the *process* of "falling in love," but he is off insofar as he confuses love as it exists in our present society with love itself. He notes that love is a reaction formation, a cycle of envy, hostility, and possessiveness: he sees that it is preceded by dissatisfaction with oneself, a yearning for something better, created by a discrepancy between the ego and the ego-ideal; that the bliss love produces is due to the resolution of this tension by the substitution, in place of one's own ego-ideal, of the other; and finally that love fades "because the other can't live up to your high ego-ideal any more than you could, and the judgment will be the harsher the higher are the claims on oneself." Thus in Reik's view love wears down just as it wound up: Dissatisfaction with oneself (whoever heard of falling in love the week one is leaving for Europe?) leads to astonishment at the other person's self-containment; to envy; to hostility; to possessive love; and back again through exactly the same process. This is the love process *today*. But why must it be this way?

Many, for example Denis de Rougemont in *Love in the Western World,* have tried to draw a distinction between romantic "falling in love" with its "false reciprocity which disguises a twin narcissism" (the Pagan Eros) and an unselfish love for the other person as that person really is (the Christian Agape). De Rougemont attributes the morbid passion of Tristan and Iseult (romantic love) to a vulgarization of specific mystical and religious currents in Western civilization.

I believe instead that *love is essentially a simple phenomenon—unless it has become complicated, corrupted, or obstructed by an unequal balance of power.* We have seen that love demands a mutual vulnerability or it turns destructive: the destructive effects of love occur only in a context of inequality. But if, as we have seen, (biological) inequality has always remained a constant, existing to varying degrees, then it is understandable that "romantic love" would develop. (It remains for us only to explain why it has steadily increased in Western countries since the medieval period, which we shall attempt to do in the following chapter.)

How does the sex class system based on the unequal power distribution of the biological family affect love between the sexes? In discussing Freudianism, we have gone into the psychic structuring of the individual within the family and how this organization of personality must be different for the male and the female because of their very different relationships to the mother. At present the insular interdependency of the mother/child relationship forces both male and female children into anxiety about losing the mother's love, on which they depend for physicial survival. When later (Erich Fromm notwithstanding) the child learns that the mother's love is conditional, to be rewarded the child in return for approved behavior (that is, behavior in line with the mother's own values and personal ego gratification—for she is free to mold the child "creatively," however she happens to define that), the child's anxiety turns into desperation. This, coinciding with the sexual rejection of the male child by the mother, causes, as we have seen, a schizophrenia in the boy between the emotional and the physical, and in the girl, the mother's rejection, occurring for different reasons, produces an insecurity about her identity in general, creating a lifelong need for approval. (Later her lover replaces her father as a grantor of the necessary surrogate identity—she sees everything through his eyes.) Here originates the hunger for love that later sends both sexes searching in one person after the other for a state of ego security. But because of the early rejection, to the degree that it occurred, the male will be terrified of committing himself, of "opening up" and then being smashed. How this affects his sexuality we have seen: To the degree that a woman is like his mother, the incest taboo operates to restrain his total sexual/emotional commitment; for him to feel safely the kind of total response he first felt for his mother, which was rejected, he must degrade this woman so as to distinguish her from the mother. This behavior reproduced on a larger scale explains many cultural phenomena, including perhaps the ideal love-worship of chivalric times, the forerunner of modern romanticism.

Romantic idealization is partially responsible, at least on the part of men, for a peculiar characteristic of "falling" in love: the change takes place in the lover almost independently of the character of the love object. Occasionally the lover, though beside himself, sees with another rational part of his faculties that, objectively speaking, the one he loves isn't worth all this blind devotion; but he is helpless to act on this, "a slave to love." More often he fools himself entirely. But others can see what is happening ("How on earth he could love her is beyond me!"). This idealization occurs much less frequently on the part of women, as is borne out by Reik's clinical studies. A man must idealize one woman over the rest in order to justify his descent to a lower caste. Women have no such reason to idealize men—in fact, when one's life depends on one's ability to "psych" men out, such idealization may actually be dangerous—though a fear of male power in general may carry over into relationships with individual men, appearing to be the same phenomenon. But though women know to be inauthentic this male "falling in love," all women, in one way or another, require proof of it from men before they can allow themselves to love (genuinely, in their case) in return. For this idealization process acts to artificially equalize the two parties, a minimum precondition for the development of an uncorrupted love—we have seen that love requires a mutual vulnerability that is impossible to achieve in an unequal power situation. *Thus "falling in love" is no more than the process of alteration of male vision—through idealization, mystification, glorification—that renders void the woman's class inferiority.*

However, the woman knows that this idealization, which she works so hard to produce, is a lie, and that it is only a matter of time before he "sees through her." Her life is a hell, vacillating between an all-consuming need for male love and approval to raise her from her class subjection, to persistent feelings of inauthenticity when she does achieve his love. Thus her whole identity hangs in the balance of her love life. She is allowed to love herself only if a man finds her worthy of love.

But if we could eliminate the political context

of love between the sexes, would we not have some degree of idealization remaining in the love process itself? I think so. For the process occurs in the same manner whoever the love choice: the lover "opens up" to the other. Because of this fusion of egos, in which each sees and cares about the other as a new self, the beauty/character of the beloved, perhaps hidden to outsiders under layers of defenses, is revealed. "I wonder what she sees in him," then, means not only, "She is a fool, blinded with romanticism," but, "Her love has lent her x-ray vision. Perhaps we are missing something." (Note that this phrase is most commonly used about women. The equivalent phrase about *men's* slavery to love is more often something like, "She has him wrapped around her finger," she has him so "snowed" that he is the last one to see through her.) Increased sensitivity to the real, if hidden, values in the other, however, is not "blindness" or "idealization" but is, in fact, deeper vision. It is only the *false* idealization we have described above that is responsible for the destruction. Thus it is not the process of love itself that is at fault, but its *political*, i.e., unequal *power* context: the who, why, when and where of it is what makes it now such a holocaust.

II

But abstractions about love are only one more symptom of its diseased state. (As one female patient of Reik so astutely put it, "Men take love either too seriously or not seriously enough.") Let's look at it more concretely, as we now experience it in its corrupted form. Once again we shall quote from the Reikian Confessional. For if Reik's work has any value it is where he might least suspect, i.e., in his trivial feminine urge to "gossip." Here he is, justifying himself (one supposes his Superego is troubling him):

> A has-been like myself must always be somewhere and working on something. Why should I not occupy myself with those small questions that are not often posed and yet perhaps can be answered? The "petites questions" have a legitimate place beside the great and fundamental problems of psychoanalysis.

> It takes moral courage to write about certain things, as for example about a game that little girls

play in the intervals between classes. Is such a theme really worthy of a *serious* psychoanalyst who has passed his 77th year? (Italics mine)

And he reminds himself:

> But in psychoanalysis there are no unimportant thoughts; there are only thoughts that pretend to be unimportant in order not to be told.

Thus he rationalizes what in fact may be the only valuable contribution of his work. Here are his patients of both sexes speaking for themselves about their love lives:

Women:

Later on he called me a sweet girl. . . . I didn't answer . . . what could I say? . . . but I knew I was not a sweet girl at all and that he sees me as someone I'm not.

No man can love a girl the way a girl loves a man.

I can go a long time without sex, but not without love.

It's like H_2O instead of water.

I sometimes think that all men are sex-crazy and sex-starved. All they can think about when they are with a girl is going to bed with her.

Have I nothing to offer this man but this body?

I took off my dress and my bra and stretched myself out on his bed and waited. For an instant I thought of myself as an animal of sacrifice on the altar.

I don't understand the feelings of men. My husband has me. Why does he need other women? What have they got that I haven't got?

Believe me, if all wives whose husbands had affairs left them, we would only have divorced women in this country.

After my husband had quite a few affairs, I flirted with the fantasy of taking a lover. Why not? What's sauce for the gander is sauce for the goose. . . . But I was stupid as a goose: I didn't have it in me to have an extramarital affair.

I asked several people whether men also sometimes cry themselves to sleep. I don't believe it.

Men (for further illustration, see **Screw**):

It's not true that only the external appearance of a woman matters. The underwear is also important.

It's not difficult to make it with a girl. What's difficult is to make an end of it.

The girl asked me whether I cared for her mind. I was tempted to answer I cared more for her behind.

"Are you going already?" she said when she opened her eyes. It was a bedroom cliché whether I left after an hour or after two days.

Perhaps it's necessary to fool the woman and to pretend you love her. But why should I fool myself?

When she is sick, she turns me off. But when I'm sick she feels sorry for me and is more affectionate than usual.

It is not enough for my wife that I have to hear her talking all the time—blah, blah, blah. She also expects me to hear what she is saying.

Simone de Beauvoir said it: "The word love has by no means the same sense for both sexes, and this is one cause of the serious misunderstandings which divide them." Above I have illustrated some of the traditional differences between men and women in love that come up so frequently in parlor discussions of the "double standard," where it is generally agreed: That women are monogamous, better at loving, possessive, "clinging," more interested in (highly involved) "relationships" than in sex per se, and they confuse affection with sexual desire. That men are interested in nothing but a screw (Wham, bam, thank you Ma'am!), or else romanticize the woman ridiculously; that once sure of her, they become notorious philanderers, never satisfied; that they mistake sex for emotion. All this bears out what we have discussed—the difference in the psychosexual organizations of the two sexes, determined by the first relationship to the mother.

I draw three conclusions based on these differences:

1) That men can't love. (Male hormones? Women traditionally expect and accept an emotional invalidism in men that they would find intolerable in a woman.)
2) That women's "clinging" behavior is necessitated by their objective social situation.
3) That this situation has not changed significantly from what it ever was.

Men can't love. We have seen why it is that men have difficulty loving and that while men may love, they usually "fall in love"—with their own

projected image. Most often they are pounding down a woman's door one day, and thoroughly disillusioned with her the next; but it is rare for women to leave men, and then it is usually for more than ample reason.

It is dangerous to feel sorry for one's oppressor—women are especially prone to this failing—but I am tempted to do it in this case. Being unable to love is hell. This is the way it proceeds: as soon as the man feels any pressure from the other partner to commit himself, he panics and may react in one of several ways:

1) He may rush out and screw ten other women to prove that the first woman has no hold over him. If she accepts this, he may continue to see her on this basis. The other women verify his (false) freedom; periodic arguments about them keep his panic at bay. But the women are a paper tiger, for nothing very deep could be happening with them anyway; he is balancing them against each other so that none of them can get much of him. Many smart women, recognizing this to be only a safety valve on their man's anxiety, give him "a long leash." For the real issue under all the fights about other women is that the man is unable to commit himself.

2) He may consistently exhibit unpredictable behavior, standing her up frequently, being indefinite about the next date, telling her that "my work comes first," or offering a variety of other excuses. That is, though he senses her anxiety, he refuses to reassure her in any way, or even to recognize her anxiety as legitimate. For he *needs* her anxiety as a steady reminder that he is still free, that the door is not entirely closed.

3) When he *is* forced into (an uneasy) commitment, he makes her pay for it: by ogling other women in her presence, by comparing her unfavorably to past girlfriends or movie stars, by snide reminders in front of his friends that she is his "ball and chain," by calling her a "nag," a "bitch," "a shrew," or by suggesting that if he were only a bachelor he would be a lot better off. His ambivalence about women's "inferiority" comes out: by being committed to one, he has somehow made the hated female identification, which he now must repeatedly deny if he is to maintain his self-respect in the (male) community. This steady derogation is not entirely put on: for in fact every other girl suddenly does look a lot better, he can't help feeling he has missed something—and, naturally, his woman is to blame. For he has never given up the search for the ideal: she has forced him to resign from it. Probably he will go to his grave feeling cheated, never realizing that there isn't much difference between one woman and the other, that it is the loving that *creates* the difference.

There are many variations of straining at the bit. Many men go from one casual thing to another, getting out every time it begins to get hot. And yet to live without love in the end proves intolerable to men just as it does to women. The question that remains for every normal male is, then, *how do I get someone to love me without her demanding an equal commitment in return?*

Women's "clinging" behavior is required by the objective social situation. The female *response* to such a situation of male hysteria at any prospect of mutual commitment was the development of subtle methods of manipulation, to force as much commitment as *could* be forced from men. Over the centuries strategies have been devised, tested, and passed on from mother to daughter in secret tête-à-têtes, passed around at "kaffeeklatsches" ("I never understand what it is women spend so much time talking about!"), or, in recent times, via the telephone. These are not trivial gossip sessions at all (as women prefer men to believe), but desperate strategies for survival. More real brilliance goes into one-hour coed telephone dialogue about men than into that same coed's four years of college study, or for that matter, than into most male political maneuvers. It is no wonder, then, that even the few women without "family obligations" always arrive exhausted at the starting line of any serious endeavor. It takes one's major energy for the best portion of one's creative years to "make a good catch," and a good part of the rest of one's life to "hold" that catch. ("To be in love can be a full-time job for a woman, like that of a profession for a man.") Women who choose to drop out of this race are choosing a life without love, something that, as we have seen, most *men* don't have the courage to do.

But unfortunately The Manhunt is characterized by an emotional urgency beyond this simple desire for return commitment. It is compounded by the very class reality that produced the male inability to love in the first place. In a male-run society that defines women as an inferior and parasitical class, a woman who does not achieve male approval in some form is doomed. To legitimate her existence, a woman must be *more* than woman, she must continually search for an out from her inferior definition;[1] and men are the only ones in a position to bestow on her this state of grace. But because the woman is rarely allowed to realize herself through activity in the larger (male) society—and when she is, she is seldom granted the recognition she deserves—it becomes easier to try for the recognition of one man than of many; and in fact this is exactly the choice most women make. Thus once more the phenomenon of love, good in itself, is corrupted by its class context: women must have love not only for healthy reasons but actually to validate their existence.

In addition, the continued *economic* dependence of women makes a situation of healthy love between equals impossible. Women today still live under a system of patronage: With few exceptions, they have the choice, not between either freedom or marriage, but between being either public or private property. Women who merge with a member of the ruling class can at least hope that some of his privilege will, so to speak, rub off. But women without men are in the same situation as orphans: they are a helpless sub-class lacking the protection of the powerful. This is the antithesis of freedom when they are still (negatively) defined by a class situation: for now they are in a situation of *magnified* vulnerability. To participate in one's subjection by choosing one's master often gives the illusion of free choice; but in reality a woman is never free to choose love without external motivations. For her at the present time, the two things, love and status, must remain inextricably intertwined.

Now assuming that a woman does not lose sight of these fundamental factors of her condition when she loves, she will never be able to love gratuitously, but only in exchange for security:

1) the emotional security which, we have seen, she is justified in demanding.

2) the emotional identity which she should be able to find through work and recognition, but which she is denied—thus forcing her to seek her definition through a man.

3) the economic class security that, in this society, is attached to her ability to "hook" a man.

Two of these three demands are invalid as conditions of "love," but are imposed on it, weighing it down.

Thus, in their precarious political situation, women can't afford the luxury of spontaneous love. It is much too dangerous. The love and approval of men is all-important. To love thoughtlessly, before one has ensured return commitment, would endanger that approval. Here is Reik:

> It finally became clear during psychoanalysis that the patient was afraid that if she should show a man she loved him, he would consider her inferior and leave her.

For once a woman plunges in emotionally, she will be helpless to play the necessary games: her love would come first, demanding expression. To pretend a coolness she does not feel, *then,* would be too painful, and further, it would be pointless: she would be cutting off her nose to spite her face, for freedom to love is what she was aiming for. But in order to guarantee such a commitment, she *must* restrain her emotions, she *must* play games. For, as we have seen, men do not commit themselves to mutual openness and vulnerability until they are forced to.

How does she then go about forcing this commitment from the male? One of her most potent weapons is sex—she can work him up to a state of physical torment with a variety of games: by denying his need, by teasing it, by giving and taking it back, by jealousy, and so forth. A woman under analysis wonders why:

> There are few women who never ask themselves on certain occasions "How hard should I make it for a man?" I think no man is troubled with questions of this kind. He perhaps asks himself only, "When will she give in?"

Men are right when they complain that women lack discrimination, that they seldom love a man for his individual traits but rather for what he has to offer (his class), that they are calculating, that

they use sex to gain other ends, etc. For in fact women are in no position to love freely. If a woman is lucky enough to find "a decent guy" to love her and support her, she is doing well—and usually will be grateful enough to return his love. About the only discrimination women *are* able to exercise is the choice between the men who have chosen them, or a playing off of one male, one power, against the other. But *provoking* a man's interest, and *snaring* his commitment once he has expressed that interest, is not exactly self-determination.

Now what happens after she has finally hooked her man, after he has fallen in love with her and will do anything? She has a new set of problems. Now she can release the vise, open her net, and examine what she has caught. Usually she is disappointed. It is nothing she would have bothered with were *she* a man. It is usually way below her level. (Check this out sometime: Talk to a few of those mousy wives.) "He may be a poor thing, but at least I've got a man of my own" is usually more the way she feels. But at least now she can drop her act. For the first time it is safe to love—now she must try like hell to catch up to him emotionally, to really mean what she has pretended all along. Often she is troubled by worries that he will find her out. She feels like an impostor. She is haunted by fears that he doesn't love the "real" her—and usually she is right. ("She wanted to marry a man with whom she could be as bitchy as she really is.")

This is just about when she discovers that love and marriage mean a different thing for a male than they do for her. Though men in general believe women in general to be inferior, every man has reserved a special place in his mind for the one woman he will elevate above the rest by virtue of association with himself. Until now the woman, out in the cold, begged for his approval, dying to clamber onto this clean well-lighted place. But once there, she realizes that she was elevated above other women not in recognition of her real value, but only because she matched nicely his store-bought pedestal. Probably he doesn't even know who she is (if indeed by this time she herself knows). He has let her in not because he genuinely loved her, but only because she played so well into his preconceived fantasies. Though she knew his love to be false, since she herself engineered it, she can't help feeling contempt for him. But she is afraid, at first, to reveal her true self, for then perhaps even that false love would go. And finally she understands that for him, too, marriage had all kinds of motivations that had nothing to do with love. She was merely the one closest to his fantasy image: she has been named Most Versatile Actress for the multi-role of Alter Ego, Mother of My Children, Housekeeper, Cook, Companion, in *his* play. She has been bought to fill an empty space in his life; but her life is nothing.

So she has not saved herself from being like other women. She is lifted out of that class only because she now is an appendage of a member of the master class; and he cannot associate with her unless he raises her status. But she has not been freed, she has been promoted to "house-nigger," she has been elevated only to be used in a different way. She feels cheated. She has gotten not love and recognition, but possessorship and control. This is when she is transformed from Blushing Bride to Bitch, a change that, no matter how universal and predictable, still leaves the individual husband perplexed. ("You're not the girl I married.")

The situation of women has not changed significantly from what it ever was. For the past fifty years women have been in a double bind about love: under the guise of a "sexual revolution," presumed to have occurred ("Oh, c'mon Baby, where have you *been?* Haven't you heard of the sexual revolution?"), women have been persuaded to shed their armor. The modern woman is in horror of being thought a bitch, where her grandmother expected that to happen as the natural course of things. Men, too, in her grandmother's time, expected that any self-respecting woman would keep *them* waiting, would play all the right games without shame: a woman who did not guard her own interests in this way was not respected. It was out in the open.

But the rhetoric of the sexual revolution, if it brought no improvements for women, proved to have great value for men. By convincing women that the usual female games and demands were despicable, unfair, prudish, old-fashioned, puritanical, and self-destructive, a new reservoir of available females was created to expand the tight supply of goods available for traditional sexual exploitation, disarming women of even the little protection they had so painfully acquired. Women today dare not make the old demands for fear of having a whole new vocabulary, designed just for this purpose, hurled at them: "fucked up," "ball-breaker," "cockteaser," "a real drag," "a bad trip,"—to be a "groovy chick" is the ideal.

Even now many women know what's up and avoid the trap, preferring to be called names rather than be cheated out of the little they can hope for from men (for it is still true that even the hippest want an "old lady" who is relatively unused). But more and more women are sucked into the trap, only to find out too late, and bitterly, that the traditional female games had a point; they are shocked to catch themselves at thirty complaining in a vocabulary dangerously close to the old I've-been-used-men-are-wolves-they're-all-bastards variety. Eventually they are forced to acknowledge the old-wives' truth: a fair and generous woman is (at best) respected, but seldom loved. Here is a description, still valid today, of the "emancipated" woman—in this case a Greenwich Village artist of the thirties—from *Mosquitoes,* an early Faulkner novel:

> She had always had trouble with her men. . . . Sooner or later they always ran out on her. . . . Men she recognized as having potentialities all passed through a violent but temporary period of interest which ceased as abruptly as it began, without leaving even the lingering threads of mutually remembered incidence, like those brief thunderstorms of August that threaten and dissolve for no apparent reason without producing any rain.
>
> At times she speculated with almost masculine detachment on the reason for this. She always tried to keep their relationships on the plane which the men themselves seemed to prefer—certainly no woman would, and few women could, demand less of their men than she did. She never made arbitrary demands on their time, never caused them to wait for her nor to see her home at inconvenient hours, never made them fetch and carry for her; she fed them and flattered herself that she was a good listener. And yet—She thought of the women she knew; how all of them

had at least one obviously entranced male; she thought of the women she had observed; how they seemed to acquire a man at will, and if he failed to stay acquired, how readily they replaced him.

Women of high ideals who believed emancipation possible, women who tried desperately to rid themselves of feminine "hangups," to cultivate what they believed to be the greater directness, honesty, and generosity of men, were badly fooled. They found that no one appreciated their intelligent conversation, their high aspirations, their great sacrifices to avoid developing the personalities of their mothers. For much as men were glad to enjoy their wit, their style, their sex, and their candlelight suppers, they always ended up marrying The Bitch, and then, to top it all off, came back to complain of what a horror she was. "Emancipated" women found out that the honesty, generosity, and camaraderie of men was a lie: men were all too glad to use them and then sell them out, in the name of *true* friendship. ("I respect and like you a great deal, but let's be reasonable. . . ." And then there are the men who take her out to discuss Simone de Beauvoir, leaving their wives at home with the diapers.) "Emancipated" women found out that men were far from "good guys" to be emulated; they found out that by imitating male sexual patterns (the roving eye, the search for the ideal, the emphasis on physical attraction, etc.), they were not only achieving liberation, they were falling into something much worse than what they had given up. They were *imitating*. And they had inoculated themselves with a sickness that had not even sprung from their own psyches. They found that their new "cool" was shallow and meaningless, that their emotions were drying up behind it, that they were aging and becoming decadent: they feared they were losing their ability to love. They had gained nothing by imitating men: shallowness and callowness, and they were not so good at it either, because somewhere inside it still went against the grain.

Thus women who had decided not to marry because they were wise enough to look around and see where it led found that it was marry or nothing. Men gave their commitment only for a price: share (shoulder) his life, stand on his pedestal, become his appendage, or else. Or else—be consigned forever to that limbo of "chicks" who mean nothing or at least not what mother meant. Be the "other woman" the rest of one's life, used to provoke his wife, prove his virility and/or his independence, discussed by his friends as his latest "interesting" conquest. (For even if she had given up those terms and what they stood for, no male had.) Yes, love means an entirely different thing to men than to women: it means ownership and control; it means jealousy, where he never exhibited it before—when she might have wanted him to (who cares if she is broke or raped until she officially belongs to him: then he is a raging dynamo, a veritable cyclone, because his property, his ego extension have been threatened); it means a growing lack of interest, coupled with a roving eye. Who needs it?

Sadly, women do. Here are Reik's patients once more:

> She sometimes has delusions of not being persecuted by men anymore. At those times of her nonpersecution mania she is very depressed.

And:

> All men are selfish, brutal and inconsiderate—and I wish I could find one.

We have seen that a woman needs love, first, for its natural enriching function, and second, for social and economic reasons which have nothing to do with love. To deny her need is to put herself in an extra-vulnerable spot socially and economically, as well as to destroy her emotional equilibrium, which, unlike most men's, is basically healthy. Are men worth that? Decidedly no. Most women feel that to do such tailspins for a man would be to add insult to injury. They go on as before, making the best of a bad situation. If it gets *too* bad, they head for a (male) shrink:

> A young woman patient was once asked during a psychoanalytic consultation whether she preferred to see a man or woman psychoanalyst. Without the slightest hesitation she said, "A woman psychoanalyst because I am too eager for the approval of a man."

Note

1. Thus the peculiar situation that women never object to the insulting of women as a class, *as long as* they individually are excepted. The worst insult for a woman is that she is "just

like a woman," i.e., no better; the highest compliment that she has the brains, talent, dignity, or strength of a man. In fact, like every member of an oppressed class, she herself participates in the insulting of others like herself, hoping thereby to make it obvious that *she* as an individual is above their behavior. Thus women as a class are set against each other ["Divide and Conquer"], the "other woman" believing that the wife is a "bitch" who "doesn't understand him," and the wife believing that the other woman is an "opportunist" who is "taking advantage" of him—while the culprit himself sneaks away free.

Our next author, Simone de Beauvoir, will give a much more philosophically extended account of how male-dominated culture has enforced inferiority on women.

ON LIBERATION—EXISTENTIAL ETHICS NEEDED

De Beauvoir points out that dualities such as man/woman lead to conflict and an ultimate winner. She asks, why should man have won? Why should women be seen as "the other"? Her answer: To facilitate winning and to stay the winner, men try to portray women as being inherently inferior. They point out that the inherency is either due to biology or to God's will. Involving religion is no surprise because religions as we know them have been invented by men and are for men. The appeal to biology, and science in general, is also one of vested self-interest by men. It is only to be expected that biology (biologists are men) shows that women are inferior. De Beauvoir points up the similarities between antifeminist views and racism and anti-Semitism. Of course, there were slave holders who valued their slaves and treated the good ones well. But what was it to be a good slave? It was to be submissive to another basically out of fear. It was to live as "the Other." To put someone in this position is unfair and immoral. De Beauvoir asks, "Should this continue?"

Naturally, just about all men hope that it will. The more unsure of himself, the more a man will appreciate the subjugation of women. Men are two-faced. In a situation where they feel comfortable with women, men stress the principle of abstract equality. But just let a woman be in a position to compete, then men begin to stress the differences between men and women. (How does this square with Firestone's idea that men can love only an abstract woman?) The differences are not just differences, they are points of inferiorities. De Beauvoir emphasizes the fact that men have insisted that women are unfit for the professions.

If there are any such inferiorities between men and women, de Beauvoir makes it plain that they are almost certainly due to social discrimination and not to inherent biological differences. This is another way of saying that the differences we see are due to nurture and not nature. De Beauvoir rejects the traditional arguments of both feminists and antifeminists. She wants a fresh start.

De Beauvoir suggests that some women are trustworthy when it comes to making the case for feminism. These trustworthy women are those who are freed from subjugation but still able to empathize with their roots as women—in a way that no man could. Such women realize that the best way to ensure true equality of the sexes is to establish social institutions which are just and fair. The mark of such institutions will be positions for women where growth and change are called for. This growth will not itself create happiness. Happiness, de Beauvoir points out, is often stagnation.

De Beauvoir calls for an existentialist ethics. This means a way of life that allows for total self-determination, which is the meaning of true freedom. One should reach out for new opportunities and make choices. In doing so, one has the possibility of making mistakes that are painful and wrenching. But without this, there is nothing. Doing this results in what she terms *transcendence*. Not doing this results in what she terms *immanence*. She puts the question this way: There is a tension between happiness and liberty. She says, Choose liberty.

Naturally, this is not a possible choice if there is no free will. (There could be no true choice if there were no free will.) If women (and men) were nothing more than their biology acting according to strict laws, then liberty, as de Beauvoir defines it, would be impossible.

from The Second Sex

SIMONE DE BEAUVOIR

Legislators, priests, philosophers, writers, and scientists have striven to show that the subordinate position of woman is willed in heaven and advantageous on earth. The religions invented by men reflect this wish for domination. In the legends of Eve and Pandora men have taken up arms against women. They have made use of philosophy and theology, as the quotations from Aristotle and St. Thomas have shown. Since ancient times satirists and moralists have delighted in showing up the weaknesses of women. We are familiar with the savage indictments hurled against women throughout French literature. Montherlant, for example, follows the tradition of Jean de Meung, though with less gusto. This hostility may at times be well founded, often it is gratuitous; but in truth it more or less successfully conceals a desire for self-justification. As Montaigne says, "It is easier to accuse one sex than to excuse the other." Sometimes what is going on is clear enough. For instance, the Roman law limiting the rights of woman cited "the imbecility, the instability of the sex" just when the weakening of family ties seemed to threaten the interests of male heirs. And in the effort to keep the married woman under guardianship, appeal was made in the sixteenth century to the authority of St. Augustine, who declared that "woman is a creature neither decisive nor constant," at a time when the single woman was thought capable of managing her property. Montaigne understood clearly how arbitrary and unjust was woman's appointed lot: "Women are not in the wrong when they decline to accept the rules laid down for them, since the men make these rules without consulting them. No wonder intrigue and strife abound." But he did not go so far as to champion their cause.

It was only later, in the eighteenth century, that genuinely democratic men began to view the matter objectively. Diderot, among others, strove to show that woman is, like man, a human being. Later John Stuart Mill came fervently to her defense. But these philosophers displayed unusual impartiality. In the nineteenth century the feminist quarrel became again a quarrel of partisans. One of the consequences of the industrial revolution was the entrance of women into productive labor, and it was just here that the claims of the feminists emerged from the realm of theory and acquired an economic basis, while their opponents became the more aggressive. Although landed property lost power to some extent, the bourgeoisie clung to the old morality that found the guarantee of private property in the solidity of the family. Woman was ordered back into the home the more harshly as her emancipation became a real menace. Even within the working class the men endeavored to restrain woman's liberation, because they began to see the women as dangerous competitors—the more so because they were accustomed to work for lower wages.[1]

In proving woman's inferiority, the antifeminists then began to draw not only upon religion, philosophy, and theology, as before, but also upon science—biology, experimental psychology, etc. At most they were willing to grant "equality in difference" to the *other* sex. That profitable formula is most significant; it is precisely like the "equal but separate" formula of the Jim Crow laws aimed at the North American Negroes. As is well known, this so-called equalitarian segregation has resulted only in the most extreme discrimination. The similarity just noted is in no way due to chance, for whether it is a race, a caste, a class, or a sex that is reduced to a position of inferiority, the methods of justification are the same. "The eternal feminine" corresponds to "the black soul" and to "the Jewish character." True, the Jewish problem is on the whole very different from the other two—to the anti-Semite the Jew is not so much an inferior as he is an enemy for whom there is to be granted no place on earth, for whom annihilation is the fate desired. But there are deep similarities between the situation of woman and that of the Negro. Both are being emancipated today from a like paternalism, and the former master class wishes to "keep them in their place"—that is, the place chosen for them. In both cases the former masters lavish more or less sincere eulogies, either on the virtues of "the good Negro" with his dormant, childish, merry soul—the submissive Negro—or on the merits of the woman who is "truly feminine"—that is, frivolous, infantile, irresponsible—the submissive woman. In both cases the dominant class bases its argument on a state of affairs that it has itself created. As George Bernard Shaw puts it, in substance, "The American white relegates the black to the rank of shoeshine boy; and he concludes from this that the black is good for nothing but shining shoes." This vicious circle is met with in all analogous circumstances; when an individual (or a group of individuals) is kept in a situation of inferiority, the fact is that he is inferior. But the significance of the verb *to be* must be rightly understood here; it is in bad faith to give it a static value when it really has the dynamic Hegelian sense of "to have become." Yes, women on the whole are today inferior to men; that is, their situation affords them fewer possibilities. The question is: should that state of affairs continue?

Many men hope that it will continue; not all have given up the battle. The conservative bourgeoisie still see in the emancipation of women a menace to their morality and their interests. Some men dread feminine competition. Recently a male student wrote in the *Hebdo-Latin:* "Every woman

student who goes into medicine or law robs us of a job." He never questioned his rights in this world. And economic interests are not the only ones concerned. One of the benefits that oppression confers upon the oppressors is that the most humble among them is made to *feel* superior; thus, a "poor white" in the South can console himself with the thought that he is not a "dirty nigger"— and the more prosperous whites cleverly exploit this pride.

Similarly, the most mediocre of males feels himself a demigod as compared with women. It was much easier for M. de Montherlant to think himself a hero when he faced women (and women chosen for his purpose) than when he was obliged to act the man among men—something many women have done better than he, for that matter. And in September 1948, in one of his articles in the *Figaro littéraire,* Claude Mauriac—whose great originality is admired by all—could[2] write regarding woman: "*We* listen on a tone [*sic!*] of polite indifference . . . to the most brilliant among them, well knowing that her wit reflects more or less luminously ideas that come from *us.*" Evidently the speaker referred to is not reflecting the ideas of Mauriac himself, for no one knows of his having any. It may be that she reflects ideas originating with men, but then, even among men there are those who have been known to appropriate ideas not their own; and one can well ask whether Claude Mauriac might not find more interesting a conversation reflecting Descartes, Marx, or Gide rather than himself. What is really remarkable is that by using the questionable *we* he identifies himself with St. Paul, Hegel, Lenin, and Nietzsche, and from the lofty eminence of their grandeur looks down disdainfully upon the bevy of women who make bold to converse with him on a footing of equality. In truth, I know of more than one woman who would refuse to suffer with patience Mauriac's "tone of polite indifference."

I have lingered on this example because the masculine attitude is here displayed with disarming ingenuousness. But men profit in many more subtle ways from the otherness, the alterity of woman. Here is miraculous balm for those afflicted with an inferiority complex, and indeed no one is more arrogant toward women, more aggressive or scornful, than the man who is anxious about his virility. Those who are not fear-ridden in the presence of their fellow men are much more disposed to recognize a fellow creature in woman; but even to these the myth of Woman, the Other, is precious for many reasons.[3] They cannot be blamed for not cheerfully relinquishing all the benefits they derive from the myth, for they realize what they would lose in relinquishing woman as they fancy her to be, while they fail to realize what they have to gain from the woman of tomorrow. Refusal to pose oneself as the Subject, unique and absolute, requires great self-denial. Furthermore, the vast majority of men make no such claim explicitly. They do not *postulate* woman as inferior, for today they are too thoroughly imbued with the ideal of democracy not to recognize all human beings as equals.

In the bosom of the family, woman seems in the eyes of childhood and youth to be clothed in the same social dignity as the adult males. Later on, the young man, desiring and loving, experiences the resistance, the independence of the woman desired and loved; in marriage, he respects woman as wife and mother, and in the concrete events of conjugal life she stands there before him as a free being. He can therefore feel that social subordination as between the sexes no longer exists and that on the whole, in spite of differences, woman is an equal. As, however, he observes some points of inferiority—the most important being unfitness for the professions—he attributes these to natural causes. When he is in a co-operative and benevolent relation with woman, his theme is the principle of abstract equality, and he does not base his attitude upon such inequality as may exist. But when he is in conflict with her, the situation is reversed: his theme will be the existing inequality, and he will even take it as justification for denying abstract equality.[4]

So it is that many men will affirm as if in good faith that women *are* the equals of man and that they have nothing to clamor for, while *at the same time* they will say that women can never be the equals of man and that their demands are in vain. It is, in point of fact, a difficult matter for man to realize the extreme importance of social discriminations which seem outwardly insignificant but which produce in woman moral and intellectual effects so profound that they appear to spring from

her original nature.[5] The most sympathetic of men never fully comprehend woman's concrete situation. And there is no reason to put much trust in the men when they rush to the defense of privileges whose full extent they can hardly measure. We shall not, then, permit ourselves to be intimidated by the number and violence of the attacks launched against women, nor to be entrapped by the self-seeking eulogies bestowed on the "true woman," nor to profit by the enthusiasm for woman's destiny manifested by men who would not for the world have any part of it.

We should consider the arguments of the feminists with no less suspicion, however, for very often their controversial aim deprives them of all real value. If the "woman question" seems trivial, it is because masculine arrogance has made of it a "quarrel"; and when quarreling one no longer reasons well. People have tirelessly sought to prove that woman is superior, inferior, or equal to man. Some say that, having been created after Adam, she is evidently a secondary being; others say on the contrary that Adam was only a rough draft and that God succeeded in producing the human being in perfection when He created Eve. Woman's brain is smaller; yes, but it is relatively larger. Christ was made a man; yes, but perhaps for his greater humility. Each argument at once suggests its opposite, and both are often fallacious. If we are to gain understanding, we must get out of these ruts; we must discard the vague notions of superiority, inferiority, equality which have hitherto corrupted every discussion of the subject and start afresh.

Very well, but just how shall we pose the question? And, to begin with, who are we to propound it at all? Man is at once judge and party to the case; but so is woman. What we need is an angel—neither man nor woman—but where shall we find one? Still, the angel would be poorly qualified to speak, for an angel is ignorant of all the basic facts involved in the problem. With a hermaphrodite we should be no better off, for here the situation is most peculiar; the hermaphrodite is not really the combination of a whole man and a whole woman, but consists of parts of each and thus is neither. It looks to me as if there are, after all, certain women who are best qualified to elucidate the situation of woman. Let us not be misled by the sophism that because Epimenides was a Cretan he was necessarily a liar; it is not a mysterious essence that compels men and women to act in good or in bad faith, it is their situation that inclines them more or less toward the search for truth. Many of today's women, fortunate in the restoration of all the privileges pertaining to the estate of the human being, can afford the luxury of impartiality—we even recognize its necessity. We are no longer like our partisan elders; by and large we have won the game. In recent debates on the status of women the United Nations has persistently maintained that the equality of the sexes is now becoming a reality, and already some of us have never had to sense in our femininity an inconvenience or an obstacle. Many problems appear to us to be more pressing than those which concern us in particular, and this detachment even allows us to hope that our attitude will be objective. Still, we know the feminine world more intimately than do the men because we have our roots in it, we grasp more immediately than do men what it means to a human being to be feminine; and we are more concerned with such knowledge. I have said that there are more pressing problems, but this does not prevent us from seeing some importance in asking how the fact of being women will affect our lives. What opportunities precisely have been given us and what withheld? What fate awaits our younger sisters, and what directions should they take? It is significant that books by women on women are in general animated in our day less by a wish to demand our rights than by an effort toward clarity and understanding. As we emerge from an era of excessive controversy, this book is offered as one attempt among others to confirm that statement.

But it is doubtless impossible to approach any human problem with a mind free from bias. The way in which questions are put, the points of view assumed, presuppose a relativity of interest; all characteristics imply values, and every objective description, so called, implies an ethical background. Rather than attempt to conceal principles more or less definitely implied, it is better to state them openly at the beginning. This will make it unnecessary to specify on every page in just what sense one uses such words as *superior, inferior, better, worse, progress, reaction,* and the like. If we survey some of the works on woman, we note that one of the points of view most frequently adopted is that of the public good, the general interest; and one always means by this the benefit of society as one wishes it to be maintained or established. For our part, we hold that the only public good is that which assures the private good of the citizens; we shall pass judgment on institutions according to their effectiveness in giving concrete opportunities to individuals. But we do not confuse the idea of private interest with that of happiness, although that is another common point of view. Are not women of the harem more happy than women voters? Is not the housekeeper happier than the workingwoman? It is not too clear just what the word *happy* really means and still less what true values it may mask. There is no possibility of measuring the happiness of others, and it is always easy to describe as happy the situation in which one wishes to place them.

In particular those who are condemned to stagnation are often pronounced happy on the pretext that happiness consists in being at rest. This notion we reject, for our perspective is that of existentialist ethics. Every subject plays his part as such specifically through exploits or projects that serve as a mode of transcendence; he achieves liberty only through a continual reaching out toward other liberties. There is no justification for present existence other than its expansion into an indefinitely open future. Every time transcendence falls back into immanence, stagnation, there is a degradation of existence into the *"en-soi"*—the brutish life of subjection to given conditions—and of liberty into constraint and contingence. This downfall represents a moral fault if the subject consents to it; if it is inflicted upon him, it spells frustration and oppression. In both cases it is an absolute evil. Every individual concerned to justify his existence feels that his existence involves an undefined need to transcend himself, to engage in freely chosen projects.

Now, what peculiarly signalizes the situation of woman is that she—a free and autonomous being like all human creatures—nevertheless finds herself living in a world where men compel her to assume the status of the Other. They propose to stabilize her as object and to doom her to immanence since her transcendence is to be overshadowed and forever transcended by another ego (*conscience*) which is essential and sovereign. The drama of woman lies in this conflict between the fundamental aspirations of every subject (ego)—who always regards the self as the essential—and the compulsions of a situation in which she is the inessential. How can a human being in woman's situation attain fulfillment? What roads are open to her? Which are blocked? How can independence be recovered in a state of dependency? What circumstances limit woman's liberty and how can they be overcome? These are the fundamental questions on which I would fain throw some light. This means that I am interested in the fortunes of the individual as defined not in terms of happiness but in terms of liberty.

Quite evidently this problem would be without significance if we were to believe that woman's destiny is inevitably determined by physiological, psychological, or economic forces. Hence I shall discuss first of all the light in which woman is viewed by biology, psychoanalysis, and historical materialism. Next I shall try to show exactly how the concept of the "truly feminine" has been fashioned—why woman has been defined as the Other—and what have been the consequences from man's point of view. Then from woman's point of view I

shall describe the world in which women must live; and thus we shall be able to envisage the difficulties in their way as, endeavoring to make their escape from the sphere hitherto assigned them, they aspire to full membership in the human race.

Notes

1. See Part II, pp. 115–17.

2. Or at least he thought he could.

3. A significant article on this theme by Michel Carrouges appeared in No. 292 of the *Cahiers du Sud.* He writes indignantly: "Would that there were no woman-myth at all but only a cohort of cooks, matrons, prostitutes, and bluestockings serving functions of pleasure or usefulness!" That is to say, in his view woman has no existence in and for herself; he thinks only of her *function* in the male world. Her reason for existence lies in man. But then, in fact, her poetic "function" as a myth might be more valued than any other. The real problem is precisely to find out why woman should be defined with relation to man.

4. For example, a man will say that he considers his wife in no wise degraded because she has no gainful occupation. The profession of housewife is just as lofty, and so on. But when the first quarrel comes, he will exclaim: "Why, you couldn't make your living without me!"

5. The specific purpose of Book II of this study is to describe this process.

Andrea Dworkin also makes a call for freedom. But for her, freedom means a totally new approach to sex and sexuality. Her philosophical view of sexual intercourse is one that de Beauvoir would almost certainly reject.

ON THE IMMORALITY OF INTERCOURSE

Dworkin would be classified as a radical feminist. To her, all intercourse is consorting with the enemy. A woman's vagina is unique biologically, psychologically, and philosophically. Men have nothing at all like it. The vagina represents a woman's personal space and personal identity.

The act of intercourse requires that this space be entered, penetrated, and occupied; as a result, privacy is impossible. Men, however, consider sexual penetration as appropriate and thus never see it as an intrinsic violation of privacy. In fact, a woman who remains celibate (for whatever reason) is thought to have repudiated sex—as if having sexual intercourse is the norm; as if the repudiation is deviant. It is as if someone decided to give up eating. What this comes down to is that for women to be used and abused are one in the same thing. It is no wonder, then, that women are seen as less than fully human.

Dworkin asks—playing on the occupation metaphor—how can an occupied people ever be free? What she is saying is that women cannot be free until they give up sexual intercourse. Of course, it is easy to claim that this is all overstated. Intercourse is private business, not really so metaphysical, great fun, and part of growing up and having lovers. Dworkin dismisses these defenses with a rhetorical flourish when she says that they are slight of hand and meant to divert from the real issue: women's freedom and equality. She also counters these defenses with facts.

If we can believe *The Hite Report,* most women do not experience orgasm through sexual intercourse. Dworkin quotes Hite, who says that to own one's body, to be truly autonomous, is best shown by the ability to have an orgasm when one so desires. (This is what Robert Solomon would characterize as a liberal American myth about sex.) Part of the reason (many) women cannot achieve orgasm through sexual intercourse is that intercourse represents and expresses the domination of men over women as well as hostility and anger. In the chapter on sexual harassment and rape, we will be reminded that according to many researchers, rape is motivated precisely by these sorts of factors. Also, because of the dominance of men over women, many women use sex as a way to barter for some extra power. This demeans women, if only in some unconscious manner.

To those feminists who write of enlightened intercourse that would not express dominance, Dworkin replies that this is a dream. In real life, men will not relinquish either their power or their way of using women sexually. Again, appealing to the occupation metaphor, Dworkin interprets intercourse as men violating women, an enemy they hate and conquer symbolically through sexual intercourse. She suggests that romance, love, and pleasurable sex are stories told by women who desperately seek meaning for their experiences—in the way that many Holocaust survivors have sought to find meaning in their horrific experiences.

Dworkin closes with the following points. Biologically, women have nothing that is really like "heat" in animals. What this should be taken to mean is that women are never ready, that is, available, for intercourse. In other contexts, feminists rail against the idea that anatomy is destiny, yet when it comes to sex, it is so hard to reject the idea that just because there is a space into which a penis can fit, that is the way sex ought to be had.

from Intercourse

ANDREA DWORKIN

Women have wanted intercourse to work and have submitted—with regret or with enthusiasm, real or faked—even though or even when it does not. The reasons have often been foul, filled with the spiteful but carefully hidden malice of the powerless. Women have needed what can be gotten through intercourse: the economic and psychological survival; access to male power through access to the male who has it; having some hold—psychological, sexual, or economic—on the ones who act, who decide, who matter. There has been a deep, consistent, yet of course muted objection to what Anaïs Nin has called "[t]he hunter, the rapist, the one for whom sexuality is a thrust, nothing more."[3] Women have also wanted intercourse to work in this sense: women have wanted intercourse to be, for women, an experience of equality and passion, sensuality and intimacy. Women have a vision of love that includes men as human too; and women want the human in men, including in the act of intercourse. Even without the dignity of equal power, women have believed in the redeeming potential of love. There has been—despite the cruelty of exploitation and forced sex—a consistent vision for women of a sexuality based on a harmony that is both sensual and possible. In the words of sex reformer Ellen Key:

> She will no longer be captured like a fortress or hunted like a quarry; now will she like a placid lake await the stream that seeks its way to her embrace. A stream herself, she will go her own way to meet the other stream.[4]

A stream herself, she would move over the earth, sensual and equal; especially, she will go her own way.

Shere Hite has suggested an intercourse in which "thrusting would not be considered as necessary as it now is . . . [There might be] more a mutual lying together in pleasure, penis-in-vagina, vagina-covering-penis, with female orgasm providing much of the stimulation necessary for male orgasm."[5]

These visions of a humane sensuality based in equality are in the aspirations of women; and even the nightmare of sexual inferiority does not seem to kill them. They are not searching analyses into the nature of intercourse; instead they are deep, humane dreams that repudiate the rapist as the final arbiter of reality. They are an underground resistance to both inferiority and brutality, visions that sustain life and further endurance.

They also do not amount to much in real life with real men. There is, instead, the cold fucking, duty-bound or promiscuous; the romantic obsession in which eventual abandonment turns the vagina into the wound Freud claimed it was; intimacy with men who dread women, coital dread—as Kafka wrote in his diary, "coitus as punishment for the happiness of being together."[6]

Fear, too, has a special power to change experience and compromise any possibility of freedom. A stream does not know fear. A woman does. Especially women know fear of men and of forced intercourse. Consent in this world of fear is so passive that the woman consenting could be dead and sometimes is. "Yeah," said one man who killed a woman so that he could fuck her after she was dead, "I sexually assaulted her after she was dead. I always see them girls laid out in the pictures with their eyes closed and I just had to do it. I dreamed about it for so long that I just had to do it."[7] A Ne-

braska appeals court did not think that the murder "was especially heinous, atrocious, cruel, or manifested exceptional depravity by ordinary standards of morality and intelligence," and in particular they found "no evidence the acts were performed for the satisfaction of inflicting either mental or physical pain or that pain existed for any prolonged period of time."[8] Are you afraid now? How can fear and freedom coexist for women in intercourse?

The role of fear in destroying the integrity of men is easy to articulate, to understand, hard to overstate. Men are supposed to conquer fear in order to experience freedom. Men are humiliated by fear, not only in their masculinity but in their rights and freedoms. Men are diminished by fear; compromised irrevocably by it because freedom is diminished by it. "Fear had entered his life," novelist Iris Murdoch wrote,

> and would now be with him forever. How easy it was for the violent to win. Fear was irresistible, fear was king, he had never really known this before when he had lived free and without it. Even unreasoning fear could cripple a man forever. . . . How well he understood how dictators flourished. The little grain of fear in each life was enough to keep millions quiet.[9]

Hemingway, using harder prose, wrote the same in book after book. But women are supposed to treasure the little grain of fear—rub up against it— eroticize it, want it, get excited by it; and the fear could and does keep millions quiet: millions of women; being fucked and silent; upright and silent; waiting and silent; rolled over on and silent; pursued and silent; killed, fucked, and silent. The silence is taken to be appropriate. The fear is not perceived as compromising or destroying freedom. The dictators do flourish: fuck and flourish.

Out of fear and inequality, women hide, use disguises, trying to pass for indigenous peoples who have a right to be there, even though we cannot pass. Appropriating Octavio Paz's description of the behavior of Mexicans in Los Angeles— which he might not like: "they feel ashamed of their origin . . . they act like persons who are wearing disguises, who are afraid of a stranger's look because it could strip them and leave them stark naked."[10] Women hide, use disguises, because fear has compromised freedom; and when a woman has intercourse—not hiding, dropping the disguise—she has no freedom because her very being has been contaminated by fear: a grain, a tidal wave, memory or anticipation.

The fear is fear of power and fear of pain: the child looks at the slit with a mirror and wonders how it can be, how will she be able to stand the pain. The culture romanticizes the rapist dimension of the first time: he will force his way in and hurt her. The event itself is supposed to be so distinct, so entirely unlike any other experience or category of sensation, that there is no conception that intercourse can be part of sex, including the first time, instead of sex itself. There is no slow opening up, no slow, gradual entry; no days and months of sensuality prior to entry and no nights and hours after entry. Those who learn to eroticize powerlessness will learn to eroticize the entry itself: the pushing in, the thrusting, the fact of entry with whatever force or urgency the act requires or the man enjoys. There is virtually no protest about entry as such from women; virtually no satire from men. A fairly formidable character in Don DeLillo's *White Noise,* the wife, agrees to read pornography to her husband but she has one condition:

"I will read," she said. "But I don't want you to choose anything that has men inside women, quote-quote, or men entering women. 'I entered her.' 'He entered me.' We're not lobbies or elevators. 'I wanted him inside me,' as if he could crawl completely in, sign the register, sleep, eat, so forth. I don't care what these people do as long as they don't enter or get entered."

"Agreed."

"'I entered her and began to thrust.'"

"I'm in total agreement," I said.

"'Enter me, enter me, yes, yes.'"

"Silly usage, absolutely."

"'Insert yourself, Rex, I want you inside me, entering hard, entering deep, yes, now, oh.'"[11]

Her protests make him hard. The stupidity of the "he entered her" motif makes her laugh, not kindly. She hates it.

We are not, of course, supposed to be lobbies or elevators. Instead, we are supposed to be wombs, maternal ones; and the men are trying to get back in away from all the noise and grief of being adult men with power and responsibility. The stakes for men are high, as Norman O. Brown makes clear in prose unusually understated for him:

Coitus successfully performed is incest, a return to the maternal womb; and the punishment appropriate to this crime, castration. What happens to the penis is coronation, followed by decapitation.[12]

This is high drama for a prosaic act of commonplace entry. Nothing is at risk for her, the entered; whereas he commits incest, is crowned king, and has his thing cut off. She might like to return to the maternal womb too—because life outside it is not easy for her either—but she has to be it, for husbands, lovers, adulterous neighbors, as well as her own children, boys especially. Women rarely dare, as we say, draw a line: certainly not at the point of entry into our own bodies, sometimes by those we barely know. Certainly they did not come from there, not originally, not from this womb belonging to this woman who is being fucked now. And so we have once again the generic meaning of intercourse—he has to climb back into some womb, maternal enough; he has to enter it and survive even coronation and decapitation. She is made for that; and what can it matter to him that in entering her, he is entering this one, real, unique individual.

And what is entry for her? Entry is the first acceptance in her body that she is generic, not individual; that she is one of a many that is antagonistic to the individual interpretation she might have of her own worth, purpose, or intention. Entered, she accepts her subservience to his psychological purpose if nothing else; she accepts being confused with his mother and his Aunt Mary and the little girl with whom he used to play "Doctor." Entered, she finds herself depersonalized into a function and worth less to him than he is worth to himself: because he broke through, pushed in, entered. Without him there, she is supposed to feel empty, though there is no vacuum there, not physiologically. Entered, she finds herself accused of regicide at the end. The king dead, the muscles of the vagina contract again, suggesting that this will never be easy, never be solved. Lovely Freud, of course, having discovered projection but always missing the point, wrote to Jung: "In private I have always thought of Adonis as the penis; the woman's joy when the god she had thought dead rises again is too transparent!"[13] Something, indeed, is too transparent; women's joy tends to be opaque.

Entered, she has mostly given something up: to Adonis, the king, the coronation, the decapitation for which she is then blamed; she has given up a dividing line between her and him. Entered, she then finds out what it is to be occupied: and sometimes the appropriate imagery is of evil and war, the great spreading evil of how soldiers enter and contaminate. In the words of Marguerite Duras, "evil is there, at the gates, against the skin."[14] It spreads, like war, everywhere: "breaking in everywhere, stealing, imprisoning, always there, merged and mingled . . . a prey to the intoxicating passion of occupying that delightful territory, a child's body, the bodies of those less strong, of conquered peoples."[15] She is describing an older brother she hates here ("I see wartime and the reign of my elder brother as one"[16]). She is not describing her lover, an older man fucking an adolescent girl. But it is from the sex that she takes the texture of wartime invasion and occupation, the visceral reality of occupation: evil up against the skin—at the point of entry, just touching the slit; then it breaks in and at the same time it surrounds everything, and those with power use the conquered who are weaker, inhabit them as territory.

Physically, the woman in intercourse is a space inhabited, a literal territory occupied literally: occupied even if there has been no resistance, no force; even if the occupied person said yes please, yes hurry, yes more. Having a line at the point of entry into your body that cannot be crossed is different from not having any such line; and being occupied in your body is different from not being occupied in your body. It is human to experience these differences whether or not one cares to bring the consequences of them into consciousness. Humans, including women, construct meaning. That means that when something happens to us, when we have experiences, we try to find in them some reason for them, some significance that they have to us or for us. Humans find meaning in poverty and tyranny and the atrocities of history; those who have suffered most still construct meaning; and those who know nothing take their ignorance as if it were a precious, rare clay and they too con-

struct meaning. In this way, humans assert that we have worth; what has happened to us matters; our time here on earth is not entirely filled with random events and spurious pain. On the contrary, we can understand some things if we try hard to learn empathy; we can seek freedom and honor and dignity; that we care about meaning gives us a human pride that has the fragility of a butterfly and the strength of tempered steel. The measure of women's oppression is that we do not take intercourse—entry, penetration, occupation—and ask or say what it means: to us as a dominated group or to us as a potentially free and self-determining people. Instead, intercourse is a loyalty test; and we are not supposed to tell the truth unless it compliments and upholds the dominant male ethos on sex. We know nothing, of course, about intercourse because we are women and women know nothing; or because what we know simply has no significance, entered into as we are. And men know everything—all of them—all the time—no matter how stupid or inexperienced or arrogant or ignorant they are. Anything men say on intercourse, any attitude they have, is valuable, knowledgeable, and deep, rooted in the cosmos and the forces of nature as it were: because they know; because fucking is knowing; because he knew her but she did not know him; because the God who does not exist framed not only sex but also knowledge that way. Women do not just lie about orgasm, faking it or saying it is not important. Women lie about life by not demanding to understand the meaning of entry, penetration, occupation, having boundaries crossed over, having lesser privacy: by avoiding the difficult, perhaps impossible (but how will we ever know?) questions of female freedom. We take oaths to truth all right, on the holy penis before entry. In so doing, we give up the most important dimension of what it means to be human: the search for the meaning of our real experience, including the sheer invention of that meaning—called creativity when men do it. If the questions make the holy penis unhappy, who could survive what the answers might do? Experience is chosen for us, then, imposed on us, especially in intercourse, *and so is its meaning.* We are allowed to have intercourse on the terms men determine, according to the rules men make. We do not have to have an orgasm; that terrible burden is on them.

We are supposed to comply whether we want to or not. *Want* is active, not passive or lethargic. Especially we are supposed to be loyal to the male meanings of intercourse, which are elaborate, dramatic, pulling in elements of both myth and tragedy: the king is dead! long live the king!—and the Emperor wears designer jeans. We have no freedom and no extravagance in the questions we can ask or the interpretations we can make. We must be loyal; and on what scale would we be able to reckon the cost of that? Male sexual discourse on the meaning of intercourse becomes our language. It is not a second language we speak, however, with perfect fluency even though it does not say what we mean or what we think we might know if only we could find the right word and enough privacy in which to articulate it even just in our own minds. We know only this one language of these folks who enter and occupy us: they keep telling us that we are different from them; yet we speak only their language and have none, or none that we remember, of our own; and we do not dare, it seems, invent one, even in signs and gestures. Our bodies speak their language. Our minds think in it. The men are inside us through and through. We hear something, a dim whisper, barely audible, somewhere at the back of the brain; there is some other word, and we think, some of us, sometimes, that once it belonged to us.

There are female-supremacist models for intercourse that try to make us the masters of this language that we speak that is not ours. They evade some fundamental questions about the act itself and acknowledge others. They have in common a glorious ambition to see women self-determining, vigorous and free lovers who are never demeaned or diminished by force or subordination, not in society, not in sex. The great advocate of the female-first model of intercourse in the nineteenth century was Victoria Woodhull. She understood that rape was slavery; not less than slavery in its insult to human integrity and human dignity. She acknowledged some of the fundamental questions of female freedom presented by intercourse in her imperious insistence that women had a *natural* right—a right that inhered in the nature of intercourse itself—to be entirely self-determining, the controlling and dominating partner, the one whose desire determined the event, the one who both initiates

and is the final authority on what the sex is and will be. Her thinking was not mean-spirited, some silly role reversal to make a moral point; nor was it a taste for tyranny hidden in what pretended to be a sexual ethic. She simply understood that women are unspeakably vulnerable in intercourse because of the nature of the act—entry, penetration, occupation; and she understood that in a society of male power, women were unspeakably exploited in intercourse. Society—men—had to agree to let the woman be the mind, the heart, the lover, the free spirit, the physical vitality behind the act. The commonplace abuses of forced entry, the devastating consequences of being powerless and occupied, suggested that the only condition under which women could experience sexual freedom in intercourse—real choice, real freedom, real happiness, real pleasure—was in having real and absolute control in each and every act of intercourse, which would be, each and every time, chosen by the woman. She would have the incontrovertible authority that would make intercourse possible:

> To woman, by nature, belongs the right of sexual determination. When the instinct is aroused in her, then and then only should commerce follow. When woman rises from sexual slavery to sexual freedom, into the ownership and control of her sexual organs, and man is obliged to respect this freedom, then will this instinct become pure and holy; then will woman be raised from the iniquity and morbidness in which she now wallows for existence, and the intensity and glory of her creative functions be increased a hundred-fold . . . [17]

The consent standard is revealed as pallid, weak, stupid, second-class, by contrast with Woodhull's standard: that the woman should have authority and control over the act. The sexual humiliation of women through male ownership was understood by Woodhull to be a concrete reality, not a metaphor, not hyperbole: the man owned the woman's sexual organs. She had to own her sexual organs for intercourse to mean freedom for her. This is more concrete and more meaningful than a more contemporary vocabulary of "owning" one's own desire. Woodhull wanted the woman's desire to be the desire of significance; but she understood that ownership of the body was not an abstraction; it was concrete and it came first. The "iniquity and morbidness" of intercourse under male dominance would end if women could exercise a materially real self-determination in sex. The woman having material control of her own sex organs and of each and every act of intercourse would not lead to a reverse dominance, the man subject to the woman, because of the nature of the act and the nature of the sex organs involved in the act: this is the sense in which Woodhull tried to face the fundamental questions raised by intercourse as an act with consequences, some perhaps intrinsic. The woman could not forcibly penetrate the man. The woman could not take him over as he took her over and occupy his body physically inside. His dominance over her expressed in the physical reality of intercourse had no real analogue in desire she might express for him in intercourse: she simply could not do to him what he could do to her. Woodhull's view was materialist, not psychological; she was the first publisher of the *Communist Manifesto* in the United States and the first woman stockbroker on Wall Street. She saw sex the way she saw money and power: in terms of concrete physical reality. Male notions of female power based on psychology or ideas would not have addressed for her the real issues of physical dominance and power in intercourse. The woman would not force or rape or physically own the man because she could not. Thus, giving the woman power over intercourse was giving her the power to be equal. Woodhull's vision was in fact deeply humane, oriented toward sexual pleasure in freedom. For women, she thought and proclaimed (at great cost to herself), freedom must be literal, physical, concrete self-determination beginning with absolute control of the sexual organs; this was a natural right that had been perverted by male dominance—and because of its perversion, sex was for women morbid and degrading. The only freedom imaginable in this act of intercourse was freedom based on an irrevocable and unbreachable female will given play in a body honestly her own. This was an eloquent answer to reading the meaning of intercourse the other way: by its nature, intercourse mandated that the woman must be lesser in power and in privacy. Instead, said Woodhull, the woman must be king. Her humanity required sexual sovereignty.

Male-dominant gender hierarchy, however, seems immune to reform by reasoned or visionary argument or by changes in sexual styles, either personal or social. This may be because intercourse itself is immune to reform. In it, female is bottom, stigmatized. Intercourse remains a means or the means of physiologically making a woman inferior: communicating to her cell by cell her own inferior status, impressing it on her, burning it into her by shoving it into her, over and over, pushing and thrusting until she gives up and gives in—which is called *surrender* in the male lexicon. In the experience of intercourse, she loses the capacity for integrity because her body—the basis of privacy and freedom in the material world for all human beings—is entered and occupied; the boundaries of her physical body are—neutrally speaking—violated. What is taken from her in that act is not recoverable, and she spends her life—wanting, after all, to have something—pretending that pleasure is in being reduced through intercourse to insignificance. She will not have an orgasm—maybe because she has human pride and she resents captivity; but also she will not or cannot rebel—not enough for it to matter, to end male dominance over her. She learns to eroticize powerlessness and self-annihilation. The very boundaries of her own body become meaningless to her, and even worse, useless to her. The transgression of those boundaries comes to signify a sexually charged degradation into which she throws herself, having been told, convinced, that identity, for a female, is there—somewhere beyond privacy and self-respect.

It is not that there is no way out if, for instance, one were to establish or believe that intercourse itself determines women's lower status. New reproductive technologies have changed and will continue to change the nature of the world. Intercourse is not necessary to existence anymore. Existence does not depend on female compliance, nor on the violation of female boundaries, nor on lesser female privacy, nor on the physical occupation of the female body. But the hatred of women is a source of sexual pleasure for men in its own right. Intercourse appears to be the expression of that contempt in pure form, in the form of a sexed hierarchy; it requires no passion or heart because it is power without invention articulating the arrogance of those who do the fucking. Intercourse is the pure, sterile, formal expression of men's contempt for women; but that contempt can turn gothic and express itself in many sexual and sadistic practices that eschew intercourse per se. Any violation of a woman's body can become sex for men; this is the essential truth of pornography. So freedom from intercourse, or a social structure that reflects the low value of intercourse in women's sexual pleasure, or intercourse becoming one sex act among many entered into by (hypothetical) equals as part of other, deeper, longer, perhaps more sensual lovemaking, or an end to women's inferior status because we need not be forced to reproduce (forced fucking frequently justified by some implicit biological necessity to reproduce): none of these are likely social developments because there is a hatred of women, unexplained, undiagnosed, mostly unacknowledged, that pervades sexual practice and sexual passion. Reproductive technologies are strengthening male dominance, invigorating it by providing new ways of policing women's reproductive capacities, bringing them under stricter male scrutiny and control; and the experimental development of these technologies has been sadistic, using human women as if they were sexual laboratory animals—rats, mice, rabbits, cats, with kinky uteri. For increasing numbers of men, bondage and torture of the female genitals (that were entered into and occupied in the good old days) may supplant intercourse as a sexual practice. The passion for hurting women is a sexual passion; and sexual hatred of women can be expressed without intercourse.

There has always been a peculiar irrationality to all the biological arguments that supposedly predetermine the inferior social status of women. Bulls mount cows and baboons do whatever; but human females do not have estrus or go into heat. The logical inference is not that we are *always* available for mounting but rather that we are never, strictly speaking, "available." Nor do animals have cultures; nor do they determine in so many things what they will do and how they will do them and what the meaning of their own behavior is. They do not decide what their lives will be. Only humans face the often complicated reality of having potential and having to make choices based on having potential. We are not driven by instinct, at least not much. We have possibilities, and we make up meanings as we go along. The meanings we create or learn do not exist only in our heads, in ineffable ideas. Our meanings also exist in our bodies—what we are, what we do, what we physically feel, what we physically know; and there is no personal psychology that is separate from what the body has learned about life. Yet when we look at the human condition, including the condition of women, we act as if we are driven by biology or some metaphysically absolute dogma. We refuse to recognize our possibilities because we refuse to honor the potential humans have, including human women, to make choices. Men too make choices. When will they choose not to despise us?

Being female in this world is having been robbed of the potential for human choice by men who love to hate us. One does not make choices in freedom. Instead, one conforms in body type and behavior and values to become an object of male sexual desire, which requires an abandonment of a wide-ranging capacity for choice. Objectification may well be the most singly destructive aspect of gender hierarchy, especially as it exists in relation to intercourse. The surrender occurs before the act that is supposed to accomplish the surrender takes place. She has given in; why conquer her? The body is violated before the act occurs that is commonly taken to be violation. The privacy of the person is lessened before the privacy of the woman is invaded: she has remade herself so as to prepare the way for the invasion of privacy that her preparation makes possible. The significance of the human ceases to exist as the value of the object increases: an expensive ornament, for instance, she is incapable of human freedom—taking it, knowing it, wanting it, being it. Being an object—living in the realm of male objectification—is abject submission, an abdication of the freedom and integrity of the body, its privacy, its uniqueness, its worth in and of itself because it is the human body of a human being. Can intercourse exist without objectification? Would intercourse be a different phenomenon if it could, if it did? Would it be shorter or longer, happier or sadder; more complex, richer, denser, with a baroque beauty or simpler with an austere beauty; or bang bang bang? Would intercourse without objectification, if it could exist, be compatible with women's equality—even an expression of it—or would it still be stubbornly antagonistic to it?

Would intercourse cause orgasm in women if women were not objects for men before and during intercourse? Can intercourse exist without objectification and can objectification exist without female complicity in maintaining it as a perceived reality and a material reality too: can objectification exist without the woman herself turning herself into an object—becoming through effort and art a thing, less than human, so that he can be more than human, hard, sovereign, king? Can intercourse exist without the woman herself turning herself into a thing, which she must do because men cannot fuck equals and men must fuck: because one price of dominance is that one is impotent in the face of equality?

To become the object, she takes herself and transforms herself into a thing: all freedoms are diminished and she is caged, even in the cage docile, sometimes physically maimed, movement is limited: she physically becomes the thing he wants to fuck. It is especially in the acceptance of object status that her humanity is hurt: it is a metaphysical acceptance of lower status in sex and in society; an implicit acceptance of less freedom, less privacy, less integrity. In becoming an object so that he can objectify her so that he can fuck her, she begins a political collaboration with his dominance; and then when he enters her, he confirms for himself and for her what she is: that she is something, not someone; certainly not someone equal.

There is the initial complicity, the acts of self-mutilation, self-diminishing, self-reconstruction, until there is no self, only the diminished, mutilated reconstruction. It is all superficial and unimportant, except what it costs the human in her to do it: except for the fact that it is submissive, conforming, giving up an individuality that would withstand object status or defy it. Something happens inside; a human forgets freedom; a human learns obedience; a human, this time a woman, learns how to goose-step the female way. Wilhelm Reich, that most optimistic of sexual liberationists, the only male one to abhor rape *really,* thought that a girl needed not only "a free genital sexuality" but also "an undisturbed room, proper contraceptives, a friend who is capable of love, that is, not a National Socialist . . ."[18] All remain hard for women to attain; but especially the lover who is not a National Socialist. So the act goes beyond complic-

ity to collaboration; but collaboration requires a preparing of the ground, an undermining of values and vision and dignity, a sense of alienation from the worth of other human beings—and this alienation is fundamental to females who are objectified because they do not experience themselves as human beings of worth except for their value on the market as objects. Knowing one's own human value is fundamental to being able to respect others: females are remade into objects, not human in any sense related to freedom or justice—and so what can females recognize in other females that is a human bond toward freedom? Is there anything in us to love if we do not love each other as the objects we have become? Who can love someone who is less than human unless love itself is domination per se? Alienation from human freedom is deep and destructive; it destroys whatever it is in us as humans that is creative, that causes us to want to find meaning in experiences, even hard experiences; it destroys in us that which wants freedom whatever the hardship of attaining it. In women, these great human capacities and dimensions are destroyed or mutilated; and so we find ourselves bewildered—who or what are these so-called persons in human form but even that not quite, not exactly, who cannot remember or manifest the physical reality of freedom, who do not seem to want or to value the individual experience of freedom? Being an object for a man means being alienated from other women—those like her in status, in inferiority, in sexual function. Collaboration by women with men to keep women civilly and sexually inferior has been one of the hallmarks of female subordination; we are ashamed when Freud notices it, but it is true. That collaboration, fully manifested when a woman values her lover, the National Socialist, above any woman, anyone of her own kind or class or status, may have simple beginnings: the first act of complicity that destroys self-respect, the capacity for self-determination and freedom—readying the body for the fuck instead of for freedom. The men have an answer: intercourse is freedom. Maybe it is second-class freedom for second-class humans.

What does it mean to be the person who needs to have this done to her: who needs to be needed as an object; who needs to be entered; who needs to be occupied; who needs to be wanted more than she needs integrity or freedom or equality? If objectification is necessary for intercourse to be possible, what does that mean for the person who needs to be fucked so that she can experience herself as female and who needs to be an object so that she can be fucked?

The brilliance of objectification as a strategy of dominance is that it gets the woman to take the initiative in her own degradation (having less freedom is degrading). The woman herself takes one kind of responsibility absolutely and thus commits herself to her own continuing inferiority: she polices her own body; she internalizes the demands of the dominant class and, in order to be fucked, she constructs her life around meeting those demands. It is the best system of colonialization on earth: she takes on the burden, the responsibility, of her own submission, her own objectification. In some systems in which turning the female into an object for sex requires actual terrorism and maiming—for instance, footbinding or removing the clitoris—the mother does it, having had it done to her by her mother. What men need done to women so that men can have intercourse with women is done to women so that men will have intercourse; no matter what the human cost; and it is a gross indignity to suggest that when her collaboration is complete—unselfconscious because there is no self and no consciousness left—she is free to have freedom in intercourse. When those who dominate you get you to take the initiative in your own human destruction, you have lost more than any oppressed people yet has ever gotten back. Whatever intercourse is, it is not freedom; and if it cannot exist without objectification, it never will be. Instead occupied women will be collaborators, more base in their collaboration than other collaborators have ever been: experiencing pleasure in their own inferiority; calling intercourse freedom. It is a tragedy beyond the power of language to convey when what has been imposed on women by force becomes a standard of freedom for women: and all the women say it is so.

If intercourse can be an expression of sexual equality, it will have to survive—on its own merits as it were, having a potential for human expression not yet recognized or realized—the destruction of male power over women; and rape and prostitution will have to be seen as the institutions that most impede any experience of intercourse as freedom—chosen by full human beings with full human freedom. Rape and prostitution negate self-determination and choice for women; and anyone who wants intercourse to be freedom and to mean freedom had better find a way to get rid of them. Maybe life is tragic and the God who does not exist made women inferior so that men could fuck us; or maybe we can only know this much for certain—that when intercourse exists and is experienced under conditions of force, fear, or inequality, it destroys in women the will to political freedom; it destroys the love of freedom itself. We become female: occupied; collaborators against each other, especially against those among us who resist male domination—the lone, crazy resisters, the organized resistance. The pleasure of submission does not and cannot change the fact, the cost, the indignity, of inferiority.

Notes

3. Anaïs Nin, *In Favor of the Sensitive Man and Other Essays* (New York: Harcourt Brace Jovanovich, 1976), p. 8.

4. Ellen Key, *Love and Marriage*, trans. Arthur G. Chater (New York: G. P. Putnam's Sons, 1911), p. 82.

5. Hite, *Hite Report*, p. 141.

6. Franz Kafka, *Diaries 1910–1913*, ed. Max Brod, trans. Joseph Kresh (New York: Schocken Books, 1965), p. 296.

7. *State v. Hunt*, 220 Neb. 707, 709–10 (1985).

8. *State v. Hunt*, 220 Neb. at 725.

9. Iris Murdoch, *Henry and Cato* (New York: The Viking Press, 1977), p. 262.

10. Paz, *Labyrinth*, p. 13.

11. Don DeLillo, *White Noise* (New York: The Viking Press, 1985), p. 29.

12. Norman O. Brown, *Love's Body* (New York: Random House, 1966), p. 133.

13. Sigmund Freud and C. G. Jung, *The Freud/Jung Letters: The Correspondence Between Sigmund Freud and C. G. Jung,* ed. William McGuire, trans. Ralph Manheim and R. F. C. Hull (Princeton, N.J.: Princeton University Press, 1974), p. 265.

14. Marguerite Duras, *The Lover,* trans. Barbara Bray (New York: Pantheon Books, 1985), p. 63.

15. Duras, *The Lover*, p. 63.

16. Duras, *The Lover*, p. 62.

17. Victoria Claflin Woodhull, *The Victoria Woodhull Reader,* ed. Madeleine B. Stern (Weston, Mass.: M&S Press, 1974), p. 40.

18. Wilhelm Reich, *The Sexual Revolution,* trans. Theodore P. Wolfe, ed. rev. (New York: Farrar, Straus & Giroux, 1970), p. 15.

There is a movement in applied ethics that stresses the use of narratives and story telling. Many ethicists claim (and have claimed for some time) that fiction is the best way to portray ethical quandaries and possible solutions. In keeping with this idea—and the fact that many feminists are proponents of this view—we present excerpts from two novels.

ON INTERCOURSE—PERFECT IF

A feminist writer has her budding feminist of a main character, Isadora Wing, tell us her fantasy of the best kind of sexual encounter. No words, no strings. Just sex and goodbye.

How would you feel about such an encounter? How many such encounters would any one person have before longing for some sort of stable sexual relation? Jong's character longs for a zipless fuck and makes a reasonable case for it. But is a zipless fuck the best kind of sex? In Chapter 2, we saw a number of answers to this question. Of those answers, which would be most persuasive to Isadora Wing?

from Fear of Flying

ERICA JONG

Five years of marriage had made me itchy for all those things: itchy for men, and itchy for solitude. Itchy for sex and itchy for the life of a recluse. I knew my itches were contradictory—and that made things even worse. I knew my itches were un-American—and that made things *still* worse. It is heresy in America to embrace any way of life except as half of a couple. Solitude is un-American. It may be condoned in a man—especially if he is a "glamorous bachelor" who "dates starlets" during a brief interval between marriages. But a woman is always presumed to be alone as a result of abandonment, not choice. And she is treated that way: as a pariah. There is simply no dignified way for a woman to live alone. Oh, she can get along financially perhaps (though not nearly as well as a man), but emotionally she is never left in peace. Her friends, her family, her fellow workers never let her forget that her husbandlessness, her childlessness—her *selfishness,* in short—is a reproach to the American way of life.

Even more to the point: the woman (unhappy though she knows her married friends to be) can never let *herself* alone. She lives as if she were constantly on the brink of some great fulfillment. As if she were waiting for Prince Charming to take her away "from all this." All what? The solitude of living inside her own soul? The certainty of being herself instead of half of something else?

My response to all this was not (not yet) to have an affair and not (not yet) to hit the open road, but to evolve my fantasy of the Zipless Fuck. The zipless fuck was more than a fuck. It was a platonic ideal. Zipless because when you came together zippers fell away like rose petals, underwear blew off in one breath like dandelion fluff. Tongues intertwined and turned liquid. Your whole soul flowed out through your tongue and into the mouth of your lover.

For the true, ultimate zipless A-1 fuck, it was necessary that you never get to know the man very well. I had noticed, for example, how all my infatuations dissolved as soon as I really became friends with a man, became sympathetic to his problems, listened to him *kvetch* about his wife, or ex-wives, his mother, his children. After that I would like him, perhaps even love him—but without passion. And it was passion that I wanted. I had also learned that a sure way to exorcise an infatuation was to write about someone, to observe his tics and twitches, to anatomize his personality in type. After that he was an insect on a pin, a newspaper clipping laminated in plastic. I might enjoy his company, even admire him at moments, but he no longer had the power to make me wake up trembling in the middle of the night. I no longer dreamed about him. He had a face.

So another condition for the zipless fuck was brevity. And anonymity made it even better. . . .

Zipless, you see, *not* because European men have button-flies rather than zipper-flies, and not because the participants are so devastatingly attractive, but because the incident has all the swift compression of a dream and is seemingly free of all remorse and guilt; because there is no talk of her late husband or of his fiancée; because there is no rationalizing; because there is no talk at *all*. The zipless fuck is absolutely pure. It is free of ulterior motives. There is no power game. The man is not "taking" and the woman is not "giving." No one is attempting to cuckold a husband or humiliate a wife. No one is trying to prove anything or get anything out of anyone. The zipless fuck is the purest thing there is.

ON MARRIAGE—PERFECT SELDOM IF EVER

In what might be a short story, French shows the crumbling of a romantic relation. It is broken down not so much by the institution of marriage but by the reality of what the man was like and how he inflicted his will on his wife—and how she allowed it.

In his book *Love: Emotion, Myth and Metaphor* (Doubleday Anchor, 1981), Robert Solomon used French's story as an example of what can go wrong with romantic love. He refers to her argument in the book as showing "the personal outrage and bitter disappointment of a million or more women, only some of whom would identify themselves as 'feminists' and few of whom would be able to articulate the precise mechanism by which they have been systematically shut out of power or what all of this has to do with love." Solomon goes on to defend the existence (and importance) of romantic love. His defense of romantic love is based on the notion that romantic roles are sex-neutral and presuppose equality. Indeed, he sees the switching of roles as central to maintaining a true romantic love relationship. Would Solomon's critique of French also stand against the arguments made by Firestone?

from The Women's Room

MARILYN FRENCH

14

Some dramatic sense, probably culled from reading plays, or female *Bildungsromane,* which always end with the heroine's marriage, makes me want to stop here, make a formal break, like the curtain going down. Marriage should mean a great change, a new life. But it was less a new beginning for Mira than a continuation. Although the external events of her life changed, the internal ones remained much the same.

Oh, Mira was able to leave her parents' tense home, and to pick out little things—towels, throw rugs, some curtains—that would turn their furnished rooms into her own "home," and she enjoyed that. She and Norm had taken a small fur-

Reprinted with the permission of Simon & Schuster from *The Women's Room* by Marilyn French, sections 14–15. Copyright © 1977 by Marilyn French.

nished place near Coburg, where Norm was in medical school. She had left school, and with few regrets. She did not want to go back there again, to have to look at those faces again. She did most of her reading on her own anyway, she reasoned, and would learn as much out of school as in it. Norm would finish med school and his internship while she worked to support them, and once he was out, the future would be secure. They had worked it all out.

After a honeymoon spent in Norm's parents' New Hampshire cottage, they returned, he to the books and she to try to find a job. She was hindered in this because she could not drive; she asked Norm to teach her. He was reluctant. In the first place, he needed the car most days, in the second, she was not mechanically apt and would be a poor driver. He took her in his arms. "I couldn't bear to live if anything happened to you." Something nagged at her, but she was so encompassed by his love, so grateful for it, that she did not probe to find out what it was. Taking buses, and begging her mother to drive her around, she finally found a job as a clerk-typist for $35 a week. They could live on that, but not well, and she decided to try to get a job in New York, commuting back and forth from New Jersey. Norm was horrified. The city! It was such a dangerous place. Commutation would eat up a third of what she earned. She would have to get up early and arrive home late. And then there would be the men . . .

Mira had never told Norm about the night at Kelley's, but he either had the same fears as she, or he had sensed that she had them, because the unspoken threat contained in the word was one he was to continue to use for the next years—indeed, until it was no longer necessary. If he had not, Mira might have learned to overcome her fears. Armed by the title of *Mrs.*, property of some man, she felt stronger in the world. They would be less likely to attack her if they knew some man had her under his protection.

She gave up the idea of the city, accepted the clerk-typist job; Norm got a part-time job, spending much of his time reading beforehand the texts he would be studying in the fall, and they settled into their life together.

She had enjoyed their honeymoon. It was incredible delight to be able to kiss and hold without

fear. Norm was using only condoms, but somehow being married made it less threatening. She was shy about revealing her body. So was Norm, for that matter. And the two of them giggled and delighted in their mutual shyness, their mutual pleasure. The only problem was, Mira did not reach orgasm.

After a month, she decided she was frigid. Norm said that was ridiculous, that she was only inexperienced. He had married friends and he knew that it would pass in time. She asked him, timidly, if it would be possible for him to hold back a little, that she felt she was on the verge, but then he would come, and lose all erectness. He said no healthy male could or should try to hold back. She asked, even more timidly, if they could try a second time. He said that would be unhealthy for him, and probably impossible. He was a medical student, and she believed him. She settled back to enjoy what she could, and waited for him to fall asleep to masturbate herself to orgasm. He always fell asleep quickly after sex.

So they went on. They entertained friends on occasion: she learned to cook. He always shared the laundry chores with her and took her grocery shopping on Friday nights, when she got paid. If she teased him enough, he would help her clean the apartment on Saturday. Sometimes she felt very grown up: when offering a drink to a guest, say, or when putting on makeup and jewelry before leaving to go out with her husband. But most of the time she felt like a child who had stumbled, bumbled into the wrong house. Her job was stultifyingly dull; the long bus rides with other gray, tired people made her feel grimy and poor. At night, Norm turned on the TV (the one large purchase they had made with wedding-gift money), and since there was only the kitchen and the bed-living room, she had no choice but to hear it. She tried to read, but her concentration was continually broken. The tube is demanding. Life felt hideously empty. But she told herself that was only because women are educated to think that marriage will be a sudden panacea to all emptiness, and although she'd fought off such notions, she had no doubt been infected by them. She told herself it was her own fault, that if she had wanted to do some real studying and intellectual work, she could. But, she argued, she was so tired after eight hours in an office, two on buses, preparing dinner, washing dishes—a job Norm simply refused to touch. Besides, Norm always had TV on at night. Well, she argued back, it would be better when he started school; then he would have to study at night. Nevertheless, she was approaching her twentieth birthday: look, her other self said, what Keats had done by twenty. And finally her whole self would rise up and wipe it all out. Oh, don't bother me with it! I do the best I can!

Part of her knew that she was simply surviving in the only way she could. Dull day by dull day she paced through her responsibilities, moving toward some goal she could not discern. The word *freedom* had dropped from her vocabulary; the word *maturity* replaced it. And dimly she sensed that maturity was knowing how to survive. She was as lonely as ever; except sometimes at night, she and Norm, cuddled up together, would talk seriously. One night she was discussing what she wanted: to go back to school and eventually get a Ph.D. and teach. Norm was horrified. He mentioned the problems, financial difficulties, her exhaustion—she would have to do all that and still cook and clean, because when he went back to school he would no longer have time to help her. She argued that they should share. He reminded her that after all he was the one responsible for earning the living: he didn't insist, he wasn't peremptory, he didn't demand. He merely stated it and asked if that weren't so. Frowning and puzzled, reluctantly, she agreed. It was what she had wanted: Norm was responsible, not like Lanny. He would never leave her to go out and get drunk with the boys while she listened to a crying baby, down on her hands and knees scrubbing the kitchen floor. Medical school was difficult, demanding, he added. She could do that, she insisted: do what he said he couldn't, go to med school and still help out in the house. He pulled his big gun: there would be guys, they would give her a hard time, male professors insisting she screw her way to a degree. He was too obvious this time. She pondered. "Sometimes I think you'd like to lock me up in a convent, Norm, where only you could visit me."

"It's true. I would." He was serious.

She turned away from him, and he fell asleep. In three months, the protection she had sought had already become oppressive. It was what she

had wanted too, wasn't it? If she had been less wretched, she would have laughed.

15

Survival is an art. It requires the dulling of the mind and the senses, and a delicate attunement to waiting, without insisting on precision about just what it is you are waiting for. Vaguely, Mira thought of "The End" as Norm's finishing both med school and his internship, but that was so far off, and five years of the boredom she was living in seemed so unendurable that she preferred not to think at all.

Norm went back to school, and as she had expected, no longer watched TV. But she found that she could not concentrate even though it was off. She suspected the problem was not just tiredness; when she picked up a serious book, one that made her think, she thought. And that was unbearable, because to think involves thinking about one's own life. She read at night, read voluminously. It was like the beginning of her adolescence. She read junk: mystery novels, light social satirists like O'Hara and Marquand and Maugham. She could not handle anything more true.

She blamed Norm for nothing. She took care of him, worried about him, cooked what he liked, and asked nothing of him. It was not Norm she hated, but her life. But what other life could she have, being the way she was? Although Norm was often ill-tempered, he insisted that he loved her and was happy with her. It was the stupid school he hated, the stupid finicky professors. He was not doing well: he got through his first year with an undistinguished record. He blamed his low grades on his being upset about her. For she was pregnant.

It was in May that she missed her period. This made her nervous because she was regular, but also because, after her first disastrous attempts with a diaphragm, Norm had insisted that they continue in the old way. He did not like her fiddling for ten minutes in the bathroom when he was full of ardor. And she suspected that he wanted control of the situation himself. She worried about the risk with condoms, but sometimes, when they were very broke, Norm used nothing at all, and withdrew before orgasm. She felt that was risky; he assured her it was all right.

The way she gave herself over to him in this area seemed strange to her in later years. The fact was she hated using a diaphragm. She had come to dislike sex entirely, for he would get her aroused and leave her dissatisfied; now, when she masturbated, she wept. She realized, looking back, that she had given her life over to him just as she had perforce given her life over to her parents. She had simply transferred her childhood. And Norm, although he was seven years older than she, had been in the army during the war and had a few adventures, was not old enough to have a twenty-year-old child. Perhaps, in some dark hidden place in her mind, she had wanted a child: perhaps what she was waiting for, what she called maturity, involved having one and getting it over with. Perhaps.

At the time, it felt like disaster. How would they live? White and drawn, she went to a gynecologist. She came home with the news on an evening when Norm was studying for an important exam. She was worn out from work, the bus rides, the hour's wait in the doctor's office. She imagined as she walked the two blocks from the bus stop that maybe Norm would have cooked some dinner. But he was studying, eating cheese and crackers when she came in, and he was irritated with her for being out so late, although he knew where she had gone and why. As she entered the apartment, she looked across the room at him: he stared mutely back. For three weeks they had discussed little else: there was no need to speak.

Suddenly he threw the book he had been holding across the room.

"You've just ruined my life, do you realize that?"

She sat down on the edge of a rocking chair. "*I* just ruined *your* life?"

"I'll have to quit school now, how else are we going to live?" He lighted a cigarette with nervous intensity. "And how am I supposed to study for this exam when you come home with this? If I flunk it, I flunk out. Did you realize that?"

She sat back, half closing her eyes, detached. She wanted to point out to him the illogic of his last sentences. She wanted to point out to him the injustice of his attack. But the fact that he felt right in making it, felt that he had legitimate grounds to treat her like a naughty child, overwhelmed her. It

was a force against which she could not struggle, for his legitimacy was supported by the entire outside world, and she knew that. She tried. She leaned forward:

"Did I chase you around the bed? You said your way was safe. *You* said it, Mr. Medical Student!"

"It is!"

"Yeah. That's why I'm pregnant."

"It is, I tell you."

She looked at him. His face was nearly blue at the edges, his mouth a tight cruel accusing line.

Her voice faltered. "Are you saying you are not the father of this child? Are you suggesting it happened some other way?"

He glared at her with bitter hate. "How should I know? You tell me you never slept with anybody but me, but how can I tell? There sure was enough talk about you and Lanny. Everybody talked about you. You were free enough in those days, why should it be different now?"

She leaned back again. She had told Norm about her fear of sex, her fear of men, her timidity in a part of the world she did not understand. And he had listened sweetly, caressing her face, holding her close to him. She had thought he understood, thought it even more because he seemed, despite his stories about army adventures, to share it—her shyness and fear and timidity. She thought she had escaped, but all she had done was to let the enemy into her house, let him into her body, he was growing there now. He thought in the same way they did; he, like them, believed he had innate rights over her because he was male and she female; he, like them, believed in things they called virginity and purity, or corruption and whoredom, in women. But he was gentle and respectful; he was among the best of men. If he was like them, there was no hope. It was not worthwhile living in such a world. She leaned back farther and closed her eyes; she began to rock gently in the chair. She went into a quiet darkened place in her mind. There were many ways to die, she did not have to think about that now. All she had to do was find a way out, and she had done that. She would die, and all this would end. It would go away. She would never again have to feel what she was feeling now, which was just like what she had been feeling for years, except stronger. The rockets were exploding all over her body. Her heart ached no more than her stomach or her brain. It was all exploding in fire and tears, and the tears were as hot and hurtful as the fires of rage. There was nothing to be said. He simply would not have understood. It went too deep, and it seemed that she was alone, that she was the only person who felt this way. It must be that, although she felt entirely right, she was wrong. It didn't matter. Nothing mattered.

After a long time, Norm approached her. He knelt down at the side of her chair. "Honey," he said sweetly. "Honey?"

She rocked.

He put his hand on her shoulder and she shuddered away from it.

"Get away from me," she said dully, her tongue cleaving to the roof of her mouth. "Just leave me alone."

He pulled a footstool over and sat close to her, putting his arms around her legs, laying his head in her lap. "Honey, I'm sorry. It's just that I don't know how I'll finish school. Maybe my folks will help us."

She knew it was true. She knew that he was just frightened, as frightened as she. But he felt he had a right to blame her. Upset as she had been when she heard the news, it had not occurred to her to blame him. She had seen it simply as a mess they were in together. She put her hand on his head. It was not his fault. It was just that everything was poisoned. It didn't matter. She would die and be out of it. When she touched him, he began to cry. He *was* as frightened as she, more frightened maybe. He clutched her legs tighter, he sobbed, he apologized. He didn't mean it, he didn't know what had got into him, it was ridiculous childishness, he was sorry. He clutched and cried and she began to caress his head. He cheered up, he looked at her, he caressed her cheek, he joked, he wiped away the water that was running down her face, he laid his head against her breast. She wept fully in great jolting sobs and he held her against him in astonishment, not having known, saying, "I'm sorry, honey, oh, God, I'm sorry," thinking, she imagined, that she was weeping about his suspicion of her fidelity, not knowing, never to know, never to understand. Finally he smiled up at her as her sobs came less often and less strong, and asked her if she weren't hungry. She understood. She rose and made dinner. And in January, she had the baby, and a year and a half later, she had another. Norm's parents lent them money on a note: eight thousand dollars to be repaid when he went into practice. After that she got another diaphragm. But by then she was a different person.

Each of the feminists in this chapter has critiqued Western monogamous marriage as it now exists. One does not have to be a feminist, have the sexual longings of Erica Jong's heroine, or feel as trapped as Marilyn French's Mira to see that current marriages as many are now practiced could be improved. The next chapter deals with marriage. The articles critique, defend, and offer suggestions for changing traditional Western monogamous marriage.

CHAPTER 4

Marriage

Marriage in the Western World, conventional monogamous heterosexual marriage, is in trouble. Symptomatic of the crisis is not only the high percentage of recent marriages ending in divorce court (some analysts place the figure at 50 percent), but also the breakdown of "family values" that seems to be permeating contemporary society and is being portrayed often approvingly in movies, talk shows, and sit-coms. Indeed, the fracturing of marriage and family values has become so widespread that restoration of family values has become a powerful slogan in the hands of resurgent political conservatism.

For several decades social analysts have been warning that all is not well with marriage. Alvin Toffler, for example, in his best-seller, *Future Shock,* published a quarter of a century ago, warned his readers that pressures for change harbored by superindustrialized society and its new reproductive technologies were straining and breaking conventional marriage and the traditional family built on it. Toffler declared that while change is inevitable, managing that change is nevertheless possible. Hampering intelligent managing of such change, however, is the paralysis of decision making with which the bewildering unexpected newness of the future can infect people, a paralysis that is appropriately described as "future shock."

A strong antidote for "future shock" is the careful critical thinking about marriage that is a part of the philosophy of sex and love. We propose to engage in just such critical thinking, and a fitting point of departure is the eminently careful analysis of conventional marriage presented by the eighteenth-century philosopher Immanuel Kant. We will encounter a number of limitations in Kant's discussion that will lead us to explore the analysis offered by the twentieth-century philosopher Lyla H. O'Driscoll, as well as some comments presented by Richard Taylor, also a contemporary philosopher. Then we will listen to a number of contemporary voices that challenge the nature and privileged position of monogamous heterosexual marriage. We will hear from Raymond Belliotti, who describes and assesses the Marxist critique of marriage; from Frederick Elliston, who presents the case for gay marriage; and from Lawrence Casler, who makes a plea for diverse forms of marriage beyond heterosexual monogamy. Finally, we will listen to Gerhard Neubeck's paean of praise for traditional marriage.

In our examination of marriage, we should keep several important questions in mind. What, for example, shall we say "marriage" is? Does the view we espouse have some sort of moral warrant? If so, what precisely is that warrant? Does our view of marriage agree with or differ from the view of marriage that has legal status in our society? Do the current laws governing marriage need to be reinforced, modified, or abandoned? And how shall we respond to those who differ from us and who claim to have moral warrant for their positions?

MONOGAMOUS HETEROSEXUAL MARRIAGE SUPPORTED

Kant begins building his case for monogamous heterosexual marriage on the basis of the sexual impulse that nature has given to all humans. That impulse is simply an appetite for enjoying the sex of another human being. As soon as the appetite is satisfied, the other person is "cast aside as one casts away a lemon which has been sucked dry." When we act in this fashion we find ourselves using another human being as an instrument or object to indulge ourselves, to satisfy our thirst for sexual pleasure. In using another person as an object in this way, however, we are violating a fundamental principle of morality: namely, that one should never treat a human being (whether oneself or another) as a means only, but should always treat a person as an end. This principle is a categorical imperative, a command of morality that must be obeyed under all circumstances. This command of morality honors the dignity, autonomy, and freedom that we all cherish for ourselves and must, therefore, cherish for others as well.

A serious puzzle now surfaces for those who are sympathetic with the Kantian point of view. Nature has given me this sexual drive. I did not ask for it. Nature gave it to me without my permission. When, however, I pursue and satisfy this desire, I find myself using another and even myself as a thing, which seems to be contrary to the commands of morality. The satisfaction of natural sexual appetite and the concerns of morality seem to be on a collision course. Is it at all possible for me to express my natural sexual desire without violating morality? Kant thinks that it is possible; but that possibility is lodged within monogamous heterosexual marriage. Let us watch how the conflict between sexual appetite and morality is resolved by Kant through marriage.

from Lectures on Ethics and The Philosophy of Law

IMMANUEL KANT

LECTURES ON ETHICS

Duties toward the Body in Respect of Sexual Impulse

Amongst our inclinations there is one which is directed towards other human beings. They themselves, and not their work and services, are its Objects of enjoyment. It is true that man has no inclination to enjoy the flesh of another—except, perhaps, in the vengeance of war, and then it is hardly a desire—but none the less there does exist an inclination which we may call an appetite for enjoying another human being. We refer to sexual impulse. Man can, of course, use another human being as an instrument for his service; he can use his hands, his feet, and even all his powers; he can use him for his own purposes with the other's consent. But there is no way in which a human being can be made an Object of indulgence for another except through sexual impulse. This is in the nature of a sense, which we can call the sixth sense; it is an appetite for another human being. We say that a man loves someone when he has an inclina-

The first selection from Immanuel Kant is taken from his *Lectures on Ethics,* translated by Louis Infield (New York: Harper Torchbooks, 1963), pp. 162–168. Copyright © Methuen & Co. Ltd., 11 New Fetter Lane, London EC4P 4EE, England. Used by permission of Methuen & Co. Ltd. The second selection from Kant is taken from *The Philosophy of Law,* translated by W. Hastie (Edinburgh: T. & T. Clark, 1887), pp. 109–113.

tion towards another person. If by this love we mean true human love, then it admits of no distinction between types of persons, or between young and old. But a love that springs merely from sexual impulse cannot be love at all, but only appetite. Human love is good-will, affection, promoting the happiness of others and finding joy in their happiness. But it is clear that, when a person loves another purely from sexual desire, none of these factors enter into the love. Far from there being any concern for the happiness of the loved one, the lover, in order to satisfy his desire and still his appetite, may even plunge the loved one into the depths of misery. Sexual love makes of the loved person an Object of appetite; as soon as that appetite has been stilled, the person is cast aside as one casts away a lemon which has been sucked dry. Sexual love can, of course, be combined with human love and so carry with it the characteristics of the latter, but taken by itself and for itself, it is nothing more than appetite. Taken by itself it is a degradation of human nature; for as soon as a person becomes an Object of appetite for another, all motives of moral relationship cease to function, because as an Object of appetite for another a person becomes a thing and can be treated and used as such by every one. This is the only case in which a human being is designed by nature as the Object of another's enjoyment. Sexual desire is at the root of it; and that is why we are ashamed of it, and why all strict moralists, and those who had pretensions to be regarded as saints, sought to suppress and extirpate it. It is true that without it a man would be incomplete; he would rightly believe that he lacked the necessary organs, and this would make him imperfect as a human being; none the less men made pretence on this question and sought to suppress these inclinations because they degraded mankind.

Because sexuality is not an inclination which one human being has for another as such, but is an inclination for the sex of another, it is a principle of the degradation of human nature, in that it gives rise to the preference of one sex to the other, and to the dishonouring of that sex through the satisfaction of desire. The desire which a man has for a woman is not directed towards her because she is a human being, but because she is a woman; that she is a human being is of no concern to the man; only her sex is the object of his desires. Human nature is thus subordinated. Hence it comes that all men and women do their best to make not their human nature but their sex more alluring and direct their activities and lusts entirely towards sex. Human nature is thereby sacrificed to sex. If then a man wishes to satisfy his desire, and a woman hers, they stimulate each other's desire; their inclinations meet, but their object is not human nature but sex, and each of them dishonours the human nature of the other. They make of humanity an instrument for the satisfaction of their lusts and inclinations, and dishonour it by placing it on a level with animal nature. Sexuality, therefore, exposes mankind to the danger of equality with the beasts. But as man has this desire from nature, the question arises how far he can properly make use of it without injury to his manhood. How far may persons allow one of the opposite sex to satisfy his or her desire upon them? Can they sell themselves, or let themselves out on hire, or by some other contract allow use to be made of their sexual faculties? Philosophers generally point out the harm done by this inclination and the ruin it brings to the body or to the commonwealth, and they believe that, except for the harm it does, there would be nothing contemptible in such conduct in itself. But if this were so, and if giving vent to this desire was not in itself abominable and did not involve immorality, then any one who could avoid being harmed by them could make whatever use he wanted of his sexual propensities. For the prohibitions of prudence are never unconditional; and the conduct would in itself be unobjectionable, and would only be harmful under certain conditions. But in point of fact, there is in the conduct itself something which is contemptible and contrary to the dictates of morality. It follows, therefore, that there must be certain conditions under which alone the use of the *facultates sexuales* would be in keeping with morality. There must be a basis for restraining our freedom in the use we make of our inclinations so that they conform to the principles of morality. We shall endeavour to discover these conditions and this basis. Man cannot dispose over himself because he is not a thing; he is not his own property; to say that he is would be self-contradictory; for in so far as he is a person he is a Subject in whom the ownership of things can be vested, and if he were his own property, he would be a thing over which he could have ownership. But a person cannot be a property and so cannot be a thing which can be owned, for it is impossible to be a person and a thing, the proprietor and the property.

Accordingly, a man is not at his own disposal. He is not entitled to sell a limb, not even one of his teeth. But to allow one's person for profit to be used by another for the satisfaction of sexual desire, to make of oneself an Object of demand, is to dispose over oneself as over a thing and to make of oneself a thing on which another satisfies his appetite, just as he satisfies his hunger upon a steak. But since the inclination is directed towards one's sex and not towards one's humanity, it is clear that one thus partially sacrifices one's humanity and thereby runs a moral risk. Human beings are, therefore, not entitled to offer themselves, for profit, as things for the use of others in the satisfaction of their sexual propensities. In so doing they would run the risk of having their person used by all and sundry as an instrument for the satisfaction of inclination. This way of satisfying sexuality is *vaga libido,* in which one satisfies the inclinations of others for gain. It is possible for either sex. To let one's person out on hire and to surrender it to another for the satisfaction of his sexual desire in return for money is the depth of infamy. The underlying moral principle is that man is not his own property and cannot do with his body what he will. The body is part of the self; in its togetherness with the self it constitutes the person; a man cannot make of his person a thing, and this is exactly what happens in *vaga libido.* This manner of satisfying sexual desire is, therefore, not permitted by the rules of morality. But what of the second method, namely *concubinatus?* Is this also inadmissible? In this case both persons satisfy their desire mutually and there is no idea of gain, but they serve each other only for the satisfaction of sexuality. There appears to be nothing unsuitable in this arrangement, but there is nevertheless one consideration which rules it out. Concubinage consists in one person surrendering to another only for the satisfaction of their sexual desire whilst retaining freedom and rights in other per-

sonal respects affecting welfare and happiness. But the person who so surrenders is used as a thing; the desire is still directed only towards sex and not towards the person as a human being. But it is obvious that to surrender part of oneself is to surrender the whole, because a human being is a unity. It is not possible to have the disposal of a part only of a person without having at the same time a right of disposal over the whole person, for each part of a person is integrally bound up with the whole. But concubinage does not give me a right of disposal over the whole person but only over a part, namely the *organa sexualia.* It presupposes a contract. This contract deals only with the enjoyment of a part of the person and not with the entire circumstances of the person. Concubinage is certainly a contract, but it is one-sided; the rights of the two parties are not equal. But if in concubinage I enjoy a part of a person, I thereby enjoy the whole person; yet by the terms of the arrangement I have not the rights over the whole person, but only over a part; I, therefore, make the person into a thing. For that reason this method of satisfying sexual desire is also not permitted by the rules of morality. The sole condition on which we are free to make use of our sexual desire depends upon the right to dispose over the person as a whole—over the welfare and happiness and generally over all the circumstances of that person. If I have the right over the whole person, I have also the right over the part and so I have the right to use that person's *organa sexualia* for the satisfaction of sexual desire. But how am I to obtain these rights over the whole person? Only by giving that person the same rights over the whole of myself. This happens only in marriage. Matrimony is an agreement between two persons by which they grant each other reciprocal rights, each of them undertaking to surrender the whole of their person to the other with a complete right to disposal over it. We can now apprehend by reason how a *commercium sexuale* [sexual reciprocity] is possible without degrading humanity and breaking the moral laws. Matrimony is the only condition in which use can be made of one's sexuality. If one devotes one's person to another, one devotes not only sex but the whole person; the two cannot be separated. If, then, one yields one's person, body and soul, for good and ill and in every respect, so that the other has complete rights over it, and if the other does not similarly yield himself in return and does not extend in return the same rights and privileges, the arrangement is one-sided. But if I yield myself completely to another and obtain the person of the other in return, I win myself back; I have given myself up as the property of another, but in turn I take that other as my property, and so win myself back again in winning the person whose property I have become. In this way the two persons become a unity of will. Whatever good or ill, joy or sorrow befall either of them, the other will share in it. Thus sexuality leads to a union of human beings, and in that union alone its exercise is possible. This condition of the use of sexuality, which is only fulfilled in marriage, is a moral condition. . . . Only under that condition can I indulge my *facultas sexualis.* . . .

THE PHILOSOPHY OF LAW

The Natural Basis of Marriage

The domestic Relations are founded on Marriage, and Marriage is founded upon the natural Reciprocity or intercommunity (*commercium*) of the Sexes. This natural union of the sexes proceeds either according to the mere animal Nature or according to Law. The latter is MARRIAGE, which is the Union of two Persons of different sex for lifelong reciprocal possession of their sexual faculties.—The End of producing and educating children may be regarded as always the End of Nature in implanting mutual desire and inclination in the sexes; but it is not necessary for the rightfulness of marriage that those who marry should set this before themselves as the End of their Union, otherwise the Marriage would be dissolved of itself when the production of children ceased.

And even assuming that enjoyment in the reciprocal use of the sexual endowments is an end of marriage, yet the Contract of Marriage is not on that account a matter of arbitrary will, but is a Contract necessary in its nature by the Law of Humanity. In other words, if a man and a woman have the will to enter on reciprocal enjoyment in accordance with their sexual nature, they *must* necessarily marry each other; and this necessity is in accordance with the juridical Laws of Pure Reason.

The Rational Right of Marriage

For, this natural *'Commercium'* [reciprocity] is an enjoyment for which the one person is given up to the other. In this relation the human individual makes himself a *'res,'* [thing] which is contrary to the Right of Humanity in his own Person. This, however, is only possible under the one condition, that as the one Person is acquired by the other as a *res,* that same Person also equally acquires the other reciprocally, and thus regains and re-establishes the rational Personality. The Acquisition of a part of the human organism being, on account of its unity, at the same time the acquisition of the whole Person, it follows that the surrender and acceptation of, or by, one sex in relation to the other, is not only *permissible* under the condition of Marriage but is further *only* really possible under that condition. But the Personal Right thus acquired is at the same time, *real in kind;* and this characteristic of it is established by the fact that if one of the married Persons run away or enter into the possession of another, the other is entitled, at any time, and incontestably, to bring such a one back to the former relation, as if that Person were a Thing.

Monogamy and Equality in Marriage

For the same reasons, the relation of the Married Persons to each other is a relation of EQUALITY as regards the mutual possession of their Persons, as well as of their Goods. Consequently Marriage is only truly realized in MONOGAMY: for in the relation of Polygamy the Person who is given away on the one side, gains only a part of the one to whom that Person is given up, and therefore becomes a mere *res.* But in respect of their Goods, they have severally the Right to renounce the use of any part of them, although only by a special Contract. . . .

Fulfilment of the Contract of Marriage

The Contract of Marriage is completed only by conjugal cohabitation. A Contract of two Persons of different sex, with the secret understanding either to abstain from conjugal cohabitation or with the consciousness on either side of incapacity for it, is a *simulated Contract;* it does not constitute a marriage, and it may be dissolved by either of the parties at will. But if the incapacity only arises after marriage, the Right of the Contract is not annulled or diminished by a contingency that cannot be legally blamed.

The Acquisition of a Spouse either as a Husband or as a Wife, is therefore not constituted . . . by Cohabitation—without a preceding Contract; nor even—by a mere Contract of Marriage, without subsequent Cohabitation; but only . . . as a juridical consequence of the obligation that is formed by two Persons entering into a sexual Union solely on the basis of a reciprocal *Possession* of each other. . . .

It would seem that Kant's resolution of the conflict between sexual appetite and the commands of morality depends on the way persons give themselves to each other. If I give myself to another only for purposes of sexual gratification and if the other does the same to me, we are not really giving our full selves to each other; instead, we are giving only a part of our selves to each other. To give ourselves partially in this fashion is to treat ourselves and each other as things, as if we were bundles of properties or things that could be dispensed now and then. But we are not bundles of things. We are human selves. We are persons, not things. To treat ourselves and others as things is to violate the commands of morality. If, however, we give our whole selves to each other, we become committed to concern for each other's total well-being and overall happiness. Indeed, we find ourselves treating each other as "ends" and not simply as "means." In such total giving we are faithful to the commands of morality. But such mutual total giving of our whole selves takes place only in marriage where two people "grant each other reciprocal rights, each of them undertaking to surrender the whole of their person to the other with a complete right to disposal over it." In devoting ourselves to each other in marriage, the right to use each other's sexual organs comes as part of the "package." Only in marriage can one's sexual impulses be satisfied without violating morality.

How convincing is Kant's case? Has he not portrayed accurately the reification of the other that is at the core of the sexual impulse? And would we not want to endorse the fundamental moral principle of treating persons as ends and not simply as means? Would we not want to stand up and cheer for Kant's high regard for human dignity, autonomy, and freedom? And would we not want to agree that he has put his finger on a genuine puzzle: namely, the apparent conflict between the reifying sexual impulse and the concerns of morality? Yet has Kant really resolved the puzzle? To be sure, if we mutually give rights to each other relative to our whole selves, then using each other's sexual organs for sexual gratification is not a violation of each other's autonomy and freedom. But are we still not using each other's sexual organs as if they were things that gratify our personal pursuit of sexual pleasure? Even though marriage may grant us the rights to use each other's sexual organs, does the granting of those rights remove the reification which Kant perhaps correctly sees is at the heart of the sexual impulse? Indeed, can the gratification of the sexual impulse ever avoid reification of the sexual partner?

Even though Kant's analysis may not neutralize or remove the reification at the heart of sexual gratification, does not his view of marriage as the reciprocal surrender of whole selves to each other, and the rights thereby entailed, present a strong case for conventional marriage as a particularly attractive form of sexual union in which the dignity, autonomy, and freedom of persons are respected? Perhaps. Yet could not the case he makes for marriage apply not only to heterosexual but also to homosexual marriage? And is his case necessarily applicable only to monogamous marriage? Is it not possible to yield mutually to several spouses simultaneously the rights to one's whole self? Questions such as these lead us to consider a broader picture of marriage than the conventional monogamous hetero-sexual model treated by Kant. Our next author, Lyla H. O'Driscoll, provides us with some windows overlooking a broader view of marriage.

A BROADER VIEW OF MARRIAGE EXAMINED

Two hundred years ago Kant was defending conventional marriage (that is, monogamous heterosexual marriage) as the social arrangement that allowed persons to gratify their sexual impulses without violating the requirements of morality. Compared with prostitution, concubinage and polygamy, conventional marriage seemed to be morally superior. Voices were soon raised, however, that questioned the moral superiority of conventional marriage. First the Marxists in the nineteenth century followed by the feminists in the twentieth century called into question that moral superiority. Marxists pointed out that conventional marriage was in fact a social construct that expressed and guaranteed the interests of bourgeois capitalists; and feminists declared that conventional marriage locked women into a relationship that oppressed them politically, exhausted them physically, exploited them sexually, and stultified them intellectually. If Marxists and feminists are correct, does not conventional marriage lose its moral warrant? And if it loses that warrant, can it survive long as the legally privileged form of sexual union? On the contemporary scene, the voices of gay activists are blending with those of many Marxists and feminists in mounting a robust critique of conventional marriage and in calling for changes in the law.

O'Driscoll seeks to contribute to the current debate about marriage by clarifying what marriage is and by identifying the values that it might serve. First, she examines marriage as a legal civil contract, then as a social institution, and finally as an interpersonal relationship.

from On the Nature and Value of Marriage

Marriage—recently condemned as psychologically destructive, as socially pointless or ineffective, as oppressive, sexist, and morally repugnant—is the focus of new and lively scholarly and popular controversy.[1] This paper is an attempt to clarify some of the issues comprehended in this debate, in particular, certain conceptual issues that seem to have been neglected or misconstrued by both advocates and critics of marriage. The marriage controversy is not merely conceptual, of course; normative issues, including the justifiability of the institution, are familiar themes in the de-bate. Formulation of normative issues involves conceptual assumptions, however, including assumptions about the kinds of value that institutions and formal relations might have.

This paper does not directly treat the justifiability of marriage. Instead, it attempts to articulate a concept of marriage and suggests that partisans on both sides of the controversy, in conceiving of marriage as an instrument, have misjudged its value. The discussion may have some significance for the issue of justification, however: without a clearly formulated concept of marriage and of the

The selection from Lyla H. O'Driscoll is taken from her article "On the Nature and Value of Marriage," in *Feminism and Philosophy,* edited by Mary Vetterling-Braggin, Frederick A. Elliston, and Jane English (Totowa, New Jersey: Rowman and Littlefield, 1977), pp. 249–263. Used by permission of Rowman & Littlefield, Publishers, Inc.

kinds of value it might have, attempts to assess its justifiability are likely to be futile.

I

One concept of marriage is the legal concept. Since the Anglo-American institution of heterosexual monogamy is frequently a target of criticism, it will be examined in order to ascertain some of the features of marriage as a legal institution.

According to Anglo-American custom and law, marriage is a social and legal status brought into existence by a civil contract. In the standard case, a marriage originates in a properly witnessed formal contract (distinct from any antenuptial financial contract) entered into by two persons, one male and one female; each party must be of legal age, must possess other requisites of contractual capacity, and must freely consent to the agreement.

The contract initiating a marriage differs in several ways from an ordinary business contract. Contracting a marriage requires the performance of special formalities; the contract cannot be terminated or rendered void except by action of a competent official. Business contractors have considerable leeway in formulating the terms of their agreement; those who contract a marriage are limited to the terms uniformly specified by law. The requirements of contractual capacity are especially stringent for marriage contracts. Marriage contractors are prohibited from having certain degrees of blood kinship and may be required to submit to a physician's examination. Furthermore, marriage contractors may have no prior marital relationship (unless legally dissolved), no concurrent marriages, and must enter the contractual relationship in pairs consisting of one male and one female.[2]

Each party to the marriage contract obtains certain rights and duties, including rights regarding support, fidelity, companionship, sexual congress, inheritance, confidentiality, and protection from interference by third parties.[3] In some cases, spouses choose not to seek enforcement of these rights; persons may even enter the legal relation intending not to seek enforcement—as in the case of a marriage of convenience or marriage to prevent the deportation of one contractor.

In jurisdictions recognizing common-law marriage, mutual rights to support, companionship, sexual congress, inheritance, etc. arise from an overt agreement to become spouses, cohabitation over a legally specified period of time, and public presentation and reputation as spouses.[4]

A leading English case characterizes marriage as "the voluntary union for life of one man and one woman, to the exclusion of all others."[5] The accuracy of the restriction, "for life," is dubious, for even at the time of the decision (1866), divorce was legal in England.[6]

English and American jurists disagree about whether procreation is a principal end of marriage. The leading English case is a 1948 ruling that one spouse's insistence on the use of contraceptives did not constitute willful refusal to consummate the marriage. The judge pointed out that

> the institution of marriage generally is not necessary for the procreation of children; nor does it appear to be a principal end of marriage as understood in Christendom. . . . In any view of Christian marriage, the essence of the matter, as it seems to me, is that the children, *if there be any,* should be born into a family, as that word is understood in Christendom generally, and in the case of a marriage between spouses of a particular faith that they should be brought up and nurtured in that faith. But this is not the same thing as saying that a marriage is not consummated or that procreation is the principal end of marriage.[7]

The judge also noted that it was not alleged in the suit that the sterility of a husband or the barrenness of a wife had some bearing on the question whether a marriage had been consummated.[8]

In the past, American jurists have regarded procreation as "the controlling purpose" of marriage, ruling that a wife's refusal to engage in uncontracepted intercourse constituted desertion of her husband or cruelty to him. In another case, the wife's refusal was adjudged a breach of her marital obligations and resulted in dismissal of her suit for separation and support.[9] Although a few jurisdictions have even ruled that a spouse's premarital sterility renders a marriage void, most have concurred with recent decisions more carefully distinguishing canon law and rejecting the claim that in civil law procreation is the chief end of marriage.[10]

A recent decision in a suit requesting legal recognition of homosexual alliances was rejected on the grounds that the common usage of the term "marriage" restricted its application to unions of persons of opposite sexes and that marriage is a union "uniquely involving procreation."[11]

The advocacy and existence of deliberately child-free marriages controverts the traditional assumption that the "unique involvement" of procreation in marriage is that it is the *purpose* of marriage. It also controverts the assumption that there is a necessary connection between the intention to become spouses and the intention to become parents. Once those assumptions are discarded, one rationale for nonrecognition of homosexual alliances is weakened.

The characterization of marriage as a legal institution is one concept of marriage; or, to be more precise, it is a concept of a form of marriage. Nonterminable, monogamous heterosexual marriage is one form of marriage. The qualifications can be variously altered to specify other logically possible forms of marriage. Legal recognition of polyandry, for example, could be accomplished by altering the rules of contractual capacity so that a female could maintain prior or concurrent marital relationships. Legal recognition of homosexual monogamy could be accomplished by abolition of the requirement that persons enter the relationship in pairs consisting of one male and one female.

A multilateral marriage, which consists of three or more partners, "each of whom considers himself/herself to be married (or committed in a functionally analogous way) to more than one of the other partners,"[12] could be legally recognized if the requirement of pairing were deleted and the requirement that spouses have no previous or concurrent marriages were deleted. (Multilateral marriage is distinct from polygyny, the marriage of one male to more than one female, and from polyandry. In polygyny, the females are not married to more than one person. It is characteristic of multilateral marriage that each spouse has more than one spouse.)

Successful criticisms of heterosexual monogamy do not suffice to demonstrate the unacceptability of the institution of marriage any more than successful criticisms of absolute monarchy demonstrate the unacceptability of the institution of government. The concept of marriage is more abstract and general than the concept of heterosexual monogamy. Thus, for example, John McMurtry's critique of heterosexual monogamy, if well taken, demonstrates at most the unacceptability of that form of marriage (and then only when it has the consequences he attributes to it.)[13]

Some constituents of the legal characterization of the institution, including the restriction of entry to male-female pairs, are not part of the concept of marriage. Other features characterize marriage as a legal institution, regardless of form: in law, marriage is a formalized relationship between legal adults, initiated by a more or less explicit agreement, and defined by legally specified rights and duties.

II

Although they are important, the legal aspects of marriage do not exhaust the concept of marriage. A broader conceptual problem remains, and it is one that cannot be resolved by a descriptive study of marriage in various cultures, a study in which common features, if any, are noted and combined as the essence of marriage.

Indeed, resolution of the broader conceptual problem is logically prior to empirical or descriptive study of the institution. The conceptual problem here is one of discerning the characteristics that distinguish a society having an institution of marriage from one lacking it. It is also a problem of determining what features of human association would have to be examined in order to resolve the question whether the institution of marriage exists.

Part of the solution to the broader conceptual problem is evident enough: whatever else it is, marriage is a social institution. The marital relation is not captured in a catalogue of changes in the spatial and temporal locations of human bodies; still less is it comprehended in a list of pieces of behavior. Marriage is a social institution that typically regulates (some) sexual activities and (in some way) the production of offspring. Marriage is of course not the only social institution that serves these functions. In order to determine whether the institution of marriage exists in a society, however, one would examine the social institutions that regulate sexual conduct and procreation.

The difference between a society with marriage and one without it is that in the former the rules constituting an existing social institution distinguish between illegitimate and legitimate progeny and characterize actual or possible instances of sexual congress as conjugal relations. The institution of marriage is partly constituted by rules that structure certain activities and define certain roles. Two-party heterosexual copulation, for example, cannot be adultery unless one of the participants is the spouse of a nonparticipant; it cannot be an instance of conjugal relations unless the participants are married to one another. Other activities structured by the rules constituting marriage include courtship, engagement, payment of dowry, divorce, and bigamy. By reference to the rules defining marriage, the bachelor can be distinguished from the husband, the spinster from the wife, the fiancée from the divorcée, the in-law from the parent, the bastard from the legitimate offspring.

Whatever its form, marriage is a social institution in which sexual intercourse is socially and legally legitimate and in which the production of socially and legally legitimate offspring is possible. Until effective contraception was generally available, it was tempting, in view of the connection between marriage and the production of *legitimate* offspring, to regard procreation as the purpose of marriage. It is important, however, to distinguish the device used to identify an institution as marriage from a specification of the purpose of the institution. The logical connection between marriage and procreation is not that procreation is the purpose of marriage but that it is in marriage that legitimate offspring can be produced.

Social and legal legitimacy are not always all-or-nothing matters. Some societies have not only marriages that confer full legitimacy on sexual intercourse and offspring but also legally recognized systems of concubinage. The legitimacy of sexual congress with a concubine and of the offspring of such a union may be more social than legal, but the relationship is nevertheless distinguished from, and more legitimate than, casual, fleeting sexual encounters or incestuous relationships.[14]

This concept of marriage, an explication by reference to the social functions of the institution, provides a general characterization compatible with the logical possibility of various forms of marriage and usable in deciding whether the institution exists in a particular society. A society lacks the institution if there is no social institution by reference to which one can distinguish conjugal and nonconjugal relations, legitimate offspring and bastards. (Such a society can nevertheless have rules to distinguish rape from consensual intercourse.)

Articulation of this concept of marriage will not end the marriage controversy, but it does indicate that the disputants may share some common ground. Critics of marriage have not generally advocated a society in which marriage does not exist, although some have ventured in the direction of such a proposal.[15] Individuals on both sides of the marriage controversy largely agree that a society will (and perhaps even should) have an institution or institutions to perform these functions.

Part of the marriage controversy is a dispute about whether the institution or institutions performing these functions should be legally defined and should be limited by law to a single form. Another aspect of the dispute focuses on the fact that if spouses become parents, they customarily take on the task of rearing the young. Some, who claim that the additional burden of child-rearing inflicts excessive strain on marriages, suggest that this function can and should be separated from the legitimating function of marriage.

The purpose of this paper is not to resolve these disputes, but to formulate the issues more clearly and precisely so that others may approach them with a greater awareness of what is at stake.

III

Participants in the marriage controversy frequently assimilate the question of the justifiability of the institution with the question of the aptness of the institution as a means to the achievement of certain good ends such as human happiness. The issue is then treated as a problem of assessing the costs and benefits of particular arrangements, a problem whose resolution depends essentially on empirical evidence regarding the effects of the arrangements on the psychological, pecuniary, legal, and social well-being of spouses and off-spring, and evidence regarding social advantages and disadvantages. Much of the feminist critique of heterosexual monogamy originates in such considerations.

But the issue of the justifiability of the institution is not as simple as this assimilation suggests. Among the complexities is the possibility that a marriage can be good even if its goodness does not lie solely in its aptness as a means of advancing good ends. Not all value is instrumental; the value of marriage, for the spouses, may lie not merely in what it *does* or can do (i.e., the effects it has) but in what it *is* or can be.

I would like to suggest that as an expression of friendship, marriage can have intrinsic value. I do not wish to deny, of course, that marriage can have instrumental value; the suggestion, rather, is that its instrumental value is not its only possible value.[16]

The thesis that marriage can have noninstrumental value for spouses is distinct from the claim that marriage is morally valuable. Something intrinsically valuable is valuable in itself, valuable because of its intrinsic properties, not because of its effects; something morally valuable is good on moral grounds, for example, its aptness as a means to morally praiseworthy ends. Something can be intrinsically good without being morally good; in the view of the hedonistic utilitarian, for example, pleasure is intrinsically and nonmorally good.[17]

It is evident that expressions of friendship can have noninstrumental value. A service performed as a gesture of friendship, for example, can be instrumentally useful, and can also be valuable because it is done by a certain person out of certain motives. In such gestures, friendship can be expressed for its own sake and not for the sake of some external objective. The pledge of marriage can be a gesture of friendship; it creates a public and relatively permanent arrangement that symbolizes the dispositions and attitudes constitutive of friendship.

It might be thought that to characterize the marriage pledge and status as expressions of friendship trivializes the relationship between spouses, reducing it to "mere friendship." To suppose this is to confuse merely being friendly and being friends. Although friendships vary in the degree of affection, intimacy, sharing, and trust involved,

these attitudes and behavior are essential to friendship; in the paradigm case—close (but not the closest possible) friendship—the depth of affection amounts to love.

IV

The difference between friendship and ordinary social associations, as described by Kant, is that in ordinary social associations

> we do not enter completely into the social relation. The greater part of our disposition is withheld; there is no immediate outpouring of our feelings, dispositions and judgments. We voice only the judgments that seem advisable in the circumstances. A constraint, a mistrust of others, rests upon all of us, so that we withhold something, concealing our weaknesses to escape contempt, or even withholding our opinions.[18]

If marriage is to express friendship, friendship must exist; if there is to be friendship, certain attitudes must exist and certain kinds of shared activities must occur.[19] Two persons are friends if and only if, first, they regard one another as worthy of respect and trust; second, they are disposed to seek one another's company (for the sake of *that person's* company, not merely for the sake of company); third, they are disposed to seek one another's well-being; and fourth, they have these dispositions because they are fond of one another.

A marriage that expresses friendship reveals and symbolizes attitudes such as affection for and commitment to a particular person. Such a relation is necessarily personal. Affection *for a person* is distinct from regard for someone's virtues and admiration for someone's characteristics, although it may be causally connected with these virtues and characteristics. Admiration and approval of a person's characteristics diminish if the characteristics dwindle; admiration of an artist's ability declines with the artist's declining skill. Affection for a person, on the other hand, does not diminish in the face of diminution of admired and approved qualities in the person. Love of a person, as Shakespeare points out, does not alter when it alteration finds. Affection for a person applies to a particular being; it cannot be automatically transferred to another instantiation of similar characteristics.[20]

Mutual trust and respect underlie the sharing of confidences that is typical of friends. Friendship between two persons entails the existence of durable tendencies; the affection of friends is not transitory fondness or attraction, nor is it unrequited.

Friends do not value one another primarily or merely as means; someone who values another primarily or merely because he has certain instrumentally useful traits values him as an instrument. If customer Jones's association with grocer Smith is primarily or solely instrumentally valuable to both parties, each individual, as far as the other is concerned, is a replaceable component in the arrangement. It is a matter of indifference to Smith whether Jones or some other equally good instrument occupies the role of customer; Jones is indifferent to the particular person occupying the grocer's role, as long as the services are efficiently provided.

In short, if people value one another's characteristics as instruments, their relation is essentially impersonal, not a valuing of a particular person, but an appreciation of the usefulness of certain traits that happen to be embodied in one person but would be equally valuable if found in another. Smith values Jones's patronage, the business he brings to the store; Smith would value equally any other instantiation of the properties that make Jones a good customer. Likewise, Jones values the performance of certain services, and would value equally another instantiation of the characteristics that make Smith a good grocer.

The importance of affection in marriage is often confined to or confused with the importance of erotic love. Although erotic love is one facet of marital affection, others include the tendency to find companionship in one's spouse's company (*philia*) and the tendency to give oneself nonsexually and unselfishly—to invest oneself in the relationship.

Activities, including sexual activities, are enhanced in value by being shared with, or done for, the sake of someone of whom the agent is fond. Sexual desire can of course be satisfied in casual encounters. But the mutual respect, trust, and affection that subsist between friends can render sexual activity intrinsically as well as instrumentally valuable—valued because it is shared with a valued individual.[21]

Friends are not necessarily of the same sex; nor are friends necessarily of opposite sexes.

Friendship is neither exclusive nor necessarily transitive. Someone may have several friends, including people who are not mutual friends. It is unlikely, however, that anyone could maintain a large number of close friendships. The problem is not conceptual but empirical: intimacy and intense affection are psychologically demanding and can probably subsist only in small groups.

Not all affectionate relationships are friendships. A parent may be fond of a newborn child. Since the affection is not reciprocated and since mutual trust and respect are not possible, the relationship is not friendship.

Friends need not have made a formal or explicit pledge of friendship. In some cases, one's commitment to a friend is simply a tendency to seek his well-being for his sake. This tendency may exist without having been deliberately cultivated; the principle of action may be unformulated, and the agent may even be unable to formulate it. If the agent's behavior, attitudes, and beliefs are generally consistent with his regarding the other's well-being as a good, and if the agent is disposed to alter his behavior, attitudes, and beliefs to conform to the belief that the other person's well-being is a good, then the person may be characterized as having an inchoate principle of action committing him to seek the other person's good for that person's sake.

Implicit commitment to a friend may consist of a tendency, should the occasion arise, upon reflection to admit the existence of activities, attitudes, and dispositions essential to friendship and to identify the other as a friend.[22] There is a sense, therefore, in which friendship can be initiated and terminated voluntarily. Upon becoming aware of the existence of the relevant attitudes, dispositions, and activities, one can choose to discontinue the activities and seek to eradicate or modify the attitudes and dispositions. Such a choice amounts to refusing to make an explicit commitment to the person, a refusal to affirm the dispositions, attitudes, and activities of friendship, and a refusal to sustain a friendship.

On the other hand, people might choose to affirm the relationship, and furthermore to formalize it in a ceremony such as the ritual of blood brotherhood. Such a public declaration is a fully explicit statement of a willingness to pursue mutual well-being; it is a joint pledge of continuing association, loyalty, and fidelity. A public declaration is not necessary in order to make such a commitment explicit, but it can serve to distinguish an especially serious and significant friendship from other associations.

At any of these levels of explicitness, the commitment of friendship need not be a commitment to the exclusivity of the friendship: even when one has publicly declared the great significance of a particular friendship, it is logically possible to ascribe (and to declare publicly) the equal significance of another friendship.

V

Marriage can single out an especially significant friendship (if monogamous) or especially significant friendships (if multilateral, polygamous, or polyandrous); it can distinguish such relationships from less profound, serious, and durable affections and commitments.

As has been pointed out, friends are disposed to seek one another's company and well-being, and they have these tendencies because they are fond of one another. Between (or among) friends, these dispositions may be manifested in the desire to share domicile and in the desire of each to participate fully in the achievement of the other's aspirations and the execution of the other's plans—the desire to share in the other's life and (good or ill) fortune. Individuals having these desires might reasonably choose a formal declaration to express, affirm, and cement their intentions, and their commitment to, and affection for, one another. They regard their relationship, and its formal expression, as having intrinsic value.

Their willingness to declare their intention to pursue joint well-being openly and in a way that creates legal and moral obligations signifies their confidence in the durability and importance of the relationship. Their willingness to make such a declaration also signifies their willingness to risk censure, from their spouses or from others, should they fail to fulfill their obligations; and it also signifies their willingness to have these obligations enforced. The willingness of friends to make such

a declaration and to undertake such obligations signifies their willingness to share in one another's good (or ill) fortune, and to incur the risks inherent in an enduring and legally recognized relationship, including the risk that pursuit of mutual well-being will necessitate some compromise and sacrifice of individual well-being.[23]

No one marries all his friends, not even all his especially significant friends. But considerations of the intrinsic value of the relationship might, in some (rare) cases, account for the decision to marry. Such considerations could provide a satisfactory reason for initiating or continuing a marriage if they were (as they usually are) conjoined with judgments about the instrumental value of a legally recognized bond (for example, the supposition that the special legal and social status accorded to spouses fosters a stable, profound, and enduring affection and enhances the attitudes and commitments of friendship).

Marriage expressive of friendship can be heterosexual, homosexual, multilateral, polygynous, or polyandrous. Thus, this account of the nature and possible value of marriage for spouses is compatible with the conceivability of a variety of forms of marriage.

This discussion is not intended as proof of the justifiability of the institution of marriage. I have considered its possible value for spouses. It may be that the intrinsic value of the relationship for spouses is insufficient to show the institution acceptable from a moral point of view; there may be overriding objections based on other considerations. I have attempted only to outline a different perspective for the assessment of marriage, to suggest that the value of marriage, for spouses, may be intrinsic as well as instrumental.

Notes

I would like to thank Robert Hollinger, Gerald P. O'Driscoll, Jr., Warren S. Quinn, Alyce Vrolyk, and Virginia Warren for helpful comments on earlier versions of this paper. [L. H. O'Driscoll]

1. Instances of such criticisms can be found in the following: Robin Morgan, ed., *Sisterhood Is Powerful* (New York: Random House, Vintage Books, 1970), pp. 438–54, 514–48; Vivian Gornick and Barbara K. Moran, eds., *Woman in Sexist Society* (New York: New American Library, Mentor Books, 1971), pp. xxvi, 145–86. On the legal effects of marriage on

women, see Leo Kanowitz, *Women and the Law* (Albuquerque: University of New Mexico Press, 1969), chap. 3.

2. P. M. Bromley, *Family Law* (London: Butterworth, 1971), pp. 11–12.

3. Morris Ploscowe, Henry H. Foster, Jr., and Doris Jonas Fried, *Family Law* (Boston: Little, Brown, 1972), p. 43.

4. Ibid., pp. 79–81. See also Stuart J. Stein, "Common Law Marriage," *Journal of Family Law* 9 (1970): 271–99.

5. Ploscowe, Foster, and Fried, pp. 16–17. The case is *Hyde* v. *Hyde*.

6. Bromley, p. 12.

7. J. C. Hall, *Sources of Family Law* (Cambridge: Cambridge University Press, 1966), p. 2. The case is *Baxter* v. *Baxter.* Emphasis added.

8. Hall, p. 2.

9. Joseph Goldstein and Jay Katz, *The Family and the Law* (New York: Free Press, 1965), pp. 823–28. The cases are *Raymond* v. *Raymond, Forbes* v. *Forbes,* and *Baretta* v. *Baretta.*

10. Goldstein and Katz, p. 816; Monrad G. Paulsen, Walter Walington, and Julius Goebel, Jr., *Domestic Relations,* 2d ed. (Mineola, NY: Foundation Press, 1974), p. 155. The cases are *Van Nierke* v. *Van Nierke* and *T.* v. *M.*

11. Paulsen, Walington, and Goebel, pp. 35–36. The case is *Baker* v. *Nelson.*

12. Larry Constantine and Joan Constantine, *Group Marriage* (New York: Macmillan, 1973), p. 28.

13. John McMurtry, "Monogamy: A Critique," *Monist* 56 (1972): 587–99; reprinted in *Philosophy and Sex,* ed. Robert Baker and Frederick Elliston (Buffalo, NY: Prometheus Books, 1975). Other relevant essays in the same anthology are David Palmer, "The Consolation of the Wedded," and Michael D. Bayles, "Marriage, Love, and Procreation."

14. See William J. Goode, *World Revolution and Family Patterns* (New York: Free Press, 1963), pp. 282–85, on concubinage in China; and idem. *The Family* (Englewood Cliffs, NJ: Prentice Hall, 1964), chap. 3.

15. David E. Engdahl, "Medieval Metaphysics and English Marriage Laws," *Journal of Family Law* 8 (1969): 381–97.

16. The thesis that formalized relationships can be intrinsically valuable is defended in John Rawls, *A Theory of Justice* (Cambridge: Harvard University Press, 1971), pp. 520–29. In *An Anatomy of Values* (Cambridge: Harvard University Press, 1971), pp. 117–21, Charles Fried also defends this claim and applies it to legal institutions in general and to marriage in particular. Fried defines an *expressive* relation as one that has intrinsic value (p. 118n). In this discussion, however, "express" is used in the sense of "serving to manifest, reveal, or symbolize."

17. On the notion of intrinsic value, see William Frankena, *Ethics,* 2d ed. (Englewood Cliffs, NJ: Prentice Hall, 1973), p. 82.

18. Immanuel Kant, *Lectures on Ethics* (New York: Harper & Row, Harper Torchbooks, 1963), p. 205.

19. This account of friendship substantially follows Elizabeth Telfer, "Friendship," *Proceedings of the Aristotelian Society* 71 (1970–71): 222–41. The view is rooted in the doctrines of Kant and Aristotle. See especially Immanuel Kant, *The Metaphysical Principles of Virtue* (Indianapolis: Bobbs-Merrill, 1964), and Aristotle, *Nichomachean Ethics* (Indianapolis: Bobbs-Merrill, 1962), book 8.

20. Cf. Gregory Vlastos, "Justice and Equality," in *Social Justice,* ed. Richard B. Brandt (Englewood Cliffs, NJ: Prentice Hall, Spectrum Books, 1962), pp. 43–44, and idem, "The Individual As an Object of Love in Plato," in *Platonic Studies* (Princeton: Princeton University Press, 1973), pp. 3–34.

21. Cf. Carl Cohen, "Sex, Birth Control and Human Life," *Ethics* 79 (1969): 257. Cohen argues for the intrinsic worth of sexual passion. In "Marriage, Love, and Procreation" (above, n. 13), pp. 197–98, Michael Bayles argues for the intrinsic value of relationships intentionally of indefinite duration, claiming that they are superior to relationships of intentionally limited duration.

22. See Fried (above, n. 16), pp. 23–24, for a formulation of the distinction between inchoate and implicit principles.

23. Bayles (above, n. 13), p. 198, adduces similar considerations in discussing the value of relationships that are intentionally of indefinite duration.

Clearly the analysis by O'Driscoll leaves us with the impression that marriage is a much broader and richer concept than the conventional concept (namely, monogamous heterosexual marriage) on which Kant focused. Not only is marriage a legal contract that specifies rights and duties, it is also a social institution that "regulates (some) sexual activities and (in some way) the production of offspring." Being aware that marriage can take diverse forms ranging from heterosexual to homosexual, from multilateral to polygynous and polyandrous helps us to be more sophisticated as we try to understand the current marriage debate. To those who criticize marriage, we must ask, "To what *form* of marriage are they reacting? Are they rejecting marriage per se as a social institution with its regulative functions? If so, why?" To those who defend marriage, we must ask, "Which *form* are they defending? Does that form merit a privileged position among other forms? If so, why?" And to both critics and defenders of marriage we must ask, "What moral warrant, if any, do they have for the positions they take?"

Before we hear from some critics in considerable detail, let us pause to hear a few words from another twentieth-century philosopher, Paul Taylor, as he provides us with an addendum to O'Driscoll's discussion of marriage as an expression of friendship.

THE NATURE OF FIDELITY ILLUSTRATED

The friendship that O'Driscoll believes marriage can shelter as an intrinsic value involves two persons who (a) regard one another as worthy of respect and trust, (b) are disposed to seek one another's company, (c) are disposed to seek one another's well-being, and (d) have these dispositions because they are fond of one another. To use Kantian terms, friends with these dispositions would, most assuredly, always seek to treat each other as ends, never simply as means. And to use Richard Taylor's terms, such friends in marriage would surely exhibit "fidelity."

Back in 1982, Richard Taylor wrote a rather lengthy treatise titled *Having Love Affairs* (published by Prometheus Books) in which he tried to contribute to human happiness by providing carefully thought-out advice for those who were involved in extramarital love affairs, as well as for those whose spouses were involved in such affairs. Taylor was seeking to preserve generally healthy marriages from the destructive forces that extramarital affairs can so easily unleash. We will be considering the topic of adultery in detail in the next chapter, but for the present, note the following brief description of fidelity taken from Taylor's book. Does it not provide a memorable gloss on O'Driscoll's notion of friendship in marriage?

from Having Love Affairs

RICHARD TAYLOR

. . . the real and literal meaning of fidelity is *faithfulness;* and what thinking person could imagine that there is only one way in which someone can fail to keep faith with another? Faithfulness is a state of one's heart and mind. It is not the mere outward conformity to rules. There are countless ways that it can fail which have nothing whatever to do with sexual intimacy nor, indeed, with outside persons. It can be fulfilled in various ways as well, even in spite of sexual nonexclusiveness, though this is sometimes more difficult to see.

To illustrate this, imagine a man who has long been married to one person, a man who has never lapsed from the rule of strict sexual constancy, nor has he ever appeared to, and who could never be suspected of this by anyone with the slightest knowledge of his character. This man, we shall imagine, assumes without doubt the rightness of his behavior, is scornful of anyone whose standards are less strict, would not permit a violation of this rule by anyone under his own roof, and would consider no circumstances to mitigate the breach of it. So far, so good; he is, it would seem to most persons, a faithful husband.

But now let us add to the picture that this same man, being of a passive nature and having somewhat of an aversion to sex, has never yielded to temptations for the simple reason that he has had no temptations placed before him. His intimacy with his own wife is perfunctory, infrequent, dutiful, and quite devoid of joy for himself or his spouse. They are, in fact, essentially strangers to each other's feelings. In this light, the nobility of his austere ethic begins to appear less impressive, does it not?

But we are not finished with our description. Let us add to the foregoing that these two persons appear to the world as hard workers, but are still quite poor. He works monotonously as a sales clerk in a declining drug store, we can suppose, while she adds what she can to the family's resources by putting in long hours assisting in the local public library. Appearances are misleading, however, for behind this facade of meager resources there are, unbeknown to anyone but the husband, and scrupulously kept secret from his wife, eight savings accounts, which have been built up over the years, each in his name only, and none containing less than thirty thousand dollars. At every opportunity—sometimes by shrewd dealing, often by sheer penuriousness, and always by the most dedicated selfishness—the husband squirrels away more savings, so that by this time the total, augmented by interest compounded over the years, adds up to a most impressive sum.

Has the rule of good faith been breached?

But to continue the description: We now suppose that the long suffering wife of this dreary marriage is stricken, let us say, with cancer, and undergoes a radical mastectomy as the only hope of saving her life. Whereupon whatever small af-fection her husband ever had for her evaporates completely. He turns sullen, distant, and only dimly aware of his wife's presence, finding all the comfort for his life in those growing and secret savings accounts. He never thinks of sexual infidelity, and congratulates himself for this, as well as for other things, such as his thrift.

Finally, let us suppose that his wife has always been a poet of considerable creative power, whose creations have never received the attention they deserve, least of all her husband's, he being only dimly aware that they even exist. Yet they are finally seen and sincerely praised by another sensitive soul having the qualities of mind necessary to appreciate them, and through his encouragement, we shall imagine, she is finally able to have a sense of meaningfulness in her life, hitherto found only meagerly in the lonely creation of poetic beauty. This same new found friend is, moreover, oblivious to the scars of her illness; he cares only for her, and, unlike her husband, his love is sincere, impulsive, passionate, imaginative, and as frequent as conditions allow.

We could expand this story, but the point of it is abundantly clear by now. It is found in answering the question: *Who has been faithless to whom?* In that answer one finds not only the essential meaning of infidelity, which is a betrayal of the promise to love, but also, by contrast, the true meaning of fidelity.

While Kant and Taylor would probably agree with O'Driscoll that the prevailing form of marriage in contemporary Western society, that is to say, monogamous heterosexual marriage, can and frequently does express friendship, others would argue that the social context of contemporary conventional marriage inhibits, if not precludes, the experience of genuine friendship. To such a critique, as exemplified in Marxism, we now turn our attention.

THE MARXIST CRITIQUE ASSESSED

Powerful critiques of marriage have been mounted by those who analyze sexual relations and marriage within their socioeconomic contexts. Such critiques have been presented by Marxists for more than a century and in recent decades by feminists. The feminist critique of sex and love is so important and powerful that we devoted the entire previous chapter to an examination of it. Here we will focus on the Marxist critique. But before doing so, it is important for us to remember that feminism has directed our attention to the powerlessness of women in conventional marriage and to the deleterious consequences that this power imbalance has especially for women but also for men. Feminism builds on, but moves beyond, the Marxist grounding of human oppression in economic realities. For feminists, not all domination, especially gender oppression, has economic origins. Now let us turn to the Marxist critique that provided considerable impetus for the feminist analysis.

Classical Marxism, the Marxism of Marx and Engels, analyzed society in terms of two major facets: the economic substructure and the social superstructure. At the heart of the economic substructure are the relations of production, the way people associate with each other to produce the goods and services of society. Marx discerned that all previous relations of production (with the possible exception of a primitive communism) had one important feature in common: They were relations of exploitation and oppression. An elite who controlled the means of production would exploit and oppress the masses. At the core of the economic substructure of any hitherto existing society was a conflictual relation of the oppressors versus the oppressed.

The social superstructure, the other facet of society, consists of all social constructs, including the educational system, marriage and the family, the prevailing morality, religion, the legal system, and especially the state. Each concrete manifestation of these constructs was developed to express and to safeguard the interests of the economic oppressors. Particularly important is the state, which is the legitimized instrument of social coercion possessing deadly force to ensure that the oppressors are free to pursue their economic exploitation. The key to understanding any social institution, then, is to discern how it serves the interests of the oppressing, ruling class. Accordingly, from the perspective of classical Marxism, the prevailing form of marriage within bourgeois capitalism is to be understood as an instrument reflecting and serving the economic interests, or greed, of bourgeois capitalism.

Marx believed that the struggle between the oppressors and the oppressed, that is, the class struggle, had become simplified during his time into a battle between the two great contending classes: the bourgeois capitalists and the proletarian workers. Marx foresaw the time when the proletarian workers would wrest control of the state from the bourgeoisie and use the coercive power of the state to establish a new form of the relations of production in which there would be no dominating oppressors and exploited oppressed. There would only be one class of workers mutually cooperating to produce the goods and services of society, giving to the productive process in accordance with their abilities and receiving from the productive process in accordance with their needs. On the basis of these new relations of production the entire social superstructure would be revolutionized to express and guarantee the interests of humankind rather than just the interests of an elite ruling class. Indeed, there would now be no ruling class and no class struggle: There would be only the community of humankind working for their mutual benefit. In this new society, the communist society, all social institutions, including marriage, would lose their oppressive character because the foundation of all oppression—economic oppression—would have been replaced by the new "humanizing" socialized relations of production.

For the Marxist, then, marriage whether in capitalistic or communistic societies must be understood in terms of the economic substructure. Raymond A. Belliotti, in his recent book, *Good Sex: Perspectives on Sexual Ethics,* renders us an important service by providing a clear, brief yet sufficiently detailed exposition of the Marxist critique of marriage based on the writings of Marx and Engels. In addition, Belliotti provides an assessment of the Marxist analysis. A somewhat shortened version of Belliotti's discussion is reproduced below.

from Good Sex: Perspectives on Sexual Ethics

RAYMOND A. BELLIOTTI

Classical Marxism conceives the bourgeois family as founded on the unremitting basis of capitalism: private gain. The rhetoric of commodities pervades the family, as women, lacking access to the public sphere, are forced to link themselves to men for financial reasons. Accordingly, sex *within* capitalist marriage is viewed as a form of prostitution. Only the destruction of the capitalist system and the establishment of communism can redeem sexuality by providing the requisite conditions of economic and social equality. . . .

. . . I argue that Marxism embodies an overly sanguine picture of sex within the proletarian class, an astounding naiveté regarding the phenomenon of nonmonogamous sex and its relation to economics, and a crude reductionism which stubbornly traces all oppression to an economic genesis.

Sexual Ethics

The classical Marxist critique of Western sexual relationships is sketched by Karl Marx (1818–1883) and Friedrich Engels (1820–1895) in their *Communist Manifesto* and in Engels's *The Origin of the Family, Private Property, and the State.* The Marxist critique observes that in bourgeois families wives provided cheap domestic labor and socially necessary tasks (e.g., care of children and the elderly) and were expected to produce identifiable and legitimate heirs for the orderly transfer of capitalist property, while husbands provided lodging and board in return. This exchange presumably explained the need for conjugal fidelity on the part of women and provided an economic basis for the existence of male prerogatives within the family.

On what foundation is the present family, the bourgeois family, based? On capital, on private gain. In its completely developed form this family exists only among the bourgeoisie. . . . The bourgeois family will vanish . . . with the vanishing of capital. . . . The bourgeois sees in his wife a mere instrument of production.[1] . . . Remove the economic considerations that now force women to submit to the customary disloyalty of men, and you will place women on an equal footing with men. All present experiences prove that this will tend much more strongly to make men truly monogamous. . . . The supremacy of man in marriage is simply the consequence of his economic superiority and will fall with the abolition of the latter.[2]

Thus, classical Marxism conceives the bourgeois family as founded on the unremitting ground of capitalism: private gain. Because bourgeois women in a capitalist society were excluded from the public workplace, they were forced to tie themselves financially to men. The emotional and personal attachments seemingly at play in marital sex in fact reduce to a series of commercial interactions where purportedly reciprocal contractual benefits are exchanged. Accordingly, the rhetoric of commodities pervades even the inner, private sanctum of capitalist life.

Monogamy arose through the concentration of considerable wealth in one hand—a man's hand—and from the endeavor to bequeath this wealth to the children of this man to the exclusion of all others. This necessitated monogamy on the woman's, but not on the man's part . . . the impending social revolution will reduce this whole care of inheritance to a minimum by changing . . . the means of production into social property . . . with the transformation of the means of production into collective property the monogamous family ceases to be the economic unit of society. The private household changes to a social industry. The care and education of children becomes a public matter.[3]

Engels retained an overly romantic vision of the proletarian marriages of his time, sanguinely insisting that such unions escaped the crass com-

The selection from Raymond A. Belliotti is taken from his book *Good Sex: Perspectives on Sexual Ethics* (Lawrence, Kansas: University Press of Kansas, 1993), pp. 111–119. Used by permission of University Press of Kansas.

mercialism and inequality of bourgeois families. He tended to ignore causes of oppression that were not directly and obviously attributable to economic sources. Because material inequalities were not striking in proletarian families, the amount of private property was insufficient to promote deep interests in inheritance, and proletarian women often worked outside the home, Engels concluded that "the material foundations of male dominance have ceased to exist [in proletarian families]."[4]

His disdain for bourgeois marriage, however, recognized few bounds. He sometimes described women's role in such marriages as akin to slavery and thus a rank below even the downtrodden proletariat wage laborer: "This [bourgeois] marriage of convenience often enough turns into the crassest prostitution—sometimes on both sides, but much more generally on the part of the wife, who differs from the ordinary courtesan only in that she does not hire out her body, like a wageworker, on piecework, but sells it once for all."[5]

Here Engels turns the Christian argument on its head: sex *within* the bourgeois family is a form of prostitution (in a pejorative sense) and is thus immoral because its genesis is the economic exploitation of the deprived by the powerful and its result is the commodification of the attributes constitutive of women's innermost selves: "What is considered a crime for women and entails grave legal and social consequences for them, is considered honorable for men.[6] ... By changing all things into commodities, [capitalist production] dissolved all inherited and traditional relations and replaced time hallowed custom and historical right by purchase and sale, by the 'free contract.'"[7]

Classical Marxism protests, however, that in a capitalist society the notion of "informed consent" is contaminated by the underlying need for economic survival. Reports of "mutual agreement" and "reciprocal benefit" may be illusions emanating from the false consciousness[8] of capitalist materialism.

> In order to make contracts, people must have full freedom over their persons, actions and possessions. They must furthermore be on terms of mutual equality. ... Marriage according to bourgeois conception was a contract, a legal business affair, and the most important one at that, because it decided the weal and woe of body and spirit of two

beings for life. At that time the agreement was formally voluntary. ... But it was only too well known how this consent was obtained and who were really the contracting parties [the families of the respective parties].[9]

The solution to the maladies of the bourgeois family is the socialization of housework, the full inclusion of women in the public arena, and, most important, the dismantling of the capitalist framework which nurtures class division and economic exploitation[10]: "The full freedom of marriage can become general only after all minor economic considerations, that still exert such a powerful influence on the choice of a mate for life, have been removed by the abolition of capitalist production and of the property relations created by it. Then no other motive will remain but mutual fondness."[11]

Engels cannot describe fully the details of sexual relations in a communist society, but he does underscore the preconditions of truly moral sex:

> a race of men who never in their lives have had any occasion for buying with money or other economic means of power the surrender of a woman; a race of women who have never had any occasion for surrendering to any man for any reason but love, or for refusing to surrender to their lover from fear of economic consequences. ... They will follow their own practice and fashion their own public opinion about the individual practice of every person—only this and nothing more.[12]

Engels, however, at times gives the clear impression that people under a communist structure would not be prone to the promiscuity, adultery, and sexual perversions endemic in capitalist regimes: "Since sexlove is exclusive by its very nature—although this exclusiveness is [under capitalism] realized for women alone—marriage founded on sexlove must be monogamous."[13] Because under communism marriage will be founded only on sexlove, it follows that relations will be monogamous because marriage will be founded on pure motivations. Clearly, Engels betrays here an incredible naiveté regarding the phenomenon of love and sexuality. Even under conditions of full economic and social equality and in the presence of mutual "sexlove," neither monogamy nor fidelity is fully ensured. Moreover, talk of the natural exclusivity of sexlove suggests an essentialism[14] that Marxists otherwise diligently avoid and stridently berate when invoked by non-Marxists.

Perhaps we should not make too much of this. It is probably better to downplay Engels's essentialist leanings and to underscore his willingness to concede the open possibilities of sexual relations under communism.[15] In any event, we can fairly describe a classical Marxist approach to sexual relations: sex is morally permissible only if the parties share a measure of equality, are not motivated by (conscious or subconscious) economic needs, and do not wrongly commodify their persons—all of which in turn require the elimination of capitalism.

Exploitation and Sexuality

How does Marxism's analysis of exploitation[16] apply to sexuality? Will eliminating the economic pressures enveloping capitalism ensure that sexual relations will be free and uncoerced? Within capitalism can two people have nonexploitative sexual relations if they are economic equals? Is the possibility of wrongful commodification eliminated once capitalist exchange disintegrates?

Presumably, Marxists suggest that once capitalism falls, or at least by the time communism is in place, many currently fashionable employment contracts and sexual relations will disappear.[17] As the coercive economic forces which underlie such agreements crumble, so too will the agreements themselves. Thus, Marxists take the relevant economic forces as necessary conditions for, among other things, the exercise of certain disapproved sexual relations such as prostitution. The elimination of necessary conditions must, therefore, imply the jettisoning of disapproved sexual relations. The problem with this interpretation is twofold: first, it may saddle Marxism with a substantive (ahistorical?) theory of human nature, which is required for Marxism to project confidently specific human activities once capitalism has evaporated; and second, it reveals Marxism's stark reductionist tendency to trace all social ills to economic causes.

Perhaps a better interpretation would take capitalist economic forces as sufficient conditions for those sexual relations of which Marxists disapprove. Under this interpretation, the presence of capitalist relations of production ensures that certain sexual maladies will occur, but the elimination of capitalism does not guarantee the disappearance of disapproved sexual relations: at the end of capitalism the forms that sexual relations will take is up for grabs. This interpretation comports better with the openness to human possibilities often displayed by Marxism, but has the disadvantage of domesticating somewhat Marxism's critical bite. Under this interpretation, capitalist economics cannot be identified antecedently as the sole cause of dysfunctional sexual relations, nor can socialist relations of production be identified as the magical elixir ensuring cure. This interpretation salvages, however, the Marxist claim that capitalism must be eliminated if economically free and psychologically salutary sex is to be possible.

But what can we do about sex within capitalism? Suppose Vittoria and Dominic are economic equals, both attorneys who hold comparable rank, experience, ability, earnings, and prestige. From a Marxist perspective, both are capitalists of a sort and thus exploiters, and both are attorneys and thus types of economic parasites. But is Dominic an exploiter of Vittoria? Is Vittoria an exploiter of Dominic?

Most non-Marxists would say, of course, that we do not have enough facts to answer adequately such questions. Lacking information about general societal conditions and the specifics of the parties' personalities and dealings, any proffered answers are lame. As for the Marxist, she might be tempted to say that the apparent absence of exploitive economic relations at least holds open the possibility of uncoerced, thus permissible, sex. After all, Engels's cheerful portrayal of proletarian sexual relations was founded on the alleged economic equality of the participants.

But Dominic and Vittoria are not members of the proletarian class, and the answer is not so clear in their case. Their economic equality is not the same as absence of economic power and coercion, as is presumably the case in proletarian relations. Dominic and Vittoria both have a measure of economic power that members of the proletariat lack. Do their comparable economic powers in effect cancel each other out and render their relationships coercion free? Or do two strong economic powers multiply the possibilities for exploitation?

Is economic equality paramount for uncoerced sexual relations? Or is absence of economic power?

Our ability to answer is complicated by the fact that Engels's excoriation of bourgeois marriage is so encompassing and his appreciation of proletarian marriage so naive. Moreover, in the capitalism of his day we would find few Vittorias with economic power and influence comparable to their male partners. With all such disclaimers in mind, I prefer to interpret Marxism as conceding the *possibility* of uncoerced sex between Vittoria and Dominic as long as they truly share a measure of equality, are not motivated by economic needs vis à vis each other, and do not wrongly commodify their persons by treating each other as mere instruments of mutual benefit. This interpretation, to be sure, reneges on the stipulation that the elimination of capitalism is required for the possibility of uncoerced, free sexual relations. Under an advanced form of capitalism unknown to Marx and Engels, however, a form in which some women have comparable economic power to their male partners, there is the possibility for nonexploitive sexual relations.[18]

In any event, the classic Marxist critique of bourgeois sexual relations depends heavily on the notions of exploitation and commodification. It is clear that Marxists take libertarian consent and mutual use as insufficient to vitiate exploitation. Libertarian notions of consent ignore pernicious class divisions and economic inequalities, while mutual use—each party knowingly and reciprocally using the other for personal benefit—multiplies, rather than erases, impermissible exploitation. The Marxist aspiration to a communism which transforms and transcends the capitalist polarities of individuality and community precludes the use of one human by another.

Reciprocity and Mutuality

It is therefore somewhat misleading to talk of Marxist sexual analysis in terms of reciprocal exchanges of benefits. Reciprocity connotes equal sacrifices or transfer of equal benefits. As such, reciprocity invokes a type of quantification that conjures images of libertarian contractualism. Marxist sexual relations are better portrayed as presupposing equality as an antecedent condition of mutuality, where the parties give and accept what they need without regard for the aggregate amount of benefits and burdens exchanged.[19]

Pious paeans to mutuality must always be carefully scrutinized, however, because where inequalities precede a relationship, the call for mutuality almost always results in the subordination of the socially disadvantaged party. That is why full social equality must be a prerequisite for mutuality, a prerequisite that is obviously a major obstacle. Still, mutuality may well embody our highest hopes for sexual relations.[20]

By highlighting social context, Marxism astutely points out that sexual relations must not be abstracted from the totality of our lives. Marxism portrays the ills of sexual relations as resulting not from wrongful acts by individuals, but from the political and social institutions allied with a particular economic structure, capitalism. But the doctrine tends to focus myopically on the relations of economic production in a society. Perhaps the most glaring omission in Marxism's analysis of sexual relations is one that generally pervades its argument: the failure to recognize clearly that economic class division is not the sole source of human oppression. By reducing the cause of all social maladies to wrongful productive relations and prescribing the transformation of capitalist economic arrangements as the omnipotent cure, Marxism leaves itself vulnerable to charges that it ignores other sources of human oppression such as racism, sexism, religious intolerance, and age discrimination. If, as one might suspect, these various forms of oppression cannot all be traced to one specific cause, then it is unlikely that economic reforms, which may be at the root of some forms, can remedy all social ills. Thus, the magic elixir of political revolution may be less dynamic than Marxists imagine.

Moreover, our observation of the actual practices of those countries purporting to be socialist confirms that Marxism's crude reductionism is faulty. Socialist regimes in practice have fallen far short of gender-equal utopias.[21] In this same vein, Marxism ignored the sexual division of labor: the biological function of women as childbearers and their social function as childrearers. The sexual division of labor is reflected in the traditional distinction between the public sphere of important social activity, the realm of male prerogatives; and the private sphere of essential but less highly regarded and compensated family activity, the realm of female performance. The abolition of private ownership of the means of production may thus be insufficient to liberate women from male oppression.[22] Accordingly, some feminists, denying the analogy of husband-wife to employer-employee, would argue that the primary source of women's oppression is not capitalism, but men. These thinkers highlight the differences in the alienation and exploitation accompanying traditional Western marriage and the alienation and exploitation accompanying capitalist employment.[23]

Notes

1. Friedrich Engels and Karl Marx, *Communist Manifesto,* ed. Frederick Engels, trans. (Chicago: Charles H. Kerr and Company, 1906). Excerpts reprinted in *Sexual Love and Western Morality,* ed. D. P. Verene (New York: Harper and Row, 1972), 194.

For Marxism generally, see Karl Marx, *Economic and Philosophical Manuscripts* (1844); Karl Marx, "Excerpts from James Mill's Elements of Political Economy" (1844) in *Writings of the Young Marx on Philosophy and Society,* ed. L. D. Easton and K. Guddat (Garden City, NY: Doubleday, 1967); Richard Schmitt, *Marx and Engels: A Critical Reconstruction* (Boulder, CO: Westview Press, 1987); and Raymond A. Belliotti, *Justifying Law* (Philadelphia: Temple University Press, 1992), 145–161.

2. Engels and Marx, *Communist Manifesto,* in Verene, *Sexual Love,* 204.

3. Ibid., 196–197.

4. Passage quoted in Michele Barrett, *Women's Oppression Today* (London: Verso, 1980), 49.

5. Friedrich Engels, *The Origin of the Family, Private Property and the State* (New York: International Publishers, 1972), 79.

6. Engels and Marx, *Communist Manifesto,* in Verene, *Sexual Love,* 196.

7. Ibid., 201.

8. Engels explicitly used the term "false consciousness" in his letter to Franz Mehring, July 14, 1893, in Marx and Engels, *Selected Works* (Moscow: Progress Publishers, 1968), 690. "Ideology is a process accomplished by the so-called thinker consciously, it is true, but with a false consciousness. The real motive forces impelling him remain unknown to him; otherwise it simply would not be an ideological process. Hence he imagines false or seeming motive forces." Some theorists claim that Marx never explicitly used the term "false consciousness," but they admit that no substantive implications follow if they are correct. See, for example, Martin Seliger, *The Marxist Conception of Ideology* (Cambridge: Cambridge University Press, 1977), 30–31.

The term "false consciousness" suggests an inverted representation of reality that is systematically misleading and socially mystifying, in that it misrepresents what are in fact the interests of the ruling class as the natural, common interests of society. This misrepresentation, which flows from superstructure, justifies, stabilizes, and reinforces the social and political status quo. A person who holds a view resulting from false consciousness is unaware of the underlying motives and causal processes by which she came to accept that view.

The term "false consciousness" is used specifically when oppressed classes adopt the dominant prevailing ideology and perceptual prism. When these dominant ideas do not truly correspond to the experience of the oppressed classes, ideological distortion occurs. See, for example, Jorge Larrain, "Ideology," in *A Dictionary of Marxist Thought,* ed. Thomas Bottomore (Cambridge, MA: Harvard University Press, 1983), 218–220; Hugh Collins, *Marxism and Law* (Oxford: Oxford University Press, 1984), 40; R. G. Peffer, "Morality and the Marxist Concept of Ideology," in *Marx and Morality,* ed. K. Nielsen and S. C. Patten (Guelph, Ont.: Canadian Association for Publishing Philosophy, 1981), 67–91.

Such distortions have a functional explanation: They legitimate the ruling class's monopoly on power by depicting current social relations as natural, appropriate, or inevitable. In this fashion, the interests of the ruling class misrepresent themselves as universal human interests.

A belief is ideological only if it would perish upon the revelation of its causal origins. Because the relationship between false consciousness and nonideological perception cannot be interpreted validly as a species of the general relationship between illusion and truth, ideological distortion cannot be overcome solely by intellectual criticism. Ideological distortion is not the opposite of truth, but is, instead, a narrow or one-sided rendering of truth that functions to preserve the practices of the ruling class.

Accordingly, false consciousness dissolves only when the internal contradictions of an economic system—especially evident when relations of production can no longer efficiently make use of developing technology—are *practically* resolved.

Marxism is not committed to the simplistic position that all members of subordinate classes, or all subjects generally, are *necessarily* victims of the mystifying effects of ideological distortion. It should be obvious that at least some (and perhaps all) of the people some of the time will be able to pierce the smokescreen of false consciousness.

Certainly, certain views may be the unconscious, conditioned reflection of economic and social oppression, and subordinate classes often become accomplices in their own torment by internalizing the very dominant ideologies which contributed to their mistreatment. But if applied relentlessly, the notion of false consciousness loses much of its critical bite. If the notion is advanced as a nonrefutable thesis, if all denials of Marxism are taken to be affirmations of the doctrine of false consciousness, then the notion of false consciousness is trivial. Any subjective report that denies any basic Marxist conclusion seems too easily and automatically to stigmatize itself. Marxists dismiss the content of a view because it allegedly can be explained by its determinants. Moreover, such a posture demeans the experiences, not merely the ideologies, of Marxism's philosophical rivals. In fact, subjective reports of one's inner condition or of one's ideological commitments are neither incorrigibly true nor self-refuting. The challenge for a Marxist is to delineate, without begging the question, under what circumstances such reports and commitments do and do not reflect veridical perceptions correlated to wider experience. Thus, Marxism cannot automatically deny the veracity of a perception or experience which does not support the conclusions of Marxism. On the other hand, critics of Marxism cannot automatically accept the veracity of such perceptions and experiences as evidence refuting Marxist conclusions.

9. Engels and Marx, *Communist Manifesto,* in Verene, *Sexual Love,* 201–202.

10. In its most general Kantian-Marxist sense, "exploitation" occurs when someone uses another person merely as an object for her own benefit without regard for the humanity of that person. In its more particular Marxist sense, exploitation occurs when one class, the proletariat, produces a surplus whose use is controlled by another class, the capitalists. See, for example, Karl Marx and Friedrich Engels, *The German Ideology* (1845); Karl Marx, *Capital,* vol. I (1867); Peter Singer, *Marx* (Oxford: Oxford University Press, 1980), 25–34.

Moreover, the capitalist economic mode differs from other economic modes in that this kind of exploitation occurs without the use of explicit duress, physical threat, or other noneconomic force. It is through the capitalists' vastly superior economic bargaining power over workers, their ownership of the means of production, and the lack of real alternatives for workers that exploitation flourishes in a capitalist regime. Finally, capitalism, shrouded by its pretensions to neutral, economic processes, is especially pernicious because it can mask the nature and effects of the exploitation of workers (ibid.).

Capitalists exploit workers by siphoning the surplus value produced by their labor. Capitalists purchase workers' labor power at its value, which is equivalent to a subsistence wage, and sell products at their value. Because the value workers create is greater than the value of labor power itself, surplus value results. The exploitive nature of the relationship is reflected in the fact that workers do not receive wages equivalent to the value they produce. (Marx, *Capital,* vol. 1; Schmitt, *Marx and Engels,* 74–85; David Conway, *A Farewell to Marx* [Harmondsworth, Eng.: Penguin, 1987], 98–105; Singer, *Marx,* 23–25, 50–54; and John Elster, *An Introduction to Karl Marx* [Cambridge: Cambridge University Press, 1986], 81–101).

Workers' labor is "forced" in the sense that only limited and equally debilitating alternatives are available for workers seeking to satisfy their subsistence requirements (ibid.).

Despite the considerable dispute over precisely which set of necessary and sufficient conditions captures the meaning of Marxist exploitation, the following elements are relevant: workers benefit capitalists; capitalists economically force, in the relevant Marxist sense of that term, workers to supply that benefit; and capitalists wrongfully fail to supply reciprocal benefits to workers. See, for example, Conway, *Farewell to*

Marx, 98–105; Allen Buchanan, *Marx and Justice* (Totowa, NJ: Rowman and Littlefield, 1982), chap. 5; Allen Wood, "The Marxian Critique of Justice," in *Marx, Justice, and History,* ed. M. Cohen, T. Nagel, and T. Scanlon, (Princeton, NJ: Princeton University Press, 1980), 3–41.

11. Engels and Marx, *Communist Manifesto,* in Verene, *Sexual Love,* 203.

12. Ibid., 205.

13. Ibid., 203.

14. Although Marx was not a proponent of a fixed, universal human nature, he viewed alienation as estrangement from historically created human possibilities. His minimalist view of species-being included the conviction that human fulfillment is intimately connected with imaginative, unshackled use of productive capacities. Labor is a distinctively human activity and possesses central normative significance. Humans presumably shape their social world and forge their personal identities through interaction with their material world and its dominant productive process. It is only through free and creative activity that a person realizes unalienated being. See, for example, Marx, *Economic and Philosophical Manuscripts* (1844); Conway, *Farewell to Marx,* 34–41.

For Marx, the conditions and reality of alienation are not dependent on workers' subjective reports. Regardless of whether workers self-consciously announce the requisite feelings of estrangement, the objective social condition of the proletariat is permeated with alienation. See, for example, Elster, *Karl Marx,* 81–101.

Conversely, nonalienated labor honors our species-being because it is freely chosen, it is collectively designed by workers without a hierarchy of power, it involves creativity and joy, its product is socially useful and appreciated by consumers, and the process of its production effaces the distinction between work and play. The allocation of the products of nonalienated labor is based on need and all surplus is a community, not individual or capitalistic, resource. It is clear that fully nonalienated labor can occur only within a communist framework which abrogates commodity relations among humans, and that Marx employs a "thin" (nonessentialist) theory of human nature.

15. Alan Soble describes the situation well: "Those who claim to know the details of human nature have a firm idea where people are headed and what human behavior will look like when human beings are free, but they have difficulty showing that this 'knowledge' is not mere ideology, simply reproduces dominant values, or flies off into utopianism. On the other hand, those who do not claim to know the details of human nature do not have to worry about putting an epistemological foot in the mouth. But they have very little to say about what human beings will be like when they are free; furthermore, whatever human desires do turn out to be, the agnostic is committed to accept them just because they are the desires of free people. The latter is Engels's preferred view" (*Pornography* [New Haven, CT: Yale University Press, 1986], 43).

16. See notes 10 and 17.

17. One of Marx's most intriguing and baffling pronouncements concerns the relationship between a society's economic

substructure ("the base") and its ideological superstructure ("the superstructure"). A society's mode of economic production includes its forces of production (natural resources, instruments and means of production, workers and their skills, raw materials) and its relations of production (the formal and informal organization of relations among people, or among people and commodities, in the productive process). The base consists, strictly speaking, of the relations of production. The superstructure consists of our political and legal institutions, and our forms of social consciousness (what we think, believe, how we understand and experience the world).

For Marx, the development of the forces of production results in changes in the relations of production. Moreover, there will come a time when the existing relations of production no longer effectively and efficiently allow the growth of the productive forces. This internal contradiction divides society and will result in revolution and the fall of the obsolete set of productive relations. See, for example, Schmitt, *Marx and Engels,* 30.

New relations of production will triumph because they have the capacity to facilitate the continued growth of society's productive forces. Thus, Marx provides an economic explanation for political revolution.

18. I have, of course, ignored here the numerous *noneconomic* sources of oppression that must be factored into any refined analysis of the Dominic-Vittoria relationship. Because of this I can talk only of the *possibility* that their relationship is noncoercive.

19. "By [mutuality] we mean a relation in which neither person uses the other, neither sees the other primarily as a means to the satisfaction of his or her own self-interest. The relation is genuinely mutual; it is only achievable together, and consciously . . . [It is] a relation in which neither the interest or self nor the interest of the other are pitted against one another, because for both persons, cooperation simultaneously replaces competition" (Virginia Held, "Marx, Sex, and the Transformation of Society," *Philosophical Forum* 5 [1973]:172–173).

20. "Genuine mutual consideration between [parties] making love is neither the joint pursuit of self-satisfaction nor the joint bestowing of charity, but the mutual pursuit of and awareness of mutual feelings and values" (ibid., 173).

21. "[The] practice, of course, in those countries claiming to base practice on the work of [Marxists] is almost as repressively sexist as in capitalist countries . . . the record of socialism in even being aware of, much less in adequately addressing itself to, the distinctive problems and concerns of women has made of socialism so far almost as dismal a social movement for women as its predecessors and competitors. And the judgment may be applied to both social democratic and communist movements and governments" (ibid., 170–171.).

22. "The sexual division of labor, rooted in the institution of heterosexuality is at least as responsible for women's oppression as is the institution of private property— a point that Engels failed to address and that led him to valorize the proletariat family . . . over the bourgeois family" (Rosemarie Tong, *Feminist Thought* [Boulder, CO: Westview Press, 1989], 51).

23. Ibid., 63.

The Marx of *The Communist Manifesto* and *Das Kapital* did not present communism as a moral solution to an immoral society. Instead, he and Engels represented communism as the inevitable goal toward which socioeconomic forces operating with inexorable necessity were driving humankind. Yet does not even a casual glance at the material presented by Belliotti suggest that Marx and Engels morally condemned capitalism in general and bourgeois marriage in particular? But what is the foundation upon which they based their moral judgments? On the basis of a number of manuscripts unpublished during Marx's lifetime, especially the *Economic and Philosophic Manuscripts of 1844,* a case can be made that Marx was a moral consequentialist who condemned bourgeois capitalism because of what it did to humankind, because its outcomes fell far short of the ideal Marx cherished for humankind. Marx embraced an ideal picture of human beings whose distinctive attribute is free, conscious activity and whose destiny is to express this activity in multifaceted creation, in creative productivity that binds humans to each other in a cooperative society that respects human individuality. In such a community, human futures would be wide open: Persons would be free, for example, to fish in the morning, hunt in the afternoon, and write poetry like a Goethe in the evening. Instead of providing the openness for humans to pursue multifaceted creative activity, bourgeois capitalism constricted human freedom by forcing workers to become mere appendages of machines in factories. Marx adopted the powerful Hegelian concept of alienation to describe the depravation, domination, and reification of the human being he discerned within capitalism. Eventually, Marx traced the origin of this alienation to economic exploitation that was set and kept in motion by human greed. Lurking behind classical Marxism's socioeconomic analysis of capitalism and bourgeois marriage, then, is this normative ideal of the human being as a multifaceted creator. The socioeconomic analysis explained why bourgeois marriage had the shape it had. The normative ideal provided the basis for the moral condemnation of that shape.

While Belliotti praises Marxism's socioeconomic analysis for drawing our attention to the social context of sexual relations and marriage, he chastises Marx for his crude economic reductionism. In other words, is not classical Marxism being overly simplistic in suggesting that all social constructs, including marriage, can be reduced to expressions of and safeguards for the interests of the economic oppressors? Are not social institutions far more complex entities than that? Is all human oppression really traceable to economic oppression? Are not Marx and Engels exhibiting considerable naivete concerning the relationship between the economic substructure and the social superstructure?

While Marxism's socioeconomic analysis might be faulted as naive and simplistic, can its moral condemnation of capitalism and bourgeois marriage similarly be faulted? Is Marx's normative ideal of the human as a multifaceted creator naive and simplistic? Was that ideal merely spun out of Marx's head, the product of wishful thinking? If so, would that render his ideal trivial? Or was that ideal rooted in actual capacities he discerned, perhaps ever so faintly, in living human beings? If so, with what warrant can he move from saying that the ideal is mirrored faintly in contemporary humans to claiming that this ideal ought to be pursued and should constitute the yardstick by which we assess the moral progress of humankind? After all, would it not be possible to see other ideals (such as the ideal of creative cruelty) mirrored however faintly in contemporary humans? Providing warrant for a moral ideal is no easy task.

While classical Marxism condemned bourgeois marriage, it did not reject marriage per se. Indeed, Engels we have seen glorified proletarian marriage (to an extreme, says Belliotti) and also affirmed monogamy. And Marx, biographers tell us, enjoyed a lifelong, satisfying marriage to Jenny von Westphalen even though they were frequently on the verge of pauperism.

Has the emergence of the postcommunist era rendered the Marxist critique of bourgeois marriage impotent and irrelevant? Perhaps. But if the Marxist critique has been incorporated into the wider critique offered by feminism, as some philosophers suggest, then can we legitimately dismiss the Marxist critique as completely passé?

THE CASE FOR GAY MARRIAGE PRESENTED

Earlier in this chapter Lyla O'Driscoll pointed out that marriage can take diverse forms ranging from heterosexual to homosexual, from multilateral to polygynous and polyandrous. Is her claim correct? Does, for example, a homosexual relationship really qualify for the "marriage" designation? If one says that it does, what case can be made to back up that claim?

Frederick Elliston attempts to provide just such a case. He does not attack conventional marriage per se. Rather, he attacks the notion that monogamous heterosexual marriage is the only morally warranted (and hence legitimately legal) form of marriage. Elliston mounts his case in two stages. First, he attacks eight different considerations that could be invoked in an attempt to justify ethically the practice of denying homosexuals the legal right to marry. Second, he presents three arguments to justify morally the legalization of homosexual marriages. His case is neatly organized and carefully crafted. But is it convincing? To that question we will return after we review his case.

from Gay Marriage

FREDERICK ELLISTON

In this essay, I want to examine one battle that has been fought and lost: the homosexual's right to marry. In 1971, two men petitioned the Minnesota Supreme Court to compel the state to grant them a marriage license.[1] The court denied their petition and the following year the United States Supreme Court dismissed their appeal.[2] My examination will not be a legal one tracing out the cases and precedents for their rights, but rather a moral one. Are there any sound ethical arguments for denying homosexuals the legal right to marry? I shall assess eight considerations that could be invoked to provide an ethical justification for the denial of such a legal right: 1) the historical function of marriage within our society; 2) the religious perspective on the very nature of marriage; 3) the suffering of innocent children; 4) the argument from shared values; 5) the law as promoter of values; 6) the argument from perversion implicit in most sodomy statutes; 7) the worry: What if everybody did that?; and 8) the "slippery slope" appeal—What next? I shall try to show that none of these arguments provides adequate moral grounds for outlawing homosexual marriages. I shall then offer three positive considerations in defense of legalization—appeals to freedom, love, and justice.

I

The Semantic Issue

Let me begin by defining a homosexual marriage. Obviously what is at issue is not the legal right of a latent homosexual to marry someone of the opposite sex. Nor is it a question of denying a practicing homosexual such a right. Though acting on such a sexual preference may constitute adultery and be grounds for divorce, it is not as such an obstacle to successful application for a marriage license. What is at stake in gay marriages is the legal right of two people of the same sex to marry one another.

For economy's sake I shall refer to the homosexual as male. But the term refers to 'homo' in the sense of *same,* as in the word "homogeneous" meaning same consistency. Thus the lesbian is a homosexual also, and the arguments to defend the right of two gay men to marry apply to two women, with slight variations.[3]

In most cases the law does not specify that the members of a marriage must be of the opposite sex. Such an assumption was, and to some extent still is, so pervasive that it was not thought necessary to build it into the law. But legal appeals of the state's refusal to grant a marriage license simply because the partners were of the same sex have failed (as documented above in footnotes one and two): heterosexuality is taken as a necessary condition of matrimony by those who enforce the law, though the law typically fails to stipulate this requirement.

One could argue that even if the state fails to stipulate this condition, its oversight is inconsequential: heterosexuality is part of the meaning of marriage in our society and monogamy is a relationship between a husband and wife, a male and female. This strategy to solve the problem by defining it out of existence is misconceived, but it does call for a careful analysis of the meaning of monogamy.

Quite literally "monogamy" means one spouse. It is a form of marriage that limits the number of participants to two. To enter into this relationship is typically to sign a legal contract.[4] No further contracts can be signed until earlier contracts have been dissolved by the state: to fail to do so is bigamy. Unlike most contracts, this one cannot be dissolved by mutual consent: though both parties may agree to a divorce, the state may in theory (though less frequently in practice) refuse to grant one, unless it is convinced that the relationship has been irreparably destroyed. The state further regulates the signing of this contract by requiring a license that is granted only if the couple satisfies several conditions—minimal age, no direct family and/or blood ties, physical and psychological health (i.e., blood tests are required, severely retarded people and those serving life sentences frequently cannot marry).

Heterosexuality is not part of the definition of monogamy. Whether or not it ought to be is better seen not as a semantic issue but as a moral one. Otherwise the problem is reduced to one of meaning, a verbal quibble that seems impossible to resolve short of linguistic fiat or an appeal to vague intuitions.[5] To keep the issue where it belongs— on the moral turf—a neutral definition of monogamy should be employed that does not beg the question of the legitimacy of homosexual marriages by loading the semantic dice at the outset. Such a minimal definition would describe monogamy as a form of marriage that limits the number of participants who may legally enter this contractual relation to two. As such, monogamy stands in contrast to other forms of marriage primarily in terms of the number of participants: polygamy allows for several husbands or wives. Should homosexuals be denied a license to enter into our form of marriage? Let me turn first to a historical justification of a negative response.

II

1. The Historical Function of Monogamy

Marriage—by which I shall henceforth mean monogamy as the form of marriage most widely practiced in our Western culture—has served a variety of functions in the past: to consolidate political power, to form international alliances, to enable men to escape the draft, to provide citizenship for bettering employment prospects, to legalize copulation, to regulate the transfer of property from one generation to another, and to legitimize offspring. The last is probably still one of the most important and prevalent functions of marriage today: it provides a secure and loving context for having and raising children.

Clearly homosexual acts are nonreproductive.

No one will ever get pregnant by engaging in sex exclusively with someone of the same sex. Accordingly, one of the objections against legalizing homosexual marriages is that such an arrangement violates one of the primary functions of marriage. People marry in order to raise a family, but couples who are exclusively homosexual will never have children. Legalizing such pairings jeopardizes the traditional function of the institution of marriage. It denies the state's interest in protecting the welfare of children by according heterosexual marriages a privileged legal position.

This argument is weak for two reasons. First the principle on which it rests cuts against too many other widely and rightly accepted social practices. If we are to deny a marriage license to homosexuals on the grounds that they will never have children, then we should also deny it in the case of the professional couple who have decided to remain childless for the sake of their careers. Admittedly, they could have children but the homosexual couple never will. But it is impossible to see a significant difference if they are determined and abortion is legal.

Or consider a marriage when the husband is sterile, and the state knows it. Should the couple be denied a marriage license on the grounds that they will never fulfil the proper historical function of holy matrimony by having children? To do so would be wrong, and by analogy, I suggest, it is equally wrong for two men to be denied a marriage license for this reason and this reason alone.

Some may object that this argument by analogy collapses because it depends on the contingency of the husband's infertility and the state's knowledge of it. But consider, then, a situation where the woman is past menopause. Should the state deny a marriage license to elderly couples, say over sixty-five years of age, where it is virtually certain that the couple will remain childless? I think to do so would be wrong, and that most people would agree. Consequently, unless we are prepared to deny a marriage license to elderly and sterile couples, it is inconsistent and hence immoral to refuse the gay couple—at least on this ground alone.

Second, I think this historical argument is anachronistic. Recent contraceptive technology has provided control over fertility that makes procreation an option many can and do reject, who still choose to marry for a variety of other good reasons. The value of companionship, intimacy, social approval and support are widely recognized and marriage plays a key role in promoting and protecting these. But these are some of the same good reasons gay couples want to marry. They wish to solidify a relation with a 'significant other' whom each cares for deeply. They seek the social support that will safeguard their relationship and foster its growth. Many of the values that make marriage attractive to heterosexual, professional couples who intend to remain childless, or to elderly couples who must remain childless make it attractive to gay couples too. . . .

2. The Religious Argument

Roman Catholicism asserts that conjugal love—sex within marriage—is inseparably and necessarily tied to procreation. The argument in defense of this assertion is put forth in "Humanae Vitae"[6] and recently reaffirmed, that marriage has two inseparable functions—spiritual union and procreation of children.

This papal encyclical issued by Pope Paul in 1968 is still binding on devout and faithful Catholics. It is primarily a condemnation of contraception within marriage. Yet the arguments provided suffice to show why the Church would not sanction homosexual marriages either. Sex within marriage is acceptable and proper only insofar as each conjugal act serves two simultaneous purposes: first to unite the husband and wife in bonds of love and affection, and second to provide for the creation and transmission of new life. Insofar as the pill, I.U.D. (or Intrauterine Device), condoms, or other contraceptive devices intrude into the divinely sanctioned natural process of reproduction, they violate the second condition of moral sex, and hence are condemned as sinful by the Church. Sexual practices other than penile-vaginal intercourse—at least if they serve as a substitute rather than supplement—would also violate the natural function of sex, and would therefore be equally condemned. Clearly homosexual practices fall into this category.[7] To marry a homosexual would be to approve of sin.

Carl Cohen has offered one of the most direct and powerful attacks on this logic.[8] He contends that the inseparability premise is unsupported by rational argument and relies instead on religious fiat, that it cannot be defended by appeal to scriptures, that it contradicts the Church's own emphasis on love and its acceptance of the rhythm method, and that it betrays an unwholesome attitude toward sex as dirty and not valuable in its own right. I find his elaboration of these points convincing though I do not wish to rehearse it here. To the extent that his attack weakens the inseparability premise, it weakens Catholic opposition to homosexual marriages. The crux of the Catholic position, however, is a view of the natural function of sex as reproduction, which I shall address later.

Let me say that whatever the merits of the Catholic position, it is inconclusive as a reason for outlawing gay marriages. For why should all of society be bound by the special teachings of one religious sect? . . . No sect has the moral right to use the law to impose its beliefs on others. The well-established doctrine of separation of religion and state prohibits the simplistic inference from that which is sinful to that which is illegal. . . .

3. The Welfare of Children

Some people may fear that homosexual marriages could have harmful consequences, not so much for the family as an institution but for children who are its weakest and most vulnerable members. The innocent offspring of homosexuals who marry may suffer from social ridicule and confusion about their sexual identity and social roles. In order to protect the welfare of children, homosexual marriages must be illegal. Let us assess this stance by examining carefully the ways the problem of harming innocent children might arise.

First, the children could be the result of a previous marriage. So the question is: Would they be better or worse off if their mother should 'marry' another woman, or their father another man?

In part the question is an empirical one, and could be answered definitively only through a social experiment: legalize gay marriages, take a representative sample of the children of such marriages, and compare them to a control group in terms of self-esteem, personal adjustment, satisfactory social relations, career successes, delinquency or deviance, and other measures of self-worth. Ideally, the study would be longitudinal and would control for all outside factors. Less definitive data could be extrapolated through a comparison of the children of gay and straight couples. But it would then be impossible to determine how much the illegality of homosexuality and homosexual marriages affected the outcome.

Behind the question is a worry: What will happen to innocent children? One way to diminish the worry is to recognize the protective mechanisms we already have. Safeguards now exist in the form of the courts who decide, and can re-decide, custody of the children of divorced parents based on the best interests of the child. In a particular case if the court were convinced that the children would be disadvantaged by the homosexual marriage of a gay parent, the judge could reassign custody. Each case could be decided on its merits by an independent arbiter, and if homosexual marriages were harmful to children, the children could be protected.

Second, the situation could arise through the death of one spouse and the remarriage of the parent. In cases where the first parent and spouse has died, the court can effectively do little to prevent the remaining parent from taking a gay lover. The question in this situation is: Would the children be better off if the parent had the legal option to marry a gay lover? Without this option, the parent has two choices: to continue the doubly illicit affair, or to end it. In view of what many straight people will risk for sex and love, a significant number would probably choose the first option nevertheless. Then the question is: Would the children be better off if the homosexual affair is not secretive and clandestine but open, recognized, and legitimate? My own view is that the answer to this question is yes. The deception, distrust, and dishonesty that are the natural concomitants of illicit conduct, sexual or not, are disruptive in any case, and when the relationship undermined holds between a parent and child, it is inevitably damaging to the child. The statistics on delinquent children and broken homes bear ample testimony to this fact. Accordingly, the legalization of gay marriages would thus remove the social stigma mistakenly attached to innocent children and would promote the interests of the innocent.

Moreover, it is again worth noting that there is already a mechanism in place to protect the interests of children: the courts. Where children are abused, neglected, or endangered, a judge can remove them from the home and take them away from the parents. If it were true that a homosexual relationship were so harmful to the interests of the child as to endanger his/her physical or mental health, then the courts could intervene. But the contingent connection between the welfare of the child and the sexual preferences of the parent needs to be established, and to be established in each case. There is ample evidence that excessive drinking, drug abuse, and, indeed, chronic unemployment and poverty are harmful to the welfare of children, but their presence in the home does not automatically justify legal intervention by the courts to remove the children. Neither should the presence of homosexuality.

Third, the situation of children living with a gay married couple could arise through adoption. Let me first insist that this is another issue entirely. Legalizing gay marriages does not logically entail granting gay couples the right to adopt children. One can support the former and oppose the latter, yet still be consistent. Moreover, the first is exclusively a legal question and the second is more a matter of social policy. It depends partly on the practices of private adoption agencies. Secondly, the problem is miniscule: few gay couples want to adopt children to begin with, and it is difficult for many straight couples to find children to adopt. Finally, I would point out that the private adoption agency can legally form its own *ad hoc* judgment about allowing any couple to adopt children. My own view is that some gay couples would make better parents than some heterosexual couples, but I think this decision should be left to competent professionals.

Lastly, the situation of children within a homosexual marriage relationship could arise through artificial insemination by a donor, a practice that is much debated among a significant but small minority of lesbian couples. Here again I think that the legalization of gay marriages is a separate issue, that this situation rarely occurs, and that it should be decided by professionals—i.e., the doctor who would perform the operation. I think that a woman who would go to the trouble and expense of becoming pregnant in this way demonstrates sufficient dedication to parenthood that she ought to be given the freedom of choice. But even if society were to decide against her (and could somehow enforce its decision), it could still consistently support her right to marry the person of her choice.

The suffering of innocent children is a serious issue. But it is difficult to formulate a utilitarian calculus about their long-term interests. Moreover what children stand to lose is as dependent on society's attitudes as the sexual orientation of their parents.

Consider an analogy with interracial marriages. Some argued that the marriage of a white man and black woman (or vice versa) should not be permitted, because innocent children suffer. They suffer social ridicule, ostracism, reprobation, and rejection. But what was the source of their suffering? It was not interracial marriage but racism—the unfair and unwarranted discrimination against someone on the basis of their race.

Similarly, to discriminate against someone on the basis of sex, the sex of their partner, is unwarranted. In the case of both interracial and homosexual marriage, the source of the harm to children is social prejudice. These prejudices are only perpetuated by social and legal disapproval of unconventional marriages. It is indeed unfortunate if the helpless and guiltless young must bear the burden of combating bigotry among their elders. But future generations of children and adults may reap the benefits of their pain.

If one could dispense with social biases against gays, a remaining objection would be the lack of role models. How could a gay couple provide a necessary socialization into the appropriate behavior for a boy or a girl, a man or a woman?

Single parents face the same problem of raising children of the opposite sex, and often manage to do so quite well. Moreover, we do not (any longer, at least) forbid them to divorce, or require them to remarry or to give up their children.

If, indeed, role models are desirable, a gay couple could still ensure that their children would learn them from other sources—e.g., friends, television, schools, the church, neighbors, and so forth. The actual parents are not the sole source, or always the most effective or appropriate one. It is for this reason that some children with very bad parents are able to be fine parents themselves. . . .

4. The Argument from Shared Morality

[Lord Patrick] Devlin has provided two general arguments to justify society's use of the law to enforce its moral code.[10] Though addressed more specifically to the recommendations of the Wolfenden Committee on homosexuality and prostitution, and the classic liberal principle on which it was based, his arguments can apply to society's refusal to legalize homosexual marriages.

He offers two arguments, the second of which has attracted more philosophical attention. His first is an *a posteriori* argument to establish that the law is and ought to be based on society's morals. Citing the refusal of courts to force payment of gambling debts or to accord legal status to murder contracts, he contends that the law could not function in fact if it were not based on a moral consensus. This consensus, where it exists, is not only necessary but sufficient to justify the law as it operates in our society today. His second argument, an *a priori* one, appeals more to the nature of society as a group of individuals bound together by their shared values. A threat to their common code is a threat to their existence as a society, or at least it could be. The right of society to defend itself entails the right to enforce its moral code.

This right is not an obligation, as Devlin realizes. Thus, he must confront the question: When should this right be exercised? Four elastic principles demarcate his answer. First, individual freedom of choice should be accorded maximum respect. Second, the law should be slow to act, since once a moral consensus has been enshrined in a legal statute it is difficult to change. Third, privacy should be respected. And fourth, the law should be concerned with minimal, not maximal, moral transgressions. As a test of society's ability to withstand deviant behavior, Devlin appeals to a combination of intense feelings of intolerance, indignation, and disgust. At concert pitch, they mark the breaking point of the moral code, the point at which legal intervention is warranted.

If Devlin's argument were sound and if the thought of homosexual marriages produced unanimous feelings of intolerance, indignation, and disgust in twelve randomly chosen people, then society's present stance on homosexual marriages would be warranted.[11] But, in the first place, I doubt that such emotional uniformity can be found in our pluralistic society. Though many people would not choose a homosexual marriage for themselves or their children, a few have done so and even larger numbers are prepared to accept it with equanimity. Accordingly, the emotional and moral consensus on which Devlin might defend current statutes does not exist. Some people approve of homosexual marriages and some disapprove, and this admixture of sentiment leaves the law without a social foundation.

But even if the consensus of feeling Devlin requires could be achieved, it would not provide a sound basis for either morality or the law. One could still ask: Are people misinformed about the meaning of homosexuality or the reality of homosexual lives? Are these individuals simply scapegoats for other feelings that the larger community lacks the courage to confront? Are people generally conceptually confused about pedophilia, inversion, and homosexuality, and thus led astray by the erroneous belief that gay men are child molesters or effeminate?

Finally, as H. L. A. Hart points out,[12] Devlin's argument fails to distinguish clearly between the incidental and the essential elements of a society's moral code; it provides no basis for contrasting a shift in society's moral code with its destruction. Possibly, even if people were unanimous in their emotional abhorrence of gay marriage, and were not deceived or misinformed, changing demographics would justify a changed morality. Homosexuality may have once been counterproductive, but may no longer be and people do not know it. A change in attitudes may therefore be warranted. Rather than annihilating our shared values, accepting gay marriages may improve them.

5. The Law As Promoter of Values

More recently Michael Bayles offered another version of Devlin's conservative stance. Though he is primarily intent on defending monogamy as an intentionally life-long and exclusive relation, the argument he develops could be extended to the heterosexual orientation of our marriage laws as well. He notes that the law serves two different functions: to prohibit some practices (the criminal law) and to promote others (the civil law). The practices prohibited by the criminal code are those thought to be wrong, largely (but not necessarily only) actions harmful to others, such as murder and rape. The practices promoted are socially approved, such as buying, selling, and marrying. These private-arranging laws are based on society's values—in the case of marriage, on the value of an intimate, intentionally life-long heterosexual relationship. Though Bayles believes that homosexuals ought not to be prohibited from engaging in private consenting acts, he might insist that they have no right to demand that society legalize and promote through marriage laws something of which it does not fully approve. The most a homosexual can demand is that he be left alone when his actions do not harm others. He cannot demand that society condone his relationship by institutionalizing it through law.

I believe that this argument, like Devlin's, is inconclusive because the final court of appeal is society's *actual* values, however misguided or ill-founded they may be. Any appeal to positive morality leaves open the question: Are these beliefs justified? Some apparatus is needed to sort out fact from fantasy, wisdom from folly. If the law is a promoter of values, which values or whose values does it promote? In a pluralistic society, different groups have different values and will use the law to realize them. On what basis can the law decide which of the competing sets of values to promote or protect? No appeal to existing values can answer this question.

Society's values and attitudes must be subject to rational scrutiny. Are they based on prejudice and rationalization or logic and experience? Do people just parrot what they are told or can they sincerely and consistently defend their position? Only if these values withstand a reasoned critique can they serve as a basis for the law. . . .

6. Homosexuality and Perversion

Underlying the Roman Catholic position, and the visceral response of many, is the sense that homosexuality is "unnatural." The term can mean many different things: unaccepted, unacceptable, unusual, abnormal, deviant, or just repugnant. In the context of sexual behavior, the terms "unnatural" or "perverted" typically and most coherently refer to acts that are nonreproductive.

Behind the Catholic position is a mythology: God created man and woman so that the first and natural sex act was with a member of the opposite sex. This mythology is buttressed by theological arguments found in Saint Thomas Aquinas.[13] Each bodily organ has its natural function, the function it performs better than any other organ to a degree of perfection none can match. Thus, the eyes are for seeing, the ears for hearing, and genitalia for reproduction—for that is what they alone can do and what they do best.

All homosexual acts are thus unnatural: they do not serve the biological function of reproduction. Like coprophila, necrophilia, and pedophilia, they are to be condemned as a violation of God's plan. To condone homosexual marriages would be as sinful as promulgating bestiality.

One immediate difficulty with this inference from the unnatural to the immoral is overkill. It rules out all forms of fetishism, voyeurism, masturbation, and petting. But few today would indiscriminately and without qualification condemn the sex appeal of almost all Hollywood movies which to some degree are voyeuristic. Far from taking masturbation as unnatural, Masters and Johnson have taken the ability to masturbate to orgasm as the condition of mature and healthy sexuality.

More significantly for "straight couples," this logic leads to a condemnation of contraception, sex among the aged or sterile, and oral-genital sex between husband and wife. . . .

The identification of the natural and the reproductive seems initially plausible because it captures some of our intuitions about perverted sex. Necrophilia, pedophilia, and bestiality seem wrong and are also nonprocreative. But is it their sterility that accounts for their immorality? What these acts also have in common is a lack of informed, voluntary consent from all participants. The paradigm of an immoral sexual act is rape—sex with another against their will. It is this failure of *consent* rather than *conception* that makes any sexual act (perverted or not) immoral. . . .

7. The Universalizability Problem

Behind some opposition to homosexuality is this worry: What if everybody did that? This concern could be made into a philosophical argument along Kantian lines. For an action to be morally right, it must be based on a principle we can recommend to all people. Yet to recommend that everyone become a homosexual, or enter a homosexual marriage, is to promulgate the termination of the human race. Since this practice fails the test of universalizability, it is properly condemned as immoral.

The most apparent difficulty with this argument is that it misses the logical mark. What is disputed is not the *obligation* to be gay or to enter a gay marriage but the *right* to do so. What is at issue is the option, not the duty of everyone to marry the person of their choice regardless of gender.

There is nothing illogical about recommending that every person has such a right, the way there is something illogical about saying that everyone should lie or have the right to do so (is this recommendation itself a lie?). Moreover the fear of the consequences from according everyone this right is also groundless. The best statistical evidence from Kinsey and his researchers suggests only a minority of the population would exercise their right to enter a homosexual marriage. If one adopts a rule utilitarian perspective in which the morality of an act is determined by the social utility of adopting the practice, then homosexual marriages are warranted: in a world in which overpopulation is a serious and growing problem, this practice promises to alleviate the increasing demand on scarce resources.

8. The Slippery Slope

The final argument I want to consider has a logical form familiar to philosophers debating abortion, euthanasia, and other contemporary issues. The major premise is that the small and perhaps plausible step we are now proposing will soon accelerate us down the slope into a moral abyss. Thus mercy killing may seem humane, but it weakens the principle of the sanctity of human life, so that soon we will also be killing deformed babies, senile men, incapacitated women, the insane, misfits, and others deemed socially unacceptable. To avoid these atrocities we must avoid the first step.

By a similar logic one might argue that legalizing homosexual marriages will lead shortly to group marriages, polygamy, polyandry—until there is nothing left of marriage as we know it. But to destroy the institution of marriage is to undermine the family and the basis of society. To avoid such a catastrophe we must avoid the first step: we must adhere resolutely to marriage as we know it—one man and one woman in holy wedlock.

In my view, such arguments rely more on scare tactics than on clear-mindedness. They invite the reassertion of the point made earlier that prevents the slide into other forms of marriage: monogamy has not been abandoned, for the homosexual marriage at issue still involves just one spouse. Moreover, I am not convinced that the abyss is so abysmal. There may be good reasons to challenge our binary frame of reference for conceptualizing legitimate sexual behavior. . . .

III

None of the first eight arguments in defense of current restrictive marriage laws have turned out to be sound. Of course it does not follow that none can be formulated: some may be forthcoming at a future time. In order to justify legalizing homosexual marriages, let me now offer three positive considerations.

1. Maximizing Freedom of Choice

Freedom is one of the things our society values, and rightly so. The ability to live one's life as one chooses is not only sought by most people, but used as a standard against which particular social practices and, indeed, entire societies can be judged. The law serves as both the protector and promoter of this freedom. Its failure to include homosexual marriages can be regarded as a failure to provide freedom in one of its most important areas—our intimate, personal sexual life. The fact that some cannot marry the partner of their choice marks a moral deficiency in our society. . . .

2. The Value of Love

However cynical one wants to be and however extreme one's view of love, it is difficult to deny that some homosexual couples do love one another and that their lives are the better for it. They make enduring commitments in word and deed to comfort and console each other, to safeguard and secure their partner's interests, and to care for their needs. Like health and wealth, such love is a good thing, something we would choose for ourselves and those close to us.

As a ceremony, marriage serves to recognize and legitimize a relationship, and to solicit social support for what is good and valuable in it. . . . Insofar as love is of value and homosexual relationships are loving, then homosexual marriages should be legal.

3. Sexless Justice

According to the popular image, justice is blindfolded, indicating that certain particularities are irrelevant to considerations of fairness. The biological identity of a person is one of these facts that I consider irrelevant: whether one's partner is male or female should make no difference in the eyes of the law. The Equal Rights Amendment, which outlaws discrimination on the basis of sex, may entail the legalization of homosexual marriages. But I do not want to argue this change as a constitutional point, but as a requirement of equity or justice.

I am not sure how to refute those who believe that gender makes a moral difference. Their view strikes me as pernicious, sexist, and chauvinistic, but I concede that this response contains more rhetoric than logic. Let me therefore offer three arguments from justice.

First, the "Golden Rule" may provide some logical leverage to budge the stubborn opponent: Do unto others as you would have others do unto you! Since all of us want to be granted the right to marry the partner of our choice, the homosexual should be accorded this same right. . . .

Second, a Rawlsian argument might be more persuasive.[13] Imagine that you did not know whether you would be born into the world preferring partners of the same sex or the opposite sex.

Imagine further that you would be condemned to frustration, embarrassment, and loneliness if you could not marry a partner with your sexual preference. Imagine finally that you are rational and concerned about your own well-being. Would you choose to have homosexual marriages legal? It seems to me that most people would and should answer yes, if this were all they knew. In short it seems to me that if we can disengage ourselves from our sexual orientation through reason or compassion, then the unfairness of discrimination against homosexuals becomes blatant. . . .

Third, consider an analogy with interracial marriages. To strengthen it I shall reverse the factors. Imagine a society of two races in which people could marry only individuals of the opposite race, because marriage is thought of as a way to legitimize a sexual relationship. Sex with someone of the same race is considered by that society to be unnatural and perverted, a cause for reprobation, condemnation, and expulsion. Confronted with such conjugal practices, it seems plausible for us to object that they are racist and hence unjust. Whether one is prevented from marrying someone of the opposite race (as in our society at one time) or someone of the same race (as in the hypothetical case) is immaterial. The biological contingencies of birth into a particular race ought not, if we are to be just, serve as a basis for social or legal practice. People cannot do anything about their race—it is given, perhaps a God given. To prevent someone from marrying another just because that person happens to be of the wrong race—namely the same race—strikes us quite rightly as grossly unfair. By the same logic the prohibition on same-sex marriages is just as unwarranted—not racist but "sexist" in the very broad sense of making gender differences per se into moral differences. Like race, our biological identity as male or female is something over which the average person has little control (transsexualism notwithstanding). Each of us is born into the world as a member of a particular race and endowed with a particular gender. Social policies that discriminate on the basis of gender alone fault us for something we cannot change. If ought implies can, if the focus of morality is free, voluntary actions, then sexist marriage laws are unjust. . . .

A racist says you cannot marry some people be-

cause of their race, and a sexist says you cannot marry some people because of their sex. Both policies are unjust: neither race nor sex should make a legal or moral difference.

The injustice would be less serious if only the right to marry were at issue. But in our society this right is tied to many other financial benefits—medical and health insurance, taxation (though now changed), and inheritance—not to mention the psychological and emotional advantages. . . . homosexual couples are denied a host of real privileges and significant advantages that accrue automatically to heterosexual pairs. This inequitable distribution based solely on the gender of the participants strikes me as a violation of the principle of justice, not a humane practice for an enlightened society. . . .

Notes

1. *Baker vs. Nelson,* 291 Minn 310, 191 N.W. 2nd 185 Minn Sup. Ct., 1971.

2. *Baker vs. Nelson,* 41 U.S.L.W. 3167 (Us Oct. 10, 1972).

3. The variations arise because of the different roles of men and women in child bearing and child rearing. See the subsequent discussion of the family.

4. The qualification "typically" is needed to cover cases of common law marriage. There is no means whereby same-sex couples who live together can acquire the rights that opposite-sex couples acquire through the institution of common law marriage. A bill in San Francisco to grant gay couples legal rights comparable to common law marriage was recently defeated.

5. I would take the same stance against those who would argue that open marriage is a contradiction in terms because exclusivity is part of the definition of monogamy. Richard Wasserstrom suggests a strategy for opposing this semantic approach that I have not adopted in "Is Adultery Immoral?", herein, pp. 93 to 106.

6. Pope Paul VI "Humanae Vitae," herein, pp. 167–184, and the recent Vatican Declaration on Ethics.

7. The position of the study commissioned by the Catholic Theological Society of America is far more humane and tolerant. See A. Kosnik et al., *Human Sexuality* (New York: Paulist Press, 1977) pp. 186–218.

8. See Carl Cohen, "Sex, Birth Control, and Human Life," in *Ethics* 19 (July, 1969), also reprinted in this volume pp. 185–199.

9. See Patrick Devlin, *The Enforcement of Morals* (New York: Oxford University Press, 1965), viz ch. 1.

10. In chapter 4, dealing with marriage laws, Devlin goes further, building on the positive converse that if society generally feels a marital practice is warranted, then it should be legal.

11. See H. L. A. Hart "Immorality and Treason" in *The Listener* (July 30, 1959), pp. 162–63, and his elaboration in *Law, Liberty and Morality* (New York: Oxford University Press, 1963).

12. Thomas Aquinas, *On the Truth of the Catholic Faith*

Book 3: Providence pt. 1, trans. Vernon J. Bourke (New York: Doubleday, 1956).

13. John Rawls, *A Theory of Justice* (Cambridge: Harvard University Press, 1971), viz. Chapter 3.

Is Elliston's case convincing? Perhaps. Yet let us revisit the argument he presents against the first consideration that some people might use to reject the legalization of homosexual marriage. Elliston claims that "unless we are prepared to deny a marriage license to elderly and sterile couples, it is inconsistent and hence immoral to refuse the gay couple—at least on this ground alone." But would such refusal necessarily be inconsistent? Suppose some critics claimed that in defining and legalizing marriage society is dealing with "classes" or "types" of people. Suppose further that they claimed that the types of people to which marriage pertains are those who when united in marriage have in principle the capacity to reproduce the species through sexual intercourse. Would that not limit marriage to the union of males and females? From this perspective, would it really be inconsistent to grant a marriage license to elderly and sterile couples but to refuse such a license to homosexuals? To be inconsistent would not society have to be treating the same types of people differently? But are homosexual couples really of the same type as heterosexual couples that are elderly and/or sterile? Or are they actually two different types? If so, is Elliston's charge of inconsistency warranted?

Now suppose we accept the critic's claim that marriage pertains to persons who when united have in principle the capacity to reproduce the species through sexual intercourse. Would not modern reproductive technologies involving artificial insemination or male pregnancy render homosexual couples in principle capable of reproducing the species? And if the critic insisted that the only reproduction that counts is reproduction involving sexual intercourse, could not a pregnant homosexual partner claim that his or her pregnancy involved sexual intercourse with his or her partner? And if the critic retorted that to count for marriage the pregnancy had to be the result of the penis of one of the partners ejaculating sperm into the vagina of another of the partners, then would not couples who, in order to overcome infertility, utilize in vitro fertilization or sperm donated by a third party fail to qualify for the designation "married"? If the critic would not wish to deny the designation of "married" to such couples, then on what grounds could the critic still deny a similar designation to homosexual couples? If such a critic persists in denying the designation of marriage to homosexual couples, would not Elliston's charge of inconsistency still stand?

If society defines marriage in a certain way to regulate procreation and promote the survival of the species and, in so doing, precludes certain spousal choices (such as a father choosing to marry his daughter, a brother choosing to marry his sister, a mother choosing to marry her son, a homosexual choosing to marry a homosexual), does the limiting of choices necessarily entail a violation of justice? Elliston would clearly answer yes.

But what is justice and when is it violated? Shall we say that justice involves simply rendering to persons what is their due, respecting their rights? If so, then injustice would involve denying persons their rights. But where do rights come from? Are they given by God? Are they simply self-evident? Do they come into existence through personal proclamation when someone declares that she has a right to something? Are they derived logically from moral theory or perhaps from the nature of human rationality? Or are rights bestowed on persons by society? Suppose someone claimed that rights are bestowed by society (and indeed many people do make such as claim). If, then, society is seen as the grantor of rights and if society chooses not to grant a right to persons to select as marriage partners whatever person, animal or thing they happen to like, can society be charged with a violation of justice when there exists no society-given right to be violated?

Yet suppose someone claimed that rights are merely recognized by society and that they are derived from and receive their warrant from natural law or morality. If so, would not such a grounding of rights in natural law or morality provide a basis from which to criticize the legally warranted rights in a particular society? Would not Elliston's case for legalizing gay marriages on the basis of justice find new strength in this view of rights?

These are complex and important questions that arise as we try to think through the issue of justice and the legalization of homosexual marriage. We find ourselves needing insight from the biological sciences about the biological basis, if any, for sexual orientation. We find ourselves needing insights from moral philosophy and the philosophy of law concerning the nature of justice, injustice, and rights. And we also find ourselves needing assistance from tough-minded analytical philosophy to construct a viable definition of "marriage," on which a great deal will hang. In the next chapter dealing with adultery, defining marriage also becomes a pivotal issue.

PERMISSIVE MATRIMONY ADVOCATED

We began this chapter with a recognition that conventional monogamous heterosexual marriage is in trouble. Lawrence Casler would rush to agree. Indeed, Casler believes that conventional marriage has "outlived its usefulness" to the extent that it is now "doing more harm than good." Conventional marriage, steeped in possessiveness and jealousy, is responsible, says Casler, for "today's prevailing neurotic climate, with its pervasive insecurity."

What is to be done? Shall we try to reform conventional marriage and breathe new life into it? Shall we abandon it entirely? Or shall we supplement it with additional marital options? Kant and perhaps classical Marxism would probably favor the first option. O'Driscoll, Taylor, and Elliston would all probably select the third option. None of the authors examined so far in this chapter would choose the second option, total abandonment of conventional marriage. Although Casler's ardent criticism of conventional marriage might suggest that he would recommend abandonment, he also chooses the third alternative.

Casler proposes a system called "permissive matrimony" that would enable persons to choose from a wide variety of legalized sexual and marital relationships ranging from conventional marriage to nonexclusive monogamy, and from trial marriage to group marriage. Casler's proposal is based on the claim that "the individual should have the right to unlimited sexual expression, provided only that his behavior does not infringe upon the rights of others." The material below is taken from his article "Permissive Matrimony: Proposal for the Future" that is based on his book *Is Marriage Necessary?*

from Permissive Matrimony: Proposals for the Future _____

LAWRENCE CASLER

Marriage, for most people, has outlived its usefulness and is doing more harm than good. The solution is not to make divorces more difficult to obtain, but to recognize the so-called divorce problem for what it is: a symptom of the marriage problem. And to get rid of a symptom, you try to do something about the underlying illness. By way of analogy, if a child fails to thrive despite daily beatings from his parents, is the solution to increase the severity of the beatings? No. If a particular practice does not seem to be working, it is appropriate to ask if the practice is necessary. Similarly, it is appropriate now to ask: Is marriage necessary?

I propose a system of "permissive matrimony" within which individuals can choose, within very broad limits, the types of human relationships they wish to experience. All individuals would be permitted to choose freely from the following options.

Conventional Monogamy

Little needs to be said at this point concerning the current mode of male-female and parent-child relationships. Anyone who wishes, for reasons of religious commitment, moral beliefs, or personality, to enter upon a conventional marriage would be perfectly free to do so—provided, of course, that he can find a willing partner. The fact that "permissive matrimony" does include this option should lay to rest any claims that I am advocating the abolition of conventional marriage.

Modified Monogamy

Nonexclusive monogamy refers to a marital arrangement by which one man and one woman are married to each other, but are under no obligation to refrain from sexual (or other) relationships with other persons. Adultery, no longer a legal ground for divorce, would, rather, be viewed as a normal and acceptable diversion.

Child-free monogamy is similar to the status quo, but minus the child-rearing function. If it is true that children are being brought up, in many cases, by the people least suited to do so (that is, their parents), and if it is true that children, in many cases, reduce the marital and/or individual satisfaction of their parents, then it follows that marriage could be improved, as an institution, if it were less closely tied to the child-rearing function. (For a more detailed account of child-rearing, see below.)

Contractual monogamy, as its name implies, involves the recognition of marriage as a civil contract. As such, the relationship could be terminable without recourse to complicated legal or religious procedures, or unseemly accusations.

Trial marriage means many things to many people, but its various forms appear to be subsumable within the general category of modified monogamy. One type of trial marriage involves the couple living together for as long as they wish, or for a stipulated period of time, after which they either separate or become married in the conventional sense.

Another type of arrangement would permit unilateral termination. This possibility is not so heartless as it may seem. As is fairly obvious, a marriage with only one willing partner is scarcely a marriage at all. What self-respecting person would want to continue a marriage in which the spouse remained solely because of legal, social, or psychological duress?

Quarternary marriage involves two married couples and their offspring living together, with the goals of companionship, division of labor, and increasing the number of adult role-models available to the children.

The selection from Lawrence Casler is taken from his article "Permissive Matrimony: Proposals for the Future," in *The Humanist*, Vol. xxxiv, No. 2 (March/April 1974), pp. 4–8. Used by permission of the publisher, American Humanist Association, copyright 1974.

The three-generation family: Most of the foregoing options (and some of those that follow) can be readily incorporated within a multigenerational framework. The "extended family" and its variants, so frequently described by cultural anthropologists, have numerous obvious advantages. With children living in the midst of grandparents as well as parents, the number of adult role-models is increased, parental ties may be beneficially weakened, a more realistic perception of the aged may be attained, and the elderly would find themselves in environments less morbid and more conducive to self-respect than the typical old-age home. But these advantages may be neutralized by the social stagnation likely to ensue.

Nonmonogamous Matrimony

Polygamy, of either the polygynous or polyandrous variety, would obviously increase the number of permissible mates. Fewer than 20 per cent of the world's societies have established monogamy as the preferred form of marriage. Nevertheless, no advocacy of polygamy will be presented here. Too often, the multiple husbands or wives can become mere possessions, rather than independent persons.

Group marriage involves the simultaneous practice of polyandry and polygyny, in which every man in the group is married to every woman. Group marriage, representing an attenuation of traditional bonds, has attracted considerable attention in recent years. A number of experiments in group marriage are currently in progress, and it should soon be possible to evaluate the effects of these attempts to reduce exclusivity and possessiveness.

Nonmarital Relationships

Included in this category are all those types of relationships which, by virtue of their freedom from legal, religious, or social constraints, are nonbinding and readily terminable. The term "free love" has the same denotation but suffers from misleading connotations. In the first place, reference to "love" is inappropriate, because that emotion may play no role in the establishment or continuation of the relationship. "Free sex" would be a preferable term, except that "free" may imply, to some, an irresponsible exploitation that does not require the consent of both partners.

• • •

Many readers may feel repugnance at the very idea of mate-sharing. Possessiveness and jealousy are part of an especially vicious cycle: marriage and family life have been largely responsible, I suggest, for today's prevailing neurotic climate, with its pervasive insecurity, and it is precisely this climate that makes so difficult the acceptance of a different, healthier way of life. Nothing could be further removed from mental health than a man's being haunted by the fear that his wife will find someone with a penis larger or more satisfying than his own; or a woman's being desperately afraid that her husband will have a casual affair that will break up the marriage (the implication being, of course, that the reason her husband has been coming home day after day is neither spiritual, emotional, nor intellectual, but merely genital). Secretly aware that her personality is not attractive enough to keep any man interested for very long—marriage itself having stunted whatever remnants of a mature self had somehow survived the onslaught of her parents' neurotic needs—she has no choice but to defend the "ideal" of sexual fidelity, even at the cost of sacrificing her own chances for pleasant sexual variety. And her husband is on her side, too, unwilling to risk the possibility of coming out second best in a sexual comparison. Thus are the bonds of matrimony woven from the threads of emotional compulsions.

Individual opposition to a system that permits more than one sexual partner may have other roots as well, but these are usually less direct, being more closely tied to social and religious pressures. If there is such a thing as hell, nobody wants to be condemned to it; and most religions teach that there is no surer path to damnation than sexual "sin." It may not be out of place to remind the reader that the rigorous sexual restrictions from which he, as a God-fearing, society-fearing, body-fearing citizen is suffering are almost without exception the restrictions laid down by the "Elders" in the ancient religious communities—men so old that they had not had, we may assume, an urgent sex drive for several years; or else men who may well have been of dubious sexuality. The answer to those who are afraid, either of genital competition or of eternal damnation, is simple: let them choose conventional monogamy. It should be clear that the proposed new system would not in any way infringe upon their legitimate rights.

Permissive matrimony need have no adverse consequences for the adults concerned, their offspring, or society at large. But it is not enough to defend a projected social change by referring only to the damage it will not do. While it may be true that a society that does not coerce its members to commit matrimony would be a society without the many ill effects of marriage, the necessity remains of indicating the likely positive benefits of this proposal.

Would people be happier under such a system? They would certainly have a greater chance for sexual happiness, no longer restricted in their choice of bedmates by a set of artificial and outmoded social prohibitions. As has already been noted, the rate of nonmarital sexual intercourse seems to be gradually rising. But so long as the "official" morality persists, guilt feelings and fear of apprehension are likely accompaniments. Also, the sexual act is often abused in a restrictive society such as ours, being flaunted by many as a symbol of nonconformity. This sort of childishness would rapidly become obsolete in a system such as the one proposed here.

It would be naive to suppose that permissive matrimony would be characterized by total promiscuity. While there would be ample opportunity (except for those who opt for conventional monogamy) to enjoy a large number of sexual partners, many couples who discover an unusually gratifying condition of sexual compatibility might decide to stay together for as long as the sexual compatibility continues. This temporarily stable relationship may seem, superficially, to resemble marriage; but it differs, in that it is contingent upon mutual satisfaction, is free of legal duties, and does not preclude what is now called infidelity. . . .

. . . At whatever age the sex drive is strongest, as well as at all other ages, the individual should have the right to unlimited sexual expression, provided only that his behavior does not infringe upon the rights of others. But as long as marriage and the monogamistic (or "monoga-mystic") ideal hold sway, premarital and extramarital sex are regarded, almost automatically, as infringements— either on the rights of specific other people or on the whole structure of public morality. Let it be noted again, however, that (1) a system of permissive matrimony would not interfere with individual rights, because sexual freedom would not be an option to anyone who had pledged fidelity to a particular mate; and (2) the fact that 80 per cent of the societies of the world permit multiple sexual partnerships strongly suggests that our society would not be risking ruin if it became equally tolerant.

For most people, conventional monogamy represents a major, and unnecessary, reduction in sexual pleasure. And if thwarted sexual desires are, as many authorities have long maintained, among the chief causes of emotional disturbance, then the message is glaringly clear. (There *are* those who maintain that there is virtually no limit to the amount of sexual variety that can be experienced between husband and wife. But how does this justify society's refusal to let a person have as many sexual partners as he wants?)

Sexual freedom is but one aspect of happiness that would be enhanced by a modification of existing marital traditions. An increasing emphasis on emotional independence, on honest human relationships, and on the full development of human potentialities may be expected, as the harmful effects of marriage—exploitation, parasitism, and a narrowing of personal horizons—gradually diminish. In short, there is no reason to believe that men and women living in a society that does not emphasize marriage would be any less happy than the men and women of today, and the most rational prediction is that they would enjoy a considerably higher degree of happiness. . . .

Individuals who are currently involved in nonmarital relationships can add to the liberating trend by finding a middle course between the blatant, antagonism-provoking display of their freedom and the abject concealment that defines the relationship as a sordid one. The proper stance to take is probably an intensely private one: your marital status, like your politics and your religion, is your own business. If the private nature of human relationships were more widely acknowledged, we would eventually reach a point at which a person's social status would be independent of his marital status. At that point, the battle for permissive matrimony would be virtually won. . . .

If a motto for the new system were necessary, "Freedom of sexual behavior" would be less accurate than "Freedom of social interaction." But even the latter is somewhat too narrow. Our marriage-mad society is so intent on linking eligible males with eligible females (while keeping "ineligibles" apart) that nearly every male-female social interaction, no matter how freely undertaken, is contaminated by its possible marital implications: "Are his intentions honorable?" "Does this relationship have a future?" The person who socializes with "too many" members of the opposite sex may be as suspect as the one who socializes with too few.

Thus, the ultimate goal of permissive matrimony is simply the freedom to be oneself. That this goal of personal freedom happens to be highly congruent with the ideals of democracy leads to the prediction that the proposal should meet with less resistance in so-called free societies than in those more totalitarian. Future events may permit the testing of this prediction.

•　•　•

The arguments presented here have been intended to indicate that permissive matrimony is a viable policy that does not deviate unduly from contemporary standards of interpersonal conduct. A few words need to be said now to those who believe that the proposal is too conservative. Trenchant demands for the total abolition of marriage and the family are by no means new, but they have become particularly vigorous in recent years because conventional matrimony is seen by some to be a major stumbling block in the path toward women's liberation. Although I sympathize fully with this view, I find myself unable to advocate the wholesale elimination of marriage at this time. One reason is a purely practical one: such a radical proposal has no chance of public acceptance, whereas the more evolutionary scheme proposed here may

well receive support, even from those who are personally opposed to some of its details.

There is a second and more basic reason for rejecting any demand for the immediate abolition of marriage. Such a demand is quite analogous to a demand for the immediate abolition of crutches. As long as there are people who are physically handicapped, there will be a need for crutches. And as long as there are people who are emotionally handicapped, there will be a need for marriage.

Finally, there is the matter of individual freedom. Just as society has absolutely no right to force people into marriage, it has no right to prevent people from getting married. Readers who hold vehemently anti-marriage views may be somewhat consoled by the recognition that if marriage is as bad as they think it is, it will probably fade into obsolescence as more and more members of succeeding generations, progressively freer from the matrimonial imperative, select more liberating life-styles.

Permissive matrimony will not solve all of society's problems. There will still be crime, exploitation, and psychopathology. It is doubtless true that a thorough overhauling of many of our social institutions—economic, religious, and political—must be undertaken if human happiness and dignity are to have a fighting chance for survival. Marriage has been singled out for special attention here for several reasons. First, it may be the most influential of all social institutions, so that marital reforms are likely to have significant effects on the other institutions that need to be modified. A second, and related, point is that the child-rearing function of marriage provides the initial medium by which other social institutions determine the lives of each successive generation. And third, individuals are more likely, through their own decision-making processes, to effect changes in marital patterns than to effect changes in political, economic, or religious domains, which have proven to be relatively impermeable to individual action.

It is possible that a "perfect" society will never exist. But a vastly improved society can exist—if, and only if, enough dedicated men and women are able to envisage, and willing to work toward, its actualization.

What shall we say about Casler's proposal? Because marriage is an immensely important social institution that impacts so many facets of society, implementing Casler's proposal would involve a veritable social transformation. Laws relating to marriage would have to undergo major revision. But how could that be done without widespread public debate? And how could such public debate be effective without socioeconomic impact studies, major attitudinal changes in society, and significant modifications in the moral and religious beliefs of a majority of citizens? Casler is aware of the magnitude of his proposal and, accordingly, recommends a slow evolutionary approach rather than a speedy revolutionary upheaval.

Our engaging Casler in public debate can begin with a few questions. First of all, how accurate is the story he tells us about contemporary conventional marriage? Suppose that Casler is correct in saying that society exhibits a "prevailing neurotic climate" with "pervasive insecurity," has he demonstrated a causal connection between marriage and that prevailing climate? Indeed, given the as yet unanswered objections to causal connection raised by the philosopher David Hume (who awakened Immanuel Kant from his dogmatic slumbers), *could* Casler really establish a causal connection between marriage and the neurotic climate; indeed, between any two or more events? Given the uncertainty associated with demonstrating conclusively the causal connection between events, why does Casler select marriage as the major cause of this condition? Why not choose, in Marxist fashion, economic oppression as the major factor? Or why not choose male dominance, or international politics, or technological innovations, or a combination of these or other factors as the major cause?

Moving now to a different concern, shall we agree with Casler's basic premise that "the individual should have the right to unlimited sexual expression, provided only that his behavior does not infringe upon the rights of others"? Once again we see the thorny issue of "rights" arising. Should society grant this right to individuals? If so, would not a couple with AIDS be allowed to procreate? On whose rights would they be infringing? The rights of the unborn? But do the unborn, do future generations have rights? What about a mentally retarded couple wishing to procreate? Would they be infringing on anyone's rights? And what about a father and daughter, a mother and son, a brother and sister all willingly procreating with each other? On whose rights would they be infringing? Casler reinforces his position with the claim that "your marital status, like your politics and your religion, is your own business." But is your marital status your own business? Does not society have a stake in the survival of the species? If so, is your marital status really your own business? Is not the interest of society in the survival of the species one of the major reasons why society regulates marital relations through its laws?

A futurist might suggest that society should consider separating the regulation of procreation from marriage entirely. For example, to procreate a couple would have to secure a license to do so, and such licensing would involve genetic screening to ensure insofar as possible babies without birth defects. Coupled with this regulation of procreation could be the regulation of child raising in which professionally trained child raisers would take over from the child bearers so that sound physical, psychological, and educational development of the offspring would be facilitated. Under such arrangements, a wide variety of marital forms would be legal and virtually any form of consensual sexual activity would be legal, with the exception that heterosexual intercourse without contraceptive measures would be illegal unless the couple had a license to procreate. What would be the advantages of such a system? What would be the disadvantages?

CONVENTIONAL MARRIAGE PRAISED

We began this chapter with a defense of conventional marriage by Immanuel Kant. In subsequent readings we have heard a growing chorus of voices challenging conventional marriage that has reached a crescendo in Casler, whose permissive marriage would disprivilege conventional marriage and legalize a multitude of alternative sexual and marital relationships. We now end this chapter with a paean of praise to conventional marriage by Gerhard Neubeck.

The reading below is Neubeck's 1978 Presidential address delivered at the annual meeting of the National Council on Family Relations. Listen to his story.

from In Praise of Marriage

GERHARD NEUBECK

I have come here this afternoon to sing the praise of marriage. My thanks to you for allowing me to do this, me a 60 year old who has been married some 37 years to the same woman who has been married 37 years to me. To sing the praise of marriage is a formidable task in light of the mess this old and venerable institution is in. I shall not spell out to you in detail the troubles I have seen and heard about, the anguish of men and women locked in deadly embraces, the tortured children of parents struggling in violence. Sanity is set aside, agonies galore, knots excruciatingly unknotted. There are, of course, the necessary breakups as well, the couples who are better off apart, survival not possible together . . . though I am haunted by Paul Simon's, "You like to sleep with the window open, I like to sleep with the window closed, so Good Bye, good bye, good bye." And all of that in spite of the helping professions and an ever increasing sophistication about the nature of bonding, pairing, communication, relating, loving and so-called love making.

Enough of this purple prose. You know very well what I am talking about, the miserable state of marriage. Yet, more people than ever are marrying today, and not withstanding other options marry for the first time, a second and even marry again. And each time they expect payoffs to follow as if they had not learned anything from the previous experience. Must there not be something right with marriage? Permanent bonding seems to be such a powerful incentive, such an eternal invitation, if not temptation to happiness that we succumb over and over again. What is it then that holds such attraction, that is so enticing that we marry, marry and marry . . . with a vengeance?

I believe that there is a universal and primitive longing to be attached. The other side of that coin is perhaps less controversial: we don't want to go it alone!

Before I go much further I might as well admit to a not very obscure bias, my romanticism. Tempered by my more objective social science trained self—and on that side let me recommend the two lead articles in both the July 1978 issue of *The Family Coordinator* and the August 1978 issue of the *Journal of Marriage and the Family*—I do profess that I am loaded with sentimentality and perhaps will shock you with a challenge: "What's wrong with promising your mate a rose garden?" Of course I want a rose garden, too, no question about that, and that brings me to my next point. No, wait a minute. I wonder if I really have been honest. Maybe it is the other way around and it is

The selection from Gerhard Neubeck is taken from his article "In Praise of Marriage" in *The Family Coordinator*, Vol. 28, No. 1 (January 1979), pp. 115–117. Copyrighted © 1979 by the National Council on Family Relations, 3989 Central Ave. NE, Suite 550, Minneapolis, MN 55421. Reprinted by permission of the National Council on Family Relations and Gerhard Neubeck.

my social science self that is tempered by my romanticism. . . . well, we shall see by the way this essay progresses what your final judgment will be.

My next point, yes. "I did promise you a rose garden." Fritz Perls' pearls, quoted all over the globe, in my estimation were poison. "You do your thing and I do mine, etc." was the grand capitulation to SELFISM. Perhaps it was not meant to do that but surely FOR BETTER OR FOR WORSE was easily abandoned in the wake of ME FIRST. Oh, I know that there is a thin line where self satisfaction ends and altruism begins . . . but when I bring my wife a cup of coffee in the morning so that she can wake up properly, I know that it gives her pleasure, but I enjoy that, too; her face lights up, she says, "Thank you," and our day is off to a good start. . . . Don't worry, this speech is not entitled INSIDE RUTH AND GERRY, but occasionally I'll have to let you know where I live.

For better or for worse. These days we are tuned in primarily on the better. The worse? Me thinks that means we have to pay a price, that for the joys there are hardships, for satisfactions—disappointments, for fun and games—frustrations. These minuses should come as no surprise or shock. That's what we pay *in* for the pay*offs*. In any system inconveniences like those exist. There are strains and stresses, pains, situations short of perfection, less than ideal. . . . and in the marital system that is par for the intercourse. Unfortunately most of us have been sold a bill of goods to the extent that a marriage furnishes perpetual, multiple ecstasies and that we have them due to us from our mates, and in spades. And if they are not forthcoming we blame these mates or marriage itself, forgetting that the roses in our garden do have thorns.

In Praise of Marriage. Oh, the feeling of security, that is knowing you are there, will be there, always, I can count on it. Too much togetherness can be a burden, we know that, but not to have you around when I come home would be a pain in the solar nexus. Ann Sexton, my favorite poet had this to say in one of her pieces:

. . . . and then
how we gnaw at the barrier because we are two.
How you come and take my blood cup
and link me together and take my brine.

We are bare. We are stripped to the bone
and we swim in tandem and go up and up
the river, the identical river called Mine
and we enter together. No one's alone.

Let me take a look at you. Do I really see you still? What a cute nose! Your eyes are brown, I have almost forgotten that. Yesterday your wrinkles didn't strike me as very appealing, they almost turned me off. But your doctor had said they couldn't be helped. I won't love them, but what the hell . . . for better or for worse, really not so worse. But I like the new jeans you bought. I like walking behind you when you wear them, you there in those jeans. Tomorrow, next week, next year.

To be married squelches, to a degree at least, that most vicious of feelings, jealousy, a primitive, troublesome and hateful emotion, but one that is universal and tenacious. To be married to each other means not to be married to anyone else. We may not belong to each other but we are primary to each other. Anyone else is down the line. We may not adhere to each other but we do come first. We may not possess each other but we owe each other first call. When we can't depend on anyone else we can depend on one another.

As I say this I am, of course, aware that these conditions are not an ever-flowing tide, an always-full cornucopia, that sometimes, occasionally, perhaps even often, throws darts into our life together or that external circumstances threaten our tranquility, and we begin to doubt that we are really so compatible. But then, with *effort* we put things in place and our world is restored to an equilibrium. The whipporwill sings again.

Phillip Roth in his novel *Professor of Desire* had one of his characters say: "At our best, our bravest and most sensible and most devoted, we try very hard to hate what divides us rather than each other." That's the stuff that marriage can be built on.

Of course it takes being on speaking terms. I am not being facetious. Talking is one thing; speaking another. When you and I speak with each other, we can express our thoughts, not merely idle chatter, not the concerns of everyday life alone but rather an exchange of interpretation of how the outer world looks and our interior one as well. And be assured that we are being listened to and are heard.

How often are there complaints that one spouse neither listens nor hears. Many spouses can be faulted for this. But there is that beautiful opportunity most of the time to get a load off my mind, a point clarified, my pipe dreams brought down to earth, my sorrow smoothed, my joy reverberated. I should be so lucky! To go to church and shopping, play tennis or scrabble, what fun!

To adventure out into the world with you, knowing that you love adventure as much as I do! Or sitting together looking at the fire in the fireplace, silently, each with our own thoughts; or cleaning up the yard and sharing messy chores; sharing unpleasant duties makes for only half a misery. Ain't that nice!

You are seldom laughing at my jokes these days; you have heard them a hundred times, after all, but we can laugh together at silly things. . . . and each other. We can giggle or break up. Our fun comes from being tuned to the same wave length. What is laughable or amusing to you is so to me, and what strikes my funny bone strikes yours, too. How divine our comedy!

And the goodies of the skin. Skin to skin. Arms to be in, lips to meet. Touchy our hands. Knees and toes, tongues and nose, and below those. Warm and comfortable. Hot and ardent. Affection and passion.

And the opportunities to make babies. Home-made little creatures who go by first names we give them and a surname that shows their linkage to their ancestors. But these kids with our genes are holding their own destiny. Their years under our tutelage are precious but few, the joys and headaches—givens. But you and I did make them. There is an old verse by Gene Fowler:

> Prudish old censors forbid it
> Reformers adroitly have hid it
> Though each person on earth
> Arrived here by birth
> To testify two people did it.

If all this spells LOVE, so be it. I don't know, perhaps I call it enjoyment, marriage enjoyment. Our research has been concerned with success and happiness, satisfaction and adjustment, what I have tried very briefly to describe are the opportunities for enjoyment. Here we are, helpmeets, spouses, mates, lovers, wives, husbands. We come in handy, don't we? We complement each other, we fit, we mesh, we mix, we dovetail, we trade and barter and exchange, we are one flesh. I do not want to knock other options but hurrah for marriage. Hurrah for building a history together. Hurrah for an institution that gives us that opportunity.

Let me finish with a poem from *A Book of Love* by Charles Vildrac, a French poet. Hank Bowman had this poem in his earlier editions of *Marriage for Moderns,* and I have always been grateful to him for introducing me to this lovely image:

> They are also with you and with me
> As in everyone else, things lacking,
> A particular weapon
> You cannot lay hands on;
> But it happens always, luckily for us,
> That I can lay hold of that weapon,
> That your garden is alive with those flowers,
> And that we go, without asking, the one to
>   the other
> To take what we need
>
> You are well aware of my wants
> And of my weaknesses;
> They turn to you unabashed,
> You receive them and love them;
> And I equally love yours,
> Which are a part of your strength.
>
> And so each of us. . . .
> Goes and may go with assurance,
> Because of a hand which is ready,
> At the least peril, to term and take hold
> Of the wandering arm of the blind man
> That you become, or that I become,
> Like everyone else, from time to time.

What shall we say about Neubeck's story? Is it just a wistful gasp from a bygone age that is irrelevant to the shape of the future society? Or is it an appealing model of marriage, a rich source of friendship? Or is it a type of therapy for fractured and alienated humans?

Conventional marriage is in trouble. What is to be done? Breathe new life into it? Abolish it? Disprivilege it and legalize a variety of alternatives? Perhaps we have more troubling questions than convincing answers. But hopefully the surplus of troubling questions will keep us looking for even more convincing answers.

CHAPTER 5

Adultery

EVER SINCE MARRIAGE APPEARED ON THE SCENE, so, too, have acts of extramarital sex, or adultery. But it was not until relatively recent research into sexual behavior that substantial nonanecdotal data revealed that extramarital sex occurs on a surprisingly large scale. Beginning with his landmark studies in the 1940s and '50s, Alfred Kinsey found that roughly 50 percent of men and 25 percent of women had engaged in extramarital sex. Later studies suggested that adultery may have increased to an even greater extent, with some researchers estimating up to 72 percent of males (*Hite Report on Male Sexuality,* 1981) and 50 percent of females (*Cosmopolitan* survey, 1980) had engaged in extramarital sex. On the other hand, a very recent study developed by researchers at the University of Chicago indicated that, when asked, 80 percent of women and 65 to 85 percent of men between the ages of 18 and 59 reported that they had never had extramarital sex (*Sex in America,* 1994). While it should be recognized that these studies encounter such methodological problems as population samples, bias, accuracy and quality of the surveys, and the veracity of the respondents, we can safely admit that in the United States alone, millions of people commit acts of adultery. These facts suggest many normative questions of interest to philosophers, not the least of which is, are all of these acts seriously immoral?

If we turn to our own country's most influential religions, the answer is clearly, Yes. Our legal traditions also consider adultery as grounds for divorce and often as a criminal offense. Whereas the religious responses are ultimately supported by appeal to authority, such as sacred texts and prominent religious figures, and the legal domain by the authority of legal precedents and legislated statutes, the philosopher has only the tools of reason and logic to approach this question.

Our first article, "Is Adultery Immoral?" by Richard Wasserstrom, illustrates how a philosopher goes about trying to answer such a question. The few philosophers who previously discussed adultery addressed the question, "Given that adultery is immoral, should it be illegal?" Or, put another way, should the law enforce morality? Wasserstrom, in typically philosophical fashion, notes that the question makes a very *basic assumption* that requires scrutiny: It assumes adultery *is* immoral. In his article, he explicates some of the most common rational arguments against adultery, as well as some of the limitations of these arguments. Wasserstrom goes on to present critical questions that he takes to be worth consideration and concludes that adultery may not be immoral under certain circumstances.

In the two articles that follow Wasserstrom's, Michael J. Wreen and Bonnie Steinbock both argue that adultery is immoral, but for very different reasons. Wreen argues that adultery is morally wrong because it represents contradictory policies and is therefore irrational. Steinbock does not claim that adultery is irrational or that it necessarily breaks a moral rule, but rather, she contends that adulterous activities detract from an *ideal* intimate relationship.

Finally, J. E. and Mary Ann Barnhart portray a more pluralistic view. They claim that different couples have different conceptions of marriage and what their marital commitment means to them. They argue that the morality of extramarital sex ought to be judged relative to these unique commitments. There is no one kind of marriage; therefore, they contend, it is inappropriate to seek one answer to the question whether adultery is immoral.

WHEN ADULTERY MIGHT NOT BE IMMORAL

In a landmark article, "Is Adultery Immoral?" Richard Wasserstrom examines the moral status of adultery. In particular, he addresses the questions, is adultery a moral matter at all, and if so, what makes it immoral?

Wasserstrom identifies two major arguments to show the *prima facie* immorality of adultery: (1) adultery is seriously wrong because it breaks an important *promise,* and (2) adultery involves *deception.* He describes an interesting mode of deception that occurs in a culture that strongly links sex with love and love with marriage. He then questions basic assumptions of this culture: namely, that almost all people believe in the intimate connection between sex and love, and that it is desirable to attribute *symbolic* meaning to sex. Some thinkers suggest that sex be demystified and treated as an intrinsically enjoyable experience—period.

Wasserstrom notes that contemporary champions of sexual liberation argue that sex should be separated from love, or if not, that love should be separated from *exclusivity.*

Finally, given the two major arguments against adultery, Wasserstrom discusses open marriages, concluding that they are simply not immoral. He anticipates the objection that an open marriage is not a marriage at all, responding with an argument that sexual exclusivity is neither a necessary nor a sufficient condition for the existence of a marriage.

from Is Adultery Immoral?

RICHARD WASSERSTROM

Many discussions of the enforcement of morality by the law take as illustrative of the problem under consideration the regulation of various types of sexual behavior by the criminal law. It was, for example, the Wolfenden Report's recommendations concerning homosexuality and prostitution that led Lord Devlin to compose his now famous lecture, "The Enforcement of Morals." And that lecture in turn provoked important philosophical responses from H. L. A. Hart, Ronald Dworkin, and others.

Much, if not all, of the recent philosophical literature on the enforcement of morals appears to take for granted the immorality of the sexual behavior in question. The focus of discussion, at least, is whether such things as homosexuality, prostitution, and adultery ought to be made illegal even if they are immoral, and not whether they are immoral.

I propose in this paper to think about the latter, more neglected topic, that of sexual morality, and to do so in the following fashion. I shall consider just one kind of behavior that is often taken to be a case of sexual immorality—adultery. I am interested in pursuing at least two questions. First, I want to explore the question of in what respects

The selection from Richard Wasserstrom is taken from his article "Is Adultery Immoral?" in *Today's Moral Problems,* edited by Richard Wasserstrom (New York: Macmillan, 1975), pp. 240–248. Used by permission of Macmillan Publishing Co.

adulterous behavior falls within the domain of morality at all: For this surely is one of the puzzles one encounters when considering the topic of sexual morality. It is often hard to see on what grounds much of the behavior is deemed to be either moral or immoral, for example, private homosexual behavior between consenting adults. I have purposely selected adultery because it seems a more plausible candidate for moral assessment than many other kinds of sexual behavior.

The second question I want to examine is that of what is to be said about adultery, without being especially concerned to stay within the area of morality. I shall endeavor, in other words, to identify and to assess a number of the major arguments that might be advanced against adultery. I believe that they are the chief arguments that would be given in support of the view that adultery is immoral, but I think they are worth considering even if some of them turn out to be nonmoral arguments and considerations.

A number of the issues involved seem to me to be complicated and difficult. In a number of places I have at best indicated where further philosophical exploration is required without having successfully conducted the exploration myself. The paper may very well be more useful as an illustration of how one might begin to think about the subject of sexual morality than as an elucidation of important truths about the topic.

Before I turn to the arguments themselves there are two preliminary points that require some clarification. Throughout the paper I shall refer to the immorality of such things as breaking a promise, deceiving someone, etc. In a very rough way, I mean by this that there is something morally wrong that is done in doing the action in question. I mean that the action is, in a strong sense, of *"prima facie"* prima facie wrong or unjustified. I do not mean that it may never be right or justifiable to do the action; just that the fact that it is an action of this description always does count against the rightness of the action. I leave entirely open the question of what it is that makes actions of this kind immoral in this sense of "immoral."

The second preliminary point concerns what is meant or implied by the concept of adultery. I mean by "adultery" any case of extramarital sex, and I want to explore the arguments for and against extramarital sex, undertaken in a variety of morally relevant situations. Someone might claim that the concept of adultery is conceptually connected with the concept of immorality, and that to characterize behavior as adulterous is already to characterize it as immoral or unjustified in the sense described above. There may be something to this. Hence the importance of making it clear that I want to talk about extramarital sexual relations. If they are always immoral, this is something that must be shown by argument. If the concept of adultery does in some sense entail or imply immorality, I want to ask whether that connection is a rationally based one. If not all cases of extramarital sex are immoral (again, in the sense described above), then the concept of adultery should either be weakened accordingly or restricted to those classes of extramarital sex for which the predication of immorality is warranted.

One argument for the immorality of adultery might go something like this: what makes adultery immoral is that it involves the breaking of a promise, and what makes adultery seriously wrong is that it involves the breaking of an important promise. For, so the argument might continue, one of the things the two parties promise each other when they get married is that they will abstain from sexual relations with third persons. Because of this promise both spouses quite reasonably entertain the expectation that the other will behave in conformity with it. Hence, when one of the parties has sexual intercourse with a third person he or she breaks that promise about sexual relationships which was made when the marriage was entered into, and defeats the reasonable expectations of exclusivity entertained by the spouse.

In many cases the immorality involved in breaching the promise relating to extramarital sex may be a good deal more serious than that involved in the breach of other promises. This is so because adherence to this promise may be of much greater importance to the parties than is adherence to many of the other promises given or received by them in their lifetime. The breaking of this promise may be much more hurtful and painful than is typically the case.

Why is this so? To begin with, it may have been difficult for the nonadulterous spouse to have kept the promise. Hence that spouse may feel the unfairness of having restrained himself or herself in the absence of reciprocal restraint having been exercised by the adulterous spouse. In addition, the spouse may perceive the breaking of the promise as an indication of a kind of indifference on the part of the adulterous spouse. If you really cared about me and my feelings—the spouse might say—you would not have done this to me. And third, and related to the above, the spouse may see the act of sexual intercourse with another as a sign of affection for the other person and as an additional rejection of the nonadulterous spouse as the one who is loved by the adulterous spouse. It is not just that the adulterous spouse does not take the feelings of the spouse sufficiently into account, the adulterous spouse also indicates through the act of adultery affection for someone other than the spouse. I will return to these points later. For the present, it is sufficient to note that a set of arguments can be developed in support of the proposition that certain kinds of adultery are wrong just because they involve the breach of a serious promise which, among other things, leads to the intentional infliction of substantial pain by one spouse upon the other.

Another argument for the immorality of adultery focuses not on the existence of a promise of sexual exclusivity but on the connection between adultery and deception. According to this argument, adultery involves deception. And because deception is wrong, so is adultery.

Although it is certainly not obviously so, I shall simply assume in this paper that deception is always immoral. Thus the crucial issue for my purposes is the asserted connection between extramarital sex and deception. Is it plausible to maintain, as this argument does, that adultery always does involve deception and is on that basis to be condemned?

The most obvious person on whom deceptions might be practiced is the nonparticipating spouse; and the most obvious thing about which the nonparticipating spouse can be deceived is the existence of the adulterous act. One clear case of deception is that of lying. Instead of saying that the afternoon was spent in bed with A, the adulterous spouse asserts that it was spent in the library with B, or on the golf course with C.

There can also be deception even when no lies are told. Suppose, for instance, that a person has sexual intercourse with someone other than his or her spouse and just does not tell the spouse about it. Is that deception? It may not be a case of lying if, for example, the spouse is never asked by the other about the situation. Still, we might say, it is surely deceptive because of the promises that were exchanged at marriage. As we saw earlier, these promises provide a foundation for the reasonable belief that neither spouse will engage in sexual relations with any other persons. Hence the failure to bring the fact of extramarital sex to the attention of the other spouse deceives that spouse about the present state of the marital relationship.

Adultery, in other words, can involve both active and passive deception. An adulterous spouse may just keep silent or, as is often the fact, the spouse may engage in an increasingly complex way of life devoted to the concealment of the facts from the nonparticipating spouse. Lies, half-truths, clandestine meetings, and the like may become a central feature of the adulterous spouse's existence. These are things that can and do happen, and when they do they make the case against adultery an easy one. Still, neither active nor passive deception is inevitably a feature of an extramarital relationship.

It is possible, though, that a more subtle but pervasive kind of deceptiveness is a feature of adultery. It comes about because of the connection in our culture between sexual intimacy and certain feelings of love and affection. The point can be made indirectly at first by seeing that one way in which we can, in our culture, mark off our close friends from our mere acquaintances is through the kinds of intimacies that we are prepared to share with them. I may, for instance, be willing to reveal my very private thoughts and emotions to my closest friends or to my wife, but to no one else. My sharing of these intimate facts about myself is from one perspective a way of making a gift to those who mean the most to me. Revealing these things and sharing them with those who mean the most to me is one means by which I create, maintain, and confirm those interpersonal relationships that are of most importance to me.

Now in our culture, it might be claimed, sexual intimacy is one of the chief currencies through which gifts of this sort are exchanged. One way to tell someone—particularly someone of the opposite sex—that you have feelings of affection and love for them is by allowing to them or sharing with them sexual behaviors that one doesn't share with the rest of the world. This way of measuring affection was certainly very much a part of the culture in which I matured. It worked something like this. If you were a girl, you showed how much you liked someone by the degree of sexual intimacy you would allow. If you liked a boy only a little, you never did more than kiss—and even the kiss was not very passionate. If you liked the boy a lot and if your feeling was reciprocated, necking, and possibly petting, was permissible. If the attachment was still stronger and you thought it might even become a permanent relationship, the sexual activity was correspondingly more intense and more intimate, although whether it would ever lead to sexual intercourse depended on whether the parties (and particularly the girl) accepted fully the prohibition on nonmarital sex. The situation for the boy was related, but not exactly the same. The assumption was that males did not naturally link sex with affection in the way in which females did. However, since women did, males had to take this into account. That is to say, because a woman would permit sexual intimacies only if she had feelings of affection for the male and only if those feelings were reciprocated, the male had to have and express those feelings, too, before sexual intimacies of any sort would occur.

The result was that the importance of a correlation between sexual intimacy and feelings of love and affection was taught by the culture and assimilated by those growing up in the culture. The scale of possible positive feelings toward persons of the other sex ran from casual liking at the one end to the love that was deemed essential to and characteristic of marriage at the other. The scale of possible sexual behavior ran from brief, passionless kissing or hand-holding at the one end to sexual intercourse at the other. And the correlation between the two scales was quite precise. As a result, any act of sexual intimacy carried substantial meaning with it, and no act of sexual intimacy was simply a pleasurable set of bodily sensations. Many such acts were, of course, more pleasurable to the participants because they were

a way of saying what the participants' feelings were. And sometimes they were less pleasurable for the same reason. The point is, however, that in any event sexual activity was much more than mere bodily enjoyment. It was not like eating a good meal, listening to good music, lying in the sun, or getting a pleasant back rub. It was behavior that meant a great deal concerning one's feelings for persons of the opposite sex in whom one was most interested and with whom one was most involved. It was among the most authoritative ways in which one could communicate to another the nature and degree of one's affection.

If this sketch is even roughly right, then several things become somewhat clearer. To begin with, a possible rationale for many of the rules of conventional sexual morality can be developed. If, for example, sexual intercourse is associated with the kind of affection and commitment to another that is regarded as characteristic of the marriage relationship, then it is natural that sexual intercourse should be thought properly to take place between persons who are married to each other. And if it is thought that this kind of affection and commitment is only to be found within the marriage relationship, then it is not surprising that sexual intercourse should only be thought to be proper within marriage.

Related to what has just been said is the idea that sexual intercourse ought to be restricted to those who are married to each other as a means by which to confirm the very special feelings that the spouses have for each other. Because the culture teaches that sexual intercourse means that the strongest of all feelings for each other are shared by the lovers, it is natural that persons who are married to each other should be able to say this to each other in this way. Revealing and confirming verbally that these feelings are present is one thing that helps to sustain the relationship; engaging in sexual intercourse is another.

In addition, this account would help to provide a framework within which to make sense of the notion that some sex is better than other sex. As I indicated earlier, the fact that sexual intimacy can be meaningful in the sense described tends to make it also the case that sexual intercourse can sometimes be more enjoyable than at other times. On this view, sexual intercourse will typically be more enjoyable where the strong feelings of affection are present than it will be where it is merely "mechanical." This is so in part because people enjoy being loved, especially by those whom they love. Just as we like to hear words of affection, so we like to receive affectionate behavior. And the meaning enhances the independently pleasurable behavior.

More to the point, moreover, an additional rationale for the prohibition on extramarital sex can now be developed. For given this way of viewing the sexual world, extramarital sex will almost always involve deception of a deeper sort. If the adulterous spouse does not in fact have the appropriate feelings of affection for the extramarital partner, then the adulterous spouse is deceiving that person about the presence of such feelings. If, on the other hand, the adulterous spouse does have the corresponding feelings for the extramarital partner but not toward the nonparticipating spouse, the adulterous spouse is very probably deceiving the nonparticipating spouse about the presence of such feelings toward that spouse. Indeed, it might be argued, whenever there is no longer love between the two persons who are married to each other, there is deception just because being married implies both to the participants and to the world that such a bond exists. Deception is inevitable, the argument might conclude, because the feelings of affection that ought to accompany any act of sexual intercourse can only be held toward one other person at any given time in one's life. And if this is so, then the adulterous spouse always deceives either the partner in adultery or the nonparticipating spouse about the existence of such feelings. Thus extramarital sex involves deception of this sort and is for this reason immoral even if no deception vis-à-vis the occurrence of the act of adultery takes place.

What might be said in response to the foregoing arguments? The first thing that might be said is that the account of the connection between sexual intimacy and feelings of affection is inaccurate. Not inaccurate in the sense that no one thinks of things that way, but in the sense that there is substantially more divergence of opinion than that account suggests. For example, the view I have delineated may describe reasonably accurately the concepts of the sexual world in which I grew up,

but it does not capture the sexual *weltanschauung* of today's youth at all. Thus, whether or not adultery implies deception in respect to feelings depends very much on the persons who are involved and the way they look at the "meaning" of sexual intimacy.

Second, the argument leaves to be answered the question of whether it is desirable for sexual intimacy to carry the sorts of messages described above. For those persons for whom sex does have these implications, there are special feelings and sensibilities that must be taken into account. But it is another question entirely whether any valuable end—moral or otherwise—is served by investing sexual behavior with such significance. That is something that must be shown and not just assumed. It might, for instance, be the case that substantially more good than harm would come from a kind of demystification of sexual behavior: one that would encourage the enjoyment of sex more for its own sake and one that would reject the centrality both of the association of sex with love and of love with only one other person.

I regard these as two of the more difficult, unresolved issues that our culture faces today in respect to thinking sensibly about the attitudes toward sex and love that we should try to develop in ourselves and in our children. Much of the contemporary literature that advocates sexual liberation of one sort or another embraces one or the other of two different views about the relationship between sex and love.

One view holds that sex should be separated from love and affection. To be sure sex is probably better when the partners genuinely like and enjoy each other. But sex is basically an intensive, exciting sensuous activity that can be enjoyed in a variety of suitable settings with a variety of suitable partners. The situation in respect to sexual pleasure is no different from that of the person who knows and appreciates fine food and who can have a very satisfying meal in any number of good restaurants with any number of congenial companions. One question that must be settled here is whether sex can be so demystified; another, more important question is whether it would be desirable to do so. What would we gain and what might we lose if we all lived in a world in which an act of sexual intercourse was no more or less significant or enjoyable than having a delicious meal in a nice setting with a good friend? The answer to this question lies beyond the scope of this paper.

The second view seeks to drive the wedge in a different place. It is not the link between sex and love that needs to be broken; rather, on this view, it is the connection between love and exclusivity that ought to be severed. For a number of the reasons already given, it is desirable, so this argument goes, that sexual intimacy continue to be reserved to and shared with only those for whom one has very great affection. The mistake lies in thinking that any "normal" adult will only have those feelings toward one other adult during his or her lifetime—or even at any time in his or her life. It is the concept of adult love, not ideas about sex, that, on this view, needs demystification. What are thought to be both unrealistic and unfortunate are the notions of exclusivity and possessiveness that attach to the dominant conception of love between adults in our and other cultures. Parents of four, five, six, or even ten children can certainly claim and sometimes claim correctly that they love all of their children, that they love them all equally, and that it is simply untrue to their feelings to insist that the numbers involved diminish either the quantity or the quality of their love. If this is an idea that is readily understandable in the case of parents and children, there is no necessary reason why it is an impossible or undesirable ideal in the case of adults. To be sure, there is probably a limit to the number of intimate, "primary" relationships that any person can maintain at any given time without the quality of the relationship being affected. But one adult ought surely be able to love two, three, or even six other adults at any one time without that love being different in kind or degree from that of the traditional, monogomous, lifetime marriage. And as between the individuals in these relationships, whether within a marriage or without, sexual intimacy is fitting and good.

The issues raised by a position such as this one are also surely worth exploring in detail and with care. Is there something to be called "sexual love" which is different from parental love or the nonsexual love of close friends? Is there something about love in general that links it naturally and appropriately with feelings of exclusivity and possession? Or is there something about sexual love, whatever that may be, that makes these feelings especially fitting here? Once again the issues are conceptual, empirical, and normative all at once: What is love? How could it be different? Would it be a good thing or a bad thing if it were different?

Suppose, though, that having delineated these problems we were now to pass them by. Suppose, moreover, we were to be persuaded of the possibility and the desirability of weakening substantially either the links between sex and love or the links between sexual love and exclusivity. Would it not then be the case that adultery could be free from all of the morally objectionable features described so far? To be more specific, let us imagine that a husband and wife have what is today sometimes characterized as an "open marriage." Suppose, that is, that they have agreed in advance that extramarital sex is—under certain circumstances—acceptable behavior for each to engage in. Suppose, that as a result there is no impulse to deceive each other about the occurrence or nature of any such relationships, and that no deception in fact occurs. Suppose, too, that there is no deception in respect to the feelings involved between the adulterous spouse and the extramarital partner. And suppose, finally, that one or the other or both of the spouses then has sexual intercourse in circumstances consistent with these understandings. Under this description, so the agreement might conclude, adultery is simply not immoral. At a minimum, adultery cannot very plausibly be condemned either on the ground that it involves deception or on the ground that it requires the breaking of a promise.

As one may expect, Richard Wasserstrom's groundbreaking essay on the morality of adultery raises a myriad of challenging questions—questions ranging from technical philosophical arguments regarding promise keeping and deception to bold inquiries concerning alternative social views on our attitudes about sex and love and love and exclusivity. What would the consequences be if our society accepted, on a large-scale basis, the demystification of the sex-love connection and, in fact, treated sex the same as it treats other human activities such as playing tennis and eating meals? Such questions stimulate our imaginations—what would a totally sexually permissive society be like? Certainly, anthropology has described some sexually permissive societies, but we may still ponder the effects of incorporating an openly permissive sexual morality into a highly industrialized, technologically advanced, ethnically/culturally heterogeneous society such as ours.

Would human relationships that separated sex and love and love and exclusivity be better relationships? As we shall see, thinkers such as Bonnie Steinbock will argue that such relationships would sacrifice the great value and ideal of deeply committed monogamous relationships.

Another interesting line of investigation is suggested in the widely held claim that adultery is *prima facie* wrong. Remember that *"prima facie* wrong" means wrong unless there are other overriding reasons. Of the millions of actual instances of adultery, could there be a significant variety of overriding reasons? Let us assume that our own society establishes the general moral rule, "Do not commit adultery." Let us also assume that contemporary lifestyles and relationships no longer embody the static and clearly defined roles they once did. Instead, they now produce an infinite variety of human and marital relationships. Would it not be likely that the general rule prohibiting adultery would prove to be inadequate because of all the exceptions to it that would seem to be warranted giving the changing times? Perhaps a general rule cannot cover all situations and should be supplemented with other rules. Perhaps there is a need for a more basic philosophical project of developing rational methods for distinguishing exceptions to moral rules. As we shall see, some of these issues will be addressed by the Barnharts in a later selection.

Moving away from complex and often speculative discussions of the effects of a more permissive sexual morality or of the consequences that may follow from the recognition of legitimizing reasons for adultery, if any, one may view the morality of adultery in more formalist or Kantian terms whereby one attempts to universalize the principles involved in marriage and in adultery. A clear examination of such an endeavor is to be found in Michael Wreen's article—to which we now turn.

WHY ADULTERY IS ALWAYS IMMORAL

Michael J. Wreen argues, "Contrary to Wasserstrom, . . . we do have good reasons for claiming that adultery is *prima facie* wrong."[1] For Wreen, the one and only commonsense concept of marriage in our culture necessarily includes sexual exclusivity. Thus, marriage requires that one accept a "policy" to have sex only with one's spouse. Further, appealing to Kant's principle of universalizability, Wreen concludes that adultery necessarily involves a contradiction in conception insofar as adultery requires adopting a policy to have sex with someone other than one's spouse, and this violates the policy required by marriage. The contradiction consists of adopting policies which cannot be consistently acted upon or universalized. Moreover, this inconsistency is morally important as it involves social and personal commitment to another person. This argument also applies to open marriage insofar as those involved are consenting to inconsistent policies. Finally, Wreen argues, contra Wasserstrom, that in our culture, sexual exclusivity *is* a necessary condition for marriage.

[1]This statement is puzzling inasmuch as Wasserstrom himself believes most instances of adultery are *prima facie* wrong since they involve either deception or promise breaking.

from What's Really Wrong With Adultery

MICHAEL J. WREEN

While philosophers are probably as interested in adultery as everyone else is—and that's pretty interested—philosophical literature on the topic is somewhat scarcer than that on golden mountains or unicorns. To my knowledge, only one paper devoted exclusively to the topic, Richard Wasserstrom's "Is Adultery Immoral?"[1] has appeared in print thus far. Hence this paper, in which I will argue that, contrary to Wasserstrom's admittedly well-considered views, we do in fact have good grounds for thinking that adultery is *prima facie* wrong.

Before I present my argument, though, a definition of adultery is in order. Wasserstrom defines adultery as "any case of extramarital sex" with "case" here apparently referring to a particular act of sexual intercourse, whether heterosexual or homosexual. My disagreement with this definition is a minor one, though one which, as will be seen, will make a difference in the argument which follows. A given "case" of adultery could involve extramarital sex on the part of one partner but not on the part of the other, namely if the second partner isn't married at all. So, I prefer to define adultery in terms of a particular individual's engaging in a particular act of sexual intercourse with another:

> X's engaging in sexual intercourse with Y at time t is an act of adultery if and only if either X or Y is married at time t, and X and Y are not married to each other at that time.[2]

Why, then, is adultery wrong? Wasserstrom argues that although many, many cases of adultery involve promise breaking, deception, or hurting others, not all do, and so none can serve as a reason for thinking that adultery *per se* is immoral. He is undoubtedly correct about this. Indeed, other reasons for thinking that adultery as such is immoral—that it involves a breach in the relations between two individuals respecting sex and feelings of deep affection (love), or love and exclu-

sivity, or that it threatens the development and maintenance of the nuclear family—all fare little better, according to Wasserstrom, since in each case the argument is incomplete. Sex without love may be not only possible but desirable, and so adultery not immoral (the proper place for love being assumed here, for the sake of argument, to be within, and only within, the confines of marriage). Or, sex without love not being possible or desirable, love with more than one person, or more than the permissible number of marital partners, may be both possible and desirable, and so adultery not immoral. And, as for the preservation of the nuclear family: this argument is predicated on the nuclear family's being desirable, but whether it really is such is far from clear.

The reason that I think that adultery is wrong, however, focuses on what adultery itself is. The key concept is *marriage,* in the common sense, and not necessarily the legal sense, of the term. Marriage, on my view, is living together (or at least a commitment to do so, other things being equal), plus a commitment to at least occasional sexual intercourse if possible—and if not possible, the fact known to both (or however many) marital partners—plus a commitment to exclusivity as far as sexual intercourse is concerned. This definition allows the newly wedded, elderly couples incapable of sexual intercourse, and those married for convenience's sake all to be married. It captures the common view that marriage is commitment, specifically the commitment to be and love as one, and explains why non-consummation is a legally sufficient ground for annulment. Even more to the point, it explains why adultery is a legally sufficient ground for divorce. It is, however, simply the commitment to sexual exclusivity that is important here.[3]

Let us assume for the present, then, that marriage involves a commitment to exclusivity as far as sexual intercourse is concerned. If so, then there

The selection from Michael J. Wreen is taken from a modified version of his article "What's Really Wrong With Adultery" in *International Journal of Applied Philosophy,* Vol. 3, No. 2 (1986), pp. 45–49. Use by permission of *International Journal of Applied Philosophy* and Michael J. Wreen.

does seem to be something wrong with adultery. For, first, such a commitment is, or at least entails, the adoption of a policy, namely the policy to have sexual congress only with a single, particular person of the opposite sex (the example of standard monogamy being used here for simplicity's sake). And secondly, the concept of adultery is logically parasitic on that of marriage; it is defined in terms of marriage, and adulterous behavior logically impossible in the absence of marriage. Given these facts, and given what adultery is, adultery necessarily involves a contradiction in the will—or, to be more accurate (and Kantian), a contradiction in conception. For marriage involves the adoption of a policy of sexual exclusivity; and adultery, by definition, is a violation of that policy, an attack on one of the conceptual cornerstones of marriage itself. The contradiction consists in adopting policies which cannot be consistently acted upon, or universalized. It is inconsistent to adopt both a policy of sexual exclusivity and a policy of engaging in sexual intercourse with a person not specified in the original policy when, for whatever reason, that seems to be a good idea. Let me put the point this way. To be married is, in part, to adopt the maxim "Whenever I engage in sexual intercourse I shall do so with person X," while to commit adultery is, in part, to adopt the maxim "Whenever I engage in sexual intercourse I shall do so for such-and-such or so-and-so reasons, regardless of my sexual commitments." The policies represented by these maxims are internally inconsistent. The immorality—irrationality, in Kant's terms—lies in the contradictoriness of the policies, indeed, the necessary contradictoriness of the policies, not in some other fact.

A succinct way to put this point is the following. Adultery is and must be wrong because, by definition, it involves the violation of a defining commitment of the very institution on which it itself is parasitic. Adultery may not be, as jealousy is, a "green-eyed monster," but it does, conceptually and morally, "mock the meat which it feeds on." It will be noticed that this is a formalist, Kantian objection to adultery. If a good objection, it holds even if the spouse of an adulterer knows of and condones his/her spouse's adulterous behavior. The fact that they are married is sufficient for such behavior to be wrong. (But, it could be replied, a spouse who knows of and condones adulterous behavior is a spouse only in the legal sense of the term. Morally speaking, it could be argued that he/she is no longer married at all, since he/she has released his/her spouse from a commitment to exclusivity. However, given the place of marriage in the architectonics of human value, it is doubtful that a commitment to sexual exclusivity is so easily banished.)

The above argument, however, would seem to apply only to married adulterers; and, as I've noted, not all adulterers are married. What of the non-married person who engages in adultery? Does he/she do anything wrong? I think so; I think the above argument applies at one remove to non-married adulterers, at least in most cases. For *if* such a person accepts the institution of marriage at all, then his/her act of adultery involves a similar contradiction in conception, one between a policy which accepts marriage, and so is committed to honoring the marital commitments of others, and a policy which permits him/her to engage in sexual intercourse whenever such-and-such or so-and-so reasons obtain, regardless of the sexual commitments of his/her partner. The first policy here commits one to respecting marriage commitments; the second allows one to disregard them; and the result is a contradiction in conception similar to that of a married adulterer. Of course, a non-married adulterer may not accept the institution of marriage at all; it is possible to reject the institution altogether. In that case, then, there would seem to be nothing wrong with adultery as such. Rebels of the above sort, though, are, like Cartesian madmen, more the product of the philosopher's imagination than the stuff of flesh and blood people.

One objection to the above argument is that it depends on a false premise: viz., that a commitment to sexual exclusivity is a necessary condition for being married. Wasserstrom, for instance, holds that "it is doubtful that there are many, if any, *necessary* conditions for marriage; but even if there are, a commitment to sexual exclusivity is not such a condition." Why? Because "counterexamples not satisfying [such a] condition are . . . easily produced." Societies in which "polygamy and polyandry are practiced" are no such counterexamples, as Wasserstrom himself recognizes, because these are not societies in which "sex is permitted with someone other than one of the persons to whom one is married." Genuine counterexamples do exist, though, according to Wasserstrom: there are societies "in which it is permissible for married persons to have sexual relations with persons to whom they are not married, for example, temple prostitutes, concubines, and homosexual lovers." And secondly, if "all of the other indicia of marriage were present [—if] the two persons were of the opposite sex . . . and had the capacity and desire to have intercourse with each other . . . and participated in a formal ceremony in which they understood themselves to be entering into a relationship with each other in which substantial mutual commitments were assumed [—then] we would not be in any doubt as to whether the two persons were married, even though they had not taken on a commitment to sexual exclusivity and even though they had agreed that extramarital sexual intercourse was permissible behavior for each to engage in."

Neither of these counterarguments convinces me, however. To take the second one first: I *do* doubt that such a couple is married. From Wasserstrom's description, what I would conclude is that the two people have entered in a public, formalized contractual agreement, one apparently regarding sexual intercourse, i.e., they had agreed to have sexual intercourse with each other, and, apparently, regarding important business matters as well—at least "business matters" is what comes to mind most readily, given that the "substantial mutual commitments" assumed don't include a commitment to sexual exclusivity. Wasserstrom's description, in short, is one of contractual sex plus other mutual services. A formalized, extended prostitute/"John" relationship, one which also included, say, health care in exchange for extensive home repair, as well as sex for money, satisfies his description, as does any other formalized, sex-plus contractual relationship.

As for societies "in which it is permissible for married persons to have sexual relations with persons to whom they are not married . . . temple prostitutes, concubines, and homosexual lovers"— and, perhaps, geisha girls: in and of itself this does not show that marriage does not involve a com-

mitment to sexual exclusivity in such societies. What it does show is that even if marriage does involve a commitment to sexual exclusivity, such societies permit, and may even promote, to some extent, extramarital sex. In point of fact, in the United States, there exist states in which prostitution is legal—and legal not just for the unmarried. There might be any number of reasons why a society condones or even encourages extramarital sex. Legal moralism might be thought objectionable; there might be laws against adultery, but society might, for whatever reason, "look the other way" whenever violations occur, e.g., violations might be pervasive but not harm the society to any appreciable extent (as is the case with widespread violations of anti-jay-walking laws in the United States); tax revenues might be needed (as is the case with legalized, state regulated prostitution in Mexico and Nevada); the general populace might be indifferent to the practice of adultery; and so on.

As a matter of fact, there are even subsectors of societies in which, for cultural reasons, the practice of "the big house" and "the little house" obtains and is enthusiastically supported.[5] In some Latin American countries (or at least parts of those countries) a man is not only expected to marry and maintain a "big house" for his wife and their legitimate offspring; he is also expected—and virtually socially required—to have at least one mistress and to maintain a "little house," which may include supporting illegitimate offspring. The practice may not be publicly proclaimed and applauded, but it is as obvious to, and as accepted by, everyone in such subsectors as the sky. Indeed, the practice is so deeply entrenched that if a husband does not have a mistress, his wife is likely to badger and insult him until he acquires one— *machismo* is that important, and that accepted, a cultural concept. Societies, like people, are complex—far too complex to infer, as Wasserstrom apparently does, that because extramarital sexual intercourse is permitted in some societies, marriage does not involve a commitment to sexual exclusivity in those societies.

A seemingly stronger counterexample, though not one mentioned by Wasserstrom, is provided by "certain cultures [which] permit extramarital sexuality [sexual intercourse, I take it] by married persons with friends, guests, or in-laws."[6] Although the author of this passage does not provide any details, or cite any sources, regarding friends or in-laws—or guests, for that matter—stories of guests being granted the privilege of sleeping with his/her host's spouse—always *his* host's *wife,* in the tales I've been told—are at least as old as European exploration of (and imperialism in) the South Pacific. Supposing the stories true, do we have a genuine counterexample of the sort Wasserstrom requires?

In other words, is *marriage* a family resemblance concept, as Wasserstrom has it? I still think not. Although the point is not generally recognized, the notion of a family resemblance concept can be interpreted, and so can cut, in either of two ways: to show that a given concept, *C,* has no necessary conditions, this being based on the (alleged) fact that *C*s resemble each other only in there being strands of similarity, but nothing common, among *C*s;[7] or—and this is the road not taken—to show that *C* does have necessary conditions, but bears a family resemblance to other concepts. *C', C", C'''*, and so on, which are in the near vicinity and may well be known, for that reason, by the same sobriquet as *C*. Which of the two routes it is best to take in a given case may well depend on a number of factors, but among them are undoubtedly the conceptual entrenchment of a putatively necessary condition, *N,* for *C,* the strength of our intuitions regarding *N,* the place of *N* in binding *C* to other concepts, and the importance of *N* and *C* in the social, scientific, moral, and personal orders. It seems to me that all of these factors argue for the second alternative as far as *marriage* is concerned; that is, they argue for saying, Yes, the South Sea Islanders in question are married—but not in our sense of the term. Family resemblance concepts, in the second sense of the term, are, like relatives, frequently spread far and wide; and again like relatives, they may well bear the same name. But lacking the necessary blood connections, they succeed to no thrones.

Two other objections to my argument can be more briefly stated and answered. First, it might be objected that there is nothing particularly immoral about conduct which entails a contradiction in conception. Contradictions in conception can arise in relation to purely prudential behavior; hence, the question of whether adultery is immoral remains unanswered. Second, it could be argued that there are many imaginable circumstances in which adultery would seem to be morally permissible or even obligatory (or at least an "ought to engage in adultery" judgment would seem to be true). For example, a married man or woman might be experiencing sexual dysfunction, and the couple might realize that the dysfunctional partner's engaging in sexual intercourse with another would help remedy the dysfunction and, in the long run, strengthen the marriage and make them both happier. Adultery would seem to be at least permissible in such circumstances, if the husband, wife, and third party knowingly and voluntarily agree to its occurrence.

The proper answer to the first of these objections, I think, is that adultery is immoral not just because a contradiction in conception is involved, but because the contradiction essentially includes a social, as well as personal, commitment to a second party. Such relationships are, or at least are close to, the paradigm of moral relationships.

The second objection is adequately answered by noting that if my argument is successful, all that it establishes is the *prima facie* wrongness of adultery. Failure of universalizability seems to me, and to most moral philosophers (but not to Kant, of course), to establish no more than the *prima facie* wrongness of a course of behavior. And *prima facie* wrongness can be overridden in some circumstances, such as, in the case of adultery, those indicated above.

Indeed, all that my argument purports to show is that adultery is *prima facie* wrong. I have only grazed the issue of how *prima facie* wrong it is, and a full moral assessment of adultery would require a determination of that, among many other things. Is the *prima facie* wrongness of adultery great, like that of killing a healthy adult, or is it relatively small, like forgetting a friend's birthday? Not as large as the former or as small as the latter, we (or at least I) tend to think; but the argument remains to be given, and would require ranging much farther and wider than space permits here.

So, as I can think of no other objections to my

argument, I conclude that adultery is indeed *prima facie* immoral.[8]

Notes

1. Originally published in Richard Wasserstrom, ed., *Today's Moral Problems* (New York: Macmillan Co., 1975); reprinted in Robert Baker and Frederick Elliston, eds., *Philosophy and Sex,* 1st ed. (Buffalo, NY: Prometheus Books, 1975), pp. 207–221. Subsequent references are to *Philosophy and Sex,* and are indicated in parentheses.

2. This definition should probably be supplemented with the clauses that *X* and *Y* are aware, or should be aware, of his/her own and the other person's marital status, and that each has given his/her consent to engage in sexual intercourse with the other. This rules out, as cases of adultery, the rape of a married woman, sexual intercourse in which, through no fault of his/her own, a person wrongly believes that he/she or his/her

partner isn't married, and so on. Throughout this paper I shall assume that the above are indeed necessary conditions for adultery.

3. And which I need to, and will, defend below.

4. Virtually the same argument is offered for a second time on p. 218.

5. I am grateful to David Decker for bringing the facts noted in this paragraph to my attention.

6. John McMurtry, "Monogamy: A Critique," reprinted in Baker and Elliston, *op. cit.,* pp. 166–177; p. 176 no. 10.

7. A partial examination of the limitations of the notion of a family resemblance concept in this, the usual sense, and a critique of its employment in the philosophy of art can be found in Maurice Mandelbaum, "Family Resemblances and Generalization Concerning the Arts," reprinted in George Dickie and Richard Sclafani, eds., *Aesthetics: A Critical Anthology* (New York: St. Martin's Press, 1977), pp. 500–515.

8. My thanks to Walter L. Weber for reading an earlier draft of this paper and keeping me out of the doghouse.

Wreen presents a tightly argued critique of Wasserstrom's essay. However, some aspects of Wreen's argument are puzzling. Wreen himself concludes that adultery is *prima facie* immoral, but isn't that exactly what Wasserstrom concluded? If, as Wasserstrom argues, adultery is *prima facie* wrong because it breaks a promise to be sexually exclusive, how is this different from Wreen's claim that adultery is wrong because it contradicts the policy adopted by married people to be sexually exclusive?

One difference may reside in Wasserstrom's view that one justification for overriding the *prima facie* wrongness of breaking a promise may be that the parties mutually agree to abandon that promise, as in his example of open marriage. Here, Wreen would argue that since sexual exclusivity is a necessary condition of being married, such people would no longer be married and therefore not committing adultery. To reject the promise of sexual exclusivity is to reject the concept of marriage.

This makes Wreen's counterargument depend entirely on his claim that sexual exclusivity is indeed a necessary condition of being married (in our society). Whether this is in fact a necessary condition for marriage in our society depends, in turn, upon our definition of marriage. One such definition may be the legal definition, but Wreen does not utilize this. Rather, his claim is based upon what he calls the 'commonsense definition.' In short, the key concept in his counterargument is the commonsense concept of marriage. This raises the question, how does Wreen prove that this *is* the commonsense definition of marriage or the one and only concept of marriage found in our society? Do we use dictionaries? Do we ask individuals in our society whether sexual exclusivity is a necessary condition for being married? As we shall see, the Barnharts do not share this claim and see nothing particularly contradictory in married couples allowing some degree of extramarital sex.

So far, the discussions between Wasserstrom and Wreen emphasize the rightness and wrongness of adultery *vis-à-vis* the violation of moral rules. Other writers may attack adultery on grounds that relate not to moral rules *per se* but rather to moral ideals—ideals of the good life. In our next reading, Bonnie Steinbock argues against adultery on the ground that it violates the high value of the ideal of monogamous love and a committed relationship.

WHEN ADULTERY CONFLICTS WITH A MORAL IDEAL

Bonnie Steinbock poses the question whether there is a rational justification for disapproving adultery that holds for everyone and answers in the affirmative. However, she does not base her view on the assumption that the prohibition of adultery is a *moral rule*; in fact, she claims that adultery is a *private* matter. Still, it is in the moral domain, not as a moral rule, but rather, as a moral *ideal*. Agreeing with Wasserstrom that open marriages are not immoral, she defends marital fidelity on a *Romeo and Juliet* model of "true love"—a valued ideal of what marriage should be, an ideal in which one chooses to forgo pleasures with other partners in order to achieve a unique relationship with one's beloved.

Adultery falls within the domain of morality insofar as it relates to a view of a good way for people to live. The prohibition of adultery is neither a moral absolute (there can be extramarital sex without betrayal) nor binding on all rational agents. Steinbock defends the value of fidelity on a particular ideal of married love that depends on what it means to love someone deeply and completely.

from Adultery

BONNIE STEINBOCK

According to a 1980 survey in *Cosmopolitan,* 54 percent of American wives have had extramarital affairs; a study of 100,000 married women by the considerably tamer *Redbook* magazine found that 40 percent of the wives over 40 had been unfaithful. While such surveys are, to some extent, self-selecting—those who do it are more likely to fill out questionnaires about it—sexual mores have clearly changed in recent years. Linda Wolfe, who reported the results of the *Cosmopolitan* survey, suggests that "this increase in infidelity among married women represents not so much a deviation from traditional standards of fidelity as a break with the old double standard." Studies show that men have always strayed in significant numbers.

Yet 80 percent of "COSMO girls" did not approve of infidelity and wished their own husbands and lovers would be faithful. Eighty-eight percent of respondents to a poll taken in Iowa in 1983 viewed "coveting your neighbor's spouse" as a "major sin." It seems that while almost nobody approves of adultery, men have always done it, and women are catching up.

The increase in female adultery doubtless has to do with recent and radical changes in our attitudes toward sex and sexuality. We no longer feel guilty about enjoying sex; indeed, the capacity for sexual enjoyment is often regarded as a criterion of mental health. When sex itself is no longer intrinsically shameful, restraints on sexual behavior are loosened. In fact, we might question whether the abiding disapproval of infidelity merely gives lip service to an ancient taboo. Is there a rational justification for disapproving of adultery which will carry force with everyone, religious and nonreligious alike?

Trust and Deception

Note first that adultery, unlike murder, theft, and lying, is not universally forbidden. Traditional Es-

The selection from Bonnie Steinbock is taken from her article "Adultery" in *QQ: Report from the Center for Philosophy and Public Policy* 6, no. 1 (Winter 1986), pp. 12–14. Reprinted by permission of Bonnie Steinbock.

kimo culture, for example, regarded sharing one's wife with a visitor as a matter of courtesy. The difference can be explained by looking at the effects of these practices on social cohesiveness. Without rules protecting the lives, persons, and property of its members, no group could long endure. Indeed, rules against killing, assault, lying, and stealing seem fundamental to having a morality at all.

Not so with adultery. For adultery is a *private* matter, essentially concerning only the relationship between husband and wife. It is not essential to morality like these other prohibitions: there are stable societies with genuine moral codes which tolerate extra-marital sex. Although adultery remains a criminal offense in some jurisdictions, it is rarely prosecuted. Surely this is because it is widely regarded as a private matter: in the words of Billie Holiday, "Ain't nobody's business if I do."

However, even if adultery is a private matter, with which the state should not interfere, it is not a morally neutral issue. Our view of adultery is connected to our thoughts and feelings about love and marriage, sex and the family, the value of fidelity, sexual jealousy, and exclusivity. How we think about adultery will affect the quality of our relationships, the way we raise our children, the kind of society we have and want to have. So it is important to consider whether our attitudes toward adultery are justifiable.

Several practical considerations militate against adultery: pregnancy and genital herpes immediately spring to mind. However, unwanted pregnancies are a risk of all sexual intercourse, within or without marriage; venereal disease is a risk of all non-exclusive sex, not just adulterous sex. So these risks do not provide a reason for objecting specifically to adultery. In any event, they offer merely pragmatic, as opposed to moral, objections. If adultery is wrong, it does not become less so because one has been sterilized or inoculated against venereal disease.

Two main reasons support regarding adultery as seriously immoral. One is that adultery is an instance of promise-breaking, on the view that marriage involves, explicitly or implicitly, a promise of sexual fidelity: to forsake all others. That there is this attitude in our culture is clear. Mick Jagger, not noted for sexual puritanism, allegedly refused to marry Jerry Hall, the mother of his baby, because he had no intention of accepting an exclusive sexual relationship. While Jagger's willingness to become an unwed father is hardly mainstream morality, his refusal to marry, knowing that he did not wish to be faithful, respects the idea that *marriage* requires such a commitment. Moreover, the promise of sexual fidelity is regarded as a very serious and important one. To cheat on one's spouse indicates a lack of concern, a willingness to cause pain, and so a lack of love. Finally, one who breaks promises cannot be trusted. And trust is essential to the intimate partnership of marriage, which may be irreparably weakened by its betrayal.

The second reason for regarding adultery as immoral is that it involves deception, for example, lying about one's whereabouts and relations with others. Perhaps a marriage can withstand the occasional lie, but a pattern of lying will have irrevocable consequences for a marriage, if discovered, and probably even if not. Like breaking promises, lying is regarded as a fundamental kind of wrongdoing, a failure to take the one lied to seriously as a moral person entitled to respect.

Open Marriage

These two arguments suffice to make most cases of adultery wrong, given the attitudes and expectations of most people. But what if marriage did not involve any promise of sexual fidelity? What if there were no need for deception, because neither partner expected or wanted such fidelity? Objections to "open marriage" cannot focus on promise-breaking and deception, for the expectation of exclusivity is absent. If an open marriage has been freely chosen by both spouses, and not imposed by a dominant on a dependent partner, would such an arrangement be morally acceptable, even desirable?

The attractiveness of extramarital affairs, without dishonesty, disloyalty, or guilt, should not be downplayed. However satisfying sex between married people may be, it cannot have the excitement of a new relationship. ("Not *better*, a friend once said defensively to his wife, attempting to explain his infidelity, "just *different*.") Might we not be better off, our lives fuller and richer, if we allowed ourselves the thrill of new and different sexual encounters?

Perhaps the expectations of sexual exclusivity in marriage stems from emotions which are not admirable: jealousy and possessiveness. That most people experience these feelings is no reason for applauding or institutionalizing them. Independence in marriage is now generally regarded as a good thing: too much "togetherness" is boring and stifling. In a good marriage, the partners can enjoy different activities, travel apart, and have separate friends. Why draw the line at sexual activity?

The natural response to this question invokes a certain conception of love and sex: sex is an expression of affection and intimacy and so should be reserved for people who love each other. Further, it is assumed that one can and should have such feelings for only one other person at any time. To make love with someone else is to express feelings of affection and intimacy that should be reserved for one's spouse alone.

This rejection of adultery assumes the validity of a particular conception of love and sex, which can be attacked in two ways. We might divorce sex from love and regard sex as a pleasurable activity in its own right, comparable to the enjoyment of a good meal. In his article "Is Adultery Immoral?"[1] Richard Wasserstrom suggests that the linkage of sex with love reflects a belief that unless it is purified by a higher emotion, such as love, sex is intrinsically bad or dirty.

But this is an overly simplistic view of the connection between sex and love. Feelings of love occur between people enjoying sexual intercourse, not out of a sense that sexual pleasure must be purified, but precisely because of the mutual pleasure they give one another. People naturally have feelings of affection for those who make them happy, and sex is a very good way of making someone extraordinarily happy. At the same time, sex is by its nature intimate, involving both physical and psychological exposure. This both requires and creates trust, which is closely allied to feelings of affection and love. This is not to say that sex necessarily requires or leads to love; but a conception of the relation between love and sex that ignores these factors is inadequate and superficial.

Alternatively, one might acknowledge the connection between sex and love, but attack the assumption of exclusivity. If parents can love all their children equally and if adults can have numerous close friends, why should it be impossible to love more than one sexual partner at a time? Perhaps we could learn to love more than one sexual partner at a time? Perhaps we could learn to love more widely and to accept that a spouse's sexual involvement with another is not a sign of rejection or lack of love.

The logistics of multiple involvement are certainly daunting. Having an affair (as opposed to a roll in the hay) requires time and concentration; it will almost inevitably mean neglecting one's spouse, one's children, one's work. More important, however, exclusivity seems to be an intrinsic part of "true love." Imagine Romeo pouring out his heart to both Juliet *and* Rosalind! In our ideal of romantic love, one chooses to forgo pleasure with other partners in order to have a unique relationship with one's beloved. Such "renunciation" is natural in the first throes of romantic love; it is precisely because this stage does *not* last that we must promise to be faithful through the notoriously unromantic realities of married life.

Fidelity As an Ideal

On the view I have been defending, genuinely open marriages are not *immoral,* although they deviate from a valued ideal of what marriage should be. While this is not the only ideal, or incumbent on all rational agents, it is a moral view in that it embodies a claim about a good way for people to live. The prohibition of adultery, then, is neither arbitrary nor irrational. However, even if we are justified in accepting the ideal of fidelity, we know that people do not always live up to the ideals they accept and we recognize that some failures to do so are worse than others. We regard a brief affair, occasioned by a prolonged separation, as morally different from installing a mistress.

Further, sexual activity is not necessary for deviation from the ideal of marriage which lies behind the demand for fidelity. As John Heckler observed during his bitter and public divorce from former Health and Human Services Secretary Margaret Heckler, "In marriage, there are two partners. When one person starts contributing far less than the other person to the marriage, that's the original infidelity. You don't need any third party." While this statement was probably a justification of his own infidelities, the point is valid. To abandon one's spouse, whether to a career or to another person, is also a kind of betrayal.

If a man becomes deeply involved emotionally with another woman, it may be little comfort that he is able to assure his wife that "Nothing happened." Sexual infidelity has significance as a sign of a deeper betrayal—falling in love with someone else. It may be objected that we cannot control the way we feel, only the way we behave; that we should not be blamed for falling in love, but only for acting on the feeling. While we may not have direct control over our feelings, however, we are responsible for getting ourselves into situations in which certain feelings naturally arise. "It just happened," is rarely an accurate portrayal of an extramarital love affair.

If there can be betrayal without sex, can there be sex without betrayal? In the novel *Forfeit,* by Dick Francis, the hero is deeply in love with his wife, who was paralyzed by polio in the early days of their marriage. Her great unspoken fear is that he will leave her; instead, he tends to her devotedly. For several years, he forgoes sex, but eventually succumbs to an affair. While his adultery is hardly praiseworthy, it is understandable. He could divorce his wife and marry again, but it is precisely his refusal to abandon her, his continuing love and tender care, that makes us admire him.

People do fall in love with others and out of love with their spouses. Ought they refrain from making love while still legally tied? I cannot see much, if any, moral value in remaining physically faithful, on principle, to a spouse one no longer loves. This will displease those who regard the wrongness of adultery as a moral absolute, but my account has nothing to do with absolutes and everything to do with what it means to love someone deeply and completely. It is the value of that sort of relationship that makes sexual fidelity an ideal worth the sacrifice.

Neither a mere religiously based taboo, nor a relic of a repressive view of sexuality, the prohibition against adultery expresses a particular conception of married love. It is one we can honor in our own lives and bequeath to our children with confidence in its value as a coherent and rational ideal.

Note

1. In Wasserstrom's *Today's Moral Problems* (New York: Macmillan, 1975), 288–300. Reprinted in R. Baker and F. Elliston, eds., *Philosophy and Sex,* 1st ed. (Buffalo, NY: Prometheus, 1975), 207–21; 2nd ed. (1984), 93–106.

Unlike Wasserstrom and Wreen, Bonnie Steinbock has fashioned a defense of the prohibition against adultery that is not based on the violation of objective moral rules, but rather, on the ground that the prohibition underwrites a rationally justified ideal that holds for everyone. However, Steinbock later concedes, ". . . this is not the only ideal, or incumbent on all rational agents. . . ." How does this square with the opening claim that this ideal holds for everyone? Why call this a *moral* ideal? She answers the latter question by adding, ". . . it embodies a claim about a good way for people to live." Here "good" could mean morally good or prudentially good—that is, good in terms of one's long-range enlightened self-interest.

Has Steinbock produced arguments to show that we rationally must accept the "morally good" interpretation? If, on the other hand, the arguments are prudential, why must we accept the moral prohibition? Even if romantic-monogamous marriage, as she admits, is one rationally justified ideal, and there may be others, why accept a general prohibition that devalues the other ideals? Could we rationally justify other ideals of what a good marriage is?

In our next selection, we shall see the Barnharts argue for this very point. Might not there be a variety of ideals that may be rationally justified relative to the actual needs and desires of the individuals involved in their respective marriages?

WHY ADULTERY NEED NOT BE IMMORAL

Noting the strong negative connotations built into the word *adultery*, J. E. and Mary Ann Barnhart discuss the moral issue of adultery in terms of extramarital sexual intimacy (EMS). EMS can be judged as either immoral, moral, or amoral. In contrast to Wreen, the Barnharts claim that even in monogamy, empirical facts show there are many types of marriages and different kinds of marital commitments as opposed to one concept of "true marriage" that requires sexual exclusivity.

The Barnharts propose that moral judgments against infidelity should be construed as breaking faith with the terms of an agreement within a particular marriage. Consequently, if a husband and wife agree to some degree of EMS (such as open marriage), there would be no unfaithfulness or deceit. In sum, the morality of marital relationships should depend on what the members of the marriage want, expect, and promise each other.

Some degree of EMS may promote personal freedom and, contra Steinbock, may be considered an *ideal* form of marriage and romantic passion. In some cases, the inclusion of EMS in a marriage may be a better way to cope in a culture that produces alienation and depersonalization, may make life more interesting and enriching, and may give some happiness to those in a troubled marriage.

The Barnharts note that romantic passion can lead to extreme possessiveness, jealousy, or hero worship, but it can also, for some, give new hope and meaning to their lives. The problem is how to retain the positive while avoiding the negative consequences of EMS. The Barnharts conclude with a plea for tolerance for those marriages that exclude EMS and those that permit it.

from Marital Faithfulness and Unfaithfulness _____

J. E. AND MARY ANN BARNHART

It is a curious fact that many persons professing a religious allegiance hold that while killing other human beings is sometimes justified (and on occasion is a positive moral imperative), committing adultery is never justified. In fact, the commandment "Thou shalt not kill" has been revised (or, as some would say, it has been better *translated*) to read "Thou shalt not commit murder." Such a revision or translation makes it possible to place perhaps the majority of killings outside the domain of the Old Testament commandment. However, no such similar revision or translation of the prohibition against adultery has gained general acceptance among Christians and Jews. In fact, Jesus, instead of narrowing the definition of 'adultery,' expanded it to include looking "upon a woman to lust after her."

In his book *The Scientific Study of Religion,* the sociologist J. Milton Tinger calls attention to the fact that it is difficult to find a neutral vocabulary in the study of religion. He bemoans the lack of objective vocabulary that plagues him and others as sociologists of religion. The term 'adultery' is charged in such a way as to evoke a negative response. And the word 'unfaithfulness,' when used in some contexts, carries the added emphasis that adultery is not only intercourse outside the marriage circle, but is also deception and, in popular parlance, "cheating" on one's spouse. The term 'unfaithfulness' usually functions to prevent prob-

The selection from J. E. and Mary Ann Barnhart is taken from their article "Marital Faithfulness and Unfaithfulness" in *Journal of Social Philosophy,* Vol. iv, No. 2 (April 1973), pp. 10–15. Reprinted by permission of the *Journal of Social Philosophy.*

ably most persons from thinking of adultery that is not also couched in deceit and deception of at least one spouse. Indeed, adultery is often so readily associated with deceit and deception of especially one's spouse that there is a strong tendency to *define* it in terms of deceit and deception. Hence the words 'unfaithfulness' and 'infidelity' become interchangeable with 'adultery.'

Now, this raises the question as to whether adultery can be engaged in without deceit. If it can, then it is adultery? The trouble with defining 'adultery' in such a way as to include deceit as a part of its *meaning* is that whenever we learn of someone's engaging in extramarital sexual intimacy, we do not know how to classify him if he has not deceived his spouse. (We will perhaps be forgiven the shorthand here. We use "him" to mean either husband or wife, as the case may be.) If someone honestly tells his spouse that he is engaging in extramarital sexual intimacy, then can he be said to be unfaithful to her? If so, then 'unfaithfulness' would, in this context, seem to *mean* the extramarital sexual intimacy itself rather than deceit or bad faith.

Extramarital sexual intercourse may conceivably be judged as either moral, amoral, or immoral. There is also extramarital intimacy of a *non-sexual* nature too, which often has considerable bearing—for good or ill—on the marriage. We will use EMN to symbolize extramarital intimacy of a non-sexual nature. We will use EMS to symbolize the extramarital intimacy that either combines both the sexual and non-sexual dimensions or is primarily sexual in nature.

Wives as Property and Possessions

In many ways the adulterer has been treated as if he were a cattle thief stealing property having another man's brand. (Until only a few decades ago in the United States the wedding ring was usually worn only by the wife and functioned somewhat as a brand bestowed by the husband.) The notion of wives as property goes back at least as far as the Old Testament. And even in our civilized times it is not uncommon in some circles to hear a woman referred to as a "piece"—as if she were a piece of property or possession for rent, use, or sale. A pop-

ular song has the words "There goes my only possession," which is, of course, his woman. The relationship is one of I-it rather than I-thou. At least some of the Old Testament gives this clear impression that a wife belongs among a man's possessions. To covet another man's wife is to covet one of his most valuable possessions, perhaps his most valuable. The Old Testament prohibition against adultery seems to be a subheading of the prohibition against coveting the possessions of another man.

The issue of the immorality of morality of EMS would seem to have a new setting (at the very least) if the view of the wife as property or possession is rejected. If a wife does not belong to a man as a piece of property, then the question arises as to whether she is bound (obligated, etc.) to him in the way of property regulations. To be sure, marriage has its strict bounds, bonds, and obligations. There can be no serious question about that. But the nature of these bonds has to be carefully unpacked.

Faithfulness According to Marital Style

Empirical data show that there are all sorts of marriages and all sorts of marital commitments even for couples, to say nothing of possible marriages of more than two. To be sure, we may decide that only one style of marriage is the "true" marriage, all the others being mere approximations of it or even fake-images of it. But what style will it be? Will it be Billy Graham's marriage? Here is a man who has traveled considerably, leaving his wife at home at long periods of time to rear their children. Is that an ideal for every couple? Some men of the cloth have chosen not to marry so that they could devote their time to their religious vocations. Dr. Graham chose to opt for a compromise. Luckily his wife Ruth agreed to the arrangement. Another woman might not have been so understanding. She might not have consented to sharing her spouse with the great demands of the Billy Graham Evangelistic Association.

'Unfaithfulness,' then, might more accurately be defined, in a marital context, as breaking faith with the terms of agreement, dedication, and commitment. That is, it is a breaking of the bonds by which the couple have obligated themselves to one another. Hence, it would seem that if a husband and wife should agree to some measure of EMS (or EMN) on the part of one or both spouses, then no unfaithfulness, deceit, or deception would be involved. The morality of marital relationships and extramarital relationships (whether sexual or nonsexual) depends considerably upon what the members of the marriage want and expect from one another and what they promise (realistically) to give to one another. Hence, a rock-bottom meaning of 'marital faithfulness' would seem to entail a clear and honest spelling out to one another those expectations, wants, promises, and capacities for keeping promises.

Extramarital Intimacy and Personal Freedom

Marriages change. But successful communication (of the kind mentioned above) can help the change to flow somewhat more smoothly and creatively. If EMS becomes a part of a couple's repertoire, then it would seem that moral rules and regulations would have to be developed between the husband and wife if they are not only to know what they are about, but also to keep EMS within the bounds appropriate to their particular marriage style. To be sure, many—perhaps most—marriages lack the social, economic, etc. means for EMS. Such a strain on these marriages would simply be too much to bear. But does that mean that EMS is in itself evil? Or does it suggest that it is evil only when the couple lack the means, capacity, and development for incorporating it into their marriage? This is not an easy question to handle. It raises the question as to whether or not a thriving marriage that permits or encourages a measure of EMS and EMN is not an *ideal* to aim at. Of course, ideals have a way of generating great frustration whenever means are not realistically at hand. Which is to say that the evangelist of EMS, in particular, may not be liberating people so much as increasing their relative deprivation. To generate expectations without realistic empirical means of fulfillment is to increase *un*freedom, not freedom; for freedom is the net *satisfaction* of wants and is not merely the bare increase of wants.

Evil Effects and Evil Causes

In the social and behavioral sciences in particular, there is a tendency to look for "evil" or "inferior" causes of effects that are judged to be "evil." This fallacy has created a considerable fog over the question of EMS. Assuming EMS to be evil, counselors and psychiatrists and others have often searched for the hidden "evil" motives that issue into EMS. It is often supposed by non-specialists that a "bad marriage" must have produced EMS in every case. Or in more scientific-sounding terms, the party guilty of EMS is regarded as "neurotic," "insecure," etc. True, some persons engaging in EMS may be bored, sexually frustrated, homosexual, fickle, or whatever. But the same may be said of many persons about to enter marriage. In fact, some of the early church fathers seemed to think that marriage is at best a necessary evil that is caused by a comparable evil, namely, sexual passion, which some Christians took in some way to be the ultimate human cause of all sin. It has, by contrast, been said of many who decline to marry that they are poorly motivated, that only "evil" causes could produce the "evil" state of bachelorhood. What causes this tendency among some social scientists to search for "evil" causes to explain "evil" effects is unclear to us, but we will resist the temptation to suppose there is some evil cause at work.

It is at least conceivable that in some cases, EMS is a more or less successful way of coping with a culture that manifests many patterns of alienation and depersonalization. In other cases, however, EMS may simply be a way of making life for at least two persons more interesting and enriching, while in still other cases it may be an attempt to gain some measure of happiness despite a marriage that is coming apart. Whether or not EMS is itself a causal factor contributing to either the dissolution or the improvement of a marriage would seem to be a matter of empirical inquiry into each specific marriage in question, for there are numerous variables at play in each marriage. This does not at all suggest that a science of marriage (and even a technology of marriage) is impossible. Doubtless, there are many marriage styles for which EMS is either ruled out by definition or is made practically impossible because of the difficulty of harmonizing excessive tension among wants and needs. In this latter case behavioral science ought to be coming up with studies and findings which can make our moral decisions better informed.

The Spouse's Right to Know

Let us assume for the present that for some persons at least, the ideal marriage style includes EMS that is not hidden from the spouse. Does this entail that if the EMS must be concealed from the spouse, then EMS ought not to be engaged in? It would be very difficult to give a general rule in answer to this question because the rule might die the death of a thousand qualifications in applying it to actual marriages. There is furthermore the question as to how much self-revelation can be demanded of a spouse, and here marriages differ greatly from one another. Some couples, for example, can reveal to one another their sexual fantasies about other persons outside the marriage. Yet even here the revelations may vary in detail. Some marriages accept more details than do others, while some could not even so much as admit verbally any fantasies at all.

The Logic of Intimacy

This raises a practical moral problem. If someone is engaged in EMS (or EMN for that matter), does not the very meaning of 'intimacy' entail that some things must remain secret? That is, if, say, Jonathan has an intimate marriage with Betty, he would seem to be bound morally not to reveal to his EMS friend, Peggy, certain details about the life of Betty. By the same token he would be obligated not to reveal to Betty certain things about Peggy. Indeed, to recognize this is simply to understand what is involved both in the primary intimacy of EMS (or EMN). To violate this obligation is either to practice deceit (unfaithfulness in the wider sense) or to fail to grasp the nature of the relationships engaged in.

Marital Rights Have Contexts and Consequences

Is it always true that the EMS which is kept wholly secret from the spouse is a case of unfaithfulness?

The answer might seem to be Yes. But perhaps there are situations in which the spouse does not have a *right* to know. We might more easily agree that while it is perfectly permissible to have at least a moderate number of fantasies regarding persons outside the marriage, the spouse has no *right* to demand that the fantasies be revealed to her (or him). Some things are private—even in marriage. Yet, even here it depends upon the nature of the given individual marriage itself. Obviously if a couple should seriously agree to reveal to one another their fantasies, then each member of the marriage would have a right to expect such revelations from the other.

It would appear that much of the talk of the "right" of one spouse to know of the other's EMS becomes talk about what the consequences would be if the secret were revealed and what the consequences would be if it were not revealed. And these consequences must include the pattern that might be established in keeping still another secret from one's spouse.

Levels of Communication

We are strongly tempted to draw the conclusion, therefore, that marriage cannot function without considerable open and efficient communication between husband and wife. But it would be a mistake to yield to this temptation. Nevertheless, it is probably safe to say that relationships of a special kind between husband and wife—relationships thought by many to be highly valuable—cannot be enjoyed without a considerable amount of honest and forthright communication between husband and wife. Yet even here the communication cannot come all at once. Communication about some matters cannot safely come about until communication about other matters first develops. In fact, there must be some measure of communication between husband and wife before they can know when and how to advance to another level of communication. Marital faithfulness might entail knowing when and how to make such an advance and when and how not to. In some cases, to reveal information, new suggestions, etc. too quickly is to break the lines of communication already established. In other cases, however, failure to reveal, suggest, etc. may be a serious mistake because the spouse feels that he (or she) has a right (i.e., rightly expects) to receive the communique. After a certain level of development, a marriage of a certain style may be viewed after the model of a highly sensitive and responsive communication system that is taking in new data without suffering an untimely overload. But of course, the marriage is more than this.

Romantic Passion and Relative Deprivation

Romantic passion is what we sometimes call "love" when we say with Shakespeare that "Love is blind." It is not easily checked by evidence and logic. It is often impulsive and its hopes and dreams seem to fly into the face of reality. It is a kind of euphoric utopianism. It is sometimes seen in hero worship and even in religious conversion. It professes total commitment, devotion, and in its extreme form becomes worship and adoration (as many of the so-called "love songs" reveal). It even promotes excessive possessiveness and resists even the most modest attempts to raise doubts about the object of one's affections. In many cases the person "loved" is transformed into a symbol of something that can best be described as an urge-for-Camelot. There is even *mysterium tremendum* that the "loved one" evokes.

In some cases the "lover" professes to be ready to sacrifice his whole being for his "loved one." He will be a "fool" for her, just as Paul spoke of being a "fool for Christ." Romantic passion sometimes develops into a kind of humanized monotheism—Thou shalt have no other men (or women) before me in any respect whatsoever! Jealousy and possessiveness—opposites of love—sometimes swell out of control.

Nevertheless, it is essential to understand that the romantic passion offers for many a hope of "new life." This seems to be essential for many people if they are to have "meaning" in their lives. We see much good in this aspect of romantic passion so long as it does not become excessive, although in some cases it is difficult to know precisely where excess begins.

Doubtless this hope for new life or new possibilities is a source of many reforms, marriages, and extramarital relations (sexual and nonsexual).

How both to extract the best from romantic passion and to eliminate the worst consequences—that would seem to be a challenge to interest behavioral scientists and counselors. By and large romantic passion generates vague expectations of great intensity. These expectations are difficult to deal with because they are vague and intense. They become a source of much frustration and disappointment. Romantic passion itself needs to be reformed if the gap of relative deprivation is to be closed. Perhaps one of the most practical ways of reforming it is to develop programs by which married people can gain real success in certain areas of their marriage—e.g., Masters and Johnson's work in sexual enjoyment—so that their interests will turn to the real successes rather than to the more hopeless promises. Whether or not actual success in various areas of marriage will tend to reduce EMS remains to be seen. It may set the stage for a low-key attitude of greater acceptance of EMS—for some marriages at least.

Tolerance of Multiple Styles

In his controversial book *Future Shock,* Alvin Toffler portrays our society as one in which change is king—even in marriage. But if change is not to become chaos, some stability factors are essential. We suggest that in our highly mobile society, *exchange* of one spouse for another via the route of divorce is often a very dear price to pay for many persons. If marriage can be conditioned and nourished in such a way as to make a mutual change and growth *within* marriage possible instead of an exchange of spouses, then perhaps the marriage relationship could itself function as a stabilizing factor in a world of high mobility, accelerated change, and estrangement.

It may be that some marriages can remain stabilized and stabilizing, as well as interesting and productive, if either EMS or EMN is allowed to enrich at least one member of the marriage without injuring the other member. There are some marriage counselors who are beginning to suggest that this is the case. It may be the case for some marriages, but it is hardly a panacea for all. What the effects of EMS are on marriage whenever a more tolerant attitude toward it prevails is a matter that more and more behavioral scientists ought to be studying. There is no useful point in presupposing that husband and wife have a kind of preestablished harmony of even sexual interest, although doubtless care in selecting spouses could better approximate this ideal. But EMS may be one way of coming to terms with the fact that this perfect preestablished harmony does not exist. The price that EMS demands needs to be made clearer before it becomes a fad with very costly consequences.

Finally, a question needs to be raised about the assumption that one's spouse ought to be the *sole* source of sexual enrichment. The husband is hardly the only source of enrichment for his wife in other areas. Why should he be expected to be so in the sexual area alone? Is there something intrinsic to sexuality to make it an exclusive relationship? On the other hand, why should a person be presumed to be pathological if he finds his own spouse to be the sole source of sexual satisfaction? One psychologist suggests that such sexual exclusiveness is "a sign of intense inhibition." In some cases it may be, but in other cases it may not. And even when it is, there may not be much that can be done to improve the situation without creating a worse situation.

Hence, a plea for tolerance would seem to be in order. Those couples who wish to be left to have their sexual relationship exclusively within the marital circle alone should not be made to endure the flirtations, etc. of others. And those who wish to participate in EMS of some sort should be allowed to do so. Currently there seems to be no efficient and unobtrusive means of communicating preferences on this matter, which means that those inclined to EMS risk being embarrassed, while those preferring no EMS risk being unnecessarily bothered or even insulted.

It is interesting to note that although the Barnharts' brief essay predates the three preceding ones, it seems to address points in each of them. With respect to Wasserstrom, the Barnharts suggest that passive deception may sometimes be justified. To Wreen, the Barnharts clearly do not accept his monolithic definition of marriage whereby nothing would count as a marriage if it did not require sexual exclusivity. Finally, as concerns Steinbock, the Barnharts argue for a pluralistic conception of the ideal marriage—one which allows for couples to create their own ideal marriages relative to their respective needs and desires.

This chapter has generated many challenging questions. Among others, we may consider the following: Can reason justify an absolute prohibition of adultery or, instead, a *prima facie* one? If reason justifies a *prima facie* prohibition, under what circumstances would given cases of adultery be morally permissible? Must a society such as ours make sexual exclusivity a necessary condition for marriage, or could society prosper with marriages in which some participants allow a degree of extramarital sex? Must society promote one kind of ideal marriage like that proposed by Steinbock? If society were to allow couples to create their own marriages and choose their own ideal relationships, would there be dire consequences? If so, can we produce rational arguments to support the prediction of these dire consequences?

While we have raised a few questions concerning adultery, it is likely that the reader will think of many others. Philosophy considers this a plus, for well-thought-out questions inspire one's journey toward wisdom.

CHAPTER 6

Prostitution

$\mathbf{P}$ROSTITUTION,[1] KNOWN AS THE WORLD'S OLDEST PROFESSION, not surprisingly raises a host of philosophical and ethical issues; nevertheless, it has been a subject almost completely ignored by academic philosophers. In this chapter, we shall focus on the investigations of several contemporary philosophers who address some of the most fundamental ethical issues concerning prostitution. Before turning to their writings, however, some preliminary remarks are in order.

To begin with, it is important to avoid simple generalizations and stereotypes. Not all prostitutes are alike, but in fact represent a wide variety of arrangements, such as high-priced call girls, house prostitutes, escorts, massage attendants, streetwalkers, some bar girls and strippers, dominatrices, lesbian prostitutes, male heterosexual and homosexual prostitutes, child prostitutes, etc.[2] Not all prostitutes are forced into "white slavery," and many freely choose "the life." Just as there are different types, prostitutes report different motivations for their activities, some of which include attraction to easy money, perceived adventure and excitement, possible contact with high status men, a sense of power, playing the role of an experienced professional, money for drugs, etc.

As prostitutes have different motives, so, too, do their male customers. Some of their stated reasons include simple sexual gratification, sexual gratification without emotional commitment or relationship, variety of partners or sexual acts, and curiosity. In addition, some male customers seek either to impress other males with their masculinity, to experience the illusion of romance, to be mothered, to relax with a sympathetic listener, to act out fantasies, to escape loneliness, to relieve the sexual frustration of not having a partner, or to engage in certain sexual acts his own partner finds objectionable.[3]

In modern Western society, prostitution is generally considered deviant and immoral behavior. The idea of sex for money sharply contrasts with Judeo-Christian ideals of love, marriage, and the purposes of sex, such as procreation, the expression of love, and shared intimacy between monogamous lovers.

Not only is prostitution considered by most to be immoral, but it is classified as a crime in all 50 states (except for a few counties in Nevada). Since many acts of prostitution are considered victimless crimes in which both parties agree to have private consensual sex, many thinkers have raised questions concerning its criminalization. The initial contemporary philosophical writings in prostitution emanated from just this issue: Is it morally right to use the law to enforce morality? The *cause célèbre* was the 1957 "Report of the

---

[1]For practical purposes, let us define prostitution as providing sexual activities in exchange for the immediate payment of money.

[2]Since the overwhelming majority of prostitutes are females, female prostitution will be the focus of this discussion, and the term *prostitution,* unless otherwise noted, will be used to refer to females.

[3]For further factual information, see *Dimensions of Human Sexuality,* Jones, Shainberg and Byer, eds. Dubuque, IA: William C. Brown Publishers, 1985, pp. 613–627.

Wolfenden Commission" in England, which contended that such private "immoral" behaviors as adultery, homosexuality, and prostitution ought not to be subjected to the criminal law. The report soon became the object of a classic confrontation of ideas between Sir Patrick Devlin and H. L. A. Hart, followed by numerous responses from other philosophers.

Some other ethical issues are raised by laws criminalizing prostitution. Do they discriminate against women? Do they make the life of the prostitute more dangerous? Do they turn otherwise law-abiding citizens into criminals? Do they invade our right to privacy? Do they encourage the expenditure of huge sums of public money that could be put to better use? As a result, many today advocate the decriminalization of prostitution or legalization regulated by the state.

The claim that prostitution is immoral has been based upon diverse assumptions ranging from religious ideals concerning sex, love, and marriage to the Kantian belief that a person should never be used as a means only. In our lead article, we find a philosopher, Lars Ericsson, refusing to *assume* prostitution is immoral. Ericsson formulates the fundamental question concerning the most basic value judgment regarding prostitution: that is, is prostitution *undesirable?* Ericsson then argues that while prostitution is *not* ultimately desirable (i.e., desirable in a perfect world), it is conditionally desirable (desirable in the imperfect real world).

Following Ericsson are two critical articles representing the feminist point of view: Carole Pateman charges that Ericsson completely misunderstands the feminist objection to prostitution, as does Laurie Schrage, who presents a feminist case for opposing prostitution.

THE CASE FOR SOUND PROSTITUTION

Unlike most discussions of prostitution, in "Charges Against Prostitution," Lars Ericsson zeroes in on the *most basic value judgment* or "unshakeable postulate" that has guided all philosophical discussions of prostitution; that is, *prostitution is undesirable.* This, in turn, leads to the proposition that prostitution ought to be eradicated. Ericsson argues that while prostitution is *not* ultimately desirable, (that is, desirable in a perfect world), it *is* conditionally desirable (desirable in the imperfect real world).

Strategically, Ericsson first attacks all the main arguments against prostitution (referred to as "charges") one by one,[4] and then more positively proposes a system of "sound prostitution." In general, Ericsson finds that most of the antiprostitution arguments are biased by society's "negative and hostile attitudes towards prostitution grounded in centuries of ignorance, superstition and blind moral and religious dogmas."

Very briefly, some of the charges examined by Ericsson include: *The Charge of Conventional Morality,* which is that prostitution is *intrinsically* evil or intrinsically immoral. Ericsson explicates several factors underlying the conventional moralists' view and concludes that in the end the charge is nothing but the dogmatic assertion of "intrinsic wrongness," which amounts to saying, "This is how I see it." As such, no arguments or justifications are even offered.

The Sentimentalist Charge is interesting insofar as it does not attack prostitution on *moral* grounds; rather, it claims that mercenary sex is just poor sex. Sex without the senti-

---

[4]Due to the sheer number of arguments presented by Ericsson, space limitations require that many go unmentioned here.

ments of love and affection is cold and impersonal.[5] Admitting that mercenary sex is usually of poorer quality than *ideal* sentimental sex, Ericsson argues that is no reason to regard mercenary sex as undesirable. This argument is no different than claiming that since a Big Mac is not of the quality of filet mignon, the Big Mac is undesirable. In fact, it is misleading to compare ideal romantic sex to mercenary sex, which fulfills wholly different social and individual functions. Moreover, most nonmercenary sexual relations fall far short of the sentimentalists' ideal.

Anticipating several other arguments, Ericsson makes three significant and highly controversial points: (1) The prostitute does not sell her body or bodily parts, but only sexual services; (2) prostitutes ought to be viewed as social service workers similar to nurses and caseworkers; and (3) sexual desire is as natural, basic, necessary, and compelling as the need for food.

The Paternalist Charge finds prostitution undesirable on the ground *not* that prostitution harms society or others, but that it harms prostitutes themselves. Prostitution involves increased physical harms, for example, STDs, beatings, etc., and emotional harm such as depression, neurosis, etc. Ericsson points out that ordinarily, when occupations are considered hazardous (coal mining, taxi driving), society attempts to improve working conditions. For Ericsson, most of the harms to the prostitute are caused by society's denigration of prostitutes. Moreover, the paternalistic argument depends on two unproven assumptions: (1) that scorn for prostitution is justified, and (2) that prostitutes do not perform a valuable service.

The Feminist Charge consists of a group of arguments concluding that prostitution is undesirable and ought to be abolished because it is a supreme example of the inequality of the sexes, where the oppression, domination, exploitation, and dehumanization of the female by the male is exemplified. When a man reduces a woman to a sexual object, he violates the moral rule against treating people as mere means to one's own selfish ends. Ericsson concurs that the central argument of inequality against women must be taken seriously. For example, in a capitalistic society, the prostitute is exploited more than other wage earners, such as an auto worker, by having to pay exorbitant rents and for protection. He suggests the conclusion to be drawn is not that prostitution is undesirable, but rather, the laws, regulations, and attitudes that cause this kind of exploitation are undesirable. On the other hand, Ericsson responds to the argument that women are oppressed, reified, and reduced to sexual objects or mere pieces of merchandise insofar as the customer is not interested in her *as a person,* by noting this is true of relations with persons who perform almost any other job or service as well, and they are not considered dehumanizing.

With regard to the Kantian injunction not to treat people as mere means to one's own ends, Ericsson acknowledges that both the prostitute and the customer treat each other as means. But because this is true of all commercial transactions, the immorality of this transaction would have to be founded on other grounds.

Against the claim that the prostitute, as a female, is oppressed, Ericsson offers an analysis of oppression that includes the act of reducing one's freedom of choice so that she acts against her will. However, this type of oppression does not hold for the typical case of prostitution. Prostitutes do not have to accept all customers or satisfy all requests. Prostitutes can make free choices in most cases.

Turning to the *constructive* stage, Ericsson offers his system of sound prostitution. To begin with, two questions are posed: (1) the factual question, "can prostitution be eradicated?" and (2) the normative moral question, "ought prostitution be eradicated?"

In addressing the first question, it must be observed that Ericsson assumes the key cause

[5]For a more detailed discussion of this topic, see Chapter 2.

of prostitution is the ever-present and powerful natural *demand* for sex. This being the case, the answer to the first question will depend on whether we can eliminate the demand. Borrowing on the works of Kingsley Davis and Benjamin and Masters, Ericsson tries to imagine a society in which the demand for prostitution would not exist. He concludes that while one might imagine a sexually perfect world where demand is eliminated, it would be a fantasy science fiction world so totally unrealistic that there is virtually no hope for its ever coming into existence (short of accepting an Orwellian *1984* world), a view buttressed by the fact that all attempts to suppress the demand for prostitution have failed throughout history.

Since none of the negative attempts at suppression have succeeded, why not try a constructive one—a program of "sound prostitution"? Sound prostitution requires (1) decriminalization of prostitution, (2) improved housing conditions for prostitutes, (3) elimination of child and teenage prostitution, and (4) a change in society's values and attitudes towards prostitution.

The latter change would be exceedingly difficult, but Ericsson contends it is easier to change attitudes than biological nature. The question then becomes, "Which attitudes need to be changed?" Negative attitudes toward prostitution, according to Ericsson, stem from two main sources. Western culture has (1) devalued women and (2) devalued sexuality. The elimination of these destructive attitudes, and those that stem from them, affect not only prostitution, but also relationships between the sexes generally, and thus must be a focal point in achieving sound prostitution. Sound prostitution would exist in a social climate devoid of blind prejudice, would involve free choice, and would be legal and free from exploitation.

from Charges Against Prostitution: An Attempt at a Philosophical Assessment

LARS O. ERICSSON

I. A Neglected Philosophical Task

The debate over prostitution is probably as old as prostitution itself. And the discussion of the oldest profession is as alive today as it ever was. New books and articles are constantly being published, new scientific reports and theories presented, and new committees and commissions formed.[1] Yet while the scientific and literary discussion is very much alive, the philosophical discussion of it seems never even to have come to life. How is this to be explained? And is there any justification for it?

Could it be that harlotry is a topic unsuitable for philosophical treatment? Or could it be that, although suitable, it does not give rise to any interesting philosophical questions? Obviously, I would not be writing this article if I thought that the answer to any of these questions was yes. But I wish to emphasize that it seems absurd to maintain that the subject is unsuitable for philosophical treatment, since it clearly involves many normative and evaluative issues. Could it be instead that prostitution as a moral question belongs to casuistry or to applied ethics rather than to moral philosophy proper? Could it be that it does not give rise to any "high-level" questions of principle? This will not do as an explanation, for the same thing could be said just as appropriately about such topics as abortion, suicide, war, or mercy killing—topics that have been intensively discussed by philosophers. Nor can the explanation

From "Charges Against Prostitution: An Attempt at a Philosophical Assessment" by Lars O. Ericsson, *Ethics,* 90 (April 1980), pp. 335–366. Used by permission of the author and The University of Chicago Press.

be that prostitution is regarded by philosophers as too unworthy or too base a subject to deal with, for that would put them in a prudish ivory tower, and this (I hope) they do not deserve.

What then is the reason for this remarkable lack of interest? In order to explain what seems to me the most plausible answer, I suggest that we return for a moment to the days of Hume. When Hume wrote his essay *Of Suicide,* suicide was primarily a religious and theological matter. Suicide was a horrendous crime and an intolerable evil; a cardinal sin. So if there were any disputes between religion and philosophy about suicide they were likely to have to do with such intricate questions as, Where exactly in hell would you end up? For how long would you have to burn? etc. To venture to suggest that perhaps suicide was not all that bad after all was unthinkable. And to have the nerve to suggest that perhaps suicide could represent a rational response to an unbearable life-situation was not only unthinkable but tantamount to heresy. Nevertheless, it was something to this effect that Hume had the courage to say in his essay.

What Hume did was to question what at the time appeared as an unshakable postulate. The evil of suicide was not a matter for discussion but the Archimedean point from which all discussion took off. To make us conscious of such alleged Archimedean points and to question them has always been an important philosophical task. In moral philosophy this amounts to the task of subjecting the canons of conventional morality to critical scrutiny.

If we return to our own time and to prostitution, we shall find that the alleged Archimedean point from which practically all discussion of harlotry takes off is the view that *prostitution is undesirable.* And on *this* presupposition, the crucial issues become scientific and political, not philosophical. Science is called in to explain the undesirable phenomenon and to invent a cure to be put in the hands of the politicians. And moralists of all shades and colors act as their cheerleaders. The philosophical contributions have mainly consisted of the discussion of such derivative issues, as, Does society have the right to pass judgment at all on matters of sexual morals? and, if so, does it also have the right to use the weapon of the law to enforce what it considers to be sexual immorality?[2]

It is the purpose of this paper to undertake a critical assessment of the view that prostitution is an undesirable social phenomenon that ought to be eradicated. I shall do this by examining what seem to me (and to others) the most important and serious charges against prostitution. I shall try to show that mercenary love per se must, upon closer inspection, be acquitted of most of these charges. Instead, I shall argue, the major culprit is the hostile and punitive attitudes which the surrounding hypocritical society adopts toward promiscuous sexual relations in general and prostitution in particular.

II. The Charge from Conventional Morality

By far the most common ground for holding that prostitution is undesirable is that it constitutes a case of sexual immorality. Society and conventional morality condemn it. The law at best barely tolerates it; sometimes, as in most states in the United States, it downright prohibits it. In order to improve prostitution, we must first and foremost improve our attitudes toward it. Contrary to what is usually contended, I shall conclude that prostitution, although not in any way *ultimately* desirable, is still conditionally desirable because of certain ubiquitous and permanent imperfections of actual human societies.

The prostitute, according to the moralist, is a sinful creature who ought to be banned from civilized society. Whoredom is "the great social evil" representing a flagrant defiance of common decency. The harlot is a threat to the family, and she corrupts the young. To engage in prostitution signifies a total loss of character. To choose "the life" is to choose a style of living unworthy of any decent human being. And so on.

There is also a less crude form of moralism, which mixes moral disapproval with a more "compassionate" and "concerned" attitude. The fate of a whole is "a fate worse than death." The hustler is a poor creature who has to debase herself in order to gratify the lusts of immoral men. Prostitution is degrading for all parties involved, but especially for the woman.

It might seem tempting to say that the best thing to do with respect to the moralistic critique is to ignore it. But this is exactly what moral philosophers have been doing for far too long. It appears that many otherwise sophisticated persons more or less consciously adhere to views of a rather unreflectively moralistic kind where prostitution is concerned. More important, to ignore conventional moralism would be philosophically unsatisfactory for the simple reason that the mere fact that an idea is conventional does not constitute a disproof of its validity. Thus, arguments are what we need, not silence.

How are the hostile and punitive attitudes of society toward prostitution to be explained? It seems to be an anthropological fact that sexual institutions are ranked on the basis of their relation to reproduction. Hence, in virtue of its intimate relation to reproduction, the monogamous marriage constitutes the sexual institution in society which is ranked the highest and which receives the strongest support from law and mores. On the other hand, the less a sexual practice has to do with the bearing and rearing of children, the less sanctioned it is. Therefore, when coitus is practiced for pecuniary reasons (the hooker), with pleasure and not procreation in mind (the client), we have a sexual practice that, far from being sanctioned, finds itself at the opposite extreme on the scale of social approval.[3]

Two other factors should be mentioned in this connection. First, wherever descent is reckoned solely through the male line, promiscuity in the female can hardly be approved by society. And the property relations associated with descent of course point in the same direction. Second, our Christian heritage—especially in its Lutheran and Calvinist versions—is both antisexual and antihedonistic. To indulge in sexual activities is bad enough, but to indulge in them for the sheer fun and pleasure of them is a major feat in the art of sin. Moreover, sex is time consuming and as such quite contrary to Protestant morals with respect to work.

An explanation of our antiprostitution attitudes and their probably prehistoric roots must not, however, be confused with a *rationale* for their continuation in our own time. That we understand why the average moralist, who is a predominantly unreflecting upholder of prevailing rules and values, regards prostitution and prostitutes as im-

moral gives us no good reason to shield those rules and values from criticism, especially if we find, upon reflection, that they are no longer adequate to our present social conditions.

That prostitution neither is nor ever was a threat to reproduction within the nuclear family is too obvious to be worth arguing for. Nor has it ever been a threat to the family itself. People marry and visit whores for quite different reasons. In point of fact, the greatest threat to the family is also the greatest threat to prostitution, namely, complete sexual liberty for both sexes. The conclusion we must draw from this is that neither the value of future generations nor the importance of the family (if it is important) warrants the view that prostitution is bad and undesirable.

It is hardly likely, however, that the moralist would be particularly perturbed by this, for the kernel of his view is rather that to engage in prostitution is *intrinsically* wrong. Both whore and customer (or at least the former) act immorally, according to the moralist, even if neither of them nor anyone else gets hurt. Mercenary love per se is regarded as immoral.

Personally, I must confess that I, upon reflection, am no more able to see that coition for a fee is intrinsically wrong than I am able to see that drunkenness is. There is something fanatic about both of these views which I find utterly repelling. If two adults voluntarily consent to an economic arrangement concerning sexual activity and this activity takes place in private, it seems plainly absurd to maintain that there is something intrinsically wrong with it. In fact, I very much doubt that it is wrong at all. To say that prostitution is intrinsically immoral is in a way to refuse to give any arguments. The moralist simply "senses" or "sees" its immorality. And this terminates rational discussion at the point where it should begin.

III. The Sentimentalist Charge

There is also a common contention that harlotry is undesirable because the relation between whore and customer must by the nature of things be a very poor relation to nonmercenary sex. Poor, not in a moral, but in a nonmoral, sense. Since the majority of the objections under this heading have to do with the quality of the feelings and sentiments involved or with the lack of them, I shall refer to this critique as "the sentimentalist charge."

Sex between two persons who love and care for one another can of course be, and often is, a very good thing. The affection and tenderness which exists between the parties tends to create an atmosphere in which the sexual activities can take place in such a way as to be a source of mutual pleasure and satisfaction. Sexual intercourse is here a way of becoming even more intimate in a relation which is already filled with other kinds of intimacies.

Now, according to the sentimentalist, mercenary sex lacks just about all of these qualities. Coitus between prostitute and client is held to be impoverished, cold, and impersonal. The association is regarded as characterized by detachment and emotional noninvolvement. And the whole thing is considered to be a rather sordid and drab affair.

In order to answer this charge, there is no need to romanticize prostitution. Mercenary sex usually *is* of poorer quality compared with sentimental sex between lovers. To deny this would be simply foolish. But does it follow from this that hustling is undesirable? Of course not! That would be like contending that because 1955 Ch. Mouton-Roths-child is a much better wine than ordinary claret, we should condemn the act of drinking the latter.

The sentimentalist's mistake lies in the comparison on which he relies. He contrasts a virtual sexual ideal with prostitutional sex, which necessarily represents an entirely different kind of erotic association and which therefore fulfills quite different social and individual functions. Only a minute share of all sex that takes place deserves to be described as romantic sex love. And if, in defending mercenary sex, we should beware of romanticizing *it,* the same caution holds for the sentimentalist when he is describing nonprostitutional sex. The sex lives of ordinary people often fall miles short of the sentimentalist's ideal. On the other hand, the sexual services performed by harlots are by no means always of such poor quality as we are conditioned to think. And we would most likely think better of them were we able to rid ourselves of the feelings of guilt and remorse that puritanism and conventional morality create in us.

In fact, the comparison between sex love and mercenary lovemaking is both pointless and naive. That lovers have very little need for the services of hustlers is at best a silly argument against prostitution. Most couples are not lovers. A great number of persons do not even have a sexual partner. And not so few individuals will, in any society, always have great difficulties in finding one. What is the point of comparing the ideal sex life of the sentimentalist with the sexual services of prostitutes in the case of someone whose only alternative to the latter is masturbation? Is there any reason to think that mercenary sex must be impersonal, cold, and impoverished compared with autosex?

By this I do not wish to contend that the typical customer is either unattractive, physically or mentally handicapped, or extremely shy. There is abundant empirical evidence showing that the prostitute's customers represent all walks of life and many different types of personalities.[4] That the typical "John" is a male who for some reason cannot find a sexual partner other than a prostitute is just one of the many popular myths about harlotry which empirical studies seem unable to kill. Approximately 75 percent of the customers are married men,[5] most of whom are "respectable" taxpaying citizens.

This brings us to another aspect of the sentimentalist charge. It is not seldom a tacit and insidious presupposition of the sentimentalist's reasoning that good sex equals intramarital sex, and that bad sex equals extramarital—especially prostitutional—sex. This is just another stereotype, which deserves to be destroyed. Concerning this aspect, Benjamin and Masters make the following comment: "The experience with a prostitute is probably ethically, and may be esthetically, on a higher level than an affectionless intercourse between husband and wife, such as is all too common in our present society."[6] The demarcation line between marital and mercenary sex is not quality but the contrasting nature of the respective legal arrangements. Furthermore, we must not think that the quality—in terms of physical pleasure—of the sex services of prostitutes varies any less than the quality of "regular" sex. The best prostitutional sex available is probably much better from the customer's point of view than average marital sex.

The sentimentalistic critique of the prostitute-customer relationship, however, has also another side to it. This consists in the notion that sex without love or affection—sex "pure and simple"—is "no good." I have already admitted the obvious here—namely, that sex love is a beautiful thing. But this seems to me no reason for embracing the romantic notion that sex without love or mutual affection must be valueless. On the contrary, satisfaction of sexual desires is, qua satisfaction of a basic need, *intrinsically good,* love or no love.

The argument fails to show that prostitution is undesirable. If it shows anything at all it shows lack of contact with reality. As I pointed out earlier, sex between lovers hardly dominates the scene of human sex quantitatively. Consequently, the argument entails that a major part of the sex that takes place between humans is worthless. And how interesting is this? Even if correct, it does not show that there is something *particularly* or *distinctively* bad about prostitution.

In conclusion, I would like to counter the charge that the prostitute-customer relationship is bad on the ground that it involves the selling of something that is too basic and too elementary in human life to be sold. This is perhaps not a sentimentalist charge proper, but since it seems to be related to it I shall deal with it here.

Common parlance notwithstanding, what the hustler sells is of course not her body or vagina, but sexual *services.* If she actually did sell herself, she would no longer be a prostitute but a sexual slave. I wish to emphasize this simple fact, because the popular misnomer certainly contributes to and maintains our distorted views about prostitution.

But is it not bad enough to sell sexual services? To go to bed with someone just for the sake of money? To perform fellatio on a guy you neither love nor care for? In view of the fact that sex is a fundamental need, is it not wrong that anyone should have to pay to have it satisfied and that anyone should profit from its satisfaction? Is it not a deplorable fact that in the prostitute-customer relationship sexuality is completely alienated from the rest of the personality and reduced to a piece of merchandise?

In reply to these serious charges I would, first, like to confess that I have the greatest sympathy for the idea that the means necessary for the satisfaction of our most basic needs should be free, or at least not beyond the economic means of anyone. We all need food, so food should be available to us. We all need clothes and a roof over our heads, so these things should also be available to us. And since our sexual desires are just as basic, natural, and compelling as our appetite for food, this also holds for them. But I try not to forget that this is, and probably for a long time will remain, an *ideal* state of affairs.

Although we live in a society in which we have to pay (often dearly) for the satisfaction of our appetites, including the most basic and natural ones, I still do not regard food vendors and the like with contempt. They fulfill an important function in the imperfect world in which we are destined to live. That we have to pay for the satisfaction of our most basic appetites is no reason for socially stigmatizing those individuals whose profession it is to cater to those appetites. With this, I take it, at least the nonfanatical sentimentalists agrees. But if so, it seems to me inconsistent to hold that prostitution is undesirable on the ground that it involves the selling of something that, ideally, should not be sold but freely given away. Emotional prejudice aside, there is on *this* ground no more reason to despise the sex market and those engaged in it than there is to despise the food market and those engaged in it.

But still, is there not an abyss between selling meat and selling "flesh"? Is there not something private, personal, and intimate about sex that makes it unfit for commercial purposes? Of course, I do not wish to deny that there are great differences between what the butcher does and what the whore does, but at the same time it seems to me clear that the conventional labeling of the former as "respectable" and the latter as "indecent" is not so much the result of these differences as of the influence of cultural, especially religious and sexual, taboos. That the naked human body is "obscene," that genitalia are "offending," that menstrual blood is "unclean," etc., are expressions of taboos which strongly contribute to the often neurotic way in which sex is surrounded with mysteriousness and secrecy. Once we have been able to liberate ourselves from these taboos we will come to realize that we are no more justified in devaluating the prostitute, who, for example, masturbates her customers, than we are in devaluating the assistant nurse, whose job it is to take care of the intimate hygiene of disabled patients. Both help to satisfy important human needs, and both get paid for doing so. That the harlot, in distinction to the nurse, intentionally gives her client pleasure is of course nothing that should be held against her!

As for the charge that in the prostitute-customer relationship sexuality is completely alienated from the rest of the personality—this is no doubt largely true. I fail to see, however, that it constitutes a very serious charge. My reason for this is, once again, that the all-embracing sex act represents an ideal with which it is unfair to compare the prostitute-customer relationship, especially if, as is often the case, such an all-embracing sex act does not constitute a realizable alternative. Moreover, there is no empirical evidence showing that sex between two complete strangers must be of poor quality.

IV. The Paternalistic Charge

It is a well-established fact that the occupational hazards connected with prostitution constitute a serious problem. The prostitute runs the risk of being hurt, physically as well as mentally. On the physical side there is always the risk of getting infected by some venereal disease. Certain forms of urosis are known to be more common among harlots than among women in general. And then there is the risk of assault and battery from customers with sadistic tendencies. On the mental side we encounter such phenomena as depression and neurosis, compulsive behavior, self-degrading and self-destructive impulses, etc.

It is therefore not uncommon to find it argued that prostitution is undesirable because it is not in the best interest of the prostitute to be what she is. It is held that society should, for the prostitutes' own good, try to prevent people from becoming prostitutes and to try to "rehabilitate" those who already are. This type of criticism I shall refer to as "the paternalistic charge."

I shall not consider the question—discussed by Mill, Devlin, Hart, and others—of whether society has the *right* to interfere with a person's liberty for his own good. I shall limit my discussion to the question of whether the fact that the hustler runs the risks that she runs is a good reason for holding that prostitution is undesirable.

A comparison with other fields clearly shows that the fact that a certain job is very hazardous is not regarded as a good reason for the view that the type of job in question is undesirable. Take, for instance, a miner: he runs considerable risks in his job, but we hardly think that this warrants the conclusion that mining should be prohibited. What we do think (or at least ought to think) is that, since the miner is doing a socially valuable job, everything possible should be done to minimize those risks by improving his working conditions by installing various safety devices, introducing shorter working hours, etc. It seems to me, therefore, that in cases like this—and there are many of them—paternalistic considerations carry no weight. The individual is not to be protected from himself (for wanting to take risks) but from certain factors in the environment. It is not the individual who should be changed but the milieu in which he has to place himself in order to be able to follow his occupational inclinations.

Unless the paternalist simply assumes what remains to be proven, namely, that what the prostitute does is of no value to society, a similar argument also applies in the case of prostitution. The individual whore does not need to be protected from herself if her hustling is voluntary in the same sense of "voluntary" as someone's choice of profession may be voluntary. What she does need protection from are detrimental factors in the social environment, especially the hostile, punitive, or condescending attitudes of so-called respectable citizens. It is not the hooker who should be changed, reformed, or rehabilitated but the social milieu in which she works.

The paternalistic charge is not an independent argument against prostitution. It only seems to work because it has already given in to conventional morality. To oppose prostitution by referring to the welfare, good, happiness, needs, or interests of the prostitute may seem very noble and humanitarian; but in reality it serves the status quo by leaving the norms and values of the surrounding society intact, viewing prostitution through the unreflected spectacles of a conservative public opinion, and placing the "blame" exclusively on the individual.

If public opinion accorded prostitutes the same status as, say, social workers, most of the hazards connected with hustling would probably disappear. And those that would remain would not be thought to make hustling undesirable. Society would try to minimize the risks rather than try to rehabilitate and reform those who run them.

The paternalist does not ask himself *why* depressions and neuroses are common among harlots, *why* they display self-degrading and self-destructive tendencies, *why* their behavior often is antisocial, and so on. Yet the answer should be obvious: the principal cause of these psychological and sociological "dysfunctions" is the social anathema attached to their way of life. Make people outcasts and they will behave like outcasts. It is thus the degradation in which the harlot is held, and as a result also often holds herself, that constitutes the greatest danger to her physical and mental health. In addition, as I shall hereafter argue, this constitutes the basis for her being exploited in various ways.

To sum up. The paternalistic charge rests on two assumptions, neither of which is valid. First, it rests on the assumption that society's scorn for whoredom is justified. Second, it rests on the assumption that the hooker is not doing a socially valuable job. From these assumptions together with the fact that harlotry is known to be a hazardous profession the paternalist jumps to the conclusion that prostitution is undesirable and that society should intervene against it for the prostitutes' own good. . . .

VI. The Feminist Charge

In this essay I have deliberately desisted from trying to *define* "prostitution." I have simply relied upon the fact that we seem to know pretty well what we mean by this term. My reason for resisting the well-known predilection of philosophers for definitional questions is that ordinary usage seems to me sufficiently precise for my present purposes.[7] In consequence I have up till now referred to the prostitute as "she" and to the customer as "he." For in ordinary parlance the whore is a woman and her customer a man. I do not think, however, that ordinary usage is such that this is true by definition. I rather suspect that our habit of thinking of the hustler as a *she* and her customer as a *he* simply reflects the empirical fact that most prostitutes are women and most customers men.

I shall in this section discuss a group of arguments in support of the thesis that prostitution is undesirable whose common feature is this fact. Prostitution is held to be undesirable on the ground that it constitutes an extreme instance of the inequality between the sexes. Whoredom is regarded as displaying the male oppression of the female in its most naked form. It is contended that the relation between hooker and "John" is one of object to subject—the prostitute being reified into a mere object, a thing for the male's pleasure, lust, and contempt. The customer-man pays to use the whore-woman and consequently has the upper hand. He is the dominating figure, the master. It is the whore's task to oblige, to satisfy his most "perverse" and secret desires, desires that the male is unable to reveal to his wife or girl friend. Prostitution, it is argued, reduces the woman to a piece of merchandise that anyone who can pay the price may buy. The unequal nature of prostitution is also contended to consist in the fact that it represents a way out of *misère sexuel* only for men. Instead of trying to solve the sexual problems together with his wife, the married man can resort to the services of the hustler; but the married woman lacks the same advantage, since there are not so many male heterosexual prostitutes around. I shall refer to this group of arguments as "the feminist charge."

Like the moralist and the Marxist, the feminist is of the opinion that prostitution can and ought to be eradicated.[8] Some feminists, like the moralist, even want to criminalize prostitution. But unlike the moralist they want to criminalize both whore and customer.

The core of the feminist charge—that prostitution is unequal and disfavors the female sex—deserves to be taken seriously. For social inequality is a serious matter both morally and politically. And inequalities based on differences with regard to race, color of skin, religious belief, sex, and the like are particularly serious. Thus, if valid, the feminist critique would constitute powerful support for the view that prostitution is undesirable.

Before I proceed to an attempt to counter the feminist charge, I would like to add a few nuancing facts to the prostitute-customer picture outlined at the beginning of this section.[9] No one denies that a majority of prostitutes are women, and no one denies that a majority of customers are men. But it is clear from the evidence that a large portion of the prostitutes, especially in metropolitan areas, are male homosexuals.[10] There is also lesbian prostitution, though this is not (at least not yet) sufficiently widespread to be of any great social importance. And finally, there is male heterosexual prostitution, the prevalence of which is also rather limited. We may sum up by saying that, rather than constituting a dichotomy between the sexes, prostitution has the characteristic that a considerable portion of the prostitutes are men, and a small minority of the customers are women. I mention this because I think that a rational assessment should not be based on an incomplete picture of the phenomenon under assessment and I consider these data to have some relevance with respect to the feminist charge against prostitution.

There are at least two types of inequalities. In the one, the inequality consists in the fact that some *benefit* is withheld from some group or individual. A typical example: only white members of a society are allowed to vote. In the other, the inequality consists in the fact that some *burden* is placed only on some group or individual. A typical example: a feudal society in which peasants and artisans are the only ones who have to pay taxes. We may also distinguish between unequal practices which, like racial discrimination, are best dealt with through a complete *abolition* of them, and unequal practices which, like male franchise, are best dealt with by *modifying* them (in the case of male franchise, by granting the franchise to women). The one type of unequal practice is always and under all conditions undesirable: there is no remedy to the inequality of apartheid but abolition. The other type of unequal practice is also undesirable, but it has the seed of something defensible or valuable in it: the franchise is some-

thing good, although the franchise restricted to males is not. Obviously, these two pairs of categories are not mutually exclusive. On the contrary, all combinations of them are possible.

After these preliminaries, we come to the question of how prostitution is to be classified. Is harlotry an unequal practice? And if so, in what precisely does its inequality consist?

If it is conceded that in exchange for his money the customer receives a service—something that at least the sentimentalist seems most reluctant to concede—it could be argued that harlotry is unequal in the sense that some benefit is withheld from or denied women that is not withheld from or denied men. This is perhaps how the argument that hustling represents a way out only for men should be understood. However, if this is what the feminist charge amounts to, two things appear to be eminently clear. The first is that prostitution is unequal in a less serious way than, for instance, male franchise. For in the latter the benefit (opportunity to vote) which is withheld from women is withheld from them in the strong sense that it is not legally possible for the women to vote, while in the former no such legal or formal obstacle stands in their way. In fact, instead of saying that the sex services of prostitutes are withheld or denied women, it would be more appropriate to say that centuries of cultural and social conditioning makes them desist from asking for them. It is after all only recently that women have begun to define their sexuality and require that their sexual needs and desires be recognized. Rowbotham reminds us that "'Nymphomania,' was actually used in the 1840s to describe any woman who felt sexual desire, and such women were seen as necessarily abandoned, women of the streets, women of the lower classes."[11] The second point is that if, through prostitution, a benefit is "withheld" the female sex, the best way to deal with this inequality would not be an attempt to stamp out the institution but an attempt to modify it, by making the benefit in question available to both sexes.

Could it be then that the inequality of whoredom consists in the fact that some burden is unequally placed on the two sexes and in disfavor of the female sex? This allegation can be interpreted in several different ways. And I shall in what follows consider those that seem to me the most important.

To begin with, this allegation can be understood in accordance with the view that it is women, and not men, who are in peril of becoming prostitutes. But first of all, this is largely untrue since, as I have argued earlier, a great many prostitutes are men. Moreover, the perils of being a prostitute, although existent today (due to factors discussed in Sec. IV), do not constitute a good reason for abolishing harlotry; rather they constitute a good reason for a social reform that will reduce the perils to a minimum tomorrow.[12]

Another way of interpreting this allegation is to say that prostitution constitutes exploitation of the female sex, since harlots are being exploited by, inter alia, sex capitalists and customers, and a majority of harlots are women. This interpretation of the allegation merits careful study, and I shall therefore in the first instance limit my discussion to the capitalist exploitation of prostitutes.

It is of course true that not all prostitutes can be described as workers in the sex industry. Some are in point of fact more adequately described as small-scale private entrepreneurs. Others are being exploited without being exploited by sex capitalists. Those who can be regarded as workers in the sex industry—the growing number of girls working in sex clubs and similar establishments for instance—are, of course, according to Marxist theory, being exploited in the same sense as any wage worker is exploited. But exploitation in this Marxist sense, although perhaps effective as an argument against wage labor in general, is hardly effective as an argument against prostitution.

There is no doubt, however, that practically all harlots—irrespective of whether they are high-class call girls, cheap streetwalkers, or sex-club performers—are being exploited, economically, in a much more crude sense than that in which an automobile worker at General Motors is being exploited. I am thinking here of the fact that all of them—there are very few exceptions to this—have to pay usury rents in order to be able to operate. Many are literally being plundered by their landlords—sex capitalists who often specialize in letting out rooms, flats, or apartments to people in the racket. Not a few prostitutes also have to pay for "protection" to mafiosi with close connections to organized crime.

What makes all this possible? And what are the implications of the existence of conditions such as these for the question of the alleged undesirability of prostitution? With respect to the first of these questions the answer, it seems to me, is that the major culprit is society's hypocritical attitude toward harlotry and harlots. It is this hypocrisy which creates the prerequisites for the sex-capitalist exploitation of the prostitutes. Let me exemplify what I mean by society's hypocritical—and, I might add, totally inconsistent—attitude here. On the one hand, most societies, at least in the West (one deplorable exception is the United States), have followed the UN declaration which recommends that prostitution in itself should not be made illegal.[13] One would therefore expect that someone who pursues a legal activity would have the right to rent the necessary premises to advertise her services, and so on. But not so! The penal code persecutes those who rent out rooms, apartments, and other premises to prostitutes. And an editor of a Swedish newspaper was recently convicted for having accepted ads from "models" and "masseuses." In what other legal field or branch would contradictions such as these be considered tolerable? None of course! One of the first to point out this double morality of society was Alexandra Kollontay, who as early as 1909 wrote: "But if the state tolerates the prostitutes and thereby supports their profession, then it must also accept housing for them and even—in the interest of social health and order—institute houses where they could pursue their occupation.[14] And the most incredible of all is that the official motivation for outlawing persons prepared to provide harlots with the premises necessary for their legal activity is a paternalistic one: so doing is in the best interest of the hustlers themselves, who would otherwise be at the mercy of unscrupulous landlords! In practice, the risk of being thrown in jail of course scares away all but the unscrupulous individuals, who can charge sky-high rents (after all they take a certain risk) and who often are associated with the criminal world. How can anyone, therefore, be surprised at the fact that not so few hustlers display "antisocial tendencies"?

The conclusion I draw from this is that the crude economic exploitation of the prostitutes is not an argument against prostitution. It rather constitutes an accusation against the laws, regulations, and attitudes which create the preconditions for that exploitation. Society cannot both allow harlotry and deprive harlots of reasonable working conditions (as a concession to "common decency") and still expect that all will be well.

A third way of interpreting the charge that prostitution is unequal in the sense that it places a burden on women that it does not place on men is to say that whores are being oppressed, reified, and reduced to a piece of merchandise by their male customers. To begin with the last version of this charge first, I have already pointed out the obvious, namely, that whores do not sell themselves. The individual hooker is not for sale, but her sexual services are. One could therefore with equal lack of propriety say of any person whose job it is to sell a certain service that he, as a result thereof, is reduced to a piece of merchandise. I cannot help suspecting that behind this talk of reduction to a piece of merchandise lies a good portion of contempt for prostitutes and the kind of services they offer for sale.

As for the version according to which the whole is reified—turned into an object, a thing—it can be understood in a similar way as the one just dealt with. But it can also be understood as the view that the customer does not look upon the prostitute as a human being but as "a piece of ass." He is not interested in her as a person. He is exclusively interested in her sexual performance. As far as I can see, this version of the charge collapses into the kind of sentimentalistic critique that I discussed in Section III. Let me just add this: Since when does the fact that we, when visiting a professional, are not interested in him or her as a person, but only in his or her professional performance, constitute a ground for saying that the professional is dehumanized, turned into an object?

The "reification charge" may, however, be understood in still another way. It may be interpreted as saying that the whore is nothing but a means, a mere instrument, for the male customer's ends. This also comes rather close to the sentimentalist charge. Its Kantian character does perhaps deserve a few words of comment, however. First of all, that the customer treats the harlot as a means to his ends is only partly true. The other part of the truth is that the prostitute treats her customer as a means to *her* ends. Thus, the complete truth (if it deserves to be called that) is that prostitute and customer treat *one another* as means rather than as ends.

I have to say, however, that I do not find much substance in this Kantian-inspired talk about means and ends. The kind of relationship that exists between prostitute and customer is one that we find in most service professions. It is simply cultural blindness and sexual taboos that prevent so many of us from seeing this. Moreover, in virtue of the prevalence of this type of relationship—a contractual relation in which services are traded—I suspect that those who talk about the badness of it in the case of prostitute-customer relationship have in fact long before decided that the relationship is bad on some *other*—not declared—ground. The means-ends talk is just a way of rationalizing a preconceived opinion.

I shall conclude this section by considering the charge that harlotry constitutes oppression of the female sex. Prostitution is here regarded as displaying male oppression of the female in its most overt and extreme form. The seriousness of this charge calls, to begin with, for a clarification of the meaning of the word "oppression." If A oppresses B, I take it that B's freedom of choice and action is severely reduced, against his will, as a result of actions undertaken by A against B. In the case of political oppression, for example, A thwarts B's desire to form unions and political parties, prevents B from expressing his political opinions, throws B in jail if he refuses to comply, and so on.

It can hardly be disputed that prostitutes are oppressed in this sense. They would not have chosen to become hustlers if some better alternative had been open to them. They are very much aware of the fact that to be a prostitute is to be socially devalued; to be at the bottom of society. To become a hooker is to make just the reverse of a career. It should be observed, however, that none of this warrants the charge that prostitution means the oppression of the female by the male sex. The oppression just described is not an oppression on the basis of sex, as male franchise would be. The "oppressor" is rather those social conditions—present in practically all known social systems—which offer some individuals (both men and women) no better alternative than hustling.

But perhaps what the charge amounts to is that the male sex's oppression of the female sex consists in the oppression of the whore by her male customer. It certainly happens that customers treat prostitutes in ways which could motivate use of the term "oppression." But this does not mean that this term typically applies to the prostitute-customer relationship. Moreover, harlots usually develop a keen eye for judging people, and that helps them to avoid many of the (latently) dangerous customers. For it is just a myth that their freedom of choice and action is reduced to a point where they have to accept customers indiscriminately. This is not even true of prostitutes in the lowest bracket, and it certainly is not true of girls in the higher ones.

It is not seldom argued from feminist quarters that the liberation of women must start with the liberation of women from exploitation of their sex. Hence the crusade against prostitution, pornography, and the use of beautiful women in commercial advertising, etc. It is argued that women's lib must have as its primary goal the abolition of the (ab)use of the female sex as a commodity. As long as the female sex is up for sale, just like any other commercial object, there can be no true liberation from oppression.

To the reader who has read this far it should be obvious that, at least in part, this type of reasoning rests on or is misguided by such misnomers as "the whore sells her body," "to live by selling oneself," "to buy oneself a piece of ass," etc. So I need not say any more about that. Instead I wish to make a comparison between a typical middle-class housewife in suburbia and her prostitute counterpart, the moderately successful call girl. And I ask, emotional prejudice aside, which of them needs to be "liberated" the most? Both are doing fairly well economically, but while the housewife is totally dependent on her husband, at least economically, the call girl in that respect stands on her own two feet. If she has a pimp, it is she, not he, who is the breadwinner in the family. Is she a traitor to her own sex? If she is (which I doubt), she is no more

a traitor to her own sex than her bourgeois counterpart. For, after all, Engels was basically right when he said that the major difference between the two is that the one hires out her body on piecework while the other hires it out once and for all.

All this does not mean that I am unsympathetic toward the aspirations of the feminist movement. It rather means that I disagree with its order of priorities.

Both men and women need to be liberated from the harness of their respective sex roles. But in order to be able to do this, we must liberate ourselves from those mental fossils which prevent us from looking upon sex and sexuality with the same naturalness as upon our cravings for food and drink. And, contrary to popular belief, we may have something to learn from prostitution in this respect, namely, that coition resembles nourishment in that if it cannot be obtained in any other way it can always be bought. And bought meals are not always the worst. . . .

VIII. The Charge of a Disturbed Emotional Life

Most of the emotional problems that often afflict prostitutes can be traced back to the social stigma that we attach to their way of life. If our attitudes to sexuality, promiscuity, and mercenary sex were different—if, for example, prostitutes were held in esteem instead of in degradation—I am convinced that they would display very little of the mental disturbances that not seldom haunt them today.

But is it not possible that certain emotional problems would always remain, no matter how the attitudes of the surrounding society changed? Is it not likely, for instance, that even a harlot whose occupation was held in esteem would find her own love life, her feelings for the man she loves, disturbed by her professional activities? Can one have a well-functioning sexual life if sex is what one lives by? Compulsive behavior apart, the sex drive is no more of an insatiable appetite than hunger. Must not, therefore, the repetitious performance of sexual acts always in the end result in nausea or total indifference? And if the prostitute tries to avoid this effect through a complete detachment, not allowing herself to feel anything when with a customer, will she be able to "switch on" her feelings when with her lover?

I must admit that I do not feel certain what to say about this charge, which we may call "the charge of a disturbed emotional life." Since those prostitutes who are active today are victims of our present scornful attitudes, we cannot but speculate what would happen to their emotional lives if those attitudes were changed in a positive direction. I am inclined to think, however, that some prostitutes, even under the best of circumstances, would run the risk of getting emotional problems. But on the other hand, some prostitutes seem capable of preserving their integrity and sensibility even under the adverse conditions of today.

Since we cannot but speculate, no definite conclusion can be drawn. I wish to add, however, that I think that if prostitution were to be reformed in accordance with the suggestions that I am presently about to make, no prostitute would have to continue in the profession, should she (or he) find that she (or he) was not suited for it.

IX. Can Prostitution Be Abolished?

Hitherto I have been exclusively concerned with the thesis that prostitution is an undesirable social phenomenon. I now come to the thesis that it can and ought to be eradicated.

The thesis that prostitution can and ought to be eradicated is, of course, relatively independent of the thesis that it is undesirable. For, even if undesirable, it neither follows that it can nor that it should be eradicated. But since this thesis usually forms an integrate part of the set of antiprostitution postulates, I think that a critical examination of it is definitely called for in the present context.

Although no entirely satisfactory scientific explanation of mercenary sex exists today, the theories and data available seem adequate enough to allow certain well-founded conclusions as regards the eradicability of prostitution. The data available, however, also seem to disconfirm some theories.

In what follows I shall argue with Kingsley Davis that "we can imagine a social system in which the motive for prostitution would be completely absent, but we cannot imagine that the system could ever come to pass."[15]

To explain a natural or social phenomenon is to state its causes. According to Marxist theory the causes of harlotry are to be found among the economic and productive arrangements of society. Briefly speaking, the sole, or at least major, cause of prostitution is, according to this type of theory, the general social condition of women under capitalist production, particularly their economic deprivation and exploitation.

If true, Marxist theory would, in my view, constitute a good reason both for the view that prostitution is undesirable and for the view that it ought to be eradicated. For it is no doubt empirically possible to do away with capitalism. And who likes economic deprivation and exploitation? Unfortunately, as I have argued elsewhere in this essay, the simplistic Marxist view seems extremely hard to square with well-established data. Let me just, in corroboration of this contention, add a few facts from the Swedish scene. During the deep recession in the 1930s a steady *decrease* of the rate of prostitution took place. But in the 1970s, in our welfare society which has few counterparts in the world, there has been a sharp *increase* in the amount of prostitution. And during this period the Swedish economic system has not undergone any drastic changes as far as capitalism is concerned. It remains as capitalistic today as it was in the 1930s.

This does not mean that I wish to deny that economic factors play a role as causes of (i) the existence of prostitutes, (ii) the rate of the demand for their services, (iii) the number of prostitutes in a particular society, (iv) any particular individual's entrance into prostitution, and (v) any particular individual's demand for mercenary sex. On the contrary, I believe that economic factors may influence all of these things. But I do believe that exclusive reference to economic factors is grossly inadequate as an explanation of so complex a phenomenon as prostitution.[16]

If economic changes of society cannot achieve the abolition of prostitution, what changes, if any, can? What would a society be like in which prostitution would be nonexistent? In theory, harlotry can be eradicated by suppressing the supply of harlots, or the demand for their services, or both. Harlotry can also be abolished in a society such that *no one has* any reason or need to use extraneous means in order to obtain gratification. Let us consider these possibilities in turn.

To be able to advocate the suppression of commercial sex, one's outlook must, I think, be completely ahistorical. For if there is one single general truth about human societies, it is that all attempts at suppressing prostitution—and they are innumerable—have failed completely. The harder and more efficacious the coercive measures, the deeper underground the mercenaries in sex are driven, but never is prostitution stamped out. History also teaches us that the effects of attempted suppressions of prostitution are usually devastating, particularly for the prostitutes. As far as I can see, it would take at least a society as repugnant as that described by Orwell in his *1984* in terms of totalitarian supervision and coercive measures to suppress prostitution. And who but a fanatic antiprostitutionist would be willing to achieve this end at that price?

Suppression, however, is a negative and destructive path to take. Could not the same end be achieved by means of some more positive or constructive method? Could not a social state of affairs be realized in which mercenary sex would be *superfluous* rather than suppressed?

Since, short of absolute and complete totalitarianism, the supply of prostitutes will not cease until there is practically no demand for the services of whores, all positive and constructive measures aiming at the abolishment of harlotry must aim at abolishing the *demand* for mercenary sex. Can we envisage a social system in which this type of demand would be absent? And what would it be like? Davis answers as follows:

> It would be a regime of absolute sexual freedom, wherein intercourse were practised solely for the pleasure of it, by both parties. This would entail at least two conditions: *First,* there could be no institutional control of sexual expression. Marriage, with its concomitants of engagement, jealousy, divorce, and legitimacy, could not exist. Such an institution builds upon and limits the sexual urge, making sex expression contingent upon non-sexual factors, and thereby paving the way for intercourse against one's physical inclinations. *Second,* all sexual desire would have to be mutually complementary. One person could not be erotically attracted to a non-responsive person, be-

cause such a situation would inevitably involve frustration and give a motive for using force, fraud, authority, or money to induce the unwilling person to co-operate.[17]

And it is, of course, totally unrealistic to think that this will ever happen.

Benjamin and Masters are also, like in fact most writers on the subject, completely pessimistic as far as the elimination of the demand is concerned: "Yet it would seem that only in a society—thoroughly abhorrent to contemplate—where every male and every female could have access upon demand to every other male and female, would the problem of frustration be solved and the demand for prostitution thus be eliminated."[18] I have no serious objections to these views, but I think that they need to be supplemented lest the full extent of the unreality of eliminating the demand be underestimated. In the passages just quoted, a central role is attributed to *frustration* of sexual needs with respect to the existence of the demand for prostitution. But unless "frustration" is taken to have a very inclusive meaning, it seems to me that not even the elimination of frustration would be sufficient to eliminate the demand for prostitution. Both Davis and Benjamin and Masters seem to be aware of this. Davis, for instance, says: "But in addition to the sheer desire for sexual satisfaction, there is the desire for satisfaction in a particular (often an unsanctioned) way. . . . The craving for variety, for perverse gratification, for mysterious and provocative surroundings, for intercourse free from entangling cares and civilized pretense, all play their part.[19] And Benjamin and Masters seem to touch upon still another factor influencing the demand when they write: "For example, it is an unfortunate truism that with the passage of the years the attractiveness of the marriage partner as a sex partner typically diminishes and often vanishes; yet there frequently remains a powerful affectional bond that neither husband nor wife would wish to break. Even the most hostile critic of the prostitute will often concede that she plays a socially valuable role in helping to preserve such marriages."[20] All these factors could (and probably will) be influenced by a growing tolerance toward promiscuous behavior by both sexes. But not even the most permissive values in the area of sexual expression could do more than diminish the demand.[21]

It is also naive to think that an open, honest, and equal relationship between partners would do away with the demand for prostitution. Sexual attraction and the lack of it are largely irrational phenomena and as such they are only marginally influenceable (thank heaven!) by open, honest discussions between equal men and women: Moreover, it is my guess that when equality between the sexes is achieved we will see an increase in the demand for male heterosexual prostitutes. The degree of female frustration that exists today (but is rarely spoken of) will then no longer be tolerated, rationalized, or sublimated, but channeled into a demand for, inter alia, mercenary sex. An outlet which always has been the privilege of men will then also be available to women.[22]

The points which have been put forward in this section may, I think, be summed up in the following way. It is a mistake to think that prostitution can be eradicated by eradicating such things as poverty, illiteracy, sex and class inequalities, broken homes, and impoverished living conditions generally. For one thing, measures such as these will be the supply of prostitutes while the existence and rate of the demand will remain untouched, and it is the demand which calls forth the supply. For another, not even the supply is due solely to economic causes. It is also a mistake to think that prostitution can be suppressed by employing various punitive and coercive methods. All such attempts are not only doomed to fail, they also create an enormous amount of avoidable suffering. Third, and most important of all, it is a mistake to think that prostitution can be made superfluous by eliminating the demand for mercenary sex. For the fact is that the social system where no one would ask for the services of harlots, although imaginable, is so totally unrealistic that no one who has carefully considered the matter can seriously believe that it will ever come to pass. This is neither pessimism nor defeatism but realism.

If someone, after careful consideration of the data, still insists upon the view that the best policy to adopt toward prostitution is to suppress it effectively, we are, I think, morally entitled to require that this person, before any part of his suggested policy is put into action, presents us with a detailed solution of the equation that no one has previously been able to solve, namely, how to prevent prostitution while preserving fundamental rights and liberties. By this I do not mean that it is a fundamental right to prostitute oneself (it is hardly a right at all). What I mean is that it has proven impossible to prevent prostitution without violating fundamental rights and liberties. And I find this price far too high to pay for almost any social change, let alone a change the value of which is highly doubtful.

But from the fact that prostitution can neither be suppressed (short of a brave new world) nor rendered superfluous (short of utopia), it does not follow that we must give in to the conservative notion that we live in the best of all worlds as far as prostitution is concerned. For it is hardly an exaggeration to say that the situation of today is highly unsatisfactory, especially with respect to those most primarily concerned: the prostitutes.

Given all this, the only reasonable conclusion is that prostitution ought not to be eradicated, but reformed. How? A few words will be said about this vast subject in the next section.

X. Some Policy Suggestions

In several of the previous sections of this essay I have had occasion to discuss the negative features of prostitution as it functions today (and has long functioned) in most societies: the great professional hazards: the economic exploitation; the antisocial tendencies of people in the racket, their frequent association with the criminal world and organized crime, and the stigma attached to their profession; etc. But in distinction to all those who hold these negative features against prostitution (as if they were intrinsic to it), I regard them as the avoidable result of values and attitudes of the society wherein prostitution occurs. And these values and attitudes are not only detrimental to prostitution, *they are also detrimental to the relations between the sexes generally.* But more of this presently.

How can I say that the negative features are the *avoidable* result of values and attitudes of the surrounding society? Is it not just as unrealistic to think that our attitudes toward sex and sexuality can be changed within a reasonable period of time as it is to think that the demand for mercenary sex can be eliminated? My answer is: Not quite. For it is after all less difficult to alter our views, attitudes, and values than to alter our physiological nature. Think, for instance, how the average American's attitudes toward Negroes have changed during recent decades.

I admit, of course, that a change in our attitudes toward prostitution must be regarded as a long-range goal that it will take a long time to realize. In the meantime a great many prostitutes will continue to suffer from our present prejudices. A program for more immediate action is therefore also called for. In this section I shall, to begin with, make some suggestions with respect to this more immediate reform program. I shall also have something to say about those values and attitudes which have negative effects on, inter alia, prostitution and prostitutes. I shall finally suggest, in outline, my conception of a sound prostitution, a prostitution which is allowed to function in a social climate freed from prejudice.

The first and most urgent step to take is to decriminalize prostitution in those places where it is still a crime to be or to visit a whore. For, as long as harlotry is lumped together with crime there are hardly any chances of improvement. Fortunately, most societies have taken this step. But even in these societies the progress made is not seldom threatened by various groups who would like to see prostitution recriminalized.

The second step is to improve the housing situation for prostitutes. The prostitute must be given the right to rent a suitable location in her/his capacity as a prostitute. The same legal rules that prohibit a landlord from refusing a tenant *in spe* should be made to apply in the case of the prostitute. Thus, that the tenant *in spe* is a harlot should not constitute adequate ground for refusal. It should also be made impossible for a landlord to evict a person simply because she/he is a hustler. Nor should it be allowed to refuse or evict someone on the ground that other tenants do not wish to live next door to a whore. People sometimes do not wish to live next door to Negroes, gypsies, and mentally retarded persons either, but just as in those cases society should not, in the case of prostitutes, attribute these wishes any legal weight. And, as a corollary to these suggestions, no land-

lord who charges normal rents should have to run the risk of being convicted for bawdry.

What positive effects would this have? First, it would greatly reduce the crude economic exploitation of harlots. Being able to rent a flat without pretense, they would no longer have to pay usury rents to unscrupulous landlords. Second, it would tend to diminish some of the occupational hazards, notably those related to the feeling of insecurity, of being secluded, deprived of the rights of ordinary citizens. Third, it would tend to weaken the association between prostitution and organized crime.

What negative effects, if any, would this have? As far as I can see, the major negative effect would be that certain "respectable" citizens would get their feelings of decency upset by having to live in the same house or neighborhood as a prostitute. But this negative effect is, in my opinion, outweighed by the fact that the customers will not have to walk so far to visit one.

A third urgent step is to develop a program intended to get rid of child and teenage prostitution. Minors should as far as possible be prevented from entrance into prostitution, not on moralistic but on paternalistic grounds. For in the case of minors, paternalistic measures seem justified for the same reason as they are justified in other social matters. Do I contradict myself when I recommend this? Not at all, for from the fact that prostitution generally is inevitable it does not follow that prostitution among minors is. The difficulties of finding an effective antidote should, however, not be underestimated. And we must beware of constructing a program that, although well intended, will make the already difficult situation of the young hustlers even worse. Punitive and coercive measures must therefore be banned from such a program. But first and foremost we must do research in order to discover more about the causes of prostitution among minors.[23] The sad truth is that we do not know enough about the causes of prostitution in general, and we know even less about the causes of child and teenage prostitution. That drug addiction constitutes one of the causes can hardly be disputed, however. Any effective program against hustling among the young must therefore be coordinated with the measures undertaken to prevent the use of narcotics. An effective program must also give due consideration to the possibility that today's minors have a different attitude toward sex and sexuality than todays' adults. For no measures can be effective without good communication.

As for adult prostitution, I have suggested that it should be reformed rather than abolished. But the most important part of that reform does not concern prostitution and prostitutes but our *attitudes* toward them. For it seems to me impossible to come to grips with the negative aspects of harlotry without a change of our values and attitudes. Which values and attitudes? And why should they be changed? It would take an essay of its own to deal with these questions exhaustively, so I shall have to confine myself to a few examples and the outlines of a justification.

In my view, contempt for whores and contempt for women are closely related. The devaluation of the female sex is a permanent part of the Western tradition of ideas, reinforced by the Christian so-called culture. As an early example, according to Aristotle we should "look upon the female state as being as it were a deformity through one which occurs in the ordinary course of nature."[24] And according to Freud, who in many respects echoes Aristotle, woman is pictured as partial man: "She [the female child] acknowledges the fact of her castration, and with it too, the superiority of the male."[25] The influence of these and numerous other similar ideas has, with the passage of the years and often in vulgarized form, been sedimented in public opinion.

In order to see the relationship between contempt for women and contempt for harlots, another important part of the Western tradition of ideas must be added, namely, the devaluation of sexuality. Both contempt for the female sex and the devaluation of sexuality have their roots in the ancient notion that man consists of two distinct parts, body and soul, of which the second is immensely more valuable than the first. As is well known, the soul, according to Plato, does not really belong here in our material world, the world of the senses. It belongs to the spiritual world, although it temporarily takes its seat (or is imprisoned) in the body. These ideas were later developed by Aristotle and the purveyor of philosophy to the Catholic church, Thomas Aquinas. The originally Orphic distinction between body and soul

was soon transformed, especially under the influence of Christian thinkers such as Saint Augustine, to a general devaluation of the body, bodily functions, and sexuality. Saint Augustine, for instance, seems to have been greatly disappointed in the Creator for not having made human reproduction possible in a less crudely bodily and pleasurable way. In the Christian tradition generally the body and its function, especially when associated with pleasure, have typically been regarded as sinful.

In a culture where both the female sex and sexuality are devaluated it is only "logical" to place the prostitute—an individual who is not only a female but who also earns her living by means of her female sex by selling sexual services—at the bottom of the scale of social approval.

It is a grave mistake to think that ideas and attitudes of this nature, in our present "enlightened" and "liberated" era, have lost their power of influence and that contemporary critics of such things as pornography and prostitution rely on entirely different sources. One common notion behind the opposition to pornography, for instance, seems to be that it reduces man (or more frequently, woman) to an object, to a certain amount of flesh. Translated into the tradition just described, this becomes: Pornography catches only the bodily aspect of man, thereby totally disregarding his soul. It is sheer self-deception to retort here that the opposition to pornography is based rather on its commercialistic character, for a nude by Picasso is just as much a commercial object as a copy of *Playboy*. In fact, scorn for pornography, erotic art, and nudity in general fits excellently into the traditional scorn for the human body. When two persons go to bed with each other for no other reason than that they are physically attracted to each other, their behavior, according to conventional standards, is *brutish*. And according to somewhat more sophisticated standards, the relation is regarded as *impoverished* (see the sentimentalist critique of prostitution). Poor of what? Well, in the Aristotelian, Augustinian tradition animals have no soul. Thus, what makes the couple's behavior brutish is its lack of "soul." Another example of a prevailing attitude, whose roots can be traced back to this tradition, is our attitude toward physical beauty and native intelligence. If a woman excels in beauty without excelling in intelligence, she is said to be *"merely"* beautiful, while if she excels in intelligence without excelling in beauty, she is hardly said to be *"merely"* intelligent. But then, after all, intelligence is excellence of the "soul," while physical beauty is no more than excellence of the body.

This list of examples could be made much longer (the reader is invited to provide examples of his own), but those given should suffice to make it clear that our outlook as far as sex roles, relations between the sexes, and sexuality are concerned is still very much under the influence of time-honored, but primitive, ideas and attitudes—ideas and attitudes which have negative effects not only on prostitution and prostitutes but also on the relations between the sexes generally. I find it particularly sad that so many feminists seem unable to understand that contempt for harlotry involves contempt for the female sex.

Our attitudes toward sexual expression in general, and mercenary sex in particular, ought to be modified or abandoned partly because of the damage that they do, partly because they represent prejudices in the sense that they are rooted in false beliefs. Women are not partial men nor is the female sex a deformity. And the distinction between body and soul, with all its metaphysical and religious ramifications, apart from being philosophically highly dubious, is the source of more human misery than almost any other.

A sound prostitution is, first of all, a prostitution that is allowed to function in a social climate freed from emotional prejudice of the kind described above. Prostitution can never be rid of its most serious negative aspects (primarily the suffering the prostitutes have to endure) in a society where females are regarded as inferior to males and where man's physical nature is regarded as inferior to his spiritual nature.

A sound prostitution is, furthermore, a prostitution such that those who become prostitutes are adults who are not compelled to prostitute themselves but who freely choose to do so in the same sense of "freely" as anyone's trade or occupation may be said to be freely chosen. A sound prostitution is, in other words, a prostitution of voluntary, not compulsive, hustlers.

A sound prostitution is, third, a prostitution that is legal, and where the prostitutes are not persecuted but attributed the same rights as ordinary citizens as a recognition of the fact that they fulfill a socially valuable function by inter alia, decreasing the amount of sexual misery in society.

A sound prostitution is, fourth, a prostitution such that the prostitutes are no more economically exploited than wage workers in general.

A sound prostitution is, finally, a prostitution that is equally available to both sexes.

Of these conditions I regard the first as the most fundamental. Without it being at least partially satisfied, the satisfaction of the others seems more difficult. Thus, if I were to sum up the principal view put forward in this concluding section, it would be formulated as follows: *in order to improve prostitution, we must first and foremost improve our attitudes toward it.*

I admit that a sound prostitution in this sense is far from easy to realize, but this does not mean that I think that it is unrealistic. As far as I can see, we have at least begun to liberate ourselves from some of the archaic strands of Western thought. But we surely still have a long way ahead of us.

In conclusion, I wish to emphasize once again that I do not regard prostitution, not even a sound prostitution, as in any way *ultimately* desirable. Its desirability is conditional upon certain ubiquitous and permanent imperfections of actual human societies. In a perfectly good society, however, it would be superfluous.

Notes

I wish to acknowledge my indebtedness to Harry Benjamin and R. E. L. Masters. Their well-argued plea for a rational reevaluation of prostitution and for an assessment of it freed from emotional prejudice has been a great source of inspiration. Their empirical studies have also provided me with a large share of my factual insights concerning mercenary sex. I also wish to thank Harald Ofstad for his valuable criticism of an earlier version of this essay.

1. For a comprehensive bibliography, see Vern Bullough et al., eds., *A Bibliography of Prostitution* (New York and London: Garland Publishers, 1977).

2. I am thinking here of the debate between Devlin and Hart which followed upon the publication of the *Wolfenden Report* on homosexual offenses and prostitution in 1957 (see Lord Devlin, *The Enforcement of Morals* [London: Oxford University Press, 1965], and H. L. A. Hart, *Law, Liberty, and Morality* [Stanford, CA: Stanford University Press, 1963]).

3. Here I am indebted to Kingsley Davis (see his "The Sociology of Prostitution," reprinted in *Deviance, Studies in the Process of Stigmatization and Social Reaction,* ed. A. C. Clarke, S. Dinitz, and R. R. Dynes (New York: Oxford University Press, 1975).

4. See Harry Benjamin and R. E. L. Masters, *Prostitution and Morality* (New York: Julian Press, 1964), chap. 6.

5. Ibid.

6. Ibid., p. 208.

7. I should perhaps stress, however, that I use the term "prostitution" in a neutral, descriptive sense, disregarding the ordinary negative value association of the term. In a later section (X) a normative concept 'sound prostitution' will be developed.

8. The empirical part of this opinion will be examined critically in the next section.

9. My major source of information has here as elsewhere been Benjamin and Masters (n. 4 above), esp. chaps. 5, 6, and 10. I have also consulted the reports of Jersild (Jens Jersild, *Buy Prostitution* [Copenhagen: G. E. C. Gad, 1956]) and Butts (W. M. Butts, "Boy Prostitutes of the Metropolis, *Journal of Clinical Psychopathology* [1947], pp. 673–81).

10. A ratio of 60/40 has been mentioned for big city areas like New York and Los Angeles. I do not regard this (or any other) figure as completely reliable, however. The empirical material available does not seem to allow any exact conclusions.

11. Rowbotham, p. 66.

12. To those who find this statement a bit too categorical I suggest a quick glance back to Sec. IV.

13. United Nations, *Study on Traffic in Persons and Prostitution* (New York, 1959).

14. Kollontai, p. 46.

15. Davis (n. 3 above), p. 391.

16. Here I am indebted to Davis.

17. Ibid., p. 391.

18. Benjamin and Masters (n. 4 above), p. 116.

19. Davis, p. 390.

20. Benjamin and Masters, pp. 435–36.

21. A fact that is often overlooked, when in the discussion a growing sexual freedom is regarded as an alternative to prostitution, is that with a larger sexual freedom and a greater tolerance toward promiscuity also follows a weakening of the social and psychological barriers that previously, rather effectively, prevented many individuals from entrance into prostitution.

22. That the lack of male heterosexual prostitutes is due to physiological factors is, of course, a myth. That inability to achieve erection would constitute an obstacle is gainsaid by the practices of male homosexual prostitutes (see Benjamin and Masters, *Prostitution and Morality,* chap. 10). Moreover, actual intercourse is only one type of sexual service, among many others, that a prostitute typically sells.

23. A Swedish public commission (Prostitutionsutredningen) formed in 1977 is presently working on, inter alia, this problem. Its results have, however, not yet been published.

24. Aristotle, *The Generation of Animals,* quoted in Caroline Whitbeck, "Theories of Sex Difference," *Philosophical Forum* 5, nos. 1 and 2 (1973–74): 54–80, quote from p. 56.

25. Sigmund Freud, *Female Sexuality,* quoted in Whitbeck, p. 69.

Upon reflection, one can recognize that Ericsson's defense of a reformed prostitution brings up many issues even more fundamental than prostitution *per se.* For example, Ericsson's article raises questions concerning the very nature of human sexuality, answers to which will influence our attitudes toward reformed prostitution.

Some thinkers conceptualize human sexuality as the most intense expression of one's body and indeed of one's most intimate self. When sex is so conceived, prostitution is characterized as the "selling of one's body" or the "selling of one's self," and as such, constitutes a form of slavery. Others, such as Ericsson, construe human sexual interactions as natural activities that may be engaged in for a variety of purposes and may have different meanings to the individuals involved—ranging from simple physical pleasure to the deepest expression of love. Most important, for our present concern, Ericsson views some sexual activity as a human service, one that may be exchanged for monetary benefits much like that of a nurse, barber, or accountant.

When one voluntarily chooses to sell their sexual services, this is no more slavery than the selling of any other service. As we shall see in the following article, the question of whether prostitution is conceived as the selling of a service or the selling of one's body is a critical factor in judging the moral permissibility of prostitution. If prostitution is characterized as the selling of oneself or one's body, we might ask what is involved in the concepts of selling or of property rights in general. For instance, if one buys a set of golf clubs, one obtains the right to exclude others from using them. One can also, in return, sell them

to anyone else for any price one wishes; further, one has the right to break them or even totally destroy them. Thus, it may be asked, when a person interacts with a prostitute, do they
obtain anything like these property rights? If not, how does a prostitute "sell" her body?

In Chapter 2, fundamental questions regarding the value of sex with love versus sex
without love were raised. Here again, it may be noted that one's response to this issue may
have a bearing on the question of prostitution. If one argues that sex without love is immoral, it logically follows that sex with prostitutes, which does not involve love, is immoral.
And if we construe the purpose of sex as procreation, then prostitution will be deemed immoral. What are your views concerning the relation between sex and love? Do you think
there is one purpose or function of sex? Is the purpose of sex the same for everyone? Is it
even the same for any individual at different times or on different occasions?

Another basic issue underlying evaluation of prostitution is whether sexual desire is a
natural and powerful biological need or impulse which, like other basic human needs,
should be satisfied, or whether sexual activity is determined by other cultural values such
as patriarchal political power or religious moralities. Some feminists, for example, argue
that sexual desires are determined by the male power structure in society and that male-female sexual relationships take place within a dominance-submission context where the male
is the master and the woman a slave. When perceived this way, some feminists regard all
male-female sexual relationships as prostitution or as otherwise immoral. Do you believe
that human sexuality is a basic and important biological need, or do you believe sexual desires are determined by your culture (as will be seen in Laurie Schrage's essay), or is sexual desire a result of many factors?

Finally, Ericsson contends that if we can rid ourselves of religious dogmas, supersti-
tions, biases, myths, and negative attitudes towards sex and towards woman's sexuality, a
reformed prostitution would be possible and desirable. Do you think this is possible? Would
it be desirable? Some argue that a reformed prostitution would not be desirable since it
would merely continue the submission of women to their male masters. For such a view, let
us turn to Carole Pateman's essay.

THE FEMINIST OBJECTION TO PROSTITUTION

In "Defending Prostitution: Charges Against Ericsson," Carole Pateman argues that Ericsson completely fails to grasp the real nature of the feminist charge. That charge is contra
Ericsson, based not merely on inequality constructed as unequal burdens and benefits, but
rather, on the place of women living in a patriarchy of male dominance and female suppression. When male abstract liberalism sees prostitution in terms of liberal ideals of individualism, free contracts, and free markets, it fails to recognize male-female transactions
occur within a social system of male domination and female subjection.

Pateman then scrutinizes Ericsson's crucial assertion that prostitution is essentially the
selling of sexual services. Here, she presents arguments to show that the prostitute actually
does sell her body in a capitalistic society. Moreover, since prostitution is more intimately
connected with the body than social service work, Ericsson's analogy between prostitution
and social service work is mistaken.

Ericsson's other major bias, according to Pateman, is his treatment of prostitution as a
female problem rather than a problem about the men who demand it. Here, Pateman makes
two counterpoints: (1) While some sexual urges may be natural and biological, the sale of

sexual service is not, and (2) sex is not so basic, natural, or compelling as the appetite for food and drink since no one dies from lack of sexual release.

To explain male demand, Pateman argues, don't look at biology, but at the cultural and psychological facts about men and women. In capitalistic society, the fundamental issue in male-female relations is *power,* and prostitution is just one more way of recognizing men as sexual masters. To understand female-male relations psychologically, Pateman reverts to recent feminist interpretations of psychoanalytic theory. She points out that Ericsson assumes men and women have a universal, homogenous sexual nature, but she argues that men and women have fundamentally different psychological natures, and male demand can be traced to the early development of the male unconscious.

Finally, Pateman argues that Ericsson fails to draw two logical implications of his position: (1) All sexual relationships should be modeled on universal prostitution, and (2) there is no reason to prohibit children from this practice. In short, what distresses feminists is what the demand for prostitution reveals about the current status of relationships between men and women.

from Defending Prostitution: Charges Against Ericsson

CAROLE PATEMAN

Ericsson's contractarian defense of prostitution[1] extends the liberal ideals of individualism, equality of opportunity, and the free market to sexual life. The real problem with prostitution, Ericsson claims, is the hypocrisy, prejudice, and punitive attitudes that surround it. Once unblinkered, we can see that prostitution is merely one service occupation among others and that, with some reforms, a morally acceptable, or "sound," prostitution could exist. This defense has its appeal at a time when strict control of sexual conduct is again being strenuously advocated. However, Ericsson's argument fails to overcome the general weaknesses of abstract contractarianism, and his claim that he has rebutted the feminist charge against prostitution cannot be granted. The central feminist argument is that prostitution remains morally undesirable, no matter what reforms are made, because it is one of the most graphic examples of men's domination of women.

Ericsson's argument illustrates nicely how liberal contractarianism systematically excludes the patriarchal dimension of our society from philosophical scrutiny. He interprets feminists as arguing that prostitution is "undesirable on the ground that it constitutes an extreme instance of the inequality between the sexes" (p. 348), and he then interprets inequality to be a matter of the distribution of benefits and burdens. It thus appears that a remedy can be found for the withholding of a benefit (access to prostitutes) from women by extending equality of opportunity to buy and sell sexual services on the market to both sexes. Ericsson ignores the fact that men earn a good deal more than women, so the latter would still have a greater incentive to be sellers than buyers (or would be confined to the cheaper end of the market as buyers; Ericsson pays no attention to the different categories of prostitution). Moreover, Ericsson notes that three-quarters of the men who are in the market for prostitutes are married. Any change in attitudes would have to be sufficient to make it acceptable that wives could spend what they save from housekeeping money, or spend part of their

From "Defending Prostitution: Charges Against Ericsson" by Carole Pateman, *Ethics,* 93 (April 1983), pp. 561–565. Used by permission of the author and The University of Chicago Press.

own earnings, on prostitutes. Second, Ericsson dismisses as meaningless the charge that prostitution unfairly burdens women because they are oppressed as prostitutes; properly understood, prostitution is an example of a free contract between individuals in the market in which services are exchanged for money. Ericsson's defense does not and cannot confront the feminist objection to prostitution. Feminists do not see prostitution as unacceptable because it distributes benefits and burdens unequally; rather, to use Ericsson's language of inequality, because prostitution is grounded in the inequality of domination and subjection. The problem of domination is both denied by and hidden behind Ericsson's assertion that prostitution is a free contract or an equal exchange.

The most striking feature of Ericsson's defense is that he makes no attempt to substantiate the key claim that prostitution *is* the sale of sexual services. His assertion relies on the conventional assumption that free wage labor stands at the opposite pole from slavery. The worker freely contracts to sell labor power or services for a specified period, whereas the person of the slave is sold for an unlimited time. Ericsson comments that if a prostitute "actually did sell herself, she would no longer be a prostitute but a sexual slave" (p. 341). More exactly since she has the civil and juridical status of a free individual in the capitalist market, she would be in a form of subjection that fell short of slavery. Ericsson avoids discussing whether this is indeed the position of the prostitute because he ignores the problems involved in separating the sale of services through contract from the sale of the body and the self. In capitalist societies it appears as if labor power and services are bought and sold on the market, but "labor power" and "services" are abstractions. When workers sell labor power, or professionals sell services to clients (and Ericsson regards some prostitutes as "small scale private entrepreneurs"),[2] neither the labor power nor services can in reality be separated from the person offering them for sale. Unless the "owners" of these abstractions agree to, or are compelled to, use them in certain ways, which means that the "owners" act in a specified manner, there is nothing to be sold. The employer appears to buy labor power; what he actually obtains is the right of command over workers, the right to put their capacities, their bodies, to use as he determines.

Services and labor power are inseparably connected to the body and the body is, in turn, inseparably connected to the sense of self. Ericsson writes of the prostitute as a kind of social worker, but the services of the prostitute are related in a more intimate manner to her body than those of other professionals. Sexual services, that is to say, sex and sexuality, are constitutive of the body in a way in which the counseling skills of the social worker are not (a point illustrated in a backhanded way by the ubiquitous use by men of vulgar terms for female sexual organs to refer to women themselves). Sexuality and the body are, further, integrally connected to conceptions of femininity and masculinity, and all these are constitutive of our individuality, or sense of self-identity. When sex becomes a commodity in the capitalist market so, necessarily, do bodies and selves. The prostitute cannot sell sexual services alone; what she sells is her body. To supply services contracted for, professionals must act in certain ways, or use their bodies; to use the labor power he has bought the employer has command over the worker's capacities and body; to use the prostitute's "services," her purchaser must buy her body and use her body. In prostitution, because of the relation between the commodity being marketed and the body, it is the body that is up for sale.

Critics of marriage have often claimed that wives are no different from prostitutes. Women who marry also contract away their bodies but (in principle) for life rather than for minutes or hours like the prostitute. However, a form of marriage in which the husband gains legal right of sexual use of his wife's body is only one possible form. The conjugal relation is not necessarily one of domination and subjection, and in this it differs from prostitution. Ericsson's defense is about prostitution in capitalist societies; that is, the practice through which women's bodies become commodities in the market which can be bought (contracted for) for sexual use. The questions his defense raises are why there is a demand for this commodity, exactly what the commodity is, and why it is *men* who demand it.

Ericsson cannot admit that the first two questions arise. The third he treats as unproblematic. He stands firmly in the patriarchal tradition which discusses prostitution as a problem about the women who are prostitutes, and our attitudes to them, not a problem about the men who demand to buy them. For Ericsson it is merely a contingent fact that most prostitutes are women and customers men.[3] He claims that the demand for prostitution could never disappear because of some "ubiquitous and permanent imperfection" of human existence arising from the sexual urge. In other words, prostitution is a natural feature of human life. Certainly, sexual impulses are part of our natural constitution as humans, but the sale of "sexual services" as a commodity in the capitalist market cannot be reduced to an expression of our natural biology and physiology. To compare the fulfillment of sexual urges through prostitution to other natural necessities of human survival, to argue from the fact that we need food, so it should be available, to the claim that "our sexual desires are just as basic, natural, and compelling as our appetite for food, [so] this also holds for them," is, to say the least, disingenuous. What counts as "food" varies widely, of course, in different cultures, but, at the most fundamental level of survival there is one obvious difference between sex and other human needs. Without a certain minimum of food, drink, and shelter, people die; but, to my knowledge, no one has yet died from want of sexual release. Moreover, sometimes food and drink are impossible to obtain no matter what people do, but every person has the means to find sexual release at hand.

To treat prostitution as a natural way of satisfying a basic human need, to state that "bought meals are not always the worst" (p. 355), neatly, if vulgarly obscures the real, social character of contemporary sexual relations. Prostitution is not, as Ericsson claims, the same as "sex without love or mutual affection." The latter is morally acceptable *if* it is the result of mutual physical attraction that is freely expressed by both individuals. The difference between sex without love and prostitution is not the difference between cooking at home and buying food in restaurants; the difference is that between the reciprocal expression of desire and unilateral subjection to sexual acts with the consolation of payment: it is the difference for women between freedom and subjection.

To understand why men (not women) demand prostitutes, and what is demanded, prostitution has to be rescued from Ericsson's abstract contractarianism and placed in the social context of the structure of sexual relations between women and men. Since the revival of the organized feminist movement, moral and political philosophers have begun to turn their attention to sexual life, but their discussions are usually divided into a set of discrete compartments which take for granted that a clear distinction can be drawn between consensual and coercive sexual relationships. However, as an examination of consent and rape makes graphically clear,[4] throughout the whole of sexual life domination, subjection, and enforced submission are confused with consent, free association, and the reciprocal fulfillment of mutual desire. The assertion that prostitution is no more than an example of a free contract between equal individuals in the market is another illustration of the presentation of submission as freedom. Feminists have often argued that what is fundamentally at issue in relations between women and men is not sex but power. But, in the present circumstances of our sexual lives, it is not possible to separate power from sex. The expression of sexuality and what it means to be feminine and a woman, or masculine and a man, is developed within, and intricately bound up with, relations of domination and subordination.

Ericsson remarks that "the best prostitutional sex available is probably much better from the customer's point of view than average marital sex." It is far from obvious that it is either "quality" or the "need" for sex, in the commonsense view of "quality" and "sex," that explains why three-quarters of these customers are husbands. In the "permissive society" there are numerous ways in which men can find sex without payment, in addition to the access that husbands have to wives. But, except in the case of the most brutal husbands, most spouses work out a modus vivendi about all aspects of their lives, including the wife's bodily integrity. Not all husbands exercise to the full their socially and legally recognized right— which is the right of a master. There is, however, another institution which enables all men to affirm themselves as masters. To be able to purchase a body in the market presupposes the existence of masters. Prostitution is the public recognition of men as sexual masters; it puts submission on sale as a commodity in the market.

The outline of an answer to the complex question of why men demand this commodity can be found in recent feminist interpretations of psychoanalytic theory. Feminist discussions of the differential development of gendered individuality suggest that the masculine sense of self is grounded in separateness, especially separation from those other (opposing) feminine selves which proclaim what masculinity is not.[5] Hegel showed theoretically in his famous dialectic of mastery and servitude that a self so conceived always attempts to gain recognition and maintain its subjective isolation through domination. When women and men are seen in their substantive individuality, and not as abstract makers of contracts, an explanation can be found for why it is *men* who demand to buy women's bodies in the market. The demand by men for prostitutes in patriarchal capitalist society is bound up with a historically and culturally distinctive form of masculine individuality. The structure of the relation between the sexes reaches into the unconscious early development of little boys and girls and out into the form of economic organization in which the capacities of individuals, and even women's bodies, become commodities to be alienated to the control and use of others.

The peculiarity of Ericsson's argument for equality of opportunity in "sound" prostitution should now be apparent. He assumes that the (sexual) selves of women and men are interchangeable. This may appear radical, but it is a purely abstract radicalism that reduces differentiated, gendered individuality to the seemingly natural, undifferentiated, and universal figure of the "individual"—which is an implicit generalization of the masculine self. The feminist exploration of gendered individuality provides the material, sociological grounding for that familiar, liberal abstraction, the possessive, atomistic self that appears as the bearer of rights and the maker of contracts in civil society. The logic of Ericsson's sexual contractarianism also leads to two unpalatable con-

clusions that he is unwilling to draw. The first is that all sexual relations should take the form of universal prostitution, the buying and selling of sexual services on the market. The equal right of access to sexual use of a body (or "sexual services") can be established more economically and advantageously for the individual through universal prostitution than through (the contract of) marriage. Second, it is unnecessary to confine the buying and selling of sexual services to adults. Ericsson is fainthearted in his contractarianism when he excludes children from the market. Strictly, the capacity to make a contract is all that is required; surely not a capacity confined to those who are statutorily adults.

Ericsson shows how complete is his misunderstanding of feminism and the feminist criticism of prostitution when he complains that "so many feminists seem unable to understand that contempt for harlotry involves contempt for the female sex." Neither contempt for women nor their ancient profession underlies feminist arguments; rather, they are sad and angry about what the demand for prostitution reveals of the general character of (private and public) relations between the sexes. The claim that what is really wrong with prostitution is hypocrisy and outdated attitudes to sex is the tribute that liberal permissiveness pays to political mystification.

Notes

1. L. O. Ericsson, "Charges against Prostitution: An Attempt at a Philosophical Assessment," *Ethics* 90, no. 3 (1980): 335–66.

2. On workers as "petty entrepreneurs," their labor power or services, see R. P. Wolff, "A Critique and Reinterpretation of Marx's Labor Theory of Value," *Philosophy and Public Affairs* 10 (1981): 89–120, esp. 109–11.

3. In cities like Sydney, male homosexual prostitutes are not uncommon. Following Ericsson, I discuss only heterosexual (genitally oriented) prostitution. It is not immediately clear that homosexual prostitution has the same social significance.

4. See my "Women and Consent," *Political Theory* 8 (1980): 149–68.

5. See, esp., J. Benjamin, "The Bonds of Love: Rational Violence and Erotic Domination," *Feminist Studies* 6 (1980): 175–96. Benjamin builds on N. Chodorow, *The Reproduction of Mothering: Psychoanalysis and the Sociology of Gender* (Berkeley and Los Angeles: University of California Press, 1978).

Carole Pateman forges several direct and relevant challenges to Ericsson's defense of a reformed prostitution. Against Ericsson's view that a prostitute engages in a kind of voluntary contractual relationship with her customer in which both are free and equal participants, Pateman argues that such seemingly free contracts take place in a larger social context in which the woman is not an equal but rather one who, due to the patriarchal institutions of society, is in a weak or powerless position. In fact, for Pateman, all male-female sexual relationships are essentially power relationships, and it is the men who have the power.

Pateman also argues that people in a capitalistic system cannot sell their services independently of selling their bodies; and since, unlike other human services, sex is inextricably connected with one's body and one's self, the prostitute cannot merely sell her services alone. Rather, for the prostitute, her body itself is up for sale. Does this claim then raise the question of what it is to sell anything in a capitalistic society? Does the purchaser of a prostitute's services get exclusive rights to her body for as long as he wants? Can he sell her to someone else? Can he destroy her completely? How does the purchaser get any more property rights than he would if he hired a secretary? How does he buy a "self"?

Prostitution, according to Pateman, is unlike marriage in that prostitution is necessarily a relationship of domination and subjection. Is this a valid generalization? Might we ask how one knows that all or most interactions between a prostitute and male customer consist of male domination? In actual instances of prostitution, dominatrices often call the shots, as do many high-priced call girls. Further, the male customers of prostitutes are often weak, shy, and submissive individuals. Many prostitutes claim that in their line of work, it is *they* and *not the male* who are in control. Could it be that this broad claim about male-female dominance is an unproven generalization and that it abstracts from actual relationships between real prostitutes and their real customers? Are all prostitutes weak, submissive victims or could some be strong, independent businesswomen who are in charge?

Finally, Pateman points out that Ericsson misunderstands the feminist criticism of prostitution, which is really driven by what the demand for prostitution tells us about the general character of the relations between the sexes, whether private or public. Is this a valid charge against Ericsson? Does Ericsson really ignore these relations or does he, too, condemn them and suggest a revolution in the cultural attitudes and practices that have produced these unsatisfactory relationships between males and females?

Whereas Pateman focuses on questions of why individuals sell or buy sexual services, others, like Laurie Schrage in the following article, attack underlying cultural principles that determine a society's form of prostitution.

THE FEMINIST OBJECTION REINFORCED

In "Should Feminists Oppose Prostitution?" Laurie Shrage, like Pateman, claims that prostitution is morally and politically objectionable insofar as it represents another instance of women's domination and degradation by men. Consequently, she argues that persons who are averse to the subordination of women ought to denounce prostitution.

It is important to note that Shrage does not discuss prostitution as a universal, historical phenomenon, but confines her argument to prostitution as it exists in contemporary Western Society. Shrage argues that when historical and cultural factors are recognized, prostitution is not the same thing in every culture.

As does Pateman, Shrage sees the problem of prostitution as a problem of demand, but rather than offer an analysis of why individuals buy and sell sexual services, Shrage focuses on what she regards as the four underlying principles that structure our culture's form of prostitution—principles that reflect "pernicious patriarchal beliefs and values, ones which are not only harmful to prostitutes but to all women in our society." Shrage claims that regardless of what an individual prostitute may think, the social practice itself underwrites morally bad principles that encourage the subordination of women.

The first principle is the belief in the *universal possession of a potent sex drive*, as evidenced by Ericsson's view of prostitution as a response to a strong, natural *biological* urge. Even Pateman assumed the naturalness of sexual impulses. In contrast, Shrage, in discussing, for example, one tribe of the Dani of New Guinea, argues that the level of sexuality is *culturally* determined. Our biological rationalization of prostitution is, she claims, a product of our modern Western culture.

Secondly, prostitution assumes the *"natural" dominance of men*. Here, Shrage argues that even feminists have uncritically assumed this dominance rather than recognize the phenomenon as based on nothing other than "arbitrary *culturally* determined beliefs."

Thirdly, referring to the writings of Robert Baker, Andrea Dworkin, and Ann Gary, Shrage argues that our culture believes that *sexual contact with men pollutes women*. In our society, we see women engaging in sex with men as harmed objects or damaged goods.

The fourth and final principle is the *reification of sexual practice*, by which Shrage means that a person's entire social identity is actually defined by their sexual behavior; that is, homosexual, loose woman, slut, prostitute, etc.

For Shrage, these four principles produce the very *social meaning* of our culture's form of prostitution, and our acceptance of prostitution implies acceptance of these sexist principles which subordinate women.

Like Ericsson, Shrage imagines specific hypothetical conditions of a society in which prostitution is sought as a high-quality sexual service and which is free from our culturally held principles. But she argues this would not be a *reformed* prostitution, but the *elimination of prostitution as we know it*.

Shrage urges feminists to attack the very principles that underlie the patriarchy, and prostitution is one dramatic case of a practice representing those principles. Therefore, prostitution ought to be opposed. Shrage notes her position is not inconsistent with decriminalization of prostitution but does make it appropriate to engage in a consumer boycott of the entire sex industry.

from Should Feminists Oppose Prostitution?

LAURIE SHRAGE

Because sexuality is a social construction, individuals as individuals are not free to experience *eros* just as they choose. Yet just as the extraction and appropriation of surplus value of the capitalist represents a choice available, if not to individuals, to society as a whole, so too sexuality and the forms taken by *eros* must be seen as at some level open to change.

[Nancy Hartsock, *Money, Sex and Power*][1]

Introduction

Prostitution raises difficult issues for feminists. On the one hand, many feminists want to abolish discriminatory criminal statutes that are mostly used to harass and penalize prostitutes, and rarely to punish johns and pimps—laws which, for the most part, render prostitutes more vulnerable to exploitation by their male associates.[2] On the other

From "Should Feminists Oppose Prostitution?" by Laurie Shrage, *Ethics*, 99 (January 1989), pp. 347–361. Used by permission of the author and The University of Chicago Press.

hand, most feminists find the prostitute's work morally and politically objectionable. In their view, women who provide sexual services for a fee submit to sexual domination by men, and suffer degradation by being treated as sexual commodities.[3]

My concern, in this paper, is whether persons opposed to the social subordination of women should seek to discourage commercial sex. My goal is to marshal the moral arguments needed to sustain feminists' condemnation of the sex industry in our society. In reaching this goal, I reject accounts of commercial sex which posit cross-cultural and transhistorical causal mechanisms to explain the existence of prostitution or which assume that the activities we designate as "sex" have a universal meaning and purpose. By contrast, I analyze mercenary sex in terms of culturally specific beliefs and principles that organize its practice in contemporary American society. I try to show that the sex industry, like other institutions in our society, is structured by deeply ingrained attitudes and values which are oppressive to women. The point of my analysis is not to advocate an egalitarian reformation of commercial sex, nor to advocate its abolition through state regulation. Instead, I focus on another political alternative: that which must be done to subvert widely held beliefs that legitimate this institution in our society. Ultimately, I argue that nothing closely resembling prostitution, as we currently know it, will exist, once we have undermined these cultural convictions.

Why Prostitution Is Problematic

A number of recent papers on prostitution begin with the familiar observation that prostitution is one of the oldest professions.[4] Such 'observations' take for granted that 'prostitution' refers to a single transhistorical, transcultural activity. By contrast, my discussion of prostitution is limited to an activity that occurs in modern Western societies— a practice which involves the purchase of sexual services from women by men. Moreover, I am not interested in exploring the nature and extension of our moral concept "to prostitute oneself"; rather, I want to examine a specific activity we regard as prostitution in order to understand its social and political significance.

In formulating my analysis, I recognize that the term 'prostitute' is ambiguous: it is used to designate both persons who supply sex on a commercial basis and persons who contribute their talents and efforts to base purposes for some reward. While these extensions may overlap, their relationship is not a logically necessary one but is contingent upon complex moral and social principles. In this paper, I use the term 'prostitute' as shorthand for 'provider of commercial sexual services,' and correspondingly, I use the term 'prostitution' interchangeably with 'commercial sex.' By employing these terms in this fashion, I hope to appear consistent with colloquial English, and not to be taking for granted that a person who provides commercial sexual services "prostitutes" her- or himself.

Many analyses of prostitution aim to resolve the following issue: what would induce a woman to prostitute herself—to participate in an impersonal, commercial sexual transaction? These accounts seek the deeper psychological motives behind apparently voluntary acts of prostitution. Because our society regards female prostitution as a social, if not natural, aberration, such actions demand an explanation. Moreover, accepting fees for sex seems irrational and repugnant to many persons, even to the woman who does it, and so one wonders why she does it. My examination of prostitution does not focus on this question. While to do so may explain why a woman will choose prostitution from among various options, it does not explain how a woman's options have been constituted. In other words, although an answer to this question may help us understand why some women become sellers of sexual services rather than homemakers or engineers, it will not increase our understanding of why there is a demand for these services. Why, for example, can women not as easily achieve prosperity by selling child-care services? Finding out why there is a greater market for goods of one type than of another illuminates social forces and trends as much as, if not more than, finding out why individuals enter a particular market. Moreover, theorists who approach prostitution in this way do not assume that prostitution is "a problem about the women who are prostitutes, and our attitudes to them, [rather than] a problem about the men who demand to buy them."[5] This assumption, as Carole Pateman rightly points out, mars many other accounts.

However, I do not attempt to construct an account of the psychological, social, and economic forces that presumably cause men to demand commercial sex, or of the factors which cause a woman to market her sexual services. Instead, I first consider whether prostitution, in all cultural contexts, constitutes a degrading and undesirable form of sexuality. I argue that, although the commercial availability of sexuality is not in every existing or conceivable society oppressive to women, in our society this practice depends upon the general acceptance of principles which serve to marginalize women socially and politically. Because of the cultural context in which prostitution operates, it epitomizes and perpetuates pernicious patriarchal beliefs and values and, therefore, is both damaging to the women who sell sex and, as an organized social practice, to all women in our society.

Historical and Cross-Cultural Perspectives

In describing Babylonian temple prostitution, Gerda Lerner reports: "For people who regarded fertility as sacred and essential to their own survival, the caring for the gods included, in some cases, offering them sexual services. Thus, a separate class of temple prostitutes developed. What seems to have happened was that sexual activity for and in behalf of the god or goddesses was considered beneficial to the people and sacred."[6] Similarly, according to Emma Goldman, the Babylonians believed that "the generative activity of human beings possessed a mysterious and sacred influence in promoting the fertility of Nature."[7] When the rationale for the impersonal provision of sex is conceived in terms of the promotion of nature's fecundity, the social meaning this activity has may differ substantially from the social significance it has in our own society.

In fifteenth-century France, as described by Jacques Rossiaud, commercial sex appears likewise to have had an import that contrasts with its role in contemporary America. According to Rossiaud:

> By the age of thirty, most prostitutes had a real chance of becoming reintegrated into society . . . .

Since public opinion did not view them with disgust, and since they were on good terms with priests and men of the law, it was not too difficult for them to find a position as servant or wife. To many city people, public prostitution represented a partial atonement for past misconduct. Many bachelors had compassion and sympathy for prostitutes, and finally, the local charitable foundations of the municipal authorities felt a charitable impulse to give special help to these repentant Magdalens and to open their way to marriage by dowering them. Marriage was definitely the most frequent end to the career of communal prostitutes who had roots in the town where they have publicly offered their bodies.[8]

The fact that prostitutes were regarded by medieval French society as eligible for marriage, and were desired by men for wives, suggests that the cultural principles which sustained commercial exchanges of sex in this society were quite different than those which shape our own sex industry. Consequently, the phenomenon of prostitution requires a distinct political analysis and moral assessment vis-à-vis fifteenth-century France. This historically specific approach is justified, in part, because commercial sexual transactions may have different consequences for individuals in an alien society than for individuals similarly placed in our own. Indeed, it is questionable whether, in two quite different cultural settings, we should regard a particular outward behavior—the impersonal provision of sexual services for fees or their equivalent—as the same practice, that is, as prostitution.

Another cross-cultural example may help to make the last point clear. Anthropologists have studied a group in New Guinea, called the Etoro, who believe that young male children need to ingest male fluid or semen in order to develop properly into adult males, much like we believe that young infants need their mothers's milk, or some equivalent, to be properly nurtured. Furthermore, just as our belief underlies our practice of breastfeeding, the Etoro's belief underlies their practice of penis-feeding, where young male children fellate older males, often their relatives.[9] From the perspective of our society, the Etoro's practice involves behaviors which are highly stigmatized—incest, sex, with children, and homosexuality. Yet, for an anthropologist who is attempting to interpret and translate these behaviors, to assume that the Etoro practice is best subsumed under the category of "sex" rather than, for example, "child rearing," would reflect ethnocentrism. Clearly, our choice of one translation scheme or the other will influence our attitude toward the Etoro practice. The point is that there is no practice, such as "sex," which can be morally evaluated apart from a cultural framework.

In general, historical and cross-cultural studies offer little reason to believe that the dominant forms of sexual practice in our society reflect psychological biological, or moral absolutes that determine human sexual practice. Instead, such studies provide much evidence that, against a different backdrop of beliefs about the world, the activities we designate as "sex"—impersonal or otherwise—have an entirely different meaning and value. Yet, while we may choose not to condemn the "child-rearing" practices of the Etoro, we can nevertheless recognize that "penis-feeding" would be extremely damaging to children in our society. Similarly, though we can appreciate that making an occupation by the provision of sex may not have been oppressive to women in medieval France or ancient Babylon, we should nevertheless recognize that in our society it can be extremely damaging to women. What then are the features which, in our culture, render prostitution oppressive?

The Social Meaning of Prostitution

Let me begin with a simple analogy. In our society there exists a taboo against eating cats and dogs. Now, suppose a member of our society wishes to engage in the unconventional behavior of ingesting cat or dog meat. In evaluating the moral and political character of this person's behavior, it is somewhat irrelevant whether eating cats and dogs "really" is or isn't healthy, or whether it "really" is or isn't different than eating cows, pigs, and chickens. What is relevant is that, by including cat and dog flesh in one's diet, a person may really make others upset and, therefore, do damage to them as well as to oneself. In short, how actions are widely perceived and interpreted by others, even if wrongly or seemingly irrationally, is

crucial to determining their moral status because, though such interpretations may not hold up against some "objective reality," they are part of the "social reality" in which we live.

I am not using this example to argue that unconventional behavior is wrong but, rather, to illustrate the relevance of cultural convention to how our outward behaviors are perceived. Indeed, what is wrong with prostitution is not that it violates deeply entrenched social conventions—ideals of feminine purity, and the noncommoditization of sex—but precisely that it epitomizes other cultural assumptions—beliefs which, reasonable or not, serve to legitimate women's social subordination. In other words, rather than subvert patriarchal ideology, the prostitute's actions, and the industry as a whole, serve to perpetuate this system of values. By contrast, lesbian sex, and egalitarian heterosexual economic and romantic relationships, do not. In short, female prostitution oppresses women, not because some women who participate in it "suffer in the eyes of society" but because its organized practice testifies to and perpetuates socially hegemonic beliefs which oppress all women in many domains of their lives.

What, then, are some of the beliefs and values which structure the social meaning of the prostitute's business in our culture—principles which are not necessarily consciously held by us but are implicit in our observable behavior and social practice? First, people in our society generally believe that human beings naturally possess, but socially repress, powerful, emotionally destabilizing sexual appetites. Second, we assume that men are naturally suited for dominant social roles. Third, we assume that contact with male genitals in virtually all contexts is damaging and polluting to women. Fourth, we assume that a person's sexual practice renders her or him a particular "kind" of person, for example, "a homosexual," "a bisexual," "a whore," "a virgin," "a pervert," and so on. I will briefly examine the nature of these four assumptions, and then discuss how they determine the social significance and impact of prostitution in our society. Such principles are inscribed in all of a culture's communicative acts and institutions, but my examples will only be drawn from a common body of disciplinary resources: the writings of philosophers and other intellectuals.

The Universal Possession of a Potent Sex Drive.—In describing the nature of sexual attraction, Schopenhauer states:

The sexual impulse in all its degrees and nuances plays not only on the stage and in novels, but also in the real world, where, next to the love of life, it shows itself the strongest and most powerful of motives, constantly lays claim to half the powers and thoughts of the younger portion of mankind, is the ultimate goal of almost all human effort, exerts an adverse influence on the most important events, interrupts the most serious occupations every hour, sometimes embarrasses for a while even the greatest minds, does not hesitate to intrude with its trash interfering with the negotiations of statesmen and the investigation of men of learning, knows how to slip its love letters and locks of hair even into ministerial portfolios and philosophical manuscripts, and no less devises daily the most entangled and the worst actions, destroys the most valuable relationships, breaks the firmest bonds, demands the sacrifice sometimes of life or health, sometimes of wealth, rank, and happiness, nay robs those who are otherwise honest of all conscience, makes those who have hitherto been faithful, traitors; accordingly to the whole, appears as a malevolent demon that strives to pervert, confuse, and overthrow everything.[10]

Freud, of course, chose the name "libido" to refer to this powerful natural instinct; which he believed manifests itself as early as infancy.

The assumption of a potent "sex drive" is implicit in Lars Ericsson's relatively recent defense of prostitution: "We must liberate ourselves from those mental fossils which prevent us from looking upon sex and sexuality with the same naturalness as upon our cravings for food and drink. And, contrary to popular belief, we may have something to learn from prostitution in this respect, namely, that coition resembles nourishment in that if it cannot be obtained in any other way it can always be bought. And bought meals are not always the worst."[11] More explicitly, he argues that the "sex drive" provides a noneconomic, natural basis for explaining the demand for commercial sex.[12] Moreover, he claims that because of the irrational nature of this impulse, prostitution will exist until all persons are granted sexual access upon demand to all other persons.[13] In a society where individuals lack such access to others, but where women are the social equals of men, Ericsson predicts that "the degree of female frustration that exists today . . . will no longer be tolerated, rationalized, or sublimated, but channeled into a demand for, inter alia, mercenary sex."[14] Consequently, Ericsson favors an unregulated sex industry, which can respond spontaneously to these natural human wants. Although Pateman, in her response to Ericsson, does not see the capitalist commoditization of sexuality as physiologically determined, she nevertheless yields to the assumption that "sexual impulses are part of our natural constitution as humans."[15]

Schopenhauer, Freud, Ericsson, and Pateman all clearly articulate what anthropologists refer to as our "cultural common sense" regarding the nature of human sexuality. By contrast, consider a group of people in New Guinea, called the Dani, as described by Karl Heider: "Especially striking is their five year post-partum sexual abstinence, which is uniformly observed and is not a subject of great concern or stress. This low level of sexuality appears to be a purely cultural phenomenon, not caused by any biological factors."[16] The moral of this anthropological tale is that our high level of sexuality is also "a purely cultural phenomenon," and not the inevitable result of human biology. Though the Dani's disinterest in sex need not lead us to regard our excessive concern as improper, it should lead us to view one of our cultural rationalizations for prostitution as just that—a cultural rationalization.

The "Natural" Dominance of Men.—One readily apparent feature of the sex industry in our society is that it caters almost exclusively to a male clientele. Even the relatively small number of male prostitutes at work serve a predominantly male consumer group. Implicit in this particular division of labor, and also the predominant division of labor in other domains of our society, is the cultural principle that men are naturally disposed to dominate in their relations with others.

Ironically, this cultural conviction is implicit in some accounts of prostitution by feminist writers, especially in their attempts to explain the social and psychological causes of the problematic demand by men for impersonal, commercial sex. For example, Marxist feminists have argued that prostitution is the manifestation of the unequal class position of women vis-à-vis men: women who do not exchange their domestic and sexual services with the male ruling class for their subsistence are forced to market these services to multiple masters outside marriage.[17] The exploitation of female sexuality is a ruling-class privilege, an advantage which allows those socially identified as "men" to perpetuate their economic and cultural hegemony. In tying female prostitution to patriarchy and capitalism, Marxist accounts attempt to tie it to particular historical forces, rather than to biological or natural ones. However, without the assumption of men's biological superiority, Marxist feminist analyses cannot explain why women, at this particular moment under capitalism, have evolved as an economic under-class, that is, why capitalism gives rise to patriarchy. Why did women's role in production and reproduction not provide them a market advantage, a basis upon which they could subordinate men or assert their political equality?

Gayle Rubin has attempted to provide a purely social and historical analysis of female prostitution by applying some insights of structuralist anthropology.[18] She argues that economic prostitution originates from the unequal position of men and women within the mode of reproduction (the division of society into groups for the purpose of procreation and child rearing). In many human cultures, this system operates by what Lévi-Strauss referred to as "the exchange of women": a practice whereby men exchange their own sisters and daughters for the sisters and daughters of other men. These exchanges express or affirm "a social link between the partners of the exchange . . . confer[ing] upon its participants a special relationship of trust, solidarity, and mutual aid."[19] However, since women are not partners to the exchange but, rather, the objects traded, they are denied the social rights and privileges created by these acts of giving. The commoditization of female sexuality is the form this original "traffic in women" takes in capitalist societies. In short, Rubin's account does not assume, but attempts to explain, the dominance of men in production, by appealing to the original dominance of men in reproduction. Yet this account does not explain why women are the objects of the original affinal exchange, rather than men or opposite sex pairs.[20]

In appealing to the principle that men naturally assume dominant roles in all social systems, feminists uncritically accept a basic premise of patriarchy. In my view such principles do not denote universal causal mechanisms but represent naturally arbitrary, culturally determined beliefs which serve to legitimate certain practices.

Sexual Contact Pollutes Women.—To say that extensive sexual experience in a woman is not prized in our society is to be guilty of indirectness and understatement. Rather, a history of sexual activity is a negative mark that is used to differentiate kinds of women. Instead of being valued for their experience in sexual matters, women are valued for their "innocence."

That the act of sexual intercourse with a man is damaging to a woman is implicit in the vulgar language we use to describe this act. As Robert Baker has pointed out, a woman is "fucked," "screwed," "banged," "had," and so forth, and it is a man (a "prick") who does it to her.[21] The metaphors we use for the act of sexual intercourse are similarly revealing. Consider, for example, Andrea Dworkin's description of intercourse: "The thrusting is persistent invasion. She is opened up, split down the center. She is occupied—physically, internally, in her privacy."[22] Dworkin invokes both images of physical assault and imperialist domination in her characterization of heterosexual copulation. Women are split, penetrated, entered, occupied, invaded, and colonized by men. Though aware of the nonliteralness of this language, Dworkin appears to think that these metaphors are motivated by natural, as opposed to arbitrary, culture features of the world. According to Ann Garry, "Because in our culture we connect sex with harm that men do to women, and because we think of the female role in sex as that of harmed object, we can see that to treat a woman as a sex object is automatically to treat her as less than fully human."[23] As the public vehicles for "screwing," "penetration," "invasion," prostitutes are reduced to the status of animals or things—mere instruments for human ends.

The Reification of Sexual Practice.—Another belief that determines the social significance of prostitution concerns the relationship between a person's social identity and her or his sexual behavior.[24] For example, we identify a person who has sexual relations with a person of the same gender as a "homosexual," and we regard a woman who has intercourse with multiple sexual partners as being of a particular type—for instance, a "loose woman," "slut," or "prostitute." As critics of our society, we may find these categories too narrow or the values they reflect objectionable. If so, we may refer to women who are sexually promiscuous, or who have sexual relations with other women, as "liberated women," and thereby show a rejection of double (and homophobic) standards of sexual morality. However, what such linguistic iconoclasm generally fails to challenge is that a person's sexual practice makes her a particular "kind" of person.

I will now consider how these cultural convictions and values structure the meaning of prostitution in our society. Our society's tolerance for commercially available sex, legal or not, implies general acceptance of principles which perpetuate women's social subordination. Moreover, by their participation in an industry which exploits the myths of female social inequality and sexual vulnerability, the actions of the prostitute and her clients imply that they accept a set of values and beliefs which assign women to marginal social roles in all our cultural institutions, including marriage and waged employment. Just as an Uncle Tom exploits noxious beliefs about blacks for personal gain, and implies through his actions that blacks can benefit from a system of white supremacy, the prostitute and her clients imply that women can profit economically from patriarchy. Though we should not blame the workers in the sex industry for the social degradation they suffer, as theorists and critics of our society, we should question the existence of such businesses and the social principles implicit in our tolerance for them.

Because members of our society perceive persons in terms of their sexual orientation and practice, and because sexual contact in most settings—but especially outside the context of a "secure" heterosexual relationship—is thought to be harmful to women, the prostitute's work may have social implications that differ significantly from the work of persons in other professions. For instance, women who work or have worked in the sex industry may find their future social prospects severely limited. By contrast to medieval French society, they are not desired as wives or domestic servants in our own. And unlike other female subordinates in our society, the prostitute is viewed as a defiled creature; nonetheless, we rationalize and tolerate prostitutional sex out of the perceived need to mollify men's sexual desires.

In sum, the woman who provides sex on a commercial basis and the man who patronizes her epitomize and reinforce the social principles I have identified: these include beliefs that attribute to humans potent, subjugating sex drives that men can satisfy without inflicting self-harm through impersonal sexual encounters. Moreover, the prostitute cannot alter the political implications of her work by simply supplying her own rationale for the provision of her services. For example, Margo St. James has tried to represent the prostitute as a skilled sexual therapist, who serves a legitimate social need.[25] According to St. James, while the commercial sex provider may be unconventional in her sexual behavior, her work may be performed with honesty and dignity. However, this defense is implausible since it ignores the possible adverse impact of her behavior on herself and others, and the fact that, by participating in prostitution, her behavior does little to subvert the cultural principles that make her work harmful. Ann Garry reaches a similar conclusion about pornography: "I may not think that sex is dirty and that I would be a harmed object; I may not know what your view is; but what bothers me is that this is the view embodied in our language and culture. . . . As long as sex is connected with harm done to women, it will be very difficult not to see pornography as degrading to women. . . . The fact that audience attitude is so important makes one wary of giving whole-hearted approval to any pornography seen today."[26] Although the prostitute may want the meaning of her actions assessed relative to her own idiosyncratic beliefs and values, the political and social meaning of her actions must be assessed in the political and social context in which they occur.

One can imagine a society in which individuals sought commercial sexual services from women in order to obtain high quality sexual experiences.

In our society, people pay for medical advice, meals, education in many fields, and so on, in order to obtain information, services, or goods that are superior to or in some respect more valuable than those they can obtain noncommercially. A context in which the rationale for seeking a prostitute's services was to obtain sex from a professional—from a person who knows what she is doing—is probably not a context in which women are thought to be violated when they have sexual contact with men. In such a situation, those who supplied sex on a commercial basis would probably not be stigmatized but, instead, granted ordinary social privileges.[27] The fact that prostitutes have such low social status in our society indicates that the society in which we live is not congruent with this imaginary one; that is, the prostitute's services in our society are not generally sought as a gourmet item. In short, if commercial sex was sought as a professional service, then women who provided sex commercially would probably not be regarded as "prostituting" themselves—as devoting their bodies or talents to base purposes, contrary to their true interests.

Subverting the Status Quo

Let me reiterate that I am not arguing for social conformism. Rather, my point is that not all non-conformist acts equally challenge conventional morality. For example, if a person wants to subvert the belief that eating cats and dogs is bad, it is not enough to simply engage in eating them. Similarly, it is unlikely that persons will subvert prevalent attitudes toward gender and sexuality by engaging in prostitution.

Consider another example. Suppose that I value high quality child care and am willing to pay a person well to obtain it. Because of both racial and gender oppression, the persons most likely to be interested in and suitable for such work are bright Third World and minority First World women who cannot compete fairly for other well-paid work. Suppose then, I hire a person who happens to be a woman and a person of color to provide child care on the basis of the belief that such work requires a high level of intelligence and responsibility. Though the belief on which this act is based may be unconventional, my action of hiring

a "sitter" from among the so-called lower classes of society is not politically liberating.[28]

What can a person who works in the sex industry do to subvert widely held attitudes toward her work? To subvert the beliefs which currently structure commercial sex in our society, the female prostitute would need to assume the role not of a sexual subordinate but of a sexual equal or superior. For instance, if she were to have the authority to determine what services the customer could get, under what conditions the customer could get them, and what they would cost, she would gain the status of a sexual professional. Should she further want to establish herself as a sexual therapist, she would need to represent herself as having some type of special technical knowledge for solving problems having to do with human sexuality. In other words, experience is not enough to establish one's credentials as a therapist or professional. However, if the industry were reformed so that all these conditions were met, what would distinguish the prostitute's work from that of a bona fide "sexual therapist"? If her knowledge was thought to be only quasilegitimate, her work might have the status of something like the work of a chiropractor, but this would certainly be quite different than the current social status of her work.[29] In sum, the political alternatives of reformation and abolition are not mutually exclusive: if prostitution were sufficiently transformed to make it completely nonoppressive to women, though commercial transactions involving sex might still exist, prostitution as we now know it would not.

If our tolerance for marriage fundamentally rested on the myth of female subordination, then the same arguments which apply to prostitution would apply to it. Many theorists, including Simone de Beauvoir and Friedrich Engels, have argued that marriage, like prostitution, involves female sexual subservience. For example, according to de Beauvoir: "For both the sexual act is a service; the one is hired for life by one man; the other has several clients who pay her by the piece. The one is protected by one male against all others; the other is defended by all against the exclusive tyranny of each."[30] In addition, Lars Ericsson contends that marriage, unlike prostitution, involves economic dependence for women: "While the housewife is totally dependent on her husband, at least economically, the call girl in that respect stands on her own two feet. If she has a pimp, it is she, not he, who is the breadwinner in the family."[31]

Since the majority of marriages in our society render the wife the domestic and sexual subordinate of her husband, marriage degrades the woman who accepts it (or perhaps only the woman who accepts marriage on unequal terms), and its institutionalization in its present form oppresses all women. However, because marriage can be founded on principles which do not involve the subordination of women, we can challenge oppressive aspects of this institution without radically altering it.[32] For example, while the desire to control the sinful urges of men to fornicate may, historically, have been part of the ideology of marriage, it does not seem to be a central component of our contemporary rationalization for this custom.[33] Marriage, at present in our society, is legitimated by other widely held values and beliefs, for example, the desirability of a long-term, emotionally and financially sustaining parental partnership. However, I am unable to imagine nonpernicious principles which would legitimate the commercial provision of sex and which would not substantially alter or eliminate the industry as it now exists. Since commercial sex, unlike marriage, is not reformable, feminists should seek to undermine the beliefs and values which underlie our acceptance of it. Indeed, one way to do this is to outwardly oppose prostitution itself.

Conclusions

If my analysis is correct, then prostitution is not a social aberration or disorder but, rather, a consequence of well-established beliefs and values that form part of the foundation of all our social institutions and practices. Therefore, by striving to overcome discriminatory structures in all aspects of society—in family, at work outside the home, and in our political institutions—feminists will succeed in challenging some of the cultural presuppositions which sustain prostitution. In other words, prostitution needs no unique remedy, legal or otherwise; it will be remedied as feminists make progress in altering patterns of belief and practice that oppress women in all aspects of their lives.

Yet, while prostitution requires no special social cure, some important strategic and symbolic feminist goals may be served by selecting the sex industry for criticism at this time. In this respect, a consumer boycott of the industry is especially appropriate.

In examining prostitution, I have not tried to construct a theory which can explain the universal causes and moral character of prostitution. Such questions presuppose that there is a universal phenomenon to which the term refers and that commercial sex is always socially deviant and undesirable. Instead, I have considered the meaning of commercial sex in modern Western cultures. Although my arguments are consistent with the decriminalization of prostitution, I conclude from my investigation that feminists have legitimate reasons to politically oppose prostitution in our society. Since the principles which implicitly sustain and organize the sex industry are ones which underlie pernicious gender asymmetries in many domains of our social life, to tolerate a practice which epitomizes these principles is oppressive to women.

Notes

I am grateful to Sandra Bartky, Alison Jaggar, Elizabeth Segal, Richard Arneson, and the anonymous reviewers for *Ethics* for their critical comments and suggestions. Also, I am indebted to Daniel Segal for suggesting many anthropological and historical examples relevant to my argument. In addition, I would like to thank the philosophy department of the Claremont Graduate School for the opportunity to present an earlier draft of this paper for discussion.

1. Nancy Hartsock, *Money, Sex, and Power* (Boston: Northeastern University Press, 1985), p. 178.

2. See Rosemarie Tong, *Women, Sex, and the Law* (Totowa, NJ: Rowman & Allanheld, 1984), pp. 37–64. See also Priscilla Alexander and Margo St. James, "Working on the Issue," National Organization for Women (NOW) National Task Force on Prostitution Report (San Francisco: NOW, 1982).

3. See Carole Pateman, "Defending Prostitution: Charges against Ericsson," *Ethics* 93 (1983): 561–65; and Kathleen Barry, *Female Sexual Slavery* (New York: Avon, 1979).

4. For example, see Gerda Lerner, "The Origin of Prostitution in Ancient Mesopotamia," *Signs: Journal of Women in Culture and Society* 11 (1986): 236–54; Lars Ericsson, "Charges against Prostitution: An Attempt at a Philosophical Assessment," *Ethics* 90 (1980): 335–66; and James Brundage, "Prostitution in the Medieval Canon Law," *Signs: Journal of Women in Culture and Society* 1 (1976): 825–45.

5. Pateman, p. 563.

6. Lerner, p. 239.

7. Emma Goldman, "The Traffic in Women," in *Red Emma Speaks,* ed. Alix Kates Shulman (New York: Schocken, 1983), p. 180.

8. Jacques Rossiaud, "Prostitution, Youth, and Society in the Towns of Southeastern France in the Fifteenth Century," in *Deviants and the Abandoned in French Society: Selections from the Annales Economies, Sociétés, Civilisations,* ed. Robert Forster and Orest Ranum (Baltimore: Johns Hopkins University Press, 1978), p. 21.

9. See Gilbert H. Herdt, ed., *Rituals of Manhood* (Berkeley and Los Angeles: University of California Press, 1982). Also see Harriet Whitehead, "The Varieties of Fertility Cultism in New Guinea: Part 1," *American Ethnologist* 13 (1986): 80–99. In comparing penis-feeding to breast-feeding rather than to oral sex, some anthropologists point out that both involve the use of a culturally erotic bodily part for parental nurturing.

10. Arthur Schopenhauer, "The Metaphysics of the Love of the Sexes," in *The Works of Schopenhauer,* ed. Will Durant (New York: Simon & Schuster, 1928), p. 333.

11. Ericsson, p. 355.

12. Ibid., p. 347.

13. Ibid., pp. 359–60.

14. Ibid., p. 360.

15. Pateman, p. 563.

16. Karl Heider, "Dani Sexuality: A Low Energy System," *Man* 11 (1976): 188–201.

17. See Friedrich Engels, *The Origin of the Family, Private Property and the State* (New York: Penguin, 1985); Goldman; Alison Jaggar, "Prostitution," in *The Philosophy of Sex,* ed. Alan Soble (Totowa, NJ: Rowman & Littlefield, 1980), pp. 353–58.

18. Gayle Rubin, "The Traffic in Women: Notes on the 'Political Economy' of Sex," in *Toward an Anthropology of Women,* ed. Rayna Reiter (New York: Monthly Review Press, 1975).

19. Ibid., p. 172.

20. In his attempt to describe the general principles of kinship organization implicit in different cultures, Lévi-Strauss admits it is conceivable that he has over-emphasized the patrilineal nature of these exchanges: "It may have been noted that we have assumed what might be called . . . a paternal perspective. That is, we have regarded the woman married by a member of the group as acquired, and the sister provided in exchange as lost. The situation might be altogether different in a system with matrilineal descent and matrilocal residence. . . . The essential thing is that every right acquired entails a concomitant obligation, and that every renunciation calls for a compensation. . . . Even supposing a very hypothetical marriage system in which the man and not the woman were exchanged . . . the total structure would remain unchanged: (Claude Lévi-Strauss, *The Elementary Structures of Kinship* [Boston: Beacon, 1969], p. 132). A culture in which men are gifts in a ritual of exchange is described in Michael Peletz, "The Exchange of Men in Nineteenth-Century Negeri Sembilan (Malayà)"; *American Ethnologist* 14 (1987): 449–69.

21. Robert Baker, "'Pricks' and 'Chicks': A Plea for 'Persons,'" in *Philosophy and Sex,* ed. R. Baker and F. Elliston (Buffalo, NY: Prometheus, 1984), pp. 260–66. In this section, Baker provides both linguistic and nonlinguistic evidence that intercourse, in our cultural mythology, hurts women.

22. Andrea Dworkin, *Intercourse* (New York: Free Press, 1987), p. 122.

23. Ann Garry, "Pornography and Respect for Women," in Baker and Elliston, eds., p. 318.

24. In "Defending Prostitution," Pateman states: "The services of the prostitute are related in a more intimate manner to her body than those of other professionals. Sexual services, that is to say, sex and sexuality, are constitutive of the body in a way in which the counseling skills of the social worker are not. . . . Sexuality and the body are, further, integrally connected to conceptions of femininity and masculinity and, all these are constitutive of our individuality, our sense of self-identity" (p. 562). On my view, while our social identities are determined by our outward sexual practice, this is due to arbitrary, culturally determined conceptual mappings, rather than some universal relationship holding between persons and their bodies.

25. Margo St. James, Speech to the San Diego County National Organization for Women, La Jolla, California, February 27, 1982, and from private correspondence with St. James (1983). Margo St. James is the founder of COYOTE (Call Off Your Old Tired Ethics) and the editor of *Coyote Howls.* COYOTE is a civil rights organization which seeks to change the sex industry from within by gaining better working conditions for prostitutes.

26. Garry, pp. 318–23.

27. According to Bertrand Russell: "In Japan, apparently, the matter is quite otherwise. Prostitution is recognized and respected as a career, and is even adopted at the instance of parents. It is often a not uncommon method of earning a marriage dowry" (*Marriage and Morals* [1929; reprint, New York: Liveright, 1970], p. 151). Perhaps contemporary Japan is closer to our imaginary society, a society where heterosexual intercourse is not felt to be polluting to women.

28. This of course does not mean we should not hire such people for child care, for that would simply be to deny a good person a better job than he or she might otherwise obtain—a job which unlike the prostitute's job is not likely to hurt their prospects for other work or social positions. Nevertheless, one should not believe that one's act of giving a person of this social description such a job does anything to change the unfair structure of our society.

29. I am grateful to Richard Arneson for suggesting this analogy to me.

30. Simone de Beauvior, *The Second Sex* (New York: Vintage, 1974), p. 619. According to Engels: "Marriage of convenience turns often enough into the crassest prostitution—sometimes of both partners, but far more commonly of the woman, who only differs from the ordinary courtesan in that she does not let out her body on piecework as a wage worker, but sells it once and for all into slavery" (p. 102).

31. Ericsson, p. 354.

32. Pateman argues: "The conjugal relation is not neces-

sarily one of domination and subjection, and in this it differs from prostitution" (p. 563). On this I agree with her.

33. Russell informs us that "Christianity, and more particularly St. Paul, introduced an entirely novel view of marriage, that it existed not primarily for the procreation of children, but to prevent the sin of fornication. . . . I remember once being advised by a doctor to abandon the practice of smoking, and he said that I should find it easier if whenever the desire came upon me, I proceeded to suck an acid drop. It is in this spirit that St. Paul recommends marriage" (pp. 44–46).

Laurie Shrage generates a thoughtful and unique critique of prostitution, not by questioning the motives and values of the individuals involved in commercial sexual transactions, but rather by illuminating the underlying cultural principles which are offensive to women and which are supported by tolerating the practice of prostitution. One of her most forceful moves is to point out the need to morally evaluate prostitution not as some universal, transcultural, abstract phenomenon but as a practice based on a particular historical and cultural framework that gives it a social meaning. In response to Ericsson, Shrage argues that a *truly* reformed prostitution is not a reformed prostitution but rather the demise of prostitution as we now know it. This claim raises the question of whether Shrage's views are really at cross-purposes with those of Ericsson. This would be true if Ericsson's ideal of a sound and reformed prostitution were similar to the kind of commercial and sexual institution that Shrage imagines would replace prostitution as we know it. Do you think the two characterizations of commercial sex are indeed similar?

Might we reflect on the respective strategies of Ericsson and Shrage? Shrage argues that the fundamental principles that underwrite the social meaning of prostitution are false and irrational; and even if the individuals engaged in the practice of commercial sex do not consciously agree with them, their actions symbolically support those principles and are, therefore, immoral. For this reason, individuals ought not to engage in such activities.

Another strategy would be to act in accordance with what individuals engaging in commercial sex believe to be morally right or justified even though others who hold those irrational and unjustified beliefs may be upset and offended. In other words, why should the free moral choices of some be limited because of others' irrational beliefs? We may also ask how much effect or influence prostitution really has in reinforcing these underlying principles as compared to other social institutions, such as education, religion, law, economics, etc. If the latter are more significant in determining the larger principles that define sex in our culture, why not, as Ericsson contends, attack the primary source of those irrational and unjustified principles?

Pateman and Shrage have formulated rigorous arguments to show that Ericsson's proposal of a sound and reformed prostitution would serve only to perpetuate the oppression of women and dominance of men. On the other hand, Ericsson argues that given the current laws and attitudes of people toward sex and prostitutes in general, most of whom are women, prostitutes are indeed oppressed and harmed. However, he favors strong reform and reconstruction of prostitution as a means of avoiding the current exploitation, oppression, and harm done to women.

Having considered the arguments on both sides, it is now up to the reader to pursue these questions, as well as others not discussed here. What policies should our country develop relative to prostitution? Should we continue to criminalize prostitution, reform it, economically boycott it? Can you think of other policies that would have moral and rational justification?

CHAPTER 7

Natural and Perverse

Consider the following list. Which of the entries on that list would you classify as natural?

1. automobiles
2. trains
3. the four-minute mile
4. anesthesia
5. heart transplants
6. antibiotics
7. pain in childbirth
8. seedless oranges
9. fruit-bearing fig trees in New York City
10. John Stuart Mill being able to read the *Decline and Fall of the Roman Empire* at age three
11. the parting of the Red Sea by God
12. the parting of the Red Sea by a unique kind of storm

Let us briefly consider anesthesia, pain in childbirth, antibiotics, and fig trees in order to enrich our understanding of the concepts of natural and unnatural.

On some interpretations of the Bible, it can be argued that God decreed that the punishment for Eve's sin is pain in childbirth for all women, for all time. Anesthesia by means of ether (invented about 1846) made pain in childbirth a matter of choice. Given the theological interpretation that pain in childbirth is God's will, anesthesia could be considered unnatural because it violates God's will. Indeed, the way God means things to be has always been one meaning for the expression "natural order." But there is another.

Fig trees that actually bear figs in the climate of New York City violate the natural order of things in the following sense. Left alone, fig trees cannot bear fruit in a temperate climate. They must be helped along considerably by people. Here "natural order" refers to nature without people doing things. In this sense, antibiotics are unnatural for it took people either to make them or to realize how naturally occurring plants could be used. In another sense, where "natural" means made or invented by people, as opposed to superhumans, antibiotics are natural. Notice that even if one sees antibiotics as unnatural, in the sense of made by people, they still can be considered good. Whereas, if one sees anesthesia as flouting the will of God, anesthesia will not be seen as anything except bad. Another sense in which antibiotics are natural is that they work according to the laws of nature. In this sense, whether anything is unnatural depends on one's views about God and miracles. Miracles are by definition breaks with the patterns of nature. They are breaks that are explainable only by supernatural intervention. If one denies the existence of the supernatural, then in this sense, everything that happens is natural; reducing what would be called "miraculous" as so statistically rare that it defies explanation. (Whether a God created nature is another issue that does not affect the distinctions being drawn here.)

What have we seen in our investigation of these cases?

1. There are many senses for the pair natural/unnatural.
2. Some natural things (e.g., disease) may be bad. Some unnatural things (e.g., antibiotics) may be good.
3. There may be implicit and, therefore, hidden values in the categorization of something as natural or unnatural.
4. To call something "natural" or "unnatural" presupposes some background assumptions. Sometimes those assumptions are theological, sometimes they are specific, and sometimes they are just common sense assumptions.

Thus, if someone says that something is not natural, our best reply is "Not natural, with respect to what?"

How can we apply the dual concepts, natural and unnatural, to sexual activities? The traditional way has been to ask if some sexual acts, lifestyles, even hopes, wishes, desires, and fantasies are unnatural/natural? We have seen that using the natural/unnatural dichotomy brings with it many complexities. For example, are we making some sort of absolute claim, or are we making a claim relative to time and place? If such characterizations are not relative, then what makes them absolute? Is it God and some special theological view, or is there something inherent in their natures that make, for example, some sexual acts natural and others unnatural?

Instead of using the natural/unnatural dichotomy, often the question is put using the terms: perverse and normal. Many candidates for sexual perversion have been proposed. Here are three general characterizations of sexual perversion.

(1) Any action which brings sexual pleasure but has little or no chance of resulting in conception may be regarded as perverse. Masturbation and homosexual acts are often mentioned. The use of contraceptives in this sense may be considered perverse. Sexual activity with nonhuman animals, plants, or inanimate objects would fall in this category. Is the bringing about of sexual pleasure a necessary part of the characterization? Could we imagine someone who often has sexual intercourse with Venus fly traps but gets no real sexual enjoyment from such engagements? One can imagine a person performing any one particular sex act out of duty (or fear) and getting no pleasure from it at all. But can one imagine this going on all or most of the time with actions as rare as sexual intercourse with horses, chickens, and potted plants—unless there were some payoff in terms of pleasure?

Here is where there may be some differences in the sexual physiologies of males and females that matter. In general, if a man's penis is stimulated enough, he will have an orgasm—which by its nature is pleasurable. So even where a man is performing sexual intercourse for God and country (e.g., the fictional character James Bond) and really finds his actions distasteful, nonetheless if he performs long enough, he will almost certainly experience the pleasure of an orgasm.

(2) Another typical candidate is any action which brings sexual pleasure to one person by means of physical contact with another person without the consent, or against the will, of that other person. Sex with corpses is an example of sex without consent. Rape is an example of sex against the will of another.

But is fantasizing about another person without consent a perversion? Is phone harassment to bring sexual gratification a perversion? Is "flashing" (exposing one's genitals or breasts [in women]) a perversion? Is being a peeping Tom a perversion? Suppose you see a man/woman undressing (or engaging in some sexual act) in a way that you can watch without being seen and it excites you sexually to watch, or for that matter, to listen. Is that a perversion?

(3) Fetishes are usually considered perversions where the objects of sexual attraction are very untraditional. A typical example would be a foot fetishist—someone who gets sexual pleasure from looking at bare feet. (At the beach, the foot fetishist needs no consent to look. The "peeping Tom," whose sexual pleasure derives from secretly watching women undress, must look in secret.) One problem here is that we are unsure what precisely is going on. Is the fetishist merely using the object to fantasize or as a proxy for a more traditional object (a person)? Or, is the fetishist finally and basically interested sexually in the object itself. Bicycle seats, underwear, silk scarves, a lock of hair are traditional examples of such objects—almost always for men. But, photographs of one's loved one, a team jacket, a fraternity pin, an engagement ring might also be examples. Is treasuring any one of these a perversion? Or do they only become perversions under certain circumstances.

Sexual desires are often more than passing whims. They can be an integral part of one's life. If this is so, it is important to remember that to talk about perversions may well be to talk not just about isolated acts or even kinds of acts, but rather to talk about whole ways of living. It is to judge one way of life. But we must remember that when we judge one way of life, we also do it relative to another way of life. This does not mean that we cannot judge; only that we should know the limits of our judgments.

In the articles that follow, we will see sexual perversion first discussed in terms of what seems naturally to lead to intercourse followed by a critique of this view. Perversion will then be analyzed in terms of basic goods and finally in terms of monstrous and deep fears.

SEXUAL PERVERSION AS INCOMPLETE COMMUNICATION

The following article seems to have set the tone for the literature in perversion. Nagel asks us to imagine a situation where two people gradually become aware that they are becoming aware of each other in a way that is sexual. At some point, when they mutually agree to do so, they are naturally ready for sexual intercourse. Anything short of reaching this level of arousal by means of a series of "he senses that she senses that he senses that she senses . . ." Nagel refers to as truncated and by his definition, perverted. Nagel uses Sartre's expression "double reciprocal relation" to refer to this sort of natural sexual relation. One's entire body becomes full of desire. One gives in willingly to the loss of control that comes with a body saturated with desire. Nagel sees sexual activity such as fetishes, bestiality, and masochism as clear examples of perversions. But he does not want to claim that perverted sex is not satisfying, pleasurable sex. Nor does he want to claim that all perverted sex is immoral. As he defines it, "perversion" is not a morally evaluative term.

Most responses to Nagel focus on this Romeo and Juliet scenario that he proposes. But there is more to Nagel's article. He points out that perversions are psychologically complex. To Nagel, eating cotton is odd and generally unhealthy, but it is not psychologically complex enough to be a perversion. However, eating pictures from cookbooks instead of the food pictured would be a perversion according to Nagel. The object of sexual attraction must be a person and not just a set of characteristics, for example, tall, dark, and handsome. This is what Nagel means when he says that the object of sexual attraction must transcend the properties that make him/her attractive.

He also suggests that natural sex is like the use of language in that we try to get another person to understand that we want him/her to understand what we are trying to say. Thus, just as three discussions at one time are unlikely to succeed in anyone getting anyone else's meaning, so a *ménage à trois* may be characterized as perverse. The exhibitionist wants only to talk and never listens. The voyeur wants only to listen and never is willing to contribute.

Is Nagel clear about what counts as truncated sex? Is premature ejaculation truncated and therefore to some degree perverse, or, is it just unfortunate and very frustrating? Does Nagel correctly describe us as "saturated with desire" when we engage (or begin to engage) in sex? As is often the case with sex, is it possible that Nagel is describing himself (or a lover or friend) and that the description cannot justifiably be generalized as he does? Is "saturated with desire" just descriptive, or it is really normative? That is, is Nagel really suggesting that we ought to be saturated with desire or else we are having truncated sex?

from Sexual Perversion

THOMAS NAGEL

There is something to be learned about sex from the fact that we possess a concept of sexual perversion. I wish to examine the concept, defending it against the charge of unintelligibility and trying to say exactly what about human sexuality qualifies it to admit of perversions. Let me make some preliminary comments about the problem before embarking on its solution.

Some people do not believe that the notion of sexual perversion makes sense, and even those who do disagree over its application. Nevertheless I think it will be widely conceded that, if the concept is viable at all, it must meet certain general conditions. First, if there are any sexual perversions, they will have to be sexual desires or practices that can be plausibly described as in some sense unnatural, though the explanation of this natural/unnatural distinction is of course the main problem. Second, certain practices will be perversions if anything is, such as shoe fetishism, bestiality, and sadism; other practices, such as un-

adorned sexual intercourse, will not be; about still others there is controversy. Third, if there are perversions, they will be unnatural sexual *inclinations* rather than merely unnatural practices adopted not from inclination but for other reasons. I realize that this is at variance with the view, maintained by some Roman Catholics, that contraception is a sexual perversion. But although contraception may qualify as a deliberate perversion of the sexual and reproductive functions, it cannot be significantly described as a *sexual* perversion. A sexual perversion must reveal itself in conduct that expresses an unnatural *sexual* preference. And although there might be a form of fetishism focused on the employment of contraceptive devices, that is not the usual explanation for their use.

I wish to declare at the outset my belief that the connection between sex and reproduction has no bearing on sexual perversion. The latter is a concept of psychological, not physiological interest, and it is a concept that we do not apply to the lower

From "Sexual Perversion" by Thomas Nagel, *The Journal of Philosophy*, Vol. LXVI, No. 1 (January 16, 1969), pp. 5–17. Used by permission of the author and *The Journal of Philosophy*.

animals, let alone to plants, all of which have reproductive functions that can go astray in various ways. (Think of seedless oranges.) Insofar as we are prepared to regard higher animals as perverted, it is because of their psychological, not their anatomical similarity to humans. Furthermore, we do not regard as a perversion every deviation from the reproductive function of sex in humans: sterility, miscarriage, contraception, abortion.

Another matter that I believe has no bearing on the concept of sexual perversion is social disapprobation or custom. Anyone inclined to think that in each society the perversions are those sexual practices of which the community disapproves, should consider all the societies that have frowned upon adultery and fornication. These have not been regarded as unnatural practices, but have been thought objectionable in other ways. What is regarded as unnatural admittedly varies from culture to culture, but the classification is not a pure expression of disapproval or distaste. In fact it is often regarded as a *ground* for disapproval, and that suggests that the classification has an independent content.

* * *

I am going to attempt a psychological account of sexual perversion, which will depend on a specific psychological theory of sexual desire and human sexual interactions. To approach this solution I wish first to consider a contrary position, one which provides a basis for skepticism about the existence of any sexual perversions at all, and perhaps about the very significance of the term. The skeptical argument runs as follows:

"Sexual desire is simply one of the appetites, like hunger and thirst. As such it may have various objects, some more common than others perhaps, but none in any sense 'natural.' An appetite is identified as sexual by means of the organs and erogenous zones in which its satisfaction can be to some extent localized, and that the special sensory pleasures which form the core of that satisfaction. This enables us to recognize widely divergent goals, activities, and desires as sexual, since it is conceivable in principle that anything should produce sexual pleasure and that a nondeliberate, sexually charged desire for it should arise (as a result of conditioning, if nothing else). We may fail to empathize with some of these desires, and some of them, like sadism, may be objectionable on extraneous grounds, but once we have observed that they meet the criteria for being sexual, there is nothing more to be said on *that* score. Either they are sexual or they are not: sexuality does not admit of imperfection, or perversion, or any other such qualification—it is not that sort of affection."

This is probably the received radical position. It suggests that the cost of defending a psychological account may be to deny that sexual desire as an appetite. But insofar as that line of defense is plausible, it should make us suspicious of the simple picture of appetites on which the skepticism depends. Perhaps the standard appetites, like hunger, cannot be classed as pure appetites in that sense either, at least in their human versions.

Let us approach the matter by asking whether we can imagine anything that would qualify as a gastronomical perversion. Hunger and eating are importantly like sex in that they serve a biological function and also play a significant role in our inner lives. It is noteworthy that there is little temptation to describe as perverted an appetite for substances that are not nourishing. We should probably not consider someone's appetites as *perverted* if he liked to eat paper, sand, wood, or cotton. Those are merely rather odd and very unhealthy tastes: they lack the psychological complexity that we expect of perversions. (Coprophilia, being already a sexual perversion, may be disregarded.) If on the other hand someone liked to eat cookbooks, or magazines with pictures of food in them, and preferred these to ordinary food—or if when hungry he sought satisfaction by fondling a napkin or ashtray from his favorite restaurant—then the concept of perversion might seem appropriate (in fact it would be natural to describe this as a case of gastronomical fetishism). It would be natural to describe as gastronomically perverted someone who could eat only by having food forced down his throat through a funnel, or only if the meal were a living animal. What helps in such cases is the peculiarity of the desire itself, rather than the inappropriateness of its object to the biological function that the desire serves. Even an appetite, it would seem, can have perversions if in addition to its biological function it has a significant psychological structure.

In the case of hunger, psychological complexity is provided by the activities that give it expression. Hunger is not merely a disturbing sensation that can be quelled by eating; it is an attitude toward edible portions of the external world, a desire to relate to them in rather special ways. The method of ingestion: chewing, savoring, swallowing, appreciating the texture and smell, all are important components of the relation, as is the passivity and controllability of the food (the only animals we eat live are helpless mollusks). Our relation to food depends also on our size: we do not live upon it or burrow into it like aphids or worms. Some of these features are more central than others, but any adequate phenomenology of eating would have to treat it as a relation to the external world and a way of appropriating bits of that world, with characteristic affection. Displacements or serious restrictions of the desire to eat could then be described as perversions, if they undermined that direct relation between man and food which is the natural expression of hunger. This explains why it is easy to imagine gastronomical fetishism, voyeurism, exhibitionism, or even gastronomical sadism and masochism. Indeed some of these perversions are fairly common.

If we can imagine perversions of an appetite like hunger, it should be possible to make sense of the concept of sexual perversion. I do not wish to imply that sexual desire is an appetite—only that being an appetite is no bar to admitting or perversions. Like hunger, sexual desire has as its characteristic object a certain relation with something in the external world; only in this case it is usually a person rather than an omelet, and the relation is considerably more complicated. This added complication allows scope for correspondingly complicated perversions.

•   •   •

The fact that sexual desire is a feeling about other persons may tempt us to take a pious view of its psychological content. There are those who believe that sexual desire is properly the expression of some other attitude, like love, and that when it occurs by itself it is incomplete and unhealthy— or at any rate subhuman. (The extreme Platonic version of such a view is that sexual practices are all vain attempts to express something they cannot

in principle achieve: this makes them all perversions, in a sense.) I do not believe that any such view is correct. Sexual desire is complicated enough without having to be linked to anything else as a condition for phenomenological analysis. It cannot be denied that sex may serve various functions—economic, social, altruistic—but it also has its own content as a relation between persons, and it is only by analyzing that relation that we can understand the conditions of sexual perversion.

I believe it is very important that the object of sexual attraction is a particular individual, who transcends the properties that make him attractive. When different persons are attracted to a single person for different reasons: eyes, hair, figure, laugh, intelligence—we feel that the object of their desire is nevertheless the same, namely that person. There is even an inclination to feel that this is so if the lovers have different sexual aims, if they include both men and women, for example. Different specific attractive characteristics seem to provide enabling conditions for the operation of a single basic feeling, and the different aims all provide expressions of it. We approach the sexual attitude toward the person through the features that we find attractive, but these features are not the objects of that attitude.

This is very different from the case of an omelet. Various people may desire it for different reasons, one for its fluffiness, another for its mushrooms, another for its unique combination of aroma and visual aspect; yet we do not enshrine the transcendental omelet as the true common object of their affections. Instead we might say that several desires have accidentally converged on the same object: any omelet with the crucial characteristics would do as well. It is not similarly true that any person with the same flesh distribution and way of smoking can be substituted as object for a particular sexual desire that has been elicited by those characteristics. It may be that they will arouse attraction whenever they recur, but it will be a new sexual attraction with a new particular object, not merely a transfer of the old desire to someone else. (I believe this is true even in cases where the new object is unconsciously identified with a former one.)

The importance of this point will emerge when we see how complex a psychological interchange constitutes the natural development of sexual attraction. This would be incomprehensible if its object were not a particular person, but rather a person of a certain *kind*. Attraction is only the beginning, and fulfillment does not consist merely of behavior and contact expressing this attraction, but involves much more.

• • •

The best discussion of these matters that I have seen appears in part III of Sartre's *Being and Nothingness*.[1] Since it has influenced my own views, I shall say a few things about it now. Sartre's treatment of sexual desire and of love, hate, sadism, masochism, and further attitudes toward others, depends on a general theory of consciousness and the body which we can neither expound nor assume here. He does not discuss perversion, and this is partly because he regards sexual desire as one form of the perpetual attempt of an embodied consciousness to come to terms with the existence of others, an attempt that is as doomed to fail in this form as it is in any of the others, which include sadism and masochism (if not certain of the more impersonal deviations) as well as several nonsexual attitudes. According to Sartre, all attempts to incorporate the other into my world as another subject, i.e., to apprehend him at once as an object for me and as a subject for whom I am an object, are unstable and doomed to collapse into one or other of the two aspects. Either I reduce him entirely to an object, in which case his subjectivity escapes the possession or appropriation I can extend to that object; or I become merely an object for him, in which case I am no longer in a position to appropriate his subjectivity. Moreover, neither of these aspects is stable; each is continually in danger of giving way to the other. This has the consequence that there can be no such thing as a *successful* sexual relation, since the deep aim of sexual desire cannot in principle be accomplished. It seems likely, therefore, that the view will not permit a basic distinction between successful or complete and unsuccessful or incomplete sex, and therefore cannot admit the concept of perversion.

I do not adopt this aspect of the theory, nor many of its metaphysical underpinnings. What interests me is Sartre's picture of the attempt. He says that the type of possession that is the object of sexual desire is carried out by "a double reciprocal incarnation" and that this is accomplished, typically in the form of a caress, in the following way: "I make myself flesh in order to impel the Other to realize *for herself* and *for me* her own flesh, and my caresses cause my flesh to be born for me in so far as it is for the Other *flesh causing her to be born as flesh*" (391; italics Sartre's). The incarnation in question is described variously as a clogging or troubling of consciousness, which is inundated by the flesh in which it is embodied.

The view I am going to suggest, I hope in less obscure language, is related to this one, but it differs from Sartre's in allowing sexuality to achieve its goal on occasion and thus in providing the concept of perversion with a foothold.

• • •

Sexual desire involves a kind of perception, but not merely a single perception of its object, for in the paradigm case of mutual desire there is a complex system of superimposed mutual perceptions—not only perceptions of the sexual object, but perceptions of oneself. Moreover, sexual awareness of another involves considerable self-awareness to begin with—more than is involved in ordinary sensory perception. The experience is felt as an assault on oneself by the view (or touch, or whatever) of the sexual object.

Let us consider a case in which the elements can be separated. For clarity we will restrict ourselves initially to the somewhat artificial case of desire at a distance. Suppose a man and a woman, whom we may call Romeo and Juliet, are at opposite ends of a cocktail lounge, with many mirrors on the walls which permit unobserved observation, and even mutual unobserved observation. Each of them is sipping a martini and studying other people in the mirrors. At some point Romeo notices Juliet. He is moved, somehow, by the softness of her hair and the diffidence with which she sips her martini, and this arouses him sexually. Let us say that *X senses Y* whenever *X* regards *Y* with sexual desire. (*Y* need not be a person, and *X*'s apprehension of *Y* can be visual, tactile, olfactory, etc., or purely imaginary; in the present example we shall concentrate on vision.) So Romeo senses Juliet, rather than merely noticing her. At this stage he is aroused by an unaroused object, so he is more in the sexual grip of his body than she of hers.

Let us suppose, however, that Juliet now senses Romeo in another mirror on the opposite wall, though neither of them yet knows that he is seen by the other (the mirror angles provide three-quarter views). Romeo then begins to notice in Juliet the subtle signs of sexual arousal: heavy-lidded stare, dilating pupils, faint flush, et cetera. This of course renders her much more bodily, and he not only notices but senses this as well. His arousal is nevertheless still solitary. But now, cleverly calculating the line of her state without actually looking her in the eyes, he realizes that it is directed at him through the mirror on the opposite wall. That is, he notices, and moreover senses, Juliet sensing him. This is definitely a new development, for it gives him a sense of embodiment not only through his own reactions but through the eyes and reactions of another. Moreover, it is separable from the initial sensing of Juliet; for sexual arousal might begin with a person's sensing that he is sensed and being assailed by the perception of the other person's desire rather than merely by the perception of the person.

But there is a further step. Let us suppose that Juliet, who is a little slower than Romeo, now senses that he senses her. This puts Romeo in a position to notice, and be aroused by, her arousal at being sensed by him. He senses that she senses that he senses her. This is still another level of arousal, for he becomes conscious of his sexuality through his awareness of its effect on her and of her awareness that this effect is due to him. Once she takes the same step and senses that he senses her sensing him, it becomes difficult to state, let alone imagine, further iterations, though they may be logically distinct. If both are alone, they will presumably turn to look at each other directly, and the proceedings will continue on another plane. Physical contact and intercourse are perfectly natural extensions of this complicated visual exchange, and mutual touch can involve all the complexities of awareness present in the visual case, but with a far greater range of subtlety and acuteness.

Ordinarily, of course, things happen in a less orderly fashion—sometimes in a great rush—but

I believe that some version of this overlapping system of distinct sexual perceptions and interactions is the basic framework of any full-fledged sexual relation and that relations involving only part of the complex are significantly incomplete. The account is only schematic, as it must be to achieve generality. Every real sexual act will be psychologically far more specific and detailed, in ways that depend not only on the physical techniques employed and on anatomical details, but also on countless features of the participants' conceptions of themselves and of each other, which become embodied in the act. (It is a familiar enough fact, for example, that people often take their social roles and the social roles of their partners to bed with them.)

The general schema is important, however, and the proliferation of levels of mutual awareness it involves is an example of a type of complexity that typifies human interactions. Consider aggression, for example. If I am angry with someone, I want to make him feel it, either to produce self-reproach by getting him to see himself through the eyes of my anger, and to dislike what he sees—or else to produce reciprocal anger or fear, by getting him to perceive my anger as a threat or attack. What I want will depend on the details of my anger, but in either case it will involve a desire that the object of that anger be aroused. This accomplishment constitutes the fulfillment of my emotion, through domination of the object's feelings.

Another example of such reflexive mutual recognition is to be found in the phenomenon of meaning, which appears to involve an intention to produce a belief or other effect in another by bringing about his recognition of one's intention to produce that effect. (That result is due to H. P. Grice,[2] whose position I shall not attempt to reproduce in detail.) Sex has a related structure: it involves a desire that one's partner be aroused by the recognition of one's desire that he or she be aroused.

It is not easy to define the basic types of awareness and arousal of which these complexes are composed, and that remains a lacuna in this discussion. I believe that the object of awareness is the same in one's own case as it is in one's sexual awareness of another, although the two awarenesses will not be the same, the difference being as great as that between feeling angry and experiencing the anger of another. All stages of sexual perception are varieties of identification of a person with his body. What is perceived is one's own or another's *subjection* to or *immersion* in his body, a phenomenon which has been recognized with loathing by St. Paul and St. Augustine, both of whom regarded "the law of sin which is in my members" as a grave threat to the dominion of the holy will.[3] In sexual desire and its expression the blending of involuntary response with deliberate control is extremely important. For Augustine, the revolution launched against him by his body is symbolized by erection and the other involuntary physical components of arousal. Sartre too stresses the fact that the penis is not a prehensile organ. But mere involuntariness characterizes other bodily processes as well. In sexual desire the involuntary responses are combined with submission to spontaneous impulses: not only one's pulse and secretions but one's actions are taken over by the body; ideally, deliberate control is needed only to guide the expression of those impulses. This is to some extent also true of an appetite like hunger, but the takeover there is more localized, less pervasive, less extreme. One's whole body does not become saturated with hunger as it can with desire. But the most characteristic feature of a specifically sexual immersion in the body is its ability to fit into the complex of mutual perceptions that we have described. Hunger leads to spontaneous interactions with food; sexual desire leads to spontaneous interactions with other persons, whose bodies are asserting their sovereignty in the same way, producing involuntary reactions and spontaneous impulses in *them*. These reactions are perceived, and the perception of them is perceived, and that perception is in turn perceived; at each step the domination of the person by his body is reinforced, and the sexual partner becomes more possessible by physical contact, penetration, and envelopment.

Desire is therefore not merely the perception of a preexisting embodiment of the other, but ideally a contribution to his further embodiment which in turn enhances the original subject's sense of himself. This explains why it is important that the partner be aroused, and not merely aroused, but aroused by the awareness of one's desire. It also explains the sense in which desire has unity and possession as its object: physical possession must eventuate in creation of the sexual object in the image of one's desire, and not merely in the object's recognition of that desire, or in his or her own private arousal. (This may reveal a male bias: I shall say something about that later.)

* * *

To return, finally, to the topic of perversion: I believe that various familiar deviations constitute truncated or incomplete versions of the complete configuration, and may therefore be regarded as perversions of the central impulse.

In particular, narcissistic practices and intercourse with animals, infants, and inanimate objects seem to be stuck at some primitive version of the first stage. If the object is not alive, the experience is reduced entirely to an awareness of one's own sexual embodiment. Small children and animals permit awareness of the embodiment of the other, but present obstacles to reciprocity, to the recognition by the sexual object of the subject's desire as the source of his (the object's) sexual self-awareness.

Sadism concentrates on the vocation of passive self-awareness in others, but the sadist's engagement is itself active and requires a retention of deliberate control which impedes awareness of himself as a bodily subject of passion in the required sense. The victim must recognize him as the source of his own sexual passivity, but only as the active source. De Sade claimed that the object of sexual desire was to evoke involuntary responses from one's partner, especially audible ones. The infliction of pain is no doubt the most efficient way to accomplish this, but it requires a certain abrogation of one's own exposed spontaneity. All this, incidentally, helps to explain why it is tempting to regard as sadistic an excessive preoccupation with sexual technique, which does not permit one to abandon the role of agent at any stage of the sexual act. Ideally one should be able to surmount one's technique as some point.

A masochist on the other hand imposes the same disability on his partner as the sadist imposes on himself. The masochist cannot find a satisfactory embodiment as the object of another's sexual desire, but only as the object of his control. He is passive not in relation to his partner's passion but in relation to his nonpassive agency. In addition, the subjection to one's body characteristic of pain and physical restraint is of a very different kind from that of sexual excitement: pain causes people to contract rather than dissolve.

Both of these disorders have to do with the second stage, which involves the awareness of oneself as an object of desire. In straightforward sadism and masochism other attentions are substituted for desire as a source of the object's self-awareness. But it is also possible for nothing of that sort to be substituted, as in the case of a masochist who is satisfied with self-inflicted pain or of a sadist who does not insist on playing a role in the suffering that arouses him. Greater difficulties of classification are presented by three other categories of sexual activity: elaborations of the sexual act; intercourse of more than two persons; and homosexuality.

If we apply our model to the various forms that may be taken by two-party heterosexual intercourse, none of them seem clearly to qualify as perversions. Hardly anyone can be found these days to inveigh against oral-genital contact, and the merits of buggery are urged by such respectable figures as D. H. Lawrence and Norman Mailer. There may be something vaguely sadistic about the latter technique (in Mailer's writings it seems to be a method of introducing an element of rape), but it not obvious that this has to be so. In general, it would appear that any bodily contact between a man and a woman that gives them sexual pleasure, is a possible vehicle for the system of multi-level interpersonal awareness that I have claimed is the basic psychological content of sexual interaction. Thus a liberal platitude about sex is upheld.

About multiple combinations, the least that can be said is that they are bound to be complicated. If one considers how difficult it is to carry on two conversations simultaneously, one may appreciate the problems of multiple simultaneous interpersonal perception that can arise in even a small-scale orgy. It may be inevitable that some of the component relations should degenerate into mutual epidermal stimulation by participants otherwise isolated from each other. There may also be a tendency toward voyeurism and exhibitionism, both of which are incomplete relations. The exhibitionist wishes to display his desire without needing to be desired in return; he may even fear the sexual attentions of others. A voyeur, on the other hand, need not require any recognition by his object at all: certainly not a recognition of the voyeur's arousal.

It is not clear whether homosexuality is a perversion if that is measured by the standard of the described configuration, but it seems unlikely. For such a classification would have to depend on the possibility of extracting from the system a distinction between male and female sexuality; and much that has been said so far applies equally to men and women. Moreover, it would have to be maintained that there was a natural tie between the type of sexuality and the sex of the body, and also that two sexualities of the same type could not interact properly.

Certainly there is much support for an aggressive-passive distinction between male and female sexuality. In our culture the male's arousal tends to initiate the perceptual exchange, he usually makes the sexual approach, largely controls the course of the act, and of course penetrates whereas the woman receives. When two men or two women engage in intercourse they cannot both adhere to these sexual roles. The question is how essential the roles are to an adequate sexual relation. One relevant observation is that a good deal of deviation from these roles occurs in heterosexual intercourse. Women can be sexually aggressive and men passive, and temporary reversals of role are not uncommon in heterosexual exchanges of reasonable length. If such conditions are set aside, it may be urged that there is something irreducibly perverted in attraction to a body anatomically like one's own. But alarming as some people in our culture may find such attraction, it remains psychologically unilluminating to class it as perverted. Certainly if homosexuality is a perversion, it is so in a very different sense from that in which shoe-fetishism is a perversion, for some version of the full range of interpersonal perceptions seems perfectly possible between two persons of the same sex.

In any case, even if the proposed model is correct, it remains implausible to describe as perverted every deviation from it. For example, if the partners in heterosexual intercourse indulge in private heterosexual fantasies, that obscures the recognition of the real partner and so, on the theory, constitutes a defective sexual relation. It is not, however, generally regarded as a perversion. Such examples suggest that a simple dichotomy between perverted and unperverted sex is too crude to organize the phenomena adequately.

• • •

I should like to close with some remarks about the relation of perversion to good, bad, and morality. The concept of perversion can hardly fail to be evaluative in some sense, for it appears to involve the notion of an ideal or at least adequate sexuality which the perversions in some way fail to achieve. So, if the concept is viable, the judgment that a person or practice or desire is perverted will constitute a sexual evaluation, implying that better sex, or a better specimen of sex, is possible. This in itself is a very weak claim, since the evaluation might be in a dimension that is of little interest to us. (Though, if my account is correct, that will not be true.)

Whether it is a moral evaluation, however, is another question entirely—one whose answer would require more understanding of both morality and perversion than can be deployed here. Moral evaluation of acts and of persons is a rather special and very complicated matter, and by no means all our evaluations of persons and their activities are moral evaluations. We make judgments about people's beauty or health or intelligence which are evaluative without being moral. Assessments of their sexuality may be similar in that respect.

Furthermore, moral issues aside, it is not clear that unperverted sex is necessarily *preferable* to the perversions. It may be that sex which receives the highest marks for perfection *as sex* is less enjoyable than certain perversions; and if enjoyment is considered very important, that might outweigh considerations of sexual perfection in determining rational preference.

That raises the question of the relation between the evaluative content of judgments of perversion and the rather common *general* distinction between good and bad sex. The latter distinction is usually confined to sexual acts, and it would seem, within limits, to cut across the other: even someone who believed, for example, that homosexuality was a perversion could admit a distinction between better and worse homosexual sex, and might even allow that good homosexual sex could be better *sex* than not very good unperverted sex. If this is correct, it supports the position that, if judgments of perversion are viable at all, they represent only one aspect of the possible evaluation of sex, even *qua sex*. Moreover it is not the only important aspect: certainly sexual deficiencies that evidently do not constitute perversions can be the object of great concern.

Finally, even if perverted sex is to the extent not so good as it might be, bad sex is generally better than none at all. This should not be controversial: it seems to hold for other important matters, like food, music, literature, and society. In the end, one must choose from among the available alternatives, whether their availability depends on the environment or on one's own constitution. And the alternatives have to be fairly grim before it becomes rational to opt for nothing.

Notes

My research was supported in part by the National Science Foundation.

1. Translated by Hazel E. Barnes (New York: Philosophical Library: 1956).

2. "Meaning," *Philosophical Review,* LXVI, 3 (July 1957): 377–388.

3. See Romans, VII, 23; and the *Confessions,* Book 8, V.

Robert Solomon offers a critique of Nagel. According to Solomon, Nagel has fallen prey to what Solomon refers to as the "liberal American sexual myth." This myth, Solomon claims, is presupposed by much of what Nagel claims about sex and perversity.

SEXUAL PERVERSION AS THE CONTENT OF COMMUNICATION

Solomon critiques Nagel by discussing what Solomon calls "liberal American sexual mythology." One of the problems with this mythology is that it sees sex as casual and meaningless, except insofar as sex leads to orgasm. Solomon asks, "Shouldn't there be at least a mention of why two people (in Nagel's scenario, Romeo and Juliet) should spend time 'making eyes at each other'?" Moreover, why should the scene end with Romeo and Juliet having sexual intercourse? Why does Nagel assume that this is the natural end of the meeting he has created?

Solomon agrees with Nagel in seeing sexual encounters as if they were communications. But Solomon faults Nagel for not being precise about the content of the communication. On the other hand, he praises Nagel for not overemphasizing the role of orgasm in sexual encounters. Orgasm and what Solomon calls the "over genitalized conception of sexuality" form another part of the liberal myth that Solomon would like to see rejected. For Solomon, seeing sex as having one aim, namely enjoyment, is actually destructive of sex and sexual pleasures. Also destructive of sex are two other views. One is that sexual activity ought to be private. The other is that sexual activities are all equally valid (so long as performed by consenting adults).

According to Solomon, Nagel assumes that arousal—what was going on between Romeo and Juliet—requires release at some point by sexual intercourse. But, again, Nagel never argues why this is so. Nagel never discusses the actual sex between Romeo and Juliet. He avoids doing so, not because he lacks imagination, but because it would be a violation of their privacy. Is Nagel committed to the view that all sexual contact between consenting adults is permissible? Solomon thinks that the answer is "probably yes." After all, Nagel does say that there need be no moral injunction made when categorizing an activity as a sexual perversion. Moreover, Nagel says that "any bodily contact" will do to satisfy his scheme. Thus it is that Nagel is upholding what Solomon has called the American liberal sexual myth.

What exactly is wrong with that myth according to Solomon? He focuses on the idea that sex is basically only for enjoyment. Enjoyment—orgasm—should not be considered the only legitimate goal of sexual contact. The enjoyment of sex should be found in sexual satisfaction, which can take many forms other than orgasm. We should not be satisfied by sexual enjoyment alone. Why have we missed this point? The reason can be seen in Nagel's analogy of sex to communication where Nagel never tells us what is to be communicated. Solomon's claim is that it is the content of the communication that makes sex the wonderful thing that it can be. Dealing only with levels of arousal, as Nagel does, hides the lack of content in Nagel's analysis. Just as one needs context to understand a sentence, so one needs context to truly appreciate sex.

If the pleasures of orgasm were all that mattered, then masturbation would be preferable to sex with partners since tests indicate rather clearly that intensity of orgasm is highest with masturbation. But sex with partners is almost always considered preferable. Solomon takes this as evidence that he is correct. If sex is a contentless language, then perversion can be categorized as Nagel does, as truncated versions of complete sentences (for example, there is no direct object). But this will not do. Perversions are more than just broken rules of grammar. Perversions say things and what they say, their messages, are worth rejecting—not necessarily because they are immoral, but rather because they stand in the way of what Solomon terms the utterly important expressive capacity of sex.

Try to work through the sex as language metaphor. Are there rules (as in grammar)?

Are there dictionaries and thesauruses? (We discussed what might count as one of these in Chapter 1.) Languages change with time. Does sexual activity also change? If so, how? Experts on language can tell you what a sentence means, given the context. Are there analogous sexual experts?

from Sexual Paradigms

Robert Solomon

It is a cocktail lounge, well-lit and mirrored, not a bar, martinis and not beer, two strangers—a furtive glance from him, shy recognition from her. It is 1950's American high comedy: boy arouses girl, both are led through ninety minutes of misunderstandings of identity and intention, and, finally, by the end of the popcorn, boy kisses girl with a clean-cut fade-out or panned clip of a postcard horizon. It is one of the dangers of conceptual analysis that the philosopher's choice of paradigms betrays a personal bias, but it is an exceptional danger of sexual conceptual analysis that one's choice of paradigms also betrays one's private fantasies and personal obsessions.[1] No doubt that is why, despite their extraprofessional interest in the subject, most philosophers would rather write about indirect discourse than intercourse, the philosophy of mind rather than the philosophy of body.

In Tom Nagel's pioneering effort* there are too many recognizable symptoms of liberal American sexual mythology. His analysis is cautious and competent, but absolutely sexless. His Romeo and Juliet exemplify at most a romanticized version of the initial phases of (hetero-)sexual attraction in a casual and innocent pick-up. They "arouse" each other, but there is no indication to what end. They "incarnate each other as flesh," in Sartre's awkward but precise terminology, but Nagel gives us no clue as to why they should indulge in such a peculiar activity. . . .

Sexual desire is distinguished, like all desires, by its aims and objects. What are those peculiarly sexual aims and objects? Notice that Nagel employs a fairly standard "paradigm case argument" in his analysis; he begins,

. . . certain practices will be perversions if anything is, such as shoe fetishism, bestiality and sadism; other practices, such as unadorned sexual intercourse will not be (5).

So we can assume that the end of Romeo and Juliet's tryst will be intercourse—we do not know whether "adorned" or not. But what is it that makes intercourse the paradigm of sexual activity—its biological role in conception, its heterosexuality, its convenience for mutual orgasm? Would Nagel's drama still serve as a sexual paradigm if Juliet turns out to be a virgin, or if Romeo and Juliet find that they are complementarily sado-masochistic, if Romeo is in drag, if they are both knee-fetishists? Why does Nagel choose two *strangers?* Why not, as in the days of sexual moralism, a happily married couple enjoying their seventh anniversary? Or is not the essence of sex, as Sartre so brutally argues, Romeo and Juliet's mutual attempts to possess each other, with each's own enjoyment only a secondary and essentially distracting effect? Are we expected to presume the most prominent paradigm, at least since Freud, the lusty ejaculation of Romeo into the submissive, if not passive, Juliet? Suppose Juliet is in fact a prostitute, skillfully mocking the signs of innocent arousal: is this a breach of the paradigm, or might not such subsequent "unadorned" intercourse be just the model that Nagel claims to defend?

To what end does Romeo arouse Juliet? And to what end does Juliet become affected and in turn excite Romeo? In this exemplary instance, I would think that "unadorned" intercourse would be perverse, or at least distasteful, in the extreme. It would be different, however, if the paradigm were our seven-year married couple, for in such cases

From "Sexual Paradigms" by Robert Solomon, *The Journal of Philosophy,* Vol. LXXI (1974), pp. 336–345. Used by permission of the author and *The Journal of Philosophy.*

"adorned" intercourse might well be something of a rarity. In homosexual encounters, in the frenzy of adolescent virginal petting, in cases in which intercourse is restricted for temporary medical or political reasons, arousal may be no different, even though intercourse cannot be the end. And it is only in the crudest cases of physiological need that the desire for intercourse is the sole or even the leading component in the convoluted motivation of sexuality. A nineteen-year-old sailor back after having discussed nothing but sex on a three-month cruise may be so aroused, but that surely is not the nature of Juliet's arousal. Romeo may remind her of her father, or of her favorite philosophy professor, and he may inspire respect, or fear, or curiosity. He may simply arouse self-consciousness or embarrassment. Any of these attitudes may be dominant, but none is particularly sexual.

Sexuality has an essential bodily dimension, and this might well be described as the "incarnation" or "submersion" of a person into his body. The end of this desire is interpersonal communication; but where Sartre gives a complex theory of the nature of this communication, Nagel gives us only an empty notion of "multi-level interpersonal awareness." Presumably the mutual arousal that is the means to this awareness is enjoyable in itself. But it is important that Nagel resists the current (W.) Reichian-American fetish for the wonders of the genital orgasm, for he does not leap to the facile conclusion that the aim of sexual activity is mutual or at least personal orgasm. It is here that Nagel opens a breach with liberal sexual mythology, one that might at first appear absurd because of his total neglect of the role of the genitalia and orgasm in sexuality. But we have an overgenitalized conception of sexuality, and, if sexual satisfaction involves and even requires orgasm, it does not follow that orgasm is the goal of the convoluted sexual games we play with each other. Orgasm is the "end" of sexual activity, perhaps, but only in the sense that swallowing is the "end" of tasting a Viennese torte.

There was a time, and it was not long ago and may come soon again, when sexuality required defending. It had to be argued that we had a right to sex, not for any purpose other than our personal enjoyment. But that defense has turned stale, and sexual deprivation is no longer our problem. The "swollen bladder" model of repressed sexuality may have been convincing in sex-scared bourgeois Vienna of 1905, but not today, where the problem is not sexual deprivation by sexual dissatisfaction. The fetishism of the orgasm, now shared by women as well as men, threatens our sex lives with becoming antipersonal and mechanical, anxiety-filled athletic arenas with mutual multiple orgasm its goal. Behind much of this unhappiness and anxiety, ironically, stands the liberal defense of sexuality as enjoyment. It is one of the virtues of Nagel's essay that he begins to overcome this oppressive liberal mythology. But at the same time he relies upon it for his support and becomes trapped in it, and the result is an account which displays the emptiness we have pointed out and the final note of despair with which he ends his essay.

Liberal sexual mythology appears to stand upon a tripod of mutually supporting platitudes: (1) and foremost, that the essential aim (and even the sole aim) of sex is enjoyment; (2) that sexual activity is and ought to be essentially private activity, and (3) that any sexual activity is as valid as any other. The first platitude was once a radical proposition, a reaction to the conservative and pious belief that sexual activity was activity whose end was reproduction, the serving of God's will or natural law. Kant, for example, always good for a shocking opinion in the realm of normative ethics, suggests that sexual lust is an appetite with an end intended by nature, and that any sexual activity contrary to that end is "unnatural and revolting," by which one "makes himself an object of abomination and stands bereft of all reverence of any kind."[2] It was Sigmund Freud who destroyed this long-standing paradigm, in identifying sexuality as "discharge of tension" (physical and psychological), which he simply equated with "pleasure," regardless of the areas of the body or what activities or how many people happened to be involved. Sex was thus defined as self-serving, activity for its own sake, with pleasure as its only principle. If Freud is now accused of sexual conservatism, it is necessary to remind ourselves that he introduced the radical paradigm that is now used against him. Since Freud's classic efforts, the conception of sexuality as a means to other ends, whether procreation or pious love, has become bankrupt in terms of the currency of opinion. Even radical sexual ideology has confined its critique to the social and political *abuses* of this liberal platitude without openly rejecting it.

The second platitude is a hold-over from more conservative days, in which sexual activity, like defecation, menstruation, and the bodily reactions to illness, was considered distasteful, if not shameful and to be hidden from view. Yet this conservative platitude is as essential as the first, for the typically utilitarian argument in defense of sexuality as enjoyment is based on the idea that sex is private activity and, when confined to "consenting adults," should be left as a matter of taste. And sex is, we are reminded by liberals, a natural appetite, and therefore a matter of taste.

The platitude of privacy also bolsters the third principle, still considered a radical principle by many, that any sexual activity is as valid as any other. Again, the utilitarian argument prevails, that private and mutually consented activity between adults, no matter how distasteful it might be to others and no matter how we may think its enthusiasts to be depraved, is "their own business."

Nagel's analysis calls this tri-part ideology to his side, although he clearly attempts to go beyond it as well. The platitude of enjoyment functions only loosely in his essay, and at one point he makes it clear that sexuality need not aim at enjoyment. ["It may be that . . . perfection *as sex* is less enjoyable than certain perversions; and if enjoyment is considered very important, that might outweigh considerations of sexual perfection in determining rational preference" (16/17).] His central notion of "arousal," however, is equivocal. On the one hand, arousal is itself not necessarily enjoyable, particularly if it fails to be accompanied with expectations of release. But on the other hand, Nagel's "arousal" plays precisely the same role in his analysis that "tension" (or "cathexis") plays in Freud, and though the arousal itself is not enjoyable, its release is, and the impression we get from Nagel, which Freud makes explicit, is that sexual activity is the intentional arousal both of self and other in order to enjoy its release. On this interpretation, Nagel's analysis is perfectly in line with post-Freudian liberal theory.

Regarding the second platitude, Nagel's analysis does not mention it, but rather it appears to be presupposed throughout that sexuality is a private affair. One might repeat that the notion of privacy is more symptomatic of his analysis itself. . . .

[Nagel] spends . . . much space giving us the preliminaries of sexuality without ever quite breaching the private sector in which sexual activity is to be found.

The third platitude emerges only slowly in Nagel's essay. He begins by chastising an approach to that same conclusion by a radical "skeptic," who argues of sexual desires, as "appetites,"

> Either they are sexual or they are not; sexuality does not admit of imperfection, or perversion, or any other such qualification (7).

Nagel's analysis goes beyond this "skepticism" in important ways, yet he does conclude that "any bodily contact between a man and a woman that gives them sexual *pleasure* [italics mine], is a possible vehicle for the system of multi-level interpersonal awareness that I have claimed is the basic psychological content of sexual interaction" (15). Here the first platitude is partially employed to support the third, presumably with the second implied. Notice again that Nagel has given us no indication what distinguishes "sexual pleasure" from other pleasures, whether bodily pleasures or the enjoyment of conquest or domination, seduction or submission, sleeping with the president's daughter or earning thirty dollars.

To knock down a tripod, one need kick out only one of its supporting legs. I for one would not wish to advocate, along with several recent sexual pundits, an increased display of fornication and fellatio in public places, nor would I view the return of "sexual morality" as a desirable state of affairs. Surprisingly, it is the essential enjoyment of sex that is the least palatable of the liberal myths.

No one would deny that sex is enjoyable, but it does not follow that sexuality is the activity of "pure enjoyment" and that "gratification," or "pure physical pleasure," that is, orgasm, is its end. Sex is indeed pleasurable, but . . . We enjoy being sexually satisfied; we are not satisfied by our enjoyment.

If sexuality does not essentially aim at pleasure, does it have any purpose? Jean-Paul Sartre has given us an alternative to the liberal theory in his *Being and Nothingness,* in which he argues that our sexual relations with others, like all our various relationships with others, are to be construed as *conflicts*, modeled after Hegel's parable of master and slave. Sexual desire is not desire for pleasure, and pleasure is more likely to distract us from sexuality than to deepen our involvement. For Sartre, sexual desire is the desire to possess, to gain recognition of one's own freedom at the expense of the other. By "incarnating" and degrading him/her in flesh, one reduces him/her to an object. Sadism is but an extension of this domination over the other. Or one allows himself to be "incarnated" as a devious route to the same end, making the other his/her sexual slave. Sexual activity concentrates its attention on the least personal, most inert parts of the body—breasts, thighs, stomach, and emphasizes awkward and immobile postures and activities. On this model, degradation is the central activity of sex, to convince the other that he/she is a slave, to persuade the other of one's own power, whether it be through the skills of sexual technique or through the passive demands of being sexually served. Intercourse has no privileged position in this model, except that intercourse, particularly in these liberated times in which it has become a contest, is ideal for this competition for power and recognition. And no doubt Sartre, who, like Freud, adopts a paradigmatically male perspective, senses that intercourse is more likely to be degrading to the woman, who thus begins at a disadvantage.

Sartre's notion of sexuality, taken seriously, would be enough to keep us out of bed for a month. Surely, we must object, something has been left out of account, for example, the two-person *Mitsein* that Sartre himself suggests in the same book. It is impossible for us to delve into the complex ontology that leads Sartre into this pessimistic model, but its essential structure is precisely what we need to carry us beyond the liberal mythology. According to Sartre, sexuality is interpersonal communication with the body as its medium. Sartre's mistake, if we may be brief, is his narrow constriction of the message of that communication to mutual degradation and conflict. Nagel, who accepts Sartre's communication model but, in line with the liberal mythology, seeks to reject its pessimistic conclusions, makes a mistake in the opposite direction. He accepts the communication model, but leaves it utterly without content. What is communicated, he suggests, is arousal. But, as we have seen, arousal is too broad a notion; we must know arousal of what, for what, to what end. Nagel's notion of "arousal" and "interpersonal awareness" gives us an outline of the grammar of the communication model, but no semantics. One might add that sexual activity in which what is aroused and intended are pleasurable sensations alone is a limiting and rare case. A sensation is only pleasurable or enjoyable, not in itself, but in the context of the meaning of the activity in which it is embedded. This is as true of orgasm as it is of a hard passion-bite on the shoulder.

This view of sexuality answers some strong questions which the liberal model leaves a mystery. If sex is pure physical enjoyment, why is sexual activity between persons far more satisfying than masturbation, where, if we accept recent physiological studies, orgasm is at its highest intensity and the post-coital period is cleansed of its interpersonal hassles and arguments? On the Freudian model, sex with other people ("objects") becomes a matter of "secondary process," with masturbation primary. On the communication model, masturbation is like talking to yourself; possible, even enjoyable, but clearly secondary to sexuality in its broader interpersonal context. (It is significant that even this carnal solipsism is typically accompanied by imaginings and pictures; "No masturbation without representation," perhaps.) If sex is physical pleasure, then the fetish of the genital orgasm is no doubt justifiable, but then why in our orgasm-cluttered sex lives are we so dissatisfied? Because orgasm is not the "end" of sex but its resolution, and obsessive concentration on reaching climax effectively overwhelms or distorts whatever else is being said sexually. It is this focus on orgasm that has made Sartre's model more persuasive; for the battle over the orgasm, whether in selfish or altruistic guise ("my orgasm first" or "I'll *give* you the best ever") has become an unavoidable medium for conflict and control. "Unadorned sexual intercourse," on this model, becomes the ultimate perversion, since it is the sexual equivalent of hanging up the telephone without saying anything. Even an obscene telephone caller has a message to convey.

Sexual activity consists in speaking what we

might call "body language." It has its own grammar, delineated by the body, and its own phonetics of touch and movement. Its unit of meaningfulness, the bodily equivalent of a sentence, is the *gesture*. No doubt one could add considerably to its vocabulary, and perhaps it could be possible to discuss world politics or the mind-body problem by an appropriate set of invented gestures. But body language is essentially expressive, and its content is limited to interpersonal attitudes and feelings—shyness, domination, fear, submissiveness and dependence, love or hatred or indifference, lack of confidence and embarrassment, shame, jealousy, possessiveness. There is little value in stressing the overworked point that such expressions are "natural expressions, as opposed to verbal expressions of the same attitudes and feelings. In our highly verbal society, it may well be that verbal expression, whether it be poetry or clumsy blurting, feels more natural than the use of our bodies. Yet it does seem true that some attitudes, e.g., tenderness and trust, domination and passivity, are best expressed sexually. Love, it seems, is not best expressed sexually, for its sexual expression is indistinguishable from the expressions of a number of other attitudes. Possessiveness, mutual recognition, "being-with," and conflict are expressed by body language almost essentially, virtually as its deep structure, and here Sartre's model obtains its plausibility.

According to Nagel, "perversion" is "truncated or incomplete versions of the complete configuration" (13). But again, his emphasis is entirely on the form of "interpersonal awareness" rather than its content. For example, he analyzes sadism as "the concentration on the evocation of passive self-awareness in others ... which impedes awareness of himself as a bodily subject of passion in the required sense." But surely sadism is not so much a breakdown in communication (any more than the domination of a conversation by one speaker, with the agreement of his listener, is a breach of language) as an excessive expression of a particular content, namely the attitude of domination, perhaps mixed with hatred, fear, and other negative attitudes. Similarly, masochism is not simply the relinquishing of one's activity (an inability to speak, in a sense), for the masochist may well be active in inviting punishment from his sadistic partner. Masochism is excessive expression of an attitude of victimization, shame, or inferiority. Moreover, it is clear that there is not the slightest taint of "perversion" in homosexuality, which need differ from heterosexuality only in its mode of resolution. Fetishism and bestiality certainly do constitute perversions, since the first is the same as, for example, talking to someone else's shoes, and the second is like discussing Spinoza with a moderately intelligent sheep.

This model also makes it evident why Nagel chose as his example a couple of strangers; one has far more to say, for one can freely express one's fantasies as well as the truth, to a stranger. A husband and wife of seven years have probably been repeating the same message for years, and their sexual activity now is probably no more than an abbreviated ritual incantation of the lengthy conversations they had years before. One can imagine Romeo and Juliet climbing into bed together each with a spectacular set of expectations and fantasies, trying to overwhelm each other with extravagant expressions and experiments. But it may be, accordingly, that they won't understand each other, or, as the weekend plods on, sex, like any extended conversation, tends to become either more truthful or more incoherent.

Qua body language, sex admits of at least two forms of perversion: one deviance of form, the other deviance in content. There are the techniques of sexuality, overly celebrated in our society, and there are the attitudes that these techniques allegedly express. Nagel and most theorists have concentrated on perversions in technique, deviations in the forms of sexual activity. But it seems to me that the more problematic perversions are the semantic deviations, of which the most serious are those involving insincerity, the bodily equivalent of the lie. Entertaining private fantasies and neglecting one's real sexual partner is thus an innocent semantic perversion, while pretended tenderness and affection that reverses itself soon after orgasm is a potentially vicious perversion. However, again joining Nagel, I would argue that perverse sex is not necessarily bad or immoral sex. Pretense is the premise of imagination as well as of falsehood, and sexual fantasies may enrich our lives far more than sexual realities alone. Perhaps it is an unfortunate comment on the poverty of contemporary life that our fantasies have become so confined, that our sexuality has been forced to serve needs which far exceed its expressive capacity. That is why the liberal mythology has been so disastrous, for it has rendered unconscious the expressive functions of sex in its stress on enjoyment and, in its platitude of privacy, has reduced sexuality to each man's/woman's private language, first spoken clumsily and barely articulately on wedding nights and in the back seats of Fords. It is thus understandable why sex is so utterly important in our lives, and why it is typically so unsatisfactory.

Notes

*"Sexual Perversion," this Journal, LXVI, 1, Jan. 16, 1969: 15–17.

1. I confess, for example, that certain male biases infiltrate my own analysis. I thank Janice Moulton for pointing this out to me.

2. *Metaphysics of Ethics,* trans. Semple (Edinburgh: Clark, 1971) IV, pt. I, ch. 1, sec. 7.

Donald Levy critiques a series of authors who have tried to characterize sexual perversion and shows how each of them has gone astray. Levy then claims that sexual perversion cannot be understood without first making a distinction between basic and nonbasic goods.

SEXUAL PERVERSION AS DENIAL OF BASIC GOODS FOR PLEASURE'S SAKE

Before he offers his characterization of sexual perversion, Levy criticizes six other accounts of sexual perversion found in the literature.

Levy begins with two criticisms of Nagel's characterization of perversion: (1) Some people want only incomplete sex just as some people always order from the a la carte section of the menu. Why does the term *perversion,* apply to one group but not the other? (2) Nagel's definition makes prostitution a perversion. Yet, Levy claims this is counterintuitive. Also, a sadomasochistic pair would not be perverted on Nagel's account. This too is counterintuitive.

After Nagel, Levy turns his critical eye to Sara Ruddick, Robert Solomon, Charles Fried, and Robert Gray. Ruddick defines perverted sex as unnatural sexual activity with natural sexual activity defined as sexual activity that can lead to reproduction. She is quick to point out that she means to make no moral judgment when she labels an act sexually perverted. Levy counters. In her view, the use of birth control would render sexual intercourse perverted. Moreover, how would she classify a molester of a thirteen-year-old girl? If this molestation leads to reproduction, is it still perverted? Levy's first comment against Ruddick is off the mark. No method of birth control is 100 percent trustworthy. (Some sterilizations fail. People who are thought to be sterile often turn out not to be.) Thus, using birth control always leaves open the possibility of reproduction.

Moreover, one could ask Levy, How about sexual intercourse between two ninety-year-old people? Why should this be perverted? An even better question has to do with the expression "can lead to reproduction." This is too vague. Suppose two lesbians decide that one should get pregnant and bear a child for them to raise. The man they want to be the father, for reasons of eccentric psychology and physiology, can ejaculate only if he is watching two females having sex. The lesbians agree to this arrangement. The man agrees to give his ejaculate to the lesbians for insemination. Is the sex of the lesbians perverted or not?

Levy faults Solomon for never offering a clear definition of perversion. Solomon may be right in his critique of Nagel, but he still leaves us wondering just when, for example, legitimate assertiveness turns into perverted domination. Charles Fried's definition cannot distinguish between sexual perversion and a conman or a practical joker. Fried is about the only author willing to say that sexual perversions are immoral. Alan Goldman, on the other hand, sees perversions as statistical anomalies and nothing more. Robert Gray takes an evolutionary slant on perversion. Something is a sexual perversion if it violates the natural adaptive function of sex. But, just what this natural adaptive function of sex is, Gray cannot tell us. (Evolutionary biologists are still working on why there is sex at all—why we don't reproduce asexually.) As we will see in the following piece, Michael Slote argues that the concept of perversion cannot be applied in the real world. It works only in imagination.

After this criticism of others, Levy offers his own views on perversion. He begins with the unnatural, claiming that the perverted is a subcategory of the unnatural. To understand the unnatural, we need a distinction between two sorts of goods: basic and nonbasic. Basic goods are easy to list. They are the ones we can never have too much of: life, health, control or freedom, the ability to gain knowledge and to love. All other goods are nonbasic. An act is unnatural if it denies anyone a basic good unless there is a necessity for doing so. An act is perverted when one person denies another (or herself) a basic good and the motive for the denial is pleasure. When the pleasure is sexual, then the act is a sexual perversion. Of course, knowing when an act has resulted in a person's becoming unable to love is difficult. Levy tries to side-step this issue in his example of child molestation. He says that a young girl is easily traumatized by the experience. He must mean that she will lose at least the capacity for love. Would a normal rational person give up a basic good for no reason? Probably not. Force or coercion would probably have to be used. Perhaps this is where the perversion lies: in the use of force to override lack of consent.

Would Levy have to classify a person who willingly gave up a basic good for pleasure alone as irrational or perverted, or are the two the same on his account? Perhaps what is important for Levy is this: As he sets up the concepts, to be involved in a perverted action is to ensure one's degradation. After all, one's baseline humanity is ensured only to the extent that one has basic goods, desires and strives for those basic goods, and makes every effort to keep those basic goods.

from Perversion and the Unnatural As Moral Categories

DONALD LEVY

For whatever reasons, the recent revival of philosophical interest in problems relating to love and sexuality began with attempts to analyze the concept of sexual perversion. Is it essentially an incoherent idea, one we moderns ought to seek to do without in thinking about sex? Is a revival of one or other of the traditional theologically based accounts of sexual perversion to be undertaken, perhaps updated, by the addition of the latest psychiatric findings? Or does the concept conceal hitherto unsuspected patterns of meaning which philosophical analysis might uncover for the first time? If sexual perversion is to be taken seriously, problems of definition demand solution at the start: What makes a sexual practice perverted? What differentiates sexual perversions from nonsexual perversions, if there are any such things? What makes a human activity perverted at all?

The range of human sexual activities commonly called sexual perversions is very wide and

From "Perversion and the Unnatural as Moral Categories" by Donald Levy, *Ethics* 90 (January 1980), pp. 191–202. Used by permission of the author and The University of Chicago Press.

vague in outline. Its vagueness will be clear from the following list, which I have adapted from Michael Balint:[1] (1) first of all, there are the various kinds of homosexuality; (2) next, the several forms of sadism and masochism; (3) then, exhibitionism, voyeurism, and the use of other parts of the body (i.e., other than the genitals); (4) fetishism, transvestism, and possibly kleptomania; (5) bestiality; and (6) finally, necrophilia and pedophilia. I should add that this list can be misleading by its abstractness—fetishism, for example, may cover a great variety of behaviors.

One can get some sense of the confusion in this field from the fact that Balint does not regard bestiality as a "proper" perversion—it never reaches the height of a proper perversion, he says, since it always comes about for want of something better. In addition, practices under necrophilia and pedophilia belong to the psychoses, he thinks. Even if we grant these unintuitive reasons for separating bestiality, necrophilia, and pedophilia from the main group, it is not at all easy to see what the first four categories have in common that nothing else in the way of sexual behavior shares.

Given the vague outlines of the classification, it is not surprising that the definitions proposed for this concept have not been very satisfactory. Ideas about various perversions can be found in Freud's writings, though it is fairly clear that he does not regard the term as a specially psychoanalytic one for whose definition he bears responsibility. In that sense, it is incorrect to speak of Freud as having a theory of the perversions at all. (Freud sometimes uses the word in quotes and once even refers to narcissism, which is, of course, not even a sexual activity as sometimes having "the significance of a perversion.")[2] If this is understood, we can say that Freud does tend to think of perversion as the undisguised expression of an infantile sexual wish.[3] Normal sex differs from the perverted variety in integrating the infantile sexual wish with other sexual wishes, not isolating them, and in gratifying it in disguised form. The difference between normal and perverted is one of degree, however.

The most acute criticism of the account I am attributing to Freud comes from within psychoanalysis itself. Balint points out that many forms of homosexuality, on the one hand, and of the sadomasochistic group, on the other, are definitely not survivals of infantile forms of sexuality but later developments. Balint's own attempt at definition focuses on perversions as ". . . attempts to escape from the two main demands of mature genitality: (1) accepting as real the intense need in ourselves for periodic regressions in the form of heterosexual coitus, and (2) accepting the necessity of the work of conquest, i.e., changing an indifferent object into a co-operative genital partner."[4] There are several reasons for doubting the adequacy of this approach. In the first place, Balint has made it clear that homosexuality is to be included among the perversions, yet he also maintains that in homosexual love "there is also the same bliss" as in heterosexual love, from which it is reasonable to infer that the need for regression is felt and fulfilled in both alike.[5] As for the second feature, Balint also asserts that "all the altruistically loving . . . features of heterosexual love can be found in homosexual love as well."[6] Besides, the first condition of Balint's definition would appear to make all celibates perverts, and the second condition would classify as perverted all selfish, crude, negligent—but heterosexual—lovers.

Recent philosophical attempts to define sexual perversion have not achieved any greater success than have the efforts of the psychoanalysts. Thomas Nagel conceives of sexual perversion in psychological terms, he says,[7] but it is nothing psychoanalytic he has in mind. Sexual perversions, according to Nagel, are incomplete versions of the "multi-level interpersonal awareness" which is "the basic psychological content of sexual interaction."[8] Perversions are incomplete versions of the complete configuration. Nagel's view seems close to the one usually ascribed to Freud, fixation on an infantile level being a kind of incompleteness. Nagel's view seems even closer to the idea contained in Catholic canon law, which defines as immoral any sex act which is "designed to be preparatory to the complete act," but which is "entirely divorced from the complete act."[9] Nagel does not indicate why it is important or noteworthy that some people seem to want only incomplete versions of sex instead of the complete ones—why do we need the classification "perversion" at all? (After all, we have no special designation for those who select their meals from the a la carte menu instead of ordering the complete dinner.) Another trouble with Nagel's view is that the prostitute, for example, who hardly participates at all in the interpersonal awareness Nagel refers to, would be perverted, yet neither ordinary usage nor any traditional classification of the perversions has such a result. (Nagel seems to be aware of this problem but does not regard it as crucial.) Besides, the sadomasochistic pair do complete the psychological process Nagel refers to, that is, there is interpersonal awareness between them on many levels, yet they would commonly be classified as perverted. It is surprising and puzzling that Nagel claims that sexual perversions ". . . will have to be sexual desires or practices that can be plausibly described as in some sense unnatural, though the explanation of this natural/unnatural distinction is of course the main problem."[10] Yet he does not attempt to explain the distinction or relate the concept of perversion to it.

Sara Ruddick defines "perverse" sex acts as deviations from the natural, the natural being defined as "of the type that can lead to reproduction."[11] Thus far, her view resembles Aquinas's account of that which is contrary to nature.[12] However, unlike Aquinas, she sees no moral significance to an act's being perverted.[13] Nevertheless, it seems odd to define masturbation or the use of birth control as perverted or unnatural, while it is unclear whether Ruddick's definition classifies the heterosexual child molester as perverted or not. (A twelve-year-old girl may be capable of reproducing, yet sex with her by an adult male counts as pedophilia, regardless of that biological fact.) Against Ruddick's view, an alternative account would be preferable if it explained why the perverted and the unnatural are not coextensive.

Robert C. Solomon faults Nagel's definition of perversion for emphasizing the form of the interpersonal awareness in sex rather than its content.[14] According to Solomon, sadism, for example, is not so much a breakdown in communication as ". . . an excessive expression of a particular content, namely the attitude of domination, perhaps mixed with hatred, fear, and other negative attitudes."[15] Solomon offers no account explaining at what point the expression of attitudes of domination becomes excessive enough to warrant being

labeled perversion; more important, it is hard to see why being excessive in the expression of domination should count as perversion at all and not merely as rudeness, perhaps.

According to Charles Fried, a case of perversion exists when an actor uses another person to attain his end, and when it is a necessary constitutive element of that end that another person he used, but it is also a necessary element of the actor's "rational principle" that the other person thereby not attain an end of his own.[16] One objection to this is that it is too broad—the nonsexual joker, swindler, or con man fit the definition, yet they are hardly perverted, certainly not sexually perverted. A sexual trickster also not excluded by Fried's definition would be the sterile man seeking sex with a woman who merely wishes to conceive by him. If he keeps his sterility a secret from her, his pursuit of her fits Fried's definition of perversion, though he would normally be called neither perverted nor sexually perverted, just malicious.[17] Second, the exclusive fetishist, transvestite, or bestialist is clearly beyond Fried's definition, yet Fried would probably accept them as being as genuine cases of perversion as any. Fried's view of perversion is unusual in providing an account of the concept apparently conceived in moral terms. (This seems to be his intent, though it is not clear that it would always be morally wrong for one person to use another in the way described in Fried's definition.) In this respect, Fried's account appears to be unique among recent philosophical discussions of perversion.

The opposite extreme is Alan H. Goldman's purely statistical interpretation, according to which those sexual desires are perverted which are statistically abnormal in form.[18] Identifying the form of a desire is problematic, however. Goldman gives the following examples of desires whose abnormality in form makes them perverted desires: ". . . desire, not for contact with another, but for merely looking, for harming or being harmed, for contact with items of clothing."[19] Desiring to engage in sex continuously for three hours is not, it seems, abnormal in form in the requisite sense.[20] Nevertheless, plausible counterexamples seem to be available; the male office worker whose lustful desires are restricted exclusively to his female superiors would seem to be one, since his sexual desires are abnormal (statistically), yet hardly perverted. It might at first appear that this example involves only an abnormality in the content of the desire, not in its form. But if the office-worker case is dismissed as a case of perversion on account of the form-content distinction, there is the danger that the heterosexual transvestite, necrophiliac, or child molester will also lie outside the definition of perversion. This problem with the form-content distinction arises again when Goldman writes that "raping a sheep may be more perverted than raping a woman, but certainly not more condemnable morally."[21] It is hard to see how raping a woman could be perverted at all on Goldman's account, since the form of the act would appear to be normal.[22] (Incidentally, I doubt that it even makes sense to speak of raping a sheep, whose consent or lack of it cannot exist.)[23]

Evolutionary theory is the basis of Robert Gray's definition of perversion and the unnatural, which he follows Ruddick in equating.[24] Like Ruddick, too, he regards these terms as descriptive and nonevaluative, carrying no moral connotations.[25] "If, then, we are able to show that there is some adaptive function or end that sexual activity evolved to fulfill, we may speak of sexual activity that departs from that function and, more clearly, of sexual activity that, by departing from that function, is maladaptive, as counterproductive and, in that sense, contrary to nature or unnatural. . . . Put more simply, those forms of sexual activity would be perverted which, in evolutionary terms, are dysfunctional."[26] For Gray, the advantage of this definition is that it alone enables us to avoid cultural relativism in defining perversion.[27] This claim is puzzling, given his later remark: "It may turn out, too, that the natural adaptive functions of human sexual activity are not culturally independent. In this case, a behavior that is maladaptive in one society may not be so in another."[28]

However, a more serious problem with Gray's definition arises when he comes to consider what "the natural adaptive function" of sex in humans is. To the suggestion (perhaps Ruddick's) that reproduction is the sole function of sexual activity, Gray's reply is unclear. On the one hand, he seems to deny it: "If reproduction were, as some think, the sole function of sexual activity, the scientist would have no further questions to ask about the matter, and all nonreproductive sexual activity might correctly be described as perverted. However, it would seem that this is not the case."[29] But on the other hand, the reasons he gives for denying it point in the opposite direction. Instead of considering other functions sex might fulfill, or the possibility that sex need not serve any function at all, his denial seems to rest on interpreting reproductive activity to include ". . . all those activities minimally necessary to bring those new individuals themselves to reproductive maturity. Among other things, this would seem to include the formation and maintenance of well organized, stable societies and the establishment and maintenance of fairly stable male-female reproductive pairs."

From this, it follows that ". . . maintenance of that degree (and kind) of social organization and stability requisite to the maintenance of human society is a function that normal sexual behavior has evolved to fulfill, and, if this is so, it is clear that the range of non-perverted sexual activity will be much broader than it has traditionally been taken to be."[30] Therefore, it would not be strained to ascribe to Gray the view that reproduction is "the natural adaptive function" of sex, but that reproduction includes very much more than usually supposed.

The trouble with this account is not, however, in its determination of what the natural adaptive function of sex is—anyway, Gray claims no special authority or expertise in the question, which he regards as answerable only by the scientist.[31] More problematic is the essentially utilitarian nature of Gray's use of evolutionary theory in defining perversion. This comes out in his appeals to "the maintenance of human society," "the maintenance of the over-all social order," and "the long-term viability of society"[32] as the crucial considerations in deciding which sexual activities are perverted.

As with any utilitarian theory, paradoxical implications can be expected, and one does seem to be implicit in Gray's view. Consider, for example, a society in which artificial insemination has become the form of reproduction most conducive to "the long-term viability of society." (Given certain global conditions, we might imagine this to be true of the whole species, i.e., of all human societies.) Then, heterosexual sex (between loving spouses in the missionary position) would turn out to be perverted by the functional criteria Gray suggests. This paradoxical result will be derivable even if some function (or functions) other than reproduction is decided upon by the experts to be "the natural adaptive function" of sex. Whatever the function or functions might be, nothing guarantees that normal, heterosexual sex performs this function more effectively than any other sexual practice (or combination of sexual and nonsexual practices). In some conditions, heterosexual sex may perform the function or functions of sex far less effectively than other practices and will then have to be categorized as a sexual perversion, according to Gray's definition.

Perhaps in despair at the problems such efforts at definition as these confront, the temptation arises to declare the concepts of perversion and the unnatural to be empty, idle, or meaningless. Such a trend (with regard to the unnatural) can be traced as far back as Mill's essay *On Nature,* Diderot's *D'Alembert's Dream,* Descartes's *Sixth Meditation,* and perhaps the ancient sophists. The most recent expression of this position is Michael Slote's "Inapplicable Concepts and Sexual Perversion."[33] The best response to this temptation would be a theory of perversion and the unnatural that succeeds in overcoming the difficulties to be found in Nagel, Ruddick, Solomon, Fried, Goldman, Gray, and Slote.

In offering the following theory, I have started by trying to do something different from what has been previously attempted. In the first place, I have tried to separate analysis of the concepts of perversion and the unnatural from the discussion of the criteria to be employed in applying these terms to particular cases. (The separation of concept analysis from consideration of criteria is at least as old as the philosophy of love and sexuality itself; in the *Symposium* Socrates proposes "first to treat of the nature of Eros and then to treat of his acts" [199C5–6; 201E1–2].) Also, I believe the account to be sketched here makes better sense of the differences between calling something unnatural and calling it perverted than have the seven philosophers I have reviewed. (Mostly, they do not concern themselves with this at all.) Second, I

have set out to provide a moral theory of perversion and the unnatural. Regardless of whether commonly held, unreflective applications of the terms "perversion" and "unnatural" are agreed to, there seems little point in providing a definition emptying them of their most obvious feature— that is, that their normal use is as terms of serious moral disapproval. I have tried accordingly to provide an account that preserves and explains this aspect of their use. To seek a theory of sexual perversion which accounts for our having such a concept at all in purely psychological, aesthetic, biological, or statistical terms seems a futile endeavor. Third, a theory of sexual perversion ought to make it possible to revise some of our moral judgments in applying the concept. It ought to enable us to make more reasoned judgments, recognizing that some of what has been labeled perversion in the past may have been mistakenly so labeled, as well as enabling us to add to the class of perversions acts that may have not been traditionally included there.

A good way to begin is to return to the historical origin of the idea of the unnatural, which is philosophical. It apparently first occurs in Plato's *Phaedrus,* where Socrates refers to "unnatural pleasure" (251A), but Plato's *Laws* (bk. 8, 836 ff.) contains the earliest occurrence of an argument for the unnaturalness of a human action, here, a sexual practice, homosexuality. Plato is thinking of male homosexuality, but male masturbation is perhaps also forbidden as unnatural, too. Two sorts of reasons are given; one (at 838E) is that since the natural purpose of the sex act is procreation an unnatural sex act is one in which the purpose is other than procreation. A quite different sort of consideration is offered earlier, however (at 836D): "Will the spirit of courage spring to life in the soul of the seduced person? Will the soul of the seducer learn habits of self-control?" the Athenian asks. Speaking of homosexuality, he says that ". . . such practices are incompatible with what in our view should be the constant aim of the legislator—that is, we're always asking 'which of our regulations encourages virtue, and which does not?' . . . Everyone will censure the weakling who yields to temptation, and condemn his all-too-effeminate partner who plays the role of the woman."[34] I believe this passage provides the basis for a defensible view of the unnatural even if its application by Plato is questioned. Certainly, the other definition of Plato's, that one that depends upon identifying the natural purpose of sex, is more familiar, having marked one dominant trend in traditional sexual morality. But in this passage, Plato speaks of an unnatural sex act as involving the denial to someone (whether oneself or another) of a vital capacity—courage or self-control—by seduction.

First of all, the traditional treatments (in Plato, Aquinas, and Kant, e.g.) discuss perversion under the heading of the unnatural, and this is where I shall begin, too. Modern philosophers tend to ignore the concept of the natural—and so, too, of the unnatural—perhaps out of verificationist concern about the apparent impossibility of giving nonemotive sense to talk about the unnatural in moral matters, and perhaps also out of considerations of the sort Sartre offers in *Existentialism Is a Humanism*. To talk of human nature, he argues, is possible only on the assumption that man is an artifact, a product of divine handicraft, made for a purpose. Apart from that framework, that view of the universe, no sense can be given to talk of human nature. I intend to take issue with that view; indeed, my argument will have the implication that, whatever may be the case with other things in the universe, man is one thing we can know has a nature—we can know man's nature regardless of whether man is seen as created for a purpose or created at all.

To define the unnatural, of which the perverted is a subcategory, I shall need first to make a distinction between a limited set of basic human goods on the one hand, and the indefinitely large set of nonbasic, nonessential goods on the other. Among the latter, I include such things as enjoying one's dinner, getting to be famous in one's profession, winning at the next drawing of the state lottery, winning at some drawing or other of the state lottery, having children of whom one can be proud. It should be clear from these examples that classifying something as a nonbasic human good is not at all to claim that it is unimportant. By contrast, what I count as the basic human goods can be rather completely listed: life, health, control of one's bodily and psychic functions, the capacity for knowledge and love. These goods seem to be basic in the (Rawlsian) sense that these will be de-

sired no matter whatever else will, insofar as they are necessary for the getting of any other human goods; but two other ways occur to me to identify the basic human goods and distinguish them from the others.

One mark of a basic human good is that it is hard to make literal sense of the claim that a person has too much of it; what is commonly called being loved too much, that is, being spoiled, is really a case of having been loved badly.[35] Hence, too, I exclude wealth from the list, I doubt that much disagreement about what belongs on the list is possible, though different cultures may order them differently in importance. My reasons for claiming that much disagreement is not possible may be connected with the other, major way of picking out the basic human goods, which is this: A basic human good is a feature of human life one can actively seek to reduce to a minimum among humans only at the expense of one's own status as a human being. For example, a creature (perhaps human in appearance) who acts out of a "moral" obligation to reduce health among humans as much as possible in the way we normally feel obliged to avoid causing disease as much as possible (i.e., on principle) would be a creature whom we would not perceive as human. (Imagine a creature who sincerely offered excuses for having failed to spread disease in a particular situation in which he had the opportunity.) It is at that point that simple people begin to speak of creatures as being possessed by evil demons, that is, the point at which a creature manifests negative concern for the basic human goods. (The zombie and Frankenstein's monster are variants of demon possession; in them, absence of awareness or care about the basic human goods is manifested.) People around the world intuitively avoid dealing with human wickedness as if it consisted of an infinite continuum with no lower end; instead, they cut off at a certain point and call whatever lies on the other side alien, nonhuman, demonic, possessed. I offer this general, though not universal, fact as evidence of a deep distinction between basic and nonbasic human goods; it also seems to me to pick out as basic those goods I listed as such. Any creature, however rational or articulate, who does not value the basic human goods is not human. The basic human goods may be defined as those aspects of human existence such that principled lack of concern for them by a creature is a sufficient condition of the creature's nonhumanity.

As a first approximation, I suggest that an unnatural act is one that denies a person (oneself or another) one or more of these basic human goods without necessity, that is, without having to do so in order to prevent losing some other basic human good. A person might intelligibly deny himself or another one or more of these basic human goods for the sake of another basic human good. A priest, for example, might adopt celibacy, admitting that it is against nature to seek to live without human love. An artist might sacrifice his health for his art. (A sacrifice is the giving up of something valued; we cannot sacrifice our garbage to the city dump.) But denying oneself or another a basic human good without some other basic human good being expected or intended to be made possible thereby is always wrong; it is also, as I shall show, a necessary condition of perversion. Sports-car racers enjoy risking their lives, partly at least for the gain in skill achieved thereby. Although the likelihood may be great that they may die in a racing accident, it is not probable that they will die in any particular race. If this were likely, they might well seem unnatural, even perverted. Similar arguments apply in the case of the smoker, the drinker, the drug user.

The perverted is a subclass of the unnatural. When a person denies himself or another one of the basic human goods (or the capacity for it) and no other basic human good is seen as resulting thereby, and when pleasure is the motive of the denial, the act is perverted. When the pleasure is sexual, the perversion is sexual. It should be clear from this definition of perversion that pleasure is assumed not to be a basic human good. First, because one can have too much of it—to see this, consider the case of a person hooked up to a machine stimulating the pleasure center of the brain. Suppose he were unwilling to disconnect himself even long enough to obtain food to sustain life. He would have died for a bit of extra pleasure. Besides, a person can seek to minimize human pleasure quite generally (perhaps as an obstacle to the maximization of knowledge or other basic human goods) without casting his humanity into doubt— a rather extreme Puritan might illustrate this.

This account distinguishes sexual from nonsexual perversions. An example of the latter would be the man who takes pleasure in frightening small children by holding them close up to speeding trains. His pleasure would be perverted, since the effects on his victims can be expected to be traumatic. Killing for pleasure, or maiming for the fun of it, would, of course, also be perverted; but neither would be a sexual perversion. A surgeon who performs operations for the excitement, when not required for the health of the patient, is perverted. In individual cases it may be difficult to determine just what motivated someone to do what he did— rationalizations may be common. But this uncertainty of verification is distinguishable from the blurring of the line *defining* perverted and nonperverted acts. I shall assume that the child molester is a case of sexual perversion, even though it is not the sort of case central to (or even mentioned in) several familiar accounts of the concept; it has the requisite completeness for natural sex in the canon law sense, its form is normal, it can lead to reproduction, so that Aquinas does not consider it in his treatment of the unnatural in sex. Nevertheless, the young girl sexually initiated by an older person can easily be traumatized; that there is no way of undoing the harmful effects with the ease and certainty with which they were induced establishes the correctness of classifying the case as one of sexual perversion. (The mere intensity of the seducer's sexual feeling can be traumatic to a child, even if the seducer is not strange or threatening.)[36]

The sort of damage I refer to is properly called degradation, corruption. That perversion degrades is a necessary truth (perhaps a trivial one) as I have defined perversion. To categorize some activity as perverted is to say something important about what is wrong with it. One advantage of this account of sexual perversion is that accepting it does not commit us to accepting any one of the common views of particular sex acts, although it does, in fact, capture many of our intuitions about what is perverted. How the concept of perversion as defined here would apply, for instance, to homosexuality is not obvious if only because homosexuality is a complex phenomenon: it can be viewed merely as an activity, one among many engaged in by those whose lives at the same time include other sexual activities, for example, heterosexual activities. But homosexuality can also occur as an institution, which it is in many societies other than our own; there, it is often typical of one stage of normal development, leading to, and compatible with, heterosexual functioning in marriage. Last, homosexuality can also be considered as a form of life when it practically excludes heterosexuality. It is this that modern gay liberation intends, and about which little can be learned from other societies. However, consideration of homosexuality as a form of life would take us far from the question of perversion and the unnatural.

Although the definition of the concept does not, by itself, produce criteria strong enough to allow us to be decisive in the important case of homosexuality,[37] the definition might seem to require rape to be included among the sexual perversions, contrary to the traditional accounts.[38] Rape does degrade—this would seem to be a necessary truth—but whether in the way the definition of perversion requires is unclear. (All perversions degrade, but not all degrading acts or experiences are cases of perversion.) What more must be added to the definition of perversion in order to generate criteria applicable to homosexuality deserves a paper of its own, as does the question of why rape has not traditionally been perceived as perversion at all.

Notes

Essential advice and assistance in writing this article was received from Marilyn M. Hamilton and David A. J. Richards. It has also benefited from criticisms by members of the CUNY Ethics Colloquium (March 1975) and by members of the Society for Philosophy and Public Affairs, New York chapter (November 1975).

1. Michael Balint, "Perversions and Genitality," in *Primary Love and Psycho-analytic Technique* (New York: Liveright Publishing Corp., 1965).

2. Sigmund Freud, "On Narcissism: An Introduction," *Standard Edition* (London: Hogarth Press, 1957), 14:73.

3. Sigmund Freud, *Standard Edition*, vol. 7, *Three Essays on the Theory of Sexuality* (London: Hogarth Press, 1953), p. 231.

4. Balint, p. 144.

5. Ibid., p. 137.

6. Ibid.

7. Thomas Nagel, "Sexual Perversion," *Journal of Philosophy* 66 (1969): 5–17, p. 6.

8. Ibid., p. 15.

9. H. C. Gardiner, S. J., "Moral Principles toward a Defin-

ition of the Obscene," *Law and Contemporary Problems* 20 (Autumn 1955): 560–620, p. 564.

10. Nagel, p. 5.

11. Sara Ruddick, "Better Sex," in *Philosophy and Sex*, ed. R. Baker and F. Elliston. Buffalo, NY: Prometheus Books, 1975), p. 91.

12. Aquinas, *On the Truth of the Catholic Faith* [Summa contra gentiles], bk. 3, *Providence*, pt. 2 (Garden City, NY: Doubleday & Co., 1956), "The Reasons Why Simple Fornication Is a Sin according to Divine Law, and That Matrimony Is Natural." trans. V. J. Bourke, chap. 22, p. 146.

13. Ruddick, p. 95.

14. Robert C. Solomon, "Sexual Paradigms," *Journal of Philosophy* 71 (1974): 336–45, p. 344.

15. Ibid.

16. Charles Fried, *An Anatomy of Values* (Cambridge, MA: Harvard University Press, 1970), p. 50.

17. I owe this example to Paul Shupack.

18. Alan H. Goldman, "Plain Sex," *Philosophy and Public Affairs* 6, no. 3 (Spring 1977): 267–87, p. 284.

19. Ibid.

20. Ibid.

21. Ibid., p. 286.

22. Alan Soble pointed this out to me.

23. Goldman ascribes to Nagel and Solomon evaluative accounts of perversion (p. 285), but the value, if it is there at all, seems not to be moral, only perhaps aesthetic. Cf. Nagel, pp. 6 and 16, and Solomon, p. 345: ". . . perverse sex is not necessarily bad or immoral sex."

24. Robert Gray, "Sex and Sexual Perversion," *Journal of Philosophy* 75 (1978): 189–99, p. 189.

25. Ibid., pp. 198–99.

26. Ibid., p. 190.

27. Ibid.

28. Ibid., p. 198.

29. Ibid., p. 197.

30. Ibid., pp. 197–98.

31. Ibid., p. 197.

32. Ibid., p. 198.

33. Michael Slote, in Baker and Elliston (n. 11).

34. Plato, *Laws*, 836D, trans. T. J. Saunders (Harmondsworth, Middlesex: Penguin Books, 1970).

35. Descartes seems to mean something like this when he says that in certain conditions love "can never be too great" (*The Passions of the Soul*, pt. 2, article 139, trans. E. S. Haldane and G. R. Ross [Cambridge: Cambridge University Press, 1931], 1:393).

36. The dominant view of the effects of pedophilia, opposed to this one, is well represented in L. Bender and A. E. Grugett, Jr., "A Follow-up Report on Children Who Had Atypical Sexual Experience," *American Journal of Orthopsychiatry* 22 (1952): 825–37. Whether coprophilia or necrophilia is covered by the definition of perversion proposed here has been questioned. What basic human good is a person deprived of in

engaging in these practices? Briefly, each involves the use of a fetish, which Charles Rycroft defines as "an object which a fetishist endows with sexual significance and in the absence of which he is incapable of sexual excitement. A sexual fetish is either an inanimate object or a nonsexual part of a person. . . ." (*A Critical Dictionary of Psycho-analysis* [Totowa, NJ: Littlefield, Adams & Co., 1973], p. 51). So, the coprophiliac or necrophiliac has lost the ability to love another human being sexually in seeking to obtain pleasure with some inanimate object.

37. This point has been pursued in David A. J. Richards' *The Moral Criticism of Law* (Encino, California: Dickenson, 1977), Ch. 3. A fuller expansion of these ideas can be found in the same author's "Unnatural Acts and the Constitutional Right to Privacy: A Moral Theory," *Fordham Law Review* XLV, No. 6 (May, 1977), pp. 1281–1348.

38. Sara Ruddick says rape "can constitute perversion if rape, rather than genital intercourse, is the aim of desire" (*op. cit.*, p. 99).

In a sense, Michael Slote picks up on this idea of basic goods defining our humanity. Slote ties together our classifying an act as a perversion with deeply hidden fears that perverse actions would actually undercut what we take our real world to be.

SEXUAL PERVERSION AS A NAME FOR FANTASIES

Slote argues that the concept of a "monster" derives its force from the fact that we do not believe that there are or ever were monsters. That is, what makes a monster so fearful is that it is our worst nightmare come true. But, of course, it can't come true, since to do so would be to give the monster a place in nature, which would then make it not a monster. Put another way, to call something monstrous or a monster is to say that it is unnatural. At least, this is Slote's position. When do we call something a monster? According to Slote, we do this when we are frightened out of our wits by something. Slote will use these points to discuss perversion.

Psychologically, we all have some deeply hidden fears about our sexual desires. (Here again we see the influence of Freud. Slote mentions that he is using what is often called depth psychology, a psychology that postulates levels of consciousness. Freud's was one of the first clearly worked-out depth psychologies.) The more we fear letting those desires come to the surface, the greater the tendency to characterize the desires as unnatural or perverse. When we characterize (a desire for) incest as perverse, what we are doing according to Slote is saying that incest is not part of our world, that it is monstrous.

For Slote, then, our use of the term *perverse* to describe a sexual act merely betrays the feelings that we have about ourselves. So it is not surprising that no one has been successful in coming up with a decent general characterization of perversion.

---

from Inapplicable Concepts

MICHAEL A. SLOTE

I

I shall argue here that the ordinary notions of a monster and of an unnatural (or perverted) act are for similar reasons inapplicable to reality, and shall offer an explanation of how such inapplicable concepts come to be frequently used.[1]

Whatever else a monster is, it has to be terrifying or frightening. And monsters may also have to be (relatively) large. Most of us think that if crea-

From "Inapplicable Concepts" by Michael A. Slote, *Philosophical Studies,* 28 (1975), pp. 265–271. Used by permission of *Philosophical Studies* and Kluwer Academic Publishers.

tures like those described in certain stories had actually existed, monsters would have actually existed. But do those creatures, imagined as actually existent, differ from dinosaurs like tyrannosaurus rex in any respect relevant to monster status? It appears not, and yet we do not think of dinosaurs as monsters. It is part of the modern world view that there never have been monsters, any more than wood nymphs or elves. Nor would scientists or other educated people call a creature a monster, if it today emerged from a dinosaur egg left frozen from the Cretaceous Period. The creature would be a dinosaur of a certain kind, no more, no less. Now it is puzzling that dinosaurs are not monsters, since they seem as appropriately monsterlike as many story-book monsters. Of course, someone might deny this and claim that dinosaurs are not rich enough in such 'monster-making' properties as voraciousness, sliminess, malevolence, and invulnerability to count as real monsters. But this view has the implausible implication that many putative story-book monsters, who are no richer in monster-making properties than the tyrannosaurus rex, are only mistakenly thought of as monsters. And it also implies that if certain dinosaurs had through evolution become sufficiently rich in monster-making properties, then some dinosaurs would have *developed into* monsters. And this seems inconsistent with our idea of what a monster is.

I think our reluctance to all dinosaurs monsters comes from our belief that they have a determinate (specific) biological place in nature. The monsters of stories—and here I may be using quantification loosely—do not have a really determinate biology or place in some natural order. It is well known that facts about fictional entities are often left indeterminate. And even if various monster stories represent certain creatures as having a determinate physiology, evolution, etc., there never is any specific physiology, evolution, etc., of which it can be truly said: "this is the physiology, evolution, etc., that the monster of this story has."[2]

This gives the sense in which story-book monsters lack a determinate (biological) nature. And I think only such a creature can be a monster. For that reason, if all the descriptions of some story-book monster had been, or turned out to be, realized in some actual creature (with an exotic biol-

ogy), that creature would have as determinate a biological nature and as little claim to be a monster as a dinosaur has.[3]

Gila monsters and 'moral monsters' like Hitler are not, I think, literally monsters in the sense of the term under consideration. But it might be said that I am mistaken in thinking that 'monster' is inapplicable, because various mutants and deformed creatures represent actual examples of monsters. Now I think that various mutants and the like count as monsters in a technical biological sense of the term. But those 'enlightened' people who believe there are no monsters (in Loch Ness or elsewhere) are usually not ignorant of or sceptical about the existence of mutants (like two-headed calves or bulls). They are using 'monster' in a 'story-book' sense that does not apply to such creatures, and indeed most dictionaries distinguish (at least) two senses of 'monster' in this way.[4]

It is my belief that at least part of the ordinary meaning of 'monster' is: '(large) terrifying creature that lacks a determinate (biological) nature', or, for brevity, '(large) terrifying unnatural creature'. Since no actual creature could lack a determinate nature, the ordinary concept of a monster is inapplicable in principle to non-fiction reality.

How, then, do we explain the fact that if a person who had never heard of dinosaurs were to come across one while strolling alone in the mountains, he might well think of it as a monster to be feared? The answer, I think, is that such uses of the term are largely a reflection of terror (fear) and ignorance. It is necessary that anything in the natural world with us have a determinate (biological) nature. And because it is easy to think of 'unnatural' as meaning 'not in nature (with us)', the idea of not being in nature (with us) is what might be called an overtone of the notion of unnaturalness as we have defined it: namely, an idea that is logically implied by and tends to be associated with that notion of unnaturalness. In saying that a creature is unnatural and lacks a determinate nature, one may, then, in effect be expressing the thought that that creature is not in nature with us.[5] And, of course, when one is frightened of something, one would like to be able to think of it as not in nature with one, as outside one's world, and thus as no longer a threat. It is my speculation, then, that calling a creature a monster involves, or would involve, a kind of 'whistling in the dark' that psychologists call 'denial'. One denies the existence of danger, by thinking of a creature as a monster that is in effect outside one's world, in order to alleviate one's fear of a given creature. What one does is much like what one does when, in frightening or unhappy circumstances, one says, with momentary belief or hope: "I must be dreaming all this."

Of course, in calling a given creature an unnatural monster, one's description cannot in principle apply, on our theory. But on any depth-psychological account of such matters, one will not realize the inapplicability of one's description, and one's claim that a certain creature is a monster will at most be the expression of a necessarily false *unconscious* or *subconscious* belief that that creature is not in nature with one and thus no threat. But such an unconscious belief could function to alleviate or repress one's fear of the creature in question in a way that true beliefs, under the circumstances, could not. If this psychological picture is on the right track, then our claim that there cannot be non-fiction monsters is not tarnished by the fact that *terrified* ignorant[6] people would tend to apply 'monster' to certain actual creatures.[7] . . .

II

I shall now argue that the notion of an unnatural act (and of sexual perversion) is inapplicable in much the same way that the concept monster is. (For that reason, our arguments about these different concepts will be mutually reinforcing.) Philosophers have long been perplexed about what is meant by calling an act or behavior unnatural. In calling a (sexual) act unnatural, we are not just saying that it is wrong, since even those who condemn adultery do not call it unnatural. Nor is an unnatural act simply an unusual or incomprehensible one. Certain feats of sexual prowess, for example, are thought of as unusual, but not as unnatural. Since even believing Christians do not think of adultery as unnatural, unnatural acts cannot just be acts contravening the natural order of sexual morality instituted by God. Nor, finally, should we be led into the swamps of teleology to think of unnatural acts as being those that go against the purpose of sex. Even if it makes sense to suppose that there is a purpose to sex, namely,

procreation, it will be hard for any teleological theory to explain how anyone could think that oral-genital sex, as part of the build-up to coitus, was any more unnatural than kissing, as part of that build-up.

My own view is that the notion of an unnatural act is inapplicable and, like the idea of a monster, only gets used through people's fear and ignorance. The words 'unnatural act' express horror just as strongly as the term 'monster' expresses terror. To say that an act is unnatural is to say, in effect, that it is outside of nature, or our world. And such a claim cannot in principle be true.

The acts we call unnatural horrify us, but why should that make us put them outside our world, beyond the pale, as it were? Idiots are pretty horrifying too, but they are not called unnatural. The difference here may be that the kinds of acts people call unnatural are those that most people have some impulse towards that they cannot admit to having. If we are to believe depth psychology, most of us have inside us at some level, desires for incest, homosexuality, and even one or another form of fetishism. But these are the kinds of impulses people almost never, without undergoing therapy, admit having anything to do with. Sexual behavior for which we ourselves have repressed impulses is typically what gets called unnatural. It is thereby thought of as banished to another world than ours, and this helps reassure us that the impulse towards such behavior is not *in us*. There is no such need to keep repressed and disarmed the thought that we have elements of idiocy within, for there is no literal idiocy in most of us, and most of us know that. Similarly, we do not call adultery unnatural, because even those who think it wrong are usually willing to admit (to themselves) that they have some desires in that direction. But desires for incest, etc., typically are repressed and so threatening that drastic means will, if necessary, be used to keep those desires unconscious. The use of inapplicable concepts is certainly drastic enough. But I think that one's claim that certain behavior is unnatural will at most be the expression of a necessarily false *unconscious* belief that that behavior is not in the world with one, and one will not consciously realize the inapplicability of one's description. And such a 'drastic' unconscious belief is one very effective means by which a person can and does defuse the thought, and allay the fear, that such behavior is something he deep down desires. Thus in saying that certain behavior is unnatural, we give ourselves the 'message' that certain behavioral tendencies are not in the world with us, and so not in us, and this helps to repress these very tendencies. Of course, in saying all this, I have used depth-psychological assumptions that will seem suspect to some people. But I also think that the most important parts of our psychological arguments can be made independent of abstruse psychological theorizing and based simply on common-sense insight about human nature.

It would seem, finally, that the ordinary notion of perversion involves the idea of unnaturalness. Perverted sexual behavior is by definition unnatural sexual behavior, and since the latter notion is inapplicable, so is the former.[8] And when we call certain behavior perverted, in the ordinary sense, we express and counteract our impulses and fears in much the same way that we do when we call behavior unnatural. Of course, the terms 'perverted' and 'perversion' also occur in psychiatric and psychoanalytic writings. But if those terms express (a) valid applicable concept(s) in such contexts, that is, I believe, only because they are used there in a technical way. In their ordinary sense, use of those terms expresses horror, because it is tied to the notion of unnatural behavior. But technical usage of 'perverted' does not express horror, because, I believe, such usage does not involve the idea of unnaturalness. Psychiatrists presumably understand and are unafraid of 'perverted behavior' more than most people, so on our theory they have less motive or need to call such behavior unnatural than most people have.[9] And what also supports the idea that technical usage of 'perverted' does not involve the idea of unnaturalness is the fact that those professionals who speak of perversions (almost) never seem to speak of unnatural behavior in any technical or non-technical sense. Of course, we have not specified the actual content of the (a?) technical psychiatric concept of perversion, and this would be difficult to do. But whatever its full delineation, such a technical notion presumably at least involves the idea of deviation from some favored explanatorily rich ideal-typic model of the development of human sexual

motivation. In any event, we have in this paper seen how the ordinary notions of perversion, unnatural behavior, and monster could come to be frequently used in everyday life despite their inapplicability in principle to the actual, non-fiction world.[10]

Notes

1. I am indebted to many people for helpful comments on this paper, but especially to Saul Kripke, David Lewis, and Thomas Nagel.

2. Saul Kripke has suggested that phrases like 'in this story (world)' can be treated as sentential or predicate operators, on the model of modal operators. And 'in this story creature *a* has a determinate biological nature' does not obviously entail 'there is a determinate biological nature *x* such that creature *a* has *x* in this story.' If a storybook monster is biologically determinate *in* the world of its story, then it is not, on our view, a monster *in* that story (world). (Consider that in that world some philosopher could arrive at the conclusion that the creature in question was not a monster via the very arguments we use in the actual world to show that dinosaurs are not monsters.) If a storyteller calls such a creature a monster, this description may not be internally accurate to the world of the story and may simply be a way of telling the reader how he or she is entitled to think of the creature *from the point of view of the actual world.*

3. Here I have ignored the possibility of acausal creatures, since acausality seems in no way to help make a creature a monster. Incidentally, I am leaving open the possibility that something should have a determinate biological *nature* without being determinate in every respect. Thus my talk of determinacy of nature has been left somewhat vague. But it can at least be said that if a story-book creature is (described as) a tyrannosaurus rex, its nature is determinate enough so that the creature is not a story-book *monster*—even if other facts about it are left indeterminate.

4. I think 'monster' cannot be an applicable epistemic term, roughly equivalent to 'terrifying creature whose nature is unknown,' for it seems incompatible with our ordinary idea of a monster that something could become or cease to be a monster without undergoing any so-called internal or intrinsic alterations.

5. However, non-existence in nature (with us) does not, in turn, entail indeterminacy of nature, since a story could give a determinate nature to some purely imaginary creature by specifying, for example, that it was a tyrannosaurus rex.

6. Presumably, someone knowledgeable about dinosaurs would not think of one as a monster even if he confronted it in a dangerous situation. It is hard to think of something as unnatural when one knows its nature.

7. For classic psychoanalytic use of the idea that unconscious beliefs can help repress certain fears, see, e.g., Freud's 'Splitting of the Ego in the Defense Process' in his *Collected Papers,* Hogarth Press, London, 1956, vol. 5, pp. 372–75; and

O. Fenichel's *The Psychoanalytic Theory of Neurosis,* Norton, NY, 1945, pp. 474–84.

8. Even those who think the notion of perversion applies seem to believe that perversion entails unnaturalness. See T. Nagel's 'Sexual Perversion,' *Journal of Philosophy* 66, 1969, 5f. One problem with Nagel's account of perversion, incidentally, is that it leaves unexplained why so many people think of homosexuality as a perversion.

9. That is also why psychologically educated people do not usually speak of homosexuality and the like as unnatural acts.

10. There may be other inapplicable concepts related to the ones we have discussed. Some possibly inapplicable concepts that I think deserve exploration are: 'uncanny', 'eerie', 'freak', and 'obscene'.

We began this chapter with a discussion of the unnatural and saw that it was not an easy concept to delineate. We began with unnatural in order to show its link to the concept of perversion. This linkage also turned out to require quite a bit of analysis. Michael Levin, a philosopher at City University of New York, has argued that one of the clearest examples of something that is natural is the literal fit of a penis into a vagina. Any male whose sexual desire is to put his penis into an orifice other than a vagina is, according to Levin, acting on an abnormal desire. Levin thinks, therefore, that he has shown that homosexuality is abnormal. This does not mean, he is quick to point out, that homosexuality is immoral—only that it is abnormal, in an evolutionary sense, since it is evolution that has "decreed" the almost perfect fit. Thus to Levin, homosexuality would be perverse, where perverse meant only evolutionarily unwise (see his article, "Why Homosexuality Is Immoral," *The Monist,* 67, 1984).

The next chapter is devoted to arguments whose main focus *is* the morality of homosexuality.

CHAPTER 8

Homosexuality

CULTURAL AND HISTORICAL STUDIES REVEAL a wide range of attitudes concerning homosexuality, defined as the dominant sexual attraction to members of one's own sex. There can be little doubt that, in the United States, powerful feelings of hostility towards gay and lesbian people are widespread. Many people consider gays to be immoral, perverted, promiscuous child molesters given to repulsive and unnatural sexual behaviors. As late as the 1960s, there was widespread hostility toward homosexuals. Such attitudes often translated into violent actions toward gays and lesbians, such as beatings and killings (now regarded as hate crimes), job discrimination in both public and private sectors, and social ostracism. In the last two decades, many such negative attitudes have changed. In the 1960s, gay activist movements blossomed following the much-publicized "Stonewall Rebellion," named after the gay bar on Christopher Street in New York City's Greenwich Village. This marked the first militant action of gays in response to police arrests and eventuated in the formation of over 800 gay rights groups by 1975.[1]

The scientific literature has varied greatly regarding the number of people who are exclusively homosexual in orientation, ranging from 2 to 10 percent of Americans. Some of the more recent studies (Fay, et al., 1970 and 1988)[2] found that 2 percent of males had engaged in homosexual behavior in the preceding year. Seidman and Riedle found that 2 percent of males were currently exclusively homosexual, and Diamond (1993) found that 6 percent of males and 3 percent of women had engaged in homosexuality since adolescence.[3] The most recent highly regarded study, *Sex in America,* developed by the University of Chicago (1994) noted that 2.8 percent of males and 1.4 percent of women identified themselves as homosexual or bisexual.[4] In short, there are millions of individuals in the United States alone who are gay and whose lives and happiness are profoundly affected by society's attitudes and actions towards them.

From a philosophical point of view, this situation has generated several important questions. For example, if homosexuality is immoral, should it be illegal? Should homosexual behavior by consenting adults in private be prosecuted as a crime? From a legal standpoint, the U.S. Supreme Court in 1986 (*Bowers* vs. *Hardwick*) ruled that states had the power to prosecute homosexuals if they chose to do so. Should gays have the same civil rights as other citizens? Various states and communities have enacted laws granting gays minority protections, only to encounter strong opposition to affording them this status; some calls for the repeal of these laws have succeeded. More recently, questions have been raised about

---

[1]*Dimensions of Human Sexuality,* pp. 579–580.

[2]"Homosexuality," Richard C. Friedman, M.D. and Jennifer I. Downey, M.D., *New England Journal of Medicine* 331, no. 14 (1994).

[3]*Ibid.*

[4]Robert T. Michael, John H. Gagnon, Edward O. Laumann, and Gina Kolata, *Sex in America: A Definitive Study* (Boston: Little, Brown and Company, 1994), pp. 174–177.

gays serving in the armed forces and the legalization of gay marriages. Is homosexuality unnatural, and if so, in what sense? Is homosexuality harmful to society and/or to gays themselves?

Michael Ruse addresses the most fundamental question: Is homosexuality immoral? Of the many reasons offered in support of an affirmative answer to this question, Ruse is most concerned with examining the charge that homosexual behavior is biologically unnatural and therefore immoral. He then argues that this charge is both factually (empirically) false and logically unsound. He also observes that no major contemporary philosophical moral theory entails the judgment that homosexuality *per se* is immoral.

In his article, Dennis Prager does not so much argue the question of naturalness but rather, the overall effects on society of encouraging the gay lifestyle. He argues that the progress of Western civilization was achieved through the heterosexual monogamous marriage ideal and that a permissive attitude toward homosexual ideals will undermine this moral progress.

A brief statement by Sara Hoagland represents the views of many others who agree that the heterosexual marital ideal did indeed shape Western civilization, but rather than moral progress, the result is a civilization that has produced many serious social evils, such as imperialism, sexism, racism, etc.

HOMOSEXUALITY IS NOT IMMORAL

In the following article, Michael Ruse focuses on the question, is homosexuality immoral? After a brief survey of Greek, Jewish, and early Christian views, he summarizes the views of two major philosophical schools originated by Immanuel Kant and Jeremy Bentham.

Bentham and his philosophy of utilitarianism judge an act to be morally right if it produces the greatest amount of happiness for the greatest number of people. If homosexual acts produce more pleasure than pain, they are morally right. Using Kant's major moral principle, the categorical imperative ("Act so that you treat humanity, whether in your own person or in that of another, always as an end and never as a means only"), Ruse observes that although Kant himself condemns homosexuality because of its biological unnaturalness, Kant's moral principle cannot be used to argue that homosexuality is morally wrong. Ruse than examines three contemporary writers on the subject of sexual perversion (Nagel, Ruddick, Goldman) and notes that none of the three finds homosexuality immoral.

Ruse himself is most concerned about attacking an argument reaching back to Plato—that homosexuality is morally wrong because it is biologically unnatural. Here, Ruse offers four counterarguments:

1. If by calling homosexuality unnatural we mean that it does not occur in the animal world, that claim is empirically false. Homosexual acts are common in the animal kingdom.
2. Using the evolutionary notion of "kin selection," Ruse suggests homosexuality may have a biological function in humans.
3. It is wrong to base moral judgments on our animal or biological nature since we are also *cultural* beings, and moral judgments should reflect that fact.
4. It is always fallacious to argue solely from empirical facts to normative conclusions as to what ought to be.

Based on these arguments and other material in his article, Ruse concludes that it is bad science to argue that homosexuality is biologically unnatural; in addition, there is nothing in standard philosophical moral theory that condemns homosexuality. He further concludes that while many consider homosexuality to be a perversion, something people, as cultural beings, view as disgusting and revolting, such judgments are subjective and relative. That is, some people find homosexuality perverted, and others do not. However, subjective judgments of perversion do not entail or justify judgments of objective moral wrongness.

from The Morality of Homosexuality

MICHAEL RUSE

Is Homosexuality Bad Sexuality Because It Is Biologically Unnatural?

A key philosophical charge against homosexual activity is that it is "unnatural." "Nature," in this context, is intended to refer to our *biological* nature. Hence, the conclusion is drawn that such activity should be condemned as immoral. This was the cry of Plato, it was echoed by Aquinas and Kant, and it is still with us today. There are a number of points I want to make about this argument.

First, if we mean by "homosexuality is unnatural" that it is never a practice to be found in the animal world—and this is certainly what Plato thought—then the claim is simply false. There is a substantial body of evidence that supports the conclusion that homosexual activity is widespread throughout the animal world. Virtually every animal whose activity has been studied in detail shows some forms of homosexual behavior. Mutual masturbation, anal intercourse, and so forth, are commonplace in the primate world. Similarly, amongst other mammals, we find all sorts of activity that can only truly be spoken of as "homosexual," in some sense. One male will mount another and come to climax. Analogously, females show deep bonds and sexual type behavior towards each other. Sometimes this behavior of animals is manifested just in young animals. In other cases, the homosexual activity is ongoing, if not exclusive (see Weinrich 1982 for details and references).

If homosexual activity is so widespread in the animal world, why has it not been noted before? In fact, it has been noted before; but, with their usual selectivity, people writing on human sexuality have failed to note it or have simply been ignorant about it. Then again, there has been such a fixed notion that homosexuality belongs exclusively to the human world, that people simply have not been able to see animal homosexuality—even when they have been presented with the clearest evidence of it.

A revealing example of this selective vision is given by a recent researcher on mountain sheep. He wrote two books on the subject: one in 1971 and the other a short time later (Geist 1971; 1975). In the first book, there was a great deal of discussion of male dominance and pecking order, with alpha males fighting and subduing beta males. In the second book, the author came right out and said what he had been seeing all along was homosexual activity. The alpha males mount the beta males, having erections and emissions, sometimes involving anal intercourse. Candidly, the author admitted that he simply had not been able to bring himself to think of this as homosexuality. In his own words: "Those magnificent animals, queers?" This case is atypical only in that the researcher was more candid than most. If one's desire is to argue that homosexuality is unnatural, the animal world is certainly not the place to look.

A second pertinent point is that homosexuality might have a biological function in humans. The basic mechanism of the central biological theory of Darwinian evolution is "natural selection"; or "the survival of the fittest." Those organisms more successful at reproducing than others pass on their units of inheritance—their genes—and are thus the organisms most represented in the next and future generations. Given enough time, this process leads to full-blown evolution.

Reproduction is the key to evolutionary success. It is possible, however, to reproduce by proxy. Suppose that, instead of reproducing oneself, one aids close relatives to reproduce more efficiently. Then, in a sense, one is increasing the representation of one's own units of inheritance in the next and future generations, simply because one shares these units of inheritance with close relatives. This vicarious reproduction is known as "kin selection," and it has been very extensively documented in the animal world, particularly in the hymenoptera (ants, bees, and wasps). (For a quick introduction to Darwinism, see Ruse 1982. For more on kin selection, see Wilson 1975 or Dawkins 1976.)

Kin selection in humans provides a possible biological explanation of the homosexual lifestyle, as an alternative reproductive strategy. Recent research has shown that, in nonindustrial societies, male homosexuals frequently fit a pattern one would expect were kin selection operating (Weinrich 1976). These males would probably not be efficient as direct reproducers, because of such factors as debilitating childhood illnesses. They do, however, hold positions in society that can significantly aid close relatives. For example, in many American Indian tribes homosexuals take on the role of the shaman—that is, of a kind of magical figure who has to be consulted by the tribe before great events like battles can take place. The shaman has considerable power and financial influence within the community. He is, thus, in a strong position to aid close relatives (siblings, nephews, nieces, and so on). There is, moreover, evidence that such help actually occurs. It seems plausible to suppose, therefore, that in such cases biology itself has promoted genes for manifesting homosexual inclinations and activity.

If indeed kin selection, or some like process, does operate in a way such as that just suggested, then biology is at least a partial cause of human homosexuality. It would therefore be odd to speak of homosexuality as being "unnatural." If by "natural," you mean that which nature has done, homosexuality would be as natural as heterosexuality. Indeed, forcing homosexuals to live heterosexual lifestyles would be unnatural from a biological point of view, not the converse. (The evidence for the biological foundations of human homosexuality is presented in detail, together with various explanatory models, in Ruse 1981.)

A third point is so obvious that it is usually overlooked. We humans do not live in a world of strict biology. We are cultural creatures, which is why we are so successful as a species. We have speech, customs, religion, literature, art—and even philosophy. To speak of humans as "just animals" is to ignore half the story. Any evaluation of human homosexuality from a natural or unnatural perspective must, therefore, take our culture into account. The fact that we do not always do the things that animals do, does not mean that it is unnatural for us not to do such things. It is simply a reflection of the fact that, by nature, we are not as other animals (Lumsden and Wilson 1981).

Hence, if homosexual activity is part of human culture—and it certainly is in many respects—then to speak of it as "unnatural," judged purely from a physiological perspective, is simply meaningless. It could indeed be true that animals do not practice homosexual activity (although, it so happens that it is not true); it could be true that humans do, in fact, practice homosexual activity (as indeed they do); but, the conclusion would not necessarily be that human homosexuality is unnatural. The conclusion could simply be that such behavior is part of our human nature and not part of animal nature.

Finally, let me point out that even if homosexuality were biologically unnatural, this need not make it immoral. Because we do something which is against our biological nature, it does not follow that the act is wrong. As many philosophers have pointed out, to argue from what *is* (i.e., biological nature) to what *ought* to be (i.e., the morally desirable) is a fallacy. Whether we do something or not is one thing. Whether it is moral or immoral is quite another. The two are not logically connected.

There are, then, four independent rejoinders to the "unnatural" argument that has dominated both classical and modern discussions of homosexuality: it is false that animals are not homosexual; it is false that homosexuality must be antireproductive and nonbiological; it is false that homosexuality is to be judged without taking note of the cultural nature of humans; and it is false that what is unnatural is necessarily immoral.

THE KANTIAN ANALYSIS

Kant was strongly against homosexuality. Obviously, apart from any religious biases Kant may have had, whatever he himself may have thought, essentially this opposition was based on the homosexuality-as-unnatural thesis. Assuming that the arguments of the last sections are effective, what then of the basic Kantian philosophy? Can one indulge in homosexual activity and yet be true to the Categorical Imperative? Kant himself did not think so. Nevertheless, my own sense of sex in general, and of homosexuality in particular, is that once St. Paul and Plato are put aside, the Categorical Imperative is far less of an impediment to variant sex than its author supposed (see also Baumrin 1975).

The Categorical Imperative demands that people be treated as ends, and not as means only. "Act so that you treat humanity, whether in your own person or in that of another, always as an end and never as a means only" (Kant 1959, p. 47). Nothing in the Imperative itself rules out the possibility of the relationship being a homosexual one, rather than heterosexual. Homosexuals, male or female, fall in love with partners and, under any meaningful sense of the term, treat those partners as ends and not simply as means. Thus, homosexual activity as such is not ruled out by the Categorical Imperative. Indeed, in the right circumstances, a Kantian should rather think that one ought to behave homosexually. (Suppose, for instance, one were faced with a choice of would-be partners, one of the same sex and one of the other sex, and one was oneself drawn homosexually to the same sex partner—and to act otherwise would involve deceit and unkindness.)[1]

The Utilitarian Analysis

Turning to the other great moral theory, let us first distinguish between the two main versions of utilitarianism. There is that associated with the name of Jeremy Bentham (1948), and there is that associated with the name of John Stuart Mill (1910). Benthan argued that the utility against which the consequences of all acts should be judged is any kind of pleasure that one finds desirable. He made no distinction between various pleasures or happinesses. John Stuart Mill, on the other hand, argued strongly that one can grade pleasures and happinesses and that some are much to be preferred to others. In particular, Mill argued that the more intellectual sorts of pleasures are more worthwhile. "Better to be Socrates dissatisfied than a fool satisfied" (Mill 1910, p. 9).

A Benthamite utilitarian appears to endorse homosexual activity just as did Bentham himself. If an individual enjoys homosexual activity, then it is a good thing for that person and she/he should strive to maximize its occurrence. Moreover, assuming that others enjoy it also, he/she should strive to let them enjoy it to the full.

What about Mill? I am not sure that a Millian would be quite as easy about sex as a Benthamite; but with regard to homosexual activity as such, the conclusion seems similar. Certainly, a Mill-type utilitarian would think that activity within a loving relationship, whether heterosexual or homosexual, was a good thing and ought to be promoted. Indeed, as with the Kantian analysis, there will be cases where a Millian (as well as a Benthamite) could urge homosexual activity on someone—not to show affection and not to act homosexually would be wrong.

Is Homosexuality Perverted?

Is homosexual behavior perverted behavior? With Nagel's critics, I would argue that he described something better called "incomplete" sex than "perverted" sex. But, like Nagel, I doubt that the notion of completeness in itself throws much moral light on sexuality—certainly, it throws no more light than that gained from the traditional moral theories just discussed. If some sex is bad sex, it is not so much because it is incomplete; rather, it is because the sex violates the Categorical Imperative or fails to lead to true happiness.

Does this mean that the notion of sexual "perversion" is an empty one? Not at all. Despite my earlier strictures about the concept of "naturalness" as it occurs in the philosophical literature, I do not want to deny that in some sense the perverted is the nonnatural or the unnatural. But, for reasons given, naturalness cannot be defined in terms of pure biology, as argued by philosophers from Plato to Ruddick. Humans are cultural beings, and what is natural must be understood in terms of culture. Hence, the unnatural—the perverted—is something that goes against cultural norms.

What exactly does this mean? A purely statistical definition, as offered by Goldman, will not do. Being in a minority is not as such nonnatural or perverse. Rather, nonnatural sex is sex that goes against our personal nature as cultural beings. It is something that we simply would not want to do even if we could. Remember the story of Gyges in Plato's *Republic.* He was the fellow who found a ring that enabled him to become invisible. As a result of this, he seized power in the kingdom, killing the king and seducing the queen. We can all understand what Gyges was up to, and even though we may not approve of his actions, we do not find them absurd or weird or nonnatural.

Unnaturalness is something that we simply would not want to do, even if we had gotten Gyges's ring. More particularly, it is something we could not imagine wanting to do. I might not want to murder, even though the ring enables me to do it. I can imagine playing Gyges's role, however. Suppose that, thanks to the ring, I could now spend my days concealed in the corner of a public lavatory, watching and smelling people defecate. I cannot imagine putting the ring to that use. In short, that activity for me, would be unnatural. It would be a "perversion." (Note that not all perversions are necessarily sexual. I am not sure that watching folks defecate would be.)

Thus, I argue that the perverse is the unnatural, where the unnatural is that which goes against what an individual finds culturally comprehensible.[2] The perverse is that which one cannot even conceive of wanting to do, even if one could. Now, this raises a number of questions. First, does the notion of perversion, as defined, have any value connotations? Second, would such value connota-tions (if they exist) necessarily be moral value connotations? Third, where does this leave the question of homosexual activity? Let me take these questions in turn, briefly.

First, the notion of perversion does have strong value connotations. There is little doubt (except perhaps in minds of academic philosophers), that when we speak of something as "perverted," we mean that it is in some way vile or disgusting. Just above, I gave an example of something I consider a perversion. Would it surprise you to learn that I found it difficult simply to write it down? It shouldn't! It's a perversion! In my opinion, hanging around the lavatories, watching and smelling others defecate, is a thoroughly disgusting thing to do. That is the whole point of my reference to Gyges and his ring. Watching and smelling people defecate is something that I cannot even conceive of wanting to do. I do not want to steal a camera from my colleague's office, but I can certainly conceive of situations where I might do something like this. I do not find the thought of stealing a friend's camera disgusting, although I do find it shameful. Hence, there are strong value connotations involved in the notion of perversion or nonnaturalness.

Second, what of the connection between perversion and morality? Undoubtedly, that which is perverted is often immoral. For instance, strangling a small child and simultaneously raping her is both perverted and grossly immoral. However, this does not mean that the notions of perversion and morality are logically connected. Certainly, that which is immoral is not always perverted. Stealing a colleague's camera would be an immoral act; but it would not be a perverted act.

Are all perverted acts immoral acts? I doubt it. Would my example above be immoral? Perhaps you would think it an invasion of privacy. But what if I waited until the lavatories were empty, and then went in to drink from the urinals? This would be perverted; but, I'm not at all sure that it would be immoral. Of course, the simple fact of the matter is that that which is perverse is often immoral because many things that we cannot even conceive of wanting to do would be immoral things to do. Any connections of this type are contingent rather than logical. Hence, although perversion has with it an element of disgust, which does surely involve values, perversion in itself does not entail a moral repulsion. Therefore, although those who argue that perversion is in some sense bad are right, they are also right when they argue that this badness is not in itself a moral badness. It is more something akin to an aesthetic badness.[3] We are revolted by perversions, but this does not necessarily entail moral condemnation.[4]

Third and finally, what about the connection between homosexuality and perversion? Note that the way in which I have characterized "perversion" makes it a subjective phenomenon, which could vary from person to person within a culture. Some people find certain things revolting, others do not. Expectedly, the same goes for perversions. Thus, for instance, I do not find oral sex a particularly revolting phenomenon. On the other hand, other people find it thoroughly disgusting. For me, therefore, oral sex is not a perversion. For others, oral sex clearly is a perversion.

What does all this mean for homosexuality, especially as it applies to contemporary North America? The answer is relativistic. For some people, homosexuality is indeed a perversion. They find it disgusting and recoil from the very thought of it. Others (not necessarily just homosexuals) do not find homosexual activity a perversion. This is not to say that everybody who finds homosexuality not to be perverted, wants to behave homosexually. But, it is to say that such people could, in some sense, imagine freely doing it—at least, they can put themselves in the place of someone who would want to do it. They are certainly not overwhelmed by a sense of disgust.[5]

Hence, I argue that there is no straightforward answer to the question of whether or not homosexuality is a perversion. Some people regard it as such; others do not. Clearly, we have had something of a change in the last fifty years, with fewer people now thinking homosexual activity perverted. Perhaps, we will continue to see a change. As things stand at the moment, for some people homosexuality is a perversion, and this is all there is to be said on the matter. As a consequence of this, for some people in our society, homosexuality is not the best kind of sex. For them, it is aesthetically inferior (more bluntly, it is revolting sex). But this is not to say that those who think this

way are therefore justified in inferring that homosexuality is immoral. (Although, I am sure that many do, in fact, conclude this.) For others, homosexuality is not a perversion; it is not in any sense inferior or worse sex.

Is Homosexuality Bad Sexuality?

Let us list the conclusions. First, it is simply bad science to go on arguing that human homosexual activity is biologically unnatural. Even if it were, this would tell us nothing of its moral status.

Second, although religion is *prima facie* hostile to homosexuality (and probably truly hostile), there is nothing in the standard philosophical theories of moral behavior that outrightly condemns homosexual activity. Both Kantians and utilitarians can and should approve of homosexual activity *per se*.

Third, the notion of perversion properly understood does have value connotations; namely, negative values or revulsion and disgust. Undoubtedly, many people in our society do find homosexual activity revolting. For them it is a perversion. However, this is not a universal feeling. There are heterosexuals, as well as homosexuals, who do not look upon such activity as a perversion. For them, homosexuality is perfectly good sexuality.

In response to the title of this essay, therefore, I reply that, in important respects, homosexuality is certainly not bad sexuality. It is perfectly good sexuality. However, many people look upon homosexual activity as a perversion. That is a fact, and no amount of empathetic philosophizing can change this. This is not to say, however, that the possibility of changing people's opinions is not open to us all. As philosophers, caring about human beings, aware of how much hatred today is directed towards homosexuals, we have a special obligation to work toward such change.

Notes

1. In this discussion, I am simply considering basic homosexual activity, essentially between two people who have some feeling for each other. I am not considering possible moral complications, like group sex, since presumably they are not distinctive homosexual matters. However, I must note that male homosexuals are often given to highly promiscuous be-

havior (Bell and Weinberg, 1978). Were one to think this a moral issue, then as a matter of fact this would be of particular concern in a full analysis of homosexual activity as it typically occurs. See Elliston (1975) for a spirited argument for the value of promiscuity; although, he does qualify his enthusiasm by allowing the promiscuity as a "limited value in the movement toward a sexual idea," which ideal involves "a full commitment to a single other" (p. 240). I am not sure that much male, promiscuous homosexual activity is properly viewed as moving towards such an ideal. Also, current health threats, such as Acquired Immune Deficiency Syndrome (AIDS), ought to be considered. See Silverstein and White 1977, and *Science 83* (April 1983), for more on these matters.

2. In this essay, I will just deal with perversion at the individual level, where society as a whole is undecided on the subject. This seems to me to be the case for homosexuality in our society today. But, a full analysis of perversion would need reference to when a society as a whole could be said to consider a practice "perverted." This would clearly need discussion of the way most people felt, but would probably also need to refer to other societal beliefs, like religion.

3. A philosophical emotivist could argue that, since ethics is all feelings, morality and perversion collapse together. Since I am not a philosophical emotivist in any usual sense, this is not my worry.

4. If, as Kant argues, one has obligations to oneself, then it might be argued that one ought not degrade oneself by performing that which one finds perverted. But, as will be seen, it does not follow that one must judge others immoral for doing what they do and not find perverted, even though the individual judging does find it to be immoral. Nor, speaking now as an enthusiast for Mill's views on liberty, does it follow that one should at once try to stop that which one would judge perverted. I thus disagree with Devlin's (1965) views about the propriety of legislating on private practices; although, as a matter of fact Devlin himself spoke out against antihomosexual laws.

5. In associating perversion with unnaturalness and disgust, my thinking parallels Slote (1975). However, I see no reason to argue as he does that "the kinds of acts people call unnatural are those that most people have some impulse toward that they cannot or will not admit to having" (p. 263). This may often be true, and perhaps in the case of homosexuality explains the violent emotions engulfing many homophobics. But I deny having even subconscious coprophilic tendencies.

Bibliography

AQUINAS, ST. T. (1968). *Summa Theologiae,* 43, *Temperance* (2a 2ae, 141–54). Trans. T. Gilby, (London: Blackfriars).

AUGUSTINE, A. (1909). *Confessions.* Trans. E. B. Pusey, (London: Dent).

BAILEY, D. S. (1955). *Homosexuality and the Western Christian Tradition.* (London: Longmans, Green and Co.)

BAKER, R., AND F. ELLISTON (EDS) (1975). *Philosophy and Sex.* (Buffalo, NY: Prometheus).

BAUMRIN, B. (1975). "Sexual Immorality Delineated." In R. Baker and F. Elliston (eds) 1975. *Philosophy and Sex.* (Buffalo, NY: Prometheus), 116–128, herein pp. 300–311.

BELL, ALAN P. AND MARTIN S. WEINBERG (1978). *Homosexualities: A Study of Diversity Among Men and Women.* (New York: Simon and Schuster).

BENTHAM, J. (1948). *An Introduction to the Principles of Morals and Legislation.* (New York: Hafner).

———, 1978). "Offences Against One's Self: Paederasty," *J. Homosexuality,* 3(4), 383–405; 1(4), 91–107, pp. 385–402.

BIEBER, I., H. J. DAIN, P. R. DINCE, M. G. DRELLICH, H. G. GRAND, R. H. GUNDLACH, M. W. KREMER, A. H. RIFKIN, C. B. WILBUR, AND T. B. BIEBER (1962). *Homosexuality: A Psychoanalytic Study of Male Homosexuals.* (New York: Basic Books).

BOSWELL, J. (1980). *Christianity, Social Tolerance, and Homosexuality.* (Chicago: Chicago University Press).

DE BEAUVOIR, S. (1953). *The Second Sex.* (New York: Knopf).

DEVLIN, P. (1965). *The Enforcement of Morals.* (Oxford: Oxford University Press).

DOVER, K. J. (1978). *Greek Homosexuality.* (Cambridge, MA: Harvard University Press).

ELLISTON, F. (1975). "In Defense of Promiscuity." In R. Baker and F. Elliston (eds) 1975. *Philosophy and Sex.* (Buffalo, NY: Prometheus), 222–243.

FREUD, S. (1905). *Three Essays on the Theory of Sexuality.* In J. Strachey (ed) *Collected Works of Freud,* 7. (London: Hogarth, 1953), 125–243.

GEIST, V. (1971). *Mountain Sheep: A Study in Behavior and Evolution.* (Chicago: University of Chicago Press).

———, 1975. *Mountain Sheep and Man in the Northern Wilds.* (Ithaca, NY: Cornell University Press).

GOLDMAN, A. H. (1977). "Plain Sex." *Philosophy and Public Affairs,* 6, 267–88.

HORNER, T. (1978). *Jonathan Loved David.* (Philadelphia: Westminster).

KANT, I. (1959). *Foundations of the Metaphysics of Morals.* Trans. L. W. Beck. (Indianapolis: Bobbs-Merrill).

———, (1963). *Lectures on Ethics.* Trans. L. Infield. (New York: Harper and Row).

KENYON, F. (1974). "Female Homosexuality: A Review." In: *Understanding Homosexuality: Its Biological and Psychological Bases,* edited by J. A. Loraine, pp. 83–119. (New York: American Elsevier).

KINSEY, A. C., B. POMEROY AND E. MARTIN (1948). *Sexual Behavior in the Human Male.* (Philadelphia: W. B. Saunders).

KINSEY, A. C. et al. (1953). *Sexual Behavior in the Human Female.* (Philadelphia: W. B. Saunders).

MILL, J. S. (1910). *Utilitarianism, Liberty, and Representative Government.* (London: Dent).

NAGEL, T. (1969). "Sexual Perversion." *Journal of Philosophy,* 66, 1–17. Reprinted in R. Baker and E. F. Elliston (eds) 1975. *Philosophy and Sex.* (Buffalo, NY: Prometheus), 247–260, herein pp. 268–279.

PLATO (1961). *The Collected Dialogues,* ed. E. Hamilton and H. Cairns. (Princeton, NJ: Princeton University Press).

Ramsay, R. W., P. M. Heringa and I. Boorsma (1974). "A Case Study: Homosexuality in the Netherlands." In J. A. Loraine (ed) *Understanding Homosexuality: Its Biological and Psychological Bases.* (New York: American Elsevier), 121–40.

Ruddick, S. (1975). "Better Sex." In R. Baker and F. Elliston (eds). *Philosophy and Sex.* (Buffalo, NY: Prometheus), 83–104, herein 280–299.

Ruse, Michael (1980). "Are Homosexuals Sick?" In *Current Concepts of Health and Disease,* ed A. Caplan, H. T. Engelhardt Jr., and J. McCartney. (Boston: Addison-Wesley), 693–723.

———. (1981). "Are There Gay Genes? Sociobiology Looks at Homosexuality," *Journal of Homosexuality,* 6(4), 5–34.

Sartre, J-P. (1962). *Saint Genet.* (Paris: Gallimard).

Silverstein, C., and E. White (1977). *The Joy of Gay Sex.* (New York: Simon and Schuster).

Slote, M. (1975). "Inapplicable Concepts and Sexual Perversion." In R. Baker and F. Elliston (eds) 1975. *Philosophy and Sex.* (Buffalo, NY: Prometheus), 261–267.

Weinrich, J. D. (1976). *Human Reproductive Strategy. I. Environmental Predictability and Reproductive Strategy: Effects of Social Class and Race. II. Homosexuality and Non-Reproduction; Some Evolutionary Models.* Unpublished Ph.D. thesis, Harvard University.

———, (1982). "Is Homosexuality Biologically Natural?" In W. Paul, J. D. Weinrich, J. C. Gonsiorek, and M. E. Hotvedt eds. *Homosexuality: Social, Psychological, and Biological Issues.* (Beverly Hills: Sage), 197–208.

Ruse has presented a variety of arguments to show that homosexuality is not immoral. He primarily targets the traditional argument from nature. Is Ruse's argument rationally persuasive? Can the reader generate counterexamples or alternative arguments to refute it?

Ruse claims there is nothing in standard philosophical moral theories that condemns homosexuality. One such theory is that of utilitarianism, which classically takes the form of hedonism, or the view that an act is right to the extent that it increases overall happiness and pleasure and wrong if it increases misery, suffering, or displeasure. Some writers have argued that homosexuality does indeed increase unhappiness and displeasure, while others claim there is no clear evidence it produces more unhappiness than heterosexuality. From a utilitarian perspective, the empirical facts of homosexuality do generate a moral conclusion. This suggests the claim that no standard moral theory condemns homosexuality may be open to question.

In the following article, Dennis Prager will argue against homosexuality in a manner that could also be put in utilitarian terms. That is, if the condemnation of homosexuality was the major cause of the growth and perpetuation of Western civilization, and Western civilization is the one that produces the greatest happiness over all alternative cultures, then the condemnation of homosexuality may be morally justified. Once again, given utilitarian moral theory, the factual claims become important. With this in mind, we turn to the argument of Dennis Prager.

HOMOSEXUALITY UNDERMINES THE BENEFITS OF HETEROSEXUALISM

In "Homosexuality, the Bible, and Us—A Jewish Perspective," Dennis Prager argues against the encouragement of homosexuality insofar as it undermines Western civilization. For Prager, the origin and development of Western civilization is based in the original sexual revolution begun by the Jewish Torah and perpetuated by Christianity. The essence of this revolution was the containment of the unrestrained, polymorphous, and promiscuous male natural sex drive, a drive so strong as to control not only his own life, but the life of society as well. The principal ideal of Judaism, which is the marital ideal of one man to one woman, and the central importance of the family are powerful tools to constrain the socially destructive male sexual desire.

Surveying several ancient cultures, Prager argues that where homosexuality is socially accepted, women are devalued and peripheral to society. Judaism began the revolution by desexualizing God and strongly condemning homosexuality. In so doing, it elevated the status of women and started the drive towards sexual equality.

According to Prager, prior to Judaism, judgments about sex were not concerned with gender, and the major distinctions about sex involved identifying the doer/penetrator and the receiver or one penetrated. For Prager, Judaism invented the concept of homosexuality to emphasize the importance of gender and the idea that sex is not merely an activity with interchangeable partners.

Prager argues that given the overwhelming importance of the heterosexual marital ideal as the bedrock of Western civilization, we should reject the tolerance of homosexuality in order to foster the family. Thus, homosexuality is wrong since it undermines socially important ideals.[1]

Having developed his general moral arguments against homosexuality, Prager then turns to several current practical issues. Although he argues for the decriminalization of homosexuality in private, he does not believe that homosexuality should be publicly encouraged as a social ideal. With regard to homosexual ordination, he advocates a "don't ask, don't tell" policy. Gay marriage should not be allowed as it subverts the heterosexual marital ideal. He argues against discrimination in employment except for two conditions discussed in his article. Finally, Prager emphasizes that although we must reject public acceptance of homosexuality, we should love, care for, and accept homosexuals within our community.

from Homosexuality, the Bible, and Us— A Jewish Perspective

DENNIS PRAGER

Of all the issues that tear at our society, few provoke as much emotion, or seem as complex, as the question of homosexuality.

Most homosexuals and their heterosexual supporters argue that homosexuality is an inborn condition, and one, moreover, that is no less valid than heterosexuality. They maintain that to discriminate in any way against a person because of his or her sexual orientation is the moral equivalent of discrimination against a person on the basis of color or religion; that is to say, bigotry plain and simple.

On the other hand there are those who feel, no less passionately, that homosexuality is wrong, that society must cultivate the heterosexual marital ideal, or society's very foundations will be threatened.

In the middle are many who are torn between these two claims. I have been one of them. Generally speaking, I do not concern myself with the actions of consenting adults in the privacy of their homes, and I certainly oppose government involvement with what consenting adults do in private. In addition, both lesbians and homosexual men have been part of my life as friends and relatives.

At the same time, I am a Jew who reveres Judaism. And my religion not only prohibits homo-

---

[1] For a Jewish debate concerning the morality of homosexuality, see Appendix A, pp. 403ff.

From "Homosexuality, the Bible, and Us—A Jewish Perspective" by Dennis Prager in *The Public Interest,* Number 112, Summer 1993, pp. 60–82, © 1993 by National Affairs, Inc. This article is based upon an earlier version titled "Judaism, Homosexuality and Civilization" appearing in *Ultimate Issues,* Volume 6, Number 2 (April–June 1990). Reprinted with the permission of the author and *The Public Interest.*

sexuality, it unequivocally, unambiguously, and in the strongest language at its disposal, condemns it. Judaism—and Christianity—hold that martial sex must be the ideal to which society aspires. Thus my instinct to tolerate all non-coercive behavior runs counter to the deepest moral claims of my source of values.

This is not all. Adding to the seeming complexity are the questions of choice and psychopathology. Current homosexual doctrine holds that homosexuals are born homosexual, and that homosexuality is in no way a psychological or emotional deviation. Are these claims true? And if they are, what are we to do with Western society's (i.e., Judaism's and Christianity's) opposition to homosexuality? What are we to do with our gut instinct that men and women should make love and marry each other, not their own sex? Have Judaism and Christianity been wrong? Is our instinctive reaction no more than a heterosexual bias? And what about those of us who have two gut instincts—one that favors heterosexual love, and one that believes "live and let live"? These two feelings seem irreconcilable, and they have caused me and millions of others anguish and confusion.

After prolonged immersion in the subject, I continue to have anguish about the subject of homosexuality, but, to my great surprise, much less confusion. I hope that the reader will undergo a similar process, and it is to this end that I devote this article.

THE NATURE OF SEX

Man's nature, undisciplined by values; will allow sex to dominate his life and the life of society. When Judaism first demanded that all sexual activity be channeled into marriage, it changed the world. It is not overstated to say that the Hebrew Bible's prohibition of non-marital sex made the creation of Western civilization possible. Societies that did not place boundaries around sexuality were stymied in their development. The subsequent dominance of the Western world can, to a significant extent, be attributed to the sexual revolution, initiated by Judaism and later carried forward by Christianity.

This revolution consisted of forcing the sexual genie into the marital bottle. It ensured that sex no longer dominated society, it heightened male-female love and sexuality (and thereby almost alone created the possibility of love and eroticism within marriage), and it began the arduous task of elevating the status of women.

It is probably impossible for us who live thousands of years after Judaism began this process to perceive the extent to which sex can dominate, and has dominated, life. Throughout the ancient world, and up to the recent past in many parts of the world, sexuality infused virtually all of society.

Human sexuality, especially male sexuality, is polymorphous, or utterly wild (far more so than animal sexuality). Men have had sex with women and with men; with little girls and young boys; with a single partner and in large groups; with immediate family members; and with a variety of domesticated animals. They have achieved orgasm with inanimate objects such as leather, shoes, and other pieces of clothing; through urinating and defecating on each other (interested readers can see a photograph of the former at select art museums in America exhibiting the works of the gay photographer Robert Mapplethorpe); by dressing in women's garments; by watching other human beings being tortured; by fondling children of either sex; by listening to a man or woman's disembodied voice (e.g., phone sex); and, of course, by looking at pictures of bodies, or parts of bodies. There is little, animate or inanimate, that has not excited some men to orgasm.

Of course, not all of these practices have been condoned by societies—parent-child incest and seducing another man's wife have rarely been countenanced—but many have, and all illustrate what the unchanneled, or in Freudian terms, the "unsublimated," sex drive can lead to.

DESEXUALIZING GOD AND RELIGION

Among the consequences of the unchanneled sex drive is the sexualization of everything—including religion. Unless the sex drive is appropriately harnessed (not squelched, which leads to its own consequences), higher religion cannot develop.

Thus, the first thing the Hebrew Bible did was

to desexualize God: "In the beginning God created the heavens and the earth"—by His will, not through any sexual behavior. This was an utterly radical break with all religion, and it alone changed human history. The gods of virtually all civilizations engaged in sexual relations. The gods of Babylon, Canaan, Egypt, Greece, and Rome were, in fact, extremely promiscuous, both with other gods and with mortals.

Given the sexual activity of the gods, it is not surprising that the religions themselves were replete with all forms of sexual activity. In the ancient Near East and elsewhere, virgins were deflowered by priests before marriage, and sacred or ritual prostitution was almost universal.

The Hebrew Bible was the first to place controls on sexual activity. It could no longer dominate religion and social life. It was to be sanctified—which in Hebrew means "separated"—from the world and placed in the home, in the bed of husband and wife. The restriction of sexual behavior by Judaism (and later Christianity) was one of the essential elements that enabled society to progress.

THE UBIQUITY OF HOMOSEXUALITY

The new restrictions were nowhere more radical, more challenging to the prevailing assumptions of mankind, than with regard to homosexuality. Indeed, for all intents and purposes, Judaism may be said to have invented the notion of homosexuality, for in the ancient world sexuality was not divided between heterosexuality and homosexuality. That division was the Bible's doing. Before the Bible, the world divided sexuality, between penetrator (active partner) and penetrated (passive partner).

As Martha Nussbaum, professor of philosophy at Brown University, has written, the ancients were no more concerned with people's gender preference than people today are with others' eating preferences:

Ancient categories of sexual experience differed considerably from our own. . . . The central distinction in sexual morality was the distinction between active and passive roles. *The gender of the object . . . is not in itself morally problematic.* Boys and women are very often treated interchangeably as objects of [male] desire. What is socially important is to penetrate rather than to be penetrated. Sex is understood fundamentally not as an interaction, but as a doing of something to someone. . . .[1] [emphasis added]

Judaism changed this. It rendered the "gender of the object" very "morally problematic"; it declared that no one is "interchangeable" sexually; and, as a result, it ensured that sex would in fact be "fundamentally interaction" and not simply "a doing of something to someone." The Hebrew Bible condemned homosexuality in the most powerful and unambiguous language it could: "Thou shalt not lie with mankind, as with womankind; it is an abomination."

To appreciate the extent of the revolution wrought by this prohibition of homosexuality, and the demand that all sexual interaction be male-female, it is first necessary to appreciate just how universally accepted and practiced homosexuality has been throughout the world.

It is biblical sexual values, not homosexuality, that have been deviant. In order to make this point clear, I will cite but a handful of historical examples. Without these examples, this claim would seem unbelievable.

Ancient Near East

Egyptian culture believed that "homosexual intercourse with a god was auspicious," writes New York University sociology professor David Greenberg in *The Construction of Homosexuality.* Having anal intercourse with a god was the sign of a man's mastery over fear of the god. Thus one Egyptian coffin text reads, "Atum [a god] has no power over me, for I copulate between his buttocks."[2] In another coffin text, the deceased person vows, "I will swallow for myself the phallus of [the god] Re."[3] In Mesopotamia, Hammurabi, the author of the famous legal code bearing his name, had male lovers.[4]

Greece

Homosexuality was not only a conspicuous feature of life in ancient Greece, it was exalted. The seduction of young boys by older men was expected and honored. Those who could afford, in time and money, to seduce young boys, did so. Graphic depictions of man-boy sex adorn countless Greek vases.

"Sexual intimacy between men was widespread throughout ancient Greek civilization. . . . What was accepted and practiced among the leading citizens was bisexuality; a man was expected to sire a large number of offspring and to head a family while engaging a male lover."[5]

As Greenberg writes, "The Greeks assumed that ordinarily sexual choices were not mutually exclusive, but rather that people were generally capable of responding erotically to beauty in both sexes. Often they could and did."

"Sparta, too, institutionalized homosexual relations between mature men and adolescent boys." In Sparta, homosexuality "seems to have been universal among male citizens."

Rome

Homosexuality was so common in Rome that Edward Gibbon in his *History of the Decline and Fall of the Roman Empire* wrote that "of the first fifteen emperors Claudius was the only one whose taste in love was entirely correct: (i.e., not homosexual)."[6]

According to psychiatrist and social historian Norman Sussman, "In contrast to the self-conscious and elaborate efforts of the Greeks to glorify and idealize homosexuality, the Romans simply accepted it as a matter of fact and as an inevitable part of human sexual life. Pederasty was just another sexual activity. Many of the most prominent men in Roman society were bisexual if not homosexual. Julius Caesar was called by his contemporaries every woman's man and every man's woman."[7]

The Arab World

Greenberg notes that a de facto acceptance of male homosexuality has prevailed in Arab lands down to the modern era. As early as the tenth century, German historians depicted Christian men as preferring martyrdom to submitting to Arab sexual demands.

In the words of one of the world's great scholars of Islam, Marshall G. S. Hodgson, "The sexual relations of a mature man with a subordinate youth were so readily accepted in upper-class circles that there was often little or no effort to conceal their existence."[8]

Edward Westermark observed that "it is a common belief among the Arabic-speaking mountaineers of Northern Morocco that a boy cannot learn the Koran well unless a scribe commits pederasty with him. So also an apprentice is supposed to learn his trade by having intercourse with his master."[9]

Greenberg writes: "In Morocco . . . pederasty has been an 'established custom,' with boys readily available in the towns. . . .

"In nineteenth-century Algeria, 'the streets and public places swarmed with boys of remarkable beauty who more than shared with the women the favor of the wealthier natives.'"[10]

As for non-Arab Islam, "the situation," Greenberg concludes, "has been little different."

And this is only a cursory review. Homosexuality was also prevalent among pre-Columbian Americans; the Celts, Gauls, and pre-Norman English; the Chinese, Japanese, and Thai; and dozens of other nationalities and cultures. Greenberg summarizes the ubiquitous nature of homosexuality in these words: "With only a few exceptions, male homosexuality was not stigmatized or repressed so long as it conformed to norms regarding gender and the relative ages and statuses of the partners. . . . The major exceptions to this acceptance seem to have arisen in two circumstances."

Both of these circumstances were Jewish.

JUDAISM AND HOMOSEXUALITY

The Hebrew Bible, in particular the Torah (the first five books of the Bible), has done more to civilize the world than any other book or idea in history. It is the Hebrew Bible that gave humanity such ideas as a universal, moral, loving God; ethical obligations to this God; the need for history to move forward to moral and spiritual redemption; the belief that history has meaning; and the notion that human freedom and social justice are the divinely desired states for all people. It gave the world the Ten Commandments and ethical monotheism.

Therefore, when this Bible makes strong moral proclamations, I listen with great respect. And regarding male homosexuality—female homosexuality is not mentioned—this Bible speaks in such clear and direct language that one does not have to be a religious fundamentalist in order to be influenced by its views. All that is necessary is to consider oneself a serious Jew or Christian.

Jews or Christians who take the Bible's views on homosexuality seriously are not obligated to prove that they are not fundamentalists or literalists, let alone bigots (though people have used the Bible to defend bigotry). The onus is on those who view homosexuality as compatible with Judaism or Christianity to reconcile this view with their Bible.

Given the unambiguous nature of the biblical attitude toward homosexuality, however, such a reconciliation is not possible. All that is possible is to declare: "I am aware that the Bible condemns homosexuality, and I consider the Bible wrong." That would be an intellectually honest approach.

But this approach leads to another problem. If one chooses which of the Bible's moral values to take seriously (and the Bible states its prohibition of homosexuality not only as a law, but as a value—"it is an abomination"), of what moral use is the Bible?

Advocates of religious acceptance of homosexuality respond that while the Bible is morally advanced in some areas, it is morally regressive in others. Its condemnation of homosexuality is cited as one example, and the Torah's acceptance of slavery as another.

Far from being immoral, however, the Torah's prohibition of homosexuality was a major part of its liberation of the human being from the bonds of unrestrained sexuality and of women from being peripheral to men's lives.

As for slavery, while the Bible declares homosexuality wrong, it never declares slavery good. If it did, I would have to reject the Bible as a document with moral relevance to our times. With its notion of every human being created in Gods' image and with its central event being liberation from slavery, it was the Torah which first taught humanity that slavery is wrong. The Torah's laws regarding slavery exist not to perpetuate it, but to humanize it. And within Jewish life, these laws worked. Furthermore, the slavery that is discussed in the Torah bears no resemblance to black slavery or other instances with which we are familiar. Such slavery, which includes the kidnapping of utterly innocent people, was prohibited by the Torah.

Another argument advanced by advocates of religious acceptance of homosexuality is that the Bible prescribes the death penalty for a multitude of sins, including such seemingly inconsequential acts as gathering wood on the Sabbath. Since we no longer condemn people who violate the Sabbath, why continue to condemn people who engage in homosexual acts?

The answer is that we do not derive our approach toward homosexuality only from the fact that the Torah made it a capital offense. We learn it from the fact that the Bible *makes a moral statement* about homosexuality. It makes no such statement about gathering wood on the Sabbath. The Torah uses its strongest term of disapprobation, "abomination," to describe homosexuality. It is the Bible's moral evaluation of homosexuality that distinguishes homosexuality from other offenses, capital or otherwise. As Professor Greenberg, who betrays no inclination toward religious belief, writes, "When the word *toevah* ("abomination") does appear in the Hebrew Bible, it is something applied to idolatry, cult prostitution, magic, or divination, and is sometimes used more generally. *It always conveys great repugnance*" [emphasis added].

Moreover, it lists homosexuality together with child sacrifice among the "abominations" practiced by the peoples living in the land about to be conquered by the Jews. The two are certainly not morally equatable, but they both characterized the morally primitive world that Judaism opposed. They both characterized a way of life opposite to the one that God demanded of Jews (and even of non-Jews—homosexuality is among the sexual offenses that is covered by one of the "seven laws of the children of Noah" which Judaism holds all people must observe).

Finally, the Bible adds a unique threat to the Jews if they engage in homosexuality and the other offenses of the Canaanites: "You will be vomited out of the land" just as the non-Jews who practice these things were vomited out of the land. Again, as Greenberg notes, this threat "suggests that the offenses were considered serious indeed."

WHY JUDAISM OPPOSES HOMOSEXUALITY

It is impossible for Judaism to make peace with homosexuality, because homosexuality denies many of Judaism's most fundamental values. It denies life; it denies God's expressed desire that men and women cohabit; and it denies the root structure that the Bible prescribes for all mankind, the family.

"Choose Life"

If one can speak of Judaism's essence, it is contained in the Torah statement, "I have set before you life and death, the blessing and the curse, and you shall choose life." Judaism affirms whatever enhances life, and it opposes or separates whatever represents death. Thus, meat (death) is separated from milk (life); menstruation (death) is separated from sexual intercourse (life); carnivorous animals (death) are separated from vegetarian, kosher animals (life). This is probably why the Torah juxtaposes child sacrifice with male homosexuality. Though they are not morally analogous, both represent death: One deprives children of life, the other prevents their having life.

Men Need Women

God's first declaration about man (the human being generally, and the male specifically) is, "It is not good for man to be alone." Now, presumably, in order to solve the problem of man's aloneness, God could have made another man, or even a community of men. However, God solved man's aloneness by creating one other person, a woman—not a man, not a few women, not a community of men and women. Man's solitude was not a function of his not being with other people; it was a function of his being without a woman.

Of course, Judaism also holds that women need men. But both the Torah statement and Jewish law have been more adamant about men marrying than about women marrying. Judaism is worried about what happens to men and to society when men do not channel their drives into marriage. In this regard, the Torah and Judaism were highly prescient: The overwhelming majority of violent crimes are committed by unmarried men.

In order to become fully human, male and female must join. In the words of Genesis, "God created the human . . . male and female He created them." The union of male and female is not merely some lovely ideal; it is the essence of the biblical outlook on becoming human. To deny it is tantamount to denying a primary purpose of life.

The Family

Throughout their history, one of the Jews' most distinguishing characteristics has been their commitment to family life. To Judaism, the family—not the nation, and not the individual—is to be the fundamental unit, the building block of society. Thus, when God blesses Abraham, He says, "Through you all the families of the earth will be blessed."

Homosexuality's Effect on Women

Yet another reason for Judaism's opposition to homosexuality is homosexuality's negative effect on women. There appears to be a direct correlation between the prevalence of male homosexuality and the relegation of women to a low societal role. At the same time, the emancipation of women has been a function of Western civilization, the civilization least tolerant of homosexuality.

In societies where men sought out men for love and sex, women were relegated to society's periphery. Thus, for example, ancient Greece, which elevated homosexuality to an ideal, was characterized, in Sussman's words, by "a misogynistic attitude." Homosexuality in ancient Greece, he writes, "was closely linked to an idealized concept of the man as the focus of intellectual and physical activities."

Classicist Eva Keuls describes Athens at its height of philosophical and artistic greatness as "a society dominated by men who sequester their wives and daughters, denigrate the female role in reproduction, erect monuments to the male genitalia, have sex with the sons of their peers. . . ."

In medieval France, when men stressed male-male love, it "implied a corresponding lack of interest in women. In the *Song of Roland*, a French mini-epic given its final form in the late eleventh or twelfth century, women appear only as shadowy, marginal figures: 'The deepest signs of affection in the poem, as well as in similar ones, appear in the love of man for man. . . .'"[11]

The women of Arab society, wherein male homosexuality has been widespread, have a notably low status. In traditional Chinese culture, as well, the low state of women has been linked to widespread homosexuality.[12]

While traditional Judaism is not as egalitarian as many late twentieth century Jews would like, it was Judaism, very much through its insistence on marriage and family and its rejection of infidelity and homosexuality, that initiated the process of elevating the status of women. While other cultures were writing homoerotic poetry, the Jews wrote the *Song of Songs,* one of the most beautiful poems depicting male-female sensual love ever written.

The Male Homosexual Lifestyle

A final reason for opposition to homosexuality is the homosexual lifestyle. While it is possible for male homosexuals to live lives of fidelity comparable to those of heterosexual males, it is usually not the case. While the typical lesbian has had fewer than ten sexual partners, the typical male homosexual in America has had over 500.[13] In general, neither homosexuals nor heterosexuals confront the fact that it is this male homosexual lifestyle, more than the specific homosexual act, that disturbs most people.

This is probably why less attention is paid to female homosexuality. When male sexuality is not controlled, the consequences are considerably more destructive than when female sexuality is not controlled. Men rape. Women do not. Men, not women, engage in fetishes. Men are more frequently consumed by their sex drive, and wander from sex partner to sex partner. Men, not women, are sexually sadistic.

The indiscriminate sex that characterizes much of male homosexual life represents the antithesis of Judaism's goal of elevating human life from the animal-like to the God-like.

THE JEWISH SEXUAL IDEAL

Judaism has a sexual ideal—marital sex. All other forms of sexual behavior, though not equally wrong, deviate from that ideal. The further they deviate, the stronger Judaism's antipathy. Thus there are varying degrees of sexual wrongs. There is, one could say, a continuum of wrong which goes from premarital sex, to adultery, and on to homosexuality, incest, and bestiality.

We can better understand why Judaism rejects homosexuality by understanding its attitudes toward these other unacceptable practices. For example, if a Jew were to argue that never marrying is as equally valid a lifestyle as marrying, normative Judaism would forcefully reject this claim. Judaism states that a life without marrying is a less holy, less complete, and a less Jewish life. Thus, only married men were allowed to be high priests, and only men who had children could sit as judges on the Jewish supreme court, the Sanhedrin.

To put it in modern terms, while an unmarried rabbi can be the spiritual leader of a congregation, he would be dismissed by almost any congregation if he publicly argued that remaining single is as Jewishly valid a way of life as married life.

Despite all this, no Jew could argue that single Jews must be ostracized from Jewish communal life. Single Jews are to be loved and included in Jewish family, social, and religious life.

These attitudes toward not marrying should help clarify Judaism's attitude toward homosexuality. First, it contradicts the Jewish ideal. Second, it cannot be held to be equally valid. Third, those publicly committed to it may not serve as public Jewish role models. But fourth, homosexuals must be included in Jewish communal life and loved as fellow human beings and as Jews.

We cannot open the Jewish door to non-marital sex. For once one argues that any non-marital form of sexual behavior is as valid as marital sex, the door is opened to *all* other forms of sexual expression. If consensual homosexual activity is valid, why not consensual incest between adults? Why is sex between an adult brother and sister more objectionable than sex between two adult men? If a couple agrees, why not allow consensual adultery? Once non-marital sex is validated, how can we draw any line? Why shouldn't gay liberation be followed by incest liberation?

Accepting homosexuality as the social, moral, or religious equivalent of heterosexuality would constitute the first modern assault on the extremely hard-won, millennia-old battle for a family-based, sexually monogamous society. While it is labeled as progress, the acceptance of homosexuality would not be new at all.

IS HOMOSEXUALITY WRONG (EVEN IF HOMOSEXUALS HAVE NO CHOICE)?

To all the previous arguments offered against homosexuality, the most frequent response is: But homosexuals have no choice. To many people this claim is so emotionally powerful than no further reflection seems necessary. How can we oppose actions that people have not chosen?

But upon a moment's reflection, the answer becomes very clear: "Homosexuals have no choice," when true, is a defense of the homosexual, not of his conduct.

It may be necessary to oppose actions even if they are not performed voluntarily. We do it all the time, and in all spheres of life. It is what keeps psychiatrists and the courts so busy.

The issue of whether homosexuals have any choice may be terribly important, but even if we were to conclude that they do not, that conclusion would in no way invalidate any of the objections Judaism raises against homosexuality. *Whether or not homosexuals choose homosexuality is entirely unrelated to the question of whether society ought to regard it as an equally valid way of life.*

If Judaism's arguments against homosexuality are valid, then even if we hold that homosexuals have no choice, we will have to conclude that nature or early nurture has foisted upon some people a tragic burden. But how to deal with a tragic burden is a very different question from whether Judaism, Christianity, and Western civilization should drop their heterosexual marital ideal.

In fact, to society at large, gays do not generally argue that a homosexual life is entirely as valid as a heterosexual life. Even if they believe this, few heterosexuals would agree with it. So, gays offer the argument that garners the most heterosexual sympathy—that homosexuals have no choice.

And to those homosexuals who truly have no choice, we do owe sympathy. But sympathy is one thing, and the denial of our value system is quite another. Chosen or not, homosexuality remains opposable. If chosen, we argue against the choice; if not chosen, we offer compassion while retaining our heterosexual marital ideals.

IS HOMOSEXUALITY CHOSEN?

The question of choice, then, is unrelated to the question of homosexuality's rightness or wrongness. But we must still try to resolve the question of whether homosexuality is chosen.

The question is always posed as, "Do homosexuals choose homosexuality?" When phrased this way, the answer usually seems obvious. One hardly imagines an adult sitting down and debating whether to become a homosexual or a heterosexual. But the question is much more instructive when posed in a more specific way: Is homosexuality biologically programmed from birth, or is it socially and psychologically induced?

There is clearly no one answer that accounts for all homosexuals. What can be said for certain is that some homosexuals were started along that path in early childhood, and that most homosexuals, having had sex with both sexes, prefer homosexual sex to heterosexual sex.

We can say "prefer" because the vast majority of gay men have had intercourse with women. As a four-year study of 128 gay men by a UCLA professor of psychology revealed, "More than 92 percent of the gay men had dated a woman at some time, two-thirds had sexual intercourse with a woman."[14]

Moreover, if homosexuality is biologically determined, how are we to account for the vastly differing numbers of homosexuals in different societies? As far as we know, most upper-class men practiced homosexuality in ancient Greece, yet we know that there has been very little homosexuality, for example, among Orthodox Jews.

Wherever homosexuality has been encouraged, far more people have engaged in it. And wherever heterosexuality has been discouraged, homosexuality has similarly flourished, as, for example, in prisons and elsewhere: as Greenberg has written, "High levels of homoeroticism develop in boarding schools, monasteries, isolated rural regions, and on ships with all-male crews."[15]

As for female homosexuality, many lesbian spokeswomen argue passionately that lesbianism is indeed a choice to be made, not a biological inevitability. To cite but two of many such examples, Charlotte Bunch, an editor of *Lesbians and the Women's Movement* (1975), wrote: "Lesbianism is the key to liberation and only women who cut their ties to male privilege can be trusted to remain serious in the struggle against male dominance." And Jill Johnson, in her book, *Lesbian Nation: The Feminist Solution* (1973), wrote: "The continued collusion of any woman with any man is an event that retards the progress of women's supremacy."

Of course, one could argue that homosexuality is biologically determined, but that society, if it suppresses it enough, causes most homosexuals to suppress their homosexuality. Yet, if this argument is true, if society can successfully repress homosexual inclinations, it can lead to either of two conclusions—that society should do so (socially, not legally) for its own sake, or that society should not do so for the individual's sake. Once again we come back to the question of values.

Or, one could argue that people are naturally (i.e., biologically) bisexual (and given the data on human sexuality, this may be true). Ironically, however, if this is true, the argument that homosexuality is chosen is strengthened, not weakened. For if we all have bisexual tendencies, and most of us successfully suppress our homosexual impulses, then obviously homosexuality is frequently both surmountable and chosen. And once again we are brought back to our original question of what sexual ideal society ought to foster—heterosexual marital or homosexual sex.

To sum up:

1) Homosexuality may be biologically induced, but is certainly psychologically ingrained (perhaps indelibly) at a very early age in some cases. Presumably, these individuals always have had sexual desires only for their own sex. Historically, they appear to constitute a minority among homosexuals.

2) In some cases, homosexuality appears not to be indelibly ingrained. These individuals have gravitated toward homosexuality from heterosexual experiences, or have always been bisexual, or live in a society that encourages homosexuality. As Greenberg, who is very sympathetic to gay liberation, writes, "Biologists who view most traits as inherited, and psychologists who think sexual preferences are largely determined in early childhood, may pay little attention to the finding that many gay people have had extensive heterosexual experience."

3) Therefore, the evidence overwhelmingly leads to this conclusion: By and large, it is society, not the individual, that chooses whether homosexuality will be widely practiced. A society's values, much more than individuals' tendencies, determine the extent of homosexuality in that society.

Thus we can have great sympathy for the exclusively homosexual individual while strongly opposing social acceptance of homosexuality. In this way we retain both our hearts and our values.

WHAT ARE WE TO DO?

We could conceivably hold that while heterosexual sex ought to be society's ideal, society should not discriminate against homosexuals. This solution, however, while tempting, is not as tidy as it sounds. For the moment one holds that homosexuality is less socially or morally desirable than heterosexuality, discrimination, in some form, becomes inevitable. For example, it is very difficult to hold that marriage and family must be society's ideal and at the same time advocate homosexual marriage.

More than other issues, homosexuality seems to force one into an extreme position. Either you accept homosexuality completely or you end up supporting some form of discrimination. The moment you hesitate to sanction homosexual marriage, or homosexual men as Big Brothers to young boys, or the ordaining of avowed homosexuals, you have agreed to discrimination against homosexuals. And then the ACLU, gay activists, and others will lump you with the religious right wing.

This is why many liberals find it difficult not to side with *all* the demands of gay activists. They terribly fear being lumped with right-wingers. And they loathe the thought of discriminating against minorities. Gay activists have been quite successful at depicting themselves as another persecuted minority, and this label tugs at the conscience of moral individuals, both liberal and conservative. Of course, in some ways this label is deserved, since gays are a minority, and they certainly have been persecuted. But they are not a persecuted minority in the same way that, let us say, blacks have been. Sexual lifestyle is qualitatively different from skin color.

Since blacks have been discriminated against for what they are and homosexuals have been discriminated against for what they do, a moral distinction between the two types of discrimination can be made in a handful of areas. This in no way exonerates gay-bashing or gay-baiting, let alone such evils as the Nazi or communist incarcerations of gays. But it does mean that a moral distinction between discrimination against behavior and discrimination against color is possible. For example, there is no moral basis to objecting to blacks marrying whites, but there is a moral basis for objecting to homosexual marriage.

That is why gay activists fight against every single vestige of discrimination against homosexuality. They intuit that even one form of discrimination—prohibiting homosexual marriages, for example—means that society differs only in degree from those who declare homosexuality "an abomination."

This is a problem with which I continue to wrestle. I want gays to have the rights that I have. But not everything I am allowed to do is a right. Marriage, for example, is not a universal right (see below), nor, even more so, is religious ordination.

DECRIMINALIZING HOMOSEXUALITY

Before dealing with areas where discriminating on behalf of marital heterosexuality may be proper, let us deal with the areas where discrimination is not morally defensible.

Twenty-three states in the United States continue to have laws against private homosexual relations. I am opposed to these laws. Whatever my misgivings about homosexuality may be, they do not undo my opposition to the state's interference in private consensual relations between adults. Those who wish to retain such laws need to explain where, if ever, they will draw their line. Should we criminalize adultery? After all, adultery is prohibited by the Ten Commandments.

What should be permitted in private, however, does not have to be permitted in all areas of society. Thus, for example, while I am for decriminalizing prostitution, I would not allow the transactions to take place in public or permit prostitutes to advertise on billboards, radio, or television.

To decriminalize an act is not to deem it as socially acceptable as any other act. But social acceptance is precisely what gay liberation aims for—and also where the majority of society disagrees with gay liberation.

I suspect that in this regard most people feel as I do—antipathy to gay-baiting, gay-bashing, and to the criminalization of private gay behavior, while simultaneously holding that homosexuality is not an equally viable alternative. Given these admittedly somewhat contradictory positions, what are we to do?

I believe that we ought to conduct public policy along these guidelines:

1) We may distinguish between that which grants homosexuals basic rights and that which honors homosexuality as a societally desirable way to live.

2) Therefore, we may discriminate on behalf of the heterosexual marital ideal, but not against the individual homosexual in the private arena—for example, where and how a homosexual lives.

HOMOSEXUAL ORDINATION

The most obvious area wherein the distinction between rights and public acceptance of homosexuality manifests itself is religion. It is, after all, Western religion that most fought confining sexual activity to marriage.

It is therefore not surprising that few Christian or Jewish mainstream denominations, even liberal ones, ordain individuals who publicly declare themselves homosexual.

The issue is only secondarily the individual's sex life. It is primarily one of values. If a candidate for ordination at any of the Jewish seminaries engaged in cross-dressing, a clear violation of a Torah law, or took a personal vow of celibacy, another violation of Jewish law (at least for men), but in neither instance announced it, it would not be the admissions committee's task to inquire about such things. But if a rabbinic student were to announce that he is a transvestite or that remaining single is as desirable to Judaism as being married, he should not be ordained.

In sexual matters, the issue is what is advocated and what is lived publicly far more than what is privately practiced. An organization should be able to choose spokesmen who publicly support its ideals; that sort of "discrimination" is perfectly legitimate.

HOMOSEXUAL MARRIAGE

Gay activists and some liberal groups such as the ACLU argue for the right of homosexuals to marry. Generally, two arguments are advanced—that society should not deny anyone the right to marry, and that if male homosexuals were given the right to marry, they would be considerably less likely to cruise.

The first argument is specious because there is no "right to marry." There is no right to marry more than one partner at a time, or to marry an immediate member of one's family. Society does not allow either practice. Though the ACLU and others believe that society has no rights, only individuals do, most Americans feel otherwise. Whether this will continue to be so, as Judaism and Christianity lose their influence, remains to be seen.

The second argument may have some merit, and insofar as homosexual marriages would decrease promiscuity among gay men, it would be a very positive development for both gays and society. But homosexual marriage would be unlikely to have such an effect. The male propensity to promiscuity would simply overwhelm most homosexual males' marriage vows. It is women who keep most heterosexual men monogamous, or at least far less likely to cruise, but gay men have no

such brake on their cruising natures. Male nature, not the inability to marry, compels gay men to wander from man to man. This is proven by the behavior of lesbians, who, though also prevented from marrying each other, are not promiscuous.

HOMOSEXUAL EMPLOYMENT

In general, not hiring a person because he or she is gay is morally indefensible. There are, however, at least two exceptions which necessitate the use of the qualifier, "in general."

In some rare cases in which sexual attraction, or non-attraction, is an absolutely relevant aspect of a job, a case can be made for discrimination against gays in hiring. The armed forces are one possible example. One reason for not admitting gays into combat units is the same reason for not allowing women and men to share army barracks. The sexual tension caused by individuals who may be sexually interested in one another could undermine effectiveness.

Big Brothers provides a second example. Just as heterosexual men are not allowed to serve as Big Brothers to girls, gay men should not be allowed to serve as Big Brothers to boys. The reason is not anti-homosexual any more than not allowing heterosexual men to be Big Brothers to girls is anti-heterosexual; it is common sense. We do not want Big Brothers to be potentially sexually attracted to the young people with whom they are entrusted. It is not because we trust homosexual men less; it is because we do not trust male sexual nature with any minor to whom a male may be sexually attracted.

My own view is that, in general, if employees work responsibly, their off-duty hours are their own business. This is not the view of many liberals and conservatives today, however. Off-hours "womanizing" ended the career of the leading contender for the Democratic Party's presidential nomination of 1988. And it was a major reason for not approving a secretary of defense-designate. Ironically, the voting public often seems far more tolerant of "manizing" than of womanizing. Rep. Barney Frank's male lover ran a male prostitution ring from the congressman's apartment, yet Frank seems to be as popular with his constituency as ever. Such behavior on the part of a heterosexual would doubtless have led to his resignation from Congress.

BEHAVIOR TOWARD HOMOSEXUALS

Violence against homosexuals has claimed numerous lives over the past decade, and too often the law seems to regard it as less of a crime than the murder of heterosexuals. In 1976, when a gay college student was beaten to death by teenagers in front of a Tucson bar, the judge imposed no penalty. In 1984, a Bangor, Maine, judge released to custody of their parents three teenage boys who had beaten and thrown a young gay man into a stream. In 1988, a Texas judge eased the sentence of a man who murdered two homosexuals because, in the judge's words, "I put prostitutes and gays at about the same level, and I'd be hard put to give somebody life for killing a prostitute."[16]

According to a National Gay Task Force study, one-fourth to one-third of gay men have been assaulted or threatened with violence. Even if the figures are exaggerated by a factor of two, they are terrible. And they may actually be understated, since many homosexuals do not wish to report such crimes for fear of embarrassment.

Unfortunately, religious opponents of homosexuality can abet this type of behavior. It should go without saying, but, unfortunately, it needs to be said that the homosexual is created in God's image as much as every other person, and that a homosexual can be as decent a human being as anyone else.

It should also go without saying but, again, it needs to be said that to hurt a homosexual, to be insensitive to a homosexual because of the person's homosexuality, is despicable. Likewise, I believe that when a parent severs relations with a child because of the child's homosexuality, it is a terrible and mutually destructive act.

Gay-bashing, gay-baiting, and jokes that mock (as opposed to poking good-natured fun at) homosexuals have no place in a decent society.

I can confirm from personal experience the truth of the gay activist claim that nearly all of us know or come into regular contact with gay people. From childhood, I was aware that a member of our family circle, one of my mother's cousins, was a gay man; my closest friend during my college year in England was a homosexual; and a proofreader of my journal for two years, one of my closest co-workers, was a lesbian.

I have regarded these people as no less worthy of friendship than my priest friends whose celibacy I do not agree with, or my bachelor friends whose decisions not to marry I disagree with.

"HOMOPHOBIA"

Just as we owe homosexuals humane, decent, and respectful conduct, homosexuals owe the same to the rest of us. Homosexuals' use of the term "homophobic," however, violates this rule as much as heterosexuals' use of the term "faggot" does.

When the term "homophobic" is used to describe anyone who believes that heterosexuality should remain Western societies' ideal, it is quite simply a contemporary form of McCarthyism. In fact, it is more insidious than the late senator's use of "communist." For one thing, there was and is such a thing as a communist. But "homophobia" masquerades as a scientific description of a phobia that does not exist in any medical list of phobias.

Yet the insidiousness of the term really lies elsewhere and abuses psychology in order to dismiss a human being with values the name-caller does not like. It dismisses a persons' views as being the product of unconscious pathological fear that is not only demeaning, it is unanswerable. Indeed, the more one denies it, the more the label sticks.

Whenever I hear the term, unless it is used to describe thugs who beat innocent homosexuals, I know that the user of the term has no argument, only McCarthy-like demagoguery, with which to rebut others. To hold that heterosexual marital sex is preferable to all other expressions of sexuality is no more "homophobic" than it is "incest-phobic" to oppose incest, or "beastphobic" to want humans to make love only to their own species.

Finally, those who throw around the term "homophobic ought to recognize the principle of "that which goes around comes around." We can easily descend into name-calling. Shall we start by labeling male homosexuals "women-phobic" and "vagina-phobic," and lesbians "men-phobic" and "penis-phobic"? It makes as much sense, and it is just as filthy a tactic.

Good people can differ about the desirability of alternative modes of sexual expression. There are many good people who care for homosexuals, and yet fear the chiseling away of the West's family-centered sex-in-marriage ideal. They merit debate, not the label "homophobic." And there are good homosexuals who argue otherwise. They, too, merit debate, not the label "faggot."

WHAT IS AT STAKE

The creation of Western civilization has been a terribly difficult and unique thing. It took a constant delaying of gratification, and a rechanneling of natural instincts; and these disciplines have not always been well received. There have been numerous attempts to undo Judeo-Christian civilization, not infrequently by Jews (through radical politics) and Christians (through antisemitism).

And the bedrock of this civilization, and of Jewish life, of course, has been the centrality and purity of family life. But the family is not a natural unit so much as it is a *value* that must be cultivated and protected. The Greeks assaulted the family in the name of beauty and Eros. The Marxists assaulted the family in the name of progress. And, today, gay liberation assaults in it the name of compassion and equality. I understand why gays would do this. Life has been miserable for many of them. What I have not understood is why Jews and Christians would join the assault.

I do now. They do not know what is at stake. At stake is our civilization. It is very easy to forget what Judaism has wrought and what Christians have created in the West. But those who loathe this civilization never forget. The radical Stanford University faculty and students who chanted, "Hey, hey, ho, ho, Western civ has go to go," were referring to much more than their university's syllabus.

And no one is chanting that song more forcefully than those who believe and advocate that sexual behavior doesn't play a role in building or eroding a civilization.

Notes

1. Martha Nussbaum, "The Bondage and Freedom of Eros," *Times Literary Supplement,* June 1–7, 1990.

2. Terence J. Deakin, "Evidence of Homosexuality in Ancient Egypt," *International Journal of Greek Love.* Cited in David E. Greenberg, *The Construction of Homosexuality* (Chicago: University of Chicago Press, 1988).

3. Raymond O. Faulkner, *The Ancient Egyptian Coffin Texts* (Aris and Phillips, 1973). Cited in Greenberg.

4. W. L. Moran, "New Evidence from Mari on the History of Prophecy," *Biblica: 50, 1969.* Cited in Greenberg.

5. Norman Sussman, "Sex and Sexuality in History," *The Sexual Experience,* eds. Sadock, Kaplan and Freedman (Baltimore: Williams & Wilkins, 1976).

6. Edward Gibbon, *History of the Decline and Fall of the Roman Empire,* Vol. 1, London, 1898. Cited in John Boswell, *Christianity, Social Tolerance, and Homosexuality* (Chicago: University of Chicago Press, 1980).

7. Sussman.

8. Marshall G. S. Hodgson, *The Venture of Islam,* Vol. 2 (Chicago: University of Chicago Press, 1974).

9. Edward Westermark, *Ritual and Belief in Morocco,* Vol. 1 (London: Macmillan, 1926). Cited in Greenberg.

10. Greenberg.

11. Greenberg.

12. Cited in Arno Karlen, *Sexuality and Homosexuality* (New York: Norton, 1971).

13. Alan Bell and Martin Weinberg, *Homosexualities,* Alfred Kinsey Institute for Sex Research (New York: Simon and Schuster, 1978).

14. Letitia Anne Peplau, "What Homosexuals Want," *Psychology Today,* March 1981.

15. Greenberg.

16. "Texas Judge Eases Sentence for Killer of 2 Homosexuals," *New York Times,* December 17, 1988.

Prager presents a passionate and thought-provoking argument for the condemnation of public approval of homosexuality. There are so many issues addressed in his essay that the reader should have a full plate upon which to reflect. For example, is it true that the condemnation of homosexuality was a major factor in the evolution of Western culture? If so, is it still a necessary sanction to sustain Western culture? Was it a predominant feature over other causal factors such as the development of science, democratic political institutions—with emphasis on individual human rights and liberties—economic organization, natural resources, etc.? If the monogamous heterosexual ideal is such a worthy ideal, is it really threatened if a small minority of people do not embrace it? Is it not possible for heterosexuals and homosexuals to coexist without the destruction of Western civilization and its achievements?

Another critical question is raised in the following brief selection by Sarah Lucia Hoagland. That is, if the condemnation of homosexuality, or what is sometimes referred to as compulsory heterosexuality, is indeed the bedrock of Western civilization, is Western civilization as we know it the morally ideal civilization? As we shall see in the next article, some argue that Western culture is far from ideal and in fact generates a host of social evils, such as racism, sexism, and imperialism.

LESBIANISM AVOIDS THE EVILS OF HETEROSEXUALISM

As we have seen, Prager's attack on homosexuality was based on two central assumptions: (1) that the ideal of heterosexual monogamy is the backbone of Western civilization, and (2) that Western civilization is itself a high point in human moral progress. The following brief selection from Sarah Lucia Hoagland's *Lesbian Ethics* is included to illustrate that many thinkers, most prominently feminist thinkers, agree that heterosexuality and heterosexual marriages are the backbone of Western civilization, but they claim this is more of a curse than a blessing. In her discussion, Hoagland cites what she takes to be many of the resultant evils engendered by compulsory heterosexual societies, including sexism, racism, and capitalism.

from Lesbian Ethics

SARAH LUCIA HOAGLAND

And I began to question the focus of u.s. feminism. Thinking about analyses developed by radical lesbians in québec and france, I have become convinced that the concept 'woman' is a created category, like the concept 'feminine', and is bankrupt. 'Woman' exists only in relation to 'man' (someone who dominates), and as long as this identity holds, male domination of women will appear socially desirable and, even, natural.

As a result, I mean to contrast lesbianism and heterosexualism. What I am talking about when I talk about heterosexualism is not simply a matter of men having procreative sex with women. I am talking about an entire way of life promoted and enforced by every formal and informal institution of the fathers' society, from religion to pornography to unpaid housework to medicine. Heterosexualism is a way of living that normalizes the dominance of one person and the subordination of another.

The relationship between women and men is considered in anglo-european thought to be the foundation of civilization. I agree. And it normalizes that which is integral to anglo-european civilization to such an extent that we cease to perceive dominance and subordination in any of their

From *Lesbian Ethics* by Sarah Lucia Hoagland (Chicago, Illinois: Institute of Lesbian Studies, 1988), pp. 7–8, 67–68. Used by permission of the Institute of Lesbian Studies, P.O. Box 25568, Chicago, Illinois 60625.

benevolent capacities as wrong or harmful: the "loving" relationship between men and women, the "protective" relationship between imperialists and the colonized, the "peace-keeping" relationship between democracy (u.s. capitalism) and threats to democracy. I believe that unless heterosexualism as a way of relating is undermined, there will always remain in social conscience concepts which validate oppression.

Thus, I focus on 'lesbian' because I am interested in exploring lesbianism as a challenge to heterosexualism, where heterosexualism is a matter of men (or the masculine) dominating women (or the feminine), whether that be as protectors or predators, whether that domination be benevolent or malevolent. And I am interested in exploring ways to work the dominance and subordination of heterosexualism out of lesbian choices.

In general, aside from the fact that the situations I write about are located in lesbian community, I dream lesbianism mostly because of certain possibilities embedded in it. More importantly, lesbian connection and creation to date move me as a lesbian—and make these possibilities I write of more than idle speculations. . . .

• • •

The need to control and be controlled in relationships is central to the dominant/subordinate values of heterosexualism, and, as I will argue, it is central to the values of the anglo-european tradition of ethics.

Through all of this, I am not trying to argue that heterosexualism is the "cause" of oppression. I do mean to suggest, however, that any revolution which does not challenge it will be incomplete and will eventually revert to the values of oppression. Heterosexualism is the form of social organization through which other forms of oppression, at times more vicious forms, become credible, palatable, even desirable. Heterosexualism—that is, the balance between masculine predation upon and masculine protection of a feminine object of masculine attention—de-skills a woman, makes her emotionally, socially, and economically dependent, and allows another to dominate her "for her own good" all in the name of "love." In no other

situation* are people expected to love, identify with, and become other to those who dominate them to the extent that women are supposed to love, identify with, and become other to men.

It is heterosexualism which makes us feel that it is possible to dominate another for her own good, that one who resists such domination is abnormal or doesn't understand what is good for her, and that one who refuses to participate in dominant/subordinate relationships doesn't exist. And once we accept all this, imperialism, colonialism, and ethnocentrism, for example, while existing all along, become more socially tolerable in liberal thought. They become less a matter of exercising over force and more a matter of the natural function of (a) social order.

Heterosexualism is a conceptual framework within which the concept of 'moral agency' independent of the master/slave virtues cannot find fertile ground. And it combines with ethical judgments to create a value whose primary function is not the moral development of individuals but rather the preservation of a patriarchal social control. Thus I want to challenge our acceptance and use of that ethics. And I will continue, in the next chapter, by discussing the feminine virtues of altruism, self-sacrifice, and vulnerability, and how we use them to gain control in relationships.

In discussing what I call Lesbian Ethics, I do not claim that lesbians haven't made many of the choices (heterosexual) women have made or that lesbians haven't participated in the consensus of straight thinking or that lesbians have withdrawn from the value of dominance and subordination and the security of established meaning we can find therein. I am not claiming that lesbians have lived under different conceptual or material conditions. I am claiming, however, that lesbian choice holds certain possibilities. It is a matter of further choice whether we go on to develop these possibilities or whether instead we try to fit into the existing heterosexual framework in any one of a number of ways.

Thus I am claiming that the conceptual category 'lesbian'—unlike the category 'woman'—is not irretrievably tied up with dominance and subordination as norms of behavior. And I am claiming that by attending each other, we may find the possibility of ethical values appropriate to lesbian existence, values we can choose as moral agents to give meaning to our lives as lesbians. In calling for withdrawal from the existing heterosexual value system, I am calling for a moral revolution, a revolution of lesbianism.

Note

*The situation of the mammy is similar. Racism and the politics of property intervened, however, to keep her from being quite so close to the master or mistress as woman is to man. Nevertheless, this did not make her situation any more palatable, and in many respects, it was worse.

In this brief passage, it is clear that some thinkers do not agree with Prager's high opinion of the value of Western civilization. Hoagland, in addition to the many forms of oppression she attributes to Western civilization, emphasizes the particular form of oppression generated by compulsory heterosexuality and the condemnation of homosexual ideals and, specifically, lesbian experiences, values, and ideals.

Her views raise many questions concerning the extent to which male patriarchal societies such as those of the Anglo-European cultures have oppressed women. Hoagland clearly challenges the value of the condemnation of homosexuality, especially as it relates to women. As you ponder her claims, it will be helpful to keep in mind the support Hoagland's thoughts receive from the materials presented in Chapter 3.

CHAPTER 9

Pornography

PORNOGRAPHY IS THE PRODUCT of a multibillion-dollar-a-year industry that is growing rapidly. It is presented in print, photographs, films, videos, telephone calls, and most recently on the "information super highway." It is firmly established in industrialized nations and is becoming entrenched in developing countries as well. Paralleling this economic growth is an increasing public debate concerning the nature, consequences, morality, and legality of pornography. Engaging in that debate is an important facet of the philosophy of sex and love.

An appropriate point of departure for becoming involved in the debate would be to try to clarify precisely what pornography is; that is, to try to define it. That is not an easy task. Indeed, one United States Supreme Court Justice said, "I can't define pornography, but I know it when I see it." We must try to do better than that. Indeed, how can we engage fruitfully in the debate about the morality and legality of pornography unless we have some understanding, some clarity, about what pornography is? Much depends on what we mean when we use the word *pornography*. We must ask ourselves a series of questions. Does pornography belong in the domain of obscenity? Does it differ from a work of art and from speech? If so, in what way? Can we come up with a "neutral" definition of it, with a definition that neither commends nor condemns it? What people and how many would have to agree with our definition before we could consider it warranted? Would we, perhaps, have to distinguish between strongly and weakly warranted definitions?

If we are able to generate a warranted definition of pornography, we could proceed to address some additional important questions. For example, what are the consequences of pornography? Does it benefit or harm society? Does it do both, and if both, do the harms outweigh the benefits or vice versa? Also, we could go on to ask if it is moral, immoral, or amoral. But if we are going to judge the morality of pornography, on what basis shall we render our judgment?

Suppose we conclude that the social harms of pornography outweigh its social benefits, and suppose that we judge it to be immoral, would we be warranted in seeking to make it illegal? Would, for example, the benefits that might be achieved by making it illegal outweigh the harms that might result from this "censorship"?

These are a few of the major questions that we must keep in mind as we examine the contributions of several authors to the current public debate. We will consider first the nature and consequences of pornography, then its morality and legality.

THE NATURE OF PORNOGRAPHY

In his 1981 article "Obscenity, Pornography, and the Arts: Sorting Things Out," selections from which appear below, Joel Feinberg attempts to distinguish pornography from obscenity and art. He sees a significant difference in the meaning ascribed by common usage to the terms *obscenity* and *pornography*. The former refers to something shockingly vulgar; while the latter refers to sexually explicit material designed to induce sexual arousal in the viewer. The former is a condemnatory term; the latter is a purely descriptive term. Given these differences, some pornography could be obscene, but not all of it is necessarily obscene, nor is all obscenity necessarily sexual. Yet the United States Supreme Court, says Feinberg, has blurred these differences. The Court has come to regard obscenity as materials designed to induce sexual arousal, thereby equating obscenity with pornography and generating a cloud of confusion. Feinberg proceeds to examine the question of whether pornography fits the classification of art. He concludes that pornographic films and books, insofar as they are purely pornographic, do not fall within the domain of dramatic and literary art. Yet, says Feinberg, pictorial art, poetry, and program music might fulfill simultaneously the goal of pornography (namely, sexual arousal) and the criteria of works of art. Feinberg concludes his exercise in conceptual clarification by commenting on the importance of the distinctions he has tried to make.

from Obscenity, Pornography, and the Arts: Sorting Things Out

JOEL FEINBERG

Should pornography be forbidden? Many say "no," if only for fear that prohibition would lead to censorship of genuine works of art. Others say "yes," at least partly on the ground that pornography is "obscene." A careful examination of the arguments on both sides often reveals a lamentable failure to communicate at all because of different and clashing understandings of what obscenity, pornography, and works of art are. Often, too, the arguments are unconvincing because of subtle equivocations in the slippery terms "obscene," "pornography," and "art." The essay that follows is primarily an exercise in definition or "conceptual analysis," an effort to obviate at least those confusions in the debate that are avoidable by carefully sorting out the key concepts involved.[1]

1. Is Pornography Obscene?

There is no more unfortunate mistake in the discussion of obscenity than simply to identify that concept, either in meaning or in scope of designation, with pornography.[2] To call something obscene, in the standard use of the term, is to condemn that thing as shockingly vulgar or blatantly disgusting. So understood, the term is used either to state that the object is apt to cause widespread offense, or to endorse offense as an appropriate reaction to it, or both. The corresponding term "pornographic," on the other hand, is a purely descriptive word referring to sexually explicit writing and pictures designed entirely and plausibly to induce sexual excitement in the reader or observer. To use the terms "obscene" and "pornographic" interchangeably, then, as if they referred to precisely the same things, is to beg the essentially controversial question of whether any or all (or only) pornographic materials really are obscene. Surely, to those thousands or millions of persons who delight in pornographic books, pictures, and films, the objects of their attachment do not seem disgusting or obscene. If these materials are nevertheless "truly obscene," they are not so merely by virtue of the definitions of the terms "obscene"

From "Obscenity, Pornography, and the Arts: Sorting Things Out," by Joel Feinberg in *Values in Conflict: Life, Liberty, and the Rule of Law,* edited by Burton M. Leiser (New York: Macmillan, 1981), pp. 237–253. It also forms part of a chapter in Joel Feinberg, *Offense to Others* (New York: Oxford University Press, 1985), pp. 127–143. Used by permission of Joel Feinberg and Oxford University Press.

and "pornography" but rather by virtue of their blatant violation of some relevant standards, and to establish their obscenity requires serious argument and persuasion. In short, whether any given acknowledged bit of pornography is *really* obscene is a logically open question to be settled by argument, not by definitional fiat.

Oddly enough the U.S. Supreme Court has committed itself to a different usage. In searching for definitions and tests of what it calls "obscenity," it has clearly had on its collective mind only verbal, pictorial, and dramatic materials and exhibitions designed effectively to be instruments of erotic arousal. "Obscene" has thus come to *mean* "pornographic" in the court's parlance. Justice Harlan quite explicitly underwrote this usage in *Cohen* v. *California* in 1971.[3] Robert Paul Cohen had been convicted in a county court of disturbing the peace by wearing a jacket emblazoned on its back with the words "Fuck the Draft." When the U.S. Supreme Court considered his appeal, Harlan wrote:

> This is not . . . an obscenity case. Whatever else may be necessary to give rise to the State's broader power to prohibit obscene expression, such expression must be, in some way, erotic. It cannot plausibly be maintained that this vulgar allusion to the Selective Service System would conjure up such psychic stimulation in anyone likely to be confronted with Cohen's crudely defaced jacket.[4]

If only erotic uses of language can be "obscene," then the most typical uses of the tabooed vocabulary of "dirty words" (for example, in angry insults) are not in the slightest degree obscene—an absurd consequence that the Court is apparently prepared to live with.

An even more bizarre instance of this distorted usage comes from a lower court that was committed to follow the Supreme Court's example. In the 1977 case *Connecticut* v. *Anonymous,*[5] a high school student appealed his conviction under a statute that declares it to be criminal to make an "obscene gesture." The youth in this case had rashly insulted the occupants of a police cruiser. The gesture in question, in which one extends the middle finger, is an ancient form of insult called "giving the finger." The appellate court decreed

that the gesture was not obscene (not even in the sense intended in the statute) because "to be obscene, the expression must be in a significant way erotic. . . . It can hardly be said that the finger gesture is likely to arouse sexual desire. The more likely response is anger." The reason why this opinion fills the ordinary reader with amazement is that, given the ordinary associations of the term "obscene" with offensiveness (disgust, shock to sensibility, etc.), the court seems to be saying that only sexy things can be offensive, a judgment that is either plainly false (if it is an empirical description of what things in fact offend people) or morally perverse (if it is a judgment about what kinds of things are appropriate objects of offense).

2. Pornographic Writing Versus Literary and Dramatic Art

A more difficult definitional tangle confronts writers who attempt to state (in a non-question-begging way) the relation between pornography, on the one hand, and the arts of literature and drama, on the other. Works of literature do have one thing in common, at least, with works of pornography: they both are found in books. But that is hardly sufficient to establish their identity, or even to relate them closely as species of some common, and theoretically interesting, genus. Books, after all, are an enormously heterogenous lot. Cookbooks contain recipes for preparing meals; telephone books enable one to discover the telephone numbers of friends or business firms; dictionaries explain meanings of words and prescribe standard spellings; pornographic books induce sexual desire; novels, plays, and short stories. . . . Well, works of literature are something else again. The question that has divided literary critics into disputing factions is, "To what extent may pornography be judged as legitimate literature rather than merely ersatz eroticism?"[6] But this question, which has also interested the courts, presupposes an inquiry into the characteristic, and hence defining, functions of pornographic and literary works, whether books, plays, or films.[7]

The three leading answers to the question whether pornography can be literature are (1) that pornography and literature are as different from one another as novels are from telephone books, but that pornography (like telephone books) can be useful, for all that, provided only that it not be confused with literature; (2) that pornography is a corruption or perversion of genuine literature, properly judged by literary standards, and always found wanting; (3) that pornography is, or can be, a form of literature properly judged by literary standards, and sometimes properly assigned high literary merit by those standards. The debate is easily confused by the fact that there can be within the same work a criss-cross or overlap of "characteristic functions." An undoubted work of literature can incidentally excite sexual longing in the reader just as it can arouse anger, pity, or any other passion. And an undoubted work of pornography—pure hard-core pornography—may here and there contain a line of poetic elegance and be "well written" throughout. Moreover, books of one kind can be put to the "characteristic use" of books of another kind: one could masturbate to passages in Joyce, Lawrence, or the Old Testament, for example.[8] But then one can also use a novel as a guide to correct spelling (though that does not make novels into cryptodictionaries), or, for that matter, to sit on, or to prop doors open. Despite these unavoidable overlaps of properties and uses, one can hope, in principle, to describe accurately the characteristic functions of works of different kinds. Novels can be used as dictionaries and works of pornography as door props, but that is not what each is primarily *for.*

The most persuasive advocate of the first view of the relation between pornography and literature (and a writer who has in fact persuaded me) is Anthony Burgess. He is well worth quoting at length.

A pornographic work represents social acts of sex, frequently of a perverse or wholly fantastic nature, often without consulting the limits of physical possibility. Such works encourage solitary fantasy, which is then usually quite harmlessly discharged in masturbation. A pornographic book is, then, an instrument for procuring a sexual catharsis, but it rarely promotes the desire to achieve this through a social mode, an act of erotic congress: the book is, in a sense, a substitute for a sexual partner.[9]

Burgess, of course, is talking about what other writers[10] have called "hard-core pornography" as opposed to "erotic realism." The former is the name of a category of materials (books, pamphlets, pictures, and films), now amounting to a flood, that make to claim, however indirect, to serious literary or artistic purpose and simply portray very graphically, and with unrestrained explicitness and enthusiasm, sexual acts and objects for all tastes. Erotic realism, on the other hand, is a category of literature in which sexual events, desires, longings, and so on are portrayed, often vividly and often at length, but always as part of a serious literary effort to be true to life. Sexual thoughts and activities are, of course, a vitally important part of the lives of most people. They often determine who we are, whom we encounter, what happens to us, and in which direction our lives develop. Hence, they are naturally important, often supremely important, elements in the characterizations and plots of novels that are concerned to render truly the human condition, comment critically upon it, and evoke appropriate emotions in response to it. Works of hard-core pornography are not intended to do any of these things. Their aim is to excite sexually, and that is an end of the matter.

Hard-core pornography, Burgess reminds us, has something in common with what he calls "didactic works" of other kinds, for example, political propaganda in the form of fiction, stories whose whole purpose is to arouse anger at a tyrant, or revolutionary ardor, or charitable assistance.

A pornographic work and a didactic work (like Smile's *Self-help*) have this in common: they stimulate, and expect the discharge of the stimulation to be effected in real-life acts—acts of masturbation or acts of social import. They differ from a work of literature in that the purpose of literary art is to arouse emotions and discharge those emotions as part of the artistic experience. This is what Aristotle meant by his implied doctrine of catharsis. . . . If we read a book or see a play or film and are then driven to discharge the aroused emotion in some solitary or social act, then we have experienced good pornography or good didacticism but very bad art.[11]

In fact (to be more generous), we have not experienced (literary) art at all, just as when we find the number we want in a phone book we have had a good "reference experience" but not a literary one. No one would think of confusing a telephone book with a novel; but the confusion of pornography with (erotic) literature is both common and pernicious. "Pornography," Burgess concludes, "is harmless so long as we do not corrupt our taste by mistaking it for literature."[12]

George Steiner, the leading spokesman for the second view, is less tolerant of pornography, perhaps because of his understandable impatience with the pretentious variety that mistakes itself for literature. To anyone who has surveyed the primary literature of hard-core pornography in any "adult" bookstore, Steiner's description of its standardly recurring features will seem right on target. He cites the limited number of basic themes and shrewdly notes how they correspond to the biological limitations on actual lovemaking, there being a severely limited number of "amorous orifices" in the human body, and "the mechanics of orgasm imply[ing] fairly rapid exhaustion and frequent intermission."[13] In any case, "dirty books are maddeningly the same."[14] Despite variations in trappings, race or class of the characters, or background settings hard-core pornography always follows "highly conventionalized formulas of low-grade sadism [where one partner rejoices in his or her abject humiliation], excremental drollery, and banal fantasies of phallic prowess or feminine responsiveness. In its own way the stuff is as predictable as a Scout manual."[15] Or, we might add, as a dictionary or a telephone book.

High-grade pornography by well-known writers with literary pretensions, insofar as it too is pure pornography, does no better. Steiner's verdict here too will seem to hit the target to anyone who has struggled through the more egregious works of Henry Miller, Jean Genet, or William Burroughs. Speaking of an all-star collection of "high porn" called the *Olympia Reader,* Steiner's patience collapses: "After fifty pages of 'hardening nipples,' 'softly opening thighs,' and 'hot rivers' flowing in and out of the ecstatic anatomy, the spirit cries out, not in hypocritical outrage, not because I am a poor Square throttling my libido, but in pure, nauseous boredom. Even fornication cannot be as dull, as hopelessly predictable, as all that."[16] Fornication, of course, is by no means dull, unless one tries to make a full-time job out of it.

That "high porn" is still pure porn, no matter how you slice it, is a point well worth making in reply to all the pretentious critical hogwash that would find some mysterious literary merit in the same old stuff when served up by fashionable names. No one has made the point better than Steiner. And no one has documented more convincingly the harm to imagination, to taste, to language itself that can come from mistaking pornography for literature. But, for all that, Steiner's essay is no answer to Burgess. Literature is one thing, and pornography is another. If, nevertheless, pornography is judged by literary standards, it must always get low marks, and if one persists in reading it and using it in the manner appropriate only to literature, then one converts it into hideously bad literature, and the results will be corrupting in a way common to *all* bad literature—slick westerns, soap operas, tear-jerkers, mass-produced mysteries, and Gothic romances. But there is no necessity that pornography be misconstrued in this way, and little evidence that it commonly is.

An able defender of the third view, Kenneth Tynan, defines pornography in the same way Burgess does, so that there is an apparent contrast between pornography and literature. Yet Tynan insists that when pornography is done well, that is to say, artfully, there is no reason to deny it the laudatory label of art. Pornography, he says, "is orgasmic in intent and untouched by the ulterior motives of traditional art. It has a simple and localized purpose: to induce an erection [or, presumably, the corresponding effect in women, a substantial consumers' group oddly forgotten by Tynan]. And the more skillfully the better."[17] So far, so good. There will be no objection yet from Burgess. Moreover, quite apart from the question of whether pornography can aspire to be literature without ceasing to be pornography, it can be quite valuable, and not merely "harmless," just for being what it is. Not everybody has a use for it, of course, any more than everybody needs a dictionary or a phone book, but it can be extremely useful for various well-defined classes of the population. Unlike some other writers,[18] Tynan fails to mention geriatric depressives and couples whose appetite lag to their own distress, but he does mention four other classes: First, those with minority tastes who cannot find like-minded mates; second, those who are "villainously ugly" of face or body and "unable to pay for the services of call girls";[19] third, "men on long journies, geographically cut off from wives and mistresses," for whom pornography can be "a portable memory, a welcome shortcut to remembered bliss, relieving tension without involving disloyalty";[20] and finally "uncommitted bachelors, arriving alone and short of cash in foreign cities where they don't speak the language."[21] This too is an important point, well made.

The next step in Tynan's argument is the one that makes a sharp break with both Burgess and Steiner:

> Because hard-core performs an obvious physical function, literary critics have traditionally refused to consider it a form of art. By their standards, art is something that appeals to such intangibles as the soul and the imagination; anything that appeals to the genitals belongs in the category of massage. What they forget is that language can be used in many delicate and complex ways to enliven the penis. It isn't just a matter of bombarding the reader with four letter words.[22]

It is a pity that Tynan neither quotes nor cites examples. The standard porn of the hard-core shops follows the patterns disclosed by Steiner so unswervingly that one suspects they were all composed by the same salacious computer. Readers are not simply bombarded with four-letter words; they are also assaulted by the same clichés—the trembling lips and cherry pink nipples, the open thighs and warm rivers of semen—in book after book. But what if hard-core pornography *were* done artfully? Would it be literature then in that (largely) hypothetical event?

There is a linguistic confusion underlying the question that is not easily sorted out. Almost *any* form of purposeful or creative human activity can be done either crudely or artfully. One can compose or perform music crudely or artfully; one can design or erect buildings crudely or artfully; one can write poems crudely or artfully. Music, architecture, and poetry are art forms. When they are done artfully, they are good music, architecture, or poetry; when done crudely, the result is (usually) bad music, architecture, or poetry. Bad art, how-

ever, is still art. A badly written novel is still a novel, and a badly composed photograph is still a photograph. On the other hand, one can make a phone book or dictionary crudely or artfully; one can mend a blouse or repair a carburetor crudely or artfully; one can throw a baseball or shoot a basket crudely or artfully. But it does not follow that reference compilation, repair work, and sports are art forms. Surely they are not among the fine arts.

Still it is possible, I suppose, for one to *think* of dictionary making, auto mechanics, and baseball as art forms. Professional practitioners may well think of their work as simply an occasion for artful enterprise and achievement. But, even if we grant that (with some reluctance), it does not follow that the artful construction of telephone books is *literature,* or that the artful repair of eroded buildings is *architecture,* or that the artful fielding of the second-base position is *ballet.* Nor does it follow that the artful "enlivening of the penis" with language is literature. "A thing is what it is, and not another thing."

3. Artful Pornography: The Film *Emmanuelle*

The recent films of the French director Just Jaeckin are perhaps as good examples of artful pornography as one can find. His 1973 film *Emmanuelle* became within a year the most profitable film in the history of the French movie industry, and his 1975 sequel, *The Story of O,* employing a similar formula, seems designed to break the record. Both films are produced with an artfulness that sets them off from almost all other essentially pornographic films. *Emmanuelle* is in many ways actually beautiful: It is set in exotic Bangkok whose picturesque streets and gorgeous gardens, and nearby jungles and mountains, are photographed with a wizardry that would win it awards if it were a travel documentary film. And, as one reviewer said of *The Story of O,* "It is filmed through delicate soft focuses and is so prettily presented that it might have been served up by Chanel."[23] The background music in *Emmanuelle* is sophisticated and erotic—perhaps the most suggestive music since Ravel's *Bolero*—and played sensitively by a full symphony orchestra. There are highly effective dance scenes, originally choreographed but in traditional Oriental patterns. For all its artfulness, however, *Emmanuelle* is no more a work of dramatic or literary art than a well-decorated and tastefully produced cookbook is a novel. Its sole theme or "plot" is the story of how the wife of an overworked French diplomat overcomes her boredom by abandoning herself to the sensual life with partners of all ages, genders, and races. Insofar as progression is suggested in the "story," it consists in her dawning appreciation at the end of the film of the attractions of group sex. Apart from that, the "story" is simply a hook on which to hang twelve or fifteen sexual adventures of the same stereotyped genres that are repeated monotonously in the literature of hard-core porn: coitus (as always punctuated with gasps and squeals) with a stranger in the darkness of a commercial airliner; coitus with another stranger in the locked restroom of the same plane; a sexual affair with another woman; a casual masturbation in a boring interval; a rough coitus act granted as a prize to the victor in a Siamese boxing match (here a touch of sadomasochism), a simultaneous sexual encounter with several men, and so on. The film clearly satisfies Steiner's criteria of pornography and equally clearly fails to satisfy the Burgess–Aristotle criterion of dramatic art. Not that it tries and fails; it fully succeeds in achieving what it sets out to do.

Pornographic as it is, however, *Emmanuelle* is in no obvious way obscene. Artfulness and obscenity do not sit easily together. Sex acts are filmed in shadowy pantomime; the details are simulated or merely suggested. There is no close-up camera work focusing on sex organs or the contact that stimulates them. Male sex organs are not shown at all. (This omission is typical of the double standard that generally prevails in works of pornography meant to sell to large general audiences. The commercial assumption is that the audiences are primarily *men* who will be titillated by scenes of female homosexuality but repelled or threatened by parallel episodes with men, or even by the unveiling of the masculine sex organ.) There is, in short, very little that is gross or obtrusive in the film, or likely to diminish its aphrodisiac effectiveness.

4. Pornographic Pictorial Art, Poetry, and Program Music

Although pornographic films and books, insofar as they are purely pornographic, can never aspire to the status of dramatic and literary art no matter how artfully they are produced, a quite different verdict seems to be required for pornographic pictorial art. That surprising result is no real paradox, however. Rather, it is explained by the empirical fact that the characteristic purposes of pictorial art and pornography can be jointly satisfied by one and the same picture. A painting of a copulating couple that satisfied the relevant standards for good painting would *ipso facto* be a work of pictorial art; it might be done in exquisitely harmonizing color, with properly balanced composition, subtlety of line, successful lighting effects, and depicted figures of memorably graceful posture and facial expressiveness. Such a painting might also be designed primarily to stimulate the genitals of the observer. Insofar as it also achieved that goal, it would be a work of pornography. The defining features of literature and pornography, however, mutually exclude one another for the reasons given by Burgess. To be sure, a long and complex literary work might contain whole sections that are purely pornographic, or contain art and pornography in various complex combinations and alternations. Such a work could be called both literary and pornographic, just as a dictionary that contained chapters of a novel between each alphabetical section would be both a dictionary *and* a novel. But the literary and pornographic parts would be separate and distinguishable, unlike the painting, which can be both pictorial art and pure pornography at the same time and as a whole. The point applies even more forcibly, I should think, to that rarer genre, pornographic program music. It is possible, I think, for a composer deliberately to set out to create a musical aphrodisiac and succeed in that aim, and also in the same work to create a genuine piece of music, even a work of high musical merit.

It is difficult to find any reason why a poem cannot in principle satisfy high literary standards and also achieve the deliberate aim of pornography, to arouse the reader. Very likely then lyric poetry should be classified with pictorial art and program music in this respect rather than with other species of literature. Still it is surpassingly difficult to find clear and noncontroversial examples of works that are at once good or at least serious poems and also effective pornographs; and that difficulty may reside in the nature of the two objectives and natural impediments to their successful cross-breeding. (Love poems, of course, are an altogether different matter.)[24] What *clearly* cannot be both literary art and pornography, if the argument thus far is sound, are works that tell *stories* and have subtly structured *plots*—short stories, novels, plays, dramatic films. Tragedies cannot be erotically arousing on balance and still achieve their essential goals, for the reasons given by Aristotle and Burgess. Pathos can be gripping, edifying, and saddening, but it is not possible for it to achieve its characteristic ends while also evoking erotic feelings in the reader or observer. Comedy is especially incapable of being pornography (though it may work its own purposes on erotic materials), because a laugh is a "discharge within the work," not a cause of further tensions to be discharged in "real life acts." The funny bone is not a sex organ.

5. Can Pornography Be Art? The Minimal Relevance of the Question

Interesting as the question may be for aestheticians and critics, why does it matter to a social philosopher whether pornography is art or something *sui generis?* Of course, insofar as American courts acknowledge a special social value, or "redeeming social importance" to works of art, even poor works of art, to that extent the relation between art and pornography is a question of vital practical importance. But interesting as the question is in its own right, and crucial as it may be for the application of American constitutional law, it has very little importance for the philosopher or social critic whose concern is to discover what restrictive legislation could be passed by an ideal legislature as determined by the morally correct principles for limiting individual liberty. One such principle is that severely offensive (disgusting, shocking, revolting) public behavior that is not reasonably avoidable may be prohibited as a kind of public nuisance. A legislature is generally thought to have the right to control offensive behavior, *within carefully circumscribed circumstances,* by means of the criminal law, even when that behavior (or depicted behavior) is not directly injurious to health or wealth. But what relevance to this right and its limits is there in the fact that the offensiveness in question is, or is not, attached inextricably to a work of art? After all, offensiveness is offensiveness whatever its source, and, if it is unavoidable offensiveness that confers the right of prohibition on the legislature, what relevance can the other characteristics of the offending object have?

There is surely *some* relevance in the fact that the offense stems from a work of art. Both the civil and the criminal law of nuisance empowers courts to weigh the degree (intensity and extent) of the offense caused by a given activity against the "reasonableness" of the offending conduct. One of the standards, in turn, for judging the reasonableness of offending or inconveniencing behavior is its general social utility, that is, "the social value which the law attaches to its ultimate purpose."[25] Just as in nuisance law offensive noises and smells are not prohibited when they are the unavoidable concomitants of the operations of a socially useful industry, but are enjoined when they are the products of merely private diversions of little social value,[26] so the criminal law might prohibit offensive materials and actions when they have no further "redeeming" social function, but permit them when the offense is the side effect of a socially useful purpose. The fact that publicly offensive, sexually explicit materials happen also to be serious works of literature is relevant to the social utility of the offending conduct (the creating and exhibiting of the offensive work) insofar as serious literary and artistic endeavors have social value and deserve to be encouraged in the public interest. The offense can be a price worth paying for the generally useful public practice of producing literary works, just as noise, smoke, and stench might be a price worth paying for the existence of boiler factories, power plants, and slaughterhouses. Where the offensiveness of pornography is not linked to a serious artistic intention, however, there may be no redeeming social value to counterbalance it (certainly none of an artistic kind), and in that case the offense principle, assuming that its other conditions are satisfied, would permit its prohibition.

But even pure hard-core pornography with no literary or dramatic pretensions, as Kenneth Tynan pointed out, can have a certain social utility, so there is no "open and shut case" derived from the offense principle for banning it. The balancing of values in its case may be a close matter. The case for banning pornography that *is* art, on the other hand, insofar as it is derived from a carefully formulated offense principle, would be very weak. However much social value we ascribe to pure pornography on Tynan-like grounds, we must concede that works of literature, drama, pictorial art, and music have a much higher social value as a class (including both successful and unsuccessful specimens) than works of pure pornography, so that *their* legal prohibition would be a much greater loss. And so long as pornographic intent in a work of music or pictorial art does not have a *negative* social value, the value of these objects as works of art is undiminished by their aphrodisiac content or function. To make criminal the production or exhibition of any subclass of art objects would be to produce a "chilling effect" on the entire artistic enterprise and threaten to diminish its contributions to our civilization.[27]

The relevance of these considerations about the "reasonableness" or "social value" of offensive materials and actions is severely restricted, however, to those untypical situations in which the standards for determining the seriousness of the offense itself have not been fulfilled. The "seriousness" of the offense is a function of (1) how widespread the susceptibility to it is,[28] (2) how severe it will be in the typical case, (3) how much inconvenience would be involved in the effort to avoid it, and (4) whether or not the offended states of mind in question were voluntarily incurred, or the risk of offense voluntarily assumed. Surely, in most controversial instances of pornographic exhibition, either the offending materials do not offend intensely, or durably, or universally, and hence are not properly judged "obscene" in the first place (or at least not obscene *enough*); *or* they are reasonably avoidable, and hence not a serious inconvenience to anyone; *or* the risk of offense is voluntarily assumed by those who witness them,

and hence no captive audience exists; *or* only those with abnormal susceptibilities to offense could have reasonably been expected to be offended in the first place. Moreover, some of these standards for determining the existence or degree of offense are often preemptive. In particular, if the only observers are willing observers, then it is wholly pointless to consider whether a film or book with explicitly sexual themes has social value or not, and the question of whether it is a genuine work of art becomes otiose. It is unfair to prohibit on pain of criminal punishment any object or behavior that is both harmless and in the circumstances inoffensive, whether it is a genuine work of art of not.

6. How Can Sex (of All Things) Be Obscene?

The final question to consider about the relation between obscenity and pornography is one whose perplexity is no less keen for being raised typically as a kind of afterthought. The question is not whether explicit depictions of sexual behavior as such are in fact obscene, but rather, how could sex, a department of life so highly valued by almost all of us, *possibly* be obscene? How is an extremely offended reaction to explicit sexual depictions even possible? In particular, how could sex, of all things, induce something like the "yuk reaction," an extreme form of disgust and repugnance? Even more puzzling at first sight, since the word "obscene" in its standard use endorses such disgust, how could the yuk reaction be the *appropriate* response to the unrestrained depiction of sexuality? These questions are profound and difficult and belong ultimately to the psychologist rather than to the philosopher, but the shadowy outline of their answers, at least, is visible to all. What is clear is that the answers must be of at least two kinds: (1) Sexual explicitness (to use a vague generic term) violates a certain type of moral sensibility, and (2) sexual explicitness when extremely coarse and obtrusive can shock by reducing "psychic distance," even when moral sensibility is not involved. I shall consider these distinct factors in turn.

The word "obscene" is commonly applied to behavior thought to be immoral. When we use the word in this way, we do not reserve it necessarily for what we consider the most immoral behavior; secret, devious, or subtle private immoralities, no matter how seriously wrong they may seem to be, are not called "obscene" at all.[29] Rather, we think of those immoralities that are absolutely open and shameless, and therefore "shocking" or "disgusting," as the typically obscene ones. The word "obscene" emphasizes how shocking they are to behold, not how flagrant they are as departures from a moral norm. Thus utterly cynical, obvious, or brazen falsehoods told with amazing aplomb before observers who know that they are intentional are "obscene lies"; bloated profits, made by exploiting public disasters and then openly bragged about, are "obscene profits." Similarly, blatant exhibitions of tabooed conduct, lewd revelings in the death or suffering of others, naked corruption, and stark depersonalizations are all proper subjects for the predicate "obscene." It is the grossly obtrusive offense to sensibility that elicits judgments of obscenity, whether the sensibility in question be moral, religious, patriotic, or merely gustatory (disgusting foods seem obscene) or sensory (disgusting smells seem obscene).

Naturally enough, persons who hold certain moral convictions about sexual conduct will find blatantly obtrusive exhibitions or depictions of tabooed sexuality obscene, not *simply* because they violate moral standards but because they do so openly and blatantly. Given that such is the case, the sensibilities of these persons would command the respect, and, if only other things were equal, the protection, of the law.

This account, however, is still too vague to allay the puzzlement that generated this psychological inquiry. Hardly anyone holds the conviction that *all* sexual behavior as such is wrong, whatever the circumstances and whoever the actors. At most, people find illicit or unlicensed sex, sex out of marriage, solitary sex, or sex at inappropriate times and places to be immoral. Yet many people find the *depiction* or explicit *description* of any sexual conduct at all, licit or illicit, to be obscene. How then could the obscenity stem from the perceived violation of moral principle?

The answer, I suspect, must employ the distinction between *what is depicted,* which is not thought to be obscene, at least not on moral grounds, and *the act of depicting it,* which may under the circumstances be a blatantly offensive violation of moral norms. What is immoral (by the standards of some offended parties) in vivid depictions or unvarnished descriptions of the sex acts of real or fictitious persons, even when those acts in the depicted circumstances are entirely licit, are the "impure thoughts" in the minds of the beholders, which are in large part "desires in the imagination" for what would be immoral if realized. When the beholder finds the depiction obscene (on this account), he finds his own spontaneous concupiscence disgusting, and it quickly curdles into shame and revulsion; or, if the beholder is part of a group, he or she may think of the inevitably impure ideas in the minds of the others as disgusting, or may take the act of showing or describing sex as itself blatantly immoral insofar as it is meant to exploit the weakness of the audience and induce impure thoughts in receptive minds. So it is not that what is depicted is thought to be immoral, but rather that the act of depicting it in those circumstances, and the spectacle of its common perception, with those motives, intentions, and likely effects, is thought to be immoral and—because the immorality is unsubtly shameless and open—obscene.

The second explanation of how sex can come to seem obscene has nothing to do with anyone's conception of morality. Even persons who utterly reject the prevailing sexual taboos may find some sexual depictions offensive to the point of obscenity. The reactions of such persons are to be sharply contrasted with those of people with prudish moral sensibilities who get trapped between their own salacity and shame. The disgust of this second group is not moral disgust. Rather, it is the spontaneous revulsion to what is overpoweringly close that is commonly produced not only by crude pornography but by other kinds of experiences as well. George P. Elliott has diagnosed the phenomenon well:

> Psychologically, the trouble with [artless] pornography is that, in our culture at least, it offends the sense of separateness, of individuality, of privacy. . . . We have a certain sense of specialness about those voluntary bodily functions each must perform for himself—bathing, eating, defecating, urinating, copulating. . . . Take eating, for exam-

ple. There are few strong taboos around the act of eating; yet most people feel uneasy about being the only one at table who is or who is not, eating, and there is an absolute difference between eating a rare steak washed down by plenty of red wine and watching a close-up movie of someone doing so. One wishes to draw back when one is actually or imaginatively too close to the mouth of a man enjoying his dinner; in exactly the same way one wishes to remove oneself from the presence of man and woman enjoying sexual intercourse.[30]

"Not to withdraw," Elliott adds, "is to peep, to pervert looking so that it becomes a sexual end in itself."[31] Here he makes a different point and a less tenable one. The point is (or should be) that if we are going to look without being disgusted, we had better look from a proper distance, not that looking at all is a "perversion." Not only erotically realistic art but also artful pornography *can* satisfy the criterion of distance, and when it does we identify imaginatively with one of the parties whom we watch rather than thinking of ourselves as intrusive third parties or embarrassed "peepers."

Pornographers whose aim is aphrodisiac rather than emetic might well consult Elliott for good tips. He tells us, with convincing examples, how the problem of distance is solved in pictorial art, while implying that the same solutions must be forever unavailable to the pornographer, but that is because he identifies pornography quite arbitrarily with the gross and artless kind. Distance is preserved in erotic pictorial art through the use of artificial stylized images, as in the throngs of erotic statues on Indian temples, by making the erotic image small, or by sketching it in with only a few details:

> One does not want to be close to a man while he is defecating nor to have a close-up picture of him in that natural, innocent act—not at all because defecating is reprehensible, only because it is displeasing to intrude upon. One would much rather have a detailed picture of a thief stealing the last loaf of bread from a starving widow with three children than one of Albert Schweitzer at stool. However, Brueghel's painting "The Netherlandish Proverbs" represents two bare rear ends sticking out of a window, presumably of people defecating into the river below, and one quite enjoys the sight—because it is a small part of a large

and pleasant picture of the world and because the two figures are tiny, sketched in, far away.[32]

What should we say—or, more to the point, what should the law say—about those persons whose psyches are not accurately described by Elliott, persons with special kinky tastes who prefer their psychic distances short and their sexual perceptions large and detailed? Tiny Gulliver (as Elliott reminds us) is "revolted by every blemish on the breast of the Brobdingnagian wet nurse suckling the baby."[33] Even though the breast was pleasingly shaped and would have been delightful to behold had its proportions been suited to persons of Gulliver's size, it extended six feet from the nurse's body and its nipple was "half the size of a man's head." Swift makes his point well, and most readers are appalled in their imaginations, but what are we to say of the special reader who is sexually excited by the very thought of this normally emetic object? The law, of course, should say nothing at all, provided that satisfaction of the quirky taste is not achieved at the cost of direct offense to unwilling observers.

The more interesting point, however, is that the overwhelming majority of people do *not* enjoy being spatially or psychologically close to the physiological organs and processes deemed "private" in our culture. To revel in these objects is about as common a pastime, I should think, as reveling in the slinky, slimy, smelly things that most of us find immediately repellant to the senses and thus in an analogous way obscene.

7. Summary

Obscenity and pornography are entirely distinct concepts that overlap in their applications to the world but by no means coincide. Obscene things are those that are apt to offend people by eliciting such reactions as disgust, shock, and repugnance. Moreover, when we call something obscene we usually wish to endorse some form of offense as the appropriate reaction to it. Pornography, on the other hand, simply consists of all those pictures, plays, books, and films whose *raison d'être* is that they are erotically arousing. Some obscene things (e.g., dirty words and insulting gestures) are not pornographic. Indeed some obscene things have nothing whatever to do with sex. Human wastes and other disgusting objects fall into that subcategory of the obscene, as do acts of rejoicing in the misfortunes of others, racial slurs, shameless lies, and other blatant but nonsexual immoralities. Some pornographic things, for example, artful paintings, are not obscene. Others, such as close-up, highly magnified photographs of sexual couplings are obscene, though their very obscenity tends to defeat their pornographic purpose.

Pornography ought to be prohibited by law only when it is obscene and then precisely because it is obscene. But obscenity (extreme offensiveness) is only a necessary condition, not a sufficient condition, for rightful prohibition. In addition, the offending conduct must not be reasonably avoidable, and the risk of offense must not have been voluntarily assumed by the beholders. (No doubt additional conditions might also be added such as, for example, that reasonable efforts have been made to exclude children.)

The defining purposes of plotted fiction and dramatic literature cannot be satisfied by a work that is also properly denominated pornographic. On the other hand, there is no contradiction in the idea of a pornographic painting, musical composition, or (perhaps) poem. But the question whether or not art can be pornographic, while obviously important for American constitutional law, which places limits on what legislatures *may* do, is of less interest to critical social philosophy, which asks what legislatures *ought* to do from among the alternative courses permitted them. The Supreme Court has interpreted the First Amendment as permitting legislatures to prohibit all obscenity that is not also art.[34] Reasonable liberty-limiting principles also give special importance to works of art but prevent legislatures from prohibiting even obscene *nonart,* provided that it is not imposed on unwilling audiences. It is quite unnecessary to determine whether (or to what degree) a given book or film is also art, when the only people who experience it are either unoffended or have voluntarily assumed the risk of offense in advance.

Finally, we considered how sexual conduct could possibly seem obscene to anyone given the universal human propensity to derive extreme pleasure from it. Those who find pornography obscene, we concluded, do so either when it is done in circumstances that render it both immoral and blatantly and shamelessly obtrusive (and thus shocking to moral sensibility) or else when it has reduced psychic distance to the threshhold of repugnance or disgust, even when no moral considerations are involved.

Notes

1. The two paragraphs that follow are drawn with only minor changes from my article "Pornography and the Criminal Law," *University of Pittsburgh Law Review* 40 (1979): 567ff.

2. High on the honor roll of those who have *not* made this pernicious error is the late Paul Goodman, who wrote in his article "Pornography, Art, and Censorship" [reprinted in D. A. Hughes, ed., *Perspectives on Pornography,* (New York: St. Martin's Press, 1970), pp. 42–60] that "The pornographic is not *ipso facto* the obscene" but, rather, simply that which is designed and used for the purpose of arousing sexual desires. But "if the stirring of desire is *defined* [emphasis added], and therefore treated, as obscene, how can a normal person's interest in sex be anything *but* shameful? This is what shame is, the blush at finding one's impulse to be unacceptable. . . . So the court [by treating pornography as *ipso facto* obscene] corrupts. It is a miserable social policy." The honor roll also includes Stanley Edgar Hyman, whose essay "In Defense of Pornography" also is reprinted in the Hughes collection; David A. J. Richards, *The Moral Criticism of Law* (Belmont, CA: Wadsworth, 1977); and Frederick F. Schauer, *The Law of Obscenity* (Washington, DC: Bureau of National Affairs, 1976).

3. 91 S.Ct. 1780 (1971).

4. *Ibid.*

5. 377 A.2d 1342.

6. Douglas A. Hughes, ed., *Introduction to Perspectives on Pornography* (New York: St. Martin's Press, 1970), p. xiv.

7. Precisely parallel questions can be raised, of course, about the characteristic features of pictorial art (painting and sculpture) and pornographic pictures.

8. There are no doubt some strange souls, somewhere or other, at some time or other, who have found even dictionaries, cookbooks, and telephone books useful aids to masturbation. See Earl Finbar Murphy, "The Value of Pornography," *Wayne Law Review* 10 (1964): 655ff. for some amazing examples. There is hardly any limit to human differences, especially sexual differences. But that fact should not hinder efforts at definitions and classification.

9. Anthony Burgess, "What is Pornography?" in Hughes, *op. cit.,* p. 5.

10. Following E. and B. Kronhausen, *Pornography and the Law* (New York: Ballantine Books, 1959).

11. Burgess, *op. cit.,* p. 6.

12. *Loc. cit.*

13. George Steiner, "Night Words: High Pornography and Human Privacy," reprinted in Hughes, *op. cit.,* p. 97.

14. *Ibid.,* p. 98.

15. *Loc. cit.*

16. *Ibid.,* p. 103.

17. Kenneth Tynan, "Dirty Books Can Stay," in Hughes, *op. cit.,* p. 111.

18. For example, Vivian Mercier, "Master Percy and/or Lady Chatterly," in Hughes, *op. cit.,* p. 24.

19. Tynan, *op. cit.,* p. 112

20. *Loc. cit.*

21. *Loc. cit.*

22. *Ibid.,* p. 113.

23. Bernard Drew's review in Westchester-Rockland Newspapers (the Gannett chain), November 17, 1975.

24. No doubt a genuine love poem of high literary merit like the biblical "Song of Songs" can be used pornographically, as any kind of thing can be used for a purpose other than that for which it is made and which defines the kind of thing it is. On this see E. F. Murphy, *op. cit.* It is more natural and less dogmatic, however, to classify artful love poems that celebrate the joy of sexual love with pornographic pictorial art that achieves genuine aesthetic merit and to attribute the relative scarcity of the former to the greater difficulty of the genre.

25. William Prosser, *Handbook of the Law of Torts,* 2nd ed. (St. Paul, MN: West Publishing Co., 1955), p. 411

26. As Prosser puts it, "The world must have factories, smelters, oil refineries, noisy machinery, and blasting, even at the expense of some inconvenience to those in the vicinity, and the plaintiff [in a civil suit] may be required to accept and tolerate some not unreasonable discomfort for the general good. . . . On the other hand, a foul pond, or a vicious or noisy dog will have little if any social value, and relatively slight annoyance from it may justify relief." *Ibid.,* p. 412.

27. In addition, attempts to create art objects, insofar as they are forms of personal expression, have a "special position" on that ground too.

28. In particular, offended states that occur only because of the offended party's abnormal susceptibility to offense are not to count as "very serious" offenses, although they surely are genuine.

29. For a detailed analysis of the concept of the obscene and its relation to the concept of immorality, see my "The Idea of the Obscene," The Lindley Lecture (Lawrence: University of Kansas Press, 1979).

30. George P. Elliott, "Against Pornography" in Hughes, *op. cit.,* pp. 75–76.

31. *Ibid.,* p. 76.

32. *Ibid.,* p. 77.

33. *Loc. cit.*

34. See Justice Brennan's opinion in *Roth* v. *United States,* 354 U.S. 476 (1957) and subsequent cases, such as *Manual Enterprises* v. *Day,* 370 U.S. 478 (1962); *Ginzburg* v. *United States,* 370 U.S. 403 (1963); *Mishkin* v. *New York,* 383 U.S. 502 (1963); *Memoirs* v. *Massachusetts,* 383 U.S. 413 (1963); *Miller* v. *California,* 413 U.S. 15 (1973); and *Paris Adult Theater I* v. *Slaton,* 413 U.S. 49 (1973). Of course expressions of opinion, scientific findings, and the like are also "absolutely protected" by the First Amendment. In the Court's verbal usage, genuine works of art, expressions of opinion, and the like are not called "obscene" in the first place. It might have been more natural to say that we have a constitutional right to attempt to create and exhibit works of art, *even obscene ones,* to express political opinions, *even obscene ones,* and so on. When the court says that the First Amendment does not protect obscenity, it means that it does not protect obscene nonart, obscene nonexpression, and the like. In short, it does not protect mere erotic stimulants or symbolic aphrodisiacs.

How convincing do you find Feinberg's definition of pornography? Would it be useful in helping us distinguish pornographic from nonpornographic material? Perhaps, but consider this problem: Suppose we agree with Feinberg that pornography is "sexually explicit" material "designed entirely and plausibly to induce sexual excitement in the reader or observer." We might encounter some difficulty in deciding what is "sexually explicit" and what is not. Would we, for example, want to say that the illustrations in a medical textbook on human anatomy or the photographs in the swimsuit edition of *Sports Illustrated* were sexually explicit? Perhaps we could remove the vagueness in the term "sexually explicit" through a carefully constructed precise definition, but would we be able to surmount the difficulties we would meet in trying to determine whether the material was "designed" to arouse sexually the consumer? When the issue of the original design or purpose of the material is raised we are in the shadowy domain of human intentions. How can we really be clear about the intentions of the creator of sexually explicit material? Perhaps the creator's intentions are simply to make money by selling material that she thinks is beautiful. Perhaps the creator's intentions are to discredit the public image of a former Miss America. Then, too, perhaps the creator's intention is to cause viewers to become sexually aroused. Perhaps the creator has all of these intentions. Who can say for certain what those intentions are? Would it not be more useful, then, to have a definition of pornography that avoided recourse to the intentions of the creator of the material? Suppose we eliminated the reference to design or intentions in Feinberg's definition and produced the following definition: "Pornography is sexually explicit material that induces sexual excitement in the reader or observer." But is there not some material (such as John Singer Sargent's 1891 painting "Nude Egyptian Girl," or Alexander Comfort's series on the joy of sex, or even certain sections of the *Land's End* catalog) that could be considered sexually explicit and that could induce sexual excitement in some people that we would not want to label pornographic? Perhaps an entirely new approach to defining pornography is needed. That is precisely what a number of feminist thinkers have attempted, and to a sample of their work we now turn.

THE NATURE OF PORNOGRAPHY

The material cited below is taken from Catherine Itzin's article "A Legal Definition of Pornography" and discusses the definition of pornography proposed by Catherine Mac-Kinnon and Andrea Dworkin in 1983. At that time, MacKinnon and Dworkin were both on the faculty of the University of Minnesota and were asked by the City Council of Minneapolis to draft an amendment to the city's Civil Rights Ordinance in order to address the issue of pornography as it related to civil rights. At the heart of their draft amendment was a definition of pornography that construed it in terms of the sexually explicit subordination of women. Pornography was, in their eyes, a violation of the due process and equal protection provisions of the Fourteenth Amendment to the Constitution. On December 30, 1983, the amendment was passed by the City Council by a vote of 7 to 6. The Mayor of Minneapolis, Donald Fraser, vetoed the amendment and its supporters could not muster the required 9 votes to override the veto. A slightly revised version of the amendment was again passed by the City Council in July 1984, and once again its supporters were unable to override Fraser's mayoral veto. As you read Itzin's review of the amendment (which she refers to as the "ordinance"), try to figure out the grounds on which an avowed liberal like Mayor Donald Fraser would veto this measure.

from A Legal Definition of Pornography

Catherine Itzin

The civil rights ordinance provided a major breakthrough in defining pornography by conceptualizing it as *a practice of sex discrimination which sexualizes the subordination of women and which eroticizes violence against women:* as "a political practice of power and powerlessness" which "eroticizes dominance and submission."[1] It then defined pornography specifically, descriptively and objectively for what it depicted and communicated about the sexualized subordination of women:

Pornography means the graphic sexually explicit subordination of women through pictures and/or words that also includes one or more of the following: (i) women are presented dehumanized as sexual objects, things, or commodities; or (ii) women are presented as sexual objects who enjoy humiliation or pain; or (iii) women are pre-

From "A Legal Definition of Pornography" by Catherine Itzin. Reprinted from *Pornography: Women, Violence and Civil Liberties,* edited by Catherine Itzin (Oxford, U.K.: Oxford University Press, 1992), pp. 435–455, by permission of Oxford University Press.

PORNOGRAPHY

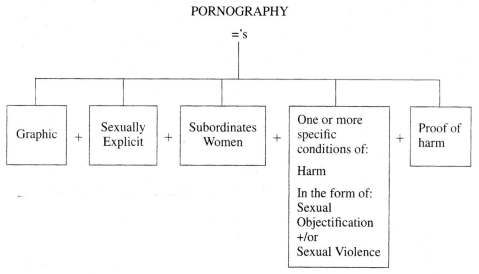

Figure 1   A legal definition of pornography—how it would work

sented as sexual objects experiencing sexual pleasure in rape, incest or other sexual assault; or (iv) women are presented as sexual objects tied up, cut up or mutilated or bruised or physically hurt, or (v) women are presented in postures or positions of sexual submission, servility, or display; or (vi) women's body parts—including but not limited to vaginas, breasts, or buttocks—are exhibited such that women are reduced to those parts; or (vii) women are presented being penetrated by objects or animals; or (viii) women are presented in scenarios of degradation, humiliation, injury, torture, shown as filthy or inferior, bleeding, bruised, or hurt in a context that makes these conditions sexual.[2]

Action could only be taken against material that could be shown to fall within this very narrow and limited definition of pornography. Anything falling within this definition of pornography would have to be *simultaneously* graphic *and* sexually explicit *and* to subordinate women; *and also* include one or more of the specific itemized characteristics which describe the content of pornography. It would *also* have to be proved to have harmed someone. This definition makes a distinction between sex and pornography. Material could not be targeted simply because it was sexually ex

plicit, as sexual explicitness is only one of four or more characteristics of pornography.

Many of the items in the specified characteristics of pornography refer to violence, but some refer "merely" to "acts of submission, degradation, humiliation and objectification." The harm, the violation, indeed the violence inherent in these acts—and in dehumanization and exploitation— have simply not been recognized as harm because these acts have traditionally been regarded as "just sex." Also, because the consumers of pornography enjoy the material sexually, and see the submission and objectification of women as both natural and "sexy," its harm has been obscured to them "even though the non-violent materials are also known to be harmful . . . for instance in their use by rapists and child molesters, in increasing the acceptability of forced sex, and in diminishing men's vision of the desirability and possibility of sex equality."[3]

Furthermore, turning women into objects and dehumanizing women is a precondition for overt violence. It is easier to hurt someone who is "less human": the function of anti-Semitic and racist representation is to dehumanize in order to enable overt acts of violence to be done. Thus the definition would include pornography in which women are "bound, battered, tortured, harassed, raped and sometimes killed." But it would also include women in "glossy men's magazines" who are "'merely' humiliated, molested, objectified and used for the entertainment and sexual pleasure of men."[4]

In practice this definition has been drafted sometimes to include only violent pornography, sometimes both sexually violent and other violating and sexually objectifying materials. The Minneapolis Ordinance included all pornography, "objectifying" as well as violent, for example "women presented dehumanized as sex objects, things or commodities." The Indianapolis Ordinance excluded that clause and restricted itself to covering violent and degrading pornography.[5] The Pornography Victims Compensation Act 1989 borrowed from this definition.[6]

Dworkin and MacKinnon based the definition on a content analysis of the materials published by the pornography industry.

> The Ordinance adopts a simple if novel strategy for definition. It looks at the existing universe of the pornography industry and simply describes what is there, including what must be there for it to work in the way that it, and only it works ... Everything in pornography is sex to someone, or it would not be there.[7]

The lowest common denominator of pornography is that it is sexually arousing to someone. However, attempts to define pornography simply in terms of sexual arousal have been inadequate because there are so many other things that produce "that definite stirring between the legs, including the violence against women and violation of women in R-rated movies or *Vogue* magazine or Calvin Klein commercials or Yeats' *Leda and the Swan*."

> It is true that pornography exists on a larger social continuum with other materials that objectify and demean women and set the stage for and reflect women's social devaluation. It is true that many materials (such as some religious works and sociobiology texts) express the same message as pornography and are vehicles for the same values. This does not mean either that pornography cannot be defined or that it does not operate in a distinctive way.[8]

It is also true that many things which are not pornography within this definition have become "pornographic" because of the existence of pornography.

> The same message of sexualized misogyny pervades the culture—indeed, it does so more and more because pornography exists. But that does not make "Dallas" and "Dynasty" into pornography, however close they come . . . in the world, a lot of people know the difference between pornography on the one hand and art, literature, mainstream media, advertisements, and sex education on the other. Such materials are not pornography—and, frankly, everyone knows they are not.[9]

Pornography is not therefore simply synonymous with sexual arousal, though "for pornography to work sexually with its major market, which is heterosexual men, it must excite the penis." Nor is pornography simply its misogynist message, though its message, what it communicates about women, is part of what makes pornography what it is. What distinguishes pornography from anything else is its combination of subordination and sexual explicitness.

Sexually Explicit Subordination

According to Dworkin and MacKinnon: "To accomplish its end, it must show sex and subordinate a woman at the same time."[10]

> From the evidence of the material itself, its common denominator is the use or abuse of a woman in an expressly sexual way. Under the Ordinance, pornography *is* what pornography *does*. What it does is subordinate women through sexually explicit pictures and words.

Just as there is sexual explicitness which is not pornography, there are also materials which show women being subordinated, but which are not sexually explicit and not pornography. "For this reason the Ordinance restricts its definition only to those sexually explicit pictures and words that actually can be proven to subordinate women in their making or use."[11] Sexually explicit subordination is the key to the definition: "Subordination is an active practice of placing someone in an unequal position or in a position of loss of power."[12]

A subordinate is not an equal: "Subordination is at the core of every systematic social inequality. It includes the practices that enforce second-class status. Subordination includes objectification, hierarchy, forced submission, and violence."[13] Pornography is "sexual subordination for sexual pleasure."[14] According to Carol Smart, "the pornographic genre succeeds by transforming the meaning of domination into (natural) sex and thereby making it invisible." She defines pornography as "the dominant, persuasive, and routine regime of representation which sexualizes and limits women."[15] According to Susan Cole, "pornography cannot exist without the subordination of women" and "pornography is active in the subordination of women"—in the material itself and in the social sphere.

Subordination is an active practice because it is something that is done, not just thought or spoken. A person would be free to think or believe or even say (i.e. speak) that women are inferior, or subordinate and should be raped or discriminated against, but within this definition and this legislation they would not be free to do it: they would not be free to subordinate or sexually violate or discriminate in the form of pornography. Therefore, as Dworkin and MacKinnon point out, "Anyone who brought a case under the Ordinance would have to *prove* that the challenged materials actually subordinated women in their making or use in order to show that the materials were pornography."[16] The civil rights ordinance therefore defines pornography as *a practice of sex discrimination* in two ways: in itself it is a form of subordination, hence sex discrimination, and it is also a cause of subordination, hence of sex discrimination.

A Practice of Sex Discrimination

Pornography is itself a form of sex discrimination in a number of ways. In pornography women are treated as sexual objects/sexually objectified/subordinate/sexualized/reduced to sexual parts/as objects of sexual use and abuse/pieces of meat/objectified for male desire. This sexual objectification is an act which dehumanizes, degrades and denies women their humanity. Pornography is often described as communicating messages of

misogyny, and it does. But its messages are not what make pornography discriminatory. It is what is done to women in the words and pictures and what the words and pictures do to women in society which make pornography itself a practice of sex discrimination. Pornography "instils the values of male dominance and female subordination,"[17] and sexualizes male power. Sexual subordination is what is done to women in and through pornography, and in and through pornography men learn how to do it.

Pornography is also a practice of sex discrimination in that it is a product manufactured and distributed by an industry. The product is made from real women, many of whom have been coerced or injured in its manufacture.[18] What happens in the making is real. The pictures are real, and the women in the pictures are real. The act of buying and looking is real, and whatever happens as a result is real and has real discriminatory consequences on the lives of women: whether it is a feeling or a "fantasy," the formulation of an attitude or belief, or whether it is a behaviour or action, or some combination of all of these. As a "real" product in which women are sexually subordinated, pornography is a practice of sex discrimination.

Pornography is also a cause of sex discrimination and subordination. The trafficking provision of the civil rights ordinance would enable women to take action against pornographers for subordinating women, to attempt to prove "a direct connection between the pornography and harm to women as a group . . . Such harm could include being targeted for rape, sexual harassment, battery, sexual abuse as children, and forced prostitution," and "the harm of being seen and treated as a sexual thing rather than as a human being." But it could also include "the harm of second-class citizenship on the basis of gender."[19]

> By making a public spectacle and a public celebration of the worthlessness of women, by valuing women as sluts, by defining women according to our availability for sexual use, pornography makes all women's social worthlessness into a public standard. Do you think such a being is likely to become Chairman of the Board? Vice President of the United States. Would you hire a "cunt" to represent you? Perform surgery on you?

Run your university? Edit your broadcast? Would you promote one above a man? . . . In creating pervasive and invisible bigotry, in addition to constituting sex discrimination in itself, pornography is utterly inconsistent with any real progress toward sex equality for women.[20]

The new definition of pornography in terms of "sexually explicit subordination" and harm marks a radical departure from the old moral view of obscenity:

> Whatever one's moral judgements, the presentations in the definition are there because there is material evidence that they do harm, and the decision has been made that the harm they do to some people is not worth the sexual pleasure they give to other people—not because the people making the laws do not like these acts sexually or disapprove of them morally.[21]

The definition is "closed, concrete and descriptive, not open-ended, conceptual, moral" or vague. It targets only pornography, but it also defines pornography narrowly rather than broadly and "takes the risk that all damaging materials might not be covered in order to try to avoid misuse of the law."[22]

Notes

1. Catherine A. MacKinnon, "Pornography, Civil Rights and Speech," *Harvard Civil Rights—Civil Liberties Law Review* 1 (11), 1985.

2. Andrea Dworkin and Catherine A. MacKinnon, *Pornography and Civil Rights: A New Day for Women's Equality* (Minneapolis, MN: Organizing Against Pornography, 1988) op. cit., pp. 138–9.

3. Ibid., p. 40. The materials used in social science research and described as non-violent often do contain acts of force or violence which men just do not see.

4. Dworkin and MacKinnon, op. cit. p. 45

5. The Indianapolis Ordinance defined pornography as follows:

> Pornography shall mean the graphic sexually explicit subordination of women, whether in pictures or in words, that also includes one or more of the following:

(1) Women are presented as sexual objects who enjoy pain or humiliation; or

(2) Women are presented as sexual objects who experience sexual pleasure in being raped; or

(3) Women are presented as sexual objects tied up or cut up or mutilated or bruised or physically hurt, or as dismembered or truncated or fragmented or severed into body parts; or

(4) Women are presented being penetrated by objects or animals; or

(5) Women are presented in scenarios of degradation, injury, abasement, torture, shown as filthy or inferior, bleeding, bruised or hurt in a context that makes those conditions sexual; or

(6) Women are presented as sexual objects for domination, conquest, violation, exploitation, possession, or use, or through postures or positions of servility or submission or display.

6. The definition in the Pornography Victims Compensation Act 1989 included some of the vocabulary of the civil rights definition, but excluded the practice of subordination as a characteristic of pornography and included sexually explicit material that was non-subordinating (i.e. masturbation and sexual intercourse).

7. Dworkin and MacKinnon, op cit., pp. 37 and 40.

8. Ibid., p. 37.

9. Ibid., pp. 37–8.

10. Ibid., p. 38

11. Ibid., pp. 38–9.

12. Ibid., p. 39.

13. Ibid.

14. Susan Cole, *Pornography and the Sex Crisis* (Toronto: Amanita Publications, 1989), pp. 64, 66, 98.

15. Carol Smart, "Theory into Practice: The Problem of Pornography," *Feminism and the Power of Law* (London: Routledge, 1989), p. 133.

16. Dworkin and MacKinnon, op. cit., p. 39.

17. Cole, op. cit., p. 102.

18. Written pornography—just words—has been shown in laboratory studies to have the same effect as pictures. Audiotaped studies have also had the same effect as pictures: see N. M. Malamuth and J. V. P. Check, "Sexual Arousal to Rape Depictions: Individual Differences," *Journal of Abnormal Psychology,* 92(1), 1983, pp. 55–67.

19. Dworkin and MacKinnon, op. cit., p. 45.

20. Ibid., p. 48.

21. Ibid., p. 40.

22. Ibid., p. 39.

Feminist authors like Itzin, Dworkin, and MacKinnon claim that by defining pornography in terms of the sexually explicit subordination of women they have set pornography squarely within the domain of politics, that is, within the context of power and powerlessness. In so doing, they claim that pornography can now be seen for what it is: a political issue rather than a moral issue. Is it really the case, however, that pornography is just a political issue? Insofar as pornography portrays women as subordinate, recommends that they be treated as sexually subordinate, and perhaps even induces men to treat them as sexually subordinate (and Itzin, Dworkin, and MacKinnon believe pornography does all of these things), would not pornography be responsible for degrading and harming human beings? Would not pornography so conceived be more than a political issue? Would it not also be a significant moral issue? Would Itzin, Dworkin, and MacKinnon perhaps reply that by grounding their amendment (with its definition) in the law, namely, the Fourteenth Amendment to the U.S. Constitution, they were trying to categorize pornography as illegal rather than trying to censor it as morally wrong? Would a legal case against pornography be stronger than a moral one?

Why did Mayor Donald Fraser veto the amendment? Fraser, a lawyer, saw the Minneapolis amendment raising important constitutional questions that he could not ignore. Fraser claimed, according to the January 6, 1984, issue of *The New York Times,* that "The definition of pornography in the ordinance is so broad and so vague as to make it impossible for a book seller, movie theater operator or museum director to adjust his or her conduct in order to keep from running afoul of its proscriptions." Do you agree with Fraser on this point? Or do you agree with Itzin, who claims that the amendment defined pornography so narrowly that it risked not covering all damaging material? In addition, Fraser seems to have construed pornography as a form of "speech" which thereby falls under the First Amendment dealing with freedom of speech and the press. Is pornography a form of speech? Does it merit protection under the First Amendment? Or does its alleged violation of the Fourteenth Amendment override any protection it might have under the First? Mayor Fraser, when discussing his veto, observed, "When in doubt I probably err on the side of the First Amendment."

THE CONSEQUENCES OF PORNOGRAPHY

Presumably human beings buy products because they desire them, and they desire them because they believe that the products will provide some sort of benefit to themselves or perhaps to others. People spend billions of dollars each year on pornographic products. The benefits they are seeking range from the pleasure derived from observing sexually explicit material, to the pleasure that accompanies masturbating while observing the material, to the enrichment of their sex lives through the new sexual techniques they learn from watching "professionals" at work in pornography. And clearly the producers and distributors of pornography and their employees benefit from the sale of their products, although it is unlikely that many consumers have the welfare of these people in mind when they consume pornography. In brief, people produce and consume pornography because of benefits they believe they will derive from it.

Yet people frequently find themselves in the position of producing and consuming products for the benefits that they hope will result only to discover that the whole process has significant attendant harms. For example, a number of years ago thalidomide appeared on the market as a sedative that seemed to function as an effective tranquilizer. Eventually, however, medical researchers linked the drug to a host of birth defects that occurred in babies whose mothers had taken the drug during pregnancy. The drug was, of course, pulled from the market. The list of products that were marketed as beneficial but turned out to have attendant harms that outweighed the benefits is long, ranging from children's toys to the Ford Pinto. Does pornography belong on that list? Does it have attendant harms?

During the past twenty-five years the United States government appointed two commissions to investigate the harms allegedly created by pornography. In 1970 *The Report of the Commission on Obscenity and Pornography* found no evidence of harm. It is important to note, however, that the Commission's mandate excluded from consideration sexually violent materials which were being assessed at the same time by the United States Commission on the Causes and Prevention of Violence that issued its report *Violence in the Media* in 1969. In addition, the research and conclusions of the 1970 report were called into question by a wide variety of social scientists who agreed that the report was fundamentally flawed. By the time the 1985 Commission reinvestigated the alleged harms of pornography, a great deal of research on the topic had been conducted by social scientists in the intervening fifteen years. The *Final Report of the Attorney General's Commission on Pornography* issued in 1986 concluded that pornography did harm some women and children. Edna F. Einsiedel provided for the Commission a detailed analysis of the social science research that had been conducted on the effects of pornography. The conclusions reached by Einsiedel, a Professor and Director of the Graduate Program in Communication Studies at the University of Calgary in Alberta, Canada, are summarized below. The catharsis theory to which she refers suggests that a person who achieves sexual climax through the use of highly arousing pornography is less likely to commit sex crimes in the future. Einsiedel writes,

> It is clear that the conclusion of "no negative effects" advanced by the 1970 Commission is no longer tenable. It is also clear that catharsis, as an explanatory model for the impact of pornography, is simply unwarranted by evidence in this area, nor has catharsis fared well in the general area of mass media effects and antisocial behaviour.
>
> This is not to say, however, that the evidence as a whole is comprehensive enough or definitive enough. While we have learned much more since 1970, even more areas remain to be explored.
>
> What do we know at this point?
>
> - It is clear that many sexually explicit materials, particularly of the commercial variety, that are obviously designed to be arousing, *are* in fact arousing, both to offenders and to non-offenders.
> - Rapists appear to be aroused by both forced as well as consenting sex depictions while non-offenders (college males) are less aroused by depictions of sexual aggression. On the other hand, when these portrayals show the victim as "enjoying" the rape, these portrayals similarly elicit high arousal levels.
> - Arousal to rape depictions appears to correlate with attitudes of acceptance of rape myths and sexual violence and both these measures likewise correlate with laboratory-observed aggressive behaviours.
> - Depictions of sexual violence also increase the likelihood that rape myths are accepted and sexual violence toward women condoned. Such attitudes have further been found to be correlated with laboratory aggression toward women. Finally, there is also some evidence that laboratory aggression toward women correlates with self-reported sexually aggressive behaviours.
>
> What we know about the effects of non-violent sexually explicit material is less clear. There are tentative indications that negative effects in the areas of attitudes might also occur, particularly from massive exposure. The mechanics of such effects need to be elaborated more fully, however, particularly in light of more recent findings that suggest that degrading themes might have effects that differ from

non-violent, non-degrading, sexually explicit materials. This is clearly an area that deserves further investigation.

- There are suggestions that pornography availability may be one of a nexus of sociocultural factors that has some bearing on rape rates in the USA. Other cross-cultural data, however, offer mixed results as well, so these findings have to be viewed as tentative at best.
- We still know very little about the causes of deviancy, and it is important to examine the developmental patterns of offenders, particularly patterns of early exposure. We do have some convergence on the data from some rapists and males in the general population in the areas of arousal and attitudes, but, again, this remains to be examined more closely.

Clearly, the need for more research remains as compelling as ever.[1]

Einsiedel's report reviewed the social science research on the consequences of pornography up to the time of the 1986 Commission's Report. James Weaver, an Associate Professor of Mass Communication and the Director of the Behavioral Research Laboratory at Auburn University, provides a review that includes research done in the early 1990s. Like Einsiedel, Weaver analyzes scores of research studies and cautiously draws some conclusions. According to Weaver, one is warranted in concluding that some pornography enhances male sexually calloused perceptions of women and in some cases promotes male aggressive behavior toward women. Weaver, then, views research as supporting *the sexual callousness model* for interpreting human responses to pornography rather than two other models; namely, *the sexual communication model,* according to which pornography is simply entertaining communication involving sexual behavior and has no negative consequences, the *violence desensitization model,* according to which only the blatant portrayal of violence against women influences asocial attitudes and behaviors towards women, whereas nonviolent pornography has innocuous effects. Here are Weaver's conclusions:

Conclusions

The fact that exposure to contemporary pornography can activate sexually callous perceptions of women and promote manipulative and, in some instances, aggressive behaviours is highlighted consistently in the research evidence. Enhanced perceptual and behavioural callousness towards women is most apparent following consumption of materials that unambiguously portray women as sexually promiscuous and undiscriminating—a depiction that dominates modern pornography. Adverse consequences resulting from exposure to coercive and/or violent sexually explicit material—especially portrayals in which women are shown tolerating, if not enjoying, abusive treatment as in the rape-myth scenario—also appear to be equally substantial. Furthermore, although findings concerning idealized-sex depictions are limited, there are some that indicate that consumption of such materials may also elevate sexual callousness towards women. However, where this has been observed, the effect appears weaker (i.e. not achieving the traditional level of statistical significance) than that produced by the other two content categories.

The nature and extent of the observed responses to contemporary sexually explicit

---

[1]Edna F. Einsiedel, "The Experimental Research Evidence: Effects of Pornography on the 'Average Individual,'" in *Pornography: Women, Violence and Civil Liberties,* ed. Catherine Itzin (Oxford, U.K.: Oxford University Press, 1992), pp. 281–283, by permission of Oxford University Press.

materials, taken together, appear most consistent with the sexual callousness model (Zillman and Weaver, 1989) while contradicting the expectations of the sexual communication and violence desensitization viewpoints. For example, although it is evident that consumers can acquire information about sexuality from pornography as suggested by the sexual communication model, it is equally apparent that they typically fail to respond to the various content themes and portrayals as fictional representations "for enjoyment only." In fact, the findings show that many viewers extract callousness-promoting information from pornography. The fact that exposure to pornography can produce significant asocial perceptual responses presents a serious challenge to the "it is not sex, but violence" (Donnerstein and Linz, 1986, p. 56) proclamation espoused by advocates of the violence desensitization model.

Consideration of the pragmatic implications of the evidence suggests first that contemporary sexually explicit materials may be, as others have argued (Russell, 1988; Chapter 17), a potent catalyst for sexually abusive behaviours such as rape. Exposure to pornography, it should be remembered, resulted in both a "loss-of-respect" for female sexual autonomy *and* the disinhibition of men in the expression of aggression against women. Extensive research evidence shows that these two factors are prominent, interwoven components in the perceptual profiles of sexually abusive and aggressive individuals (e.g. Briere, 1987; Costin, 1985; Kanin, 1969, 1985; Koss, Leonard, Beezley and Oros, 1985; Rapaport and Burkhart, 1984).

A second implication concerns the extent to which pornography induces misogynist perceptions which negatively influence the welfare of women in everyday, non-sexual circumstance. Many writers (e.g. Garry, 1978; Lederer, 1980) have suggested that the most damaging consequences of the essentially unrestricted availability of pornography are evident in the ill-treatment of women (employment discrimination, economic exploitation, etc.) simply because of their gender. Although empirical evidence addressing this issue is lacking, the occurrence of such effects seems, at least to some degree, probably given that pornographic productions typically present women as socially and sexually subordinate and inferior to men (cf. Brosius, Staab and Weaver, 1991) in a manner consistent with sexual stereotypes which permeate Western cultures (Belk and Snell, 1987; Garry, 1978; Rimmer, 1986).

Finally, there is reason to suspect that pornography—with its seemingly factual, documentary-style presentation of sexual behaviours—has usurped most other socialization agents to become a primary institution of sexual indoctrination in many societies (Zillman and Weaver, 1989). Research shows, for example, that a substantial proportion of young people in North America become consumers of sexually explicit materials during pre-adolescence (Bryant and Frown, 1989). Clearly, in light of the research findings, the desirability of pornography as a rudimentary "educator" about sex must be contemplated.[2]

The research conducted by social scientists summarized by Einsiedel and Weaver uses, among other things, self-reports (in the form of responses to questionnaires and anecdotal reports) given by the people whose reactions to pornography are being studied. A self-report given by an infamous serial sex killer in which he implicated pornography in his development appeared three years after the 1986 Commission issued its report utilizing Einsiedel's findings, and three years before the publication of Weaver's analysis in 1992 in

[2]James Weaver, "The Social Science and Psychological Research Evidence: Perceptual and Behavioural Consequences of Exposure to Pornography," in *Pornography: Women, Violence and Civil Liberties,* ed. Catherine Itzin (Oxford, U.K.: Oxford University Press, 1992), pp. 306–308, by permission of Oxford University Press.

Catherine Itzin's book. The serial sex killer, Theodore Bundy, allowed the psychologist James Dobson to interview him on January 23, 1989, the day before Bundy was executed in the Florida State Prison for the sex slaying of a twelve-year-old child, Kimberly Leach. Bundy granted the interview to Dobson with the stipulation that the interview would be used to criticize pornography and its impact on society. What follows is a transcript of the interview with Dr. Dobson.

from Exclusive Interview with Serial Sex Killer Theodore Bundy, Executed January 24, 1989

JAMES DOBSON

DR. DOBSON: Ted, it is about 2:30 in the afternoon. You are scheduled to be executed tomorrow morning at seven o'clock if you don't receive another stay. What is going through your mind? What thoughts have you had in these last few days?

TED BUNDY: Well, I won't kid you to say that it's something that I feel than I'm in control of, or something that I've come to terms with, because I haven't. It's a moment-by-moment thing. Sometimes I feel very tranquil, and other times I don't feel tranquil at all. What's going through my mind right now is to use the minutes and hours that I have left as fruitfully as possible, and see what happens. It helps to live in the moment in the essence that we use it productively. Right now, I'm feeling calm and in large part because I'm here with you.

DR. DOBSON: For the record, you are guilty of killing many women and girls.

BUNDY: Yes, Yes. That's true.

DR. DOBSON: Ted, how did it happen? Take me back. What are the antecedents of the behavior we've seen? So much grief, so much sorrow, so much pain for so many people. Where did it start? How did this moment come about?

BUNDY: That's the question of the hour and one that not only people much more intelligent than I have been working on for years, but one that I've been working on for years and trying to understand. Is there enough time to explain it all?

I don't know. I think I understand it though . . . understand what happened to me to the extent that I can see how certain feelings and ideas that developed in me to the point where I began to act out on them—certain very violent and very destructive feelings.

DOBSON: Let's go back, then, to those roots. First of all, you, as I understand it, were raised in what you consider to have been a healthy home.

BUNDY: Absolutely.

DOBSON: You were not physically abused; you were not sexually abused; you were not emotionally abused.

BUNDY: No. No way. That's part of the tragedy of this whole situation, because I grew up in a wonderful home with two dedicated and loving parents. I'm one of five brothers and sisters. [It was] a home where we as children were the focus of my parents' lives, where we regularly attended church; [I had] two Christian parents who did not drink, they did not smoke, there was no gambling, there was no physical abuse or fighting in the home. I'm not saying this was "Leave it to Beaver."

DOBSON: It wasn't a perfect home.

BUNDY: No, I don't know that such a home even exists, but it was a fine, solid Christian home, and I hope no one will try to take the easy way out and blame or otherwise accuse my family of contributing to this because I know, and I'm trying to tell you as honestly as I know how, what happened. I think this is the message I want to get across. But as a young boy—and I mean a boy of 12 or 13 certainly—I encountered outside the home again ... in the local grocery store and the local drug stores the soft-core pornography, what people call "soft core." But as I think I explained to you last night, Dr. Dobson, in an anecdote, that as young boys do, we explored the back roads and side ways and by-ways of our neighborhood, and often times people would dump the garbage and whatever they were cleaning out of the house. From time to time we'd come across pornographic books of a harder nature, more graphic you might say, [of] a more explicit nature than we would encounter, let's say, in your local grocery store. And this also included such things as detective magazines ...

DOBSON: And those that involved violence, then.

BUNDY: Yes, and this is something I think I want to emphasize as the most damaging kinds of pornography, and again I'm talking from personal experience—hard, real, personal experience. The most damaging kinds of pornography are those that involve violence and sexual violence. Because the wedding of those two forces, as I know only too well, brings about behavior that is just too terrible to describe.

DOBSON: Now, walk me through that. What was going on in your mind at that time?

BUNDY: Okay, but before we go any further, I think it's important to me that people believe what I'm saying. I'm not blaming pornography; I'm not saying that it caused me to go out and do certain things. And I take full responsibility for whatever I've done and all the things that I've done. That's not the question here. The question and the issue is how this kind of literature contributed and helped mold and shape these kinds of violent behavior.

DOBSON: It fueled your fantasies.

BUNDY: In the beginning it fuels this kind of thought process. Then at a certain time it's instrumental in what I would say crystallizing it, making it into something which is almost like a separate entity inside. At that point you're at

the verge, or I was at the verge of acting out on these kinds of thoughts.

DOBSON: Now I really want to understand that. You had gone about as far as you could go in your own fantasy life with printed material, and then there was the urge to take that little step or big step over to a physical event.

BUNDY: Right. And it happened in stages, gradually. It doesn't necessarily, not to me at least, happen overnight. My experience with pornography that deals on a violent level with sexuality is that once you become addicted to it—and I look at this as a kind of addiction—like other kinds of addiction ... I would keep looking for more potent, more explicit, more graphic kinds of materials. Like an addiction, you keep craving something which is harder, harder. Something which gives you a greater sense of excitement. Until you reach the point where the pornography only goes so far. You reach that jumping-off point where you begin to wonder if maybe actually doing it will give you that which is beyond just reading about it or looking at it.

DOBSON: How long did you stay at that point before you actually assaulted someone?

BUNDY: That is a very delicate point in my own development. And we're talking about something ... we're talking about having reached the point or a gray area that surrounded that point over a course of years.

DOBSON: You don't remember how long that was?

BUNDY: I would say a couple years. What I was dealing with there were strong inhibitions against criminal behavior—violent behavior—that had been conditioned into me, bred into me, in my environment, in my neighborhood, in my church, in my school. Things which said no, this is wrong. I mean, even to think of this is wrong, but certainly to do it is wrong. And I'm on that edge, and these last ... you might say, the last vestiges of restraint—the barriers to actually doing something were being tested constantly, and assailed through the kind of fantasy life that was fueled largely by pornography.

DOBSON: Do you remember what pushed you over that edge? Do you remember the decision to go for it? Do you remember where you decided to throw caution to the wind?

BUNDY: Again, when you say pushed, I know what you're saying ... I don't want to infer again that I was some helpless kind of victim. And yet, we're talking about an influence which—that is the influence of violent types of media and violent pornography—which was an indispensable link in the chain of behavior, the chain of events that led to the behavior, to the assaults, to the murders, and what have you. It's a very difficult thing to describe. The sensation of reaching that point where I knew that it was like something had snapped, that I knew that I couldn't control it anymore, that these barriers that I had learned as a child, that had been instilled in me, were not enough to hold me back with respect to seeking out and harming somebody.

DOBSON; Would it be accurate to call that a frenzy, a sexual frenzy?

BUNDY: Well, yes. That's one way to describe it. A compulsion, a building up of destructive energy. Again, another fact here that I haven't mentioned is the use of alcohol. But I think that what alcohol did in conjunction with, let's say, my exposure to pornography [is that] alcohol reduced my inhibitions, at the same time. The fantasy life that was fueled by pornography eroded them further, you see.

DOBSON: In the early days, you were nearly always about half-drunk when you did these things. Is that right?

BUNDY: Yes. Yes.

DOBSON: Was that always true?

BUNDY: I would say that was generally the case. Almost without exception.

DOBSON: Alright, if I can understand it now, there's this battle going on within. There are the conventions that you've been taught. There's the right and wrong that you learned as a child. And then there is this unbridled passion fueled by your plunge into hard-core, violent pornography. And those things are at war with each other.

BUNDY: Yes.

DOBSON: And then with the alcohol diminishing the inhibitions, you let go.

BUNDY: Well, yes. And you can summarize it that way, and that's accurate, certainly. And it just occurred to me that some people would say that, well, I've see that stuff, and it doesn't do anything to me. And I can understand that. Virtually everyone can be exposed to so-called pornography, and while they were aroused to it one degree or another, not go out and do anything wrong.

DOBSON: Addictions are like that. They affect some people more than they affect others. But there is a percentage of people affected by hard-core pornography in a very violent way, and you're obviously one of them.

BUNDY: That was a major component, and I don't know why I was vulnerable to it. All I know is that it had an impact on me that was just so central to the development of the violent behavior that I engaged in.

DOBSON: Ted, after you committed your first murder, what was the emotional effect on you? What happened in the days after that?

BUNDY: Again, please understand that even all these years later, it's very difficult to talk about it, and reliving it through talking about it. It's difficult, to say the least, but I want you to understand what happened. It was like coming out of some kind of horrible trance or dream. I can only liken it to, and I don't want to overdramatize it, but to have been possessed by something so awful and so alien, and then the next morning wake up from it, remember what happened and realize that basically, I mean, in the eyes of the law, certainly, and in the eyes of God, you're responsible. To wake up in the morning and realize what I had done, with a clear mind and all my essential moral and ethical feelings intact at that moment. [I was] absolutely horrified that I was capable of doing something like that.

DOBSON: You really hadn't known that before?

BUNDY: There is just absolutely no way to describe—first the brutal urge to do that kind of thing, and then what happens. I want people to understand this, too, and I'm not saying this gratuitously because it's important that people understand this. That basically, I was a normal person. I wasn't some guy hanging out at bars, or a bum. Or I wasn't a pervert in the sense that people look at somebody and say I know there's something wrong with him and just tell. But I was essentially a normal person. I had good friends. I lived a normal life except for this one small, but very potent, very destructive segment of it that I kept very secret, very close to myself, and didn't let anybody know about it. And part of the shock and horror for my dear friends and family, years ago when I was first arrested, was that there was no clue. They looked at me, and they looked at the All-American boy. I mean, I wasn't perfect, but I want to be quite candid with you, I was okay. The basic humanity and basic spirit that God gave me was intact, but it unfortunately became overwhelmed at times. And I think people need to recognize that those of us who have been so much influenced by violence in the media—in particular pornographic violence—are not some kinds of inherent monsters. We are your sons, and we are your husbands. And we grew up in regular families. And pornography can reach out and snatch a kid out of any house today. It snatched me out of my home 20, 30 years ago, as diligent as my parents were, and they were diligent in protecting their children. And as good a Christian home as we had—and we had a wonderful Christian home—there is no protection against the kinds of influences that there are loose in a society that tolerates.

DOBSON: You feel this really deeply, don't you? Ted, outside these walls right now there are several hundred reporters that wanted to talk to you.

BUNDY: Yeah.

DOBSON: And you asked me to come here from California because you had something you wanted to say. This hour that we have together is not just an interview with a man who is scheduled to die tomorrow morning. I'm here and you're here because of this message that you're talking about right here. You really feel that hard-core pornography and the doorway to it, soft-core pornography, is doing untold dam-

age to other people, and causing other women to be abused and killed the way you did it.

BUNDY: Listen, I'm no social scientist, and I haven't done a survey. I mean, I don't pretend that I know what John Q. Citizen thinks about this. But I've lived in prison for a long time now. And I've met a lot of men who were motivated to commit violence just like me. And without exception, every one of them was deeply involved in pornography—without question, without exception—deeply influenced and consumed by an addiction to pornography. There's no question about it. The FBI's own study on serial homicide shows that the most common interest among serial killers is pornography.

DOBSON: That's true.

BUNDY: And it's real. It's true.

DOBSON: Ted, what would your life have been like without that influence? You can only speculate.

BUNDY: I know it would have been far better, not just for me—and excuse me for being so self-centered here, [but] it would have been a lot better for me and lots of other people. It would have been a lot better. There is no question but that it would have been a fuller life. Certainly a life that would not have involved—I'm absolutely certain—would not have involved this kind of violence that I have committed.

DOBSON: I'm sure, Ted, if I were able to ask you the questions that are being asked out there, one of the most important as you come down to perhaps your final hours: Are you thinking about all those victims out there and their families who are so wounded? You know, years later their lives have not returned to normal. They will never return to normal.

BUNDY: Absolutely.

DOBSON: Are you carrying that load, that weight? Is there remorse there?

BUNDY: Again, I know that people will accuse me of being self-serving, but we're beyond that now, I mean, I'm just telling you how I feel. But through God's help, I have been able to come to the point where I—much too late, but better late than never—feel the hurt and the pain that I am responsible for. Yes, absolutely. In the past few days, myself and a number of investigators have been talking about unsolved cases—murders that I was involved in. And it's hard to talk about all these years later because it revives in me all those terrible feelings and those thoughts that I have steadfastly and diligently dealt with—I think successfully, with the love of God. And yet, it's reopened that. And I've felt the pain, and I've felt the horror again of all that. And I can only hope that those who I have harmed and those who I have caused so much grief—even if they don't believe my expression of sorrow and remorse—will believe what I'm saying now, that there is loose in their towns, in their communities, people like me today whose dangerous impulses are being fueled day in and day out by violence in the media in its various forms, particularly sexualized violence. And what scares me—and let's come into the present now because what I'm talking about happened 20, 30 years ago, that is, in my formative stages. And what scares and appalls me, Dr. Dobson, is when I see what's on cable TV, some of the movies, some of the violence in the movies that come into homes today was stuff that they wouldn't show in X-rated adult theaters 30 years ago.

DOBSON: The slasher movies that you're talking about.

BUNDY: The stuff is—I'm telling you from personal experience—the most that is graphic violence on the screen. Particularly as it gets into the home to the children who may be unattended or unaware that they may be a Ted Bundy who has that vulnerability to that predisposition to be influenced by that kind of behavior, by that kind of movie and that kind of violence. There are kids sitting out there switching the TV dial around and come upon these movies late at night, or I don't know when they're on, but they're on, and any kid can watch them. It's scary when I think what would have happened to me if I had seen [them]. [Or] to know that children are watching that kind of thing today, or can pick up their phone and dial away for it, or send away for it.

DOBSON: Can you help me understand this desensitization process that took place? What was going on in your mind?

BUNDY: Well, by desensitization, I describe it in specific terms. Each time I harmed someone, each time I killed someone, there would be an enormous amount of—especially at first—enormous amount of horror, guilt, remorse afterward. But then that impulse to do it again would come back even stronger. The unique thing about how this worked, Dr. Dobson, is that I still felt, in my regular life, the full range of guilt and remorse about other things. Regret and . . .

DOBSON: You had this compartmentalized . . .

BUNDY: . . . compartmentalized, very well focused, very sharply focused area where it was like a black hole. It was like a crack. And everything that fell into that crack just disappeared. Does that make sense?

DOBSON: Yes, it does. One of the final murders that you committed, of course, was apparently little Kimberly Leach, 12 years of age. I think the public outcry is greater there because an innocent child was taken from a playground. What did you feel after that? Were there the normal emotions three days later? Where were you, Ted?

BUNDY: I can't really talk about that right now. I would like to be able to convey to you what that experience is like, but I can't. I won't be able to talk about that. I can't begin to understand. Well, I can try, but I, I'm aware that I can't begin to understand the pain that the parents of these children that I have—and these young women—that I have harmed, feel. And I can't restore really much to them, if anything. And I won't pretend to. And I don't even expect them to forgive me, and I'm not asking for it. That kind of forgiveness is of God. And if they have it, they have it. And if they don't, well, maybe they'll find it someday.

DOBSON: Do you deserve the punishment the state has inflicted upon you?

BUNDY: That's a very good question, and I'll answer it very honestly. I don't want to die. I'm not going to kid you. I'll kid you not. I deserve, certainly, the most extreme punishment society has, and I think society deserves to be protected from me and from others like me. That's for sure. What I hope will come of our discussion is (that) I think society deserves to be protected from itself because as we've been talking there are forces at loose in this country—particularly again, this kind of violent pornography—where on the one hand, well-meaning, decent people will condemn behavior of a Ted Bundy, while they're walking past a magazine rack full of the very kinds of things that send young kids down the road to be Ted Bundys. That's the irony. We're talking here not just about morals. What I'm talking about is going beyond retribution, which is what people want with me. Going beyond retribution and punishment, because there is no way in the world that killing me is going to restore those beautiful children to their parents and correct and soothe the pain. But I'll tell you, there are lots of other kids playing in streets around this country today who are going to be dead tomorrow and the next day and the next day and next month, because other young people are reading the kinds of things and seeing the kinds of things that are available in the media today.

DOBSON: Ted, as you would imagine, there is tremendous cynicism about you on the outside, and I suppose for good reason. I'm not sure that there is anything that you could say that people would believe. And yet, you told me last night, and I have heard this through our mutual friend, John Tanner, that you have accepted the forgiveness of Jesus Christ, and are a follower and a believer in Him. Do you draw strength from that, as you approach these final hours?

BUNDY: I do. I can't say that being in the valley of the shadow of death is something that I've become all that accustomed to, and that I'm strong and nothing's bothering me. Listen, it's no fun. It gets kind of lonely, and yet, I have to remind myself that every one of us will go through this someday in one way or another . . .

DOBSON: It is appointed unto man.

BUNDY: . . . and countless millions who have walked this earth before us have, so this is just an experience which we all share. Here I am.

How trustworthy shall we regard Bundy's self-report? Assuredly, he was a smooth talker capable of luring many young women to their deaths. Is he deceiving us in these last hours of his life? Is he trying to wrest some pity, compassion, or forgiveness from us through his report? Are his final remarks the ultimate in self-serving? Bundy recognized that people might discount his remarks as self-serving. But is it not the mark of an expert "con man" to disarm his victims by answering their objections to his "snow job" in advance? But what would Bundy, as a "con man," have to gain from lying at this point? People are divided on how seriously to take Bundy's final comments. Yet there is a point in his interview worth noting. Does he not seem to focus again and again on pornography that displays sexual violence? Is he not reinforcing the distinction, already used by Einsiedel and Weaver, between violent and nonviolent pornography? If we are going to make headway in assessing the consequences of pornography, are we perhaps going to need to divide pornography into various genres, some of which might be harmless while others of which might be harmful?

Ann Garry tries to draw such a distinction in her article, "Pornography and Respect for Women." The main focus of her discussion, however, is the morality of pornography, and that is the next topic we must consider.

THE MORALITY AND LEGALITY OF PORNOGRAPHY

Is pornography morally right or wrong? Is it morally permissible or impermissible? There are two basic approaches we could take in trying to assess the morality of pornography. We could adopt a *consequentialist* approach (also referred to as *teleological*) in which we would focus on the consequences of pornography. We would ask: Does pornography generate more beneficial than harmful consequences? Or is the reverse the case? Does it produce more harmful than beneficial outcomes? Presumably if the scale tips in favor of beneficial outcomes, then pornography would be morally permissible. If, however, the scale is weighted more heavily on the side of harmful outcomes, then pornography would appear to be morally impermissible. If we focused on consequences to assess the morality of pornography, we would have to look not only at the way pornography affects the consumers of it, but also at the consequences of pornography for those involved in its production. In the research summarized by Einsiedel and Weaver, as well as in the self-report of Bundy, the focus was on the consequences of pornography for those who consume it and for those who are or might be impacted by those consumers. What about those who are involved in its production? Clearly, the financial benefits for the producers are enormous. What about the actors in pornographic photographs and films? Some of them perhaps fare quite well. Others might be subjected to significant harms. Consider, for example, the following comments of Catherine Itzin, writing about her reactions to the Williams Committee in the United Kingdom:

> My interest in pornography dates from an article by Polly Toynbee published in the *Guardian* on 30 October 1981, describing what she had seen as a member of the Williams Committee on Obscenity and Film Censorship. "These included scenes of castration, cannibalism, flaying, the crushing of breasts in vices, exploding vaginas packed with hand grenades, eyes gouged out, beatings, dismembering, burnings, multiple rape and every other horror that could befall the human body." She had also witnessed "women engaged in sexual intercourse with pigs and dogs" and heard of women killed on screen in snuff movies. However, she, together with the other members of the Williams Committee, concluded that there was no evidence that pornography harmed people, except in a few cases where participants in the photos might have come to harm: "the poor, unhealthy, unhappy, many Third World children" or the "South American prostitutes who were actually sexually murdered in films."
>
> What she described was burned into my brain. I was completely bewildered as to how anyone could look at that material and not see that the "people" in the pictures were real women who were actually harmed. . . .[1]

Although the amount of pornography in which the actors are physically harmed in the ways described above by Itzin might be small in comparison with all the pornography produced, is it appropriate to ignore these harms if we are going to assess the moral consequences of pornography? In addition, would it not be helpful to distinguish one type or genre of pornography from another type? Some genres might cause harm while other genres might not. Then, too, the causal connection between pornography and harm is seldom so clear as opponents of pornography declare. In the case of "snuff movies" where a performer is filmed while being subjected to sexual violence and murder, the presumption of harm being done to the performer by pornography is very high. Yet, in cases like Ted Bundy, how clear is the causal connection between pornography and the harm done to women? In situations like this, are there not other hereditary and environmental variables that enter the picture? Furthermore, as David Hume demonstrated long ago, temporal sequence does not establish causal connection. That is to say, the mere occurrence of event B after event A is

---

[1]Catherine Itzin, "Introduction: Fact, Fiction and Faction," in *Pornography: Women, Violence and Civil Liberties,* ed. Catherine Itzin (Oxford, U.K.: Oxford University Press, 1992), pp. 1–2.

insufficient grounds for claiming that A caused B. Given problems of this nature in the consequentialist approach, let us consider the other major strategy for assessing the morality of pornography.

The other method is the *deontological* approach in which we would judge the content of pornography irrespective of its consequences. We would ask: What is the message being conveyed by pornography? Does that message violate a moral value or a moral principle? This is the approach preferred by Ann Garry. She distinguishes the content from the form of pornography and argues that while the content of pornography might be immoral because it degrades people, treats them as sex objects, and advocates doing harm to women, the form of pornography is not necessarily immoral. Indeed, Garry suggests that it is possible to construct nondegrading content that would result in morally permissible pornography. The prerequisite to producing such content, however, is the alteration of some of society's fundamental views about sex. Thus, for Garry, morally objectionable, human-degrading content is not a necessary feature of pornography. It is noteworthy that Garry's case supports the suggestion that in order to think clearly and correctly about pornography we might have to discuss it in terms of different genres, depending on its content.

from Pornography and Respect for Women

ANN GARRY

Pornography, like rape, is a male invention, designed to dehumanize women, to reduce the female to an object of sexual access, not to free sensuality from moralistic or parental inhibition. . . . Pornography is the undiluted essence of anti-female propaganda.

Susan Brownmiller, *Against Our Will: Men, Women and Rape*[1]

It is often asserted that a distinguishing characteristic of sexually explicit material is the degrading and demeaning portrayal of the role and status of the human female. It has been argued that erotic materials describe the female as a mere sexual object to be exploited and manipulated sexually. . . . A recent survey shows that 41 percent of American males and 46 percent of the females believe that "sexual materials lead people to lose respect for women." . . . Recent experiments suggest that such fears are probably unwarranted.

Presidential Commission on Obscenity and Pornography[2]

The kind of apparent conflict illustrated in these passages is easy to find in one's own thinking as well. For example, I have been inclined to think that pornography is innocuous and to dismiss "moral" arguments for censoring it because many such arguments rest on an assumption I do not share—that sex is an evil to be controlled. At the same time I believe that it is wrong to exploit or degrade human beings, particularly women and others who are especially susceptible. So if pornography degrades human beings, then even if I would oppose its censorship I surely cannot find it morally innocuous.

In an attempt to resolve this apparent conflict I discuss three questions: Does pornography degrade (or exploit or dehumanize) human beings? If so, does it degrade women in ways or to an extent that it does not degrade men? If so, must pornography degrade women, as Brownmiller thinks, or could genuinely innocuous, nonsexist pornography exist? Although much current pornography

From "Pornography and Respect for Women" by Ann Garry. This article first appeared in *Social Theory and Practice* 4 (Spring 1978). It is reprinted here as it appears in Sharon Bishop and Marjorie Weinzweig, eds., *Philosophy and Women* (Wadsworth, 1979). Reprinted by permission of the author.

does degrade women, I will argue that it is possible to have nondegrading, nonsexist pornography. However, this possibility rests on our making certain fundamental changes in our conceptions of sex and sex roles.

First, some preliminary remarks: Many people now avoid using "pornography" as a descriptive term and reserve "obscenity" for use in legal contexts. Because "pornography" is thought to be a judgmental word, it is replaced by "explicit sexual material," "sexually oriented materials," "erotica," and so on.[3] I use "pornography" to label those explicit sexual materials intended to arouse the reader or viewer sexually. I seriously doubt whether there is a clearly defined class of cases that fits my characterization of pornography. This does not bother me, for I am interested here in obvious cases that would be uncontroversially pornographic—the worst, least artistic kind. The pornography I discuss is that which, taken as a whole, lacks "serious literary, artistic, political, or scientific merit."[4] I often use pornographic films as examples because they generate more concern today than do books or magazines.

What interests me is not whether pornography should be censored but whether one can object to it on moral grounds. The only moral ground I consider is whether pornography degrades people; obviously, other possible grounds exist, but I find this one to be the most plausible.[5] Of the many kinds of degradation and exploitation possible in the production of pornography, I focus only on the content of the pornographic work. I exclude from the discussion (i) the ways in which pornographic film makers might exploit people in making a film, distributing it, and charging too much to see it; (ii) the likelihood that actors, actresses, or technicians will be exploited, underpaid, or made to lose self-respect or self-esteem; and (iii) the exploitation and degradation surrounding the prostitution and crime that often accompany urban centers of pornography.[6] I want to determine whether pornography shows (expresses) and commends behavior or attitudes that exploit or degrade people. For example, if a pornographic film conveys that raping a woman is acceptable, then the content is degrading to women and might be called morally objectionable. Morally objectionable content is not peculiar to pornography; it can also be found in nonpornographic books, films, advertisements, and so on. The question is whether morally objectionable content is necessary to pornography.

• • •

The . . . argument I will consider is that pornography is morally objectionable, not because it leads people to show disrespect for women, but because pornography itself exemplifies and recommends behavior that violates the moral principle to respect persons. The content of pornography is what one objects to. It treats women as mere sex objects "to be exploited and manipulated" and degrades the role and status of women. In order to evaluate this argument, I will first clarify what it would mean for pornography itself to treat someone as a sex object in a degrading manner. I will then deal with three issues central to the discussion of pornography and respect for women: how "losing respect" for a woman is connected with treating her as a sex object: what is wrong with treating someone as a sex object: and why it is worse to treat women rather than men as sex objects. I will argue that the current content of pornography sometimes violates the moral principle to respect persons. Then, in Part IV of this paper, I will suggest that pornography need not violate this principle if certain fundamental changes were to occur in attitudes about sex.

To many people, including Brownmiller and some other feminists, it appears to be an obvious truth that pornography treats people, especially women, as sex objects in a degrading manner. And if we omit "in a degrading manner," the statement seems hard to dispute. How could pornography *not* treat people as sex objects?

First, is it permissible to say that either the content of pornography or pornography itself degrades people or treats people as sex objects? It is not difficult to find examples of degrading content in which women are treated as sex objects. Some pornographic films convey the message that all women really want to be raped, that their resisting struggle is not to be believed. By portraying women in this manner, the content of the movie degrades women. Degrading women is morally objectionable. While seeing the movie need not cause anyone to imitate the behavior shown, we can call the content degrading to women because of the character of the behavior and attitudes it recommends. The same kind of point can be made about films (or books or TV commercials) with other kinds of degrading, thus morally objectionable, content—for example, racist messages.[7]

The next step in the argument is to infer that, because the content or message of pornography is morally objectionable, we can call pornography itself morally objectionable. Support for this step can be found in an analogy. If a person takes every opportunity to recommend that men rape women, we would think not only that his recommendation is immoral but that he is immoral too. In the case of pornography, the objection to making an inference from recommended behavior to the person who recommends is that we ascribe predicates such as 'immoral' differently to people than to films or books. A film vehicle for an objectionable message is still an object independent of its message, its director, its producer, those who act in it, and those who respond to it. Hence one cannot make an unsupported inference from "the content of the film is morally objectionable" to "the film is morally objectionable." Because the central points in this paper do not depend on whether pornography itself (in addition to its content) is morally objectionable. I will not try to support this inference. (The question about the relation of content to the work itself is, of course, extremely interesting: but in part because I cannot decide which side of the argument is more persuasive. I will pass.[8]) Certainly one appropriate way to evaluate pornography is in terms of the moral features of its content. If a pornographic film exemplifies and recommends morally objectionable attitudes or behavior, then its content is morally objectionable.

Let us now turn to the first of our three questions about respect and sex objects: What is the connection between losing respect for a woman and treating her as a sex object? Some people who have lived through the era in which women were taught to worry about men "losing respect" for them if they engaged in sex in inappropriate circumstances find it troublesome (or a least amusing) that feminists—supposedly "liberated" women—are outraged at being treated as sex ob-

jects, either by pornography or in any other way. The apparent alignment between feminists and traditionally "proper" women need not surprise us when we look at it more closely.

The "respect" that men have traditionally believed they have for women—hence a respect they can lose—is not a general respect for persons as autonomous beings; nor is it respect that is earned because of one's personal merits or achievements. It is respect that is an outgrowth of the "double standard." Women are to be respected because they are more pure, delicate, and fragile than men, have more refined sensibilities, and so on. Because some women clearly do not have these qualities, thus do not deserve respect, women must be divided into two groups—the good ones on the pedestal and the bad ones who have fallen from it. One's mother, grandmother, Sunday School teacher, and usually one's wife are "good" women. The appropriate behavior by which to express respect for good women would be, for example, not swearing or telling dirty jokes in front of them, giving them seats on buses, and other "chivalrous" acts. This kind of "respect" for good women is the same sort that adolescent boys in the back seats of cars used to "promise" not to lose. Note that men define, display, and lose this kind of respect. If women lose respect for women, it is not typically a loss of respect for (other) women as a class but a loss of self-respect.

It has now become commonplace to acknowledge that, although a place on the pedestal might have advantages over a place in the "gutter" beneath it, a place on the pedestal is not at all equal to the place occupied by other people (i.e., men). "Respect" for those on the pedestal was not respect for whole, full-fledged people but for a special class of inferior beings.

If a person makes two traditional assumptions—that (at least some) sex is dirty and that women fall into two classes, good and bad—it is easy to see how that person might think that pornography could lead people to lose respect for women or that pornography is itself disrespectful to women.[9] Pornography describes or shows women engaging in activities inappropriate for good women to engage in—or at least inappropriate for them to be seen by strangers engaging in.

If one sees these women as symbolic representatives of all women, then all women fall from grace with these women. This fall is possible, I believe, because the traditional "respect" that men have had for women is not genuine, wholehearted respect for full-fledged human beings but halfhearted respect for lesser beings, some of whom they feel the need to glorify and purify.[10] It is easy to fall from a pedestal. Can we imagine 41 percent of men and 46 percent of women answering "yes" to the question, "Do movies showing men engaging in violent acts lead people to lose respect for men?"?

Two interesting asymmetries appear. The first is that losing respect for men as a class (men with power, typically Anglo men) is more difficult than losing respect for women or ethnic minorities as a class. Anglo men whose behavior warrants disrespect are more likely to be seen as exceptional cases than are women or minorities (whose "transgressions" may be far less serious). Think of the following: women are temptresses: Blacks cheat the welfare system: Italians are gangsters: but the men of the Nixon administration are exceptions—Anglo men as a class did not lose respect because of Watergate and related scandals.

The second asymmetry concerns the active and passive roles of the sexes. Men are seen in the active role. If men lose respect for women because of something "evil" done by women (such as appearing in pornography), the fear is that men will then do harm to women—not that women will do harm to men. Whereas if women lose respect for male politicians because of Watergate, the fear is still that male politicians will do harm, not that women will do harm to male politicians. This asymmetry might be a result of one way in which our society thinks of sex as bad—as harm that men do to women (or to the person playing a female role, as in a homosexual rape). Robert Baker calls attention to this point in "'Pricks' and 'Chicks': A Plea for 'Persons.'"[11] Our slang words for sexual intercourse— "fuck," "screw," or older words such as "take" or "have"—not only can mean harm but have traditionally taken a male subject and a female object. The active male screws (harms) the passive female. A "bad" woman only tempts men to hurt her further.

It is easy to understand why one's proper grandmother would not want men to see pornography or lose respect for women. But feminists reject these "proper" assumptions: good and bad classes of women do not exist: and sex is not dirty (though many people believe it is). Why then are feminists angry at the treatment of women as sex objects, and why are some feminists opposed to pornography?

The answer is that feminists as well as proper grandparents are concerned with respect. However, there are differences. A feminist's distinction between treating a woman as a full-fledged person and treating her as merely a sex object does not correspond to the good-bad woman distinction. In the latter distinction, "good" and "bad" are properties applicable to groups of women. In the feminist view, all women are full-fledged people—some, however, are treated as sex objects and perhaps think of themselves as sex objects. A further difference is that, although "bad" women correspond to those thought to deserve treatment as sex objects, good women have not corresponded to full-fledged people; only men have been full-fledged people. Given the feminist's distinction, she has no difficulty whatever in saying that pornography treats women as sex objects, not as full-fledged people. She can morally object to pornography or anything else that treats women as sex objects.

One might wonder whether any objection to treatment as a sex object implies that the person objecting still believes, deep down, that sex is dirty. I don't think so. Several other possibilities emerge. First, even if I believe intellectually and emotionally that sex is healthy, I might object to being treated *only* as a sex object. In the same spirit, I would object to being treated *only* as a maker of chocolate chip cookies or *only* as a tennis partner, because only one of my talents is being valued. Second, perhaps I feel that sex is healthy, but it is apparent to me that you think sex is dirty; so I don't want you to treat me as a sex object. Third, being treated as any kind of object, not just as a sex object, is unappealing. I would rather be a partner (sexual or otherwise) than an object. Fourth, and more plausible than the first three possibilities, is Robert Baker's view mentioned above.

Both (i) our traditional double standard of sexual behavior for men and women and (ii) the linguistic evidence that we connect the concept of sex with the concept of harm point to what is wrong with treating women as sex objects. As I said earlier, "fuck" and "screw," in their traditional uses, have taken a male subject, a female object, and have had at least two meanings: harm and have sexual intercourse with. (In addition, a prick is a man who harms people ruthlessly; and a motherfucker is so low that he would do something very harmful to his own dear mother.)[12] Because in our culture we connect sex with harm that men do to women, and because we think of the female role in sex as that of harmed object, we can see that to treat a woman as a sex object is automatically to treat her as less than fully human. To say this does not imply that no healthy sexual relationships exist; nor does it say anything about individual men's conscious intentions to degrade women by desiring them sexually (though no doubt some men have these intentions). It is merely to make a point about the concepts embodied in our language.

Psychoanalytic support for the connection between sex and harm comes from Robert J. Stoller. Stoller thinks that sexual excitement is linked with a wish to harm someone (and with at least a whisper of hostility). The key process of sexual excitement can be seen as dehumanization (fetishization) in fantasy of the desired person. He speculates that this is true in some degree of everyone, both men and women, with "normal" or "perverted" activities and fantasies.[13]

Thinking of sex objects as harmed objects enables us to explain some of the first three reasons why one wouldn't want to be treated as a sex object: (1) I may object to being treated only as a tennis partner, but being a tennis partner is not connected in our culture with being a harmed object; and (2) I may not think that sex is dirty and that I would be a harmed object; I may not know what your view is; but what bothers me is that this is the view embodied in our language and culture.

Awareness of the connection between sex and harm helps explain other interesting points. Women are angry about being treated as sex objects in situations or roles in which they do not intend to be regarded in that manner—for example, while serving on a committee or attending a discussion.

It is not merely that a sexual role is inappropriate for the circumstances; it is thought to be a less fully human role than the one in which they intended to function.

Finally, the sex-harm connection makes clear why it is worse to treat women as sex objects than to treat men as sex objects, and why some men have had difficulty understanding women's anger about the matter. It is more difficult for heterosexual men than for women to assume the role of "harmed object" in sex: for men have the self-concept of sexual agents, not of passive objects. This is also related to my earlier point concerning the difference in the solidity of respect for men and for women; respect for women is more fragile. Despite exceptions, it is generally harder for people to degrade men, either sexually or nonsexually, than to degrade women. Men and women have grown up with different patterns of self-respect and expectations regarding the extent to which they deserve and will receive respect or degradation. The man who doesn't understand why women do not want to be treated as sex objects (because he'd sure like to be) would not think of himself as being harmed by that treatment; a woman might.[14] Pornography, probably more than any other contemporary institution, succeeds in treating men as sex objects.

Having seen that the connection between sex and harm helps explain both what is wrong with treating someone as a sex object and why it is worse to treat a woman in this way, I want to use the sex-harm connection to try to resolve a dispute about pornography and women. Brownmiller's view, remember, was that pornography is "the undiluted essence of anti-female propaganda" whose purpose is to degrade women.[15] Some people object to Brownmiller's view by saying that, since pornography treats both men and women as sex objects for the purpose of arousing the viewer, it is neither sexist, antifemale, or designed to degrade women; it just happens that degrading of women arouses some men. How can this dispute be resolved?

Suppose we were to rate the content of all pornography from most morally objectionable to least morally objectionable. Among the most objectionable would be the most degrading—for example, "snuff" films and movies which recommend that men rape women, molest children and puppies, and treat nonmasochists very sadistically.

Next we would find a large amount of material (probably most pornography) not quite so blatantly offensive. With this material it is relevant to use the analysis of sex objects given above. As long as sex is connected with harm done to women, it will be very difficult not to see pornography as degrading to women. We can agree with Brownmiller's opponent that pornography treats men as sex objects, too, but we maintain that this is only pseudoequality; such treatment is still more degrading to women.[16]

In addition, pornography often exemplifies the active/passive, harmer/harmed object roles in a very obvious way. Because pornography today is male-oriented and is supposed to make a profit, the content is designed to appeal to male fantasies. Judging from the content of the most popular legally available pornography, male fantasies still run along the lines of stereotypical sex roles—and, if Stoller is right, include elements of hostility. In much pornography the woman's purpose is to cater to male desires, to service the man or men. Her own pleasure is rarely emphasized for its own sake; she is merely allowed a little heavy breathing, perhaps in order to show her dependence on the great male "lover" who produces her pleasure. In addition, women are clearly made into passive objects in still photographs showing only close-ups of their genitals. Even in movies marketed to appeal to heterosexual couples, such as *Behind the Green Door,* the woman is passive and undemanding (and in this case kidnapped and hypnotized as well). Although many kinds of specialty magazines and films are gauged for different sexual tastes, very little contemporary pornography goes against traditional sex roles. There is certainly no significant attempt to replace the harmer/harmed distinction with anything more positive and healthy. In some stag movies, of course, men are treated sadistically by women; but this is an attempt to turn the tables on degradation, not a positive improvement.

What would cases toward the least objectionable end of the spectrum be like? They would be increasingly less degrading and sexist. The genuinely nonobjectional cases would be nonsexist and nondegrading; but commercial examples do not readily spring to mind.[17] The question is: Does or could any pornography have nonsexist, nondegrading content?

• • •

I want to start with the easier question: Is it possible for pornography to have nonsexist, morally acceptable content? Then I will consider whether any pornography of this sort currently exists.

Imagine the following situation, which exists only rarely today: Two fairly conventional people who love each other enjoy playing tennis and bridge together, cooking good food together, and having sex together. In all these activities they are free from hang-ups, guilt, and tendencies to dominate or objectify each other. These two people like to watch tennis matches and old romantic movies on TV, like to watch Julia Child cook, like to read the bridge column in the newspaper, and like to watch pornographic movies. Imagine further that this couple is not at all uncommon in society and that nonsexist pornography is as common as this kind of nonsexist sexual relationship. The situation sounds fine and healthy to me. I see no reason to think that an interest in pornography would disappear in these circumstances.[18] People seem to enjoy watching others experience or do (especially do well) what they enjoy experiencing, doing, or wish they could do themselves. We do not morally object to people watching tennis on TV: why would we object to these hypothetical people watching pornography?

Can we go from the situation today to the situation just imagined? In much current pornography, people are treated in morally objectionable ways. In the scene just imagined, however, pornography would be nonsexist, nondegrading, morally acceptable. The key to making the change is to break the connection between sex and harm. If Stoller is right, this task may be impossible without changing the scenarios of our sexual lives—scenarios that we have been writing since early childhood. (Stoller does not indicate whether he thinks it possible for adults to rewrite their scenarios or for social change to bring about the possibility of new scenarios in future generations.) But even if we believe that people can change their sexual scenarios, the sex-harm connection is deeply entrenched and has widespread implications. What is needed is a thorough change in people's deep-seated attitudes and feelings about sex roles in general, as well as about sex and roles in sex (sexual roles). Although I cannot even sketch a general outline of such changes here, changes in pornography should be part of a comprehensive program. Television, children's educational material, and nonpornographic movies and novels may be far better avenues for attempting to change attitudes: but one does not want to take the chance that pornography is working against one.

What can be done about pornography in particular? If one wanted to work within the current institutions, one's attempt to use pornography as a tool for the education of male pornography audiences would have to be fairly subtle at first; nonsexist pornography must become familiar enough to sell and be watched. One should realize too that any positive educational value that nonsexist pornography might have may well be as short-lived as most of the effects of pornography. But given these limitations, what could one do?

Two kinds of films must be considered. First is the short film with no plot or character development, just depicted sexual activity in which nonsexist pornography would treat men and women as equal sex partners.[19] The man would not control the circumstances in which the partners had sex or the choice of positions or acts; the woman's preference would be counted equally. There would be no suggestion of a power play or conquest on the man's part, no suggestion that "she likes it when I hurt her." Sexual intercourse would not be portrayed as primarily for the purpose of male ejaculation—his orgasm is not "the best part" of the movie. In addition, both the man and woman would express their enjoyment; the man need not be cool and detached.

The film with a plot provides even more opportunity for nonsexist education. Today's pornography often portrays the female characters as playthings even when not engaging in sexual activity. Nonsexist pornography could show women and men in roles equally valued by society, and sex equality would amount to more than possession of equally functional genitalia. Characters would customarily treat each other with respect and consideration, with no attempt to treat men or women brutally or thoughtlessly. The local Pussycat The-

ater showed a film written and directed by a woman (*The Passions of Carol*), which exhibited a few of the features just mentioned. The main female character in it was the editor of a magazine parody of *Viva*. The fact that some of the characters treated each other very nicely, warmly, and tenderly did not detract from the pornographic features of the movie. This should not surprise us, for even in traditional male-oriented films, lesbian scenes usually exhibit tenderness and kindness.

Plots for nonsexist films could include women in traditionally male jobs (e.g., long-distance truckdriver) or in positions usually held in respect by pornography audiences. For example, a high-ranking female Army officer, treated with respect by men and women alike, could be shown not only in various sexual encounters with other people but also carrying out her job in a humane manner.[20] Or perhaps the main character could be a female urologist. She could interact with nurses and other medical personnel, diagnose illnesses brilliantly, and treat patients with great sympathy as well as have sex with them. When the Army officer or the urologist engage in sexual activities, they will treat their partners and be treated by them in some of the considerate ways described above.

In the circumstances we imagined at the beginning of Part IV of this paper, our nonsexist films could be appreciated in the proper spirit. Under these conditions the content of our new pornography would clearly be nonsexist and morally acceptable. But would the content of such a film be morally acceptable if shown to a typical pornography audience today? It might seem strange for us to change our moral evaluation of the content on the basis of a different audience, but an audience today is likely to see the "respected" urologist and Army officer as playthings or unusual prostitutes—even if our intention in showing the film is to counteract this view. The effect is that, although the content of the film seems morally acceptable and our intention in showing it is morally flawless, women are still degraded.[21] The fact that audience attitude is so important makes one wary of giving wholehearted approval to any pornography seen today.

The fact that good intentions and content are insufficient does not imply that one's efforts toward change would be entirely in vain. Of course, I could not deny that anyone who tries to change an institution from within faces serious difficulties. This is particularly evident when one is trying to change both pornography and a whole set of related attitudes, feelings, and institutions concerning sex and sex roles. But in conjunction with other attempts to change this set of attitudes, it seems preferable to try to change pornography instead of closing one's eyes in the hope that it will go away. For I suspect that pornography is here to stay.[22]

Notes

1. (New York: Simon & Schuster, 1975), p. 394.

2. *The Report of the Commission on Obscenity and Pornography* (Washington, DC, 1970), p. 201. Hereinafter, *Report*.

3. *Report*, p. 3, n. 4; and p. 149.

4. *Roth* v. *United States*, 354 U.S. 476, 489 (1957).

5. To degrade someone in this situation is to lower her/his rank or status in humanity. This is morally objectionable because it is incompatible with showing respect for a person. Some of the other moral grounds for objecting to pornography have been considered by the Supreme Court: Pornography invades our privacy and hurts the moral tone of the community. See *Paris Adult Theatre I* v. *Slaton*, 413 U.S. 49 (1973). Even less plausible than the Court's position is to say that pornography is immoral because it depicts sex, depicts an immoral kind of sex, or caters to voyeuristic tendencies. I believe that even if moral objections to pornography exist, one must preclude any simple inference from "pornography is immoral" to "pornography should be censored" because of other important values and principles such as freedom of expression and self-determination.

6. See Gail Sheehy, *Hustling* (New York: Dell, 1971) for a good discussion of prostitution, crime, and pornography.

7. Two further points need to be mentioned here. Sharon Bishop pointed out to me one reason why we might object to either a racist or rapist mentality in film: it might be difficult for a Black or a woman not to identify with the degraded person. A second point concerns different uses of the phrase "treats women as sex objects." A film treats a subject—the meaninglessness of contemporary life, women as sex objects, and so on—and this use of "treats" is unproblematic. But one should not suppose that this is the same use of "treats women as sex objects" that is found in the sentence "David treats women as sex objects"; David is not treating the *subject* of women as sex objects.

8. In order to help one determine which position one feels inclined to take, consider the following statement: It is morally objectionable to write, make, sell, act in, use, and enjoy pornography; in addition, the content of pornography is immoral; however, pornography itself is not morally objectionable. If this statement seems extremely problematic, then one

might well be satisfied with the claim that pornography is degrading because its content is.

9. The traditional meaning of "lose respect for women" was evidently the one assumed in the Abelson survey cited by the Presidential Commission. No explanation of its meaning is given in the report of the study. See H. Abelson et al., "National Survey of Public Attitudes Toward and Experience with Erotic Materials," *Tech. Report*, vol. 6, pp. 1–137.

10. Many feminists point this out. One of the most accessible references is Shulamith Firestone, *The Dialectic of Sex: The Case for the Feminist Revolution* (New York: Bantam, 1970), especially pp. 128–32.

11. In Richard Wasserstrom, ed., *Today's Moral Problems* (New York: Macmillan, 1975), pp. 152–71; see pp. 167–71. Also in Robert Baker and Frederick Elliston, eds., *Philosophy and Sex* (Buffalo, NY: Prometheus Books, 1975).

12. Baker, in Wasserstrom, *Today's Moral Problems*, pp. 168–169.

13. "Sexual Excitement," *Archives of General Psychiatry* 33 (1976): 899–909, especially p. 903. The extent to which Stoller sees men and women in different positions with respect to harm and hostility is not clear. He often treats men and women alike, but in *Perversion: The Erotic Form of Hatred* (New York: Pantheon, 1975), pp. 89–91, he calls attention to differences between men and women especially regarding their responses to pornography and lack of understanding by men of women's sexuality. Given that Stoller finds hostility to be an essential element in male-oriented pornography, and given that women have not responded readily to such pornography, one can speculate about the possibilities for women's sexuality; their hostility might follow a different scenario; they might not be as hostile, and so on.

14. Men seem to be developing more sensitivity to being treated as sex objects. Many homosexual men have long understood the problem. As women become more sexually aggressive, some heterosexual men I know are beginning to feel treated as sex objects. A man can feel that he is not being taken seriously if a woman looks lustfully at him while he is holding forth about the French judicial system or the failure of liberal politics. Some of his most important talents are not being properly valued.

15. Brownmiller, *Against Our Will*, p. 394.

16. I don't agree with Brownmiller that the purpose of pornography is to dehumanize women; rather it is to arouse the audience. The differences between our views can be explained, in part, by the points from which we begin. She is writing about rape; her views about pornography grow out of her views about rape. I begin by thinking of pornography as merely depicted sexual activity, though I am well aware of the male hostility and contempt for women that it often expresses. That pornography degrades women and excites men is an illustration of this contempt.

17. Virginia Wright Wexman uses the film *Group Marriage* (Stephanie Rothman, 1973) as an example of "more enlightened erotica." Wexman also asks the following questions in an attempt to point out sexism in pornographic films:

Does it [the film] portray rape as pleasurable to women? Does it consistently show females nude but present men fully clothed? Does it present women as childlike creatures whose sexual interests must be guided by knowing experienced men? Does it show sexually aggressive women as castrating viragos? Does it pretend that sex is exclusively the prerogative of women under twenty-five? Does it focus on the physical aspects of lovemaking rather than the emotional ones? Does it portray women as purely sexual beings? ("Sexism of X-rated Films," *Chicago Sun-Times,* 28 March 1976.)

18. One might think, as does Stoller, that since pornography today depends on hostility, voyeurism, and sado-masochism (*Perversion,* p. 87) that sexually healthy people would not enjoy it. Two points should be noticed here, however: (1) Stoller need not think that pornography will disappear because hostility is an element of sexual excitement generally; and (2) voyeurism, when it invades no one's privacy, need not be seen as immoral; so although enjoyment of pornography might not be an expression of sexual health, it need not be immoral either.

19. If it is a lesbian or male homosexual film, no one would play a caricatured male or female role. The reader has probably noticed that I have limited my discussion to heterosexual pornography, but there are many interesting analogues to be drawn with male homosexual pornography. Very little lesbian pornography exists, though lesbian scenes are commonly found in male-oriented pornography.

20. One should note that behavior of this kind is still considered unacceptable by the military. A female officer resigned from the U.S. Navy recently rather than be court-martialed for having sex with several enlisted men whom she met in a class on interpersonal relations.

21. The content may seem morally acceptable only if one disregards such questions as, "Should a doctor have sex with her patients during office hours?" More important is the propriety of evaluating content wholly apart from the attitudes and reactions of the audience; one might not find it strange to say that one film has morally unacceptable content when shown tonight at the Pussycat Theater but acceptable content when shown tomorrow at a feminist conference.

22. Three "final" points must be made:

1. I have not seriously considered censorship as an alternative course of action. Both Brownmiller and Sheehy are not averse to it. But as I suggested in note 5, other principles seem too valuable to sacrifice when options are available. In addition, before justifying censorship on moral grounds one would want to compare pornography to other possibly offensive material: advertising using sex and racial stereotypes, violence in TV and films, and so.

2. If my nonsexist pornography succeeded in having much "educational value," it might no longer be pornography according to my definition. This possibility seems too remote to worry me, however.

3. In discussing the audience for nonsexist pornography, I have focused on the male audience. But there is no reason why pornography could not educate and appeal to women as well.

Earlier versions of this paper have been discussed at a meeting of the Society for Women in Philosophy at Stanford University, California State University, Los Angeles, Claremont Graduate School, Western Area Meeting of Women in Psychology, UCLA Political Philosophy Discussion Group, and California State University, Fullerton Annual Philosophy Symposium. Among the many people who made helpful comments were Alan Garfinkel, Jackie Thomason, and Fred Berger. This paper grew out of "Pornography, Sex Roles, and Morality," presented as a responding paper to Fred Berger's "Strictly Peeking: Some Views on Pornography, Sex, and Censorship" in a Philosophy and Public Affairs Symposium at the American Philosophical Association, Pacific Division Meeting, March, 1975.

Suppose we agree with consequentialists that some pornography causes harm to the actors and some pornography increases the sexual callousness of some people. Also, suppose that we agree with deontologists that the content of some pornography degrades and demeans human beings. Suppose further that on these grounds we claim that some pornography is immoral. Does the immorality of such pornography give us warrant to pass legislation to outlaw such pornography? At first glance we might be inclined to say that it does. Yet the matter is really complex and fraught with conflicting moral concerns. Consider the situation in the United States. Clearly, this nation has laws prohibiting murder because murder inflicts irremediable harm on the victim. Accordingly, the production of "snuff movies" is regarded as both immoral and illegal. Also, pornography that uses children as the performers is regarded as immoral and illegal. Why? Is it because we think that children in pornography are being victimized, unfairly exploited, inasmuch as they are not mature enough to give free and informed consent to the display of their bodies in sexually explicit ways? Is it also because we think that such children are somehow psychologically harmed in ways that are difficult to demonstrate? At any rate, the United States Congress passed in 1977 the Protection of Children Against Sexual Exploitation Act, which because of its vague language and loose grammar has recently come under severe criticism by Supreme Court Justices.

But what about the majority of pornography that uses adult performers (who presumably consent freely to their performance and who are presumably not afflicted with irremediable harm) but is judged to be immoral because its content degrades human beings and/or its consequences involve an increase in sexual callousness? Shall we make this kind of pornography illegal because we think it is immoral?

We have already noted the frustrated attempts of the City Council of Minneapolis to pass legislation against pornography. The conflict between the Council's majority who supported the legislation and Mayor Fraser who vetoed it can be seen as a conflict between the democratically cherished value of freedom of speech harbored in the First Amendment and the democratically cherished value of equality nested in the Fourteenth Amendment. Consider the wording of those amendments:

Amendment I

Congress shall make no law respecting an establishment of religion, or prohibiting the free exercise thereof; or abridging the freedom of speech, or of the press; or the right of the people peaceably to assemble, and to petition the government for a redress of grievances.

Amendment XIV

Section 1. All persons born or naturalized in the United States, and subject to the jurisdiction thereof, are citizens of the United States and of the State wherein they reside. No State shall make or enforce any law which shall abridge the privileges or immunities of citizens of the United States; nor shall any State deprive any person of life, liberty, or property, without due process of law; nor deny to any person within its jurisdiction the equal protection of the laws.

Shall we consider pornography to be a form of speech? If so, does it fall within the domain of speech and the press sheltered by the First Amendment? First Amendment absolutists like Justice Hugo L. Black claimed that the First Amendment allowed no law whatsoever to abridge the right of freedom of speech and the freedom of the press. But Justice Black and his followers also construed "speech" and "press" in a strict sense. That is to say, "speech" and "press" are not the same thing as nonverbal conduct which, for the absolutists, would not be protected under the First Amendment. Would the absolutist position allow no pornography, or all pornography, or some pornography protection under the First Amendment?

While many contemporary jurists have embraced an absolutist position on the First Amendment, they have not followed in the steps of Justice Black by insisting on a strict interpretation of "speech" and "press." If we agree with these contemporary jurists and adopt a modified absolutist position on the First Amendment, then we might be prepared to consider pornography to be a form of speech. If so, shall we claim that pornography is protected speech under the First Amendment? Clearly not all speech has been considered protected under the First Amendment. For example, shouting "Fire!" in a crowded theater when one knows there is no fire is not protected speech because of the clear and present danger which such words harbor. Shouting "Fire!" under such circumstances would be both immoral and illegal. What about that type of pornography that we might judge immoral because it degrades persons and/or increases sexual callousness among its consumers? Would it be analogous to our shout of "Fire!"? Would we be able to demonstrate that such immoral pornography harbored a clear and present danger to society such that its protection under the First Amendment should be lifted? Would we not have an extremely difficult time persuading the courts of the land to remove that protection? Remember that the Illinois Supreme Court and the U.S. Court of Appeals ruled that the neo-Nazi march in 1978 through Skokie, Illinois (the Chicago suburb that was home to forty thousand Jews, including several thousand Holocaust survivors), although morally reprehensible, was nevertheless protected speech under the First Amendment. Although we might judge this pornography to be immoral, would we perhaps find ourselves siding with the courts and with Mayor Fraser of Minneapolis? Would we perhaps conclude that the harm done by abridging the freedom of speech in this instance would outweigh the immoralities of the speech (that is, the pornography)?

Suppose, however, that we adopt the approach of Itzin, Dworkin, and MacKinnon and build a case against this pornography (that we have assessed as immoral) on the basis of the Fourteenth Amendment. Not only would we claim that this type of pornography degrades persons and increases sexual callousness, but we would also claim that this pornography portrays women as subordinate to men and advocates that they be treated as subordinates. Thereby we could claim that this pornography violates the democratic value of equality harbored in the due process and equal protection clauses of the Fourteenth Amendment. This Amendment has been used successfully to oppose various types of discrimination as well as to support the ruling in *Roe* v. *Wade* that legalized abortion within certain limits. But in those cases was the Fourteenth Amendment pitted against the First? In the case of pornography we encounter a moral and constitutional dilemma. Surely we all prize freedom of speech and also equality under the law. But we cannot serve two masters: If we allow pornography to be protected speech, then we sacrifice a measure of equality for women under the law; but if we enforce equality, then we abridge freedom of speech with all the attendant problems that would generate. Which Amendment will prevail in this matter? Currently, the First Amendment seems to have the edge. But there is mounting pressure from religious coalitions, conservative politicians, and feminist thinkers to deny pornography the status of protected speech and to ground legal opposition to it in the Fourteenth Amendment. While the debate continues, shall we perhaps heed Garry's call to generate and disseminate throughout society a nonsexist and nonharmful sexuality that could provide a basis for a new genre of nondegrading pornography?

CHAPTER 10

Sexual Harassment
and
Rape

IMAGINE A BASEBALL TEAM in which the catcher constantly needles the hitters with wise-cracks about their ability to hit ("No hitter! No hitter!"), about their ability to drive, about their mother's sexual habits, etc. The batters get so distracted that they strike out. This is just part of the game. It always has been. Is it fair? Should there be regulations against all such needling or only some particular kinds of needling? A complaining player would probably be called a bad sport, a sore loser, a crybaby.

Suppose your brother (or sister) needles you about being short (or getting low grades or being uncoordinated). Or worse, just constantly refers to you as ugly, stupid, or fat. At first, it's just needling. But then it gets on your nerves. And then, without being conscious of it, you actually start to believe it. There is a standard parental reply to a complaint about such name-calling: "He wouldn't do it if he didn't love you."

Newly hired assistant professors (without tenure) are often referred to as junior faculty—even if they are forty years old. They have to endure jokes by the senior faculty about how they might not get tenure unless they agree to mow lawns or serve dinner for the chair. Every time they agree with a senior member at a faculty meeting they are subject to comments about how they are really looking ahead to a tenure decision. This is just how it goes.

Shannon Faulkner is a young woman who wants to be a cadet at The Citadel. As of this writing, The Citadel's cadet corps is all male. At The Citadel first-year students in the cadet corps are treated as if they were nonpersons by the upperclass students. Freshmen hazing can be physically exhausting (sometimes it has been brutal). This is just part of the deal.

The treatment of assistant professors as described above can be called harassment. The treatment of the first-year students in the corps at The Citadel is definitely harassment. The difference, on the face of it, is that in the first case, the behavior of senior faculty toward junior faculty is not really institutionally sanctioned. In the second case, it is. Indeed, it is felt that this kind of behavior is what contributes to the making of a good military officer.

Women are often treated like the assistant professor mentioned above. Sometimes they are treated more like a first-year student at The Citadel. Why are women treated this way? How often are they treated this way? Should they accept such treatment? If not, then why not? After all, hasn't the system proved its worthiness? Aren't these complainers just sore losers and bad sports? That is the issue to be discussed by the articles in this chapter that deal with sexual harassment and rape.

No matter now contentious philosophers have been, there is little argument supporting the morality of rape. (That little argument is from the Marquis de Sade.) There are two questions that are asked (especially recently) about rape. What should the definition of rape be?

What is date rape? To get a sense of the date rape question, consider the following types of situations.

Imagine a case where a teenager begs and badgers and whines and snivels, wanting to get permission to go to a rock concert. Usually the teenager bargains with a promise: I'll clean my room; I won't ask for the car again for a month; I'll get on the honor roll. The parents finally give in and say, "All right, leave us alone. You can go." Have the parents really given consent or have they just given up? Does the teen really have permission? Now imagine a case where a boy begs and badgers, whines and snivels for "permission" to have sex with his girlfriend. He might say something like, "How else can I know that you love me?" She gives in and says, "All right. Let's just do it." Does he really have permission? Did his girlfriend give consent or did she just give up?

Rather than discuss the nature and extent of rights, both individual and social, both legal and moral, we will focus on the practical questions as they have been raised in real-life contexts. The articles that follow address the issues:

When is being annoyed an instance of harassment?

What makes a case of harassment sexual?

What should the remedies be for sexual harassment?

Can there be an objective distinction between an insensitive comment and sexual harassment?

How should (date) rape be defined? Should it include coercion more subtle than knife-point?

Precisely what should count as "coercion"?

What is the true nature of rape? Once this is determined, how can rapes be prevented?

How should institutions protect their members from sexual harassment (and rape)?

What do the various answers given imply about how we view men and women? Do some answers fit better with certain forms of feminism than do others?

The questions asked above parallel some of those asked in the chapter on pornography. For example, can there be an objective definition of "pornography"? Is there a sharp distinction between erotic and pornographic, between pornography and bad art? Can any artwork be interpreted as pornographic? Should institutions regulate pornography? What does the content and popularity of pornography say about men and how men view women?

HARASSMENT—DEFINITION AND LEGAL RESPONSES

Rosemarie Tong begins by listing four conditions characteristic of most sexual harassment. To be sexually harassing, an action ought to

1. be annoying or unwelcome;
2. bring about a negative response;
3. have an element of coercion or intimidation, since the harasser usually has more power than the person harassed;
4. make it clear (perhaps by context) that consequences will ensue from the harassment—either rewards or penalties and that these rewards or penalties will not be in keeping with otherwise accepted rules and regulations.

The sex of the harasser is irrelevant in this characterization. Also, same-sex harassment is possible. Usually, however, the harasser is male and the harassed is female. Tong goes on to offer a feminist refinement of the definition of sexual harassment. There are two types of sexual harassment. In one type, there is a clear reward or punishment as part of the harassment—for example, if you want to get an A, you will have to have sex with me. In the other type, there is only annoyance—for example, purposely brushing against a woman's breasts (what might be called "copping a feel"). Since this sense of harassment also covers a one-time attempt to look down a blouse or a one-time leer at the swimming pool, it is hard to maintain that coercion is really involved in this second type of harassment.

The law provides remedies for both types of harassment. So do the rules and regulations of many institutions. Tong looks at the law. Criminal law is constrained by very strict rules of evidence which make it notoriously difficult to prosecute cases where it is "my word against yours." Civil law with its preponderance of evidence definition of proof is more open to harassment proceedings. Yet there are problems here as well. Often, the defense used is that the harassed woman really gave consent and so was not harassed at all. Here we get to the issue not so much of when "no" means "no," but rather of what counts as consent in general. Another defense is that the harasser had no prior knowledge that the woman would be annoyed by his seemingly innocent comments (for example, "Hi, Babe!"). After all, no one had ever complained before. A third problem is that civil law (tort law) requires that the claimant show that damages were caused and that the damages can be compensatable (usually by money). This is often very difficult to show.

Because of these problems with criminal and civil law, some feminists (most notable among them, Catherine MacKinnon) have suggested that harassment be seen as a way of discriminating against women. Harassment on this view is a way of taking advantage of any woman's general lack of power and authority. Here we might better refer to gender harassment as opposed to sexual harassment. So far the courts are uneven in their findings, although there are now government regulations such as Title VII and Title IX, against sexual discrimination that require specific rules and grievance procedures to be in place.

Most sexual harassment is done by men against women. Is this because men are in positions of power and feel that they can get away with it? Or is it because men are just naturally (or socialized into being) more interested in sex and more aggressive than women? As with rape, is the motivation primarily violence or primarily uncontrolled sexual passion?

from Sexual Harassment

ROSEMARIE TONG

A March 1980 article in *Newsweek* begins:

It may be as subtle as a leer and a series of off-color jokes, or as direct as grabbing a woman's breast. It can be found in typing pools and factories, Army barracks and legislature suites, city rooms and college lecture halls. It is fundamentally a man's problem, an exercise of power almost analogous to rape, for which women pay with their jobs, and sometimes their health. It's as traditional as underpaying women—and now appears to be just as illegal. Sexual harassment, the boss's dirty little fringe benefit, has been dragged out of the closet.[1]

From "Sexual Harassment" by Rosemarie Tong in *Women, Sex and the Law,* edited by Rosemarie Tong (Totowa, New Jersey: Rowman and Littlefield, 1984), pp. 65–89. Used by permission of the author and Rowman & Littlefield, Publishers, Inc.

Indeed, sexual harassment has been brought out into the open and, unlike pornography and prostitution, which have been perceived as feminist issues, sexual harassment has been labeled a woman's issue: an issue that can directly affect any woman in this country. It is surely odd to distinguish between feminist and women's issues, as if the two were mutually exclusive.

But this is the way the public tends to think. Nonetheless, had it not been for feminists, the problem of sexual harassment would never have been named, let alone confronted.

Before the 1970s women largely accepted as an unpleasant fact of life what some of them called the "little rapes." With the emergence of consciousness-raising groups, many women (especially working women and students) began to feel that they need not and should not have to submit to these nagging violations of their persons. Speaking to women, Andrea Medea and Kathleen Thompson observed:

> If you are subjected . . . to this kind of violation every day, a gradual erosion begins—an erosion of your self-respect and privacy. You lose a little when you are shaken out of your daydreams by the whistles and comments of the construction workers you have to pass. You lose a little when a junior executive looks down your blouse or gives you a familiar pat at work. You lose a little to the obnoxious drunk at the next table, to that man on the subway, to the guys in the drive-in.[2]

As a result of people realizing that such abuses are common, the problem of sexual harassment was named in 1975. No sooner was the problem named than its seriousness as well as pervasiveness became apparent. For example, a 1976 issue of *Redbook* (by no means a feminist publication) reported that out of a sample of 9,000 readers, 88 percent had experienced some form of sexual harassment, and 92 percent considered the problem of sexual harassment serious.[3] Most women find that their job or academic performance degenerates as they are forced to take time and energy away from work or school to deal with sexual harassers. Indeed, fending off offensive sexual advances, especially if they are sustained over several weeks, months, or years, causes women ten-

sion, anxiety, frustration, and above all anger. Unfortunately, many women turn this anger not against their harassers, but against themselves. Gradually, they transform their initial feelings of righteous indignation into feelings of shame or guilt. Shame is experienced when a woman feels that she has not lived up to a self-imposed ideal image of herself as a person who can control men's reactions to her body. In contrast, guilt is experienced when a woman feels that she has not lived up to society's standards for female behavior, one of which instructs women to meet men's sexual wants and needs with grace, generosity, and good humor. Plagued by intense feelings of shame (failure) or guilt (transgression), an increasing number of women workers and students suffer from what has been termed "sexual harassment syndrome." Victims of this syndrome can experience psychological depression, if not also physical ailments, such as "stomachaches, headaches, nausea, involuntary muscular spasms, insomnia, hypertension, and other medical illnesses."[4]

Unfortunately, victims of sexual harassment syndrome are sometimes scoffed at. When five women students and a male assistant professor filed a class-action suit at Yale, contending that male faculty members had engaged in sexually offensive behavior, resulting in a multitude of harms, university officials responded in a defensive manner. As one spokesman for Yale said, "It's not a new thing, but it is also not a major problem." Another university official added, "There is a stronger argument that if women students aren't smart enough to outwit some obnoxious professor, they shouldn't be here in the first place. Like every other institution, Yale has its share of twisted souls."[5]

Given such varied reactions to sexual harassment and its deleterious consequences, it poses problems of definition analogous to those posed by pornography and prostitution. This article will discuss recent attempts to define sexual harassment and to distinguish it clearly from sexual attraction. Standard as well as preferred feminist legal responses to sexual harassment will be evaluated, noting that the former tend to invoke versions of both the offense principle and the harm principle, whereas the latter tend to invoke only the harm principle. Finally, the discussion will focus on when the appropriate response to an incident of sexual harassment is a legal remedy and when it is an extralegal remedy, arguing that the law is best invoked when the price one must pay for her sexual integrity is an education or occupational opportunity/position.

THE UBIQUITOUS PHENOMENON

Although definitions of sexual harassment are by no means uniform, many feminist antiharassers agree that sexual harassment involves four conditions: (1) an annoying or unwelcome sexual advance or imposition; (2) a negative response to this sexual advance/imposition; (3) the presence of intimidation or coercion when the sexual harasser holds more power than the person sexually harassed and, frequently, (4) the suggestion that institutionally inappropriate rewards or penalties will result from compliance or refusal to comply.

This preliminary definition, critics point out, leaves much to be desired. First, it fails to illuminate the connection between the sexual advance/imposition, the negative response, and the institutional consequences. For instance, how forceful must the response be? How serious must the consequences be? Second, the definition fails to make clear who this society's power-holders are. Must one be an employer or a professor in order to have power over a woman employee or a woman student? Or does the mere fact that a person is male give him an automatic power over a female's fate? Third, it fails to distinguish between the kind of coercion that consists of a threatened penalty and the kind that consists of a promised reward. Properly speaking, is not the latter form of coercion more aptly described as a pressure tactic or an incentive technique? Fourth, and most important, the definition fails to indicate which of the four conditions are necessary for sexual harassment and which are sufficient.

In response to these criticisms, but especially the last one, feminists have refined their definition of sexual harassment. As they see it, there are two types of sexual harassment: coercive and noncoercive. Coercive sexual harassment includes

(1) sexual misconduct that offers a benefit or reward to the person to whom it is directed, as well as (2) sexual misconduct that threatens some harm to the person to whom it is directed. An example of the first instance would be offering someone a promotion only if she provides a sexual favor. An example of the second instance would be stating that one will assign a student a failing grade unless she performs a sexual favor. In contrast, noncoercive sexual harassment denotes sexual misconduct that merely annoys or offends the person to whom it is directed. Examples of noncoercive sexual misconduct are repeatedly using a lewd nickname ("Boobs") to refer to an attractive co-worker, or prowling around the women's dormitory after midnight. What coercive and noncoercive modes of sexual harassment have in common, of course, is that they are unsolicited, unwelcome, and generally unwanted by the women to whom they are directed.[6]

Coercive Sexual Harassment

According to feminists, a coercive act is "one where the person coerced is made to feel compelled to do something he or she would not normally do."[7] This compulsion is accomplished by the coercer's "adversely changing the options available for the victim's choosing."[8] The paradigm case of coercion is, of course, the use of physical or psychological restraint, but *threats* of physical or psychological restraint/reprisal are also coercive to a lesser degree. Although it is difficult to determine whether a sexual harasser has in fact narrowed for the worse the options available for a woman's choosing, John Hughes and Larry May provide two tests to facilitate such determinations: would the woman have "freely chosen" to change her situation before the alleged threat was made for her situation after the broaching of the alleged threat; and, would the woman be made "worse off" than she otherwise would be by not complying with the offer?[9]

Relying on Hughes and May's twofold test, feminists maintain that sexual advances/impositions that threaten some harm to the person to whom they are directed are clearly coercive. "If you don't go to bed with me, Suzy, I'll fail you in this course." Assuming that Suzy has not been secretly longing to sleep with her professor or to flunk her course, she would not freely choose to change her situation to one in which the only way she can attain a passing grade is by sleeping with him. Therefore, because Suzy's professor has adversely altered her options, he has coerced her into a very tight corner; and since a coercive sexual advance is by definition an instance of sexual harassment, Suzy's professor is guilty of sexual harassment.

In contrast to sexual advances backed by threats, feminists admit that sexual advances backed by offers do not constitute clear cases of sexual harassment. Nonetheless, like sexual threats, sexual offers are coercive. It is just that the bitter pill of coercion is coated with a sugary promise: "If you go to bed with me, Suzy, I'll give you a 'A' in this course." According to critics, however, feminists confuse seduction with sexual harassment when they conflate sexual offers with sexual threats—when they insist that every time a man pressures a women for a sexual favor by promising her a reward he coerces her into saying an unwilling yes to his request. In this connection, Michael Bayles asks feminists to ponder the following hypothetical case:

> Assume there is a mediocre woman graduate student who would not receive an assistantship. Suppose the department chairman offers her one if she goes to bed with him, and she does so. In what sense has the graduate student acted against her will? She apparently preferred having the assistantship and sleeping with the chairman to not sleeping with the chairman and not having the assistantship . . . the fact that choice has undesirable consequences does not make it against one's will. One may prefer having clean teeth without having to brush them; nonetheless, one is not acting against one's will when one brushes them.[10]

As Bayles sees it, the department chairman has not coerced the graduate student to sleep with him. Rather he has seduced her to sleep with him. Consequently, whatever the chairman is guilty of, it is not sexual harassment. Bayles's reasons for insisting that the graduate student has not been coerced are two. First, she would have freely chosen to move from the preoffer stage (no chance of an assistantship) to the postoffer stage (a chance of an assistantship). Second, her options after the sexual offer are not worse than before. If she refuses the sexual offer, she will not lose a chance for an assistantship because she was never in the running; and if she accepts the sexual offer, she will have not only a chance for an assistantship, but an assistantship. Despite the superficial plausibility of Bayles's analysis, feminists (once again following Hughes and May) insist that a deeper reading of the graduate student's dilemma indicates that she has in fact been coerced by her department chairman. In the first place, assuming the graduate student has not been dying to go to bed with her chairman, and that she is not a calculating mercenary who has been hoping for a sexual offer to bail her out of a dead-end career trajectory, it is not clear that she would have freely chosen to move from the preoffer stage to the postoffer stage. The best reason for her not wishing to move to the postoffer stage is that it places her in a "damned if you do, damned if you don't" predicament.

On the one hand, if the graduate student refuses to sleep with her chairman, she will of course *not* receive an undeserved assistantship. In addition, she will place herself at considerable risk. Perhaps the chairman is talking sweetly today only because he thinks the graduate student will be in his bed tomorrow. Should she disappoint him, he may turn against her. This is a real possibility, given the unpredictable character of sexual feelings and the history of reprisals against women who turn down sexual offers. On the other hand, if the graduate student agrees to sleep with the chairman—either because she wants an assistantship or because she fears angering him (a possibility that Bayles overlooks)—she increases her vulnerability to other professors as well as to the chairman. Other professors might imitate their chairman's behavior—after all, he got away with it—adding a degree of instability and potential for arbitrary treatment not only to this particular student's future, but to all female graduate students' futures. Once such considerations are factored in, feminists observe that the chairman has in fact boxed his graduate student into a corner from which she cannot emerge unscathed. Consequently, whatever else the chairman is guilty of (such as depriving a worthy candidate of an assistantship), he is also guilty of sexual harassment.

Noncoercive Sexual Harassment

Clear cases of coercive sexual harassment affect a woman's options so adversely that she gives in to her harasser's threats or offers simply because her other options seem so much worse. Unlike the sexual seducer who showers a woman with gifts so that she will at long last *willingly* leap into his arms, the coercive sexual harasser waves his stick or carrot in front of a woman, not caring how *unwilling* she is when she jumps into his bed. Significantly, what distinguishes the noncoercive sexual harasser from both the sexual seducer and the coercive sexual harasser is that his primary aim is not to get a woman to perform sexually for him, but simply to annoy or offend her.

Although it is possible to argue that the ogler's, pincher's, or squeezer's sexual misconduct is coercive, it is difficult. Many women fear calling attention not only to the sexual misconduct of their employers and professors, who can cost them their jobs or academic standing, but also to the sexual misconduct of strangers—strangers who have no long-term economic or intellectual power over them, but who nonetheless have the short-term power of physical strength over them. For example, in a recent *New York Times* article, Victoria Balfour reported that although women are frequently sexually harassed at movie theaters, they very rarely complain to theater managers. One highly educated woman who had been afraid to report an incident of sexual harassment to the theater manager commented: "He might think that somehow I had done something that made the man want to bother me, that I had provoked him. To me, harassment has its implications, like rape."[11] Two other women silently endured a harasser for the duration of another film. Although their harasser's behavior was extremely offensive, they did not report the incident: "He was staring heavily, breathing heavily and making strange noises. We didn't move because we were afraid if we got somebody to deal with him, he'd be waiting outside afterward with a knife."[12] All three of these women

kept silent because they feared provoking their harassers to some heinous deed.

To claim that these theatergoers were *coerced* into silence is, according to feminists, to accomplish some good at the risk of effecting considerable harm. On the one hand, the public ought to realize that, for women, being bothered at the movies, in the subways, and on the streets by youthful girl-watchers, middle-aged creeps, and dirty old men is a routine occurrence. On the other hand, women ought not to think of themselves as helpless victims who dare not confront their harassers for fear of retaliatory violence. Therefore, on balance, feminists are of the opinion that it is best to reserve the term *coercive* for cases of sexual harassment that involve specific threats or offers, especially if these threats or offers are made in the context of the workplace or academy. This is not to suggest, however, that feminists think that cases of noncoercive sexual harassment are always less serious than cases of coercive sexual harassment. No woman wants to be coerced into a man's bed; but neither does a woman want to be hounded by a man who takes delight in insulting, belittling, or demeaning her, and who may even find satisfaction in driving her to distraction. This being the case, feminists insist that the law attend to cases of unwanted *noncoercive* as well as unwanted coercive sexual harassment. But this is no light request to make of a law that, like some Freudians, is still wondering what women really want.

STANDARD LEGAL RESPONSES

Although the law is better suited to deal with cases of coercive sexual harassment than with cases of noncoercive sexual harassment, it has attempted to provide remedies for both types of misconduct. Traditionally, the two major legal avenues open to victims of sexual harassment have been criminal proceedings and civil suits, which invoke tort law. The rationale behind the criminal-proceedings approach depends straightforwardly on the harm principle, whereas the rationale behind civil suits relies on a mixture of the harm and offense principles. The fact that these two rationales differ is not without consequence. The civil law (=tort law) tends to take sexual harassment even less seriously than the criminal law does.

Criminal Proceedings: Invoking the Harm Principle

Criminal proceedings are now, as in the past, less frequently employed than civil suits. This is not surprising given that the criminal sanction is appropriate only if the sexually harassed woman is a victim of rape, indecent assault, common assault, assault causing bodily harm, threats, intimidation, or solicitation. That is, unless a woman is *seriously* harmed by her harasser, a prosecutor is not likely to press criminal charges, and if she is seriously harmed, the prosecutor is not likely to charge her harasser with sexual harassment but with rape, indecent assault, and so on.

The prosecutor's course of action is prima facie rational. If a woman's "harasser" is in no way connected with her place of education or employment, it is confusing and trivializing to describe his rape of her as an extreme incident of sexual harassment. But if a woman is coerced to submit to sexual intercourse as a condition of successful employment or education, then her rape is technically best described as aggravated sexual harassment. If the prosecutor wishes to be precise about the whole affair, then he should work toward an aggravated sexual harassment conviction rather than a rape conviction. But be this as it may, a victim of sexual harassment who seeks the aegis of the criminal law is not likely to get very far. Should an adult working woman or an adult student complain of indecent assault, the police are not likely either to lay charges for her or to pursue her case absent of witnesses, other than herself, to the episode. Says one police officer:

> If a girl came to us and told us her boss had called her into the office, put his arm around her, and grabbed her breast, we would first investigate to see if there was some additional evidence. No judge would convict without further evidence. Our practice is that we will not deal with complaints of this kind without some corroborating evidence. It's just too easy for her employer, an upstanding man in the community, to testify that she had asked him for a raise, that he had turned

her down, and that this false cry of assault was her ploy to get even.[13]

If a victim of sexual harassment encounters such a police officer, she may, in absence of his support, lay criminal charges herself. Should she pursue this course of action, however, the district attorney would probably not argue her case. She would be forced to hire a private prosecutor to do her arguing and "it is common knowledge that the judges who hear private prosecutors treat them with much less concern than they do police-laid charges."[14] Realizing this, victims of sexual harassment have tended to bypass the criminal sanction unless they are able to find other women who have been similarly harassed by the particular man involved. The sole victim of *even* extreme forms of sexual harassment is unlikely to be taken seriously. Oftentimes police officers and prosecutors are unable to recognize the special coercion, the extra harm, inherent in extreme forms of sexual harassment that occur in the workplace or the academy. They are apt to think that such cases are episodes of mutually agreeable sexual relations gone awry: "A guy and a gal are together—she's prepared to go along for a few months—after that she wants to cut it off and he doesn't."[15] In short, male members of the criminal justice system are quite reluctant to invoke the harm principle against sexual harassers because they remain unconvinced, on some level, that sexual harassment can indeed constitute a serious harm to a woman's physical or psychological integrity.

Civil Torts: Invoking the Harm and Offense Principles

Given the criminal law's limitations, victims of sexual harassment have turned instead to the civil law, which seems better suited to succor the individual woman who has been sexually harassed. Whereas criminal liability exists to exact a penalty from a wrongdoer in order to protect society as a whole, tort liability exists primarily to compensate the injured person by requiring the wrongdoer to pay for the damage he or she has done. Like criminal law, tort law designates that liability is progressively greater as the defendant's actions range from mere inadvertence, to negligence of likely consequences, to intentional invasion of another's rights under the mistaken notion that no harm is being committed, to instances where the motive is a "malevolent desire to do harm."[16] Because tort law is oriented to victim compensation in a way that the criminal law is not, and because guilty tort-feasors are punished less severely than guilty criminal offenders, in many more instances than the criminal law, tort law will take a strict liability approach, often requiring even the person who merely acted inadvertently or negligently to compensate the individual(s) harmed by his or her thoughtless or careless action(s). Likewise, tort law will, in many more instances than the criminal law, address what I have termed "offenses" (behavior that embarrasses, shames, disgusts, or annoys someone), sometimes requiring the merely offensive person to compensate his or her victim.

1. *Types of Torts:* While new torts are emerging all the time, there are several existing torts that may be particularly applicable to cases of sexual harassment: battery, assault, and the intentional infliction of mental or emotional disturbance.

a. *The Battery Tort:* Battery is defined as "an intentional and unpermitted contact, other than that permitted by social usage."[17] While contact must be intentional, intent to cause all the damages that resulted from the contact is not necessary to establish liability. In other words, a harasser may be guilty of battery simply because he intended to touch a woman without her consent, even though he meant her no harm or offense. So, for example, battery includes instances in which a compliment is intended. Absent her consent, it is tortious, for example, to kiss an "unappreciative woman" under the mistletoe. Because the battery tort considers contact with the body or anything already in contact with the body (such as clothing), it is a useful tort for victims to use against harassers who go beyond verbal abuse. Usually physical contact is not tortious unless it represents socially unacceptable behavior ("breast squeezing" or "fanny-pinching"). Nonetheless, in some cases, socially acceptable behavior ("cheek kissing" or "hand pressing") may be tortious if it is known by the harassers that the receiver of such contacts objects to

and does not permit them. In either event, the victim of battery may win her suit especially since she need not prove—as the victim of rape has had to prove until recently—her lack of consent through some show of resistance.

b. *The Assault Tort:* Where physical contact has not occurred, the tort of assault may be actionable. Assault is "an intentional act, short of contact, which produces *apprehension* of a battery."[18] As Catherine MacKinnon notes, the tort of assault applies to the person placed in fear of an immediately harmful and minimally offensive "touching of the mind, if not the body." Since the invasion is mental, the defendant must have intended at least to arouse psychic apprehension in his victim. Although the fear-producing event must consist of "more than words alone," without words the intentions of the harasser may remain equivocal.[19]

Because the lines between psychic and physical battery are easily crossed, battery and assault doctrines are frequently combined in practice. Catherine MacKinnon provides several examples of successful torts brought under this combined doctrine in the early 1900s. In an age of heightened sexual sensibilities, it was not unusual for cases to be brought forward such as the one in which "a railroad was found responsible for the embarrassment and humiliation of a woman passenger caused when a drunken man, of whose boisterous conduct and inebriated condition the railroad was aware, fell down on top of her and kissed her on the cheek."[20] In another case, "a woman recovered damages for assault and battery against a man who squeezed her breast and laid his hand on her face."[21]

The Intentional Infliction of Mental or Emotional Disturbance Tort

Contemporary sexual mores make it difficult to take altogether seriously the cases MacKinnon describes in today's courts. Unlike her early twentieth-century counterpart, today's woman does not take umbrage at every peck on the cheek or laying on of hands. This does not mean, however, that today's woman either *does* or *should* take in stride every obnoxious ogle, every offensive touch, and every suggestive gesture. As in the past, unwanted or annoying sexual advances/impositions can affect a woman adversely. For this reason, the tort of intentional infliction, in words or acts, of mental or emotional disturbance is gaining currency. Although this tort may be the most difficult to use against sexual harassers, because it includes only those offenses that cause "purely emotional disturbance,"[22] it is also the most promising in that it probably covers those forms of sexual harassment calculated to wear down a woman's resistance.

Consider, for example, the specific tort of intentional infliction of nervous shock. In order for this tort to apply, the sexual harasser must have either purposely, knowingly, or recklessly desired to cause alarm or fright in his victim. Moreover, his conduct must have been serious enough to cause nervous shock in a normal person (unless he was aware of his victim's peculiar susceptibility to emotional shock), and the victim's nervous shock must have physical or psychopathological consequences. Given that sexual harassers often badger their victims systematically over a long period of time, some women do suffer from nervous shock, or sexual harassment syndrome. An example may clarify matters. Over an eight-month period, David Eccles had "persistently telephoned" Marcia Samms at all hours of the night or day, begging her to have sexual intercourse with him. Although Mrs. Samms repeatedly told Eccles to stop bothering her, he kept on soliciting her. Eventually, Mrs. Samms became so emotionally distressed that she brought suit against Eccles for three thousand dollars in damages. The Supreme Court of Utah in *Samms* v. *Eccles* (1961) found that Mrs. Samms had grounds for suit (cause of action).[23] The court decision reads:

We quite agree with the idea that under usual circumstances, the solicitation to sexual intercourse would not be actionable even though it may be offensive to the offeree. It seems to be a custom of longstanding and one which in all likelihood will continue. The assumption is usually indulged that most solicitations occur under such conditions as to fall within the well known phrase of Chief Judge Magruder that "there is no harm in asking." The Supreme Court of Kentucky has observed

that an action will not lie in favor of a woman against a man who, without trespass or assault, makes such a request; and that the reverse is also true: that a man would have no right of action against a woman for such a solicitation. But the situation just described, where tolerance for the conduct referred to is indulged, is clearly distinguishable from the aggravated circumstances the plaintiff claims existed here.[24]

1. Problems with the Tort Approach: This case is important in that it offers recourse to women who are subjected to both aggravated and severely disturbing sexual harassment. Nonetheless, for at least three reasons the tort approach is problematic not only in this form, but in its battery and assault forms.

a. The Issue of Consent: At least in battery cases, the harasser may claim that the woman consented to his sexual advances. This objection is significant because the harasser is not liable for his actions if the woman agreed to submit to them. Unfortunately, it is no easy matter to determine if a woman consented to a sexual advance. For this reason, in cases of sexual harassment, as in cases of rape and woman-battering, the law has straddled between two approaches: One focuses on whether the sexual misconduct was clearly consented to; the other focuses on the consequences of the sexual misconduct without emphasizing issues of consent. Where the law has favored the consent strategy, it has adopted methods similar to those it uses in rape cases. That is, it has sought to establish consent (a mental state) by looking to the victim's resistance or lack thereof (a behavioral manifestation).

In some sense the victim who fails to resist the man who paws her does consent to his pawing. But given that women are still socialized to be "nice" to men, it will take a strong woman to say a loud "No, thank you" to a man who has more arms than an octopus has tentacles. Andrea Medea and Kathleen Thompson report that one woman went so far as to follow her eventual rapist into a dark alley because she feared "offending" him by implying that he might rape her. Rather than berating the woman for her naivete, Medea and Thompson ask their female readers to recall all those times and places in which they paid attention to a man for fear of hurting his feelings.

Realizing that many women are currently unable to express forcefully their nonconsent to an unwanted sexual advance/imposition, the law has recently experimented with the so-called consequences approach. This approach assumes that it is easier to measure the effect that unwanted sexual propositions have on female victims than it is to determine whether a female victim's lack of overt resistance to them is a sign of her tacit consent to them. If Jane experiences depression, anxiety, frustration, and even nausea or vomiting as a result of being repeatedly manhandled by Dick, she has been sexually harassed whether or not she was able to communicate her nonconsent to Dick by telling him to "shove off" or by splashing a glass of ice water on his face.

The consequences approach is an *effective* way to handle sexual harassment cases. But critics wonder whether it is a *fair* way to handle such cases, since Dick, for example, may have sincerely believed that Jane was enjoying his pawings and pattings. Under such circumstances, it does not seem unambiguously just to penalize Dick, since much of Anglo-American law teaches that unless a man knowingly or recklessly harms someone, he is not to be sanctioned for the harm he effects, unless, of course, a standard of negligence is employed. This being the case, even when the consequences approach is employed and the harassed woman does not have to prove her lack of consent, her case is strengthened where she has made her dissent quite clear through words and actions.

b. *The Issue of Hypersensitivity:* Where consent is not an issue, the harasser may claim that he had no reason to believe that the woman he touched or threatened to touch would be offended or frightened. That is, he had no reason to believe that his target was a hypersensitive individual. In such cases, the harasser will be liable only if his conduct would have been offensive to a person of ordinary sensibilities. So, for example, Dick is liable for the battery of Jane, whom he patted on the posterior, if, but only if, a person of ordinary sensibilities would have been offended by such phys-

ical contact. But since this person of ordinary sensibilities is generally termed "the ordinary *man,*" problems could arise for the female victim of sexual harassment. As Catherine MacKinnon notes:

> Ordinary women probably find offensive sexual contact and proposals that ordinary men find trivial or sexually stimulating coming from women. Sex is peculiarly an area where a presumption of gender sameness, or judgments by men of women, are not illuminating as standards for equal treatment, since to remind a man of his sexuality is to build his sense of potency, while for a man to remind a woman of hers is often experienced as intrusive, denigrating, and depotentiating.[25]

To summarize, although a typical man in this culture may like it when a strange woman squeezes muscles, a typical woman will probably not like it when a strange man squeezes her breasts or buttocks. And there will be times when a man will not be able to understand, say, why a woman does not always (or usually) appreciate wolf whistles. Of course, these differences of perspective could be remedied by a supplemental ordinary *woman* test, but this would require the law to confront squarely its male-biases—a major review for which it may not be ready.

2. *The Issue of Harm:* Where neither consent nor hypersensitivity is an issue, the harasser may argue that his victim did not suffer the harm she claims to have suffered. Such a defense is likely to set off a battle between *his* medical experts and *her* medical experts, the former arguing that Jane is of sound body and mind, the latter insisting that Jane is the shell of her former self. Unless such battles can be avoided, it may not be worth the victim's time, energy, and reputation to sue her harasser.

FEMINIST LEGAL RESPONSES: ANTIDISCRIMINATION LAW

Even if it can be shown that a woman has not consented to her harasser's sexual advances, that she is not a hypersensitive individual, and that she has indeed suffered harm as a result of her harasser's sexual misconduct, it is not clear that the tort approach best serves sexually harassed women's interests. Catherine MacKinnon notes that the "aura of the pedestal," more properly viewed as a "cage," distorts cases such as the one in which a judge preached, "every woman has the right to assume that a passenger car is not a brothel and that when she travels in it, she will meet nothing, see nothing, hear nothing, to wound her delicacy or insult her womanhood."[26] But to construe resistance to sexual harassment as a return to prudery is, according to feminists, to miss the point: Sexual harassment is not so much an issue of offensive behavior as an issue of abusive power.

But if sexual harassment is more an issue of power than an issue of offense, the tort approach, which emphasizes unseemly sexual conduct, must, in the estimation of feminists, be supplemented by a legal approach stressing that women often submit to unwanted sexual advances simply because their position in society is inferior relative to men. Not only are most men physically more powerful than most women, but it is men and not women who hold the balance of power in the political, economic, and social institutions that govern us all. Because antidiscrimination law is sensitive to these power dynamics, it can accomplish more for sexually harassed women that tort law. Whereas tort law views sexual harassment as an outrage to an individual woman's sensibilities and to a society's purported values, antidiscrimination law casts the same act either as one of *economic* coercion, in which the material survival of women in general is threatened, or as one of *intellectual* coercion, in which the spiritual survival of women in general is similarly jeopardized. If a woman wishes to argue that she has been sexually harassed not because she is vulnerable Sally Jones, but because she is a woman, a member of a gender that suffers from institutionalized inferiority and relative powerlessness, then the antidiscrimination approach obviously suits her purposes best.

Discriminatory Sexual Harassment: A Historical Survey

Despite the cogency of this line of reasoning, feminists were *initially* unable to convince the courts that sexual harassment could in fact constitute sex-based discrimination in the workplace and in the academy. The workplace decisions, resting on Ti-

tle VII, which prohibits sex-based discrimination in employment, represent an upward struggle from the first case brought under it, *Corne* v. *Bausch and Lomb, Inc.,*[27] through several subsequent cases (*Miller* v. *Bank of America*[28] and *Tomkins* v. *Public Service Electric and Gas Co.,*[29] to the landmark case *Barnes* v. *Costle*).[30] To a greater or lesser extent all these cases reveal two attitudes the courts had to overcome on the way to recognizing discriminatory sexual harassment: (1) sexual attraction between a man and a woman is a personal matter in which the courts should not intervene; and (2) the practice of sexual harassment is so prevalent that if courts became involved they would be flooded with complaints, many of which might be false or trivial.

In *Corne* v. *Bausch and Lomb, Inc.,* two female clerical workers sued for a violation of their civil rights based on sex discrimination. As a result of the offensive and unwelcome sexual liberties their male supervisor had taken with them, these two women were forced to resign their positions. In dismissing their complaint, the court gave several reasons, the chief of which was that sexual harassment is a "personal proclivity, peculiarity, or mannerism," which employers can not be expected to extirpate in their employees.[31] Said the court, "The only sure way an employer could avoid such charges would be to have employees who were asexual."[32] Incidentally, the trial judge found unimaginable precisely what Margaret Mead has encouraged; namely, that society establish a sexual taboo in the workplace (and by parity of reasoning, in the academy). Flatly stated, Mead's incest taboo asserts that "You don't make passes at or sleep with the people you work with."[33]

Although many feminists think Mead's asexual approach is too drastic, it gains strength in view of *Miller* v. *Bank of America*. In this case the court dismissed the complaint of a female bank worker who was fired when she refused to be "sexually cooperative" with her male supervisor. The court concluded that "The attraction of males to females and females to males is a natural sex phenomenon and it is probable that this attraction plays at least a subtle part in most personnel decisions. Such being the case, it would seem wise for the courts to refrain from delving into these matters."[34] This decision is particularly distressing not only because it conflates sexual attraction (a desirable social phenomenon) with sexual harassment (an undesirable social phenomenon), but because it suggests that unwanted manhandling is something that "big girls" must accept unless the company that employs their harassers *explicitly* endorses such hanky panky as a matter of policy (or some sort of fringe benefit for male employees).

That the courts have had trouble taking sexual harassment seriously as well as distinguishing between sexual attraction and sexual harassment is even more apparent in a case that followed *Miller.* In *Tomkins* v. *Public Service Electric and Gas Co.,* the court dismissed Tomkins's complaint, commenting that a sexually motivated assault that takes place in a "corporate corridor" is no more the concern of Title VII than a sexually motivated assault that takes place in a "back alley."[35] Title VII does not address the labyrinthine issue of sexual desires, and were the courts to encourage women to sue male co-workers and employees whose sexual attentions they had tired of, "an invitation to dinner could become an invitation to a federal lawsuit, if some harmonious relationship turned sour at a later time."[36] This court decision supposes that vindictive women would sue their male subordinates on trumped-up charges; similarly, hysterical or hypersensitive women would sue their male superordinates for the most trivial of reasons.

Fortunately, not all courts are as benighted as those that ruled in *Corne, Miller,* and *Tomkins.* In *Barnes* v. *Train (Costle),* the Washington, D.C., District Court originally found against the plaintiff, a woman who was first denied promotion and then fired for having refused the sexual advances of her supervisor. Ironically, the woman's supervisor was none other than the director of the Environmental Protection Agency's Equal Employment Opportunities Division. The suit was initially rejected on the grounds that sexual harassment does not constitute sex discrimination. The court contended that the woman plaintiff had been denied promotion not because of her sex, but because of her refusal to accede to the director's sexual demands. Conceding that the supervisor's behavior may have been inexcusable, the court nonetheless insisted that the behavior did not constitute an "arbitrary barrier to continued employment based on plaintiff's sex."[37] On appeal, the D.C. circuit court

reversed, declaring that discrimination *was* involved, since the declined invitation had been issued only because the plaintiff was a woman. Said Judge Robinson for the court:

> But for her womanhood, from aught that appears, her participation in sexual activity would never have been solicited. To say, then, that she was victimized in her employment simply because she declined the invitation is to ignore the asserted fact that she was invited only because she was a woman subordinate to the inviter in the hierarchy of agency personnel. Put another way, she became the target of her superior's sexual desires because she was a woman, and was asked to bow to his demands as the price for holding her job.[38]

As a result of this decision, the courts now seem prepared to find sex-based discrimination in the workplace.

In the same way that Title VII is an available remedy for sexually harassed working women, Title IX (1972 Education Amendments) is an available remedy for sexually harassed students. With the exception of the still-pending *Alexander* v. *Yale* case, in which five women students and a male assistant professor filed a class-action suit, contending that male faculty members had engaged in sexually offensive conversations and behavior resulting in a multitude of harms, the courts have not, as yet, handled Title IX cases.[39] However, should such cases be generated and processed, they will probably follow Title VII precedents. Such litigations explicitly promise to reveal the limits of antidiscrimination law as it has developed so far. In handling the grievances of working women and also of female students (who are sexually harassed more frequently by their fellow students than by their male professors), the courts will have to confront squarely the problem of peer-on-peer sexual harassment, a type of harassment that they have already encountered in *Continental Can Co.* v. *Minnesota.*[40] In this case, the Minnesota Supreme Court extended employer liability beyond the actions of supervisory personnel to those of co-workers. To the degree that *Continental Can Co.* sets a precedent for other jurisdictions, it requires the courts to rethink the three major conditions for discriminatory sexual harassment outlined in *Barnes.* There the court ruled that sex-based discrimination may be found only (1) when the victims of sexual harassment are of only one sex; (2) when the harasser is in a position to affect the terms or conditions of the victim's employment; and (3) when the harassment has a verifiably adverse impact on the victim (that is, it is not trivial).

Discriminatory Sexual Harassment: A Doctrinal Analysis

The first major condition for discriminatory sexual harassment is that it does not exist unless *only women* or *only men* are being harassed by a particular supervisor or professor. Arguably, neither Title VII nor Title IX prohibits a bisexual male supervisor/professor from sexually harassing his employees/students—provided that he harasses men as well as women.

1. *The Disparate Treatment Approach:* Regarding Title VII, sexual harassment is discriminatory when a male supervisor, for example, sexually pursues a woman simply because she is a woman, pawing and patting her when there is nothing except her sexuality to separate her from similarly situated male employees. Likewise, it is discriminatory when a female supervisor sexually pursues a man simply because he is a man, coming on to him when there is nothing except his sexuality to separate him from similarly situated female employees. Much the same could be said about male homosexual or lesbian supervisors with the necessary adjustments.

The problem with the "disparate-treatment" approach is that only a fraction of women/men present in an employment situation is likely to be victimized by any particular incident of sexual harassment. As a result, there will be a tendency to detach the incident from the group referent necessary to establish a case under Title VII. This is precisely what happened in the cases preceding *Barnes* v. *Costle*. In these cases the courts suggested that the female employees had been singled out for sexual attention not so much because they were members of the gender group women, but either because of their unique personal characteristics, such as red hair, or because of their sex-specific characteristics, such as large breasts. (A sex-specific characteristic is one that is not shared by both genders and which is possessed by only a subset of the gender class in question.) Since there is no sex discrimination unless a plaintiff can show that her personal injury contains a sufficient gender referent, a red-headed, large-breasted, sexually harassed woman employee must be able to explain why her employer has not harassed similarly situated blond, flat-chested women, if all he was interested in was *a woman* and not a specific kind of woman with red hair and large breasts. Supposedly, if she cannot explain this, she does not have cause to invoke Title VII, although she may have grounds for an assault or battery tort action.

But all this seems rather ludicrous. The sexually harassed red-haired or large-breasted woman does have an explanation for her employer's conduct: He would not be sexually harassing her were she a man or were she her employer's boss. In other words, when a woman invokes Title VII rather than slapping her harasser with an assault or battery suit, she wants to stress that had she not been a female employee in a subordinate position she would not have been sexually harassed.

Implicit in this argument is the suggestion that harassment is not an expression of sexual lust, but a show of power. Contrary to the *Tomkins* court, there is a difference, at least of degree, between an incident of sexual harassment that occurs in a "corporate corridor" and one that occurs in a "back alley." An employer has control over one's life in a way that a stranger does not. And when a company tolerates the sexual harassment of one female employee, it makes an implicit statement to all female employees, telling them that their merits are to be measured not in terms of their skills or job performance, but in terms of their sexual attractiveness and compliance. In short, when a heterosexual male employer harasses only one female employee, he not only treats her disparately but also affects her reference group disparately.

2. *The Disparate-Impact Approach:* According to the "disparate-impact" approach to discriminatory sexual harassment, the motivating impetus for harassment is indeed sexuality (whether male or female), which results in discrimination "only when conjoined with social traditions of male heterosexual predominance in academic and employment hierarchies."[41] Therefore, this approach suggests that when an individual male employee is sexually harassed by a female employer, the discrimination he experiences is of the disparate-treatment rather than the disparate-impact variety. Given the way society is still structured, men are less likely than women to become fearful as a group when one of their number is sexually harassed by an employer of the opposite sex.

3. Comparing the Disparate-Treatment and Disparate-Impact Approaches:

Regarding women, the disparate-impact approach to discriminatory sexual harassment seems more serviceable and promising than the disparate-treatment approach. Because the disparate-impact approach focuses on structural considerations (women's general position in society), it reminds the courts that women have yet to achieve parity with men either in the workplace or in the academy. In the past, the courts were either not served this reminder or they chose to ignore it. More recently, the courts have taken off their blinders. Increasingly, they are realizing that sexual harassment is a serious problem for many working and learning women. For example, the female worker may find herself at the mercy of her male supervisor, who, in an attempt to avoid liability and follow the letter of his company's official antiharassment policy, may not discharge or demote her, but may instead make working conditions so intolerable for her that she will "voluntarily" resign. Fortunately, the courts have come to see these "voluntary" resignations for what they are: "constructive discharges."

As a result of such realizations, the courts are taking a stronger line with respect to those institutions that fail to protect their employees from even the more subtle forms of adverse consequences attendant upon discriminatory sexual harassment: the assignment of undesirable work, close surveillance of performance, failure to enlist co-worker cooperation where necessary, unwillingness to provide adequate training, and failure to release recommendations for promotion. Despite a history of vacillation, the courts now seem prepared to hold employers liable for all acts of sexual harassment perpetrated by their employees, "regardless of whether the employer knew or should have known of their occurrence" except sexual harass-

ment by co-workers.[42] In other words, if Tilly is sexually harassed by her foreman, then the foreman's employer is liable for his actions. It matters not that the employer did not know, or should not have been expected to know, what his foreman was doing. The employer is strictly liable. In contrast, if Tilly is harassed by her co-worker Joe, then the employer must have *actual* or constructive knowledge of Joe's misbehavior in order to be liable for it.

This last point is worth developing because most sexual harassment occurs between peers. There is no reason to view such sexual harassment as discriminatory, however offensive it may be, unless an employer (such as a corporation or a university) is understood to tolerate, endorse, or condone it. By failing to sanction the sexually-harassing conduct of its nonmanagerial and non-supervisory employees, the employer lets them poison the work atmosphere. If the men on the assembly line are making passes at Rosy the Riveter and Betty the Bolter, and the employer, Cast Iron Works, does nothing to stop them, even though its managers and supervisors either know or should know what is going on, then Cast Iron Works is liable for their misbehavior where the other tests of liability under Title VII are met. Similarly, if the fraternity boys are sexually harassing members of the Feminist Alliance and the university does nothing to stop them, even though its deans and professors either know or should know what is going on, then the university is liable for their misbehavior when the other tests of liability under Title IX are met.

EXTRALEGAL REMEDIES

The current trend of the courts is to hold employers (corporations or universities) responsible for what goes on in the workplace or in the academy. In fact, Title IX already requires universities to adopt and publish grievance procedures providing for prompt and equitable resolution of student complaints of sexual harassment. Because sexual harassment has been kept in the closets of colleges and universities for many years, most grievance procedures are not capable of providing prompt and equitable resolution of student complaints. In the past, students have complained about members of the faculty or school who have harassed them, and some of this harassment has been explicitly sexual; however, quite a bit of it has been so-called gender harassment.

Gender harassment is related to sexual harassment as genus is to species: Sexual harassment is a form of gender harassment. Catherine MacKinnon comments "Gender *is* a power division and sexuality is one sphere of its expression. One thing wrong with sexual harassment . . . is that it eroticizes women's subordination. It acts out and deepens the powerlessness of women as a gender, *as women.*"[43] Whereas gender harassment is a relatively abstract way to remind women that their gender role is one of subordination, sexual harassment is an extremely concrete way to remind women that their subordination as a gender is intimately tied to their sexuality, in particular to their reproductive capacities and in general to their bodily contours.

Examples of verbal sexual harassment include those comments (in this case, written comments) to which female coal miners were subjected at the Shoemaker Mine in the late 1970s. Because women had never worked in the mine before, they were, from the moment they appeared on the scene, scrutinized by male eyes. Although the tension between the female and male coal miners was considerable, it was bearable until a rash of graffiti appeared on the mine walls. The graffiti focused on the women's physical characteristics. For example, one woman who had small breasts was called "inverted nipples," and another woman who supposedly had protruding lower vaginal lips was called the "low-lip express."[44] Subjected to such offensive social commentary on this and other occasions, the female miners found it increasingly difficult to maintain their sense of self-respect, and their personal and professional lives began to deteriorate.

In contrast to these examples of verbal sexual harassment stand more sanitized but not necessarily less devastating examples of verbal gender harassment. Unlike instances of verbal sexual harassment that focus on women's bodies, these latter comments, illustrations, and jokes call attention to women's gender traits and roles. It is interesting that a gender harasser may describe female gender traits and roles either in negative terms (women are irrational, hysterical, defective) or in seemingly positive terms (women are nurturing, self-sacrificing, closer to nature). In both cases, however, the gender harasser will add credence to the "*kinder, kirche, kuche*" theory of womanhood, according to which women's biology and psychology naturally suit them for bearing and raising children, praying in church, and cooking.

Although women are routinely subjected to gender harassment, society as a whole remains unconvinced that female students, for example, should take umbrage when their professors gender harass them. Nonetheless, given the educational mission of academic institutions, and the fact that women students may be more vulnerable to their professors' sexist remarks ("Women can't do math") than their professors' sexual innuendoes ("It's a joy having your body—oops! your *person*—in this class, Miss Jones"), Title IX should, and probably does, cover cases of gender harassment.

In this connection, it is important to note that Title VII has already covered several gender-harassment cases. Recently, for example, a woman named Ms. Bay, who was employed by EFCS (Executive Financial Counselling Service) in Philadelphia, won a successful sex-discrimination suit against her boss, Gordon Campbell. Although Mr. Campbell never sexually harassed Ms. Bay by calling attention to or touching her body in any way, he did gender-harass her. On one occasion Mr. Campbell asked Ms. Bay whether her husband would "suffer for food and clean clothes while she was away on business trips." On other occasions he contacted clients, on his own initiative, to inquire whether they objected to dealing with a woman and to see what they thought of Ms. Bay, "although such evaluations had never been requested for a male member of the EFCS staff." On still another occasion he arranged a seminar training program for a male employee while providing no such training program for Ms. Bay, despite her requests and despite Mr. Campbell's private comments to his superiors that her seminar performance was weak and in need of improvement. After listening to the recounting of these and other incidents, the judge ruled that, although Ms. Bay quit, she was really fired because "any reasonable person would have reacted to the situation at EFCS much as she did."[45]

Realizing that liability for sexual harassment and gender harassment belong to them as well as to authorities in the workplace, academic deans and other college personnel have tried to handle student harassment complaints informally. Their attempts have not always been successful. Not wanting to make mountains out of molehills, and arguing that young women frequently "imagine" things, some college officials have downplayed student reports of gender and sexual harassment. Even where they have taken such reports seriously and acted upon them, they have tended to keep them quiet in the name of discretion, preferring to let things "cool off" or "work themselves out." As a result of the student' rights movement, students have pressed their respective colleges and universities to handle such matters in a more formal and public manner. Students have also become much more concerned about student-on-student sexual harassment, which is a very pervasive fact of campus life. Understandably, deans and professors, who have by and large abandoned their *in loco parentis* roles, fear to invade their students' privacy. Realizing that students who come from diverse backgrounds will, as a matter of course, experience some difficulty in adjusting to one another's sexual mores, they fear making an issue out of what may be nothing more than normal social adjustment. And even when college officials discern a problem on campus, they resist setting up quasi-legal procedures to handle it. Predictably, deans and professors tend to argue that the way to handle sensitive problems such as sexual harassment is through educational forums rather than litigation.

Indeed, education is needed. Despite the breakdown of many sexual stereotypes, the macho ideal of the strong man lives on, as does the ideal of the vulnerable female. In large measure, this fact explains the growing incidence of "date-rape" on campuses. Crossed signals and mixed messages characterize many student sexual relations. Says one man:

> I get told "no," . . . and I keep going. I guess if someone said, "Look, sorry, I thought I wanted to, but I changed my mind, no way!" I'd listen, but if

we're lying on the bed and she puts her little hands up in front of her chest and says, "Oh, please, no, I'm not sure about this," I ignore it. Nobody complains afterward."[46]

Women have to learn to say no, and men have to learn to take a *no* at face value. Moreover, women have to stop blaming themselves when men sexually harass them. This may be particularly difficult for a young woman to do. She may not have met enough different types of men to realize that it's not always something about her or her body that turns a man on, but something about his need to assert himself. Arguably, the more secure a man is about his masculinity, the less need he will have to harass women sexually or otherwise. Failing to understand this, a young woman may berate herself for her harasser's conduct. She may punish herself for being sexed by starving or neglecting her body. The epidemic of anorexia on many campuses is not unrelated to young women's fear of their own sexuality; and the unkempt appearance of some young women is often evidence of their attempt to kill the "temptress" in themselves.

Not surprisingly, educators want to help students escape these destructive prisons. But, as always, education is a long-term process. In the interim, college officials must set up and enforce internal grievance procedures to handle both faculty-on-student and student-on-student sexual harassment. Such quasi-legal remedies are not in opposition to a college's educational mission. On the contrary, they serve to remind the college community that it is susceptible to the same human foibles and power plays that characterize society in general.

Internal grievance procedures have been set up in many workplaces as well as at many academic institutions even though Title VII does not require employers to *maintain* grievance procedures. Since agreement has arisen in Title VII sexual harassment cases that there is no cause for judicial action *if* the employer takes prompt and remedial action upon acquiring knowledge of an incident, prudent employers have decided to set up mechanisms that can facilitate quick and corrective action. Unfortunately, these internal grievance procedures can be subverted. Company officials can convince all but the most determined of women that it is in her best interest to keep things quiet. One government official, who was interviewed by Constance Back-house and Leah Cohen, opined that women should avoid both internal grievance procedures and complaints made directly to a personnel manager or management:

> The personnel director will most likely go to the sexual harasser and have a quiet little chat and a good laugh and express any number of the following statements:
> She brought it on herself.
> She can take care of herself.
> She was obviously willing.
> She is vindictive, as a result of a love affair gone sour.
> In fact, this is an isolated incident, not a serious problem.
> She is a troublemaker.[47]

This official went on to add that, if at all possible, the sexually harassed woman should either start looking for another job—"A woman is in real jeopardy if she can't get along in government. Who will hire you in private industry, if you are fired by the government?"—or if this is not a viable option, she should start looking for a "tough feminist lawyer" who will take the case as a "personal challenge."[48]

CONCLUSION

Sexual harassment is a phenomenon deeply rooted in the sexist assumptions that women can turn men "on" and "off" at will, and that sexual harassment is nothing more serious than old-fashioned flirtation. As such, it clearly must be approached on social and cultural as well as legal levels. However, because of its intangible or blurry-edged nature, sexual harassment often seems to be a problem with which the law, in its insistence on clear definitions and consistent guidelines, does not seem best suited to deal. The broad concept of institutional liability, which encourages the development of internal grievance procedures and internal education programs, may thus be the ideal way of confronting and remedying cases of sexual harassment. But the ideal is not always realized, and women—especially women workers and students—find themselves without effective reme-

dies, short of quitting their jobs or leaving school. As Catherine MacKinnon has noted, the sexual subordination of women interacts with other forms of social power that men have over women. To be precise: "Economic power is to sexual harassment as physical force is to rape."[49] And regarding Title IX, intellectual power is to gender harassment on the campus as economic power is to gender or sexual harassment in the workplace as physical force is to rape anywhere. Rape and harassment are abuses of power as well as expressions of male sexuality. The power that makes rape or harassment effective derives from the superior position that the rapist or harasser holds by virtue of his social position.

As in the past, men remain powerful today. Their power is currently derived not so much from their brawn or their brains as from the fact that the major institutions of society—law, education, medicine, government, business, and science—are still largely controlled by them. Only when these institutions, for whatever reasons, begin to evolve in ways that allow women full access to them will the balance of power between men and women equalize. Fortunately, this institutional evolution is already in process.

In particular, the law is being tailored to fit women's as well as men's needs. Avenues of legal action against sexual harassers are both a powerful educational tool and an important means for women to assert and protect their rights to personal respect and self-determination, especially in the workplace and in the academy, while they wait for those rights to be accepted into the canon of cultural assumptions.

Faced with the possibility of legal consequences, men may be forced to reconsider their assumptions about women, employers may be forced to recognize their workers as workers rather than sexually exploitable conveniences, and institutes of higher education may be forced to extend their promise of an environment supportive rather than inhibitive of intellectual growth to female students. Once this happens, the incidences of gender harassment, especially its sexual forms, are likely to decrease. Where neither men nor women have superior power as a group, there is no need to use "sexuality" as a cruel weapon, reminding the powerless just how limited their options are.

Notes

1. A. Press et al., "Abusing Sex at the Office," *Newsweek,* March 10, 1980, p. 81.

2. Andrea Medea and Kathleen Thompson, *Against Rape* (New York: Farrar, Straus and Giroux, 1974), p. 50.

3. Constance Backhouse and Leah Cohen, *Sexual Harassment on the Job* (Englewood Cliffs, NJ: Prentice Hall, 1982), p. 34.

4. Ibid., pp. 38–39.

5. Ibid., pp. 39–40.

6. John C. Hughes and Larry May, "Sexual Harassment," *Social Theory and Practice* 6 (Fall 1980): 251.

7. Ibid., p. 252.

8. Ibid.

9. Ibid.

10. Ibid., p. 249, cf. Michael Bayles, "Coercive Offers and Public Benefits," *The Personalist* 55 (Spring 1974): 142–43.

11. Victoria Balfour, "Harassment at Movies: Complaints Rare," *New York Times,* November 17, 1982, p. C24.

12. Ibid.

13. Backhouse and Cohen, *Sexual Harassment on the Job,* p. 101.

14. Ibid.

15. Ibid., p. 103.

16. Frank J. Till, *Sexual Harassment: A Report on the Sexual Harassment of Students* (Washington, DC: National Advisory Council on Women's Educational Programs, 1980), pt. II, p. 13.

17. Ibid.

18. Ibid.

19. Catherine MacKinnon, *Sexual Harassment of Working Women* (New Haven, CT: Yale University Press, 1979), pp. 165–66.

20. Ibid., p. 166.

21. Ibid.

22. Ibid., p. 167.

23. *Samms* v. *Eccles* (1961), in Wright I. Linden, *Canadian Tort Law,* 6th ed. (Toronto: Butterworths, 1975), pp. 52–54.

24. Ibid.

25. MacKinnon, *Sexual Harassment of Working Women,* p. 171.

26. Ibid., p. 172.

27. 390 F. Supp. 161 (1975), U.S. Dist. Ct., D. Arizona.

28. 418 F. Supp. 233 (1976), U.S. Dist. Ct., N.D. California.

29. 422 F. Supp. 553 (1976), U.S. Dist. Ct., New Jersey.

30. 561 F. 2nd 983 (1977), U.S. Ct. of Appeals, D.C. Circuit.

31. Backhouse and Cohen, *Sexual Harassment on the Job,* p. 119.

32. Ibid.

33. Margaret Mead, "A Proposal: We Need Taboos on Sex at Work," *Redbook,* April 1978, p. 31.

34. *Miller* v. *Bank of America,* 418 F. Supp. 233 (1976), U.S. Dist. Ct., N.D. California.

35. Backhouse and Cohen, *Sexual Harassment on the Job,* p. 121.

36. Ibid., p. 122.

37. *Barnes* v. *Train* (Costle), 13 FEP Cases 123, 124 (D.D.C. 1974).

38. *Barnes* v. *Costle,* 561 F. 2d at 992, n. 68 (D.C. Cir. 1977).

39. *Alexander et al.* v. *Yale University,* 459 F. Supp. 1 (D. Conn. 1977).

40. *Continental Can Co.* v. *Minnesota* (Minn. S.C. 1980).

41. Ibid., pp. 260–61.

42. Till, *Sexual Harassment,* pt. II, p. 9.

43. MacKinnon, *Sexual Harassment of Working Women,* pp. 220–21.

44. Raymond M. Lane, "A Man's World: An Update on Sexual Harassment," *The Village Voice,* December 16, 1981, p. 20.

45. *Philadelphia Inquirer,* September 9, 1982, p. 1A.

46. Karen Barrett, "Sex on a Saturday Night," *Ms.,* September 1982, p. 50.

47. Backhouse and Cohen, *Sexual Harassment on the Job,* p. 72.

48. Ibid.

49. MacKinnon, *Sexual Harassment of Working Women,* pp. 217–18.

Sexual harassment creates an atmosphere that makes it difficult, if not impossible, to be ourselves. It violates our sense of autonomy, which according to some philosophers, is central to the idea of being a person. Mike Martin sees rape in just this way.

RAPE—ITS HARMS

Rape is probably the clearest case of a moral wrong. It is vicious and aims at the degradation of a person. According to Susan Griffin, rape causes at least three kinds of harm to the woman raped: It violates a right to self-determination, it inflicts suffering, and it creates a general sense of fear (because rape is so widespread). Martin suggests another reason. Because sexuality is one of the most integral, and private, parts of our psyches—it in part defines who and what we are—rape is an intrusion into one's sexual life and is thus a severe personal violation. This view is akin to Dworkin's which, as we have seen, leads to the claim that all sexual intercourse is rape.

Martin turns to a brief discussion of date (acquaintance) rape. He offers two scenarios in order to highlight the issue of consent. For example, what counts as consent? Put another way, when is it clear that "no" means "no"? If there has been no literal "no," does this count as implied consent? Should consent ever be taken to have been given—unless literally asked for and literally given?

He quotes Susan Brownmiller to show the feminist answer to the claim that some women "ask for it" (and are therefore in part blameworthy) by the way they dress or act or by being naive in whom they trust.

Later in this chapter, we will pursue the issue of date rape and harassment with documents from Antioch College, the American Swimming Coaches Association, and a statement on sexual misconduct in the practice of medicine written by the Council on Ethical and Judicial Affairs of the American Medical Society. These documents raise the issue of what counts as consent and intentional action. The latter two documents put the question in terms of professional duties. The codes make us realize that trust is an important part of a relationship—from something as complex and important as the doctor-patient relation to what might be seen as just a simple date.

from Rape and Sexual Harassment

MIKE MARTIN

Fear of rape is part of the daily life of many women. Unfortunately, the fear is fully warranted: It is believed that one in three women alive today will be raped, and the percentage of rapes is even higher in some American cities already. These statistics represent estimates, because only about one in ten rapes is even reported. Whatever the exact statistics, rape is as shockingly common as it is horrifying. Recent studies have suggested that sexual harassment is also a problem on a much greater scale than is commonly believed.

Rape is both cruel and coercive. Sexual harassment is coercive and frequently cruel. As such, rape and sexual harassment constitute failures to maintain minimal standards of decency; they involve direct assaults on the dignity of people. We will preface our discussion with some general comments on cruelty and coercion.

COERCION AND THE RIGHT TO PERSONAL AUTONOMY

Coercion entails unjustified interference with another person's freedom. It is an infringement on one's legitimate efforts to determine one's own destiny, a violation of one's right to personal autonomy.

Personal autonomy is a wider notion than moral autonomy, a concept introduced in our discussions of Kohlberg, Gilligan, and Kant. Recall that moral autonomy means exercising the ability to make one's own moral judgments based on some degree of moral caring. Personal autonomy focuses on moral reasoning and judging rather than on action per se, although reasoning, judging, and acting certainly are closely connected. *Personal autonomy,* by contrast, pertains to all reasoning and acting, not just moral reasoning. Its close synonyms are *self-determination* and *self-governance*.

As Lawrence Haworth points out, "personal autonomy" (and its synonyms) has two senses, one purely descriptive and one normative. The descriptive sense refers to certain facts about people who exercise personal autonomy:

> In some contexts, saying a person is autonomous is a way of attributing to him the personal characteristic of being in charge of his own life. He is not overly dependent on others and not swamped by his own passions; he has the ability to see through to completion those plans and projects he sets for himself. He has, one may say, procedural independence, self-control, and competence. In these contexts, "autonomy" is a descriptive term. It is an empirical [i.e., purely factual] question whether, in what respects, and to what degree a person is autonomous.[1]

According to this definition personal autonomy has three main aspects. First, it involves "procedural independence." This means that the person is not coerced into doing things by force, duress, fraud, deception, or other forms of constraints imposed by individuals or society. The idea is that the procedures used by the autonomous person in making decisions are not undetermined by external intervention.

Second, autonomous persons are competent to guide their own lives. They have the ability to choose their actions by exercising capacities for making rational decisions and acting on them. Their reasoning is not, for example, distorted by major biases that deflect them from the truth, and they are able to live up to their convictions without frequent weakness of will.

Third, they have "substantive independence" in that they are not overly dependent on other people. "Overly dependent" is a vague term, but it refers, for example, to persons who willingly give up any attempt to think for themselves, relying on someone else to think for them. This is vividly illustrated by the persons who join cults in order to escape the difficulties they have found in governing their own lives.

The normative sense of personal autonomy refers to the moral right to exercise personal autonomy in the descriptive sense. When we claim that someone has violated our autonomy, we mean they have violated our right to guide our own lives. We can also fail to be autonomous by improperly exercising our right to autonomy: Weakness of will and self-deception undermine personal autonomy just as much as do manipulators and deceivers. In discussing rape and sexual harassment, however, our focus will be on violations of another person's right to personal autonomy.

Why is the right to personal autonomy morally important? In Kant's view, violating that right amounts to treating persons as mere means to one's own ends, thereby violating the duty to respect their dignity. In Mill's view (expressed in *On Liberty*) personal autonomy is the primary avenue to pursuing happiness, and hence to undermine autonomy is to lessen the opportunities for finding happiness. In Locke's view, the right to personal autonomy is essentially the same as the right to liberty—the fundamental human right that needs no further justification. While Locke would view it as a negative right (a right to not be interfered with), Melden might say it implies a positive right to have society create an environment where rape and sexual harassment are strongly discouraged.

Haworth believes that personal autonomy is intrinsically good—good in and of itself. The ability and willingness to guide one's own life is desirable for its own sake, apart from any further appeal to duties, happiness, or human rights. We might say it is a virtue: It is a human excellence that should be preserved despite pressures from other people and temptations from within. For it makes possible creativity, individuality, and innovative personal relationships.

CRUELTY

We can be briefer in introducing cruelty, even though it takes innumerable forms. One form is omitted actions, such as when we speak of the "cruel indifference" of an insensitive bureaucrat or of the callousness of some people concerning world hunger. There are cruel emotions, such as the enjoyment of the suffering of an innocent victim (a form of sadism); cruel attitudes, such as those of the racist and sexist; cruel hopes, such as the hope to see an innocent child hurt; and cruel motives and desires, such as the desire to augment one's reputation by unfairly criticizing someone.

The most familiar type of cruelty is deliberate infliction of suffering without justification. When the suffering is one's own, masochism is involved. When the suffering is that of another person, as in rape and some sexual harassment, sadism—that is, the enjoyment of the suffering of another person—may be involved.

Most modern moral perspectives, from the Renaissance on, have regarded cruelty as the worst form of immorality. It is noteworthy, however, that this was not true of the predominant attitudes during the Middle Ages. In particular, medieval Christianity viewed pride, not cruelty, as the worst sin. Cruelty was not even listed as one of the Seven Deadly Sins, even though lesser vices like gluttony and lust were. Much of contemporary moral thought consists of identifying subtle forms of cruelty as well as blatant forms that have been unduly tolerated. Some sexual harassment falls into the first category, while rape falls into the second category.

MOTIVATIONS TO RAPE

A rapist may have a variety of motives in committing his act, but most of them fall into four general categories: (1) maliciousness, that is, cruelty prompted by the desire to hurt; (2) means-to-end motivation, that is, cruelty as the means to some further desired purpose; (3) unintended cruelty that arises incidentally to the pursuit of other purposes; and (4) cruelty based on indifference to the suffering of the victim. (Note: In our discussion we refer to the rapist using male pronouns because the overwhelming majority of rapes are committed by men against women. Even though homosexual and lesbian rapes do occur, especially in prisons, and rape of men by women is possible, these instances are comparatively rare.)

Malice is the motive when the rapist deliberately seeks to degrade and injure the victim and (sadistically) takes pleasure in dominating her and causing her to suffer. Means-to-end motivation occurs when the rapist seeks some further goal, for example, when he seeks peer approval from fellow gang members who have dared him to commit the rape. Unintended cruelty results when the rapist thinks he is not using coercion, as when he believes that a woman wants him to engage in forcible intercourse with her despite her protestations. And cruelty based on indifference is illustrated by a sociopathic rapist who is completely indifferent to the feelings of the victim.

According to the traditional male-oriented perspective the act of rape depended primarily on means-to-end motivation. Rape was regarded as a sex-oriented crime in which the rapist used the victim as the means to attain his own sexual satisfaction. Both feminists and experimental psychologists have refuted this view, however, asserting that nearly all rapes are malicious or intentionally cruel acts of violence against women. The end sought is not sexual satisfaction per se. Instead, it is either (1) pleasure in the violence or (2) self-esteem derived from power over the victim (often vicariously experienced as power over all women).

Of course, the rapist often deceives himself about his malice. For example, he embraces the myth that women secretly want to be raped and that their protests are not genuine. Or he convinces himself that a particular woman invites the rape by her clothing and behavior. As we saw in Chapter 6, self-deception does not mitigate culpability. In fact, it compounds guilt, because the rapist is blameworthy both for cruelty and for easing his conscience at the expense of the victim and the truth.

WHAT IS WRONG WITH RAPE?

Rape is a clear-cut paradigm of immorality. But precisely why is it immoral? Part of the answer has already been given: The rapist's motives are vicious, such as enjoyment of the suffering of the victim and derivation of self-esteem from seeking to degrade an innocent person. Most of the answer, however, pertains to the act of rape itself and its effects on the victim rather than to the motives for it.

In an insightful essay on rape Susan Griffin offered the following explanation of why it is immoral:

Rape is an act of aggression in which the victim is denied her self-determination. It is an act of violence which, if not actually followed by beatings or murder, nevertheless always carries with it the threat of death. And finally, rape is a form of mass terrorism, for the victims of rape are chosen indiscriminately, but the propagandists for male supremacy broadcast that it is women who cause rape by being unchaste or in the wrong place at the wrong time, by behaving as though they were free.[2]

Griffin suggests that rape is immoral because it causes at least three kinds of harm to women. First, the act is a violation of a woman's right to self-determination or personal autonomy, a view that follows logically from the definition of rape as sexual intercourse against or without a person's consent. Second, rape inflicts suffering of several kinds: terror, fear for one's life, immediate physical pain, and trauma that endures years after the assault. Third, because rape is widespread, it creates warranted fear that restricts the range of women's activities, thereby again violating their right to autonomy.

There is yet another reason why rape is deeply immoral. In our culture sexuality is regarded as central to a person's identity. Sexuality is also an area where freedom and self-determination are very highly valued. In violating this area of private life, the rapist directly assaults the self-respect of his victim. Usually he is well aware of this fact, and he intends to communicate utter disrespect and contempt for the victim *as* a woman.

DATE RAPE VERSUS CONSENT

Susan Griffin's essay, which appeared in 1971, focused on rapists who choose their victims indiscriminately. Since then it has been learned that many, perhaps most, rapists are acquainted with their victims prior to the rape. This is especially true when the victim is a college student. Such "acquaintance rape" frequently occurs on dates, as in the following examples taken from studies done by the sociologist William B. Sanders:*

Case 4. A blind date had been arranged between the victim and suspect. The couple went out to dinner together and then for drinks. At the apartment, the man began making overtures to the victim, and she declined. Then the suspect began slapping the victim and took her into the bedroom where he raped her.

Case 13. Victim picked up suspect in a bar and drove him in her car to a college parking lot. The suspect propositioned the victim, and the victim said she was "in the mood for some loving." At the parking lot, the victim changed her mind since the man's demeanor became ugly—he offered her money. The suspect then grabbed the victim and demanded she take her pants off, which she did after repeated demands and in fear for her safety, and he raped her.[3]

In the first case there is clearly no consent at any time. What should be said, however, about the second case, in which there is initial consent that is later withdrawn? Does the victim's initial agreement constitute a tacit consent to the man's subsequent conduct, especially if they had already voluntarily engaged in some sexual activity? Surely not. Agreeing to a pleasurable game of tennis does not constitute consent to having one's partner force one to finish the game against one's subsequent wishes. And the same is even more true of sexual activity.

Is the woman nevertheless partially responsible and blameworthy for "precipitating" the rape with provocative behavior? Susan Brownmiller offers the following answer in *Against Our Will: Men, Women, and Rape,* a book that has drawn increased attention to rape:

Some men might consider a housewife who lets a strange man into her house for a glass of water guilty of precipitant behavior, and more men would consider a female hitchhiker who accepts a ride from an unknown male guilty of precipitant behavior. Rape-minded men would consider both actions tantamount to an open invitation. I, on the other hand, consider the housewife and hitchhiker insufficiently wary, but in no way would I consider their actions provocative or even mildly precipitant. Similarly, most men seem to consider a woman who engages in sex play but stops short of intercourse guilty not only of precipitant behavior, but of cruel, provocative behavior with no excuse, yet I and my sister feminists would argue that her actions are perfectly allowable and quite within the bounds of human decency and rational decisions.[4]

Brownmiller here argues that women have the same right to control over their lives and sexual conduct that men take for granted over theirs. The right to self-determination is held equally by women and men, despite the unfair double standard concerning sexual activities.

This double standard, we might add, has even entered into the traditional legal definition of rape. That definition explicitly excluded forcible and violent intercourse within marriage after a wife refused her husband's sexual advances. The exclusion was based on the assumption that wives are the sexual property of their husbands, and it also presupposed that consenting to marriage entailed a sweeping consent to sexual intercourse at any time. Laws are changing, but it remains difficult to prove in court that a rape took place when a married or unmarried victim consented on previous occasions to sexual intercourse with the rapist.

SEXUAL HARASSMENT

Sexual harassment is any sexually oriented act or practice involving intimidation, coercion, or unfair sexual conduct.** In everyday speech the work *harassment* suggests repeated aggravation or persistent annoyance. But as part of the expression "sexual harassment" it carries the special connotation of misuse of power or authority, and this can occur in a single episode that is not repeated. The primary habitat of sexual harassment is authority relationships, in particular at work and school. Before focusing on these authority contexts, however, let us mention cases involving unequal power that do not involve authority (that is, institutionally granted forms of power).

When a man leers, jeers, or whistles at a woman in a public setting, he may be "hassling" her, that is, bothering or irritating her. Hassling becomes sexual harassment when similar acts occur in threatening situations. One such situation is when the two are strangers alone on an isolated street at night; another is when the man is part of a group of men confronting and blocking the path of the woman. Whatever the actual intentions of the man, his conduct is reasonably interpreted in such situations as involving danger or disruption of the woman's life.

The Workplace

Sexual harassment by an employer (usually though not always male) of an employee (usually female) involves abuse of institutional authority, that is, the abuse of power given to the employer by the institution. Recent legislation and Supreme Court rulings define sexual harassment in the workplace as essentially any sexually oriented practice that threatens jobs or job performance.

Obvious examples include threats to fire or demote an employee unless sexual favors are granted, deliberate touching in unwanted ways, and inappropriate comments on the clothing and physical appearance of an employee. A different kind of sexual harassment occurs when employers reveal details about their personal sex lives to their employees against their wishes. And the courts have also ruled that harassment occurs when a male supervisor or colleague posts *Playboy* centerfolds in an office to which woman have access. All these forms of behavior are restricted by sex discrimination laws prohibiting differential treatment of women and men in unfair ways.

Academia

Academia, like the workplace, is structured according to authority relationships. This fact is occasionally overlooked on campuses where faculty are encouraged to give personal attention to students, where there is general trust between students and professors, and where eccentric behavior is tolerated. Thus, we must emphasize that professors have considerable control over their students through grading practices as well as because of their general authority to guide the educational process. In addition, professors are granted an exceptionally high degree of personal autonomy in carrying out their functions.

As was noted, sexual harassment need not involve assault on or physical restraint of persons against their will. In what way or ways, then, is sexual harassment in academia coercive? Let us consider three types of sexual harassment: (1) threats of penalties, (2) annoyance, and (3) offers of rewards.

Sexual threats are the clearest example of coercion. In extreme cases, professors either hint or directly state that unless students sleep with them, the students will not receive as high grades as their work warrants. This interferes with the agency of the student in that a threat suggests that something unwanted will occur unless one complies. When students do not want to have sex with professors, their situation has been worsened by the threat: Either they must accede to the professor's wishes and do something unwanted or they run the risk of not getting the grade deserved. If the student does want to sleep with the professor, the professor is nevertheless trying to manipulate unfairly, using means outside the bounds of understood professional ethics. The threat is coercive, even when the student does not experience it as such.

Sexual annoyance occurs when a professor's sexual overtures cause a student to feel uncomfortable or anxious, or when the overture in any other way creates a climate that distracts from the learning process. Such an overture normally raises (quite reasonable) fears that the professor might retaliate if the student objects to the advance. Sexual annoyance is wrong precisely because it impedes or threatens to impede the learning relationship between student and professor. In this way it also violates the right to self-determination of the student who has chosen to be in that situation to learn. Sexual annoyance is also wrong because of the disrespect demonstrated by focusing attention on one aspect of the student—the sexual one—in a context where that is understood to be inappropriate.

Sexual offers represent attempts to influence behavior by promising a benefit. For example, the professor who offers to raise a student's deserved grade from a C to an A on the condition that the student agree to a date has acted unethically. Not only is the professor violating the standards of integrity required in grading, but the professor is treating all students in the class unfairly. But is there coercion involved in such cases? After all, a desired good (the higher grade) is being offered, and the student seemingly is free to accept or re-

ject the offer. Indeed, Michael Bayles argues that such offers are not coercive when the student wants what is offered:

> Assume there is a mediocre woman graduate student who would not receive an assistantship. Suppose the department chairman offers her one if she goes to bed with him, and she does so. In what sense has the graduate student acted against her will? She apparently preferred having an assistantship and sleeping with the chairman to not sleeping with him and not having an assistantship. So it would appear that she did what she wanted in the situation. . . . The fact that a choice has an undesirable consequence [i.e., having to sleep with the chairman] does not make it against one's will. One may prefer to have clean teeth without having to brush them; nonetheless, one is not acting against one's will when one brushes them.[5]

Bayles concludes that the student's situation is actually improved by the offer because her options are preferable (in her eyes) to what they were before, and in any case Bayles claims that she is free without coercion to choose either way.

This view fails to take account of the fact that such situations often generate fear. In particular, there is fear that the professor might penalize the student for refusing the offer, a valid fear considering the professor has already (in making the offer) violated the professional standards of fairness in allocating assistantships. Moreover, such bribes exert an undue influence that distorts the choices the student should have to confront. In addition, as John Hughes and Larry May argue, such offers constitute a form of sex discrimination. As such, they directly hurt the victim, who is usually a woman, and also indirectly hurt all women:

> Sexual harassment is a form of sex discrimination because (1) the policy is based on a sex-plus criterion of classification, which adversely affects members of only one sex-class, and (2) the policy is based on and perpetuates a sex stereotype [of women as weak and vulnerable] which stigmatizes the class of women and thus, potentially, all of its members.[6]

Here is one final situation. What should be said of the professor who flirts with students and, upon receiving a positive response, asks them to bed? Assume there are no threats, no annoying overtures, and no offers amounting to undue influence. Can we then conclude that this is not sexual harassment, but rather the exercise of free choice in sexual matters? Before accepting that conclusion, the following argument by Billie Dziech and Linda Weiner should be considered:

> Whatever the intent, sexual give-and-take is based on mutual consent of equals. This is obviously not the case in sexual harassment. Normal sexual give-and-take is not possible in student-teacher relationships because the power imbalance and role disparity are too great.[7]

Later, Dziech and Weiner add the following comment:

> Attraction between professor and student may occur, but it is almost impossible for that attraction to be acted on successfully given the average campus environment and the restrictions on student-teacher roles. If legitimate attractions do occur, the couple's regard for the relationship should lead them to restrain themselves until their roles change.[8]

Is this excessive caution? Is it perhaps an infringement of the rights of both students and faculty in matters of sex and love? Or does the risk of coercion in student-faculty relationships warrant the restraint recommended by Dziech and Weiner? We will return to these questions in the "Discussion Topics" section.

SUMMARY

Whereas *character-respect* means admiring specific individuals for their good character or virtues, *minimal-respect* entails recognizing the value of all moral beings, that is, persons having a sense of moral values. Minimal-respect for other people requires honoring their right to personal autonomy of self-determination. This right creates obligations not to interfere in people's legitimate areas of personal prerogative, as well as obligations to contribute to making society supportive of personal autonomy. *Personal autonomy* includes *moral autonomy* (the ability and willingness to form reasonable moral judgments and to act on

them), but it encompasses much more. It requires procedural independence (not being coerced or deceived by others), competence (self-control and the exercising of rationality), and substantive independence (not being overly dependent on others).

Rape violates personal autonomy by violating sexual choice, an area of self-determination central to personal identity and self-respect. This is true of individual acts of rape, which by definition involve the violation of consent. But it is equally true of rape as a widespread practice, because the very real threat of rape forces women to restrict their activities.

Rape is also a form of cruelty in which suffering is deliberately and without any justification inflicted on a person. The suffering includes immediate physical pain, terror and fear for one's life, and trauma that lasts for years afterward. The rapist's intentions are violent rather than primarily sexual per se and involve the cruel motives of enjoying the violent subjugation of women and deriving self-esteem though sexual dominance.

Although sexual harassment often involves cruelty, it is of special interest because of the ways it violates self-determination. It can be defined as any sexually oriented act or practice involving intimidation, coercion, or unfair sexual conduct. Most often it involves abuse of authority relationships at work and school. Sexual harassment is most commonly exhibited through sexual threats, sexual annoyance, and sexual offers, each of which creates conditions that disrupt work and learning. . . .

Notes

*From *Rape and Woman's Identity* by William B. Sanders. © 1980 by Sage Publications, Inc. Reprinted by permission of the publisher.

**This definition applies to sexual assault, although sexual assault is sometimes treated as an offense distinct from sexual harassment.

References

1. Lawrence Haworth, *Autonomy: An Essay in Philosophical Psychology and Ethics* (New Haven, CT: Yale University Press, 1986), p. 1.
2. Susan Griffin, *Rape: The Politics of Consciousness,* 3rd ed. (New York: Harper & Row, 1986), pp. 23–24.

3. WILLIAM B. SANDERS, *Rape and Woman's Identity* (Beverly Hills, CA: Sage, 1980), pp. 50–51.

4. SUSAN BROWNMILLER, *Against Our Will: Men, Woman, and Rape* (New York: Simon & Schuster, 1975), p. 354.

5. MICHAEL D. BAYLES, "Coercive Offers and Public Benefits," *Personalist*, vol. 55 (1974): 142–143.

6. JOHN C. HUGHES, and LARRY MAY, "Sexual Harassment," *Social Theory and Practice*, vol. 6 (1980): 273–274.

7. BILLIE WRIGHT DZIECH and LINDA WEINER, *The Lecherous Professor: Sexual Harassment on Campus* (Boston: Beacon Press, 1984), p. 25.

8. IBID., p. 77.

Why would someone sexually harass another? What lies at the bottom of rape? Until fairly recently, the answer was thought to be uncontrolled sexual desire. Now, much evidence points to a desire to do violence to the victim. But the debate continues, as our next two selections show.

RAPE: ITS MOTIVATION

Groth and Birnbaum's essay presents data to show that the best explanation for rape is that it is a crime of violence—an acting out of a desire for power over women.

Palmer's essay finds fault with twelve reasons often cited by those who defend the "crime of violence" interpretation for rape. In this selection, he is attacking a position and showing its weaknesses; he does not make any claim about what the true cause of rape might be.

from Anger, Power, and Sadism Are the Primary Motives for Rape

A. NICHOLAS GROTH AND H. JEAN BIRNBAUM

One of the most basic observations one can make regarding men who rape is that not all such offenders are alike. They do not do the very same thing in the very same way or for the very same reasons. In some cases, similar acts occur for different reasons, and in other cases, different acts serve similar purposes. From our clinical experience with convicted offenders and with victims of reported sexual assault, we find that in *all* cases of forcible rape, three components are present: power, anger, and sexuality. The hierarchy and interrelationships among these three factors, together with the relative intensity with which each is experienced and the variety of ways in which each is expressed, vary from one offender to another. Nevertheless, there seems to be sufficient

clustering within the broad spectrum of sexual assault so that distinguishable patterns of rape can be differentiated based on the descriptive characteristics of the assault and the dynamic characteristics of the offender.

Rape is always and foremost an aggressive act. In some offenses, the assault appears to constitute a discharge of anger; it becomes evident that rape is the way the offender expresses and discharges a mood state of intense anger, frustration, resentment, and rage. In other offenses, the aggression seems to be reactive; that is, when the victim resists the advances of her assailant, he retaliates by striking, hitting, or hurting her in some way. Hostility appears to be quickly triggered or released, sometimes in a clear, consciously experienced state of anger or, in other cases, in what appears to be a panic state. In still other offenses, the aggression becomes expressed less as an anger motive and more as a means of dominating, controlling, and being in charge of the situation—an expression of mastery and conquest. And in a fourth vissicitude, the aggression itself becomes eroticized so that the offender derives pleasure from both controlling his victim and hurting her/him—an intense sense of excitement and pleasure being experienced in this context whether or not actual sexual contact is made. These variations on the theme of aggression are not mutually exclusive, and, in any given instance of rape, multiple meanings may be expressed in regard to both the sexual and the aggressive behaviors.

In every act of rape, both aggression and sexuality are involved, but it is clear that sexuality becomes the means of expressing the aggressive needs and feelings that operate in the offender and underlie his assault. Three basic patterns of rape can be distinguished in this regard: (1) the *anger rape,* in which sexuality becomes a hostile act; (2) the *power rape,* in which sexuality becomes an expression of conquest; and (3) the *sadistic rape,* in which anger and power become eroticized.

Rape is complex and multidetermined. It serves a number of psychological aims and purposes. Whatever other needs and factors operate in the commission of such an offense, however, we have found the components of anger, power, and sexuality always present and prominent. Moreover, in our experience, we find that either anger or power is the dominant component and that rape, rather than being primarily an expression of sexual desire, is, in fact, the use of sexuality to express these issues of power and anger. Rape, then, is a pseudosexual act, a pattern of sexual behavior that is concerned much more with status, hostility, control, and dominance than with sensual pleasure or sexual satisfaction. It is sexual behavior in the primary service of nonsexual needs.

Anger Rape

In some cases of sexual assault, it is very apparent that sexuality becomes a means of expressing and discharging feelings of pent-up anger and rage. The assault is characterized by physical brutality.

Far more actual force is used in the commission of the offense than would be necessary if the intent were simply to overpower the victim and achieve sexual penetration. Instead, this type of offender *attacks* his victim, grabbing her, striking her, knocking her to the ground, beating her, tearing her clothes, and raping her. He may use a blitz style of attack, a violent surprise offensive, in which the victim is caught completely off guard. Or he may use a confidence-style approach to gain access to the victim and then launch a sudden, overpowering attack. In the former situation, the offender approaches the victim directly by hitting her. In the latter situation, victims often relate that at first the assailant seemed pleasant enough, but that at some point he changed. Suddenly and without warning he became mean and angry. His later behavior was in sharp contrast to the initial impression:

> Listening to how the victims described me in court, the impression that I got was almost a Jekyll and Hyde. I approached all of my victims in a very acceptable manner, but then I seemed to change suddenly. When I went into these bars, I was looking for someone that would be comfortable. I was looking for people to talk to, and these women were willing to talk to me. But during the course of sitting and talking, something would happen inside of me, the anger would erupt. The assault with intent to rape wasn't it—I was trying to kill them!

The rape experience for this type of offender is one of conscious anger and rage, and he expresses his fury both physically and verbally. His aim is to hurt and debase his victim, and he expresses his contempt for her through abusive and profane language. If his primary motive is one of anger, and if he is not sexually motivated, why doesn't this offender confine his assault to a battering of the victim? Why does he also rape her? The answer seems to be that such a man considers rape the ultimate offense he can commit against another person. Sex becomes his weapon, and rape constitutes the ultimate expression of his anger:

> I wanted to knock the woman off her pedestal, and I felt rape was the worst thing I could do to her.

Often this type of offender forces the victim to submit to or to perform additional sexual acts that he may regard as particularly degrading, such as sodomy or fellatio. In some cases, contempt for the victim is expressed by urinating or by masturbating and ejaculating onto her.

Characteristically, this type of offender does not report being in a state of sexual excitement or arousal. In fact, he may be initially impotent during the assault and able to achieve an erection only by masturbating himself or having the victim perform oral sex on him. Sexuality itself is typically regarded by this type of offender as something basically "dirty" and offensive at some level of his subjective experience, and, therefore, it becomes a weapon, a means by which he can defile, degrade, and humiliate his victim. The anger rapist typically finds little or no sexual gratification in the rape—in fact, his subjective reaction to the sexual act itself is frequently one of revulsion and disgust. Satisfaction and relief result from the discharge of anger rather than from sexual gratification:

> I was enraged when I started out. I lost control and struck out with violence. After the assault I felt relieved. I felt I had gotten even. There was no sexual satisfaction; in fact, I felt a little disgusted. I felt relieved of the tension and anger for a while, but then it would start to build again, little things, but I couldn't shake them off.

Typically, such an offender reports that he did not anticipate committing a rape. It was not something he fantasized or thought about beforehand—it was, instead, something that happened on the spur of the moment. Sometimes he will say that he felt "something was going to happen" but could not identify or anticipate what course of action his feelings would lead to. Even during the offense itself the offender may psychologically dissociate himself from the assault as if he were in a trance or were more an observer than a participant; the event is experienced as unreal, and the offender may not fully appreciate the extent of his aggression:

> It wasn't until afterwards, it wasn't until after I had been able to get rid of all the anger and all the feelings that I had inside of me that I could in some ways come back to the real situation and to what I had done. And, in that way, I did in a sense sort of feel like I became an animal and it was only then that I felt very upset by what I had done.

Relatively speaking, such attacks tend to be of short duration. The offender strikes, assaults, and flees. Such assaults appear to be more impulsive or spontaneous than premeditated, and the offender finds it difficult to account for his assault, when he cannot deny it, except to rationalize that he was intoxicated or on drugs, or that he just "flipped out":

> My offense was pretty bad. I believe I was flipped out at the time. I have no defense at all. I was drunk. I was standing on the corner and—I don't know. I don't know what the hell happened. I just was standing around, and I saw this girl pull up in her car, and I didn't see her face or anything. I just saw her pull up to the stoplight, and I walked up to the car, opened the door, pushed her over to the passenger side, and I took off with her in the car. And I can't be sure why I did it, but, anyway, I took off with her and got her to an area that I thought was a good place, and I got out of the car and hit her. I hit her right in the eye, and I still don't know why I raped her.

In describing the evolution of the assault, the offender typically reports being in an upset and distressed frame of mine at the time of the offense. His predominant mood state appears to be a combination of anger, distress, frustration, and depression, and the offense itself is typically preceded by some upsetting event, often, but not invariably, involving some significant woman in the assailant's life. The assault is in response to some identifiable precipitating stress. For example, some offenders reported a serious dispute with their wives prior to the offense. These arguments revolved around a number of marital issues, such as the wife's threatening to or, in fact, leaving him, arguments over his drinking, complaints about her housekeeping skills, suspicions of infidelity, and the like. Others felt aggravated with their parents for imposing unfair restrictions on their activities or unjust punishments for their misbehavior. Some offenders cited conflicts with their girlfriends, such as being stood up, rejected, taunted, or sexually frustrated. Others reported feeling upset over such things as being rejected from military service, being fired, being burdened by financial debts, or being harassed in some fashion by other people. The common theme appeared to be one in which the offender felt that he had been wronged, hurt, put down, or treated unjustly in some fashion by some individual, situation, or event. Rape served to discharge the resulting anger, resentment, and frustration. In this fashion, the anger rapist revenges himself for what he perceives to be wrongs done him by others, especially women.

The anger rapist's relationships to important persons in his life are frequently fraught with conflict, irritation, and aggravation. The anger, resentment, hostility, and frustration engendered in these relationships is often displaced onto other individuals, and, therefore, the victim may be a complete stranger to the offender, someone who has been unfortunate enough to be in his presence at the point at which his controls begin to fail and his rage erupts. Although she has done nothing to warrant it, she becomes the target of his revenge—not revenge in a calculated, planned fashion but, instead, the recipient of an impulsive reaction precipitated by a situation she has had no part in. . . .

Power Rape

In another pattern of rape, power appears to be the dominant factor motivating the offender. In these assaults, it is not the offender's desire to harm his victim but to possess her sexually. Sexuality becomes a means of compensating for underlying feelings of inadequacy and serves to express issues of mastery, strength, control, authority, identity, and capability. His goal is sexual conquest, and he uses only the amount of force necessary to accomplish this objective. His aim is to capture and control his victim. He may accomplish this through verbal threat ("Do what I say and you won't get hurt!"), intimidation with a weapon ("I came up behind her and put a knife to her throat and told her to come with me"), and/or physical force ("I told her to undress, and when she refused I struck her across the face to show her I meant business"). Physical aggression is used to overpower and subdue the victim, and its use is directed toward achieving sexual submission. The intent of the offender usually is to achieve sexual intercourse with his victim as evidence of conquest, and to accomplish this, he resorts to whatever force he finds necessary to overcome his victim's resistance and to render her helpless. Very

often, the victim is kidnapped or held captive in some fashion, and she may be subjected to repeated assaults over an extended period of time.

Such offenders entertain obsessional thoughts and masturbatory fantasies about sexual conquest and rape. The characteristic scenario is one in which the victim initially resists the sexual advances of her assailant; he overpowers her and achieves sexual penetration; in spite of herself, the victim cannot resist her assailant's sexual prowess and becomes sexually aroused and receptive to his embrace:

> The fantasies began with going out to a nightclub or bar and picking up a girl, and these changed to increasingly more drastic attempts. I'd think about either going to big parking lots or to a quiet area where there might be girls walking and confronting them. I began to have the thought that perhaps sometime if I did this, that the woman would agree or perhaps almost attack me—perhaps just my appearance of whatever would just turn her on and she would almost literally attack me in a complete state of sexual excitement, and she would rape me as if I were just what she had been waiting for. I would fantasize about confronting a girl with a weapon, a knife or a gun, and that she would tell me that I didn't need it and that she wanted me, and that she wanted me sexually. She would say, "No, you don't need it, you don't need a gun, you don't need any of this, you're enough."

Since it constitutes a test of his competency, the rape experience for this type of offender is a mixture of excitement, anxiety, anticipated pleasure, and fear:

> I don't know how to explain the feeling I got. My heart just started to pound, and I got sort of a funny feeling in the pit of my stomach, sort of like the feeling I had the first time I ever had sexual intercourse, and I felt that I had to go out and get her. I didn't have an erection at all; I just had the feeling and desire to have a woman.

In reality, the offender tends to find little sexual satisfaction in the rape. The assault is disappointing, for it never lives up to his fantasy:

> It never came down the way I imagined it would. In the fantasy, after the initial shock of the attack,

I thought the victim would be more accepting and responsive, but, in reality, that was not the case. I did not have the good feelings I fantasized about. I felt let down. I didn't experience the same feelings in the actual assault that I had expected to feel. Everything was pleasurable in the fantasy, and there was acceptance, whereas in the reality of the situation, it wasn't pleasurable, and the girl was scared, not turned on to me.

Whatever he may tell himself to explain the situation, at some level of experience he senses that he has not found what he is looking for in the offense—something he cannot clearly identify or define is missing or lacking. He does not feel reassured by either his own performance or his victim's response to the assault, and, therefore, he must go out and find another victim, this time "the right one." His offenses become repetitive and compulsive, and he may commit a whole series of rapes over a relatively short period of time:

I felt I needed something more. I just felt that there was something more, and that I had to have it. I really felt a compulsion, I mean a strong . . . something. It's funny. Even when these assaults happened, my life, my wife, my responsibilities, my parents, and so forth would flash in front of my mind, but it seemed to be of no consequence. I mean, I just had to no matter what. The crime itself just frustrated me more. I wasn't sexually aroused. I had to force myself. I felt some relief coming off because there was some tension release, but very shortly afterwards the feelings were worse. I blamed the victim and felt it was her fault and that a different girl would give me the satisfaction I craved, so I went out looking for another victim.

The amount of force used in the assaults may vary depending in part on situational factors, but there may be an increase in aggression over time as the offender becomes more desperate to achieve that indefinable experience that continues to elude him:

Somehow I felt that I had not accomplished what I wanted to. The first three victims I approached resisted in some way or other—they just sort of laughed in my face—so the next time I went out, I took a knife with me. And even when I succeeded in committing a rape, the fantasies

didn't go away; they just intensified, and I got more and more aggressive.

The offenses themselves are either premeditated (the offender goes out in search of a victim with the clear intent of sexual assault) or opportunistic (a situation presents itself in which the offender unexpectedly finds that he has access to a victim and this access activates his propensity for sexual assault).

The victim of the power rapist may be of any age but generally tends to be within the same age range as the offender or younger. The choice of a victim is predominantly determined by availability, accessibility, and vulnerability. As one offender put it, "I always looked for a victim who was smaller than me."

Although the power rapist may report that his offense was prompted by a desire for sexual gratification, careful examination of his behavior typically reveals that efforts to negotiate the sexual encounter or to determine the woman's receptiveness to a sexual approach are noticeably absent, as are any attempts at lovemaking or foreplay. Instead, the aim of the offender is to capture, conquer, and control his victim. Sexual desire, in and of itself, is not the primary or paramount issue operating in this assailant. If it were, there are a number of opportunities available in our society for consensual sex. In fact, sexual assaults always coexist with consenting sexual relations in the life of the offender. In no case have we ever found that rape was the first or only sexual experience in the offender's sexual history, or that he had no other alternatives or outlets for his sexual desires. To the question, "If what you wanted was sex, why didn't you just go to a prostitute?" the power rapist is likely to reply, "A real man never pays for it," revealing that one of the dynamics in the assault is reaffirmation of his manhood. Such offenders feel insecure about their masculinity or conflicted about their identity. . . .

One of the key issues in working with victims of power rapes is their anger at themselves and self-blame for being victimized and not being able to escape the assault. It is important to help them realize that no strategy would necessarily have been more effective than the one they tried. What deters one assailant only encourages another, but frequently the victim feels that if she had said or done something different, she could have discouraged the assault. And it is this feeling of not having achieved her primary goal—that of escaping the offender—that affects the victim and retards her recovery from the trauma of sexual assault.

Sadistic Rape

In a third pattern of rape, both sexuality and aggression become fused into a single psychological experience known as *sadism*. There is a sexual transformation of anger and power so that aggression itself become eroticized. This offender finds the intentional maltreatment of his victim intensely gratifying and takes pleasure in her torment, anguish, distress, helplessness, and suffering. The assault usually involves bondage and torture and frequently has a bizarre or ritualistic quality to it. The offender may subject his victim to curious actions, such as clipping her hair, washing or cleansing her body, or forcing her to dress in some specific fashion or behave in some specified way. Such indignities are accompanied by explicitly abusive acts, such as biting, burning the victim with cigarettes, and flagellation. Sexual areas of the victim's body (her breasts, genitals, and buttocks) become a specific focus of injury and abuse. In some cases, the rape may not involve the offender's sexual organs. Instead, he may use some type of instrument or foreign object, such as a stick or bottle, with which to penetrate his victim sexually:

> My intention from the outset was to give my victims an enema and follow it with anal sex, but in most cases I "came off" during the enema without requiring anal entry. I have found as much pleasure, if not more, reaching a climax with masturbation during the administration of the enema—sodomy or coitus being unnecessary.

In extreme cases—those involving sexual homicide—there may be grotesque acts, such as the sexual mutilation of the victim's body or sexual intercourse with her corpse. Eric, an infamous sex killer, committed four grisly murders in the span of one summer. As described in the pathologist's report, each victim had been dismembered into five parts. The skin was peeled off the breasts and vagina. On the legs and buttocks, there were multiple stab wounds and punctures. Stab wounds were also present in the anterior chest wall. Sperm were found in both the vagina and the rectum of the body, and findings were consistent with its having being deposited postmortem. . . .

Multiple Motives Underlying Rape

Regardless of the pattern of the assault, rape is a complex act that serves a number of retaliatory and compensatory aims in the psychological functioning of the offender. It is an effort to discharge his anger, contempt, and hostility toward women—to hurt, degrade, and humiliate. It is an effort to counteract feelings of vulnerability and inadequacy in himself and to assert his strength and power—to control and exploit. It is an effort to deny sexual anxieties and doubts and reaffirms his identity, competency, and manhood. It is an effort to retain status (in gang rape) among male peers, and it is an effort to achieve sexual gratification. Rape is equivalent to symptom formation in that it serves to defend against anxiety, to express a conflict, and gratify an impulse. It is symptomatic of personality dysfunction, associated more with conflict and stress than with pleasure and satisfaction. Sexuality is not the only—nor the primary—motive underlying rape. It is, however, the means through which conflicts surrounding issues of anger and power become discharged. Rape is always a combination of anger, power, and sexuality, and each of these components must be examined in evaluating the offender and assessing the impact of the assault on the victim and the nature of her trauma.

from The "Not Sex" Explanation of Rape Is Flawed

CRAIG T. PALMER

The first step in evaluating the "not sex" explanation of rape is to establish exactly what the debate is over. Thanks to the feminist movement, no one any longer defends the dangerous claim that rape is a sexually arousing or sought-after experience on the part of the *victim*. Neither does anyone deny that male sex organs are necessarily involved in the act. The debate is over the motivation of the rapist in using his sex organs in a way that constitutes rape. Motivation refers to the purpose or goal of a behavior. Proponents of the "not sex" explanation hold that the occurrence of rape cannot be accounted for by the hypothesis that sexual stimulation is the *goal* of rapists. These authors hold that the occurrence of rape can only be explained by the hypothesis that sex is just a *means* used to attain the goals of power, control, domination, and violence.

Unfortunately, motivation is a covert entity, existing solely in the minds of individuals (either consciously or unconsciously). The problem with viewing motivation as covert is that such an entity is not externally identifiable. Statements about motivation *in this sense* are completely untestable. No data of any kind could falsify a statement about such a "motivation."

Vague semantics have also clouded the issue of whether sex is a "means" or an "end" for rapists. For example, Bercovitch et al. state that "Human rape seems to be an outcome of status assertive by males which acts as a form of power domination used to copulate with a female who could not be attained with conventional methods" (Bercovitch et al., in press). This statement appears to imply that sex (i.e., "copulation") is the sought-after goal of rape, since "power" is "used to" accomplish this goal. However, the authors use this statement to support the claim that "Rape is probably not primarily a sexually motivated phenomenon" (ibid.).

While the literature of rape motivation is often clouded by vague semantics and uncheckable claims, the issue "is an important one, and how the verdict is rendered determines whether fundamental matters are obfuscated or come into more useful analytical light" (Geis & Huston, 1980, p. 187). Consequently, the present paper attempts to resolve this controversy by examining 12 arguments given to support the "not sex" explanation.

Supporting Arguments for the "Not Sex" Explanation

Argument 1

When they say sex or sexual, these social scientists and feminists mean the *motivation,* moods, or drives associated with honest courtship and pair bonding. In such situations, males report feelings of tenderness, affection, joy and so on. . . . It is this sort of pleasurable motivation that the socioculturists (and feminists) denote as sexuality. . . . (Shields & Shields, 1983, p. 122; original emphasis)

The validity of this argument depends on the accuracy of its definition of "sex," and there appears to be considerable evidence that this definition of sex is unduly limiting. First,

it is abundantly self evident . . . that a large percentage of males have no difficulty in divorcing sex from love. Whistles and wolf-calls, attendance at burlesque shows, patronizing of call girls and prostitutes—all of these are probably manifestations of a sexual urge totally or largely bereft of romantic feelings. (Hagen, 1979, pp. 158–159)

More fundamentally, the word "sexual" (but not "tenderness," "affection," or "joy") is routinely used to refer to the motivation of non-human animals involved in reproductive acts.

Argument 2

Rape is not sexually motivated because of the "fact that most rapists have stable sexual partners." (Sanford & Fetter, 1979, p. 8)

From "Twelve Reasons Why Rape Is Not Sexually Motivated: A Skeptical Examination" by Craig T. Palmer, *Journal of Sex Research,* Vol. 25, no. 4 (November 1988), pp. 512–530. Copyright © 1988 by *Journal of Sex Research.* Used by permission of *Journal of Sex Research.*

This widely mentioned argument (Brownmiller, 1975, Finkelhor & Yllo, 1985, Groth, 1979a; Groth & Hobson, 1983; Medea & Thomson, 1974; Queen's Bench Foundation, 1978; Rada, 1978a; Rodabaugh & Austin, 1981; Shields & Shields, 1983) hinges on the assumption that a male's sexual desire is exhausted by a single "outlet." Symons points out that this does not appear to be true: "Most patrons of prostitutes, adult bookstores, and adult movie theatres are married men, but this is not considered evidence for lack of sexual motivation" (Symons, 1979, p. 280).

Argument 3

Rape is not sexually motivated because rapes are often "premeditated." (See Brownmiller, 1975; Griffin, 1971.)

The fact that many rapes are premeditated does not nullify that many rapes are also spontaneous. However, this argument presumes that all sexually motivated behavior is spontaneous. Obviously, this is untrue since there are many kinds of consenting sexual acts (affairs, rendezvous, seductions) which are highly planned and still considered to be sexually motivated (see Symons, 1979, p. 279).

Argument 4

The age distribution of rapists demonstrates that rape is a crime of violence and aggression instead of sex:

> the violence prone years for males extend from their teenage years into their late forties, this is the age range into which most rapists fall. *Unlike sexuality,* aggression does diminish with age and, therefore, a male's likelihood of committing a rape diminishes with the onset of middle age. (Groth and Hobson, 1983, p. 161; my emphasis.)

It is unfortunate that the authors of this argument do not cite the basis for their claim that the human male sexual drive does *not* decrease with age. There is abundant evidence that numerous types of male sexual activity peak in the late teens and then slowly diminish (Kinsey, Pomeroy, & Martin, 1948; Goethals, 1971). Not only does the age of most rapists fail to disprove that rape is sexually motivated, the general correlation between the age distribution of rapists and the general level of sexual activity of males is very consistent with the view that rape *is* sexually motivated.

Argument 5

The common occurrence of rape in war shows that rape is motivated by hostility instead of sex. (See Brownmiller, 1975, pp. 23–118; Shields & Shields, 1983.)

The prevalance of rape during war has indeed been well documented by Brownmiller and others. However, the writers who see this as evidence of a lack of sexual motivation are often the same ones who stress that vulnerability is a critical variable in victim selection (see Shields & Shields, 1983). Females in war situations are vulnerable to an exceptional degree. While hostility may be involved in any rape, the tremendously high degree of female vulnerability is both a sufficient and more parsimonious explanation of the high frequency of rape in war situations. Thus, the high frequency of rape during war is not evidence for the absence, or even unimportance, of sexual motivation. In fact, Brownmiller herself implies the importance of sexual motivation by reporting that: "In some of the camps, pornographic movies were shown to the soldiers, 'in an obvious attempt to work the men up'" (Brownmiller, 1975, p. 83; see also Medea & Thompson, 1974, p. 32).

Argument 6

Instead of being a sexually motivated act, rape is a form of "social control" because it is used as a form of punishment in some societies. (See Brownmiller, 1975, p. 319.)

Symons clearly demonstrates the problem with this argument by pointing out that the use of rape as a punishment "does not prove that sexual feelings are not also involved, any more than the deprivation of property as punishment proves that the property is not valuable to the punisher" (Symons, 1979, p. 280).

Argument 7

"Men have been asked why they raped and many have said it was not out of sexual desire but for power and control over their victims." (Dean & de Bruyn-kopps, 1982, p. 233; citing evidence from Groth, 1979a; see also Shields & Shields, 1983, p. 121.)

This might appear to be the simplest way to decide the issue—just ask rapists. However, such an approach requires the problematical assumption that one clearly experiences, remembers, and truthfully reports his motives. Such an assumption is especially troublesome when the subjects in question are convicts: "It is difficult to avoid the conclusion that the men's conscious attempts to emphasize their correct attitudes and to minimize their sexual impulsiveness were to some extent calculated to foster the impression that they no longer constituted a threat" (Symons, 1979, p. 283).

Even if the truthfulness of rapists' statements could be assumed, there is still the problem of *interpretation*. Symons (1979, pp. 282–283) cites several questionable interpretations present in the literature at that time (also see the Queen's Bench Foundation, 1978). This problem became particularly crucial with the subsequent publication of Groth's influential book *Men Who Rape*. Not only did Groth's interpretations go against other findings such as those by Smithyman (1978, p. iv) in which 84% of the rapists cited sexual motivation "solely or in part" as the cause of their acts (see also Ageton, 1983; Geis, 1977; Katz & Mazur, 1979; Rada, 1978a; Russell, 1975; Sussman & Bordwell, 1981), but even the examples Groth selected to support his argument make his interpretations questionable. One rapist explains his behavior by saying, "She stood there in her nightgown, and you could see right through it—you could see her nipples and breasts and, you know they were just waiting for me, and it was just too much of a temptation to pass up" (Groth, 1979a, p. 38). Another rapist reported that "I just wanted to have sex with her and that was all" (Groth, 1979a, p. 42; see also Groth, 1979a, pp. 50, 55, 93, 159, 161, 181, and 183).

Groth's reasons for not considering such statements as evidence for sexual motivation being primary in rape are interesting in light of some of the previously discredited arguments:

Although the power rapist [by far the most common type in Groth's classification] may report that his offense was prompted by a desire for sex-

ual gratification, careful examination of his behavior typically reveals that efforts to negotiate the sexual encounter or to determine the woman's receptiveness to a sexual approach are noticeably absent, as are any attempts at lovemaking or foreplay. (Groth, 1979a, p. 28)

Here again we see an attempt to redefine "sex." This time it must include concern for the other person's arousal to "really" be sexual. Even if this was true, some of Groth's own examples show evidence of negotiation and foreplay (Groth, 1979a, p. 29). Other studies on victims have found that many rapes, particularly "date rapes," often involve extensive negotiation and foreplay (e.g., Ageton, 1983; Katz & Mazur, 1979; Kirkpatrick & Kanin, 1957; Rada, 1978a). It appears that the data gathered from the statements of convicted rapists are inconclusive at best. Such "evidence" does not demonstrate the absence of sexual motivation in rape.

Argument 8

"The high incidence (1 out of 3 cases) of sexual dysfunction is further evidence for the relative unimportance of sexual desire in the act of rape." (Groth & Hobson, 1983, p. 171; see also Groth, 1979a; Harding, 1985)

The evidence of dysfunction during rape has been subject to questionable definitions (see Thornhill & Thornhill, 1983) and varies greatly between different studies (see Rada, 1978a). Hence, despite the claims of Harding (1985), sexual dysfunction in rape has not been conclusively shown to be significantly higher in rapes than in consenting acts. Even if a higher rate of actual dysfunction was conclusively demonstrated, it could be easily accounted for by the adverse circumstances under which rape often occurs. Symons (1980) points out that even the most sexually motivated rapist might experience dysfunction due to anxiety over the possibility of severe punishment and the existence of conflicting emotions. There is also the fact that offenders are often under the influence of drugs. Groth reports that 50% of the rapists in his study were drunk or on drugs at the time of the assault (1979a, p. 96). Smithyman reports that 32% of the rapists in his study were intoxicated in some way (1978, p. 60). The Queen's Bench Foundation found that 61.6% of the rapists had consumed alcohol before the rape (1978, p. 773).

Argument 9

Rape is motivated by aggression instead of sex because "changes in number of rapes and assault showed similar seasonal patterns, suggesting that rape comprised a subcategory of aggressive behavior" (Michael & Zumpe, 1983, p. 883; cited as evidence of the unimportance of sexual motivation in rape by Bercovitch et al., in press).

Rape and non-sexual assault both appear to occur most frequently in the summer months (Michael & Zumpe, 1983). The conclusion that this is evidence for a lack of sexual motivation in rape is seriously flawed in a number of ways. First, it ignores numerous alternative explanations of why rape might occur most frequently in the summer, such as greater social interaction and greater visual cues which are quite compatible with the assumption that sex is an important motivation in rape (see Chappell et al., 1977). Second, if seasonality of occurrence is an indicator of motivation, then all aggressive behaviors should follow the same pattern. The same study that reports a correlation between assault and rape reports a dramatic difference in the seasonal pattern of rape and murder (Michael & Zumpe, 1983). Finally, this argument ignores the drastic differences in other patterns of assault and rape. Many of these patterns, especially the age and sex of victims, are much more likely to be related to the motivation of the offenders than is seasonality (see Thornhill & Thornhill, 1983).

Argument 10

The real motivation in rape is violence instead of sex because castrated rapists just find other ways of doing violence to women. (See Cohen et al., 1971; Dusek, 1984; Groth, 1979a, p. 10; Katz & Mazur, 1979; LeGrand, 1973; MacDonald, 1971; Rada, 1978a.)

All data on the effects of castration must be viewed skeptically because of the many uncontrolled variables involved (Greene, 1979). Existing data suggest that castrated sex offenders have significantly lower recidivism rates in regard to *sexual* offenses (Bremer, 1959; MacDonald, 1971;

Rada, 1978b; Sturup, 1960, 1968). Proponents of the "not sex" argument have refused to see this as evidence of rape being sexually motivated. This is because "Those who view rape as primarily an aggressive offense do not believe that castration will cure the rapist's aggressive impulses" (Rada, 1978b, p. 143). People holding this view would predict that castrated offenders would simply replace their "sexual" assaults with "non-sexual" assaults.

Argument 11

Rape is clearly an act of aggression. McCahil et al. (1979) in their study of 1,401 rape victims show that: (1) a majority of victims (64%) reported being pushed or held during the incident, (2) victims are often slapped (17%), beaten (22%), and/or choked (20%), and (3) 84% of victims experienced some kind of nonphysical force during the incident (threat of bodily harm, etc.). (Thornhill & Thornhill, 1983, p. 163)

To determine the significance of data on rapist violence and victim injury, it is crucial to make the distinction between instrumental force used to accomplish the rape (and possibly to influence the female not to resist and/or not to report the rape), and excessive violence that appears to be an end in itself. This distinction is necessary because only excessive force is a possible indication of violent motivation on the part of the rapist.

Harding makes the following claim: "In many cases of rape in humans, assault seems to be the important factor, not sex. . . . [because] . . . In most cases the use of force goes beyond that necessary to compel the victim's compliance with the rapist's demands" (Harding, 1985, p. 51). However, existing evidence, including that cited by Harding (1985, p. 51), indicates that excessive force is actually only used in a minority of cases. Consistent with the previously cited figures by McCahil, Meyer and Fischman (1979), Chappell and Singer found only 15 to 20 percent of rape victims required hospital treatment for physical injuries (1977). Katz and Mazur also report the following: "Although most rape victims encountered some form of physical force, few experienced severe lasting [physical] injuries" (1979, p. 171; see also Burgess & Holmstrom, 1974; Schiff, 1971). Amir even found that "In a large number of cases (87%), only temptation and verbal coercion were used to subdue the victim" (Amir, 1975, p. 7).

Other evidence also indicates that it is only in a minority of cases that violence and injury are even one of the goals of a rapist.

Argument 12

"IT IS NOT A CRIME OF LUST BUT OF VIOLENCE AND POWER [because] . . . RAPE VICTIMS ARE NOT ONLY THE 'LOVELY YOUNG BLONDS' OF NEWSPAPER HEADLINES—RAPISTS STRIKE CHILDREN, THE AGED, THE HOMELY—ALL WOMEN." (Brownmiller, 1975, back cover; original emphasis)

It is fitting that Brownmiller chose this argument to place in bold type on the cover of her milestone book. Whether rapists prefer sexually attractive victims, or only select victims who are most vulnerable, forms a major argument of those on both sides of the debate (e.g., Alcock, 1983; Brownmiller, 1975; Dean & de Bruyn-kopps, 1982; Denmark & Friedman, 1985; Groth, 1979a; Groth & Hobson, 1983; Rodabaugh & Austin, 1981; Symons, 1979).

The argument that rape is not sexually motivated because rapists allegedly do not prefer attractive victims begins with the accurate observation that "Any female may become a victim of rape" (Brownmiller, 1975, p. 388). This is then taken as evidence that sexual attractiveness of victims is unimportant: "I already knew that the rapist chooses his victim with a striking disregard for conventional 'sex appeal'—she may be seventy-four and senile or twelve and a half with braces on her teeth" (Brownmiller, 1975, p. 376). This alleged unimportance of attractiveness is then understandably assumed to demonstrate the unimportance of sexual motivation in the act of rape: "Only young attractive women are raped. This myth is another that stems from the belief that rape is a crime of passion and sex rather than what it is: a crime of violence" (Dean & de Bruyn-kopps, 1983, p. 36; see also Brownmiller, 1975, pp. 131–132).

The weak link in this argument is the assumption that the rape of unattractive females implies that rapists lack a preference for attractive victims. This conclusion is unjustified because it ignores the fact that rape victims are not a representative cross-section of all women. It also ignores the possibility that victim selection is based on *both attractiveness and vulnerability.*

Perhaps the most consistent finding of studies on rape, and one not likely to be merely the result of reporting bias (see Hindelang, 1977), is that women in their teens and early twenties are vastly overrepresented among rape victims (Amir, 1971; Hindelang & Davis, 1977; Kramer, 1987; MacDonald, 1971; Miyazawa, 1976; Svalastoga, 1962; Thornhill & Thornhill, 1983). This fact is crucial because age can be used as at least a rough indicator of female attractiveness: "Physical characteristics that vary systematically with age appear to be universal criteria of female physical attractiveness; Williams (1975), in fact, remarks that age probably is the most important determinant of human female attractiveness" (Symons, 1979, p. 188). It also appears reasonably certain that "Judgments of female physical attractiveness will correspond in females closely to the age of maximum reproductive value or fertility, which peaks in the mid-teens and early 20's respectively and drops off sharply in the late 30's" (Buss, 1987, p. 342; see also Shields & Shields, 1983; Symons, 1979, 1987; Thornhill & Thornhill, 1983; Williams, 1975). This means there is a strong correlation between attractiveness and the likelihood of becoming a rape victim.

The existence of such a correlation would appear to be conclusive evidence that rapists prefer attractive victims (see Alcock, 1983; Symons, 1979). However, backers of the "not sex" explanation continue to claim that rapists do not prefer attractive victims.

The high vulnerability of the elderly is indeed reflected in their high susceptibility to a number of types of violent crimes (Hindelang, 1977). However, contrary to the claims of Katz and Mazur (1979), the age distribution of rape victims is vastly different from the age distributions of victims of nonsexual violent crimes (Lennington, 1985; Thornhill & Thornhill, 1983). In fact, the age distributions are so different that studies, including Groth's own study, consistently find that *less than five percent of rape victims are over the age of fifty.* The fact that elderly woman are very rarely raped *despite* being "particularly vulnerable" is strong evidence that rapists have a very definite preference for younger (and therefore more attractive) victims.

This does not mean that vulnerability is irrelevant to victim selection. It only means that vulnerability must be combined with attractiveness in order to account for the age distribution of rape victims.

Conclusion

Public awareness of the violence and horror of the act of rape *as experienced by the victim* has been crucial to facilitating social change. However, at present, the evidence does not justify the denial of sexual motivation on behalf of the *rapist*. This point is significant since adherence to the "not sex" explanation may have the unintended consequence of hindering attempts to prevent rape. For example, the effectiveness of instruction manuals on how to avoid rape (see Crook, 1980), treatment programs for rapists (see Brecher, 1978), and public policy perspectives are potentially compromised by the denial of the sexual aspect of the crime.

Although there may be evidence of the unimportance of sexual motivation in the act of rape, such evidence cannot be unskeptically adopted. Rape is prevented by accurate knowledge about its causes, and accurate knowledge can only be obtained by the objective examination of evidence and the skeptical evaluation of conclusions based on that evidence. The preceding twelve arguments have gone unquestioned for nearly twenty years, suggesting that skepticism has been noticeably absent from recent research on rape.

Perhaps the reason for this lack of skepticism and accurate knowledge about rape is that "rape" the behavior has become obscured by the politics of "rape" the "master symbol of women's oppression" (Schwendinger & Schwendinger, 1985, p. 93). An objective and accurate approach to the prevention of rape requires that the subject of rape be "depoliticized." Unfortunately, many researchers on rape fear such an objective approach: "To use the word *rape* in a de-politicized context functions to undermine ten years of feminist consciousness-raising" (Blackman, 1985, p. 118; original emphasis). Surely such fears are unfounded. "Consciousness-raising" is the act of falsifying unsupported dogma. Adherence to unsup-

ported dogma like the "not sex" explanation of rape not only prohibits true "consciousness-raising" but potentially does so at the expense of an increased number of rape victims.

References

AGETON, S. (1983). *Sexual assault among adolescents.* Lexington, Massachusetts: Lexington Books.

ALCOCK, J. (1983). *Animal behavior: An evolutionary approach, third edition.* Sunderland, MA: Sinaur Associates.

AMIR, M. (1975). Forcible rape. In L. G. Schultz (Ed.), *Rape victimology* (pp. 43–58). Springfield, Illinois: Charles C. Thomas.

BERCOVITCH, F. B., SLADKY, K.K., ROY, M. M., & GOY, R. W. (in press). Intersexual aggression and male sexual activity in captive Rhesus Macaques. *Aggressive Behavior.*

BRECHER, E. M. (1978). *Treatment Programs for Sex Offenders.* Washington, DC: U.S. Government Printing Office.

BREMER, J. (1959). *Asexualization.* New York: Macmillan.

BROWNMILLER, S. (1975). *Against our will: Men, women, and rape.* New York: Simon and Schuster.

BURGESS, A. W., & HOLMSTROM, L. L. (1974). *Rape: Victims of crisis.* Bowie, Maryland: Brady.

BUSS, D. M. (1987). Sex differences in human mate selection criteria: An evolutionary perspective. In C. Crawford, M. Smith, & D. Krebs (Eds.), *Sociobiology and psychology: Ideas, issues, and applications* (pp. 335–352). Hillsdale, New Jersey: Lawrence Erlbaum Associates.

CHAPPELL, D., GEIS, G., SCHAFER, S., & SIEGEL, L. (1977). A comparative study of forcible rape offenses known to the police in Boston and Los Angeles. In D. Chappell, R. Geis, & G. Geis (Eds.), *Forcible rape, the crime, the victim, and the offender* (pp. 169–187). New York: Columbia University Press.

CHAPPELL, D., & SINGER, S. (1977). Rape in New York City: A study of material in the police files and its meaning. In D. Chappell, R. Geis, & G. Geis (Eds.), *Forcible rape, the crime, the victim, and the offender* (pp. 245–271). New York: Columbia University Press.

CROOK, D. (1980). *What every woman should know about rape.* South Deerfield, MA: Channing L. Bete Co. Inc.

DEAN, C., & DE BRUYN-KOPPS, M. (1982). *The crime and consequences of rape.* Springfield, Illinois: Charles C. Thomas Publisher.

DENMARK, F. L., & FRIEDMAN, S. B. (1985). Social psychological aspects of rape. In S. R. Sunday & E. Tobach (Eds.), *Violence against women: A critique of the sociobiology of rape* (pp. 59–84). New York: Gordian Press.

FINKELHOR, D., & YLLO, K. (1985). *License to rape: Sexual abuse of wives.* New York: Holt, Rinehart and Winston.

GEIS, G. (1977). Forcible rape: An introduction. In D. Chappell, R. Geis, & G. Geis (Eds.), *Forcible rape, the crime, the victim, and the offender* (pp. 1–37). New York: Columbia University Press.

GEIS, G., & HUSTON, T. L. (1980). Forcible rape and human sexuality. In Multiple book reviews of Donald Symon's The evolution of human sexuality. *The Behavioral and Brain Sciences, 3,* 171–214.

GOETHALS, G. (1971). Factors affecting permissive and nonpermissive rules regarding premarital sex. In J. M. Henslin (Ed.), *Studies in the sociology of sex* (pp. 9–25). New York: Basic Books.

GRIFFIN, S. (1971). Rape: The all-American crime. *Ramparts, 10,* 26–36.

GROTH, N. A. (1979a). *Men who rape.* New York: Plenum Press.

GROTH, N. A., & HOBSON, W. (1983). The dynamics of sexual thought. In L. Schlesinger & E. Revitch (Eds.), *Sexual dynamics of anti-social behavior* (pp. 129–144). Springfield, IL: Charles C. Thomas Publishing

HAGEN, R. (1979). *The biosexual factor.* New York: Doubleday.

HARDING, C. F. (1985). Sociobiological hypotheses about rape: A critical look at the data behind the hypotheses. In S. R. Sunday & E. Tobach (Eds.), *Violence against women: A critique of the sociobiology of rape* (pp. 23–58). New York: Gordian Press.

HINDELANG, M. J., & DAVIS, B. J. (1977). Forcible rape in the United States: A statistical profile. In D. Chappell, R. Geis, & G. Geis (Eds.), *Forcible rape: The crime, the victim, and the offender* (pp. 87–114). New York: Columbia University Press.

KATZ, S., & MAZUR, M. A. (1979). *Understanding the rape victim.* New York: Wiley.

KINSEY, A. C., POMEROY, W. B., & MARTIN, C. E. (1948). *Sexual behavior in the human male.* Philadelphia: Saunders.

KIRKPATRIC, C., & KANIN, E. J. (1957). Male sex aggression on a university campus. *American Sociological Review, XXII,* 52–58.

KRAMER, L. L. (1987). Albuquerque rape crisis center: Annual report. Bernalillo County Mental Health/Mental Retardation Center.

LEGRAND, C. E. (1973). Rape and rape laws: Sexism in society and law. *California Law Review, 8,* 263–294.

LENNINGTON, S. (1985). Sociobiological theory and the violent abuse of women. In S. R. Sunday & E. Tobach (Eds.), *Violence against women: A critique of the sociobiology of rape* (pp. 13–22). New York: Gordian Press.

MCCAHILL, T. W., MEYER, L. C., & FISCHMAN, A. M. (1979). *The aftermath of rape.* Lexington, MA: D. C. Heath and Company.

MACDONALD, J. M. (1971). *Rape offenders and their victims.* Springfield, Illinois: Charles C. Thomas.

MEDEA, A., & THOMPSON, K. (1974). *Against rape.* New York: Straus and Giroux.

MICHAEL, R. P., & ZUMPE, D. (1983). Sexual violence in the United States and the role of the season. *American Journal of Psychiatry, 140,* 883–886.

MIYAZAWA, K. (1976). Victimological studies of sexual crimes in Japan. *Victimology, 1*(Spring), 107–129.

QUEEN'S BENCH FOUNDATION. (1978). The rapist and his victim. In L. D. Savitz & N. Johnson (Eds.), *Crime and society* (pp. 767–787). New York: Wiley.

RADA, R. T. (1978a). Psychological factors in rapist behavior. In R. T. Rada (Ed.), *Clinical aspects of the rapist* (pp. 21–58). New York: Grune and Stratton.

RODABAUGH, B. J., & AUSTIN, M. (1981). *Sexual assault: A guide for community action.* New York: Garland STPM.

RUSSELL, D. E. H. (1975). *The politics of rape: The victim's perspectives.* New York: Stein and Day.

SANFORD, L. T., & FETTER, A. (1979). *In defense of ourselves.* New York: Doubleday.

SCHIFF, A. F. (1971). Rape and other countries. *Medicine, Science, and Law, 11,* 139–143.

SCHWENDINGER, J. R., & SCHWENDINGER, H. (1985). Homo economicus as the rapist. In S. R. Sunday & E. Tobach (Eds.), *Violence against women: A critique of the sociobiology of rape* (pp. 85–114). New York: Gordian Press.

SHIELDS, W. M., & SHIELDS, L. M. (1983). Forcible rape: An evolutionary perspective. *Ethology and Sociobiology, 4,* 115–136.

SMITHYMAN, S. D. (1978). The undetected rapist. Ph.D. Dissertation, Claremont Graduate School. University Microfilms International: Ann Arbor, MI.

STURUP, G. K. (1960). Sex Offenses: The Scandinavian experience. *Law and Contemporary Problems, 25,* 361–375.

STURUP, G. K. (1968). Treatment of sexual offenders in Hestedvester, Denmark. *Acta Psychiatric Scandinavia, Supplement, 204.*

SUSSMAN, L., & BORDWELL, S. (1981). *The rapist file.* New York: Chesea House.

SVALASTOGA, K. (1962). Rape and social structure. *Pacific Sociological Review, 5,* 48–53.

SYMONS, D. (1979). *The evolution of human sexuality.* New York: Oxford University Press.

SYMONS, D. (1987). *If we're all Darwinians, what's the fuss about?* In C. Crawford, M. Smith, & D. Krebs (Eds.), *Sociobiology and psychology: Ideas, issues and applications* (pp. 121–146). Hillsdale, NJ: Lawrence Erlbaum Associates.

THORNHILL, R., & THORNHILL, N. W. (1983). Human rape: An evolutionary analysis. *Ethology and Sociobiology, 4,* 137–173.

WILLIAMS G. (1975). *Sex and evolution.* Princeton, NJ: Princeton University Press.

Palmer has presented no positive thesis of his own about the motivations for rapists. But he does claim that the politics (the values) now associated with rape because of the women's movement makes an objective study of it very difficult. We will see that Katie Roiphe argues that the politics of the women's movement has made rational discussion difficult.

AN UNCOMMON FEMINIST ANALYSIS OF RAPE

Roiphe has two arguments. One is that data on rape are being manipulated to show that there is much more rape than there really is. The other—and this is the more philosophical of her points—is that the feminist hard line against rape and sexual harassment carries with it the Victorian view that women are frail creatures unable to take responsibility for themselves and unable to defend themselves.

Is Roiphe right? Are women being forced, by feminists, to see themselves as sexless creatures who must constantly be on the lookout for men on the prowl for sex? Roiphe, of course, finds this counterproductive to achieving true equality. She does not, however, stress that men may be treated unfairly by the feminist hard line.

from The Morning After

KATIE ROIPHE

The Rape Crisis, or "Is Dating Dangerous?"

Radical feminists aren't the only ones talking about the rape crisis anymore. Since the mideighties the media have been kindling public interest in rape with a series of alarming revelations. In 1985, *Ms.* magazine published the startling results of an early study on rape in universities in a story dramatically entitled "Date Rape: The Story of an Epidemic and Those Who Deny It."[1] That same year, the *New York Times* ran an article called "A New Recognition of the Realities of 'Date Rape.'"[2] After William Kennedy Smith's televised date-rape trial, in 1991, there was a flurry of articles and editorials about rape. As everyone waited to see what would happen to the Kennedy name and his word against hers, a new discussion of the rape crisis opened up on the front pages, capturing public attention.

According to the widely quoted *Ms.* survey, one in four college women is the victim of rape or attempted rape. One in four. I remember standing outside the dining hall in college looking at a purple poster with this statistic written in bold letters. It didn't seem right. If sexual assault was really so pervasive, it seemed strange that the intricate gossip networks hadn't picked up more than one or two shadowy instances of rape. If I was really standing in the middle of an epidemic, a crisis, if 25 percent of my female friends were really being raped, wouldn't I know it? The answer is not that there is a conspiracy of silence. The answer is that measuring rape is not as straightforward as it seems.

Neil Gilbert, professor of social welfare at the University of California at Berkeley, has written several articles attacking the two sociological studies that are cornerstones of the rape-crisis movement, the *Ms.* magazine study and one done in the early eighties by Diana Russell. Having taken a closer look at the numbers, he questions the validity of the one-in-four statistic. He points out that in the *Ms.* study, which is the one most frequently quoted, 73 percent of the women categorized as rape victims did not define their experience as "rape."[3] It was Dr. Mary Koss, the psychologist conducting the study, who did. These are not self-proclaimed victims, then—these are victims according to someone else. From Koss's point of view, these women were suffering from what they used to call false consciousness. The way it is usually and tactfully phrased these days is that they don't recognize what has really happened to them.

Gilbert also points out that 42 percent of the

women identified in this study as rape victims later had sex with the man who supposedly raped them *after* the supposed rape.[4] As Gilbert delves further into the numbers, he does not necessarily disprove the one-in-four statistic, but he does help clarify what it means. He reveals that the so-called "rape epidemic" on campuses is more a way of interpreting, a way of seeing, than a physical phenomenon. It is more about a change in sexual politics than a change in sexual behavior.

According to Gilbert, in the *Ms.* study one of the questions used to define rape was "Have you had sexual intercourse when you didn't want to because a man gave you alcohol or drugs?"[5] The strange phrasing of this question itself raises the issue of agency. Why aren't college women responsible for their own intake of alcohol or drugs? A man may *give* a woman drugs, but she herself decides to take them. A pamphlet about acquaintance rape gives the following as an example of a rape scenario: "A woman is at a party and is very drunk. A man, whom she knows through a friend, has had a few drinks with her. He leads her into an unoccupied room in the house. They begin to make out and he feels as if she is responding to him. They have intercourse. He leaves her in the room, asleep or passed out, and returns to the party."[6]

The idea is that women get too drunk to know what they are doing, while men stay sober and lucid. If we assume women are not all helpless and naive, then shouldn't they be held responsible for their choice to drink or take drugs? If a woman's judgment is impaired, as they say, and she has sex, it isn't necessarily always the man's fault; it isn't necessarily always rape. Many of these instances, as Gilbert points out, are simply too vague for statistical certainty. Classifying a positive answer to Koss's ambiguous question as rape further explains how she could have reached the conclusion that one in four women on college campuses has been raped . . .

Feminist definitions of rape do not exist in a realm completely separate from the law. In 1992 New Jersey's Supreme Court upheld its far-reaching rape laws. Ruling against a teenager charged with raping his date, the court concluded that signs of force or the threat of force is not necessary to prove the crime of rape—no force, that is, beyond

that required for the physical act of penetration. Both the plaintiff and the defendant admitted that they were sexually involved, but the two sides differed on whether what happened that night was rape. It's hard to define anything that happens in that strange, libidinous province of adolescence, but this court upheld the judgment that the girl was raped. If the defendant had been an adult he could have gone to jail for up to ten years. Susan Herman, deputy public defender in the case, remarked, "You not only have to bring a condom on a date, you have to bring a consent form as well."[13]

The idea of consent has gone beyond the simple assertion that no means no. Politically correct sex involves a yes, and a specific yes at that: a new standard pamphlet on acquaintance rape warns men that "hearing a clear sober 'yes' to the question 'Do you want to make love?' is very different from thinking, 'Well, she didn't say no.'"[14] The yes must be clear, the yes must be sober. The idea of explicit permission has crept into rape-crisis feminism and into the standard literature on the subject.[15] . . .

In an essay entitled "Nonviolent Sexual Coercion," psychologists Charlene Muelenhard and Jennifer Schrag include the remarks "He said he'd break up with me if I didn't," "He said I was frigid," and "He said everyone's doing it" in the category of verbal coercion. They go on to explain that "a woman with low self-esteem might feel that if she refuses her partner's sexual advances she will lose him, and her value will be lessened because she is no longer associated with him."[26] This is a portrait of the cowering woman, knocked on her back by the barest feather of peer pressure. Solidifying this image of women into policy implies an acceptance of the passive role. By protecting woman against verbal coercion, these feminists are promoting the view of women as weak-willed, alabaster bodies, whose virtue must be protected from the cunning encroachments of the outside world. The idea that women can't withstand verbal or emotional pressure infantilizes them. The suggestion lurking beneath this definition of rape is that men are not just physically but intellectually and emotionally more powerful than women. Printing pamphlets about verbal coercion institutionalizes an unacceptable female position . . .

A manners guide from 1848 warns young women about the perils of verbally coercive men:

> The more attractive his exterior, the more dangerous he is as a companion for a young and inexperienced girl, and the more likely to dazzle and bewilder her mind. . . . He can with a subtlety almost beyond the power of her detection, change her ordinary views of things, confuse her judgements, and destroy her rational confidence in discriminating the powers of her own mind.[27]

The fear of verbal coercion, then, does not have its origins in modern feminism. The idea that young girls will be swayed, their judgment overturned, their mind dazzled and bewildered, by the sheer force of masculine logic has been included in date-rape pamphlets for more than a century . . .

Rape-crisis feminists reproduce the idea that guarding women's bodies from male violation is a life-or-death issue. To call date-rape victims "survivors," like survivors of a fire, a plane crash, or the Holocaust, is to compare rape to death. If date rape is as destructive as many feminists would have us believe, if women's lives really are *always* shattered by physically or emotionally forced sex, or intoxicated sex, then perhaps rape does become a crime comparable to murder . . .

On the not-so-distant edge of the spectrum, carrying this rhetoric to its logical conclusion, some feminists actually collapse the distinction between rape and sex. Catherine MacKinnon writes, "Compare victims' reports of rape with women's reports of sex. They look a lot alike. . . . In this light, the major distinction between intercourse (normal) and rape (abnormal) is that the normal happens so often that one cannot get anyone to see anything wrong with it."[40] . . .

Going against the current of much rape-crisis feminism, Marjorie Metsch, Columbia's director of peer education, also distinguishes between rape and bad sex. "Most of the time when someone comes in and says 'I was really really drunk and I shouldn't have had sex last night,' it is not the same as saying 'I was raped.' My attitude is that you do not use language that the person herself is not using. It could be that it was just bad sex." Metsch reasons that the social and psychological weight of the word "rape" eclipses its descriptive value in cases of regretted sex. With this approach,

she avoids injecting everyday college life with the melodrama of the rape crisis . . .

Reckless Eyeballing: Sexual Harassment on Campus

. . . A Princeton pamphlet declares that "sexual harassment is unwanted sexual attention that makes a person feel uncomfortable or causes problems in school or at work, or in social settings."[1] The word "uncomfortable" echoes through all the literature on sexual harassment. The feminists concerned with this issue, then, propose the right to be comfortable as a feminist principle.

The difficulty with these rules is that, although it may infringe on the right to comfort, unwanted sexual attention is part of nature. To find wanted sexual attention, you have to give and receive a certain amount of unwanted sexual attention. Clearly, the truth is that if no one was ever allowed to risk offering unsolicited sexual attention, we would all be solitary creatures.

The category of sexual harassment, according to current campus definitions, is not confined to relationships involving power inequity. Echoing many other common definitions of sexual harassment, Princeton's pamphlet warns that "sexual harassment can occur between two people regardless of whether or not one has power over the other."[2] The weight of this definition of sexual harassment, then, falls on gender instead of status.[3]

In current definitions of sexual harassment, there is an implication that gender is so important that it eclipses all other forms of power. The driving idea behind these rules is that gender itself is a sufficient source of power to constitute sexual harassment. Catherine MacKinnon, an early theorist of sexual harassment, writes that "situations of co-equal power—among co-workers or students or teachers—are difficult to see as examples of sexual harassment unless you have a notion of male power. I think we lie to women when we call it not power when a woman is come on to by a man who is not her employer, not her teacher."[4] With this description, MacKinnon extends the province of male power beyond that of tangible social power. She proposes using the words "sexual harassment" as a way to name what she sees as a fundamental social and political inequity between men and women . . .

Even if you argue, as many do, that *in this society* men are simply much more powerful than women, this is still a dangerous train of thought. It carries us someplace we don't want to be. Rules and laws based on the premise that all women need protection from all men, because they are so much weaker, serve only to reinforce the image of women as powerless . . .

The university, with its emphasis on intellectual exchange, on the passionate pursuit of knowledge, with its strange hours and unworldly citizens, is theoretically an ideal space for close friendships. The flexible hours combined with the intensity of the academic world would appear to be fertile ground for connections, arguments over coffee. Recently, reading a biography of the poet John Berryman, who was also a professor at Princeton in the forties, I was struck by stories about his students crowding into his house late into the night to talk about poetry. These days, an informal invitation to a professor's house till all hours would be a breach of propriety. As the authors of *The Lecherous Professor* warn, "Contacts outside of class deserve thought. Student-teacher conferences should be held in appropriate settings."[8] . . .

Many foreigners think that concern with sexual harassment is as American as baseball, New England Puritans, and apple pie. Many feminists in other countries look on our preoccupation with sexual harassment as another sign of the self-indulgence and repression in American society. Veronique Neiertz, France's secretary of state for women's rights, has said that in the United States "the slightest wink can be misinterpreted." Her ministry's commonsense advice to women who feel harassed by co-workers is to respond with "a good slap in the face."[14]

Once sexual harassment includes someone glancing down your shirt, the meaning of the phrase has been stretched beyond recognition. The rules about unwanted sexual attention begin to seem more like etiquette than rules. Of course it would be nicer if people didn't brush against other people in a way that makes them uncomfortable. It would also be nicer if bankers didn't bang their briefcases into people on the subway at rush hour.

But not nice is a different thing than against the rules, or the law. It is a different thing than oppressing women. Etiquette and politics aren't synonyms . . .

Instead of learning that men have no right to do these terrible things to us, we should be learning to deal with individuals with strength and confidence. If someone bothers us, we should be able to put him in his place without crying into our pillow or screaming for help or counseling. If someone stares at us, or talks dirty, or charges neutral conversation with sexual innuendo, we should not be pushed to the verge of a nervous breakdown. In an American College Health Association pamphlet, "unwanted sexual comments, jokes or gestures" are characterized as "a form of sexual assault."[18] Feminists drafting sexual harassment guidelines seem to have forgotten childhood's words of wisdom: sticks and stones may break my bones, but names will never harm me.

Someone I knew in college had an admirable flair for putting offenders in their place. Once, when she was playing pinball in Tommy's Lunch, the coffee shop across from Adams House, a teenage boy came up to her and grabbed her breast. She calmly went to the counter and ordered a glass of milk and then walked over and poured it over his head. She would intimidate obscene phone callers with the line "Listen, honey, I was blow job queen of my high school," and they would inevitably hang up. Most of us probably have less creative ways of handling "sexual harassment," but we should at least be able to handle petty instances like ogling, leering, and sexual innuendo on the personal level.

I would even go so far as to say that people have the right to leer at whomever they want to leer at. By offering protection to the woman against the leer, the movement against sexual harassment is curtailing her personal power. This protection implies the need to be protected. It paints her as defenseless against even the most trivial of male attentions. This protection assumes that she never ogles, leers, or makes sexual innuendoes herself.

Notes: The Rape Crisis, or "Is Dating Dangerous?"

1. *Ms.*, October 1985.

2. *New York Times*, 23 October 1985.

3. Neil Gilbert, "Realities and Mythologies of Rape," *Society 29* (May-June 1992).

4. Ibid.

5. Ibid.

6. "Acquaintance Rape." Rockville, Md.: American College Health Association, 1992.

13. "Acquaintance Rape: 'Is Dating Dangerous?'" Rockville, Md.: ACHA, 1991.

14. Mrs. John Farrar, *The Young Lady's Friend* (New York: Samuel S. And William Wood, 1857), 263.

15. Charlene L. Muelenhard and Jennifer L. Schrag, "Nonviolent Sexual Coercion," in Parrot and Bechhofer, 122.

27. T. S. Arthur, *Advice to Young Ladies* (Boston: Phillips and Sampson, 1848), 151.

40. Catharine MacKinnon, *Toward a Feminist Theory of the State* (Cambridge: Harvard University Press, 1989), 146.

Notes: Reckless Eyeballing:
Sexual Harassment on Campus

1. "What You Should Know About Sexual Harassment." Princeton, N.J.: SHARE.

2. Ibid.

3. A standard definition given by a book about sexual harassment affirms that "harassment can also occur when no such formal [power] differential exists, if the behavior is unwanted by or offensive to the woman." Michele A. Paludi, ed., *Ivory Power: Sexual Harassment on Campus* (Albany: State University of New York Press, 1990), 38.

4. Catharine MacKinnon, *Feminism Unmodified* (Cambridge: Harvard University Press, 1987), 89.

8. Dziech and Weiner, 180.

14. *New York Times,* 3 May 1992.

18. "Acquaintance Rape." Rockville, Md.: ACHA, 1992.

Not only does Katha Pollitt disagree with Roiphe, she also tries to make the case that Roiphe is both wrong and wrongheaded.

A FEMINIST CRITIQUE OF ROIPHE'S STYLE OF FEMINISM

In her review of Roiphe's book, Katha Pollitt points out that Roiphe depends too much on anecdote and not enough on fact and logic. Pollitt defends the studies on rape that Roiphe criticized. She also makes it clear that Roiphe has missed a central point. Women now feel upset and degraded by behavior that many men seem to think is acceptable. There is no reason for this to continue. Why, Pollitt asks, should women continue to play by the rules of men? Why can't the rules be changed out of civility, generosity, and sensitivity toward women? If men refuse to change the rules, then why shouldn't women have recourse to the law and other means of institutional redress?

Pollitt's discussion of an anecdote related by Roiphe illustrates a characteristic of feminist philosophy. Roiphe tells about a friend who would rebuff obscene phone callers with the comment "I was the blow job queen of my high school." The point of Roiphe's anecdote is that women can take control of a situation and deal with it successfully. The comment worked in getting the obscene caller to hang up (and not call again) because it showed that the woman was not one to be offended by dirty words. In a way, the story is also meant to be humorous.

Pollitt realizes all this but makes a much deeper analysis of the comment. According to Pollitt, what the comment really shows is that the tough girls still define their sexual prowess only in terms of male orgasms. The point we want to make here is that feminism uses depth psychology in ways that are uncommon in traditional philosophy.

Pollitt has criticized Roiphe for being a poor scholar and for using poor logic. What precisely are the philosophical differences that separate the Pollitt and Roiphe? Do they differ only on the facts? Would Pollitt agree with Roiphe about how women and men should relate if it turned out that many fewer women were raped than Pollitt believes? Is there any way to get data about sexual harassment or rape that does not presuppose some values? Try to define "rape" in such a way that there is no judgment made in the defining terms. Can it be done? Is it necessary that it be done?

from Not Just Bad Sex

Katha Pollitt

"The Morning After," although Roiphe denies this, goes beyond her own privileged experience to make general claims about rape and feminism on American campuses, and it is also, although she denies this, too, a "political polemic." In both respects, it is a careless and irresponsible performance, poorly argued and full of misrepresentations, slapdash research, and gossip. She may be, as she implies, the rare grad student who has actually read "Clarissa," but when it comes to rape and harassment she has not done her homework.

• • •

Have radical feminists inundated the nation's campuses with absurd and unfounded charges against men? Roiphe cites a few well-publicized incidents: at Princeton, for example, a student told a Take Back the Night rally that she had been date-raped by a young man she eventually admitted she had never met. But Roiphe's claim that such dubious charges represent a new norm rests on hearsay and a few quotations from the wilder shores of feminist theory. "Recently," she writes, "at the University of Michigan, a female teaching assistant almost brought a male student up on charges of sexual harassment," because of some mildly sexist humor in a paper. When is "recently"? In what department of the vast University of Michigan did this incident occur? How does Roiphe know about it—after all, it only "almost" happened—and know that she got it right? Roiphe ridicules classmates for crediting and magnifying every rumor of petty sexism, but she does the same: hysterical accusations are always being made at "a prominent university." Don't they

teach the students at Harvard and Princeton anything about research anymore?

Where I was able to follow up on Roiphe's sources, I found some fairly misleading use of data. Roiphe accuses the legal scholar Susan Estrich of slipping "her ideas about the nature of sexual encounters into her legal analysis" in "Real Rape," her study of acquaintance rape and the law—one such idea being that women are so powerless that even "yes" does not necessarily constitute consent to sex. In fact, in the cited passage Estrich explicitly lays that view aside to pursue her own subject, which is the legal system's victimization of women who say *no.* Nowhere does Roiphe acknowledge that—whatever may happen in the uncritical, emotional atmosphere of a Take Back the Night rally or a support-group meeting for rape survivors (a term she mocks)—in the real world women who have been raped face enormous obstacles in obtaining justice in the courts or sympathy from their friends and families. Nor does she seem to realize that it is the humiliation and stigmatization and disbelief reported by many rape victims, and documented in many studies, that have helped to produce the campus climate of fear and credulity she deplores. Indeed, the only time Roiphe discusses an actual court case it is to argue that the law veers too far to the victim's side:

> In 1992 New Jersey's Supreme Court upheld its far-reaching rape laws. Ruling against a teenager charged with raping his date, the court concluded that signs of force or the threat of force is [*sic*] not necessary to prove the crime of rape—no force, that is, beyond that required for the physical act of penetration. Both the plaintiff and

The selection from Katha Pollitt is taken from her review-essay "Not Just Bad Sex," which appears in her collection, *Reasonable Creatures: Essays on Women and Feminism* (New York: Alfred A. Knopf, 1994). It was originally published in *The New Yorker,* Vol. LXIX (October 4, 1993), pp. 220–224. Used by permission of the author.

the defendant admitted that they were sexually involved, but the two sides differed on whether what happened that night was rape. It's hard to define anything that happens in that strange, libidinous province of adolescence, but this court upheld the judgment that the girl was raped. If the defendant had been an adult he could have gone to jail for up to ten years. Susan Herman, deputy public defender in the case, remarked, "You not only have to bring a condom on a date, you have to bring a consent form as well."

Roiphe should know better than to rely on a short item in the Trenton *Times* for an accurate account of a complicated court case, and she misrepresents even the sketchy information the article contains: the girl was not the boy's "date," and they did not both "admit" they were "sexually involved." The two, indeed, disagreed about the central facts of the case. The article does mention something Roiphe chose to omit: the girl was fifteen years old. The Supreme Court opinion further distinguishes this case from Roiphe's general portrait of date-rape cases: the hypersensitive female charging an innocently blundering male with a terrible crime for doing what came naturally and doing it without a peep from her. The offender, it turns out, was dating another girl living in the house where the rape took place, and not the victim, who, far from passively enduring his assault, did what Roiphe implies she did not: she slapped him, demanded that he withdraw, and, in the morning, told her mother, whereupon they went immediately to the police. It is absurd to use this fifteen-year-old victim—who had surely never heard of Catharine MacKinnon or Take Back the Night— as an example of campus feminism gone mad. And it is equally absurd to suggest that the highly regarded New Jersey Supreme Court, which consists of one woman and six middle-aged men, issued a unanimous decision in the victim's favor because it had been corrupted by radical feminism.

The court did affirm that "signs of force or the threat of force"—wounds, torn clothes, the presence of a weapon—were not necessary to prove rape. This affirmation accords with the real-life fact that the amount of force necessary to achieve penetration is not much. But it is not true that the court opened the door to rape convictions in the kinds of cases Roiphe takes for the date-rape norm: sex in which the woman says yes but means no, or says yes, means yes, but regrets it later. The court said that consent, which need not be verbal, must be obtained for intercourse. It's easy to parody this view, as the defense counsel did with her joke about a "consent form"—but all that it really means is that a man cannot penetrate a woman without some kind of go-ahead. Roiphe ridicules this notion as "politically correct" and objects to educational materials that remind men that "hearing a clear sober 'yes' to the question 'Do you want to make love?' is very different from thinking, 'Well, she didn't say no.'" But is that such terrible advice? Roiphe herself says she wants women to be more vocal about sex, yet here she is dismissive of the suggestion that men ought to listen to them.

Roiphe's attempt to debunk statistics on the frequency of rape is similarly ill-informed. A substantial body of research, by no means all of it conducted by feminists, or even by women, supports the contention that there is a staggering amount of rape and attempted rape in the United States, and that most incidents are not reported to the police— especially when, as is usually the case, victim and offender know each other. For example, the National Women's Study, conducted by the Crime Victims Research and Treatment Center at the Medical University of South Carolina, working under a grant from the National Institute of Drug Abuse, which released its results last year, found that thirteen per cent of adult American women— one in eight—have been raped at least once, seventy-five per cent by someone they knew. (The study used the conservative legal definition of rape which Roiphe favors: "an event that occurred without the woman's consent, involved the use of force or threat of force, and involved sexual penetration of the victim's vagina, mouth or rectum.") Other researchers come up with similar numbers or even higher ones, and are supported by studies querying men about their own behavior: in one such study, fifteen per cent of the college men sampled said they had used force at least once to obtain intercourse.

Roiphe does not even acknowledge the existence of this sizable body of work—and it seems she hasn't spent much time studying the scholarly journals in which it appears. Instead, she concentrates on a single 1985 article in *Ms.* magazine, which presented a preliminary journalistic account of an acquaintance-rape study conducted by Dr. Mary Koss, a clinical psychologist now at the University of Arizona. Relying on opinion pieces by Neil Gilbert, a professor of social welfare at Berkeley, Roiphe accuses Koss of inflating her findings—one in eight students raped, one in four the victims of rape or attempted rape—by including as victims women who did not describe their experience as rape, although it met a widely accepted legal definition. It is unclear what Roiphe's point is—that women don't mind being physically forced to have sex as long as no one tells them it's rape? Surely she would not argue that the victims of other injustices—fraud, malpractice, job discrimination—have suffered no wrong as long as they are unaware of the law. Roiphe also accuses Koss of upping her numbers by asking respondents if they had ever had sex when they didn't want to because a man gave them alcohol or drugs. "Why aren't college women responsible for their own intake of alcohol or drugs?" Roiphe asks, and it may by fair to say that the alcohol question in the study is ambiguously worded. But it's worth noting that the question doesn't come out of feminist fantasyland. It's keyed to a legal definition of rape which in many states includes sex obtained by intentional incapacitation of the victim with intoxicants. . . .

. . . Be that as it may, what happens to Koss's figures if the alcohol question is dropped? The number of college women who have been victims of rape or attempted rape drops from one in four to one in five.

• • •

One in five, one in eight—what if it's "only" one in ten or twelve? Social science isn't physics. Exact numbers are important, and elusive, but surely what is significant here is that lots of different studies, with different agendas, sample populations, and methods, tend in the same direction. Rather than grapple with these inconvenient data, Roiphe retreats to her own impressions: "If I was really standing in the middle of an epidemic, a crisis, if 25 per cent of my female friends were really being raped, wouldn't I know about it?" (Roiphe

forgets that the one-in-four figure includes attempts, but let that pass.) As an experiment, I applied Roiphe's anecdotal method myself, and wrote down what I knew about my own circle of acquaintance: eight rapes by strangers (including one on a college campus), two sexual assaults (one Central Park, one Prospect Park), one abduction (woman walking down street forced into car full of men), one date rape involving a Mickey Finn, which resulted in pregnancy and abortion, and two stalkings (one ex-lover, one deranged fan); plus one brutal beating by a boyfriend, three incidents of childhood incest (none involving therapist-aided "recovered memories"), and one bizarre incident in which a friend went to a man's apartment after meeting him at a party and was forced by him to spend the night under the shower, naked, while he debated whether to kill her, rape her, or let her go. The most interesting thing about this tally, however, is that when I mentioned it to a friend he was astonished—he himself knew of only one rape victim in his circle, he said—but he knows several of the women on my list.

It may be that Roiphe's friends have nothing to tell her. Or it may be that they have nothing to tell *her.* With her adolescent certainty that bad things don't happen, or that they happen only to weaklings, she is not likely to be on the receiving end of many painful, intimate confessions. The one time a fellow-student tells her about being raped (at knifepoint, so it counts), Roiphe cringes like a high-school vegetarian dissecting her first frog: "I was startled. . . . I felt terrible for her. I felt like there was nothing I could say." Confronted with someone whose testimony she can't dismiss or satirize, Roiphe goes blank.

• • •

Roiphe is right to point out that cultural attitudes toward rape, harassment, coercion, and consent are slowly shifting. It is certainly true that many women today, most of whom would not describe themselves as feminists, feel outraged by male behavior that previous generations—or even those women themselves not so long ago—quietly accepted as "everyday experience." Roiphe may even be right to argue that it muddies the waters when women colloquially speak of "rape" in referring to sex that is caddish or is obtained through verbal or emotional pressure or manipulation, or when they label as "harassment" the occasional leer or off-color comment. But if we lay these terms aside we still have to account for the phenomenon they point to: that women in great numbers—by no means all on élite campuses, by no means all young—feel angry at and exploited by behavior that many men assume is within bounds and no big deal. Like many of those men, Roiphe would like to short-circuit this larger discussion, as if everything that doesn't meet the legal definition of crime were trivial, and any objection to it mere paranoia. For her, sex is basically a boys' game, with boys' rules, like football, and if a girl wants to make the team—whether by "embracing experience" in bed or by attending a formerly all-male college—she has to play along and risk taking some knocks. But why can't women change the game, and add a few rules of their own? What's so "utopian" about expecting men to act as though there are two people in bed and two sexes in the classroom and the workplace?

Roiphe gives no consistent answer to this question. Sometimes she dismisses the problems as inconsequential: coerced intercourse is bad sex, widespread sexual violence a myth. Sometimes she suggests that the problem is real, but is women's fault: they should be more feisty and vociferous, be more like her and her friends, one of whom she praises for dumping a glass of milk on a boy who grabbed her breast. (Here, in a typical muddle, Roiphe's endorsement of assertive behavior echoes the advice of the anti-rape educational materials she excoriates.) Sometimes she argues that the women's movement has been so successful in moving women into the professions that today's feminists are whining about nothing. And sometimes she argues that men, if seriously challenged to change their ways and habits, will respond with a backlash, keeping women students at arm's length out of a fear of lawsuits, retreating into anxious nerdhood. . . .

Coming from a self-proclaimed bad girl and sexual rebel, this last bit of counsel is particularly fainthearted: now who's warning women about the dangers of provoking the savage male? When Roiphe posits a split between her mother's generation of feminists—women eager to enter the world and seize sexual freedom—and those of to-day, who emphasize the difficulties of doing either, she has it wrong, and not just historically. (Sexual violence was a major theme of seventies feminism, in whose consciousness-raising sessions women first realized that rape was something many of them had in common.) The point she misses is that it was not the theories of academics or of would-be Victorian maidens masquerading as Madonna fans that made sexual violence and harassment an issue. It was the movement of women into male-dominated venues—universities, professions, blue-collar trades—in sufficiently great numbers to demand real accommodation from men both at work and in private life. If Roiphe's contention that focussing on "victimhood" reduces women to passivity were right, the experience of Anita Hill would have sent feminists off weeping, en masse, to a separatist commune. Instead, it sparked a wave of activism that revitalized street-level feminism and swept unprecedented numbers of women into Congress.

Roiphe is so intent on demonizing the anti-rape movement that she misses an opportunity to address a real deficiency of much contemporary feminism. The problem isn't that acknowledging women's frequent victimization saps their get-up-and-go and allows them to be frail flowers; it's that the discourse about sexuality says so little about female pleasure. Unfortunately, Roiphe, too, is silent on this subject. We hear a lot about heavy drinking, late nights, parties, waking up in strange beds, but we don't hear what made those experiences worth having, except as acts of rebellion. In a revealing anecdote, she cites with approval a friend who tells off obscene phone callers by informing them that she was her high school's "blow job queen." Not to detract from that achievement, but one wonders at the unexamined equation of sexual service and sexual selfhood. Do campus bad girls still define their prowess by male orgasms rather than their own?

It's sad for Roiphe and her classmates that they are coming of age sexually at a time when sex seems more fraught with danger and anxiety than ever. Indeed, AIDS is the uneasily acknowledged spectre hovering over "The Morning After": the condom, not the imaginary consent form, is what really put a damper on the campus sex scene. Certainly AIDS gives new urgency to the feminist campaign for female sexual self-determination, and has probably done a lot, at both conscious and unconscious levels, to frame that quest in negative rather than positive terms. But that's just the way we live now—and not only on campus. Rape, coercion, harassment, the man who edits his sexual history and thinks safe sex kills passion, the obscene phone call that is no longer amusing because you're not in the dorm anymore but living by your-

self in a not so safe neighborhood and it's three in the morning: it's not very hard to understand why women sometimes sound rather grim about relations between the sexes.

It would be wonderful to hear more from women who are nonetheless "embracing experience," retaining the vital spark of sexual adventure. Roiphe prefers to stick to the oldest put-down of all: Problems? What problems? It's all in your head.

It is not surprising that colleges as well as professional organizations have created guidelines concerning sexual harassment. We offer three sets of current guidelines.

SEXUAL MISCONDUCT, GUIDELINES AND CODES OF ETHICS FOR THE AMERICAN MEDICAL ASSOCIATION, AMERICAN SWIMMING COACHES ASSOCIATION, AND ANTIOCH COLLEGE

Guidelines and codes of ethics reflect a mix of current standards and philosophical analysis. Read through these guidelines, asking where you think they are right on target, where they have missed the mark, where they need clarification. Would you feel comfortable bound by the rules, regulations, and suggestions? Do they offer real protection to patients, swimmers, or students? How would Roiphe and Pollitt answer these questions?

from Sexual Misconduct in the Practice of Medicine

COUNCIL ON ETHICAL AND JUDICIAL AFFAIRS,
AMERICAN MEDICAL ASSOCIATION

The American Medical Association's Council on Ethical and Judicial Affairs recently reviewed the ethical implications of sexual or romantic relationships between physicians and patients. The Council has concluded that (1) sexual contact or a romantic relationship concurrent with the physician-patient relationship is unethical; (2) sexual contact or a romantic relationship with a former patient may be unethical under certain circumstances; (3) education on the ethical issues involved in sexual misconduct should be included

throughout all levels of medical training; and (4) in the case of sexual misconduct, reporting offending colleagues is especially important.

(*JAMA.* 1991;266:2741–2745)

There is a long-standing consensus within the medical profession that sexual contact or sexual relations between physicians and patients are unethical. The prohibition against sexual relations with patients was incorporated into the Hippocratic oath: ". . . I will come for the benefit of the

The selection from the report of the Council on Ethical and Judicial Affairs, American Medical Association is taken from "Sexual Misconduct in the Practice of Medicine," *The Journal of the American Medical Association,* Vol. 266, No. 19 (November 20, 1991), pp. 2741–2745. Copyright © 1991, American Medical Association. Used by permission of *JAMA.*

sick, remaining free of all intentional injustice, of all mischief and in particular of sexual relations with both female and male persons. . . ."[1]

Current ethical thought uniformly condemns sexual relations between patients and physicians.[2-4] In addition, the laws of many states prohibit sexual contact between psychiatrists or other physicians and their patients.[5-9] The ban on physician-patient sexual contact is based on the recognition that such contact jeopardizes patients' medical care.

PHYSICIAN-PATIENT SEXUAL CONTACT

Incidence

A number of studies have tried to establish the incidence of physician-patient sexual contact. Much of the research done on the prevalence of physician-patient sexual contact is based on studies that survey physicians about their own behavior.[10-13] The general stigma attached to sexual contact with patients and the professional repercussions that may result from admitting to such contact have led many researchers to believe that the occurrence of patient-physician sexual contact is underreported.[10,14,15]

Studies indicate that there is a small minority of physicians who have reported having sexual contact with patients.[10,11,16,17] Psychiatrists have been particularly diligent in examining the phenomenon of sexual contact with patients. Consequently, the majority of existing studies on physician-patient sexual contact examine sexual contact between psychiatrists and their patients. Studies of psychiatrists indicate that between 5% and 10% reported having sexual contact with patients.[10,11,16,18] Data for all specialties are not available, but a 1976 study suggested that the percentages may be comparable for other specialties.[11] While much of the discussion in this report centers on sexual misconduct by psychiatrists, it is clear that sexual misconduct is a problem not confined to any particular specialty.

Sexual contact between physician and patient can occur in a variety of ways: (1) physicians may become involved in personal relationships with patients that are concurrent with but independent of treatment[10]; (2) some physicians may use their position to gain sexual access to their patients by representing sexual contact as part of care or treatment[19]; and (3) others may assault patients by engaging in sexual contact with incompetent or unconscious patients. There seems to be little or no data indicating the prevalence of each type of sexual misconduct.

Physicians Who Engage in Sexual Contact with Patients

Failure to Handle the Emotional Content of the Therapeutic Relationship.—For some physicians, sexual contact with a patient is a result of a temporary failure to constructively manage the emotions arising from the physician-patient relationship. The professional physician-patient relationship frequently evokes strong and complicated emotions in both the physician and the patient.[20-22] It is not unusual for sexual attraction to be one of these emotions. Many commentators agree that sexual or romantic attraction to patients is not uncommon or abnormal.[2,23]

However, sexual attraction to a patient, while not necessarily detrimental to the physician-patient relationship, can also lead to sexual contact or a sexual relationship between the patient and physician. The emotions of admiration, affection, and caring that are a part of the physician-patient relationship can become particularly powerful when either party is experiencing intense pressures or traumatic or major life events. The usual professional restraint exhibited by physicians may falter under such profound emotional influences, resulting in the transformation of sexual attraction into sexual contact.

Currently, the research on sexual misconduct is insufficient to determine how many sexual interactions between physicians and patients occur under these circumstances. Although figures vary widely, one nationwide study of psychiatrists showed that 67% of psychiatrists who reported sexual contact with a patient indicated that the contact occurred with only one patient.[10] This study showed that approximately 50% of psychiatrists who reported sexual contact with only one patient sought help or consultation for the matter.[10] However, engaging in sexual contact with a patient because of temporary impairment of proper judgment or perspective is not ethically excusable or condonable.

Sexual Contact Under Exploitative Conditions.

For some physicians, sexual misconduct is the conscious (and usually repeated) use of their professional positions in order to manipulate or exploit their patients' vulnerabilities for their own gratification. Presumably, most physicians who represent sexual contact to patients as part of treatment would belong to this category. Certainly, self-gratification is the only basis for the behavior of physicians who engage in sexual contact with incompetent or unconscious patients.

Several researchers have compared the occurrence of sexual misconduct with sexual assault and incest.[15,19,24,25] It is clear that, for at least some offenders, sexual misconduct with patients results from an impulse to assert power over or to humiliate another person.[26(pp60–61)] Masters and Johnson[27] advocated that therapists who exploit their power in order to have sexual intercourse with their patients should be charged with rape.[28] Four states classify sexual exploitation by a psychotherapist as sex offenses under criminal statutes.[4,5,8,9]

The comparison with sexual assault is most easily understood when a physician represents sexual contact to the patient as being an appropriate medical or therapeutic procedure or an appropriate part of the therapeutic relationship. For health professionals engaged in a therapeutic relationship with patients, sexual misconduct is also often a manifestation of the health professional's own need to control or subjugate the patient or the sexual relationship.[26(pp60–61)] In such situations, a physician uses his or her status as a physician to influence or coerce the patient into accepting sexual contact. For instance, one researcher examined the responses of 16 women who had been sexually molested during routine gynecological examinations by the same physician.[19] The majority of the women did not stop the physician even after becoming uncomfortable with the length and nature of his examination since they trusted that their physician would not conduct an unethical examination.[19]

Several elements of the physician-patient relationship can combine to give the physician dis-proportionate influence over the patient. Within the physician-patient relationship, the physician possesses considerable knowledge, expertise, and status. A person is often most vulnerable, both physically and emotionally, when seeking medical care.[1,25] When a physician acts in a way that is not to the patient's benefit, the relative position of the patient within the professional relationship is such that it is difficult for the patient to give meaningful consent to such behavior, including sexual contact or sexual relations.[15,25] It is the lack of reliable or true consent on the part of the patient that has led researchers to compare physician-patient sexual contact with other sexually exploitative situations such as sexual assault and incest.[15,24,26(p47)] It is noteworthy that several states specify that consent of the patient or client cannot be used as a defense to charges of sexual misconduct.[6,7]

In fact, instances of sexual contact with patients do seem to occur most commonly where there is considerable disparity in power, status, and emotional vulnerability between physician and patient. Physicians who engage in sexual contact with patients are typically older and male, while patients are typically younger and female. Studies among psychiatrists indicate that approximately 85% to 90% of sexual contact involves a male psychiatrist and a female patient.[10] In one study of psychiatrists, a majority admitted that sexual contact with a patient was for their own emotional or sexual gratification.[10] Other studies of patient-psychiatrist sexual contact showed that the patients who were involved in sexual contact with their psychiatrists were also the ones most likely to be particularly vulnerable emotionally.[15] Patients who had sexual contact with psychiatrists were more likely than other patients to consider exploitative relations with an authority figure to be normal.[15]

A significant amount of sexual contact with patients does not seem to be an isolated instance of mismanaging the emotions of the professional relationship.[10,19] In one study, 33% of psychiatrists who reported sexual contact with patients also reported repeated instances of sexual contact with patients.[10] Despite considerable evidence to the contrary, repeat offenders were the most likely of all psychiatrists to claim that their conduct was beneficial to patients. These repeat offenders were also the least likely to seek help or consultation regarding the sexual contact.[10]

Effects of Sexual Contact Between Patients and Physicians

Some early attempts were made to show that sexual contact between patient and physician is or could be beneficial to the patient.[28,29] However, most researchers agree that the effects of physician-patient contact are almost universally negative or damaging to the patient.[15,19,24,26(pp24,39–45),30,31] (and *Boston Globe.* June 18, 1990:29, health science section). Studies show that 85% to 90% of patients experience such sexual contact as damaging.[32] Similar to the reactions of women who have been sexually assaulted, female patients tended to feel angry, abandoned, humiliated, mistreated, or exploited by their physicians.[14,26(p205),30,31] Victims have been reported to experience guilt, severe distrust of their own judgment, and mistrust of both men and physicians.[15,26(pp41,43,205),33] Patients who have been involved in therapist-patient sexual relationships can suffer from depression, anxiety, sexual disorders, sleeping disorders, and cognitive dysfunctions and are at risk for substance abuse.[15,26(pp43,45,205),34] While most researchers agree that sexual contact between patient and physician is potentially deleterious, it is important to note that most research has been based on patients who have initiated disciplinary action against physicians or on patients whom subsequent psychiatrists or therapists have identified as being harmed by the sexual contact with a physician. Patients not harmed by sexual contact with a physician may have escaped the attention of researchers. Also, assessing damage to patients may be complicated by the existence of preexisting conditions that are exacerbated by sexual involvement with the physician.[26(pp48,53,206)]

Most studies that have examined the effects of physician-patient sexual contact have focused on psychiatrists or therapists and their patients. However, one study found that the psychological impact of physician-patient sexual contact was negative for the patient regardless of the type of practitioner involved.[30] The study suggests that it is at least in part the betrayal of the patient's trust in the physician that produces negative psychological consequences for the patient. In addition, the risks posed to patient well-being due to loss of professional objectivity are equal regardless of the physician's specialty.

ETHICAL CONSIDERATIONS

Serving the Needs of the Patient

The satisfaction or gratification that a physician derives from treating patients is a fortunate benefit of the physician-patient alliance. However, the physician's professional obligation to serve the needs of the patient means that the physician's own needs or gratification cannot become a consideration in decisions about the patient's medical care. Regard for the physician's needs or gratifications may interfere with efforts to address the needs of the patient. At the very least, the emotional factors that accompany sexual involvement may affect or obscure the physician's medical judgment, thus jeopardizing the patient's diagnosis or treatment. Sexual contact or relationships between patient and physician are unethical because the physician's gratification inappropriately becomes part of the professional relationship.[16,30,35]

Trust Integral to the Physician-Patient Relationship

From ancient times, members of the medical profession have accepted the special responsibility that is accorded them by virtue of their unique skills of healing. The degree of knowledge, training, and expertise required to practice the art of medicine is highly sophisticated and complex. Physicians recognize that the health of individuals and society depends on their willingness to employ their knowledge, expertise, and influence solely for the welfare of patients. Patients who seek medical care must, in turn, be able to trust in the physician's dedication to the patient's welfare in order for the physician-patient alliance to succeed.[25]

A physician who engages in sexual contact with a patient seriously compromises the patient's welfare. The patient's trust that the physician will work only for the patient's welfare is violated. Consequently, sexual contact and sexual relationships between physicians and their patients are unethical.

Ethical Implications of Nonsexual Physical Contact with Patients

The ethical prohibition against romantic relationships or sexual contact with patients is not meant to bar nonsexual touching of patients by physicians. In addition to its role in physical examination, nonsexual touching may be therapeutic or comforting to patients. However, even nonsexual contact with patients should be approached with caution. It may be difficult to identify a strict boundary between nonsexual and sexual touching. Either the patient or the physician may misinterpret the touching behavior of the other.[32] There is also some concern that what may begin as benign, nonsexual contact may eventually lead to sexual contact.[11,12]

If a physician feels that a patient may misinterpret the nature of physical contact or if a physician's nonsexual touching behavior may be leading to sexual contact, then the contact should be avoided.

Termination of the Professional Relationship

It is of course possible for a physician and a patient to be genuinely attracted to or have genuine romantic affection for each other. However, any relationship in which a physician is (or risks) taking advantage of a patient's emotional or psychological vulnerability would be unethical. Therefore, before initiating a dating, romantic, or sexual relationship with a patient, a physician's minimum duty would be to terminate his or her professional relationship with the patient.[16] In addition, it would be advisable for a physician to seek consultation with a colleague before initiating a relationship with the former patient. Termination of the professional relationship would also be appropriate if a sexual or romantic attraction to (as opposed to contact with) a patient threatens to interfere with the judgment of the physician or to jeopardize the patient's care.

SEXUAL CONTACT AFTER TERMINATION OF THE RELATIONSHIP

Posttermination Relationship May Also Be Unethical

Termination of the physician-patient relationship does not eliminate the possibility that sexual contact between a physician and a former patient might be unethical. Sexual contact between a physician and a patient with whom professional relations had been terminated would be unethical if the sexual contact occurred as a result of the use or exploitation of trust, knowledge, influence, or emotions derived from the former professional relationship. The ethical propriety of a sexual relationship between a physician and a former patient, then, may depend substantially on the nature and context of the former relationship.

In most patient-psychiatrist relationships, the intense and emotional nature of treatment makes it difficult for a romantic relationship between a psychiatrist and a former patient not to be affected by the previous professional relationship. The American Psychiatric Association has accordingly stated that "sexual involvement with one's former patients generally exploits emotions deriving from treatment and is therefore almost always unethical."[4]

Relationships between patients and other types of physicians may also include considerable trust, intimacy, or emotional dependence. The length of the former professional relationship, the extent to which the patient has confided personal or private information to the physician, the nature of the patient's medical problem, and the degree of emotional dependence that the patient has on the physician, all may contribute to the intimacy of the relationship. In addition, the extent of the physician's general knowledge about the patient (ie, the patient's past, the patient's family situation, and the patient's current emotional state) is also a factor that may render a sexual or romantic relationship with a former patient unethical.

Prohibiting Sexual Contact with Former Patients

Some commentators have suggested that the amount of time that has elapsed since the termination of the professional relationship and the initiation of the sexual or romantic relationship may be pertinent to the ethical propriety of physician–former patient relationships.[24]

It may be that a sexual or romantic relationship that immediately follows the termination of the physician-patient relationship may be more suspect than one that occurs after considerable time has passed. Yet, some emotions and dependencies that were created during the professional relationship may not disappear even after a considerable amount of time has passed. Research on psychotherapists has shown that patients experience strong feelings about their therapists for 5 to 10 years after the termination of treatment.[26(pp116–118),32]

For these reasons, it is not useful to determine the appropriateness of a sexual relationship between a physician and a former patient based on the amount of time that has elapsed since the termination of the professional relationship. Rather, the relevant standard is the potential for misuse of emotions derived from the former professional relationship.

PREVENTION AND DISCIPLINE OF SEXUAL MISCONDUCT

Education

There is evidence that the issue of sexual misconduct and sexual or romantic attraction to patients is not adequately covered in many medical training programs.[23,36] However, almost all commentators agree that the issues surrounding sexual misconduct need attention during medical education.[23,33,37,38]

Education may serve to distinguish sexual or romantic attraction to patients, which is a common and normal experience, from inappropriate behavior, such as acting on the attraction or allowing the attraction to jeopardize the care of the patient. Education may also promote appropriate responses to sexual attraction to patients, such as seeking consultation with colleagues or counseling, when patient care is potentially jeopardized.[23] Obviously education about sexual misconduct would also inform physicians and medical students about the ethical implications of physician-patient sexual contact as well as the potential harm to patient well-being.

Detection and Reporting of Sexual Misconduct of Colleagues

Sexual misconduct is unlikely to be brought to the attention of the proper authorities by many of the usual means of exposing deficiencies in the practice of medicine. Other transgressions can be detected through the analysis of records or may be brought to the attention of the authorities by hospital staff or peer review processes. However, the discovery and investigation of sexual misconduct is unlikely unless victims of sexual misconduct initiate and pursue disciplinary or ethical review procedures.[37]

Unfortunately, patients who have had sexual contact with their physicians may be hindered from reporting the misconduct. There is some evidence that offenders tend to refer patients to colleagues whom they know to be sympathetic to their actions.[37] Patients may thus be discouraged from reporting instances of sexual misconduct. Also, while the rate of dismissals of cases alleging sexual intimacy between psychologists and clients is decreasing, many psychiatrists continue to express misgivings about the effectiveness of disciplinary bodies in this area.[26(pp24–25),37]

Further, some patients may not be able emotionally to report instances of sexual misconduct or to undergo the process of review and investigation required to discipline an offending physician. When the sexual relationship was a result of the physician's mishandling of the emotional influences of the professional relationship, the patient may not be able to recognize that the physician's behavior was improper or inappropriately motivated. Victims of sexual misconduct through medical deception may be incapable of reporting the offense because of the emotions of shame, humiliation, degradation, and blame that also often make it difficult for victims of sexual assault to report their assaults.

One of the few remaining avenues for identifying offending physicians is reporting by colleagues. Consequently, reporting of transgressions by peers is especially important in the case of sexual misconduct. Unfortunately, physicians are often reluctant to report instances of sexual transgression by their colleagues. A 1987 survey of 1423 practicing psychiatrists (a response rate of 26%) revealed that 65% of them reported treating patients who had been sexually involved with previous therapists, and 87% of those psychiatrists believed that the previous involvement was harmful to the patient. However, only 8% of them reported their colleagues' behavior to a professional organization or legal authority.[37]

Literature that has studied the reporting practices of physicians indicates that reluctance to report may involve concerns over confidentiality, either in the physician-patient relationship or among colleagues. Reluctance to take action contrary to a patient's wishes or concern that a patient's recovery process may be damaged also may affect the reporting practices. Some physicians may also regard the patient's allegations as hearsay and therefore unreportable.[37] Other physicians may feel that reporting laws lack sufficient clarity or immunity for good-faith reporting.

The American Medical Association includes among its Principles of Medical Ethics the standard that "[a] physician shall . . . strive to expose those physicians deficient in character or competence, or who engage in fraud or deception." Because the nature of sexual misconduct is such that most victims are rendered reluctant or unable to report the misconduct on their own, physicians should be particularly vigilant in exposing colleagues who commit sexual misconduct. Presently, four states have mandatory reporting laws specific to the reporting of sexual misconduct by colleagues.[32] The Council on Ethical and Judicial Affairs believes that physicians who learn of sexual misconduct by a colleague must report the misconduct to the local medical society, the state licensing board, or other appropriate authorities. Exception may be made if a physician learns of the misconduct while treating the offending physician for the misconduct, provided that the offending physician is not continuing the misconduct and does not resume the misconduct in the future. An exception may also be made in cases in which a patient refuses to consent to reporting or in cases where the treating physician believes that reporting would significantly harm the patient's treatment. Physicians who make good-faith reports of the sexual misconduct of a colleague should be protected from potential legal, professional, or personal repercussions.

Discipline

Some commentators have expressed concern that existing disciplinary bodies have not been sufficiently effective in dealing with sexual misconduct.[37] While the frequency of false accusations of sexual misconduct seems to be extremely low[32,38] (and *Boston Globe*. June 18, 1990:29, health science section), the rate at which practitioners are disciplined for ethical violations of this kind does not seem commensurate with the number of accusations.[37,39] There may be myriad concerns that limit the efficiency of investigative and disciplinary bodies, including the difficulties inherent in ensuring procedural fairness to the accused physician while remaining sensitive to the needs of the patient who reports physician sexual misconduct. For instance, procedural mechanisms must be in place that would prevent the leveling of baseless accusations against innocent physicians. However, procedures must also be flexible and sensitive enough so that victims are not so daunted or intimidated by the procedural requirements that they decline to proceed with complaints.

There are some ways, however, to structure disciplinary bodies that would maximize both effectiveness in detecting and disciplining offenders and sensitivity to patients who report sexual misconduct. For instance, some research has shown that women who experienced sexual contact with male psychotherapists showed an increased distrust both of men and of psychotherapists.[37] Patients should therefore be given the option of a preliminary interview with a member of the disciplinary board with whom or with whose gender they feel most comfortable. In addition, it is important that a disciplinary panel hearing sexual misconduct charges have equal gender distribution among its members.

Members of disciplinary bodies that deal with

reports of sexual misconduct should undergo training and education specific to the problem.[37] Patients may face greater obstacles in reporting and pursuing legal action in the case of sexual misconduct than with other medical transgressions. Some institutions may consider establishing a special disciplinary body to handle allegations of sexual misconduct, one whose members are educated and sensitized to the particular difficulties facing victims of sexual misconduct.[32] Alternatively, an institution might establish special procedures for handling sexual misconduct complaints.

Finally, physicians who commit sexual misconduct must be able to get help. Physicians are subject to many pressures and influences, including attraction to patients, the emotional influences of the physician-patient interaction, and the effect of their own emotional problems or conflicts on their professional lives. Many physicians who commit sexual misconduct may benefit from rehabilitation for their problem. Currently, there is virtually no research regarding the efficacy of therapy for physicians who engage in sexual misconduct. However, programs similar to those that help other kinds of physician impairments, such as alcohol and drug addiction, should be developed and made available for sexual misconduct offenders.[23,33]

CONCLUSIONS

The Council on Ethical and Judicial Affairs concludes that sexual contact or a romantic relationship with a patient concurrent with the physician-patient relationship is unethical. Sexual or romantic relationships with former patients are also unethical if the physician uses or exploits trust, knowledge, emotions, or influence derived from the previous professional relationship.

In addition, education on the issue of sexual attraction to patients and sexual misconduct should be included throughout all levels of medical training. Disciplinary bodies must be structured to maximize effectiveness in dealing with the problem of sexual misconduct. Physicians who learn of sexual misconduct by a colleague must report the misconduct to the local medical society, the state licensing board, or other appropriate authorities.

Exceptions to reporting may be made in order to protect patient welfare. It should be noted that many states have legal prohibitions against relationships between physicians and current or former patients.

References

1. Campbell M. The oath: an investigation of the injunction prohibiting physician-patient sexual relations. *Perspect Biol Med.* 1989;32:300–308.

2. Gartell N, Herman J, Olarte S, Localio R, Feldstein M. Psychiatric residents' sexual contact with educators and patients: results of a national survey. *Am J Psychiatry.* 1988;145:690–694.

3. Council on Ethical and Judicial Affairs, American Medical Association. *Current Opinions of the Council on Ethical and Judicial Affairs 1989, Opinion 8.14, Sexual Misconduct.* Chicago, Ill: American Medical Association; 1989.

4. American Psychiatric Association. *The Principles of Medical Ethics With Annotations Especially Applicable to Psychiatry.* Washington, DC: American Psychiatric Association; 1989.

5. Minn Stat Ann §609.344 (1990).

6. SD Codified Laws Ann §36–4–30 (1989).

7. Fla Stat §458.331 (1988).

8. Colo Rev Stat §18-3–405.5 (1989).

9. Wis Stat §940.22 (1986).

10. Gartrell N, Herman J, Olarte S, Feldstein M, Localio R. Psychiatrist-patient sexual contact: results of a national survey, I: prevalence. *Am J Psychiatry.* 1986;143:1126–1231.

11. Kardener SH, Fuller M, Mensh IN. Characteristics of 'erotic' practitioners. *Am J Psychiatry.* 1976;133:1324–1325.

12. Perry JA. Physicians' erotic and nonerotic physical involvement with patients. *Am J Psychiatry,* 1976;133:838–840.

13. Kardener SH, Fuller M, Mensh IN. A survey of physicians' attitudes and practices regarding erotic and nonerotic contact of patients. *Am J Psychiatry.* 1973;130:1077–1081.

14. Holroyd JC, Brodsky AM. Psychologists' attitudes and practices regarding erotic and nonerotic physical contact with patients. *Am Psychologist.* 1977;32:843–849.

15. Kluft RP. Treating the patient who has been exploited by a previous therapist. *Psychiatr Clin North Am.* 1989;12:483–500.

16. Rapp MS. Sexual misconduct. *Can Med Assoc J.* 1987;137:193–194.

17. Derosis H, Hamilton JA, Morrison E, Strauss M. More on psychiatrist-patient sexual contact. *Am J Psychiatry.* 1987;144:688–689.

18. Belote B. *Sexual Intimacy Between Female Clients and Male Psychotherapists: Masochistic Sabotage.* San Francisco; California School of Professional Psychology; 1974. Unpublished doctoral dissertation.

19. Burgess A. Physician sexual misconduct and patients' responses. *Am J Psychiatry.* 1981;138:1335–1342.

20. Zinn WM. Doctors have feelings too. *JAMA.* 1988;259:3296–3298.

21. Groves JE. Taking care of the hateful patient. *N Engl J Med.* 1978;298:883–887.

22. Gorlin R, Zucker HD. Physicians' reactions to patients. *N Engl J Med.* 1983;308:1059–1063.

23. Pope KS, Keith-Speigel P, Tabachnick BG. Sexual attraction to clients: the human therapist and (sometimes) inhuman training system. *Am Psychologist.* 1986;41:147–158.

24. Herman JL, Gartrell N, Olarte S, Feldstein M, Localioi R. Psychiatrist-patient sexual contact: results of a national survey, II: psychiatrists' attitudes. *Am J Psychiatry.* 1987;144:164–169.

25. Kardener SH. Sex and physician-patient relationship. *Am J Psychiatry.* 1974;131:1134–1136.

26. Gabbard GO. *Sexual Exploitation in Professional Relationships.* Washington, DC: American Psychiatric Press; 1989.

27. Masters WH, Johnson VE. Principles of the new sex therapy. *Am J Psychiatry.* 1976;133:548–554.

28. McCartney J. Overt transference. *J Sex Res.* 1966;2:227–237.

29. Shepard M. *The Love Treatment: Sexual Intimacy Between Patients and Psychotherapists.* New York, NY: Peter Wyden; 1971.

30. Feldman-Summers S, Jones G. Psychological impacts of sexual contact between therapists or other health care practitioners and their clients. *J Consult Clin Psychol.* 1984;52:1054–1061.

31. Bouhoutsos J, Holroyd J, Lerman H, Forer B, Greenberg M. Sexual intimacy between psychotherapists and patients. *Professional Psychol Res Pract.* 1983;14:185–196.

32. Bemmann KC, Goodwin, J. New laws about sexual misconduct by therapists: knowledge and attitudes among Wisconsin psychiatrists. *Wis Med J.* 1989;88(5):11–16.

33. Zelen SL. Sexualization of therapeutic relationships: the dual vulnerability of patient and therapist. *Psychotherapy.* 1985;22:178–185.

34. California Legislature. *Report of the California Senate Task Force on Psychotherapist and Patients Sexual Relations.* Prepared for the California Senate Rules Committee, March 1987.

35. Seeman MV. Sexual misconduct. *Can Med Assoc J.* 1987;137:699–700.

36. Glaser RD, Thorpe JS. Unethical intimacy: a survey of sexual contact and advances between psychology educators and female graduate students. *Am Psychol.* 1986;41:43–51.

37. Gartrell N, Herman J, Olarte S, Feldstein M, Localio R. Reporting practices of psychiatrists who knew of sexual misconduct by colleagues. *Am J Orthopsychiatry.* 1987;57:287–295.

38. Gutheil TG. Borderline personality disorder, boundary violations, and patient-therapist sex: medicolegal pitfalls. *Am J Psychiatry.* 1989;146:597–602.

39. Moore RA. Ethics in the practice of psychiatry update on the results of enforcement of the code. *Am J Psychiatry.* 1985;142:1043–1046.

from Criteria for Full ASCA Membership

AMERICAN SWIMMING COACHES ASSOCIATION

As of September, 1993, FULL MEMBERSHIP in the ASCA will consist of those coaches who meet the following criteria. (Associate memberships will be available to all other coaches at the same membership fee.)

These criteria are predicated on the premise that Professionalism is based on the concept of credentials that demonstrate the most current training, and behavior that demonstrates our concern for the well-being of our clients, and fellow professionals.

Criteria #1—Technical Proficiency

All new ASCA Members shall have completed the Certification Course work through Level 4. They shall have met education & experience criteria to be fully certified at Level 2 and above. They will have 1 year from the date of application to complete these 4 courses.

Note: This means COURSE WORK ONLY, NOT FULLY CERTIFIED WITH ACHIEVEMENTS. This is not necessary for membership. Level 1 is for our apprentice coaches. Currently Certified Coaches will not lose any present status. New applicants may "test out" without actually taking the coursework.

Criteria #2—Professional Behavior

An ASCA Member shall meet the following requirements in regard to Professional Behavior:

From "Criteria for Full ASCA Membership" by the American Swimming Coaches Association. Used by permission of the American Swimming Coaches Association.

A. Agreement to abide by the Code of Ethics, follow the procedures involved in its enforcement, and accept the due process of its enforcement. Written signature of the code of Ethics will constitute informed consent.

B. Statement of professional contributions. These may include publication, committee work at the national or local level, clinic instruction or administration, or other contributions to professional development of the sport and other swimming professionals.

CODE OF ETHICS AND CONDUCT OF THE ASCA

The conduct and ethical behavior of a professional is determined by the degree of respect with which he interacts with the public that he serves. This public consists of both client and peer. The intent of the following code is to define the parameters of that interaction, and to provide for adherence to the following components.

Compliance with this code, as with all law in an open society, depends primarily upon understanding and voluntary compliance, secondarily upon reinforcement by peer and public opinion, and finally, when necessary, upon enforcement through disciplinary proceedings. The code does not exhaust the moral and ethical considerations that should inform an ASCA Member professional swim coach, for no worthwhile human activity can be completely defined by rules. This simply provides a framework for the ethical coaching of the sport of swimming.

Section A. Personal Conduct

Article #1. A Coach Member of the American Swimming Coaches Association shall not abuse alcohol in the presence of athletes. A Coach Member of the ASCA shall not use illegal or recreational drugs. A legal conviction for possession or sale of any illegal substance shall be an automatic violation of this rule.

Article #2. All professional communications shall be conducted in an honest, open manner consistent with the best interests of the sport, and the profession. Integrity is a basic part of coaching, whether financial or dealing with swimming events and entries. A member is accurate at all times to the best of their knowledge.

Section B. Coach to Coach

Article #1. In all professional matters regarding the changing of organizational affiliation of athletes, the initial discussion of any such change in affiliation should be initiated by the athlete, and not by the coach, or direct agent acting on behalf of the coach.

Section C. Coach to Athlete

Article #1. A coach member of the American Swimming Coaches Association will always make decisions based on the best interest of the athlete.

Article #2. A coach member of the American Swimming Coaches Association shall not engage in sexual relations with any minor.

Article #3. Sexual misconduct consists of any behavior that utilizes the influence of the coaching position to encourage inappropriate intimacy between coach and athlete.

Article #4. Coaches of Collegiate age athletes shall not engage in sexual relations with athletes that they coach, even of legal age.

Section D. Coach to Community

Article #1. Any legal felony conviction will constitute a violation of the Code of Conduct. See Also Article A above.

ENFORCEMENT OF THE CODE OF ETHICS

The Ethics Committee shall be elected by the ASCA membership in the Olympic Year. Four positions shall be elected for a four year term. A fifth shall be appointed by the ASCA President, to chair this committee. This Chair shall be an ASCA Vice-President. The first four positions may be Board Members or non-Board Members. Each candidate for a position on the Ethics Committee must have 5 years of experience as an ASCA Member. Responsibilities of the Ethics Committee shall be:

1. To develop each month, a sample case regarding ethics and conduct to act as a case-book when accumulated, to delineate conduct that is acceptable and unacceptable within the context of the four areas of the Code of Ethics and Conduct. This casebook example shall be published each month in the ASCA Newsletter and Magazine as part of ongoing education in Professional Ethics and Conduct.

2. To receive and investigate complaints pertaining to matters of ethical behavior among the members of the Association.

3. In regard to said investigative responsibility, develop procedures to ensure the individual's right to due process is protected at all times in the procedure.

4. To develop within the due process system, a series of potential penalties for those members found in violation of our code of ethics. These will be of varying degrees of severity and may include temporary or permanent revocation of membership or certification.

5. To deliver said penalties in such cases as may be necessary to protect the integrity of our membership.

"DUE PROCESS" FOR CASES OF ETHICAL MISCONDUCT

Definitions: Due Process is the procedure that ensures that if you are charged with an ethical violation, your rights are protected in the following manner:

✓ You receive notice, in writing, of those specific offenses with which you are charged.

✓ You have an opportunity to defend yourself, and reasonable period of time to prepare that defense.

✓ You have the right to legal counsel if you wish it.

✓ You have a right to a hearing before an objective body, (ASCA Ethics Committee) at a specific time that will allow you full opportunity to present your defense.

✓ You have notice of how to appeal the decision, if the judgment is against you.

PROCEDURE

The following are the general procedures involved in the ASCA Code of Ethics Due Process proceedings

1. Only a coach member of the ASCA may bring ethical charges against another coach member. In the case of criminally charged offenses, the association itself will be considered the complainant.

2. Ethical complaints brought by one coach against another that are found to be essentially of a spurious nature, will itself be considered to be a very serious breach of ethical conduct, and will be an automatic complaint. This is meant specifically to prevent "nuisance" complaints, or issues arising from personal animosities.

3. An ethical complaint is brought to the attention of chairman of the Ethics Committee, in writing by the complainant.

4. A preliminary evaluation of the nature of the complaint will be conducted by the Chairman of the Ethics Committee, the President of the Association, and the Executive Director. If the complaint is found to represent a potential ethical violation, it is immediately sent to the full Ethics Committee, and notification by certified mail of the action and specific charges are sent in writing to the coach so accused. An invitation to respond is included, with a reasonable time frame for the accused to present a written response. It is possible that the initial screening process may decide that no ethical violation has occurred. If so, the chairman of the Ethics Committee will so inform the complainant, immediately following such a decision.

5. Following a reasonable opportunity for written response, the committee may choose to:

   a) Accept the response. No further action. Notification of the complainant.

   b) Propose simple disciplinary action, (likely to be accepted by the accused). Accused is notified, and may accept proposal, or may insist upon a full hearing.

   c) Schedule a full hearing for the complaint. In this case, a full written explanation of the hearing process and place, time, etc. will be mailed to the accused.

7. Should the accused party wish to appeal, such appeal request must be submitted to the President of the ASCA, and the appeal board will be the Board

of Directors of the ASCA. The appeal will be heard at the next regularly scheduled Board of Directors meeting or at a special meeting called for that purpose. The same procedures will then be followed as for the formal hearing by the Ethics Committee. Any member of the Ethics Committee who is also a member of the ASCA Board of Directors, shall be excused from this appeal process.

AUTHORITY OF THE ETHICS COMMITTEE TO IMPOSE PENALTIES

In the case of a decision that an Ethics Violation has occurred, the Ethics Committee may impose penalty(s) from among the following options:

1. A letter of reminder of ethical conduct to the coach.
2. A letter of reprimand directly to the offending coach.
3. A letter of reprimand to the offending coach, with copies to the employer of the coach.
4. A letter as above, with additional copies to the LSC Chairman in the cases of USS Swimming Coaching, or similar body in other situations.
5. Permanent letter in the file of the offending coach, to become a part of that permanent certification record, and distributed with information on the certification status.
6. Temporary suspension of ASCA Membership for a defined period of time.
7. Revocation or suspension of ASCA Certification.
8. Indefinite suspension of ASCA Membership, to be reviewed at a future time.

It is understood that the above are representative penalties only, and may be modified to appropriately fit any situation of ethical violation, by the Ethics Committee, and that they are presented in order of severity.

from Sexual Violence and Safety and Sexual Offense Policy

ANTIOCH COLLEGE

SEXUAL VIOLENCE AND SAFETY

The statistics on the frequency of sexual violence on college campuses today are alarming. While we try to make Antioch a safe environment for everyone, we still have problems here. There is date and acquaintance rape, and stranger rape, and, while the majority of perpetrators are men and the majority of victims are women, there are also female perpetrators and male victims. There are also many students who have already experienced sexual violence before arriving at Antioch; healing from that experience may be an integral part of their personal, social and academic lives while they are here.

Antioch has a Sexual Offense Prevention and Survivor's Advocacy Program which consists of an Advocate and trained Peer Advocates and Edu-

cators. They can talk with you confidentially about any questions or concerns you have, provide or arrange for counseling, and help you access resources about healing from sexual violence. They also provide advocacy for rape victims dealing with a hospital, police, the courts, and/or campus administrative procedures. The program is located on the second floor of Long Hall, next to Maples and above the infirmary. The telephone number is PBX xxx (xxx-xxxx). There is also a Rape Crisis Line at PBX xxx (xxx-xxxx) which you can call in an emergency. If you experience sexual harassment or assault on co-op, you can call us for support through x-xxx-xxx-xxxx.

Antioch has two policies, a sexual harassment policy and a sexual offense policy, which have been designed to help deal with these problems when they occur on campus and/or when they involve an Antioch community member. Read these policies; you are held responsible for knowing them. Under the sexual offense policy:

— All sexual contact and conduct between any two people must be consensual;
— Consent must be obtained verbally before there is any sexual contact or conduct;
— If the level of sexual intimacy increases during an interaction (i.e., if two people move from kissing while fully clothed—which is one level—to undressing for direct physical contact, which is another level), the people involved need to express their clear verbal consent before moving to that new level;
— If one person wants to *initiate* moving to a higher level of sexual intimacy in an interaction, *that person is responsible for getting the verbal consent of the other person(s) involved before moving to that level;*
— If you have had a particular level of sexual intimacy before with someone, you must still ask each and every time;
— If you have a sexual transmitted disease, you must disclose it to a potential sexual partner.

Don't ever make any assumptions about consent; they can hurt someone and get you in trouble. Also, do not take silence as consent; it isn't. Consent must be clear and verbal (i.e., saying: yes, I want to kiss you also).

Special precautions are necessary if you, or the person with whom you would like to be sexual, are under the influence of alcohol, drugs, or prescribed medication. Extreme caution should always be used. Consent, even verbal consent, may not be meaningful. Taking advantage of someone who is "under the influence" is never acceptable behavior. If, for instance, you supply someone with alcohol and get her/him drunk so that person will consent to have sex with you (figuring you wouldn't get "as far" if that person were sober), then their consent may be meaningless and you may be charged under the sexual offense policy. If you are so drunk that you act with someone totally inappropriately (in a way maybe you wouldn't if you were sober), or if you are so drunk you don't hear "no," you may still be charged under the sexual offense policy.

If you have a hard time knowing or setting your own personal boundaries, or respecting other people's boundaries, you may have a harder time if alcohol or drugs are involved. For truly consensual sex, you and your partner(s) should be sober to be sexual.

Sexual harassment should be reported to the Advocate; depending on the wishes of the complainant, mediation may be attempted or the charge may be referred to the Hearing Board. Other forms of sexual offenses are also reported to the Advocate, and depending on the wishes of the victim/survivor may be referred for mediation or to the Hearing Board which hears cases of sexual offenses where the alleged offender is a student. If the accused violator is not a student, the case may be referred for follow-up to the appropriate person. In cases of rape and sexual assault, reporting to law enforcement authorities is also encouraged. Anonymous reports may also be made. Complaint forms are in a box outside the program offices in Long Hall, or you can make a report directly to the Advocate, either in person or at xxx. All reports are treated confidentially; every attempt is made to treat everyone involved fairly, and to honor the wishes of the victim regarding what is done (or not done).

If you are raped or sexually assaulted:

— Get somewhere safe.
— Contact a friend you trust, a hall advisor, or HAC and/or
— Contact a peer advocate or the Advocate directly, or through the Rape Crisis Line at xxx.
— You may also wish to notify the police.
— Do not bathe, change clothes, or otherwise cleanup yet.

The peer advocate or Advocate will provide emotional support, help you to understand your thoughts and feelings at the time, explain your options to you, and support you in whatever decisions you choose to make.

If you have been sexually harassed at a co-op site, tell your co-op advisor and the Advocate. You can call to report the harassment from out-of-town at 1-xxx-xxx-xxxx.

If you have been victimized sexually in the past and you would like some assistance in working on these issues, there is help available. See a counselor at the Counseling Center or contact the Advocate or a peer advocate. If it's appropriate for you to see a therapist off-campus, we will try to help you find someone suitable. There are also support groups available each term for men and women who are survivors of sexual abuse.

There are ways to help prevent sexual violence on campus. A few tips:

— *Always* lock your room door when you're going to undress, sleep, or if you're under the influence of a substance which might impair your ability to react quickly. It's a good idea to get in the habit of locking your door whenever you're inside.

— *Never* prop outside doors open—strangers can enter buildings, as well as friends.

— If you're walking or running on the bike path at times when you might be the only one around, take a friend.

— Learn Self-Defense.

— Know your sexual desires and boundaries and communicate them clearly to any (potential) sexual partner; "listen" to your boundaries and honor them. If you're not sure, say "no" rather than "yes" or "maybe."

— Ask what a (potential) sexual partner's desires and boundaries are; listen to and respect them.

— If someone violates a sexual boundary, confront him/her on it. That may mean telling them directly, or, as a first step, talking with your hall advisor or HAC, the Advocate or a peer advocate, a counselor, or the Dean of Students.

THE ANTIOCH COLLEGE SEXUAL OFFENSE POLICY

All sexual contact and conduct on the Antioch College campus and/or occurring with an Antioch community member must be consensual.

When a sexual offense, as defined herein, is committed by a community member, such action will not be tolerated.

Antioch College provides and maintains educational programs for all community members, some aspects of which are required. The educational aspects of this policy are intended to prevent sexual offenses and ultimately to heighten community awareness.

In support of this policy and community safety, a support network exists that consists of the Sexual Offense Prevention and Survivors' Advocacy Program, an Advocate, Peer Advocates, and victim/survivor support groups through the Sexual Offense Prevention and Survivors' Advocacy Program and Counseling Services.

The Advocate (or other designated administrator) shall be responsible for initiation and coordination of measures required by this policy.

The implementation of this policy also utilizes established Antioch governance structures and adheres to contractual obligations.

Consent

1. For the purpose of this policy, "consent" shall be defined as follows: the act of willingly and verbally agreeing to engage in specific sexual contact or conduct.

2. If sexual contact and/or conduct is not mutually and simultaneously initiated, then the person who initiates sexual contact/conduct is responsible for getting the verbal consent of the other individual(s) involved.

3. Obtaining consent is an on-going process in any sexual interaction. Verbal consent should be obtained with each new level of physical and/or sexual contact/conduct in any given interaction, regardless of who initiates it. Asking "Do you want to have sex with me?" is not enough. The request for consent must be specific to each act.

4. The person with whom sexual contact/conduct is initiated is responsible to express verbally and/or physically her/his willingness or lack of willingness when reasonably possible.

5. If someone has initially consented but then stops consenting during a sexual interaction, she/he should communicate withdrawal verbally and/or through physical resistance. The other individual(s) must stop immediately.

6. To knowingly take advantage of someone who is under the influence of alcohol, drugs and/or prescribed medication is not acceptable behavior in the Antioch community.

7. If someone verbally agrees to engage in specific contact or conduct, but it is not of her/his own free will due to any of the circumstances stated in (a) through (d) below, then the person initiating shall be considered in violation of this policy if:

a) the person submitting is under the influence of alcohol or other substances supplied to her/him by the person initiating;

b) the person submitting is incapacitated by alcohol, drugs, and/or prescribed medication;

c) the person submitting is asleep or unconscious;

d) the person initiating has forced, threatened, coerced, or intimidated the other individual(s) into engaging in sexual contact and/or sexual conduct.

Offenses Defined

The following sexual contact/conduct are prohibited under Antioch College's Sexual Offense Policy and, in addition to possible criminal prosecution, may result in sanctions up to and including expulsion or termination of employment.

Rape: Non-consensual penetration, however slight, of the vagina or anus; non-consensual fellatio or cunnilingus.

Sexual Assault: Non-consensual sexual conduct exclusive of vaginal and anal penetration, fellatio and cunnilingus. This includes, but is not limited to, attempted non-consensual penetration, fellatio, or cunnilingus; the respondent coercing or forcing the primary witness to engage in non-consensual sexual contact with the respondent or another.

Sexual Imposition: Non-consensual sexual contact. "Sexual contact" includes the touching of thighs, genitals, buttocks, the pubic region, or the breast/chest area.

Insistent and/or Persistent Sexual Harassment: Any insistent and/or persistent emotional, verbal or mental intimidation or abuse found to be sexually threatening or offensive. This includes, but is not limited to, unwelcome and irrelevant comments, references, gestures or other forms of personal attention which are inappropriate and which may be perceived as persistent sexual overtones or denigration.

Non-Disclosure of a Known Positive HIV Status: Failure to inform one's sexual partner of one's known positive HIV status prior to engaging in high risk sexual conduct.

Non-Disclosure of a Known Sexually Transmitted Disease: Failure to inform one's sexual partner of one's known infection with a sexually transmitted disease (other than HIV) prior to engaging in high risk sexual conduct.

Procedures

1. To maintain the safety of all community members, community members who are suspected of violating this policy should be made aware of the concern about their behavior. Sometimes people are not aware that their behavior is sexually offensive, threatening, or hurtful. Educating them about the effects of their behavior may cause them to change their behavior.

If someone suspects that a violation of this Sexual Offense Policy may have occurred, she/he should contact a member of the Sexual Offense Prevention and Survivors' Advocacy Program or the Dean of Students.

It is strongly encouraged that suspected violations be reported, and that they be reported as soon as is reasonable after a suspected violation has occurred. Where criminal misconduct is involved, reporting the misconduct to the local law enforcement agency is also strongly encouraged.

Any discussion of a suspected violation with a member of the Sexual Offense Prevention and Survivors' Advocacy Program or the Dean of Students will be treated as confidential.

2. When a suspected violation of this policy is reported, the person who receives the report with the Sexual Offense Prevention and Survivors' Advocacy Program or the Dean of Students office will explain to the person reporting all of her/his options (such as mediation, the Hearing Board, and criminal prosecution) which are appropriate to the suspected offense.

3. If the person reporting a suspected policy violation wishes to arrange for mediation, then the Advocate, the Dean of Students, or a staff member of the Sexual Offense Prevention and Survivors'

Advocacy program shall arrange for mediation consistent with the mediation guidelines used by the Sexual Offense Prevention and Survivors' Advocacy Program.

a) If the Dean of Students arranges mediation, the Dean shall notify the Advocate of the mediation session.

b) A written agreement with educational and/or behavioral requirements may be part of the outcome of a mediation session. Copies of this agreement shall be given to the parties involved, the Advocate and the Dean of Students.

c) Should a student persist in sexual threatening or offensive behavior after mediation has been attempted, the Sexual Harassment Committee or the Advocate should refer the case to the Hearing Board.

d) If a satisfactory conclusion is not reached through mediation, or if the mediation agreement is not adhered to by any of its participants, then the case may be referred to the Hearing Board.

4. In the event that an action taken by the Dean of Students regarding a sexual offense is appealed, the appeal shall be made to the Hearing Board.

5. If the primary witness wishes the Hearing Board to make a finding regarding an alleged policy violation, the primary witness must file a written complaint with the Advocate. The Advocate shall inform the primary witness of her/her rights regarding procedure and appeal under this policy.

6. When a written complaint is filed, if the respondent is an employee, the Advocate shall inform the President or the President's designee of the reported violation of the Sexual Offense Policy. The matter will be promptly investigated by the appropriate administrator or other supervisor with the assistance of the Advocate. If whatever review process appropriate to the employee results in a determination that the policy has been violated, then the remedy should be commensurate with the seriousness of the violation, and procedures specified in College and University policies should be followed.

7. When an official report is filed, if the respondent is a student, then the following procedures shall be followed:

A. The Advocate shall notify the Dean of Students, or another senior College official, who shall have the respondent report to the Dean of Students' office within a reasonable period of time, not to exceed the next business day the College is open that the respondent is on campus. When the respondent reports, the respondent will then be informed by the Advocate and/or the Dean of Students of the report of the sexual offense, the policy violation which is being alleged, and her/his rights regarding procedure and appeal. The respondent will be given an opportunity to present her/his side of the story at that time. If the respondent does not report as directed, then implementation of this policy shall proceed.

B. Based on the information available, the Advocate, or the Dean of Students in the Advocate's absence, will determine whether there is reasonable cause to believe that a policy violation may have occurred.

C. In the event that the respondent is situated on campus, if (1) there is reasonable cause to believe that a policy violation may have occurred, and (2) there is reasonable cause to believe that the respondent may pose a threat or danger to the safety of the community, the Hearing Board will be convened as soon as possible, preferably within 24 hours from the time of the report to the Advocate, to determine whether the respondent shall be removed from campus until the conclusion of the Hearing process. If the Hearing Board cannot be convened within 24 hours but there is reasonable cause as stated in (1) and (2) above, the Dean of Students or the Advocate in the Dean of Students' absence, can act to remove the respondent from campus.

If the respondent is living on-campus and is temporarily banned from campus, the College will help arrange housing if the respondent is unable to locate any on her/his own.

If the respondent is taking classes on-campus and is temporarily banned from attending classes, the College will help provide alternative instruction.

The emergency removal of the respondent from campus shall not constitute a determination that the respondent has violated this policy.

D. The Hearing Board will then convene for a Hearing, to hear the case. Consistent with this policy, the Hearing Board will take into account the primary witness's story, the respondent's story, witnesses, the past history of the respondent, and other relevant evidence, and will determine whether or not a policy violation has occurred and which aspect of the policy has been violated.

E. The Hearing shall take place as soon thereafter as is reasonable, no longer than seven days from the date of filing or the notification of the respondent, whichever is later, unless the Advocate determines that reasonable cause exists for convening the meeting at a later, still reasonable time, in which event the Advocate shall so notify the Chair of the Hearing Board.

F. If the primary witness chooses, she/he may have a representative at all hearings of the Hearing Board and/or through any appeals process. The primary witness's advocate is to provide advocacy and emotional support for the primary witness. When appropriate, if the primary witness chooses, the Advocate or a Peer Advocate may act as the primary witness's representative at all hearings of the Hearing Board and/or through any appeals process. The primary witness may also choose to have someone outside the Sexual Offense Prevention and Survivor's Advocacy Program serve as her/his representative. Choosing a representative from within the Antioch community is encouraged.

G. If the respondent chooses, she/he may have a representative at all hearings of the Hearing Board and/or through any appeals process. The respondent's advocate is to provide advocacy and emotional support for the respondent. When appropriate, if the respondent chooses, the respondent may select an advocate from the list maintained by the Dean of Student's office of administrators and tenured faculty who have agreed to serve in this role. This advocate may act as the respondent's representative at all hearings of the Hearing Board and/or through any appeals process.

The respondent may also choose to have someone outside this list serve as her/his representative. Choosing a representative from within the Antioch community is encouraged.

8. The Hearing Board and any appellate body which hears a case under this policy shall administer its proceedings according to these fundamental assumptions:

A. There will be no reference to the past consensual, non-violent sexual contact and/or conduct of either the primary witness or the respondent.

B. No physical evidence of a sexual offense is necessary to determine that one has occurred, nor is a visit to the hospital or the administration of a rape kit required. The primary witness shall be supported by the Advocate in whatever decisions she/he makes, and be informed of legal procedures regarding physical evidence.

C. The fact that a respondent was under the influence of drugs or alcohol or mental dysfunction at the time of the sexual offense will not excuse or justify the commission of any sexual offense as defined herein, and shall not be used as a defense.

9. This policy is intended to deal with sexual offenses which occurred in the Antioch community, and/or with an Antioch community member, on or after February 7, 1991. Sexual offenses which occurred prior to that date were still a violation of community standards, and should be addressed through the policies and governance structures which were in effect at the time of the offense.

The Hearing Board

1. The Hearing Board's duties are:

a) to hear all sides of the story;

b) to investigate as appropriate;

c) to determine if a violation of this policy has occurred;

d) to develop, in consultation with the Dean of Students and the Advocate, an appropriate remedy in cases where mandatory remedies are not prescribed in this policy;

e) to prepare a written report setting forth its findings which it distributes to the parties involved and the Dean of Students.

2. The Hearing Board will consist of three community representatives as voting members and the Dean of Students as an ex-officio member.

3. By the end of each Spring quarter, nine representatives will be chosen to form a Hearing Board pool to begin serving at the beginning of the next academic year (Fall quarter) for the duration of that academic year: three each from the categories of students, faculty, and administrators/staff members.

A. The nine members of the Hearing Board pool shall be appointed by ADCIL from the following recommended candidates:

1) Six students recommended by COMCIL;
2) Six faculty members recommended by the Dean of Faculty and FEC;
3) Six administrators/staff members who shall be recommended by the President of the College.

B. At least five members of the Hearing Board pool shall be women.

C. Three of the representatives shall be appointed by ADCIL to serve each quarter as a Hearing Board. One Hearing Board member must be from each of the three categories listed above, and at least one member must be a person of color.

For every case which is heard, at least one Hearing Board member must be the same sex as the primary witness, and at least one Hearing Board member must be the same sex as the respondent.

D. One member of the Hearing Board shall be designated by ADCIL to serve as Chair. The Chair shall preside for all Hearing Board meetings that quarter, and shall make the necessary physical arrangements to convene the Hearing Board (i.e., contact Hearing Board members, notify all parties involved of date, time, place, etc).

E. The six representatives who are not serving in a particular quarter shall be alternates in case an active member is not available or has a conflict of interest.

F. If an active member of the Hearing Board has a conflict of interest in the case, that member is responsible to report the conflict as soon as possible. ADCIL shall be responsible to determine if the conflict requires replacing the member, with an alternate chosen by ADCIL to immediately take

her/his place. If convening ADCIL for this purpose would serve to delay the Hearing Board process, then the President shall make a determination regarding conflict and, if necessary, appoint an alternate.

4. All members of the Hearing Board pool shall receive training by the Advocate and the College attorney regarding this policy and pertinent legal issues.

5. The Hearing Board is expected to follow the procedures outlined in Appendix D. Any procedures not covered in this policy, including Appendix D, shall be determined according to the discretion of the Hearing Board.

Remedies

1. When a policy violation by a student is found by the Hearing Board, the Hearing Board shall also determine a remedy which is commensurate with the offense, except in those cases where mandatory remedies are prescribed in this policy.

When a remedy is not prescribed, the Hearing Board shall determine the remedy in consultation with the Dean of Students and the Advocate, and shall include an educational and/or rehabilitation component as part of the remedy.

2. For Rape: In the event that the Hearing Board determines that the violation of rape has occurred, as defined under this policy, then the respondent must be expelled immediately.

3. For Sexual Assault: In the event that the Hearing Board determines that the violation of sexual assault has occurred, as defined under this policy, then the respondent must: a) be suspended immediately for a period of no less than six months; b) successfully complete a treatment program for sexual offenders approved by the Director of Counseling Services before returning to campus; and c) upon return to campus, be subject to mandatory class and co-op scheduling so that the respondent and primary witness avoid, to the greatest extent possible, all contact, unless the primary witness agrees otherwise.

In the event that the Hearing Board determines

that a second violation of sexual assault has occurred, with the same respondent, then the respondent must be expelled immediately.

4. For Sexual Imposition: In the event that the Hearing Board determines that the violation of sexual imposition has occurred, as defined under this policy, then the recommended remedy is that the respondent: a) be suspended immediately for a period of no less than three months; b) successfully complete a treatment program for sexual offenders approved by the Director of Counseling Services before returning to campus; and c) upon return to campus, be subject to mandatory class and co-op scheduling so that the respondent and primary witness avoid, to the greatest extent possible, all contact, unless the primary witness agrees otherwise.

In the event that the Hearing Board determines that a second violation of sexual imposition has occurred, with the same respondent, then the recommended remedy is that the respondent: a) be suspended immediately for a period of no less than six months; b) successfully complete a treatment program for sexual offenders approved by the Director of Counseling Services before returning to campus; and c) upon return to campus, be subject to mandatory class and co-op scheduling so that the respondent and primary witness avoid, to the greatest extent possible, all contact, unless the primary witness agrees otherwise.

In the event that the Hearing Board determines that a third violation of sexual imposition has occurred, with the same respondent, then the respondent must be expelled immediately.

5. For Insistent and/or Persistent Sexual Harassment: In the event that the Hearing Board determines that the violation of insistent and/or persistent sexual harassment has occurred, as defined under this policy, then the recommended remedy is that the respondent: a) be suspended immediately for a period of no less than six months; b) successfully complete a treatment program for sexual offenders approved by the Director of Counseling Services before returning to campus; and (c) upon return to campus, be subject to mandatory class and co-op scheduling so that the respondent and primary witness avoid, to the

greatest extent possible, all contact, unless the primary witness agrees otherwise.

In the event that the Hearing Board determines that a second violation of insistent and/or persistent sexual harassment has occurred, with the same respondent, then the respondent must be expelled immediately.

6. For Non-Disclosure of a Known Positive HIV Status: In the event that the Hearing Board determines that there has been non-disclosure of a known positive HIV status, as defined under this policy, then the recommended remedy is that the respondent be expelled immediately.

7. For Non-Disclosure of a Known Sexually Transmitted Disease: In the event that the Hearing Board determines that there has been non-disclosure of a known sexually transmitted disease, as defined under this policy, then the recommended remedy is that the respondent be suspended immediately for a period of no less than three months.

In the event that the Hearing Board determines that there has been a second failure to disclose one's known sexually transmitted disease, as defined under this policy, then the recommended remedy is that the respondent be suspended immediately for a period of no less than six months.

In the event that the Hearing Board determines that there has been a third failure to disclose one's known sexually transmitted disease, as defined under this policy, then the recommended remedy is that the respondent be expelled immediately.

8. In all cases, *a second offense* under this policy, regardless of category, must receive a more severe consequence than did the first offense if the second offense occurred after the Hearing Board's first finding of a respondent's violation of this policy.

9. The remedy for *a third offense* of this policy, regardless of category, must be expulsion, if the third offense occurred after the Hearing Board's first or second finding of a respondent's violation of this policy.

10. It is the responsibility of the Dean of Students to ensure that the Hearing Board's remedies are carried out.

The Appeals Process

1. In the event that the respondent or primary witness is not satisfied with the decision of the Hearing Board, then she/he shall have the right to appeal the Hearing Board's decision within seventy-two hours of receiving that decision.

2. In the event of an appeal, the College shall secure the services of a hearing review officer with experience in conducting arbitrations or administrative agency or other informal hearings. A hearing review officer, who is not a current member of the Antioch College community, shall be selected by ADCIL in consultation with the Advocate for the purpose of handling such appeals.

3. The hearing review officer shall review the record(s) and/or written report(s) of the Hearing, any briefs or other written materials supplied to her/him by any of the involved parties, and meet with any of the involved parties which she/he determines appropriate, to determine if there was fundamental fairness in the Hearing process.

The hearing review officer's analysis shall include a determination of whether the respondent was fully apprised of the charges against her/him; that the appealing party had a full and fair opportunity to tell her/his side of the story; and whether there was any malfeasance by the Hearing Board. The hearing review officer will present her/his finding and recommendation for action, if any, to the President of the College.

Confidentiality

1. All of the proceedings of the Hearing Board, and all testimony given, shall be kept confidential.

2. For the duration of the Hearing process and any appeals process, the primary witness, the respondent, and any witnesses coming forward shall have the right to determine when and if their names are publicly released. No one shall make a public release of a name not their own while the process is underway. Any public breach of confidentiality may constitute a violation of community standards and be presented to the Community Standards Board for debate.

A. The name of the primary witness shall not be considered public knowledge until such time that the primary witness releases her/his name publicly.

B. The name of the respondent shall not be considered public knowledge until such time that the respondent releases her/his name publicly, unless the respondent is found in violation of the policy, at which time the release of the respondent's name may be included with the release of the Hearing Board's findings. The name of the respondent will be released with the Hearing Board's findings if a violation is found and the remedy includes the suspension or expulsion of the respondent.

C. The names of any witnesses who testify to the Hearing Board shall not be released publicly until such time that each witness chooses to release her/his own name publicly.

3. In the event of an appeal, the appealing party (or the party considering the appeal) shall have the right to review any written and/or audio records of the hearing. Such review shall take place on the Antioch campus with a member of the Hearing Board present. No materials are to be duplicated by any party; no materials are to be removed from the Antioch campus except to be given to the hearing review officer or to the College attorneys.

4. All members of the Hearing Board, including any note-takers, are bound to keep the contents of the proceedings confidential.

5. All written and/or audio records of the process which are kept by the Hearing Board are to be turned over to the College Attorneys at the conclusion of the appeals process, and shall be stored in their offices, to be disposed of when and as they see fit.

Educational and Support Implementation Procedures

1. A minimum of one educational workshop about sexual offenses, consent, and the nature of sexual offenses as they pertain to this policy will be incorporated into each quarterly orientation program for new students. This workshop shall be conducted by the Advocate or by a person designated by the Advocate. Attendance shall be required of all students new to the Antioch community.

2. Workshops on sexual offense issues will also be offered during all study quarters. The content of these workshops shall be determined by the Advocate. Each student shall be required to attend at least one workshop each academic year for which she/he is on campus for one or more study quarters, effective Fall 1992. Attendance records shall be maintained, and given to the Registrar's office. This requirement must be completed for graduation [pending approval by the faculty].

a. It is recommended to the faculty that it develop a policy encouraging all faculty members to attend workshops on sexual offenses.

b. Further, it is recommended to the College and University administration that all employees working on the Antioch College campus be encouraged to attend workshops on sexual offenses.

3. A one-credit P.E. self-defense course with an emphasis on women's self-defense will be offered each quarter. This course should be open to all Antioch community members free of charge.

4. Permanent support groups for female and male survivors of sexual offenses will be established and maintained through Counseling Services and/or the Sexual Offense Prevention and Survivors' Advocacy Program.

5. A Peer Advocacy Program will be maintained that shall consist of both female and male community members, recruited and trained by the Advocate. The Peer Advocates shall provide information and emotional support for sexual offense victims/survivors and primary witnesses. The peer advocates shall work with the Advocate in educating the community about sexual offenses and sexual wellness.

6. A support network for students who are on Co-op will be maintained by the Advocate and the Sexual Offense Prevention and Survivors' Advocacy Program, with trained crisis contact people available.

Contemporary
Religious Discussions

THE PHILOSOPHY OF SEX AND LOVE involves critical thinking based on and constrained by a number of presuppositions, such as the belief that there is an external world, that some if not all events are causally connected, and that the rules of logic are appropriate guides for thinking. On the basis of such presuppositions we attempt to build a network of justified beliefs about matters pertaining to the human experience of sex and love.

Critical thinking takes place also within many religious communities where additional presuppositions are frequently affirmed to guide and constrain thinking. Such presuppositions frequently involve belief in the existence of a divine being or beings, belief in the existence and authority of divine revelation, and belief in the authority of sacred texts. Technological developments, changing social conditions, and the emergence of new lifestyles have forced many religious communities to rethink their traditional interpretations of sex and love. This rethinking has fomented major intellectual debates within a number of religious communities because changing traditional views about sex and love can involve the modification of a community's crucial sense of identity. And clearly significant changes in the shared identity of a community can threaten the survival of that community.

We have selected readings that illustrate the intellectual engagement that is currently taking place in four major religious communities. These are merely windows into the discussions. Space limitations prevent us from providing a comprehensive view of these debates. The first selection represents the debate within Islam, and involves some of the introductory comments prepared by Fatima Mernissi for the 1975 and 1987 editions of her book *Beyond the Veil: Male-Female Dynamics in Modern Muslim Society.* The second selection, "Homosexuality and The Rabbinate," is a series of three brief addresses given at the 100th Convention of the Central Conference of American Rabbis in June 1989. The third selection, "A Bonfire in Baltimore," published in the journal *Christianity and Crisis,* is a report describing the turmoil produced by a report on human sexuality presented to the 203rd General Assembly of the Presbyterian Church (U.S.A.) in June 1991. The report was hotly debated and rejected by the General Assembly. The fourth and final selection is taken from *Catechism of the Catholic Church* published in 1994 in which the Roman Catholic Church defines and clarifies its position on human sexuality for the contemporary scene.

We have here illustrations of the intellectual struggles being experienced by many Muslims, Jews, Protestants, and Catholics. An important question to ponder as you read these selections is whether these religious communities are likely to modify their traditional stances on sex and love. If they do, are their communities likely to be shattered and perhaps destroyed? If they don't, are their communities likely to be made up of people who are divided souls: on the one hand, affirming the traditional teachings of their religious leaders;

on the other hand, conducting their lives at odds with those teachings? If so, how long can humans endure such tension?

ISLAM

from Beyond the Veil

FATIMA MERNISSI

When Indiana University Press decided to publish a new edition of *Beyond the Veil*, the editor asked me to write a new introduction in which I would "identify the most important changes that have occurred in women's situation since 1975, when the first edition came out." I think that one of the major trends affecting women is the wave of fundamentalist conservatism. But if we are to assess correctly women's prospects and future in Muslim societies, we have to relinquish simplistic stereotypes that present fundamentalism as "an expression of regressive medieval archaisms," and read it on the contrary as a political statement about men undergoing bewildering, compelling changes affecting their economic and sexual identity—changes so profound and numerous that they trigger deep-seated, irrational fears.

The wonder about the Muslim world is that people still manage in these apocalyptic, revolutionary times to make sense out of absurd, despotic forces scavenging their lives, that they still have an unshakable belief in a powerful future. And this despite the near collapse (or maybe because of it!) of their centuries-old defense mechanisms.

To familiarize the reader with the present-day Muslim world and how women fit into the conflicting political forces (including religion), I guess the best way is not to overwhelm you with data. On the contrary, what is most needed is some kind of special illumination of the structural dissymmetry that runs all through and conditions the entire fabric of social and individual life—the split between acting and reflecting on one's actions. The split between what one does and how one speaks about oneself. The first has to do with the realm of reality; the second has to do with the realm of the psychological elaborations that sustain human beings' indispensable sense of identity. Individuals die of physical sickness, but societies die of loss of identity, that is, a disturbance in the guiding system of representations of oneself as fitting into a universe that is specifically ordered so as to make life meaningful. Why do we need our lives to make sense? Because that's where power is. A sense of identity is a sense that one's life is meaningful, that, as fragile as one may be, one can still have an impact on one's limited surroundings. The fundamentalist wave is a statement about identity. And that is why their call for the veil for women has to be looked at in the light of the painful but necessary and prodigious reshuffling of identity that Muslims are going through in these often confusing but always fascinating times.

The split in the Muslim individual between what one does, confronted by rapid, totally uncontrolled changes in daily life, and the discourse about an unchangeable religious tradition that one feels psychologically compelled to elaborate in order to keep a minimal sense of identity is, as far as I am concerned, the key point to focus on in order to understand the dynamics of Muslim life of the late seventies and the eighties.

The selection from Fatima Mernissi is taken from her book *Beyond the Veil: Male-Female Dynamics in Modern Muslim Society,* Revised Edition (Bloomington: Indiana University Press, 1987), pp. viii–xxx, 17–20. Used by permission of Indiana University Press.

The ideas that we entertain about ourselves as individuals or as members of national communities are not to be confused with our pragmatic behavior. The latter expresses our reality as acting entities, the former expresses us as reflecting entities. We all know how wide is the discrepancy between what we do and what we say to others (or worse, to ourselves) that we are doing. Reality and the representation of reality are always far apart. But the gap between the two reaches a breaking point when a society experiences a deep crisis in which individuals don't have enough time to formulate discourses to explain to themselves what they are doing.

Everyone is afraid of change, but Muslims are more so, because what is at stake are their fantasies about power. And women all over the world know very well how important power fantasies are to one's self-empowerment. The secret of Islam's sweeping resurgence today is that it gives men at birth an inherited right to claim world hegemony as a horizon and a guiding dream. It gives, of course, also many other, more constraining limits and hierarchies. But the ability of Islam to equip its members to see the entire universe as their playground is stunning to anyone who takes the time to go through the classical religious literature.

Fundamentalism suddenly becomes intelligible when one comes across an early imam's description of the concept of the mosque. The prophet Muhammad is the only prophet who identified the whole earth as a mosque: "The prophet said: 'The whole earth was made for me a mosque. Whenever time for prayer catches a purified man from my *umma*, there is his mosque.'"[1] You can pray anywhere, you can always situate yourself by reference to Mecca. Indonesians turn their face westward to Mecca, and we Moroccans face east to the same spot. Islam is, among other things, a set of psychological devices about self-empowerment and making oneself at home everywhere around the globe, in unfamiliar as well as familiar surroundings, without having to know the language or the culture. Its prodigious world expansion in the seventh century would not be understandable without taking into account its spatial component.

Islam today is expanding without missionaries. At the same time it is a rooting, a grounding device, and a way to order the world around you. It is a compass in a universe of ever expanding horizons, a guide for navigating terrestrial space and to prepare you to jump into unknown territories. Only if we understand this will we understand why youth by the millions are claiming it as their unshakable referent and forcing it on women, who obviously face different problems and who need to mirror themselves in different power fantasies.

If fundamentalists are calling for the return to the veil, it must be because women have been taking off the veil. We are definitely here in a situation where fundamentalist men and non-fundamentalist women have a conflict of interest. We have to identify who the fundamentalist men are, and who are the non-fundamentalist women who have opted to discard the veil. Class conflicts do sometimes express themselves in acute sex-focused dissent. And contemporary Islam is a good example of this, because, beyond the strong obsession with religion, the violent confrontations going on in the Muslim world are about two eminently materialistic pleasures: exercise of political power, and consumerism.

Fundamentalists and unveiled women are the two groups that have emerged with definite disturbing claims and aspirations in the postcolonial era. Both have the same age range—youth—and the same educational privilege—a recent access to formalized institutions of knowledge. But while the men seeking power through religion and its revivification are mostly from newly urbanized middle- and lower-middle-class backgrounds, unveiled women on the contrary are predominantly of the urban upper and middle class. . . .

Before these last few decades, women in our Muslim societies were not allowed a future. They only grew old. Between these two states of mind—growing old and designing a future—lies the most important challenge of human civilization as history, that is, time-bound events, condensed, recorded, and frozen in carefully selected writings destined for later consumption by coming generations. Man-written history is what constitutes our "national" or "cultural" heritage, in spite of the claim by the theocracies that it is of divine origin. We know that it is very difficult for a woman to design for herself a past. Ironically, any other task, including designing a future, seems more feasible, and definitely more rewarding. Writing the past is a highly coded and serious act, thought of, up to now, as an exclusively male endeavor, burden, and privilege.

But what Muslim women (and, of course, all others) are discovering, in this apocalyptically shifting and thrilling galaxy in which we live, is that stretching in the direction of the future is more operational than focusing on the past. And that is what I plan to do in this introduction: What is women's future in Muslim societies, as, of course, it can be discerned from today's crisis?

Are we all going back to the veil, back to the secluded house, back to the walled city, back to the national, proudly sealed, imaginary boundaries? Of course, that would be the dream of many Muslim men. But, without taking on the role of a psychic, I can predict that it is very unlikely. . . . the main event, according to me, is the politicization of Muslim women and the new perception they have gained of their problems.

Muslim women, illiterate and educated alike, are coming to diagnose and verbalize their problems—previously identified and labeled as being emotional—as being essentially political. A woman's anger and sorrow at being repudiated are no longer interpreted as being solely due to her incapacity to please her rejecting husband or because a vamp came along who dazzled him and took him away. Women are starting to wonder about the law: "I left my village and my family, where I had some security, to come with my husband to the city," explains a twenty-three-year-old slum dweller interviewed in *Le Maroc raconté par ses femmes.*[2] "But what guarantees do I have if my husband's love fades with age? Why does he have the right to repudiate me without my having done any wrong? The family no longer takes care of me, the state doesn't care about me at all. The only thing I have left is my husband and my children. The children will grow up and go away. And my husband can repudiate me and remarry. Why? Is that God's law? Never. He can't be so unjust."

This for me is the substance of the revolutionary process that is taking place in the Muslim world. It is a process not much talked about, because it does not have the spectacular aspects that attract media coverage. It does not have the theatrical dimension that accompanies our romantic images of revolution. Revolution is noisy, it means huge demonstrations with slogans and flags and blood and police repression—and, of course, the cameras and microphones of the national and international media right there on the spot.

In this introduction I am not going to try to impress readers by overwhelming them with facts, dates, and political events.[3] The media do that. I am trying to share with you some impressions and reflections that have been slowly maturing in my mind. I do this as someone who is a passionate and partisan observer-participant in Muslim society, as well as someone who is incorrigibly addicted to life-savoring and joy-seeking in that society. One thing which has become evident to me is that you have to be careful, when dealing with the Muslim world, not to confuse the symptom, that is, the event (the only dimension the media are interested in), with the diagnosis, that is, the specific combination of forces, tendencies, compromises, and alliances which produce it.

As a symptom, the call for the veil tells us one thing. Telling us another thing is the specific conjuncture of the forces calling for it, that is, the conservative forces and movements, their own quest, and how they position themselves within the social movements dominating the national and international scene.

As a woman and sometimes a sociologist, I have learned to give great importance to unspoken forces, unexpressed desires, suppressed dreams, unverbalized claims. I know as a woman, from my ordinary daily interaction as a professional or emotional person, that silence does not mean consent or surrender. I know that acts, what you do, do not express you and your desires totally. Every daily act we perform is embedded in an incredibly intricate network of pressures, constraints, necessary compromises. Nevertheless, in spite of all these obstacles and forces blocking our way to happiness, we still manage to have our say about our inner desire for self-fulfillment, self-nourishment, self-enhancement, and self-empowerment.

Every event, every act regarding women and how others, mostly politicians, react to them, has to be decoded and read on two distinct levels: what it expresses in its manifest meaning, and what it does not tell or tries to suppress from expression. Whence my proposal to approach the fundamentalist call for the veil, because that is one of the most salient events of the late seventies and the eighties, on two levels: its manifest significance, that is, its factual dimension; and its unspoken, latent dimension. But first let's go back to *Beyond the Veil* and find out if its key idea—space as an important component of sexuality (or, if you prefer, sexuality as a component of space)—has aged and lost its pertinence with time.

Women and the Sacred Threshold: Allah's Boundaries and Men's Obedience

Beyond the Veil is a book about sexual space boundaries. It tries to grasp sex as it materializes, as it melts into and with space and freezes it in an architecture. It started from a harmless question: Why can't I stroll peacefully in the alleys of the Medina that I like and enjoy so much? I came to wonder how Muslim society designs sexual space, how it projects into space a specific vision of female sexuality.

The book illustrates an important dimension of religion that is often ignored, since religion is usually confused with and reduced to spirituality: Islam is, among other things, an overwhelmingly materialistic vision of the world. Its field is not the heavens so much as terrestrial space and terrestrial power and access to all kinds of plain worldly pleasures, including wealth, sex, and power. That is the reason, I guess, why *Beyond the Veil,* in spite of dozens of other books treating the same topic of women and Islam, still makes sense to students and other readers. It does not treat Islam and women from a factual point of view, but rather it identifies one of the key components of the system—namely, the way Islam uses space as a device for sexual control.

Beyond the Veil does not seem to age, because it is not so much about facts as data as it is about an ageless problem: the way societies manage space to construct hierarchies and allot privileges. One can easily trace, through the concept of threshold, of boundaries, of limits, the hidden hierarchies determining the use of space, as well as the laws and mechanisms of control that underlie Islam as a sexual philosophy, as a vision of both virility and femininity as sacred architecture.

I did not understand why of all my books *Beyond the Veil* has been the most in demand for translations and reprints (French in 1983, British and Dutch in 1985, German and Urdu scheduled for 1987), until I realized that, in fact, I have been working on the same theme for the last decade— women and space, because it is a rather practical magnifying glass to use for looking at the system's functioning. The tentative title of my latest book is *Le Harem politique,* which means that I am still grappling with the same old topic: women and their space boundaries.

Islam is definitely one of the modern political forces competing for power around the globe. At least that is how many of us experience it. How can a "medieval religion," ask Western students raised in a secular culture, be so alive, so challenging to the effects of time, so renewable in energy? How can it be meaningful to educated youth? We'll soon see that one of the characteristics of fundamentalism is the attraction Islam has for high achievers among young people today. In Cairo, Lahore, Jakarta, and Casablanca, Islam makes sense because it speaks about power and self-empowerment. As a matter of fact, worldly self-enhancement is so important for Islam that the meaning of spirituality itself has to be seriously reconsidered. But what was not clear for me in the early seventies was that all the problems Muslims were to be faced with in recent decades are more or less boundary problems, from colonization (trespassing by a foreign power on Muslim community space and decision making) to contemporary human rights issues (the political boundaries circumscribing the ruler's space and the freedoms of the governed). The issue of technology is a boundary problem: how can we integrate Western technological information, the recent Western scientific memory, without flooding our own Muslim heritage? International economic dependency is, of course, eminently a problem of boundaries: the International Monetary Fund's intervention in fixing the price of our bread does not help us keep a sense of a distinct national identity. What are the boundaries of the sovereignty of the Muslim state vis-à-vis voracious, aggressive transnational corporations? These are some of the components of the crisis that is tearing the Muslim world apart, along, of course, definite class lines.

Naive and serious as only a dutiful student can be, I did not know in 1975 that women's claims were disturbing to Muslim societies not because they threatened the past but because they augured and symbolized what the future and its conflicts are about: the inescapability of renegotiating new sexual, political, economic, and cultural boundaries, thresholds, and limits. Invasion of physical territory by alien inimical nations (the invasions of Afghanistan and Lebanon); invasion of national television by "Dallas" and "Dynasty"; invasion of children's desires by Coca-Cola and special brands of walking shoes, etc., are some of the political and cultural boundary problems facing the Muslim world today.

However, we have to remember that societies do not reject and resist changes indiscriminately. Muslim societies integrated and digested quite well technological innovations: the engine, electricity, the telephone, the transistor, sophisticated machinery and arms, all this without much resistance. But the social fabric seems to have trouble absorbing anything having to do with changing authority thresholds: freely competing unveiled women; freely competing political parties; freely elected parliaments; and, of course, freely elected heads of state who do not necessarily get 99 percent of the votes. Whenever an innovation has to do with free choice of the partners involved, the social fabric seems to suffer some terrible tear. Women's unveiling seems to belong to this realm. For the last one hundred years, whenever women tried or wanted to discard the veil, some men, always holding up the sacred as a justification, screamed that it was unbearable, that the society's fabric would dissolve if the mask is dropped. I do not believe that men, Muslims or not, scream unless they are hurt. Therefore, the ones calling for the reimposition of the veil surely have a reason and a good one. What is it that Muslim society needs to mask so badly?

Anatomy of a Fundamentalist

How do you picture a fundamentalist? If one did a survey by asking this one question of average Americans, I suppose the answers would all reflect the single image that the mighty, all-knowing, all-observing, quasi-divine American media give of the Muslim fundamentalist. And that would be of an unscrupulous, uneducated, uncultured, archaic, bloodthirsty, woman-hating, economically deprived, politically frustrated (of course, inevitably Muslim) terrorist, loaded with guns and bombs. And strangely enough, this monstrous creature has eyes fixed on one single enemy target: America and its lovely peace-loving, democratic, scientifically minded, highly ethical, spontaneously moral, prosperous citizens.

Well, the Americans who would have given that answer to the imaginary questionnaire would have been wrong on at least four key characteristics of the fundamentalist: he is neither uneducated, nor unscrupulous, nor primarily anti-American, nor necessarily antiwoman. And certainly he is not archaic; he is the product of two extremely modern phenomena: rapid urbanization and state-funded (therefore democratic) mass education.

The fundamentalist is neither uneducated nor uncultured. He is, on the contrary, a well-educated and particularly brilliant high achiever. . . .

Not only [are] Islamic militants . . . nice boys, their fathers are just like yours and mine—decent, educated citizens. They are men (with wives, who are the unknown element of the equation; who are the mothers? no information available on that yet!) who strive to raise good, honest families who can smoothly reproduce the system. . . .

The idea one often hears about fundamentalism is that it is an archaic phenomenon, a desire to return to medieval thinking. It is frequently presented as a revivalist movement: bring back the past. And the call for the veil for women furthers slipping into this kind of misleading simplification. If we take the Egyptian town of Asyut as an example, we have to admit that it is a modern town with a totally new cultural feature that Muslim society never knew before: mass access to knowledge. In our history, universities and knowledge were privileges of the elite. The man of knowledge enjoyed a high respect precisely because he was a repository of highly valued and aristocratically gained information. Acquisition of knowledge took years, and often included a period of initiation that compelled the student to roam through Muslim capitals from Asia to Spain for decades. Mass access to universities, therefore, constitutes a total shift in the accumulation, distribution, management, and utilization of knowledge and information. And of course we know that knowledge is power. One of the reasons the fundamentalist will be preoccupied by women is that state universities are not open just for traditionally marginalized and deprived male rural migrants, but for women as well.

Women's Access to Universities: State-Funded Education as a Blurring of Class and Sex Privileges

The fundamentalist is not so much unscrupulous as self-centered. Women become an issue with him because they interfere in his newly acquired modern identity as an educated person who has the qualifications required to make a person fit to run the world. As the class-background analysis has shown, fundamentalists are primarily the manifestation of the structural social democratization of Muslim society. . . .

While a few decades ago the majority of women married before the age of twenty, today only 22.0 percent of that age group in Egypt and 38.4 percent in Iran are married.[4] To get an idea of how perturbing it is for Iranian society to deal with an army of unmarried adolescents one has only to remember that the legal age for marriage for females in Iran is thirteen and for males fifteen.[5] The idea of an adolescent unmarried woman is a completely new idea in the Muslim world, where previously you had only a female child and a menstruating woman who had to be married off immediately so as to prevent dishonorable engagement in premarital sex. The whole concept of patriarchal honor was built around the idea of virginity, which reduced a woman's role to its sexual dimension: to reproduction within early marriage. The concept of an adolescent woman, menstruating and unmarried, is so alien to the entire Muslim family system that it is either unimaginable or necessarily linked with *fitna* (social disorder). And the Arab countries are a good example of this demographic revolution in sex roles.

Young men, faced with job insecurity or failure of the diploma to guarantee access to the desired job, postpone marriage. Women, faced with the pragmatic necessity to count on themselves instead of relying on the dream of a rich husband,

see themselves forced to concentrate on getting an education. The average age at marriage for women and men in most Arab countries has registered a spectacular increase. . . .

Is this rise in the age of both men and women at marriage due to education or to other factors? The *World Fertility Survey* report on Egypt, like many others, shows that there is "a definite positive relationship between level of education and age at first marriage. It may be inferred that increasing education opportunities for young Egyptian women are largely responsible for the recent decline in early marriage and the upward trend in age at marriage, particularly in urban areas."[6]

Education for women in the West did not have such a rapid and revolutionary impact. For decades women in America and Europe had access to education but still conformed to traditional roles. Betty Friedan's *The Feminine Mystique* is an eloquent statement about that. Therefore, to understand the fanatic rejection of women's liberation in the Muslim world, one has to take into account the time factor. Most of us educated women have illiterate mothers. Access to education seems to have an immediate, tremendous impact on women's perception of themselves, their reproductive and sexual roles, and their social mobility expectations. . . .

The main thing to remember is that women's education disturbs the traditional sexual identity reference points and sex roles in Muslim countries, which are obsessed with virginity and childbearing. The way these countries tried to prevent premarital sex was by segregating the sexes and institutionalizing early marriage. Early marriage limited women's life and expectations, regardless of class, to fantasizing about acquiring a rich husband and about childbearing. Both processes took place in a female hysterical atmosphere of magic and superstitious rituals. The hysteria of a search for a husband and for begetting sons is more than ever present today, precisely because men marry late. It shows itself in the thriving business of psychics and sorcery in many Muslim capitals, as well as in the continuation of marriage and fertility cults. . . .

The conservative wave against women in the Muslim world, far from being a regressive trend, is on the contrary a defense mechanism against profound changes in both sex roles and the touchy subject of sexual identity. The most accurate interpretation of this relapse into "archaic behaviors," such as conservatism on the part of men and resort to magic and superstitious rituals on the part of women, is as anxiety-reducing mechanisms in a world of shifting, volatile sexual identity.

Fundamentalists are right in saying that education for women has destroyed the traditional boundaries and definitions of space and sex roles. Schooling has dissolved traditional arrangements of space segregation even in oil-rich countries where education is segregated by sex, simply because, to go to school, women have to cross the street! Streets are spaces of sin and temptation, because they are both public and sex-mixed. And that is the definition of *fitna*, disorder! Fundamentalists are right when they talk about the dissolution of women's traditional function as defined by family ethics; postponed age of marriage forces women to turn pragmatically toward education as a means for self-enhancement. And if one looks at some of the education statistics, one understands why newly urbanized and educated rural youth single out university women as enemies of Islam and its tradition of women's exclusion from knowledge and decision making. . . .

What dismays the fundamentalists is that the era of independence did not create an all-male new class. Women are taking part in the public feast. And that is a definite revolution in the Islamic concept of both the state's traditional relation to women and women's relation to the institutionalized distribution of knowledge.

. . .

The Need to Be Muslim

In the seventh century, Muhammad created the concept of the *umma*, or "community of believers." There was nothing familiar about this in the minds of his contemporaries, deeply rooted in their tribal allegiances. He had to transfer the believers' allegiance from the tribe, a biological group with strong totemic overtones, to the *umma*, a sophisticated ideological group based on religious belief.[7] Islam transformed a group of individuals into a community of believers. This community is defined by characteristics that determine the relations of the individuals within the *umma* both with each other and with non-believers:

"In its internal aspect the *umma* consists of the totality of individuals bound to one another by ties, not of kinship or race, but of religion, in that all its members profess their belief in the one God, Allah, and in the mission of his prophet, Muhammad. Before God and in relation to Him, all are equal without distinction of race . . . In its external aspect, the *umma* is sharply differentiated from all other social organizations. Its duty is to bear witness to Allah in the relations of its members to one another and with all mankind. They form a single indivisible organization, charged to uphold the true faith, to instruct men in the ways of God, to persuade them to the good and to dissuade them from evil by *word and deed*."[8]

One of the devices the Prophet used to implement the *umma* was the creation of the institutions of the Muslim family, which was quite unlike any existing sexual unions.[9] Its distinguishing feature was its strictly defined monolithic structure.

Because of the novelty of the family structure in Muhammad's revolutionary social order, he had to codify its regulations in detail. Sex is one of the instincts whose satisfaction was regulated at length by religious law during the first years of Islam. The link in the Muslim mind between sexuality and the *shari'a* has shaped the legal and ideological history of the Muslim family structure[10] and consequently of relations between the sexes. One of the most enduring characteristics of this history is that the family structure is assumed to be unchangeable, for it is considered divine.

Controversy has raged throughout this century between traditionalists who claim that Islam prohibits any change in sex roles, and modernists who claim that Islam allows for the liberation of women, the desegregation of society, and equality between the sexes. But both factions agree on one thing: Islam should remain the sacred basis of society. In this book I want to demonstrate that there is a fundamental contradiction between Islam as interpreted in official policy and equality between the sexes. Sexual equality violates Islam's premiss, actualized in its laws, that heterosexual love is dangerous to Allah's order. Muslim marriage is based on male dominance. The desegregation of the sexes violates Islam's ideology on women's position in the social order: that women should be under the authority of fathers, brothers, or husbands. Since women are considered by Allah to be a destructive element, they are to be spatially confined and excluded from matters other than those of the family. Female access to non-domestic space is put under the control of males.

Paradoxically, and contrary to what is commonly assumed, Islam does not advance the thesis of women's inherent inferiority. Quite the contrary, it affirms the potential equality between the sexes. The existing inequality does not rest on an ideological or biological theory of women's inferiority, but is the outcome of specific social institutions designed to restrain her power: namely, segregation and legal subordination in the family structure. Nor have these institutions generated a systematic and convincing ideology of women's inferiority. Indeed, it was not difficult for the male-initiated and male-led feminist movement to affirm the need for women's emancipation, since traditional Islam recognizes equality of potential. The democratic glorification of the human individual, regardless of sex, race, or status, is the kernel of the Muslim message.

In Western culture, sexual inequality is based on belief in women's biological inferiority. This explains some aspects of Western women's liberation movements, such as that they are almost always led by women, that their effect is often very superficial, and that they have not yet succeeded in significantly changing the male-female dynamics in that culture. In Islam there is no such belief in female inferiority. On the contrary, the whole system is based on the assumption that women are powerful and dangerous beings. All sexual institutions (polygamy, repudiation, sexual segregation, etc.) can be perceived as a strategy for containing their power.

This belief in women's potence is likely to give the evolution of the relationship between men and women in Muslim settings a pattern entirely different from the Western one. For example, if there are any changes in the sex status and relations, they will tend to be more radical than in the West and will necessarily generate more tension, more conflict, more anxiety, and more aggression. While the women's liberation movement in the West focuses on women and their claim for equality with men, in Muslim countries it would tend to focus on the mode of relatedness between the sexes and thus would probably be led by men and women alike. Because men can see how the oppression of women works against men, women's liberation would assume the character of a generational rather than sexual conflict. This could already be seen in the opposition between young nationalists and old traditionalists at the beginning of the century, and currently it can be seen in the conflict between parents and children over the dying institution of arranged marriage.

At stake in Muslim society is not the emancipation of women (if that means only equality with men), but the fate of the heterosexual unit. Men and women were and still are socialized to perceive each other as enemies. The desegregation of social life makes them realize that besides sex, they can also give each other friendship and love. Muslim ideology, which views men and women as enemies, tries to separate the two, and empowers men with institutionalized means to oppress women. But whereas fifty years ago there was coherence between Muslim ideology and Muslim reality as embodied in the family system, now there is a wide discrepancy between that ideology and the reality that it pretends to explain. This book explores many aspects of that discrepancy and describes the *sui generis* character of male-female dynamics in Morocco, one of the most striking mixtures of modernity and Muslim tradition.

Notes

1. al-Nisa'i, *Al Sunan*, "The Book of the Mosque," Vol. 2 (Cairo: Al-Matba'a al-Misriya, al-Azhar, n.d.), p. 26.

2. Fatima Mernissi, *Le Maroc raconté par ses femmes* (Rabat: Société Marocaine des Editeurs Réunis, 1984); English translation, London: The Women's Press, forthcoming.

3. For the specific data included in *Beyond the Veil*, I updated the statistics in 1983 for the French edition, *Sexe, idéologie, islam* (Paris: Tierce, 1983), and these have been included in this edition.

4. "People's Wallchart," *People's Magazine*, vol. 12 (1985).

5. Ibid.

6. *World Fertility Survey*, No. 42, "The Egyptian Survey," November 1983.

7. Montgomery Watt, *Muhammad at Medina,* Oxford 1956, p. 239.

8. H. A. R. Gibb, "Constitutional Organization" in *Origin and Development of Islamic Law,* ed. M. Khaduri and H. J. Liebesny, Vol. I, Washington, D.C. 1955, p. 3.

9. Gertrude Stern, *Marriage in Early Islam,* London 1931, p. 71.

10. Joseph Schacht, *An Introduction to Islamic Law,* London 1964, p. 161.

JUDAISM: HOMOSEXUALITY AND THE RABBINATE

from Introduction

SELIG SALKOWITZ

Some weeks ago I was discussing this presentation with a rabbinic friend, and I was telling him about the process that the Committee on Homosexuality and the Rabbinate had gone through. It was often a painful process during these past three years. I told him of the many draft resolutions we had attempted, and of the one we presented to the CCAR Executive Board last year—one which, at first, had the unanimous agreement of the committee, and then, on second consideration, parts of which were found unacceptable by a number of our members. After lengthy discussion it was sent back to committee by the Executive Board. The Executive Board was appreciative of the committee's attempts, but determined that the report presented more problems than solutions.

My friend reminded me of a story—supposedly true—about Thomas A. Edison and his attempts to invent the storage battery. Edison, we are told, went through more than 50,000 experiments before he produced a functional storage battery. He was asked how he had overcome those thousands of failures and found the courage and will to continue. He replied that he did not consider all those unsuccessful attempts failures, but rather successes. "Each one taught me," he is reported as saying, "what *didn't* work, and I proceeded from there."

I believe that this is a thoughtful description of the work of our committee over these past three years. In my cover letter which you received with the background papers prepared by four of our colleagues at the invitation of the committee (papers that are scholarly and thought-encouraging), I described some of the process that the committee had gone through—from its initial creation in response to a resolution submitted by two of our colleagues, through the unanimous decision that a resolution and vote was *not* the solution to the task presented to us, and finally to a process of study and consciousness raising.

That decision was reached after we had studied the many disciplines relating to our subject. We read in the fields of medicine, psychology, law, and biology. We considered current policy decisions by Jewish and Christian groups. We reviewed traditional and contemporary Jewish scholarship and interpretation.

The initial process of argument and defense developed into mutual understanding and respect for differing approaches and conclusions and for the sincerity of those who hold them. But no unanimity or even overwhelming consensus could be attained.

Permit me to share with you the significant areas of unresolvable disagreement among the committee members. These will help you to understand our considered judgment that this is not a time for parliamentary resolutions but for sensitive and considered study. It is a time for discus-

This and the following two selections are taken from *Homosexuality and the Rabbinate: Papers Delivered at the 100th Convention of the Central Conference of American Rabbis,* June 1989. Used by permission of the Central Conference of American Rabbis.

sion of the sources and their implications for the Reform movement as a Jewish religious community in the United States, and for its influence on Reform Jewry.

A primary area of disagreement is the *nature* of homosexuality. Is it a genetic condition over which the individual has no control, or is it a learned expression of sexuality and therefore a matter of personal choice? The literature, other than the traditional Jewish sources, is divided. Scholarship and integrity demand our awareness to this fact. Selective quotations can support either position, but that is not helpful in attempting to arrive at an objective conclusion. Some see homosexuality and heterosexuality as equal alternative life styles; others hold that heterosexuality is the ideal and homosexuality is not.

A second area of unresolved disagreement concerned the manner in which to interpret the halachic material available to us. Some hold that over time the Halacha has been accepted and rejected, modified, loosely and strictly interpreted by Reform scholars and this Conference, and therefore should not be a significant resource in our deliberations and decisions. Others hold that our interpretation of Halacha has indeed been modified—it has been both loosely and strictly understood—but that was in matters in which there were disagreeing positions held by different rabbinic sources and authorities. In our case there is *no* disagreement in the rabbinic positions anywhere in the tradition. Therefore, it is argued, the weight of tradition is stronger and needs to be considered in that context.

A third, very painful, area of disagreement was the *effect* a resolution could have on our gay and lesbian colleagues. A supportive resolution might encourage colleagues who have concealed their homosexuality to express it more openly, relying on the support of the Conference.

Committee members argued that the freedom of homosexuals to express themselves and their sexuality as openly as heterosexual colleagues would ease the pain of isolation and secretive love relationships, and the fear of discovery. Others held that our Conference—no matter how supportive a resolution it passed—could not ensure the positive response of congregation and community and the certainty that positions would not

be lost and careers endangered. Others held that such a position was paternalistic and inappropriate. Still others maintained that such a concern was appropriate and collegial.

There was further discussion of the effect of *any* statement on congregational selection committees. Would it have them asking questions they do not now ask? What would be the effect on those choosing not to discuss their sexual lives? What might it do to the entire interviewing process?

Perhaps you can now appreciate better the difficult and necessary wrestling that went on within the committee.

A position on homosexuality would need to address the matter of the sanctity of homosexual marriages. Some argued that such a relationship could not be considered *kiddushin,* while others held that there was no reason it could not be. We could not even seek the asylum of civil law, since civil law does not address itself to the sanctity of marriage, only its legality. To the best of our knowledge, no state legalizes homosexual marriages. If rabbis officiate at them as religious ceremonies, would this be in conflict with the law?

We struggled with the question of the reaction of *Kelal Yisrael*—what would the effects be? How would *amcha*—the Reform community—respond? Would a supportive resolution be seen as a further wedge between Reform and non-Reform Judaism? Again, some held that this should not be an issue. Others maintained that we should be concerned about the total Jewish community and not become a schism outside the mainstream of American Jewry. The effect on MaRaM and the Israeli Reform community were similarly debated.

Good colleagues, after three years of arduous, intensive, and sincere study and debate, your committee recognizes that what is needed is *not* a resolution which at best would be a pyrrhic victory to whatever group might narrowly achieve a parliamentary majority. We would serve ourselves, our movement, and the Jewish community best by entering into, and encouraging among our congregational bodies, programs of study and heightened awareness of the available sources, resources, and disciplines. Some congregations have begun the process with positive results. It should be our goal to seek understanding, not coercion; reason, not emotion; unity within diversity.

To begin the implementation of this process, this morning you will hear two presentations. Each speaker has been asked to address two questions: (1) Since Judaism teaches, and Reform Judaism has affirmed, that monogamous heterosexual marriage is the ideal relationship for sanctification and sexual expression, is it Judaically possible to grant spiritual value to monogamous homosexual relationships? (2) How do you react to the claim that sexual orientation is not chosen; and how does your conclusion affect your position on question one?

We know each speaker will interpret them from differing approaches to tradition. That is the purpose. We will then adjourn into smaller groups to discuss the general theses and to consider some real scenarios which will require your thought and your willingness to respond to them in your rabbinate. Recorders will take notes of the points raised. The committee plans to meet following this convention and before the Seattle convention and to take your responses into account. It is hoped that together with the other institutions of Reform Judaism we will develop a program of education

in its broadest sense which will elicit your support and cooperation.

Our speakers are Yoel H. Kahn, Rabbi of Shaar Zahav Congregation in San Francisco, and Leonard S. Kravitz, Professor of Midrash and Homiletics at the New York School of our seminary.

May I be permitted two personal comments. First, I sincerely hope that the process suggested by the committee will be encouraged and implemented. I hope that the members of our Conference will allow adequate time for the process to develop and that no resolutions be presented for a few years. I believe that members of the Conference need, as the committee needed, time for thought, introspection, and interaction in CCAR *Kallot,* UAHC regional meetings, and congregational programs. Second, I publicly thank and praise the members of our committee. You have worked diligently, thoughtfully, and unsparingly on a sensitive and provocative subject. You have been open, considerate, and accepting during the give and take of the discussion. You have supported and encouraged me, and joined together to reach this day.

from The *Kedusha* of Homosexual Relationships _____

Yoel H. Kahn

I am deeply honored by this opportunity to address our Conference and am appreciative of the special efforts some of you made in order to be here this morning. Today is a most appropriate date for our consideration of Judaism and homosexuality. This convention commemorates the 100th anniversary of the founding of our Conference. This year—in fact, yesterday—also marked the 20th anniversary of the modern gay and lesbian liberation movement in this country. Tens and hundreds of thousands marched in cities throughout the country in Freedom Day parades. The congregation I serve, and other members of the World Congress of Gay and Lesbian Jewish Organizations, observed this weekend as Shabbat Freedom.

My linkage of these two anniversaries may seem inappropriate. But the proximity of their observance can remind us of the common heritage of liberal Judaism and the contemporary struggle for

gay and lesbian rights. The pioneering Jewish model of a minority battling for—and securing—civil rights, and then going on to full social and political integration as a distinct community within the general culture has been an inspiration to many others. Today, gay and lesbian people seek recognition of their humanity and equality, in both the civic and religious realms. To that end, in 1983 the CCAR Committee on Justice and Peace called for our "individual and collective involvement in achieving political, social and religious freedom [for all], regardless of sexual orientation."[1] As we consider the pleas of the gay and lesbian Jews among us, let us remember those of the Jewish people as a whole in years gone by.[2]

The status of the homosexual in the Jewish community in general, and the rabbinate in particular, is the topic of my paper which you have already received.[3] I will limit my remarks this morning, at the request of our committee's chair, to what is essentially a prior question: Can we affirm the place of the homosexual Jew in the synagogue and among the Jewish people? Specifically, if the goal of Jewish life is to live in *kedusha,* can we sanctify and bless homosexual relationships without compromising the integrity of our tradition? If we wish to bless these relationships, can we reconcile this new stand with the historical Jewish teaching in favor of heterosexual, procreative marriage as the normative and ideal form of Jewish family life? This morning, we will examine this question in relation to God, Torah, and Israel.

God

I begin with the most fundamental, yet unanswerable, question: What does God want of us? As a liberal Jew, I am usually reluctant to assert that I know precisely what "God wants." For me to begin by stating that "God calls us to affirm the sanctity of homosexual relationships" (a statement I believe to be true) would be to assert a privileged claim as little open to dispute as the counterassertion by Rabbi David Bleich that these relationships today remain "*to-eiva.*"[4] How would one respond to such an argument?

Thus, although our assertion of what God wants properly begins our debate, in fact it cannot. Our conclusions about God's expectations of us in a particular matter develop against the background of our unfolding, wider understanding of what God summons us to do—rooted in what we know about God and God's nature. In the foreground is all that we have learned from the scientific disciplines, from universal ethics, from Jewish tradition, and from our own prayerful conscience. It is when they touch, where the background of what we have already learned of God's expectations of us and God's nature meets foreground of knowledge, prayer, and conscientious reflection about a subject that we may discern God's will.

My teacher Eugene Borowitz writes that he does not hear a clear message from God about homosexuality, as he has in other areas.[5] I differ with Rabbi Borowitz. I believe that we can hear and affirm what God expects of us in this matter. My understanding of what God wants emerges from the background of God's justice and compassion, and

is shaped in the foreground by religious interpretation of the insights of modern science. It is this foreground that has changed in recent years and leads me to dissent from the teachings of our received tradition.

The overwhelming consensus of modern science—in every discipline—is that homosexual relations are as "natural" to us as heterosexuality is. Now, to call something "natural" is a descriptive act; what occurs in nature is not inherently good or bad. Assigning of meaning is a religious act. I, along with many others, have come to recognize sexual orientation as a primary, deep part of the human personality, inseparably bound up with the self. Science does not know what creates homosexual attraction in some people, heterosexual attraction in others; yet today we recognize that some people can only be fulfilled in relationships with people of the same sex. What do we say to them? What does God expect of them and of us?

I do not believe that God creates in vain. Deep, heartfelt yearning for companionship and intimacy is not an abomination before God. God does not want us to send the gays and lesbians among us into exile—either cut off from the Jewish community or into internal exile, living a lie for a lifetime. I believe that the time has come; I believe that God summons us to affirm the proper and rightful place of the homosexual Jew—and her or his family—in the synagogue and among the Jewish people.

I cannot prove my claim that homosexuality and the homosexual are an organic part of the divine plan unfolding in nature. I am making a religious faith statement that, like all such statements, requires a leap of faith before its assent, but one that is not inconsistent with all that we have learned of the meaning of faith in Judaism. My leap of faith, though, begins on solid ground.[6] The premises on which it rests meet the scientific criteria for a probable hypothesis of most simply and elegantly explaining the facts; and it is consistent with what we learn from our extra-Judaic sources of scientific knowledge. These are the publicly verifiable warrants for my private religious intuition: God does not create in vain. And if God does not create in vain but with purpose, we thwart God's purpose when we turn away from the homosexual Jews who turn to us. I believe, therefore, that God does not want us to discriminate against homosexuals; that lesbian and gay people are created and live *betselem Elohim*. And I do believe that homosexual relationships contribute to, and do not diminish, God's *kedusha*. Our responsibility as Jews is to find a route to the expression of full covenantal fulfillment and responsibility for the homosexual Jew.

The Jew meets God in Torah, and it is to a consideration of *kedusha* in the light of Torah that we now turn.

Torah

When we confront the text honestly, we face a twofold challenge: first, we must dissent from an explicit biblical injunction that has been in force until modern times. Now, dissenting from Leviticus has not been an obstacle for us before; Reform Judaism has long abandoned the biblical and rabbinic proscriptions in the area of ritual purity in marriage.[7] Robert Kirschner, in his paper which you received, argues convincingly that the biblical and rabbinic injunctions forbidding male homosexual acts are no longer applicable to the situation of homosexuals today.[8] It is important for us to realize that the biblical authors proscribed particular sexual acts, the motivation for which they could only understand as sinful.

We begin from an entirely different perspective than our ancestors did. If we grant that homosexual acts are not inherently sinful, then can a homosexual relationship be sanctified? When two Jews, graduates of our schools, alumni of our camps and youth movements, members of our synagogues, promise to establish a Jewish home, pledge to live together in faithfulness and integrity, and ask for God's blessing and our own on their union, is this *toeiva* or is it *kedusha*?

Do we look at this committed and loving couple from an I-It perspective, which sees a particular act and condemns it, or with I-Thou understanding, which affirms the propriety of sexual intimacy in the context of holistic and enduring relationship? Let me be clear: I do not propose merely that we politely overlook the historical Jewish teaching condemning homosexual behavior, but that we explicitly affirm its opposite: the movement from *toeiva* to *kedusha*. This transfor-

mation in our Jewish standard, from a specific act to the evaluation of the context in which acts occur, seems to me entirely consistent with Reform Jewish thought and practice.

Many are prepared to affirm that for some Jews, homosexuality is the proper expression of the human need for intimacy and fulfillment. Still, I know that some are reluctant to endorse *kiddushin* for same sex couples because these relationships apparently disregard the historical and continuing Jewish preference for what Eugene Borowitz and others have called "the procreative family."[9] How can we grant Jewish sanctity, they ask, to a form of family which by its essence precludes procreation, a primary purpose of *kiddushin*?

My reply has three parts. First, we cannot hold homosexual families to a higher standard than we do heterosexual ones. We do not require proof of fertility or even an intention to become parents before we are willing to marry a heterosexual couple. Is the homosexual couple who uses adoption, artificial insemination, or other means to fulfill the Jewish responsibility to parent so different from the heterosexual family who does the same?

Second, does *kiddushin* require procreation? While Judaism has always had a preference for procreative marriage, our tradition has also validated the possibility that some unions will not produce children. Halacha states that a woman who does not bear children after ten years can be divorced by her husband.[10] But the evidence that this law was reluctantly or negligibly enforced is precisely the type of historical example Reform responsa often cite to support the explicit expansion of a value we find implicit in our historical tradition. The Jewish tradition has never insisted that the sole purpose of sexual expression is procreation, as evidenced by the numerous rabbinic discussions on the mitzvah of sexual intimacy and pleasure.[11]

Third, the situation of the gay and lesbian Jews among us points out the need for new categories in our thinking. Reform Judaism is committed to affirming the responsibility of the individual. Can we not teach that a heterosexual relationship is the proper form of *kedusha* for many and a homosexual relationship may be a proper form for others? Can we not create a plurality of expressions of covenantal responsibility and fulfillment, and teach that different Jews will properly fulfill their Jewish communal and religious responsibilities in different ways?[12]

Finally, I would like to introduce into this discussion of Torah a text different from those that have shaped our debate so far. Mine is a classic Jewish text, the record of a uniquely Jewish form of revelation—the text of our history. The history of our people, writ large, has been a continuing source of revelation. For our own generation, the recollection of events that we witnessed has assumed the force of Torah, and makes demands upon us as a people and as individual Jews. But our history is not only writ large; history is also written in the small, daily events of our lives. I come then today bearing not only the scrolls of our sacred texts, halachic and aggadic, but also another scroll—the scroll of our people's history. And it, too, makes claims upon me.

When I arrived to assume my pulpit in San Francisco four years ago, deep down I still believed that gay and lesbian relationships and families were, somehow, not as real, not as stable, not as committed as heterosexual marriages. I could tell many stories of what I have learned since. There are the two women who have lived together for many years without familial or communal support, who have endured long distances and job transfers because employers thought them both single, and admitting their homosexuality would have endangered their livelihoods; women who have cared for each other without benefit of insurance coverage or health benefits or any legal protection. They came to me one Friday night and simply asked: "Rabbi, this is our 25th anniversary, will you say a blessing?"

Mine is a synagogue living with AIDS. I have been humbled by the unquestioning devotion of the man who, for more than two years, went to work each morning, calling intermittently throughout the day to check in on his partner, and spent each night comforting, talking, preparing meals, and waking in the middle of the night to carry his loved one to the bathroom. Who would have imagined, when they first chatted 12 years earlier, that their life together would take this path? The loving caregiver stayed at his partner's side throughout the period of his illness and until his death.

These many lives have taught me about the possibility of enduring loyalty, the meaning of commitment, and the discovery of reservoirs of strength in the face of unimaginable pain and suffering. If the Covenant people are summoned to be God-like, then these Jews live their lives *betselem Elohim* and these relationships are surely of true covenantal worth. *Kiddushin* is, in Eugene Borowitz's words, "Judaism's preferred condition in which to work out one's destiny. . . . Because it is a unique fusion of love and demand, of understanding and judgment, of personal giving and receiving, nothing else can teach us so well the meaning of covenant." If "[i]t is the situation where we are most thoroughly challenged to be a Jew and where . . . we may personally exemplify what it means to be allied with God in holiness," then the Torah scroll of lived history records the *kedusha* of these relationships.[13]

Israel

I would like to conclude with a word about *kiddushin* and the Jewish people. I have been repeatedly asked: If we elevate homosexual families to an equal status with heterosexual families, will we not undermine the already precarious place of the traditional family? I do not believe that encouraging commitment, stability, and openness undermines the institution of family—it enhances it. At present, many gay and lesbian Jews are estranged from the synagogue, the Jewish community, and their families of origin because of continued fear, stigma, and oppression. Welcoming gay and lesbian families into the synagogue will strengthen all our families, by bringing the exiles home and by reuniting children, parents, and siblings who have been forced to keep their partners and innermost lives hidden. *Kelal Yisrael* is strengthened when we affirm that there can be more than one way to participate in the Covenant.

I speak to you today on behalf of many Jews—members of our people, members of our congregations, members of our Conference—who are unable to speak themselves. They each seek, as best they are able, to establish a home that will be a *mikdash me-at*. The gay and lesbian Jews amongst us seek to live their lives in loyalty to the Covenant and as members of the Covenant people and its community. Turning to us, they offer themselves, their lives, and their sacred commitments as stones with which to build the *sanctuary of the House of Israel.*

Notes

1. "Statement of Purpose and Function, Report of the Committee on Justice and Peace," *Yearbook* XCIII (New York: CCAR, 1983).

2. This comparison was first suggested by Sanford Ragins in "An Echo of the Pleas of Our Ancestors," *CCAR Journal* 20:3 (1973). Throughout European history "the fate of Jews and gay people has been almost identical" (John Boswell, *Christianity, Social Tolerance and Homosexuality* [Chicago: University of Chicago, 1980], p. 15). Although often unmentioned or ignored in Holocaust commemorations and studies, homosexuals in Nazi Germany were beaten in the streets, sent to camps, enslaved, and killed.

3. Yoel H. Kahn, "Judaism and Homosexuality," in *Homosexuality, the Rabbinate, and Liberal Judaism: Papers Prepared for the Ad-Hoc Committee on Homosexuality and the Rabbinate* (New York: CCAR, 1989).

4. J. David Bleich, *Judaism and Healing: Halakhic Perspectives* (New York: Ktav, 1981), p. 69.

5. Eugene B. Borowitz, "On Homosexuality and the Rabbinate, a Covenantal Response," in *Homosexuality, the Rabbinate, and Liberal Judaism,* p. 2.

6. See Milton Steinberg, "The Common Sense of Religious Faith," *Anatomy of Faith* (New York: Harcourt, Brace, 1960), pp. 80ff.

7. E.g., *nidda* and *shefichat zera.*

8. Robert Kirschner, "Halakhah and Homosexuality: A Reappraisal" *Judaism* 37:4 (Fall 1988), reprinted in *Homosexuality, the Rabbinate, and Liberal Judaism,* p. 2.

9. Borowitz, *op. cit.,* p. 9.

10. Yevamot 64a; *Shulchan Aruch,* EH 154:6.

11. See David Feldman, *Marital Relations, Birth Control and Abortion in Jewish Law* (New York: Schocken, 1968), chaps. 2, 4, 5 *passim,* esp. pp. 65–71, 103–105.

12. Consider the Centenary Perspective's statement on *aliya:* "We encourage *aliyah* for those who wish to find maximum personal fulfillment in the cause of Zion." Eugene Borowitz, *Reform Judaism Today* (New York: Behrman House, 1978), p. xxiii.

13. Eugene Borowitz, *Liberal Judaism* (New York: UAHC, 1984), pp. 448–449. This section ("Accepting the Single Jew") begins, "It will not do, however, to give the impression that one must be married to be a good Jew."

from Address

LEONARD S. KRAVITZ

To speak of "homosexual marriages," to seek to apply the term *kiddushin* to same sex relationships is—to say the least and to use the most neutral terms—to stand at a cultural interface. It is more, of course: a matter of pain for some and a matter of profound discomfort for others. For some, *kiddushin,* as word and symbol, is a stamp of acceptance for behaviors which to others cannot be accepted. For each side of the interface, *kiddushin* is that which touches and hurts. That interface itself stands at the center of the arena in which we as Liberal or Reform Jews live and decide, an arena with the general culture on the one side and Jewish tradition on the other.

In truth, it is not the general culture as it is, but the general culture as we perceive it, as members of a particular cohort of college-educated middle-class people. For that cohort sexual activity of whatever kind, at least among consenting adults, is a private matter. Being private, the only authority figures who may speak to it are those who deal

with private concerns—the psychologist, the psychiatrist, and the sex therapist. If one of these worthies were to declare that a particular behavior is psychologically unhealthy, or psychiatrically problematical, or sexually dysfunctional (all internal private matters), then, perhaps, that behavior would be proscribed. If, on the other hand, a particular behavior were to be declared to be not unhealthy, then for some, it might be viewed as acceptable. Hence, when the American Psychiatric Association declared that homosexuality *per se* was no longer a pathology,[1] for many such behavior became licit and indeed acceptable.

Jewish tradition, on the other side of the arena, is not that which we follow blindly. We are, after all, Liberal or Reform. Yet we are Jews, and the Torah as a Book and a Tradition is our heritage, giving us our attitudes, our values, and our sense of self. By our study of it and our reflection on it, we have given the Torah a vote in our decision making, an *a priori* commitment in the way we live our lives. As Liberal Jews, we use the literature of the Jewish past as a means of guidance for the Jewish present and future.[2] Those who feel that they follow the tradition would hold that the term *kiddushin* could hardly be applied to behaviors proscribed by Torah texts.[3] Indeed, the notion of *homosexual marriage* is touched upon by the Midrash. We read that

> Rabbi Huna stated in the name of Rabbi Joseph: The generation of the flood was not blotted out from the world until they wrote wedding contracts (*gemomsiyot*) for males and animals.[4]

As might have been expected, there is no discussion of homosexual marriage in traditional sources. There have been two discussions in Reform Jewish sources. Our teacher Solomon Freehof has written that

> Homosexuality is deemed in Jewish Tradition to be a sin—not only in law, but in Jewish life practice . . . [and] it is hardly worth mentioning that to officiate at a so-called "marriage" of two homosexuals and to describe their mode of life as "Kiddushin" (i.e., sacred in Judaism) is a contravention of all that is respected in Jewish life.[5]

Our colleague Walter Jacob, who, as chairman of the Responsa Committee has served as Dr. Freehof's successor as decisor in the Reform movement, has written that

> . . . we cannot accommodate the relationship of two homosexuals as a "marriage" within the context of Judaism, for none of the elements of *qiddushin* normally associated with marriage can be invoked for this relationship. A rabbi cannot, therefore, participate in the "marriage" of two homosexuals.[6]

For those for whom texts are decisive, the Midrash and the responsa of Freehof and Jacob have said all that need be said.

For those for whom their perception of the general culture is decisive, to raise the issue of *kiddushin* for homosexuals is to follow the trajectory of change that has occurred with regard to the view of homosexuality itself within some sectors of the liberal Jewish community. By incremental steps, each containing its own logic, homosexuality and all that could be associated with it became acceptable. The Jewish past viewed homosexuality as a sin and hence proscribed it. Some in the Jewish present would make changes. At first, homosexuality ceased being a sin; it became a disease. As a disease, there could be no penalties or disabilities. How could you punish a disease? If it were a matter of *ones* and not *ratson,* of compulsion and not volition, how could there be discrimination against those compelled to be homosexuals?[7] Then it became a matter of life style, to be "understood" but not accepted[8]; then as something to be accepted but as some kind of disability; then to be accepted as something given in nature, equivalent in its own terms as heterosexuality is accepted in its own terms.[9] Following the logic of such development, the UAHC has passed a resolution calling upon full civil rights for homosexuals in the civic sphere, and some members of the CCAR made proposals to the CCAR for full acceptance of homosexuals even in leadership roles in the Jewish religious sphere.[10] Beyond that, the HUC-JIR has decided that homosexuality *per se* is no longer grounds for non-acceptance into the rabbinic program. That decision has been described by Eugene Borowitz as "passive acceptance."[11] With all these changes, some would argue: Why should there not be marriage forms for homosexual couples, and, indeed, why should not the traditional term *kiddushin* be applied?

In truth, both sides of the interface make selections; both are not totally consistent. Those who, from their perception of the general culture and the modern world, argue the case of the homosexual, would not, I think, argue that the other sexual behaviors described and proscribed in Leviticus 18 and 20 (such as incest, bestiality, and adultery) are now acceptable. I would hope that as Liberal Jews and as rabbis, we are not *wertfrei* in the sexual realm! On the other side, those of us who hold a more traditional view would hardly go along with the draconian punishments described in the Torah text or indeed any punishment. We, too, hold in many ways that illicit sexual behavior is a private matter, we would hope amenable to persuasion, but nothing more.

Gufa! The question stands: Why not? Why am I opposed to marriage ceremonies for homosexual couples? I should think it fair to give my own assumptions of this discussion. Whether or not homosexuality is natural is to me irrelevant. All behaviors, including all sexual behaviors, are natural in that they statistically occur in nature. People—alas, or perhaps hurray—do everything. That which is natural is not necessarily that which should be done. Indeed, I would hold that all of human culture is the attempt to transcend that which is natural. What is natural is not necessarily Jewish.[12] Indeed, it might be argued that that which is natural is that which is universal, touching all persons as persons. As a Jew, I am involved with the particular. As a Liberal Jew, I am also involved with the universal as it casts light upon the Jewish particular, but the particular makes me what I am as a Jew and as a rabbi. As a modern Jew and as a Reform rabbi, I listen to the universal, but as a Jew and as a rabbi I listen to what others might call "the voice of Sinai" and I would call "the voice of the Jewish past." My world is formed by the books that have created the Jewish ethos; my time is spent reading and teaching those books; my associations are with other Jews who read those books and attempt—in their way, as I attempt in mine—to live by them. Thus the Jewish past and the Jewish present speak to me.

My view of homosexuality is in part formed by Jewish books, the Jewish past; it is formed in part by other Jews, both within and without our movement, the Jewish present. As I read the record of that past, homosexuality is not acceptable behavior; as for the present: as I interact with other Jews, I hear the message that it is not acceptable behavior. Now, it is often argued that there are other things, such as women rabbis and patrilineality, that are not acceptable to some in the Jewish present. For them I can use the Jewish past to give analogues so as to argue for change. I can say, "You don't like women rabbis? What do you do with women prophets like Miriam and Deborah? You don't like patrilineality? What do you do with Menasseh and Ephraim with whom you bless your sons? They were the sons of Yosef ha Tzaddik and Osnat bat Potiphera Kohen On! What do you do with the sons of Mosheh Rabbenu and Tziporah bat Yitro Kohen Midyan?" (Translate that into Yiddish, you begin to cry: both Yosef ha Tzaddik and Mosheh Rabbenu *hat gehayrat mit a galach's atochter!*) With homosexuality, I can give no analogues; indeed, the past provides counter arguments!

But what if homosexuality were something given, something so grounded in personality that it could not be changed? Would that make a difference? We are at another interface: of nature and nurture, of genetics and environment, of determinism and free will. Here I make another assumption, based on my reading of history and my understanding of psychology,[13] that homosexuality is not as locked-in behavior as some would hold. There have been some cultures, e.g., Classic Greece, where such behaviors have been more prevalent and other cultures where they have not.[14] There are situations, such as in prisons, where those who are generally heterosexual may act in a homosexual manner. As I read the past and the present, admittedly in a particular way, I have come to the conclusion that homosexuality in terms of homosexual acts manifests a kind of bell curve phenomenon: at the one end are those who never under any circumstance would act in a homosexual manner, and at the other end there are those who under all circumstances would; and there is the vast majority of people who, depending on circumstances, might.

For me, circumstances are the issue. If the relationship between two homosexuals is granted the status of *kiddushin,* a public matter, we are changing the circumstances, so that those who previously might not have acted in a homosexual manner, now might. Since, as a consequence of my reading of the Jewish past, I do not accept such behavior, I therefore would wish that those who are not involved with homosexual behavior continue not to be involved.

If I have a difficulty in adjudicating the claims of nature and nurture, of compulsion as opposed to volition with regard to sexual behavior, I am in good company. Maimonides, it will be remembered, observed in the *Guide* that

> one whose testicles have a hot and humid temperament . . . in whom the seminal vessels abundantly generate semen . . . it is unlikely that such a man, even if he subject his soul to the most severe training, should be chaste.[15]

Nonetheless, in the *Code,* Maimonides spoke of the need of self-control,[16] indicated sanctions,[17] and gave the refraining from an illicit sexual liaison as the very model of repentance. (You remember the case: the same woman, same town, same desire. If you don't, that is true repentance . . . [18])

Kiddushin is a public act. It is a declaration that a particular sexual behavior is Jewishly acceptable. At a time when there is no unanimity in the general culture that homosexual behavior is acceptable; when there have been important voices in the Reform Jewish community[19] saying that it is not; when there are many voices in the general Jewish community saying that it is not[20]—it would be a mistake for the Central Conference to create any form of sanctification for homosexual relationships or to apply the term *kiddushin* to such relationships.

Notes

1. I do not enter into the question of the political nature of the decision nor the absolute number of psychiatrists who voted for this position against the total number of psychiatrists.

2. All four papers in *Homosexuality, the Rabbinate, and Liberal Judaism: Papers Prepared for the Ad-Hoc Committee on Homosexuality and the Rabbinate* (New York: CCAR, 1989) implicitly or explicitly make the claim that they follow some aspect of the Jewish past.

3. Leviticus 18:23, 20:13. What might be asked of all participants in the discussion is which of the other sexual behaviors proscribed in the two chapters of Leviticus they would be willing to see allowed and which proscribed.

4. B.R. 26:9, Lev. R. 23:9, MHG Noah 6:11.

5. Solomon Freehof, "Judaism and Homosexuality," CCAR *Yearbook,* vol. 83, 1973, pp. 115–119, reprinted in *American Reform Responsa,* Collected Responsa of the Central Conference of American Rabbis (New York, 1983), pp. 51, 52. This responsum is also quoted in the most complete listing by Yoel H. Kahn.

6. Walter Jacob, "Responsum on Marriage," quoted in Yoel H. Kahn, "Judaism and Homosexuality," in *Homosexuality, the Rabbinate, and Liberal Judaism,* p. 20.

7. One can think of the evolution of the thinking of Hershel Matt in this regard (cf. citations given by Kahn, p. 7 of his paper).

8. Cf. the view of the Rabbinical Assembly which Kahn gives (p. 14 of his paper).

9. Note Kahn's summary of the views of John Boswell, *Homosexuality, Christianity, and Social Tolerance* (p. 15 of his paper).

10. Yoel H. Kahn, "Judaism and Homosexuality," in *Homosexuality, the Rabbinate, and Liberal Judaism,* p. 10. We are beholden to Rabbi Kahn for his most comprehensive presentation of relevant material. We should note that this suggestion flies in the face of the Responsum "Homosexuals in Leadership Positions," CCAR *Yearbook,* vol. 91 (1981), pp. 67–69, reprinted in Walter Jacob, editor, *American Reform Responsa* (New York: CCAR, 1983), pp. 52–54.

11. "Addendum: A correction to 'On Homosexuality and the Rabbinate'" by Eugene Borowitz, in *Homosexuality, the Rabbinate, and Liberal Judaism.*

12. Cf. the discussion of circumcision in the Midrash, B.R. 11:7 and B.R. 46:2.

13. My reading of the statement of Mortimer Ostoff as expressed in a letter to *Conservative Judaism* 40:1, pp. 103–106, cited in Kahn, p. 25, and in my private conversation with him.

14. There is the claim by Lamm that "the very scarcity of Halakhic (i.e. Jewish legal) deliberations on homosexuality, and the quite explicit insistence of the various halakhic authorities, provide sufficient evidence of the relative absence of this practice among Jews from ancient times down to the present," quoted in Kahn, p. 1. On the other hand, the discussion by Saadia's *Beliefs and Opinions,* Ideal Human Conduct, Chapter Six, suggests that, at least in one period, homosexuality was enough of a problem that a philosopher devoted part of his discussion to it.

15. *Guide* I:34, p. 77.

16. *Hilchot De-ot* 3:2, 3; 4:19.

17. *Hilchot Ishut* I: 4, 5.

18. *Hilchot Teshuva* II:1.

19. Not only the aforementioned statements of Freehof and Jacob, but also the statements in the position papers of Eugene Borowitz and Peter S. Knobel in *Homosexuality, the Rabbinate, and Liberal Judaism.*

20. Cf. the summary given by Kahn, pp. 1–5 in his paper.

PROTESTANTISM: THE PRESBYTERIAN CHURCH (U.S.A.)

from A Bonfire in Baltimore: Presbyterian Task Force Reports on Sexuality

JIM GITTINGS

Presbyterians are caught up in a brushfire, perhaps a conflagration. In just two weeks from publication of this article, the 203rd General Assembly of the Presbyterian Church (U.S.A.), meeting in Baltimore, will take into its hands the report of a Special Task Force on Human Sexuality created in 1987 by commissioners (delegates) to the 199th General Assembly and beefed-up (and its two-year timeline extended) by the 200th General Assembly in 1988.

The task force, more appropriately called the Special Committee on Human Sexuality, has produced, after 13 public hearings held in as many cities, an explosive 173-page, 7,779-line report. Its key recommendation to the General Assembly is that it approve the report "for study and response . . . for the next two years."

The body of the report contains suggestions that bid church members to:

- Struggle to end the prevailing "patriarchal sexual code."
- Ordain practicing homosexuals who are called to ministry.
- Cease to condemn cohabitation without marriage.
- Remove the spirit of legalism from traditional church insistence upon fidelity in marriage.
- Recognize and honor the right of sexual expression for all who are physically and intellectually impaired except for those at the most dysfunctional end of the mental or behavioral spectrum.
- Excoriate clergy who violate counseling relationships for the sake of sexual satisfaction.

Pulled from context, as everyone is doing nowadays, the above list of desiderata culled from the report conveys a blunt, thumb-to-nose impression, as though the committee had determined to set teeth on edge among over-50 Presbyterians of, say, Blooming Glen, Pennsylvania, or Travellers' Rest, South Carolina.

Yet these items from the report are nowhere expressed frivolously, or created to shock. Each such suggestion derives from, and (where a relationship is described) is to be disciplined by, a new or almost new sexual ethic (echoes are to be found in Tillich and Niebuhr) that the committee would have Presbyterians apply to all sexual relationships.

"Justice/Love," the 16-member committee calls its approach; and "Justice/Love" is what committee members hope Presbyterians will strive for in their pairings, make the hallmark of their family life, treasure in the loves of people of all sexual orientations and identities, and look for in their approaches to Scripture for guidance. "Right Relatedness" is the alternative word for Justice/Love employed by the committee. Any pair or group, of any gender, may be "rightly related" within the suggested ethic; it is a matter of the spirit in which persons come together and live with each other.

Widespread Reaction

Opposition to the paper began even before it was released. First shots were fired in columns of the 280,000-circulation *Presbyterian Layman,* and in the December newsletter of Presbyterians for Renewal, a moderately conservative evangelical group led by Louisville Seminary's Professor Virgil Cruz. Criticism in *The Layman* and in the

These selections are taken from Jim Gittings, "A Bonfire in Baltimore," and Karen Lebacqz, "Sex: Justice in Church and Society," *Christianity and Crisis* (May 27, 1991), pp. 172–177. Used by permission of *Christianity and Crisis.*

newsletter was directed to the alleged departure from "biblical morality" and surprised nobody, according to committee members interviewed, since both groups are on record as viewing homosexuality as sin.

The report went to press on February 4. Between that date and May 3, when this article was written, 89 of 171 presbyteries voted to register opposition or concern over the effect of the committee's document. Some of these presbyteries did not bother to read the text. Foothills Presbytery, in my own (S.C.) area, proceeded on March 21 to vote despite the fact that only 10 percent of those present had examined the document and none could claim to have read it closely. Declared the presbytery, "The study will lead inevitably to confusion, tension, unrest, disharmony, and disunion"; therefore, the General Assembly should "reject the recommendations," "dissolve" the committee, and "suspend" all further funding.

Neither traditional conservative strength among Presbyterians nor the subject matter under discussion quite explains the speed with which presbyteries found themselves able to act. What does explain the rush to judgment is that informal coalitions of presbytery and synod executives in almost every region concluded even before release of the document that their church could not afford to undergo an extended public debate on such a document, labeled "Presbyterian," absent of expressions of other Presbyterian views. These executives, the civil service of the church, got to work with great swiftness. "Damage control" was their banner, and prompt presbytery action aimed at disowning the document was in most places their instrument.

David Snellgrove, moderator of the Synod of Living Waters (Alabama, Tennessee, Mississippi, and Kentucky) and an executive of St. Andrew Presbytery (Mississippi), took a lead in convening a February 25 meeting of presbytery leaders at Nashville. North Alabama Presbytery exec Houston Hodges led the group through a hurried process that focused on how to defeat the report. That meeting was followed on March 2 and 3 at Hilton Head, South Carolina by another gathering, this one involving 100 leaders from across the country. At Hilton Head, Stated Clerk Jim Andrews interpreted the report and South Alabama Presbytery

exec John Kimbiri preached on the Ten Commandments as the only viable ethical standard for modern times.

From the Hilton Head meeting onward, opposition to the report has rolled forward on a fast track. In the Synod of the Trinity (Pennsylvania and West Virginia), for example, executives followed the Living Waters pattern by forming a similar "damage control" committee. This one, according to Lake Erie Presbytery (Pennsylvania) Executive Henry Borchardt, at one and the same time urged clergy and elders to "trust the General Assembly" processes and to make their individual feelings known to commissioners.

While the presbytery and synod executives were setting presbytery agenda items on the report in place, some of the church's former moderators also raised their voices in condemnation. First came a letter from six: Ken Hall, Bill Wilson, Jim Anderson, James Costen, Charles Hammond, Clinton Marsh. Their word was followed, later, by similar negative sentiments from former Presbyterian Church U.S. moderators Ben Lacey Rose and Jewell C. Spach. Not on the two negative lists are the names of recent women moderators: Thelma Adair, Joan Salmon-Campbell, Isabel Rogers, and Sarah Bernice Moseley. But Price Gwynn, the current moderator, has been active. Of late he has been publicly urging that the General Assembly vote *against* a task force recommendation that the church enter upon a two-year study period on the subject.

The unfortunate part of all this is that little attention has been paid to how the committee came to the decision to say what it has said, and why it said it. As President David Ramage of McCormick Theological Seminary told *C&C*, "Somebody, somewhere has got to see the poignancy involved in a committee of the poor old Presbyterian Church feeling that it has got to put so candid a report before the membership and, in fact, daring to do so."

Heard Pain

Why did the committee feel it had to speak so clearly? According to Chairperson John J. Carey, professor of religion at Agnes Scott College, it began by listening carefully to folk who felt alienated. These included gay and lesbian persons, of course. But their number also included young unmarried persons living together, and women trapped in—or newly broken free from—destructive marriages. Older single adults. The aged. Working women. Men. "We heard a lot of pain," reports Carey. "More than you can imagine."

The committee searched in church practice and the Scriptures for "a Word" of relief for the pain these people so obviously were enduring. In church practice, truth to say, they found little of comfort. Presbyterians in the former UPCUSA acted at their 1978 General Assembly to bar practicing homosexuals from ministry and the eldership, and declared same-sex relationships sinful. A year later the former PCUS did likewise. Eleven years after that, in 1990, a scientifically controlled study by the church's Presbyterian Panel research organization found that 86 percent of the church's lay members, 90 percent of elders and deacons, and 83 percent of pastors continued to oppose ordination of practicing homosexuals.

In other modern church areas examined by the committee, studies by the Council on Women and the Church (COWAC) in 1982 turned up numerous instances of sexual harassment of women by ministers and church executives. Scandals arising from pastoral counseling situations periodically rocked the church even as the task force was meeting. The church had never, the committee found, dealt seriously with ethical questions arising from the fact that thousands of its members, of all age groups, are choosing to live together in unions not blessed by the church. Almost 40 percent of adult Presbyterians are single and the only word of the church about their sexuality is abstinence.

"They are not 'other' people who were talking to us," reports Carey. "They were our own. And we found little on the record that we could say to them by way of either recognition of their pain or of comfort."

Scriptural Authority

To the Scriptures, then, the committee turned. It found the condemnatory passages regarding homosexuals limited in application, always subject to contextual and situational interpretation or application, and, in the biblical hermeneutic used, not necessarily inerrant or (most frequently) of much use in forming a modern ethic. Further, where such strictures appeared abhorrent to or at variance with the Jesus example, the committee dismissed them.

At this point the committee may have unintentionally fallen into two kinds of trouble, neither of its own making. First of all, the "experts" available to the committee in doing its work with the Scriptures did not include any of the prevailing "stars" of the Presbyterian theological faculties—two who were nominated found reason not to serve—and none of its systematic theologians. More damaging—if one may dare to mention in polite company a continuing Presbyterian parochialism—the scholars that were on or serving in advisory roles to the committee bore the colors, personally or by locus of employment, of the (by many Presbyterians) theologically mistrusted United Church of Christ and its seminaries. From the outset, almost, the committee's theological thinking and biblical work was therefore bound to be greeted by suspicion.

But that is the lesser of the two troubles. More important is a 60-year-old still unresolved Presbyterian quarrel.

Since the winding-down of the bitter John Machen controversy in the early 1930s, Presbyterians have ducked serious discussion of how the Scripture is to be handled in their churches, confining themselves to *description* (the paper *Biblical Authority and Interpretation,* GA 1982) of the varieties of ways of approach in use. The Scripture is the "Rule of Life and Faith" to Presbyterians, and (the language of this report) holds "centrality" in the denomination.

Within that framework Presbyterian laypersons by the tens of thousands gather daily or weekly to search out in their prayer meetings and Sunday Schools the meaning of individual passages. Presbyterian ministers are handed and agree to be guided by a "Book of Confessions" in which each proposition and declaration have their roots in particular passages of Scripture that are noted and codified. The phrase "Word of God" is still in use throughout the church for Scripture, and if in Sunday worship the reader says "Listen for" rather than "Listen to," as of yore, it is a rare congregation in which the difference receives comment.

The point is that ordinary Presbyterians are permitted to believe that the Bible is the "Word of God" in a 19th-century evangelical sense.

In fact, however, the courts and the overwhelming majority of Presbyterian ministers of the Presbyterian Church use the Scripture quite differently. Prooftexting is held by the scholars to be utterly unacceptable. The range of methodologies used in handling Scripture range from the historico/critical (the majority) through David Tracy's back-and-forth questions and answers between culture and Scripture to, on the extreme margin, French deconstruction criticism in which authorial intent has little bearing on contemporary meaning. The task force operated well within the frames set by the first two of these. But for the sake of internal peace and unity the Presbyterian Church has avoided a necessary education of its lay persons in these matters. The simplicity of approach in use among the laity makes no difference when a paper deals with, say, qualifications for ordination, a decision which is handled at presbytery level anyway. But when the task force crosses over into the most intimate areas of lay persons' lives, many if not most lay persons—as Tom Parker of McCormick Theological Seminary said in a telephone interview—"cannot recognize the scriptural bridge provided by the committee."

Family Matters

That is not the only bridge left unbuilt, or half-built. The committee, says Andrew Purvis of Pittsburgh Theological Seminary, with Chairperson Carey somewhat abashedly agreeing, "failed until the final draft to deal with the family." For Purvis this amounted, at the least, to "political incompetence"—to "not taking the family seriously," and is the third of three major flaws he finds in the report (the others: absence of an adequate anthropology that answers the question, Who is the human?, and failure to sense a need to argue adequately for the "dominance of the Justice/Love concept over against the Covenant Concept").

Others of the committee agree that they "came late" to the family. "We started with the marginal people, the most hurt," says Marilyn Washburn. "Much that we had to say about family life got said in the introduction and in other aspects of the report." This is true, but as Mary-Anne Wolfe, stated clerk of Pittsburgh Presbytery, told *C&C*, "I and many others find it unacceptable to give chapters to special groups and not to speak in similar fashion to the subject of marriage. People need a place to start."

A minority report, originally signed by six members of the committee, is also traveling to the Assembly. It is an unevenly written document unlikely to please anyone. One of the reasons for that "unevenness," in addition to lack of preparation time—it was drafted in three days—is that its core material was originally intended to be inserted into the majority document, not to replace any of it but precisely to serve as the "bridge" from the familiar to the new whose absence is being lamented. But there is another reason for the minority document: The only "medical members" of the committee—Grady Crossland, Marilyn Washburn, Jean Kennedy—felt that the main document dealt inadequately with sexually transmitted diseases, teen pregnancies, biological purposes, and other medical aspects related to sexuality and sexual practice. "We scientists use data differently than theologians," says Washburn. "Often we talked past each other."

From the above it is evident that much discussion and debate must occur before the General Assembly of the Presbyterian Church (U.S.A.) will find it comfortable to release to its people a document of guidance in sexual matters. The 700 commissioners are tailors and preachers and farmers and teachers and merchants. To deal with an always crowded agenda and also to devise codes of ethics for responsible Christians in nine days is an imposing task.

That the debate could be rich can be seen from what some are even now wanting to talk about. For example:

> This report comes to us like a message from "outside"; it doesn't have a family resemblance to what Presbyterians are used to handling. We've got to go back to find a theological language for it if ownership is ever to take place.
>
> Tom Parker
> McCormick Theological Seminary

I have not seen any sustained argument on the question of whether God creates *at least some* homosexual persons. How should we think today about God's action in relation not only to the genetic process involved in conception and human development, but the socializing processes that shape the emergent selfhood? I have not seen any serious *theological* discussion of these questions. . . . The church ought to find some theologians who are willing to work on this. I mean *systematic* theologians. . . .

George H. Kehm
Pittsburgh Theological Seminary

But will further discussion and study of the report actually occur in Presbyterian churches? The process through which the report travels includes several steps at which it can be killed. The Assembly, moreover, may choose not to receive the report, or it may appoint a successor committee to carry the study further.

While all this is going on, the committee's report is "out there" with more than 15,000 copies in circulation. For some it has been received as good, good news. Among those who rejoice:

Patsy Correll, grandmother of Spartanburg, S.C.: I just don't track the argument that this is "not Reformed." The document will frighten only those who are scared to death of justice in *any* form.

More than 150 representatives from 50 "More Light" Presbyterian churches (who welcome persons of all sexual orientations into their congregations) meeting in Rochester May 3–5: This report is long overdue. The church historically was slow to include blacks and women into full membership. The full inclusion of lesbians and gay men may also be slow in coming, but it will come.

George Morgan, executive, Synod of the Covenants (Ohio and Michigan): I am very grateful that *someone* broke the silence and paralysis of our church about several sexually related issues—

especially the "sex and persons with disabilities" sections in chapters three and four.

Pat de Jong, pastor, Des Moines: How people view the report has something to do with how they choose to see God. Do we see God as someone who is disconnected from us, and waiting for us to do something wrong? Or are we living with a God who is incarnate, embodied, a friend with us in the world?

Meantime, some serve the God who is *"waiting for us to do something wrong."* Stated Clerk Jim Andrews reports he has received a query on how to bring to trial ordained members of the committee for alleged violation of their ordination vows involved in their signing the report.

In a Pittsburgh Presbytery meeting, committee member Bernadine McRipley underwent savage questioning regarding her membership on the committee in connection with presbytery confirmation hearings on her employment as associate presbytery executive. She was not confirmed.

And in North Puget Sound Presbytery, some churches are reported to be withholding funds in an attempt to force discharge of a committee member who lives in Everett, Washington.

First-century Christians were the last, possibly, to attempt creation of a truly revolutionary interpersonal ethic. They fell into trouble at the point where that ethic collided with obligations of citizenship embodied in folk rituals recognizing Caesar. Now the Presbyterians—who would have thought it?—are trying again with Justice/Love. They are, in some ways, just as weak as the first-century bunch. So where will the arenas be? The floors of 171 presbyteries? General Assembly committee rooms? And who are the lions, who are the saints?

from Sex: Justice in Church and Society

KAREN LEBACQZ

AT LAST: A report on sexuality worth reading. AT LAST a report that places sexuality squarely within the framework of concerns for *justice* in church and society. AT LAST a report that names the realities of sexual *violence* which permeate our soci-

ety. AT LAST a report that seeks *truth* by attending to voices of the marginalized. AT LAST a report that tries to "keep body and soul together" by honoring the joy, the pain, the gift, the struggle of human sexuality. Kudos to the Special Committee on

Human Sexuality of the Presbyterian Church, USA!

This is a report that deserves to be read—in full. This is a report that deserves to be studied—carefully. This is a report that will discomfit, dislocate, challenge, and ultimately move the church. This is a report that asks nothing more than Christian witness: gratitude for God's love, commitment to God's justice, and fidelity to the story of Jesus whom we call the Christ.

Fidelity to that story is centered in what the Committee calls "justice-love" or "right-relation." These rather awkward terms are meant to convey the notion that God demands nothing more nor less than justice and love intertwined, and that *any* human activity that does not exhibit both love and justice is wrong. This means that sex is not right just because it takes place inside a heterosexual marriage: violent sexuality, abusive sexuality, dishonest sexuality is wrong even when hidden within the confines of church-sanctioned marriage. This also means that sex is not wrong just because it takes place outside those confines. It is not the *form* that makes sex right or wrong, but the *content*—whether it is genuinely loving, life-serving, and just.

Such a perspective is not altogether new in church circles. Both the United Church of Christ in its *Human Sexuality: A Preliminary Study* and the Catholic Theological Society of America in its major study of *Human Sexuality* have argued much the same. All three church bodies would judge sexual acts by whether they are honest, fair, loving, life-giving, joyful, and expressive of the love and justice witnessed in Scripture and embodied in the life of Christ. All three eschew any easy formulas ("celibacy in singleness, fidelity in marriage") that ignore the core of God's intentions for the human community. That core lies in our willingness to be vulnerable, to connect and be committed to each other, to expand our circles to include not only our partners but children and others as well, and to bring about justice for and with those who are marginalized.

Tighter Ethical Demands

As the committee makes clear, to root ethical sexuality in the demands of "justice-love" or "right relationship" is not to *loosen* ethical demands but rather to *tighten* them. Many relationships that have previously been accepted will be accepted no longer, for they do not exhibit true justice and love. Judged by these criteria, many traditional marriages fail to exhibit God's purposes: the sexual contact is violent and abusive, or cold and condemning; the marriages are patriarchal and unjust to women. As William Countryman puts it in *Dirt, Greed, and Sex,* some "marriages" never really were marriages—they never expressed the spirit of God's love and justice, never embodied the internal goods of sexuality.

The churches have been singularly reluctant to acknowledge this reality. The Presbyterian Committee is to be commended for its clarity of judgment in seeing that marriage alone does not make sex acceptable, and that love and joy and justice of God are sometimes better expressed in relationships that have not received the church's official stamp of marriage. While the Special Committee is not the first church group to make this attempt, it is the most successful thus far in articulating a clear and cogent theological and scriptural stand from which to assess sexual relationships.

Ironic, then, that it is primarily charged with two failures. The first charge is moral laxness. A group of former moderators suggests that in making "justice-love" the primary consideration, "the report makes all sexual conduct subjective and free from all external guidance or restraint." This is patently false. The demands of justice and love are not merely subjective, as the committee's report demonstrates.

Rather, those demands are exacting: Justice and love require relationships that challenge patriarchal structures, that refuse to eroticize domination and violence, that operate out of mutuality and vulnerability, that expand the circle of love to include others, and so on. To do all of this is much harder than simply getting married! If the Presbyterian Church affirmed these standards, it would be establishing a harder and higher standard than it currently affirms.

Accommodating Culture

Second, the committee is charged with ignoring Scripture. The minority report accuses the majority of a "wish for accommodation" to the culture, and urges that Christians "live by the authority of God's word in sexual matters." The assumption of the minority is that God's word simply requires monogamous, heterosexual marriage. Any acceptance of sexual relations outside of this form must therefore be an accommodation to culture.

But it is the minority group, not the majority, that has accommodated to culture. The minority reads Scripture with eyes that have clearly accommodated to the 20th century. Why else could it proclaim that "the total picture of human sexuality" as given in Scripture is captured in the "lifelong commitment of husband and wife to each other"?

Only eyes blinded by 20th-century nuclear families could ignore the practice of polygamy among ancient Israelites and the affirmation of nonmarital sexual love in the Song of Songs ("Holy of Holies"). Only eyes blinded by 20th-century homophobia could assume that the church has spoken with a "single voice" on issues such as homosexuality. Only eyes blinded by 20th-century assumptions about the "privacy" of sexuality could so ignore the links between sexuality and vi-olence in this culture, and the need for a true return to the core of biblical witness: the movement of the spirit in overcoming cultural purity claims in order to place sexuality within a context of justice.

The committee, with its call for ever more demanding standards for sexual relating, has not accommodated to culture. The minority has, with its failure to allow 20th-century assumptions to be challenged by Scripture. The committee, with its return to the core Gospel message of right relation, has not neglected Scripture; the minority has, with its neglect of the total biblical record and context of biblical passages. (Although I commend the Presbyterian Church for its consistent commitment to publishing minority reports, this minority report is an embarrassment to the church.)

The Presbyterian Church (U.S.A.) should be proud to own the majority Special Committee report. The report is offered as a guide to reflection and decision—a study document, to be perused over the next two years. This it surely deserves. But it deserves more than study. It deserves adoption and enactment. *At last* we have a beginning toward a truly Christian sexual ethic.

ROMAN CATHOLICISM

from Catechism of the Catholic Church

ARTICLE 6
THE SIXTH COMMANDMENT

You shall not commit adultery.[112]

You have heard that it was said, "You shall not commit adultery." But I say to you that every one who looks at a woman lustfully has already committed adultery with her in his heart.[113]

I. "Male and Female He Created Them . . . "

2331 "God is love and in himself he lives a mystery of personal loving communion. Creating the human race in his own image . . . , God inscribed in the humanity of man and woman the *vocation,* and thus the capacity and responsibility, *of love* and communion."[114]

These selections are taken from *Catechism of the Catholic Church* (Mahwah, New Jersey: Paulist Press, 1994), paragraphs 2331 to 2400. Used by permission of Paulist Press.

"God created man in his own image . . . male and female he created them";[115] He blessed them and said, "Be fruitful and multiply";[116] "When God created man, he made him in the likeness of God. Male and female he created them, and he blessed them and named them Man when they were created."[117]

2332 Sexuality affects all aspects of the human person in the unity of his body and soul. It especially concerns affectivity, the capacity to love and to procreate, and in a more general way the aptitude for forming bonds of communion with others.

2333 Everyone, man and woman, should acknowledge and accept his sexual *identity*. Physical, moral, and spiritual *difference* and *complementarity* are oriented toward the goods of marriage and the flourishing of family life. The harmony of the couple and of society depends in part on the way in which the complementarity, needs, and mutual support between the sexes are lived out.

2334 "In creating men 'male and female,' God gives man and woman an equal personal dignity."[118] "Man is a person, man and woman equally so, since both were created in the image and likeness of the personal God."[119]

2335 Each of the two sexes is an image of the power and tenderness of God, with equal dignity though in a different way. The *union of man and woman* in marriage is a way of imitating in the flesh the Creator's generosity and fecundity: "Therefore a men leaves his father and his mother and cleaves to his wife, and they become one flesh."[120] All human generations proceed from this union.[121]

2336 Jesus came to restore creation to the purity of its origins. In the Sermon on the Mount, he interprets God's plan strictly: "You have heard that it was said, 'You shall not commit adultery.' But I say to you that every one who looks at a woman lustfully has already committed adultery with her in his heart."[122] What God has joined together, let not man put asunder.[123]

The tradition of the Church has understood the sixth commandment as encompassing the whole of human sexuality.

II. The Vocation to Chastity

2337 Chastity means the successful integration of sexuality within the person and thus the inner unity of man in his bodily and spiritual being. Sexuality, in which man's belonging to the bodily and biological world is expressed, becomes personal and truly human when it is integrated into the relationship of one person to another, in the complete and lifelong mutual gift of a man and a woman.

The virtue of chastity therefore involves the integrity of the person and the integrality of the gift.

The Integrity of the Person

2338 The chaste person maintains the integrity of the powers of life and love placed in him. This integrity ensures the unity of the person; it is opposed to any behavior that would impair it. It tolerates neither a double life nor duplicity in speech.[124]

2339 Chastity includes an *apprenticeship in self-mastery* which is a training in human freedom. The alternative is clear: either man governs his passions and finds peace, or he lets himself be dominated by them and becomes unhappy.[125] "Man's dignity therefore requires him to act out of conscious and free choice, as moved and drawn in a personal way from within, and not by blind impulses in himself or by mere external constraint. Man gains such dignity when, ridding himself of all slavery to the passions, he presses forward to his goal by freely choosing what is good and, by his diligence and skill, effectively secures for himself the means suited to this end."[126]

2340 Whoever wants to remain faithful to his baptismal promises and resist temptations will want to adopt the *means* for doing so: self-knowledge, practice of an ascesis adapted to the situations that confront him, obedience to God's commandments, exercise of the moral virtues, and fidelity to prayer. "Indeed it is through chastity that we are gathered together and led back to the unity from which we were fragmented into multiplicity."[127]

2341 The virtue of chastity comes under the cardinal virtue of *temperance,* which seeks to permeate the passions and appetites of the senses with reason.

2342 Self-mastery is a *long and exacting work.* One can never consider it acquired once and for all. It presupposes renewed effort at all stages of life.[128] The effort required can be more intense in certain periods, such as when the personality is being formed during childhood and adolescence.

2343 Chastity has *laws of growth* which progress through stages marked by imperfection and too often by sin. "Man . . . day by day builds himself up through his many free decisions; and so he knows, loves, and accomplishes moral good by stages of growth."[129]

2344 Chastity represents an eminently personal task; it also involves a *cultural effort,* for there is "an interdependence between personal betterment and the improvement of society."[130] Chastity presupposes respect for the rights of the person, in particular the right to receive information and an education that respect the moral and spiritual dimensions of human life.

2345 Chastity is a moral virtue. It is also a gift from God, a *grace,* a fruit of spiritual effort.[131] The Holy Spirit enables one whom the water of Baptism has regenerated to imitate the purity of Christ.[132]

The Integrality of the Gift of Self

2346 Charity is the *form* of all the virtues. Under its influence, chastity appears as a school of the gift of the person. Self-mastery is ordered to the gift of self. Chastity leads him who practices it to become a witness to his neighbor of God's fidelity and loving kindness.

2347 The virtue of chastity blossoms in *friendship.* It shows the disciple how to follow and imitate him who has chosen us as his friends,[133] who has given himself totally to us and allows us to participate in his divine estate. Chastity is a promise of immortality.

Chastity is expressed notably in *friendship with one's neighbor.* Whether it develops between persons of the same or opposite sex, friendship represents a great good for all. It leads to spiritual communion.

The Various Forms of Chastity

2348 All the baptized are called to chastity. The Christian has "put on Christ,"[134] the model for all chastity. All Christ's faithful are called to lead a chaste life in keeping with their particular states of life. At the moment of his Baptism, the Christian is pledged to lead his affective life in chastity.

2349 "People should cultivate [chastity] in the way that is suited to their state of life. Some profess virginity or consecrated celibacy which enables them to give themselves to God alone with an undivided heart in a remarkable manner. Others live in the way prescribed for all by the moral law, whether they are married or single."[135] Married people are called to live conjugal chastity; others practice chastity in continence:

> There are three forms of the virtue of chastity: the first is that of spouses, the second that of widows, and the third that of virgins. We do not praise any one of them to the exclusion of the others. . . . This is what makes for the richness of the discipline of the Church.[136]

2350 Those who are *engaged to marry* are called to live chastity in continence. They should see in this time of testing a discovery of mutual respect, an apprenticeship in fidelity, and the hope of receiving one another from God. They should reserve for marriage the expressions of affection that belong to married love. They will help each other grow in chastity.

Offenses Against Chastity

2351 *Lust* is disordered desire for or inordinate enjoyment of sexual pleasure. Sexual pleasure is morally disordered when sought for itself, isolated from its procreative and unitive purposes.

2352 By *masturbation* is to be understood the deliberate stimulation of the genital organs in order to derive sexual pleasure. "Both the Magisterium of the Church, in the course of a constant tradition, and the moral sense of the faithful have been in no doubt and have firmly maintained that masturbation is an intrinsically and gravely disordered action."[137] "The deliberate use of the sexual faculty, for whatever reason, outside of marriage is essentially contrary to its purpose." For here sexual pleasure is sought outside of "the sexual relationship which is demanded by the moral order and in which the total meaning of mutual self-giving and human procreation in the context of true love is achieved."[138]

To form an equitable judgment about the subjects' moral responsibility and to guide pastoral action, one must take into account the affective immaturity, force of acquired habit, conditions of anxiety, or other psychological or social factors that lessen or even extenuate moral culpability.

2353 Fornication is carnal union between an unmarried man and an unmarried woman. It is gravely contrary to the dignity of persons and of human sexuality which is naturally ordered to the good of spouses and the generation and education of children. Moreover, it is a grave scandal when there is corruption of the young.

2354 Pornography consists in removing real or simulated sexual acts from the intimacy of the partners, in order to display them deliberately to third parties. It offends against chastity because it perverts the conjugal act, the intimate giving of spouses to each other. It does grave injury to the dignity of its participants (actors, vendors, the public), since each one becomes an object of base pleasure and illicit profit for others. It immerses all who are involved in the illusion of a fantasy world. It is a grave offense. Civil authorities should prevent the production and distribution of pornographic materials.

2355 Prostitution does injury to the dignity of the person who engages in it, reducing the person to an instrument of sexual pleasure. The one who pays sins gravely against himself: he violates the chastity to which his Baptism pledged him and defiles his body, the temple of the Holy Spirit.[139] Prostitution is a social scourge. It usually involves women, but also men, children, and adolescents (The latter two cases involve the added sin of scandal.). While it is always gravely sinful to engage

in prostitution, the imputability of the offense can be attenuated by destitution, blackmail, or social pressure.

2356 Rape is the forcible violation of the sexual intimacy of another person. It does injury to justice and charity. Rape deeply wounds the respect, freedom, and physical and moral integrity to which every person has a right. It causes grave damage that can mark the victim for life. It is always an intrinsically evil act. Graver still is the rape of children committed by parents (incest) or those responsible for the education of the children entrusted to them.

Chastity and Homosexuality

2357 Homosexuality refers to relations between men or between women who experience an exclusive or predominant sexual attraction toward persons of the same sex. It has taken a great variety of forms through the centuries and in different cultures. Its psychological genesis remains largely unexplained. Basing itself on Sacred Scripture, which presents homosexual acts as acts of grave depravity,[140] tradition has always declared that "homosexual acts are intrinsically disordered."[141] They are contrary to the natural law. They close the sexual act to the gift of life. They do not proceed from a genuine affective and sexual complementarity. Under no circumstances can they be approved.

2358 The number of men and women who have deep-seated homosexual tendencies is not negligible. They do not choose their homosexual condition; for most of them it is a trial. They must be accepted with respect, compassion, and sensitivity. Every sign of unjust discrimination in their regard should be avoided. These persons are called to fulfill God's will in their lives and, if they are Christians, to unite to the sacrifice of the Lord's Cross the difficulties they may encounter from their condition.

2359 Homosexual persons are called to chastity. By the virtues of self-mastery that teach them inner freedom, at times by the support of disinterested friendship, by prayer and sacramental grace, they can and should gradually and resolutely approach Christian perfection.

III. The Love of Husband and Wife

2360 Sexuality is ordered to the conjugal love of man and woman. In marriage the physical intimacy of the spouses becomes a sign and pledge of spiritual communion. Marriage bonds between baptized persons are sanctified by the sacrament.

2361 "Sexuality, by means of which man and woman give themselves to one another through the acts which are proper and exclusive to spouses, is not something simply biological, but concerns the innermost being of the human person as such. It is realized in a truly human way only if it is an integral part of the love by which a man and woman commit themselves totally to one another until death."[142]

> Tobias got out of bed and said to Sarah, "Sister, get up, and let us pray and implore our Lord that he grant us mercy and safety." So she got up, and they began to pray and implore that they might be kept safe. Tobias began by saying, "Blessed are you, O God of our fathers. . . . You made Adam, and for him you made his wife Eve as a helper and support. From the two of them the race of mankind has sprung. You said, 'It is not good that the man should be alone; let us make a helper for him like himself.' I now am taking this kinswoman of mine, not because of lust, but with sincerity. Grant that she and I may find mercy and that we may grow old together." And they both said, "Amen, Amen." Then they went to sleep for the night.[143]

2362 "The acts in marriage by which the intimate and chaste union of the spouses takes place are noble and honorable; the truly human performance of these acts fosters the self-giving they signify and enriches the spouses in joy and gratitude."[144] Sexuality is a source of joy and pleasure:

> The Creator himself . . . established that in the [generative] function, spouses should experience pleasure and enjoyment of body and spirit. Therefore, the spouses do nothing evil in seeking this pleasure and enjoyment. They accept what the Creator has intended for them. At the same time, spouses should know how to keep themselves within the limits of just moderation.[145]

2363 The spouses' union achieves the twofold end of marriage: the good of the spouses themselves and the transmission of life. These two meanings or values of marriage cannot be separated without altering the couple's spiritual life and compromising the goods of marriage and the future of the family.

The conjugal love of man and woman thus stands under the twofold obligation of fidelity and fecundity.

Conjugal Fidelity

2364 The married couple forms "the intimate partnership of life and love established by the Creator and governed by his laws; it is rooted in the conjugal covenant, that is, in their irrevocable personal consent."[146] Both give themselves definitively and totally to one another. They are no longer two; from now on they form one flesh. The covenant they freely contracted imposes on the spouses the obligation to preserve it as unique and indissoluble.[147] "What therefore God has joined together, let not man put asunder."[148]

2365 Fidelity expresses constancy in keeping one's given word. God is faithful. The Sacrament of Matrimony enables man and woman to enter into Christ's fidelity for his Church. Through conjugal chastity, they bear witness to this mystery before the world.

> St. John Chrysostom suggests that young husbands should say to their wives: I have taken you in my arms, and I love you, and I prefer you to my life itself. For the present life is nothing, and my most ardent dream is to spend it with you in such a way that we may be assured of not being separated in the life reserved for us. . . . I place your love above all things, and nothing would be more bitter or painful to me than to be of a different mind than you.[149]

The Fecundity of Marriage

2366 Fecundity is a gift, an *end of marriage,* for conjugal love naturally tends to be fruitful. A child does not come from outside as something added on to the mutual love of the spouses, but springs from the very heart of that mutual giving, as its fruit and fulfillment. So the Church, which "is on the side of life"[150] teaches that "each and every marriage act must remain open to the transmission of life."[151] "This particular doctrine, expounded on numerous occasions by the Magisterium, is based on the inseparable connection, established by God, which man on his own initiative may not break, between the unitive significance and the procreative significance which are both inherent to the marriage act."[152]

2367 Called to give life, spouses share in the creative power and fatherhood of God.[153] "Married couples should regard it as their proper mission to transmit human life and to educate their children; they should realize that they are thereby *cooperating with* the love of *God the Creator* and are, in a certain sense, its interpreters. They will fulfill this duty with a sense of human and Christian responsibility."[154]

2368 A particular aspect of this responsibility concerns the *regulation of births*. For just reasons, spouses may wish to space the births of their children. It is their duty to make certain that their desire is not motivated by selfishness but is in conformity with the generosity appropriate to responsible parenthood. Moreover, they should conform their behavior to the objective criteria of morality:

> When it is a question of harmonizing married love with the responsible transmission of life, the morality of the behavior does not depend on sincere intention and evaluation of motives alone; but it must be determined by objective criteria, criteria drawn from the nature of the person and his acts, criteria that respect the total meaning of mutual self-giving and human procreation in the context of true love; this is possible only if the virtue of married chastity is practiced with sincerity of heart.[155]

2369 "By safeguarding both these essential aspects, the unitive and the procreative, the conjugal act preserves in its fullness the sense of true mutual love and its orientation toward man's exalted vocation to parenthood."[156]

2370 Periodic continence, that is, the methods of birth regulation based on self-observation and the use of infertile periods, is in conformity with the objective criteria of morality.[157] These methods respect the bodies of the spouses, encourage tenderness between them, and favor the education of an authentic freedom. In contrast, "every action which, whether in anticipation of the conjugal act, or in its accomplishment, or in the development of its natural consequences, proposes, whether as an end or as a means, to render procreation impossible" is intrinsically evil:[158]

> Thus the innate language that expresses the total reciprocal self-giving of husband and wife is overlaid, through contraception, by an objectively contradictory language, namely, that of not giving oneself totally to the other. This leads not only to a positive refusal to be open to life but also to a falsification of the inner truth of conjugal love, which is called upon to give itself in personal totality. . . . The difference, both anthropological and moral, between contraception and recourse to the rhythm of the cycle . . . involves in the final analysis two irreconcilable concepts of the human person and of human sexuality.[159]

2371 "Let all be convinced that human life and the duty of transmitting it are not limited by the horizons of this life only: their true evaluation and full significance can be understood only in reference to *man's eternal destiny*."[160]

2372 The state has a responsibility for its citizens' well-being. In this capacity it is legitimate for it to intervene to orient the demography of the population. This can be done by means of objective and respectful information, but certainly not by authoritarian, coercive measures. The state may not legitimately usurp the initiative of spouses, who have the primary responsibility for the procreation and education of their children.[161] It is not authorized to promote demographic regulation by means contrary to the moral law.

The Gift of a Child

2373 Sacred Scripture and the Church's traditional practice see in *large families* a sign of God's blessing and the parents' generosity.[162]

2374 Couples who discover that they are sterile suffer greatly. "What will you give me," asks Abraham of God, "for I continue childless?"[163] And Rachel cries to her husband Jacob, "Give me children, or I shall die!"[164]

2375 Research aimed at reducing human sterility is to be encouraged, on condition that it is placed "at the service of the human person, of his inalienable rights, and his true and integral good according to the design and will of God."[165]

2376 Techniques that entail the dissociation of husband and wife, by the intrusion of a person other than the couple (donation of sperm or ovum, surrogate uterus), are gravely immoral. These techniques (heterologous artificial insemination and fertilization) infringe the child's right to be born of a father and mother known to him and bound to each other by marriage. They betray the spouses' "right to become a father and a mother only through each other."[166]

2377 Techniques involving only the married couple (homologous artificial insemination and fertilization) are perhaps less reprehensible, yet remain morally unacceptable. They dissociate the sexual act from the procreative act. The act which brings the child into existence is no longer an act by which two persons give themselves to one another, but one that "entrusts the life and identity of the embryo into the power of doctors and biologists and establishes the domination of technology over the origin and destiny of the human person. Such a relationship of domination is in itself contrary to the dignity and equality that must be common to parents and children."[167] "Under the moral aspect procreation is deprived of its proper perfection when it is not willed as the fruit of the conjugal act, that is to say, of the specific act of the spouses' union. . . . Only respect for the link between the meanings of the conjugal act and respect for the unity of the human being make possible procreation in conformity with the dignity of the person."[168]

2378 A child is not something *owed* to one, but is a *gift*. The "supreme gift of marriage" is a human person. A child may not be considered a piece of property, an idea to which an alleged "right to a child" would lead. In this area, only the child possesses genuine rights: the right "to be the fruit of the specific act of the conjugal love of his parents," and "the right to be respected as a person from the moment of his conception."[169]

2379 The Gospel shows that physical sterility is not an absolute evil. Spouses who still suffer from infertility after exhausting legitimate medical procedures should unite themselves with the Lord's Cross, the source of all spiritual fecundity. They can give expression to their generosity by adopting abandoned children or performing demanding services for others.

IV. Offenses Against the Dignity of Marriage

Adultery

2380 *Adultery* refers to marital infidelity. When two partners, of whom at least one is married to another party, have sexual relations—even transient ones—they commit adultery. Christ condemns even adultery of mere desire.[170] The sixth commandment and the New Testament forbid adultery absolutely.[171] The prophets denounce the gravity of adultery; they see it as an image of the sin of idolatry.[172]

2381 Adultery is an injustice. He who commits adultery fails in his commitment. He does injury to the sign of the covenant which the marriage bond is, transgresses the rights of the other spouse, and undermines the institution of marriage by breaking the contract on which it is based. He compromises the good of human generation and the welfare of children who need their parents' stable union.

Divorce

2382 The Lord Jesus insisted on the original intention of the Creator who willed that marriage be indissoluble.[173] He abrogates the accommodations that had slipped into the old Law.[174]

Between the baptized, "a ratified and consummated marriage cannot be dissolved by any human power or for any reason other than death."[175]

2383 The *separation* of spouses while maintaining the marriage bond can be legitimate in certain cases provided for by canon law.[176]

If civil divorce remains the only possible way of ensuring certain legal rights, the care of the children, or the protection of inheritance, it can be tolerated and does not constitute a moral offense.

2384 Divorce is a grave offense against the natural law. It claims to break the contract, to which the spouses freely consented, to live with each other till death. Divorce does injury to the covenant of salvation, of which sacramental marriage is the sign. Contracting a new union, even if it is recognized by civil law, adds to the gravity of the rupture: the remarried spouse is then in a situation of public and permanent adultery:

> If a husband, separated from his wife, approaches another woman, he is an adulterer because he makes that woman commit adultery; and the woman who lives with him is an adulteress because she has drawn another's husband to herself.[177]

2385 Divorce is immoral also because it introduces disorder into the family and into society. This disorder brings grave harm to the deserted spouse, to children traumatized by the separation of their parents and often torn between them, and because of its contagious effect which makes it truly a plague on society.

2386 It can happen that one of the spouses is the innocent victim of a divorce decreed by civil law; this spouse therefore has not contravened the moral law. There is a considerable difference between a spouse who has sincerely tried to be faithful to the sacrament of marriage and is unjustly abandoned, and one who through his own grave fault destroys a canonically valid marriage.[178]

Other Offenses Against the Dignity of Marriage

2387 The predicament of a man who, desiring to convert to the Gospel, is obliged to repudiate one or more wives with whom he has shared years of conjugal life, is understandable. However *polygamy* is not in accord with the moral law. "[Conjugal] communion is radically contradicted by polygamy; this, in fact, directly negates the plan of God which was revealed from the beginning, because it is contrary to the equal personal dignity of men and women who in matrimony give themselves with a love that is total and therefore unique and exclusive."[179] The Christian who has previously lived in polygamy has a grave duty in justice to honor the obligations contracted in regard to his former wives and his children.

2388 Incest designates intimate relations between relatives or in-laws within a degree that prohibits marriage between them.[180] St. Paul stigmatizes this especially grave offense: "It is actually reported that there is immorality among you . . . for a man is living with his father's wife. . . . In the name of the Lord Jesus . . . you are to deliver this man to Satan for the destruction of the flesh. . . ."[181] Incest corrupts family relationships and marks a regression toward animality.

2389 Connected to incest is any sexual abuse perpetrated by adults on children or adolescents entrusted to their care. The offense is compounded by the scandalous harm done to the physical and moral integrity of the young, who will remain scarred by it all their lives; and the violation of responsibility for their upbringing.

2390 In a so-called *free union,* a man and a woman refuse to give juridical and public form to a liaison involving sexual intimacy.

The expression "free union" is fallacious: what can "union" mean when the partners make no commitment to one another, each exhibiting a lack of trust in the other, in himself, or in the future?

The expression covers a number of different situations: concubinage, rejection of marriage as such, or inability to make long-term commitments.[182] All these situations offend against the dignity of marriage; they destroy the very idea of the family; they weaken the sense of fidelity. They are contrary to the moral law. The sexual act must take place exclusively within marriage. Outside of marriage it always constitutes a grave sin and excludes one from sacramental communion.

2391 Some today claim a *"right to a trial marriage"* where there is an intention of getting married later. However firm the purpose of those who engage in premature sexual relations may be, "the fact is that such liaisons can scarcely ensure mutual sincerity and fidelity in a relationship between a man and a woman, nor, especially, can they protect it from inconstancy of desires or whim."[183] Carnal union is morally legitimate only when a definitive community of life between a man and woman has been established. Human love does not tolerate "trial marriages." It demands a total and definitive gift of persons to one another.[184]

In Brief

2392 "Love is the fundamental and innate vocation of every human being" (*FC* 11).

2393 By creating the human being man and woman, God gives personal dignity equally to the one and the other. Each of them, man and woman, should acknowledge and accept his sexual identity.

2394 Christ is the model of chastity. Every baptized person is called to lead a chaste life, each according to his particular state of life.

2395 Chastity means the integration of sexuality within the person. It includes an apprenticeship in self-mastery.

2396 Among the sins gravely contrary to chastity are masturbation, fornication, pornography, and homosexual practices.

2397 The covenant which spouses have freely entered into entails faithful love. It imposes on them the obligation to keep their marriage indissoluble.

2398 Fecundity is a good, a gift and an end of marriage. By giving life, spouses participate in God's fatherhood.

2399 The regulation of births represents one of the aspects of responsible fatherhood and motherhood. Legitimate intentions on the part of the spouses do not justify recourse to morally unacceptable means (for example, direct sterilization or contraception).

2400 Adultery, divorce, polygamy, and free union are grave offenses against the dignity of marriage.

Notes

112. *Ex* 20:14; *Deut* 5:18.
113. *Mt* 5:27–28.
114. *FC* 11.
115. *Gen* 1:27.
116. *Gen* 1:28.
117. *Gen* 5:1–2.
118. *FC* 22; cf. *GS* 49 § 2.
119. *MD* 6.
120. *Gen* 2:24.
121. Cf. *Gen* 4:1–2, 25–26; 5:1.
122. *Mt* 5:27–28.
123. Cf. *Mt* 19:6.
124. Cf. *Mt* 5:37.
125. Cf. *Sir* 1:22.
126. *GS* 17.
127. St. Augustine, *Conf.* 10, 29, 40: PL 32, 796.
128. Cf. *Titus* 2:1–6.
129. *FC* 34.
130. *GS* 25 § 1.
131. Cf. *Gal* 5:22.
132. Cf. *1 Jn* 3:3.
133. Cf. *Jn* 15:15.
134. *Gal* 3:27.
135. CDF, *Persona humana* 11.
136. St. Ambrose, *De viduis* 4, 23: PL 16, 255A.
137. CDF, *Persona humana* 9.
138. CDF, *Persona humana* 9.
139. Cf. *1 Cor* 6:15–20.
140. Cf. *Gen* 19:1–29; *Rom* 1:24–27; *1 Cor* 6:10; *1 Tim* 1:10.
141. CDF, *Persona humana* 8.
142. *FC* 11.
143. *Tob* 8:4–9.
144. *GS* 49 § 2.
145. Pius XII, Discourse, October 29, 1951.
146. *GS* 48 § 1.
147. Cf. CIC, can. 1056.
148. *Mk* 10:9; cf. *Mt* 19:1–12; *1 Cor* 7:10–11.
149. St. John Chrysostom, *Hom. in Eph.* 20, 8: PG 62, 146–147.
150. *FC* 30.
151. *HV* 11.
152. *HV* 12; cf. Pius XI, encyclical, *Casti connubii*.
153. Cf. *Eph* 3:14; *Mt* 23:9.
154. *GS* 50 § 2.
155. *GS* 51 § 3.
156. Cf. *HV* 12.
157. *HV* 16.
158. *HV* 14.
159. *FC* 32.
160. *GS* 51 § 4.
161. Cf. *HV* 23; *PP* 37.
162. Cf. *GS* 50 § 2.
163. *Gen* 15:2.

164. *Gen* 30:1.

165. CDF, *Donum vitae* intro., 2.

166. CDF, *Donum vitae* II, 1.

167. CDF, *Donum vitae* II, 5.

168. CDF, *Donum vitae* II, 4.

169. CDF, *Donum vitae* II, 8.

170. Cf. *Mt* 5:27–28.

171. Cf. *Mt* 5:32; 19:6; *Mk* 10:11; *1 Cor* 6:9–10.

172. Cf. *Hos* 2:7; *Jer* 5:7; 13:27.

173. Cf. *Mt* 5:31–32; 19:3–9; *Mk* 10:9, *Lk* 16:18; *1 Cor* 7:10–11.

174. Cf. *Mt* 19:7–9.

175. CIC, can. 1141.

176. Cf. CIC, cann. 1151–1155.

177. *St. Basil, Moralia* 73, 1: PG 31, 849–852.

178. Cf. *FC* 84.

179. *FC* 19; cf. *GS* 47 § 2.

180. Cf. *Lev* 18:7–20.

181. *1 Cor* 5:1, 4–5.

182. Cf. *FC* 81.

183. CDF, *Persona humana* 7.

184. Cf. *FC* 80.

Psychology
and
Sex

T HE PSYCHOLOGY OF SEX has been implicit in many of the discussions so far. For example, we have asked: Do men and women think about and experience sex and love differently. If there are such differences, what is their source? One set of answers is to be found in psychological theories of personality development. We have also pointed out that feminist critiques of many current views of sex and love turn on the validity of depth psychology and the idea that we often misunderstand our own true motivations. Love and sex are so intimately involved with all of our feelings and emotions that it would be helpful to get an overview of at least some traditional psychological theories that deal with the development of personality.

Freud is often credited with having changed the entire way we view ourselves. After Freud, it is difficult to think that we are at any time free of sexual desire. We are at rock bottom, as Freud is often interpreted, sexual creatures, seeking the pleasures of sex or at least the release of tension that comes from sex. Some feminists claim that Freud also was influential in legitimizing the low status of women. After all, Freud claimed that women were partial men in that they lacked penises. Because they lacked a penis, women never fully matured morally. Their clitoris, a sad replica of a penis, could give them great sexual pleasure. But according to Freud, to get pleasure this way was to be immature. It is easy to see why Freud would be the nemesis of many feminists. Yet depth psychology, the view that human motives can be hidden from consciousness, is a necessary condition for the feminist approach. And without Freud, the acceptance of depth psychology—even if not a Freudian depth psychology—would never have been so widespread.

Freud's psychology is not the only theory about human sexuality. To illustrate this, we will focus on the Oedipus complex, for to Freud, it was crucial in understanding human sexuality. After reading Freud's discussion of the Oedipus complex, which is embedded in his essay "Femininity," we will read a very different account of early childhood development by Havelock Ellis, a pioneer in the study of sex and its development. Ellis, as you will see, thought that Freud was mistaken to think that the Oedipus complex was a universal aspect of childhood development. After the Ellis selection, we will outline the views on the Oedipus complex of four other early psychologists who differed with Freud: Carl Jung, Alfred Adler, Otto Rank, and Karen Horney.

THE OEDIPUS COMPLEX

A boy's first love object is his mother. Freud means by "love" sexual love. The boy so loves his mother that he sees his father as an enemy. The boy wishes his father dead. Of course the father is seen as much stronger than the boy. The boy fears that he will be punished for lusting after his mother. How will he be punished? The father will take the one thing the boy prizes most: his penis. Thus fear of castration is what allows the young boy to put aside his sexual longings for the mother and gradually identify with the father.

A young girl has a more difficult time getting over (resolving) the Oedipus stage. She must wind-up with her father as representative of her love object without at the same time continuing to love him sexually. The young girl must turn from attachment to her mother. This happens in two ways. In simple development, the girl is weaned and toilet trained. Both of these cause her to become annoyed with her mother. But worse, the girl realizes that she has no penis. Why not? Her mother must have taken it away. Where can the little girl get a penis? From her father. When this happens properly, the girl sees her father not as a real possible lover but as representative—by virtue of having a penis—of possible lovers.

from Lecture XXXIII: Femininity[1]

SIGMUND FREUD

Ladies and Gentlemen,—All the while I am preparing to talk to you I am struggling with an internal difficulty. I feel uncertain, so to speak, of the extent of my license. It is true that in the course of fifteen years of work psycho-analysis has changed and grown richer; but, in spite of that, an introduction to psycho-analysis might have been left without alteration or supplement. It is constantly in my mind that these lectures are without a *raison d'être*. For analysts I am saying too little and nothing at all that is new; but for you I am saying too much and saying things which you are not equipped to understand and which are not in your province. I have looked around for excuses and I have tried to justify each separate lecture on different grounds. The first one, on the theory of dreams, was supposed to put you back again at one blow into the analytic atmosphere and to show you how durable our views have turned out to be. I was led on to the second one, which followed the paths from dreams to what is called occultism, by the opportunity of speaking my mind without constraint on a department of work in which prejudiced expectations are fighting to-day against passionate resistances, and I could hope that your judgement, educated to tolerance on the example of psycho-analysis, would not refuse to accompany me on the excursion. The third lecture, on the dissection of the personality, certainly made the hardest demands upon you with its unfamiliar subject-matter; but it was impossible for me to keep this first beginning of an ego-psychology back from you, and if we had possessed it fifteen years ago I should have had to mention it to you then. My last lecture, finally, which you were probably able to follow only by great exertions, brought forward necessary corrections—fresh attempts at solving the most important conundrums; and my introduction would have been leading you astray if I had been silent about them. As you see, when one starts making excuses it turns out in the end that it was all inevitable, all the work of destiny. I submit to it, and I beg you to do the same.

To-day's lecture, too, should have no place in

From *New Introductory Lectures on Psycho-Analysis* by Sigmund Freud, translated by James Strachey. Translation copyright © 1965, 1964 by James Strachey. Reprinted by permission of W. W. Norton & Company, Inc.

an introduction; but it may serve to give you an example of a detailed piece of analytic work, and I can say two things to recommend it. It brings forward nothing but observed facts, almost without any speculative additions, and it deals with a subject which has a claim on your interest second almost to no other. Throughout history people have knocked their heads against the riddle of the nature of femininity—

Häupter in Hieroglyphenmützen,
Häupter in Turban und schwarzem Barett,
Perückenhäupter und tausend andre
Arme, schwitzende Menschenhäupter. . . .[2]

Nor will *you* have escaped worrying over this problem—those of you who are men; to those of you who are women this will not apply—you are yourselves the problem. When you meet a human being, the first distinction you make is "male or female?" and you are accustomed to make the distinction with unhesitating certainty. Anatomical science shares your certainty at one point and not much further. The male sexual product, the spermatozoon, and its vehicle are male; the ovum and the organism that harbours it are female. In both sexes organs have been formed which serve exclusively for the sexual functions; they were probably developed from the same [innate] disposition into two different forms. Besides this, in both sexes the other organs, the bodily shapes and tissues, show the influence of the individual's sex, but this is inconstant and its amount variable; these are what are known as the secondary sexual characters. Science next tells you something that runs counter to your expectations and is probably calculated to confuse your feelings. It draws your attention to the fact that portions of the male sexual apparatus also appear in women's bodies, though in an atrophied state, and vice versa in the alternative case. It regards their occurrence as indications of *bisexuality*,[3] as though an individual is not a man or a woman but always both—merely a certain amount more the one than the other. You will then be asked to make yourselves familiar with the idea that the proportion in which masculine and feminine are mixed in an individual is subject to quite considerable fluctuations. Since, however, apart from the very rarest cases, only one kind of sexual product—ova or semen—is nevertheless

present in one person, you are bound to have doubts as to the decisive significance of those elements and must conclude that what constitutes masculinity or femininity is an unknown characteristic which anatomy cannot lay hold of.

• • •

Can psychology do so perhaps? We are accustomed to employ "masculine" and "feminine" as mental qualities as well, and have in the same way transferred the notion of bisexuality to mental life. Thus we speak of a person, whether male or female, as behaving in a masculine way in one connection and in a feminine way in another. But you will soon perceive that this is only giving way to anatomy or to convention. You cannot give the concepts of "masculine" and "feminine" *any* new connotation. The distinction is not a psychological one; when you say "masculine," you usually mean "active," and when you say "feminine," you usually mean "passive." Now it is true that a relation of the kind exists. The male sex-cell is actively mobile and searches out the female one, and the latter, the ovum, is immobile and waits passively. This behaviour of the elementary sexual organisms is indeed a model for the conduct of sexual individuals during intercourse. The male pursues the female for the purpose of sexual union, seizes hold of her and penetrates into her. But by this you have precisely reduced the characteristic of masculinity to the factor of aggressiveness so far as psychology is concerned. You may well doubt whether you have gained any real advantage from this when you reflect that in some classes of animals the females are the stronger and more aggressive and the male is active only in the single act of sexual union. This is so, for instance, with the spiders. Even the functions of rearing and caring for the young, which strike us as feminine *par excellence,* are not invariably attached to the female sex in animals. In quite high species we find that the sexes share the task of caring for the young between them or even that the male alone devotes himself to it. Even in the sphere of human sexual life you soon see how inadequate it is to make masculine behaviour coincide with activity and feminine with passivity. A mother is active in every sense towards her child; the act of lactation itself may equally be described as the mother suckling the baby or as her being sucked by it. The further you go from the narrow sexual sphere the more obvious will the "error of superimposition"[4] become. Women can display great activity in various directions, men are not able to live in company with their own kind unless they develop a large amount of passive adaptability. If you now tell me that these facts go to prove precisely that both men and women are bisexual in the psychological sense, I shall conclude that you have decided in your own minds to make "active" coincide with "masculine" and "passive" with "feminine." But I advise you against it. It seems to me to serve no useful purpose and adds nothing to our knowledge.[5]

One might consider characterizing femininity psychologically as giving preference to passive aims. This is not, of course, the same thing as passivity; to achieve a passive aim may call for a large amount of activity. It is perhaps the case that in a woman, on the basis of her share in the sexual function, a preference for passive behaviour and passive aims is carried over into her life to a greater or lesser extent, in proportion to the limits, restricted or far-reaching, within which her sexual life thus serves as a model. But we must beware in this of underestimating the influence of social customs, which similarly force women into passive situations. All this is still far from being cleared up. There is one particularly constant relation between femininity and instinctual life which we do not want to overlook. The suppression of women's aggressiveness which is prescribed for them constitutionally and imposed on them socially favours the development of powerful masochistic impulses, which succeed, as we know, in binding erotically the destructive trends which have been diverted inwards. Thus masochism, as people say, is truly feminine. But if, as happens so often, you meet with masochism in men, what is left to you but to say that these men exhibit very plain feminine traits?

And now you are already prepared to hear that psychology too is unable to solve the riddle of femininity. The explanation must no doubt come from elsewhere, and cannot come till we have learnt how in general the differentiation of living organisms into two sexes came about. We know nothing about it, yet the existence of two sexes is

a most striking characteristic of organic life which distinguishes it sharply from inanimate nature. However, we find enough to study in those human individuals who, through the possession of female genitals, are characterized as manifestly or predominantly feminine. In conformity with its peculiar nature, psycho-analysis does not try to describe what a woman is—that would be a task it could scarcely perform—but sets about enquiring how she comes into being, how a woman develops out of a child with a bisexual disposition. In recent times we have begun to learn a little about this, thanks to the circumstance that several of our excellent women colleagues in analysis have begun to work at the question. The discussion of this has gained special attractiveness from the distinction between the sexes. For the ladies, whenever some comparison seemed to turn out unfavourable to their sex, were able to utter a suspicion that we, the male analysts, had been unable to overcome certain deeply-rooted prejudices against what was feminine, and that this was being paid for in the partiality of our researches. We, on the other hand, standing on the ground of bisexuality, had no difficulty in avoiding impoliteness. We had only to say: "This doesn't apply to *you*. You're the exception; on this point you're more masculine than feminine."

• • •

We approach the investigation of the sexual development of women with two expectations. The first is that here once more the constitution will not adapt itself to its function without a struggle. The second is that the decisive turning-points will already have been prepared for or completed before puberty. Both expectations are promptly confirmed. Furthermore, a comparison with what happens with boys tells us that the development of a little girl into a normal woman is more difficult and more complicated, since it includes two extra tasks, to which there is nothing corresponding in the development of a man. Let us follow the parallel lines from their beginning. Undoubtedly the material is different to start with in boys and girls: it did not need psycho-analysis to establish that. The difference in the structure of the genitals is accompanied by other bodily differences which are too well known to call for mention. Differences emerge too in the instinctual disposition which give a glimpse of the later nature of women. A little girl is as a rule less aggressive, defiant and self-sufficient; she seems to have a greater need for being shown affection and on that account to be more dependent and pliant. It is probably only as a result of this pliancy that she can be taught more easily and quicker to control her excretions: urine and faeces are the first gifts that children make to those who look after them . . . and controlling them is the first concession to which the instinctual life of children can be induced. One gets an impression, too, that little girls are more intelligent and livelier than boys of the same age; they go out more to meet the external world and at the same time form stronger object-cathexes. I cannot say whether this lead in development has been confirmed by exact observations, but in any case there is no question that girls cannot be described as intellectually backward. These sexual differences are not, however, of great consequence: they can be outweighed by individual variations. For our immediate purposes they can be disregarded.

Both sexes seem to pass through the early phases of libidinal development in the same manner. It might have been expected that in girls there would already have been some lag in aggressiveness in the sadistic-anal phase, but such is not the case. Analysis of children's play has shown our women analysts that the aggressive impulses of little girls leave nothing to be desired in the way of abundance and violence. With their entry into the phallic phase the differences between the sexes are completely eclipsed by their agreements. We are now obliged to recognize that the little girl is a little man. In boys, as we know, this phase is marked by the fact that they have learnt how to derive pleasurable sensations from their small penis and connect its excited state with their ideas of sexual intercourse. Little girls do the same thing with their still smaller clitoris. It seems that with them all their masturbatory acts are carried out on this penis-equivalent, and that the truly feminine vagina is still undiscovered by both sexes. It is true that there are a few isolated reports of early vaginal sensations as well, but it could not be easy to distinguish these from sensations in the anus or vestibulum; in any case they cannot play a great part. We are entitled to keep to our view that in the

phallic phase of girls the clitoris is the leading erotogenic zone. But it is not, of course, going to remain so. With the change to femininity the clitoris should wholly or in part hand over its sensitivity, and at the same time its importance, to the vagina. This would be one of the two tasks which a woman has to perform in the course of her development, whereas the more fortunate man has only to continue at the time of his sexual maturity the activity that he has previously carried out at the period of the early efflorescence of his sexuality.

We shall return to the part played by the clitoris; let us now turn to the second task with which a girl's development is burdened. A boy's mother is the first object of his love, and she remains so too during the formation of his Oedipus complex and, in essence, all through his life. For a girl too her first object must be her mother (and the figures of wet-nurses and foster-mothers that merge into her). The first object-cathexes occur in attachment to the satisfaction of the major and simple vital needs,[6] and the circumstances of the care of children are the same for both sexes. But in the Oedipus situation the girl's father has become her love-object, and we expect that in the normal course of development she will find her way from this paternal object to her final choice of an object. In the course of time, therefore, a girl has to change her erotogenic zone and her object—both of which a boy retains. The question then arises of how this happens: in particular, how does a girl pass from her mother to an attachment to her father? or, in other words, how does she pass from her masculine phase to the feminine one to which she is biologically destined?

It would be a solution of ideal simplicity if we could suppose that from a particular age onwards the elementary influence of the mutual attraction between the sexes makes itself felt and impels the small woman towards men, while the same law allows the boy to continue with his mother. We might suppose in addition that in this the children are following the pointer given them by the sexual preference of their parents. But we are not going to find things so easy; we scarcely know whether we are to believe seriously in the power of which poets talk so much and with such enthusiasm but which cannot be further dissected analytically. We have found an answer of quite another sort by means of laborious investigations, the material for which at least was easy to arrive at. For you must know that the number of women who remain till a late age tenderly dependent on a paternal object, or indeed on their real father, is very great. We have established some surprising facts about these women with an intense attachment of long duration to their father. We knew, of course, that there had been a preliminary stage of attachment to the mother, but we did not know that it could be so rich in content and so long-lasting, and could leave behind so many opportunities for fixations and dispositions. During this time the girl's father is only a troublesome rival; in some cases the attachment to her mother lasts beyond the fourth year of life. Almost everything that we find later in her relation to her father was already present in this earlier attachment and has been transferred subsequently on to her father. In short, we get an impression that we cannot understand women unless we appreciate this phase of their pre-Oedipus attachment to their mother.

We shall be glad, then, to know the nature of the girl's libidinal relations to her mother. The answer is that they are of very many different kinds. Since they persist through all three phases of infantile sexuality, they also take on the characteristics of the different phases and express themselves by oral, sadistic-anal and phallic wishes. These wishes represent active as well as passive impulses; if we relate them to the differentiation of the sexes which is to appear later—though we should avoid doing so as far as possible—we may call them masculine and feminine. Besides this, they are completely ambivalent, both affectionate and of a hostile and aggressive nature. The latter often only come to light after being changed into anxiety ideas. It is not always easy to point to a formulation of these early sexual wishes; what is most clearly expressed is a wish to get the mother with child and the corresponding wish to bear her a child—both belonging to the phallic period and sufficiently surprising, but established beyond doubt by analytic observation. The attractiveness of these investigations lies in the surprising detailed findings which they bring us. Thus, for instance, we discover the fear of being murdered or poisoned, which may later form the core of a paranoic illness, already present in this pre-Oedipus

period, in relation to the mother. Or another case: you will recall an interesting episode in the history of analytic research which caused me many distressing hours. In the period in which the main interest was directed to discovering infantile sexual traumas, almost all my women patients told me that they had been seduced by their father. I was driven to recognize in the end that these reports were untrue and so came to understand that hysterical symptoms are derived from phantasies and not from real occurrences. It was only later that I was able to recognize in this phantasy of being seduced by the father the expression of the typical Oedipus complex in women. And now we find the phantasy of seduction once more in the pre-Oedipus prehistory of girls; but the seducer is regularly the mother. Here, however, the phantasy touches the ground of reality, for it was really the mother who by her activities over the child's bodily hygiene inevitably stimulated, and perhaps even roused for the first time, pleasurable sensations in her genitals.[7]

I have no doubt you are ready to suspect that this portrayal of the abundance and strength of a little girl's sexual relations with her mother is very much overdrawn. After all, one has opportunities of seeing little girls and notices nothing of the sort. But the objection is not to the point. Enough can be seen in the children if one knows how to look. And besides, you should consider how little of its sexual wishes a child can bring to preconscious expression or communicate at all. Accordingly we are only within our rights if we study the residues and consequences of this emotional world in retrospect, in people in whom these processes of development had attained a specially clear and even excessive degree of expansion. Pathology has always done us the service of making discernible by isolation and exaggeration conditions which would remain concealed in a normal state. And since our investigations have been carried out on people who were by no means seriously abnormal, I think we should regard their outcome as deserving belief.

We will now turn our interest on to the single question of what it is that brings this powerful attachment of the girl to her mother to an end. This, as we know, is its usual fate: it is destined to make room for an attachment to her father. Here we come upon a fact which is a pointer to our further advance. This step in development does not involve only a simple change of object. The turning away from the mother is accompanied by hostility; the attachment to the mother ends in hate. A hate of that kind may become very striking and last all through life; it may be carefully overcompensated later on; as a rule one part of it is overcome while another part persists. Events of later years naturally influence this greatly. We will restrict ourselves, however, to studying it at the time at which the girl turns to her father and to enquiring into the motives for it. We are then given a long list of accusations and grievances against the mother which are supposed to justify the child's hostile feelings; they are of varying validity which we shall not fail to examine. A number of them are obvious rationalizations and the true sources of enmity remain to be found. I hope you will be interested if on this occasion I take you through all the details of a psycho-analytic investigation.

The reproach against the mother which goes back furthest is that she gave the child too little milk—which is construed against her as lack of love. Now there is some justification for this reproach in our families. Mothers often have insufficient nourishment to give their children and are content to suckle them for a few months, for half or three-quarters of a year. Among primitive peoples children are fed at their mother's breast for two or three years. The figure of the wet-nurse who suckles the child is as a rule merged into the mother; when this has not happened, the reproach is turned into another one—that the nurse, who fed the child so willingly, was sent away by the mother too early. But whatever the true state of affairs may have been, it is impossible that the child's reproach can be justified as often as it is met with. It seems, rather, that the child's avidity for its earliest nourishment is altogether insatiable, that it never gets over the pain of losing its mother's breast. I should not be surprised if the analysis of a primitive child, who could still suck at its mother's breast when it was already able to run about and talk, were to bring the same reproach to light. The fear of being poisoned is also probably connected with the withdrawal of the breast. Poison is nourishment that makes one ill. Perhaps children trace back their early illnesses too to this frustration. A fair amount of intellectual education

is a prerequisite for believing in chance; primitive people and uneducated ones, and no doubt children as well, are able to assign a ground for everything that happens. Perhaps originally it was a reason on animistic lines. Even to-day in some strata of our population no one can die without having been killed by someone else—preferably by the doctor. And the regular reaction of a neurotic to the death of someone closely connected with him is to put the blame on himself for having caused the death.

The next accusation against the child's mother flares up when the next baby appears in the nursery. If possible the connection with oral frustration is preserved: the mother could not or would not give the child any more milk because she needed the nourishment for the new arrival. In cases in which the two children are so close in age that lactation is prejudiced by the second pregnancy, this reproach acquires a real basis, and it is a remarkable fact that a child, even with an age difference of only 11 months, is not too young to take notice of what is happening. But what the child grudges the unwanted intruder and rival is not only the suckling but all the other signs of maternal care. It feels that it has been dethroned, despoiled, prejudiced in its rights; it casts a jealous hatred upon the new baby and develops a grievance against the faithless mother which often finds expression in a disagreeable change in its behaviour. It becomes "naughty," perhaps, irritable and disobedient and goes back on the advances it has made towards controlling its excretions. All of this has been very long familiar and is accepted as self-evident; but we rarely form a correct idea of the strength of these jealous impulses, of the tenacity with which they persist and of the magnitude of their influence on later development. Especially as this jealousy is constantly receiving fresh nourishment in the later years of childhood and the whole shock is repeated with the birth of each new brother or sister. Nor does it make much difference if the child happens to remain the mother's preferred favourite. A child's demands for love are immoderate, they make exclusive claims and tolerate no sharing.

An abundant source of a child's hostility to its mother is provided by its multifarious sexual wishes, which alter according to the phase of the libido and which cannot for the most part be satisfied. The strongest of these frustrations occur at the phallic period, if the mother forbids pleasurable activity with the genitals—often with severe threats and every sign of displeasure—activity to which, after all, she herself had introduced the child. One would think these were reasons enough to account for a girl's turning away from her mother. One would judge, if so, that the estrangement follows inevitably from the nature of children's sexuality, from the immoderate character of their demand for love and the impossibility of fulfilling their sexual wishes. It might be thought indeed that this first love-relation of the child's is doomed to dissolution for the very reason that it is the first, for these early object-cathexes are regularly ambivalent to a high degree. A powerful tendency to aggressiveness is always present beside a powerful love, and the more passionately a child loves its object the more sensitive does it become to disappointments and frustrations from that object; and in the end the love must succumb to the accumulated hostility. Or the idea that there is an original ambivalence such as this in erotic cathexes may be rejected, and it may be pointed out that it is the special nature of the mother-child relation that leads, with equal inevitability, to the destruction of the child's love; for even the mildest upbringing cannot avoid using compulsion and introducing restrictions, and any such intervention in the child's liberty must provoke as a reaction an inclination to rebelliousness and aggressiveness. A discussion of these possibilities might, I think, be most interesting; but an objection suddenly emerges which forces our interest in another direction. All these factors—the slights, the disappointments in love, the jealousy, the seduction followed by prohibition—are, after all, also in operation in the relation of a *boy* to his mother and are yet unable to alienate him from the maternal object. Unless we can find something that is specific for girls and is not present or not in the same way present in boys, we shall not have explained the termination of the attachment of girls to their mother.

I believe we have found this specific factor, and indeed where we expected to find it, even though in a surprising form. Where we expected to find it, I say, for it lies in the castration complex. After all, the anatomical distinction [between the sexes]

must express itself in psychical consequences. It was, however, a surprise to learn from analyses that girls hold their mother responsible for their lack of a penis and do not forgive her for their being thus put at a disadvantage.

As you hear, then, we ascribe a castration complex to women as well. And for good reasons, though its content cannot be the same as with boys. In the latter the castration complex arises after they have learnt from the sight of the female genitals that the organ which they value so highly need not necessarily accompany the body. At this the boy recalls to mind the threats he brought on himself by his doings with that organ, he begins to give credence to them and falls under the influence of fear of castration, which will be the most powerful motive force in his subsequent development. The castration complex of girls is also started by the sight of the genitals of the other sex. They at once notice the difference and, it must be admitted, its significance too. They feel seriously wronged, often declare that they want to "have something like it too," and fall a victim to "envy for the penis," which will leave ineradicable traces on their development and the formation of their character and which will not be surmounted in even the most favourable cases without a severe expenditure of psychical energy. The girl's recognition of the fact of her being without a penis does not by any means imply that she submits to the fact easily. On the contrary, she continues to hold on for a long time to the wish to get something like it herself and she believes in that possibility for improbably long years; and analysis can show that, at a period when knowledge of reality has long since rejected the fulfilment of the wish as unattainable, it persists in the unconscious and retains a considerable cathexis of energy. The wish to get the longed-for penis eventually in spite of everything may contribute to the motives that drive a mature woman to analysis, and what she may reasonably expect from analysis—a capacity, for instance, to carry on an intellectual profession—may often be recognized as a sublimated modification of this repressed wish.

One cannot very well doubt the importance of envy for the penis. You may take it as an instance of male injustice if I assert that envy and jealousy play an even greater part in the mental life of women than of men. It is not that I think these characteristics are absent in men or that I think they have no other roots in women than envy for the penis; but I am inclined to attribute their greater amount in women to this latter influence. Some analysts, however, have shown an inclination to depreciate the importance of this first instalment of penis-envy in the phallic phase. They are of opinion that what we find of this attitude in women is in the main a secondary structure which has come about on the occasion of later conflicts by regression to this early infantile impulse. This, however, is a general problem of depth psychology. In many pathological—or even unusual—instinctual attitudes (for instance, in all sexual perversions) the question arises of how much of their strength is to be attributed to early infantile fixations and how much to the influence of later experiences and developments. In such cases it is almost always a matter of complemental series such as we put forward in our discussion of the aetiology of the neuroses.[8] Both factors play a part in varying amounts in the causation; a less on the one side is balanced by a more on the other. The infantile factor sets the pattern in all cases but does not always determine the issue, though it often does. Precisely in the case of penis-envy I should argue decidedly in favour of the preponderance of the infantile factor.

The discovery that she is castrated is a turning-point in a girl's growth. Three possible lines of development start from it: one leads to sexual inhibition or to neurosis, the second to change of character in the sense of a masculinity complex, the third, finally, to normal femininity. We have learnt a fair amount, though not everything, about all three.

The essential content of the first is as follows: the little girl has hitherto lived in a masculine way, has been able to get pleasure by the excitation of her clitoris and has brought this activity into relation with her sexual wishes directed towards her mother, which are often active ones; now, owing to the influence of her penis-envy, she loses her enjoyment in her phallic sexuality. Her self-love is mortified by the comparison with the boy's far superior equipment and in consequence she renounces her masturbatory satisfaction from her clitoris, repudiates her love for her mother and at

the same time not infrequently represses a good part of her sexual trends in general. No doubt her turning away from her mother does not occur all at once, for to begin with the girl regards her castration as an individual misfortune, and only gradually extends it to other females and finally to her mother as well. Her love was directed to her *phallic* mother; with the discovery that her mother is castrated it becomes possible to drop her as an object, so that the motives for hostility, which have long been accumulating, gain the upper hand. This means, therefore, that as a result of the discovery of women's lack of a penis they are debased in value for girls just as they are for boys and later perhaps for men.

You all know the immense aetiological importance attributed by our neurotic patients to their masturbation. They make it responsible for all their troubles and we have the greatest difficulty in persuading them that they are mistaken. In fact, however, we ought to admit to them that they are right, for masturbation is the executive agent of infantile sexuality, from the faulty development of which they are indeed suffering. But what neurotics mostly blame is the masturbation of the period of puberty; they have mostly forgotten that of early infancy, which is what is really in question. I wish I might have an opportunity some time of explaining to you at length how important all the factual details of early masturbation become for the individual's subsequent neurosis or character: whether or not it was discovered, how the parents struggled against it or permitted it, or whether he succeeded in suppressing it himself. All of this leaves permanent traces on his development. But I am on the whole glad that I need not do this. It would be a hard and tedious task and at the end of it you would put me in an embarrassing situation by quite certainly asking me to give you some practical advice as to how a parent or educator should deal with the masturbation of small children.[9] From the development of girls, which is what my present lecture is concerned with, I can give you the example of a child herself trying to get free from masturbating. She does not always succeed in this. If envy for the penis has provoked a powerful impulse against clitoridal masturbation but this nevertheless refuses to give way, a violent struggle for liberation ensues in which the girl, as it were, herself takes over the role of her deposed mother and gives expression to her entire dissatisfaction with her inferior clitoris in her efforts against obtaining satisfaction from it. Many years later, when her masturbatory activity has long since been suppressed, an interest still persists which we must interpret as a defence against a temptation that is still dreaded. It manifests inself in the emergence of sympathy for those to whom similar difficulties are attributed, it plays a part as a motive in contracting a marriage and, indeed, it may determine the choice of a husband or lover. Disposing of early infantile masturbation is truly no easy or indifferent business.

Along with the abandonment of clitoridal masturbation a certain amount of activity is renounced. Passivity now has the upper hand, and the girl's turning to her father is accomplished principally with the help of passive instinctual impulses. You can see that a wave of development like this, which clears the phallic activity out of the way, smooths the ground for femininity. If too much is not lost in the course of it through repression, this femininity may turn out to be normal. The wish with which the girl turns to her father is no doubt originally the wish for the penis which her mother has refused her and which she now expects from her father. The feminine situation is only established, however, if the wish for a penis is replaced by one for a baby, if, that is, a baby takes the place of a penis in accordance with an ancient symbolic equivalence. . . . It has not escaped us that the girl has wished for a baby earlier, in the undisturbed phallic phase: that, of course, was the meaning of her playing with dolls. But that play was not in fact an expression of her femininity; it served as an identification with her mother with the intention of substituting activity for passivity. *She* was playing the part of her mother and the doll was herself: now she could do with the baby everything that her mother used to do with her. Not until the emergence of the wish for a penis does the doll-baby become a baby from the girl's father, and thereafter the aim of the most powerful feminine wish. Her happiness is great if later on this wish for a baby finds fulfilment in reality, and quite especially so if the baby is a little boy who brings the longed-for penis with him.[10] Often enough in her combined picture of "a baby from

her father" the emphasis is laid on the baby and her father left unstressed. In this way the ancient masculine wish for the possession of a penis is still faintly visible through the femininity now achieved. But perhaps we ought rather to recognize this wish for a penis as being *par excellence* a feminine one.

With the transference of the wish for a penis-baby on to her father, the girl has entered the situation of the Oedipus complex. Her hostility to her mother, which did not need to be freshly created, is now greatly intensified, for she becomes the girl's rival, who receives from her father everything that she desires from him. For a long time the girl's Oedipus complex concealed her pre-Oedipus attachment to her mother from our view, though it is nevertheless so important and leaves such lasting fixations behind it. For girls the Oedipus situation is the outcome of a long and difficult development; it is a kind of preliminary solution, a position of rest which is not soon abandoned, especially as the beginning of the latency period is not far distant. And we are now struck by a difference between the two sexes, which is probably momentous, in regard to the relation of the Oedipus complex to the castration complex. In a boy the Oedipus complex, in which he desires his mother and would like to get rid of his father as being a rival, develops naturally from the phase of his phallic sexuality. The threat of castration compels him, however, to give up that attitude. Under the impression of the danger of losing his penis, the Oedipus complex is abandoned, repressed and, in the most normal cases, entirely destroyed, . . . and a severe super-ego is set up as its heir. What happens with a girl is almost the opposite. The castration complex prepares for the Oedipus complex instead of destroying it; the girl is driven out of her attachment to her mother through the influence of her envy for the penis and she enters the Oedipus situation as though into a haven of refuge. In the absence of fear of castration the chief motive is lacking which leads boys to surmount the Oedipus complex. Girls remain in it for an indeterminate length of time; they demolish it late and, even so, incompletely. In these circumstances the formation of the super-ego must suffer; it cannot attain the strength and independence which give it its cultural significance, and feminists are not pleased when we point out to them the effects of this factor upon the average feminine character.

To go back a little. We mentioned . . . as the second possible reaction to the discovery of female castration the development of a powerful masculinity complex. By this we mean that the girl refuses, as it were, to recognize the unwelcome fact and, defiantly rebellious, even exaggerates her previous masculinity, clings to her clitoridal activity and takes refuge in an identification with her phallic mother or her father. What can it be that decides in favour of this outcome? We can only suppose that it is a constitutional factor, a greater amount of activity, such as is ordinarily characteristic of a male. However that may be, the essence of this process is that at this point in development the wave of passivity is avoided which opens the way to the turn towards femininity. The extreme achievement of such a masculinity complex would appear to be the influencing of the choice of an object in the sense of manifest homosexuality. Analytic experience teaches us, to be sure, that female homosexuality is seldom or never a direct continuation of infantile masculinity. Even for a girl of this kind it seems necessary that she should take her father as an object for some time and enter the Oedipus situation. But afterwards, as a result of her inevitable disappointments from her father, she is driven to regress into her early masculinity complex. The significance of these disappointments must not be exaggerated; a girl who is destined to become feminine is not spared them, though they do not have the same effect. The predominance of the constitutional factor seems indisputable; but the two phases in the development of female homosexuality are well mirrored in the practices of homosexuals, who play the parts of mother and baby with each other as often and as clearly as those of husband and wife.

• • •

What I have been telling you here may be described as the prehistory of women. It is a product of the very last few years and may have been of interest to you as an example of detailed analytic work. Since its subject is woman, I will venture on this occasion to mention by name a few of the women who have made valuable contributions to this investigation. Dr. Ruth Mack Brunswick

[1928] was the first to describe a case of neurosis which went back to a fixation in the pre-Oedipus stage and had never reached the Oedipus situation at all. The case took the form of jealous paranoia and proved accessible to therapy. Dr. Jeanne Lampl-de Groot [1927] has established the incredible phallic activity of girls towards their mother by some assured observations, and Dr. Helene Deutsch [1932] has shown that the erotic actions of homosexual women reproduce the relations between mother and baby.

It is not my intention to pursue the further behaviour of femininity through puberty to the period of maturity. Our knowledge, moreover, would be insufficient for the purpose. But I will bring a few features together in what follows. Taking its prehistory as a starting-point, I will only emphasize here that the development of femininity remains exposed to disturbance by the residual phenomena of the early masculine period. Regressions to the fixations of the pre-Oedipus phases very frequently occur; in the course of some women's lives there is a repeated alternation between periods in which masculinity or femininity gains the upper hand. Some portion of what we men call "the enigma of women" may perhaps be derived from this expression of bisexuality in women's lives. But another question seems to have become ripe for judgement in the course of these researches. We have called the motive force of sexual life "the libido." Sexual life is dominated by the polarity of masculine-feminine; thus the notion suggests itself of considering the relation of the libido to this antithesis. It would not be surprising if it were to turn out that each sexuality had its own special libido appropriated to it, so that one sort of libido would pursue the aims of a masculine sexual life and another sort those of a feminine one. But nothing of the kind is true. There is only one libido, which serves both the masculine and the feminine sexual functions. To it itself we cannot assign any sex; if, following the conventional equation of activity and masculinity, we are inclined to describe it as masculine, we must not forget that it also covers trends with a passive aim. Nevertheless the juxtaposition "feminine libido" is without any justification. Furthermore, it is our impression that more constraint has been applied to the libido when it is pressed into the service of the feminine function, and that—to speak teleologically—Nature takes less careful account of its [that function's] demands than in the case of masculinity. And the reason for this may lie—thinking once again teleologically—in the fact that the accomplishment of the aim of biology has been entrusted to the aggressiveness of men and has been made to some extent independent of women's consent.

The sexual frigidity of women, the frequency of which appears to confirm this disregard, is a phenomenon that is still insufficiently understood. Sometimes it is psychogenic and in that case accessible to influence; but in other cases it suggests the hypothesis of its being constitutionally determined and even of there being a contributory anatomical factor.

I have promised to tell you of a few more psychical peculiarities of mature femininity, as we come across them in analytic observation. We do not lay claim to more than an average validity for these assertions; nor is it always easy to distinguish what should be ascribed to the influence of the sexual function and what to social breeding. Thus, we attribute a larger amount of narcissism to femininity, which also affects women's choice of object, so that to be loved is a stronger need for them than to love. The effect of penis-envy has a share, further, in the physical vanity of women, since they are bound to value their charms more highly as a late compensation for their original sexual inferiority.[11] Shame, which is considered to be a feminine characteristic *par excellence* but is far more a matter of convention than might be supposed, has as its purpose, we believe, concealment of genital deficiency. We are not forgetting that at a later time shame takes on other functions. It seems that women have made few contributions to the discoveries and inventions in the history of civilization; there is, however, one technique which they may have invented—that of plaiting and weaving. If that is so, we should be tempted to guess the unconscious motive for the achievement. Nature herself would seem to have given the model which this achievement imitates by causing the growth at maturity of the pubic hair that conceals the genitals. The step that remained to be taken lay in making the threads adhere to one another, while on the body they stick into the skin

and are only matted together. If you reject this idea as fantastic and regard my belief in the influence of lack of a penis on the configuration of femininity as an *idée fixe,* I am of course defenceless.

The determinants of women's choice of an object are often made unrecognizable by social conditions. Where the choice is able to show itself freely, it is often made in accordance with the narcissistic ideal of the man whom the girl had wished to become. If the girl has remained in her attachment to her father—that is, in the Oedipus complex—her choice is made according to the paternal type. Since, when she turned from her mother to her father, the hostility of her ambivalent relation remained with her mother, a choice of this kind should guarantee a happy marriage. But very often the outcome is of a kind that presents a general threat to such a settlement of the conflict due to ambivalence. The hostility that has been left behind follows in the train of the positive attachment and spreads over on to the new object. The woman's husband, who to begin with inherited from her father, becomes after a time her mother's heir as well. So it may easily happen that the second half of a woman's life may be filled by the struggle against her husband, just as the shorter first half was filled by her rebellion against her mother. When this reaction has been lived through, a second marriage may easily turn out very much more satisfying.[12] Another alteration in a woman's nature, for which lovers are unprepared, may occur in a marriage after the first child is born. Under the influence of a woman's becoming a mother herself, an identification with her own mother may be revived, against which she had striven up till the time of her marriage, and this may attract all the available libido to itself, so that the compulsion to repeat reproduces an unhappy marriage between her parents. The difference in a mother's reaction to the birth of a son or a daughter shows that the old factor of lack of a penis has even now not lost its strength. A mother is only brought unlimited satisfaction by her relation to a son; this is altogether the most perfect, the most free from ambivalence of all human relationships.[13] A mother can transfer to her son the ambition which she has been obliged to suppress in herself, and she can expect from him the satisfaction of all that has been left over in her of her masculinity complex.

Even a marriage is not made secure until the wife has succeeded in making her husband her child as well and in acting as a mother to him.

A woman's identification with her mother allows us to distinguish two strata: the pre-Oedipus one which rests on her affectionate attachment to her mother and takes her as a model, and the later one from the Oedipus complex which seeks to get rid of her mother and take her place with her father. We are no doubt justified in saying that much of both of them is left over for the future and that neither of them is adequately surmounted in the course of development. But the phase of the affectionate pre-Oedipus attachment is the decisive one for a woman's future: during it preparations are made for the acquisition of the characteristics with which she will later fulfil her role in the sexual function and perform her invaluable social tasks. It is in this identification too that she acquires her attractiveness to a man, whose Oedipus attachment to his mother it kindles into passion. How often it happens, however, that it is only his son who obtains what he himself aspired to! One gets an impression that a man's love and a woman's are a phase apart psychologically.

The fact that women must be regarded as having little sense of justice is no doubt related to the predominance of envy in their mental life; for the demand for justice is a modification of envy and lays down the condition subject to which one can put envy aside. We also regard women as weaker in their social interests and as having less capacity for sublimating their instincts than men. The former is no doubt derived from the dissocial quality which unquestionably characterizes all sexual relations. Lovers find sufficiency in each other, and families too resist inclusion in more comprehensive associations.[14] The aptitude for sublimation is subject to the greatest individual variations. On the other hand I cannot help mentioning an impression that we are constantly receiving during analytic practice. A man of about thirty strikes us as a youthful, somewhat unformed individual, whom we expect to make powerful use of the possibilities for development opened up to him by analysis. A woman of the same age, however, often frightens us by her psychical rigidity and unchangeability. Her libido has taken up final positions and seems incapable of exchanging them for others. There are no paths open to further development; it is as though the whole process had already run its course and remains thenceforward insusceptible to influence—as though, indeed, the difficult development to femininity had exhausted the possibilities of the person concerned. As therapists we lament this state of things, even if we succeed in putting an end to our patient's ailment by doing away with her neurotic conflict.

• • •

That is all I had to say to you about femininity. It is certainly incomplete and fragmentary and does not always sound friendly. But do not forget that I have only been describing women in so far as their nature is determined by their sexual function. It is true that that influence extends very far; but we do not overlook the fact that an individual woman may be a human being in other respects as well. If you want to know more about femininity, enquire from your own experiences of life, or turn to the poets, or wait until science can give you deeper and more coherent information.

Notes

1. [This lecture is mainly based on two earlier papers: "Some Psychical Consequences of the Anatomical Distinction between the Sexes" (1925*j*) and "Female Sexuality" (1931*b*). The last section, however, dealing with women in adult life, contains new material. Freud returned to the subject once again in Chapter VII of the posthumous *Outline of Psycho-Analysis* (1940*a* [1938]).]

2. Heads in hieroglyphic bonnets,
   Heads in turbans and black birettas,
   Heads in wigs and thousand other
   Wretched, sweating heads of humans. . . .
   (Heine, *Nordsee* [Second Cycle, VII, "Fragen"].)

3. [Bisexuality was discussed by Freud in the first edition of his *Three Essays on the Theory of Sexuality* (1905*d*). The passage includes a long footnote to which he made additions in later issues of the work.]

4. [I.e. mistaking two different things for a single one. The term was explained in *Introductory Lectures*, XX.]

5. [The difficulty of finding a psychological meaning for "masculine" and "feminine" was discussed in a long footnote added in 1915 to Section 4 of the third of his *Three Essays* (1905*d*), and again at the beginning of a still longer footnote at the end of Chapter IV of *Civilization and its Discontents* (1930*a*).]

6. [Cf. *Introductory Lectures*, XXI.]

7. [In his early discussions of the aetiology of hysteria Freud often mentioned seduction by adults as among its com-

monest causes (see, for instance, Section I of the second paper on the neuro-psychoses of defence (1896c), and Section II (b) of "The Aetiology of Hysteria" (1896c). But nowhere in these early publications did he specifically inculpate the girl's father. Indeed, in some additional footnotes written in 1924 for the *Gesammelte Schriften* reprint of *Studies on Hysteria,* he admitted to having on two occasions suppressed the fact of the father's responsibility. He made this quite clear, however, in the letter to Fliess of September 21, 1897 (Freud, 1950a, Letter 69), in which he first expressed his scepticism about these stories told by his patients. His first published admission of his mistake was given several years later in a hint in the second of the *Three Essays* (1905d), but a much fuller account of the position followed in his contribution on the aetiology of the neuroses to a volume by Löwenfeld (1906a). Later on he gave two accounts of the effects that this discovery of his mistake had on his own mind—in his "History of the Psycho-Analytic Movement" (1914d), and in his *Autobiographical Study* (1925d), (Norton, 1963). The further discovery which is described in the

present paragraph of the text had already been indicated in the paper on "Female Sexuality" (1931b).]

8. [See *Introductory Lectures,* XXII and XXIII.]

9. [Freud's fullest discussion of masturbation was in his contributions to a symposium on the subject in the Vienna Psycho-Analytical Society (1912f).]

10. [See pp. 440–441 below.]

11. [Cf. Section II of "On Narcissism" (1914c).]

12. [This had already been remarked upon earlier, in "The Taboo of Virginity" (1918a).]

13. [This point seems to have been made by Freud first in a footnote to Chapter VI of *Group Psychology* (1921c). He repeated it in the *Introductory Lectures,* XIII, and in Chapter V of *Civilization and its Discontents* (1930a). That exceptions may occur is shown by the example above, p. 66.]

14. [Cf. some remarks on this in Chapter XII (D) of *Group Psychology* (1921c).]

THE OEDIPUS COMPLEX IS NOT UNIVERSAL

Ellis points out that the more Freud was taken to task for claiming that children had incestuous desires, the more he pursued his ideas, putting the Oedipus complex at the center of morality as well as at the base of neuroses. But, according to Ellis, the development of an Oedipus complex requires a patriarchal family. The Oedipus complex grows out of the family structure. Since many other family structures exist, there is no reason to believe that the Oedipus complex as described by Freud can be so universally important in the development of the psyche.

Freud assumed that the desire for incest was natural and self-destructive and therefore in need of taming. But Ellis is not so sure that incest is clearly natural or unnatural (although anthropologists disagreed with him at the time). Ellis argues that the sexual attraction for the parent of the opposite sex is natural—due to close contact—but is weak compared to the sexual feelings stirred by the usual outside objects of sexual interest. Other little boys and girls make for much better sexual objects than one's mother or father. Familiarity just does not breed strong enough sexual feelings to culminate in a desire for incest.

The Oedipus complex is nothing more than what we would expect. A child grows to have some weak sexual love toward the parent of the opposite sex. It is only to be expected that there will be jealousy toward the other parent for interfering with the love-relationship. Jealousy is just as natural as the love. Ellis appeals to our remembering how we felt when we first had to deal with a new sibling. We are jealous because we are no longer first. But after a time, it is only normal for stronger feelings of interest and desire to help take over. They replace the feelings of jealousy. And so it is for the (weak) feelings of sexual desire for the parent of opposite sex. Obviously, Ellis points out, if there is a problem with the resolution of these weak feelings, emotional problems will ensue.

from The Sexual Impulse in Youth

Havelock Ellis

. . . At this point it is necessary to refer to a psychological trait to which psycho-analysts, above all Freud, who first called attention to it, have in the past, and to some extent still, attached supreme importance: the so-called Oedipus complex. It is not, on the surface, quite happily so called, for what we hereby mean psychologically is simply an attraction of love (a "wish to marry") the parent of opposite sex, on the part of the young child, with a corresponding jealousy of the parent of the same sex. Whereas in the myth Oedipus experienced no such feelings, but was compelled by the oracle and the gods to marry his mother and kill his father unwittingly, in spite of all his own struggles to avoid these crimes; but this opposition Freud explains away by saying that oracle and gods were a glorified embodiment of the Unconscious. Freud's Oedipus complex, when he first put it forward some thirty years ago—certainly in an incautious way and with a misapplied use of the word "incest"—was, as he frequently stated, greeted with horror and execration. That attitude, to one of his strong and combative temperament, merely aroused a more emphatic assertion of the doctrine. In some degree, in some form or another, even an inverted form, the Oedipus complex, Freud declared, "is a regular and very important factor in the mental life of the child." He went on to find that "it does not seem impossible" that the Oedipus complex is the source of all perversions and also "the actual nucleus of the neuroses." Rank, at the time closely associated with him, showed with the help of his wide literary culture how frequently and variously this motive had entered dramatic poetry. Finally in 1913, in *Totem and Taboo,* Freud developed a conception of the Oedipus complex as lying at the root of primitive morality, furnishing that sense of guilt which to Freud seems "the ultimate source of religion and morality," the earliest form of Kant's categorical imperative, and the first embodiment of the great cosmic figures, which, beginning as Parents became God, Fate, Nature, what we will.

But the psycho-analysts who have thus placed the Oedipus complex at the foundation of a large part of human culture have failed to realize that that complex can only be associated, if at all, with a particular family constitution, and that the family, far from having only one single form of constitution, has varied widely. A patriarchal family, such as we have had during historical times in the parts of Europe best known to us, is essential for an Oedipus complex. But that is far from being a kind of family always and everywhere known. The substance of the family is biological but its forms are socially molded. This is made clear by Malinowski (who started with a bias favorable to psycho-analysis) in his book *Sex and Repression in Savage Society.* The complexes which are supposed to mold culture could only have arisen under culture, and cultures are of various kinds. Nor can we accept a "primeval horde equipped with all the bias, maladjustments and ill-tempers of a middle-class European family and then let loose in a prehistoric jungle." Every type of civilization cannot but have a special type of complex as its necessary by-product.

The Oedipus complex, further, rests on the belief that there is a strong natural human tendency, appearing at the earliest age, to sex love towards near relations which can only be overcome by stern laws and severe repressions. It is agreed by all authorities that the free exercise of incestuous impulses is incompatible with a family order, and that on such a basis no developed culture would be likely to arise. But authorities differ as to the natural or unnatural character of incestuous impulses. Westermarck held originally that there is a definite natural instinct averse in incest; Freud holds that there is from infancy a strong natural instinct to incest; Malinowski does not accept the aversion to incest as natural but as introduced by culture, "a

The selection from Havelock Ellis is taken from his book *The Psychology of Sex* (New York: Emerson Books, 1937), pp. 91–106. Used by permission of Emerson Books, Inc.

complex scheme of cultural reactions." The position I have long held largely harmonizes these opposing views. There is a sexual attraction towards persons with whom there is close contact, such persons being often relations, and the attraction being therefore termed "incestuous." But this is a weak attraction under normal circumstances (there are always exceptions) and is quickly overcome when a fascinating new object of desire from outside his own circle strikes the young beholder. There is no anti-incestuous instinct, no natural aversion, but a deep stirring of the sexual instinct needs a strong excitement, and for this a new object is required, not one that has become commonplace by familiarity. This is a view to which Westermarck shows himself favorable in the later edition of his great work on marriage and had previously been accepted by Crawley, as well as by Heape. It is clear to any one who grasps the physiology of the sexual process and the psychology of courtship. A typical illustration may be quoted from Restif de la Bretonne's autobiography, *Monsieur Nicolas,* a precious document for erotic psychology. We here learn how an extremely precocious child was from the age of four in some degree sexually excitable by his female companions and playmates, though he received their caresses with much shyness. It was not till the age of eleven that he became highly aroused, even to the extent of attaining coitus, and losing all his early shyness, and this was with *a girl who was a stranger* and belonging to another village. Many bad theories might have been avoided had this psychological fact been clearly understood. There is no "aversion to incest," but under natural conditions a deep sexual attraction requires a powerful stimulus, and this cannot normally arise out of familiarity.

Various objections have been brought against my statement of the psychological basis of exogamy, but they are due to misunderstandings and also a failure to allow for many highly relevant considerations. Some critics have been misled by too exclusively thinking of the conditions among civilized man and domesticated animals. Some have failed to see that there is no question of absolute indifference to the sexual stimulus of familiar persons which may easily exist and sometimes indeed is peculiarly strong. Others have

rightly insisted that incest is unlikely to produce the best offspring or to result in domestic peace, and that exogamy is a highly important factor in social evolution. These influences may very well be responsible for the incest-taboo and remained responsible for maintaining it. But they could hardly have arisen except upon the foundation and by the support of the undoubted psychic tendency to which I have called attention. Social institutions are never unnatural in origin; they can only arise on a natural basis. In primitive life, moreover, we find, as Crawley points out, a naïve desire to assist Nature, as it were, by adding to what is normal the categorical imperative of custom and law.

Today we may look back serenely on the Oedipus complex and the ferocious reactions it seems to have evoked. When the facts are viewed directly and simply, without any attempt to make them look either terrifying or grandiloquent, or to generalize them into universal doctrines, it is easy to discover the very natural fact that the young boy is attracted to his mother (the corresponding phenomenon is the attachment of the young girl to her father) and is jealous at first of what distracts his mother's attention away from him. Jealousy is an entirely natural primitive emotion; every dog is inclined to growl at a seeming attempt to share his bone; any cat may be displeased at the effort of a strange cat to share her plate. Many of us—even the most normal and least neurotic—can recall, or have been told, that in early childhood we disapproved at first of the appearance of a baby brother or sister. But we can also recall that in a very short time we were completely reconciled to the new phenomenon and were even proud to assist in lovingly tending it. Any feeling of hostility to the father seldom, under normal conditions, entered at any stage. The reason is fairly obvious. The baby is new and arouses new feelings; the father has been there from the first; nothing occurs to change the attitude towards him; he is accepted as a matter of course.

But, we see also, the situation is undoubtedly favorable to morbid and emotional developments in constitutionally neurotic subjects, especially under the influence of injudicious parental behavior, such as favoritism or careless neglect. We may then have the whole chain of manifestations described by psycho-analysts. It is necessary to be alive to these possibilities, and prepared to unravel such a case fearlessly, for the path of psychology cannot be followed except with courage. But it is not necessary to generalize from a single case or even from many cases. And it is fatal to all sound conclusions to set out with a predetermined pattern and to attempt to fit every case on to it.

All this is now becoming clearer and is beginning to be admitted even by psycho-analysts. Thus Rank, who was so active in developing the conception of the Oedipus complex in its early stages, twenty years later, in his suggestive work on *Modern Education* remarks that "the Oedipus complex, as the attraction to the parent of the opposite sex and jealousy of the parent of the same sex, is not so clearly found in practice as mythology represents it and as Freud at first believed," adding that it has not been easily possible even for psycho-analysts to maintain it. Elsewhere Rank observes that the famous "mother complex" is not so much a real fixation of the child on the mother as merely a sign of the prevalence today of the belief in the influence of the mother in the child's education.

The castration-complex is associated by psycho-analysts with the Oedipus complex, Freud regarding it as primarily a reaction to intimidation in the field of sex, and any restraint on infantile activity being ultimately ascribed to the father. It sometimes happens that mothers and nurses, seeing the young child handling his penis, playfully threaten to cut it off, and the child may possibly take the threat seriously, especially if he observes that his sister has no penis; while the little girl may feel it a deprivation to lack an organ her brother possesses. It is not easy to assert that those feelings count for much in ordinary children, though Freud has gone so far as to claim, not only that the castration-complex may play a large part in the formation of neuroses but even in the formation of character in the healthy child. That the castration complex is influential in some neurotic persons there can be no doubt. Some persons of keen intelligence but neurotic disposition, when able to review their early development, have found much significance in the influence upon them of foolish nurses in arousing a castration complex.

The definite manifestation that has always most prominently attracted attention in connection with this aspect of early life is that which from old time has been termed "masturbation." Here it is convenient and possibly legitimate to speak of *sexuality,* although it is not strictly correct for we are concerned with an act which may, and often does, begin in a merely generalized and instinctive search for pleasurable sensations. But since it is an act that is not confined to early life but may occur at any age, often in connection with the most developed ideas of sex, it would be hypercritical to attempt to draw a line of distinction.

The ancient and common name of the act indicates the excitation of the sexual zone in either sex by means of the hand. But commonly and quite inevitably, the word is employed to cover all methods by which friction can be employed to produce pleasurable sensations in the genital sphere. No doubt the hand is the most frequent instrument and that which, in the absence of mental inhibitions and physical impediments, is most naturally employed. But there are many other ways: in boys, games, sports, gymnastics, even the accidental pressure of the clothes may suffice, especially under condition of general erethism, to produce erection and even orgasm, frequently to the surprise, and sometimes the alarm or the horror, of the subject to whom this experience comes; states of tension and apprehension, and spectacles arousing emotions of horror or of pleasure, may produce the same results, as well as actual experience of a similar kind, such as the punishment of whipping, the classical example of this being the experience of young Rousseau at the hands of his governess, which had, as he believed, a permanent influence on his highly sensitive psychic disposition. In girls, the action of the hands, though as in boys it is the most common method, is even less essential; a casual contact of the sexual parts may prove pleasurable even in the first childhood and be one of a girl's earliest memories; later, contact and friction with external objects may be instinctively sought; small girls will, without concealment, rub themselves against the corner of a chair, or the handle of a chest of drawers; young women will develop and continue a similar habit and even be able to excite themselves against the leg of a table at public restaurants. Without any extraneous help at all, it is sometimes possible for a girl to obtain excitement and orgasm by rubbing the thighs together, or, when in a favorable emotional state, by pressing them tightly together. And, as in boys, the same results may occur almost or quite spontaneously, under the influence of exciting spectacles or seductive thoughts. This, we see, is hardly distinguishable from what may happen, in a normal manner, between two lovers.

In boys who have had no earlier spontaneous impulses of sexual activity and no initiation from companions, the first orgasm usually occurs at puberty during sleep, with or without dreams, sometimes causing the boy much anxiety or shame, until in the course of years he learns to accept it as the almost inevitable accompaniment of adult life when it is being lived continently. In girls, however, it is not inevitable under similar conditions.It is rare (as I have frequently pointed out though the statement has not always been accepted) for girls to have their *first* experience of sexual excitement (with or without orgasm) in sleep, and the supposition that they commonly do is due to ignorance. The boy awakes sexually in sleep, spontaneously. The girl must be actively awakened, by others or herself, though after that, even if it may not occur until long after she has reached adult age, she will be liable to experience the most vivid erotic dreams. We probably have here an interesting psychic sexual difference, the greater sexual activity of the male, the greater sexual quiescence of the female, which does not, however, mean superior sexuality of the male, or inferior sexual needs of the female; it may be indeed the reason why the girl is more liable to hysterical and other nervous symptoms, if we regard these as manifestations of latent sexual energy.

Robie, in America, among a large number of persons of both sexes found few or none who had not had experience of masturbation or other form of auto-erotic activity at some period of their lives and often before the age of eight. His observations were not always very precise. Dr. Katharine Davis, who gave special attention to this point, found, among 1,000 American college women above the age of 22 that 60 per cent. gave definite histories of masturbation. She investigated the whole question, perhaps with more thoroughness and in greater detail than any other worker. Among unmarried college women graduates she found

that 43.6 per cent. began the practice from the 3rd to the 10th years inclusive; 20.2 per cent. from 11 to 15 inclusive; 13.9 per cent. from 16 to 22 inclusive; 15.5 per cent. from 23 to 29 inclusive. Comparing her results with those of other investigators dealing with men the results are as follows:

	Men	Women
Up to and including 11 yrs.	20.9	49.1
Up to and including 12–14 yrs.	44.3	14.6
Up to and including 15–17 yrs.	30.3	6.2
Up to 18 yrs. and over	4.5	30.1

These results carry weight because the groups include about 500 men to about 900 women. They show, to an unexpected degree, that girls masturbate early more often than boys, and that during adolescence it is the boys who largely predominate, while after adult age is reached, as we should anticipate, women are in a large majority.

Dr. Hamilton, in his careful study of 100 married men and 100 married women of good social standing, found that 97 per cent. of the men and 74 per cent. of the women had at some period masturbated. These results are fairly in accordance with the more general conclusion of Moll, whose work on *The Sexual Life of the Child* (1908) was the earliest comprehensive study of the subject and is still among the most judicious. Moll remarks, however, that masturbation is not as common as is sometimes supposed in Germany, and I may add that it seems not so common in England or even in France as the American percentage might lead us to anticipate.

It will be seen that these manifestations extend far beyond the classic conception of "masturbation" in its literal and commonly accepted sense, which cannot really be said to constitute a separate group for it blends with the larger group without definite frontiers.

When we thus view this group of manifestations as a whole it is seen why we cannot properly term them "perverse." They are natural; they are the inevitable result of the action of the sexual impulse when working in the absence of the object of sexual desire, occurring, under such conditions, even in some of the lower animals; and they are emphatically natural when they occur before adult